MW01259957

Introduction
to
Programming in Python

Introduction to Programming in Python

An Interdisciplinary Approach

Robert Sedgewick
Kevin Wayne
Robert Dondero

Princeton University

Addison-Wesley

New York • Boston • Indianapolis • San Francisco
Toronto • Montreal • London • Munich • Paris • Madrid
Capetown • Sydney • Tokyo • Singapore • Mexico City

For information about buying this title in bulk quantities, or for special sales opportunities (which may include electronic versions; custom cover designs; and content particular to your business, training goals, marketing focus, or branding interests), please contact our corporate sales department at corpsales@pearsoned.com or (800) 382-3419.

For government sales inquiries, please contact governmentsales@pearsoned.com.

For questions about sales outside the United States, please contact international@pearsoned.com.

Visit us on the Web: informit.com/aw

Library of Cataloging-in-Publication Data
Sedgewick, Robert, 1946-
Introduction to programming in Python : an interdisciplinary approach / Robert Sedgewick, Kevin Wayne, Robert Dondero.
pages cm
Includes indexes.
ISBN 978-0-13-407643-0 (hardcover : alk. paper)—ISBN 0-13-407643-5
1. Python (Computer program language) 2. Computer programming. I. Wayne, Kevin Daniel, 1971- II. Dondero, Robert. III. Title.
QA76.73.P98S43 2015
005.13'3—dc23

2015011936

ISBN-13: 978-0-13-407643-0
ISBN-10: 0-13-407643-5

Text printed in the United States on recycled paper at Edwards Brothers Malloy in Ann Arbor, Michigan.
First printing, June 2015

9 2022

To Adam, Andrew, Brett, Robbie,

Henry, Iona, Rose, Peter,

and especially Linda

To Jackie and Alex

To my family,

especially Ellen and Meghan

Contents

Programs

Elements of Programming

Functions and Modules

Object-Oriented Programming

Algorithms and Data Structures

Preface

THE BASIS FOR EDUCATION IN THE last millennium was "reading, writing, and arithmetic"; now it is reading, writing, and *computing*. Learning to program is an essential part of the education of every student in the sciences and engineering. Beyond direct applications, it is the first step in understanding the nature of computer science's undeniable impact on the modern world. This book aims to teach programming to those who need or want to learn it, in a scientific context.

Our primary goal is to *empower* students by supplying the experience and basic tools necessary to use computation effectively. Our approach is to teach students that composing a program is a natural, satisfying, and creative experience. We progressively introduce essential concepts, embrace classic applications from applied mathematics and the sciences to illustrate the concepts, and provide opportunities for students to write programs to solve engaging problems.

We use the Python programming language for all of the programs in this book—we refer to "Python" after "programming in the title to emphasize the idea that the book is about *fundamental concepts in programming*, not Python per se. This book teaches basic skills for computational problem solving that are applicable in many modern computing environments, and is a self-contained treatment intended for people with no previous experience in programming.

This book is an *interdisciplinary* approach to the traditional CS1 curriculum, in that we highlight the role of computing in other disciplines, from materials science to genomics to astrophysics to network systems. This approach emphasizes for students the essential idea that mathematics, science, engineering, and computing are intertwined in the modern world. While it is a CS1 textbook designed for any first-year college student interested in mathematics, science, or engineering, the book also can be used for self-study or as a supplement in a course that integrates programming with another field.

Coverage The book is organized around four stages of learning to program: basic elements, functions, object-oriented programming, and algorithms . We provide the basic information readers need to build confidence in composing programs at each level before moving to the next level. An essential feature of our approach is to use example programs that solve intriguing problems, supported with exercises ranging from self-study drills to challenging problems that call for creative solutions.

Basic elements include variables, assignment statements, built-in types of data, flow of control , arrays, and input/output, including graphics and sound.

Functions and modules are the student's first exposure to modular programming. We build upon familiarity with mathematical functions to introduce Python functions, and then consider the implications of programming with functions, including libraries of functions and recursion. We stress the fundamental idea of dividing a program into components that can be independently debugged, maintained, and reused.

Object-oriented programming is our introduction to data abstraction. We emphasize the concepts of a data type and their implementation using Python's class mechanism. We teach students how to *use*, *create*, and *design* data types. Modularity, encapsulation, and other modern programming paradigms are the central concepts of this stage.

Algorithms and data structures combine these modern programming paradigms with classic methods of organizing and processing data that remain effective for modern applications. We provide an introduction to classical algorithms for sorting and searching as well as fundamental data structures and their application, emphasizing the use of the scientific method to understand performance characteristics of implementations.

Applications in science and engineering are a key feature of the text. We motivate each programming concept that we address by examining its impact on specific applications. We draw examples from applied mathematics, the physical and biological sciences, and computer science itself, and include simulation of physical systems, numerical methods, data visualization, sound synthesis, image processing, financial simulation, and information technology. Specific examples include a treatment in the first chapter of Markov chains for web page ranks and case studies that address the percolation problem, *n*-body simulation, and the small-world phenomenon. These applications are an integral part of the text. They engage students in the material, illustrate the importance of the programming concepts, and provide persuasive evidence of the critical role played by computation in modern science and engineering.

Our primary goal is to teach the specific mechanisms and skills that are needed to develop effective solutions to any programming problem. We work with complete Python programs and encourage readers to use them. We focus on programming by individuals, not programming in the large.

Use in the Curriculum This book is intended for a first-year college course aimed at teaching novices to program in the context of scientific applications. Taught from this book, prospective majors in any area of science and engineering will learn to program in a familiar context. Students completing a course based on this book will be well prepared to apply their skills in later courses in science and engineering and to recognize when further education in computer science might be beneficial.

Prospective computer science majors, in particular, can benefit from learning to program in the context of scientific applications. A computer scientist needs the same basic background in the scientific method and the same exposure to the role of computation in science as does a biologist, an engineer, or a physicist.

Indeed, our interdisciplinary approach enables colleges and universities to teach prospective computer science majors and prospective majors in other fields of science and engineering in the *same* course. We cover the material prescribed by CS1, but our focus on applications brings life to the concepts and motivates students to learn them. Our interdisciplinary approach exposes students to problems in many different disciplines, helping them to choose a major more wisely.

Whatever the specific mechanism, the use of this book is best positioned early in the curriculum. First, this positioning allows us to leverage familiar material in high school mathematics and science. Second, students who learn to program early in their college curriculum will then be able to use computers more effectively when moving on to courses in their specialty. Like reading and writing, programming is certain to be an essential skill for any scientist or engineer. Students who have grasped the concepts in this book will continually develop that skill through a lifetime, reaping the benefits of exploiting computation to solve or to better understand the problems and projects that arise in their chosen field.

Prerequisites This book is suitable for typical science and engineering students in their first year of college. That is, we do not expect preparation beyond what is typically required for other entry-level science and mathematics courses.

Mathematical maturity is important. While we do not dwell on mathematical material, we do refer to the mathematics curriculum that students have taken in high school, including algebra, geometry, and trigonometry. Most students in our target audience automatically meet these requirements. Indeed, we take advantage of their familiarity with the basic curriculum to introduce basic programming concepts.

Scientific curiosity is also an essential ingredient. Science and engineering students bring with them a sense of fascination with the ability of scientific inquiry to help explain what goes on in nature. We leverage this predilection with examples of simple programs that speak volumes about the natural world. We do not assume any specific knowledge beyond that provided by typical high school courses in mathematics, physics, biology, or chemistry.

Programming experience is not necessary, but also is not harmful. Teaching programming is our primary goal, so we assume no prior programming experience. But composing a program to solve a new problem is a challenging intellectual task, so students who have written numerous programs in high school can benefit from taking an introductory programming course based on this book . The book can support teaching students with varying backgrounds because the applications appeal to both novices and experts alike.

Experience using a computer is not necessary, but also is not at all a problem. College students use computers regularly, to communicate with friends and relatives, listen to music, to process photos, and as part of many other activities. The realization that they can harness the power of their own computer in interesting and important ways is an exciting and lasting lesson.

In summary, virtually all students in science and engineering fields are prepared to take a course based on this book as a part of their first-semester curriculum.

Goals What can *instructors* of upper-level courses in science and engineering expect of students who have completed a course based on this book?

We cover the CS1 curriculum, but anyone who has taught an introductory programming course knows that expectations of instructors in later courses are typically high: each instructor expects all students to be familiar with the computing environment and approach that he or she wants to use. A physics professor might expect some students to design a program over the weekend to run a simulation; an engineering professor might expect other students to be using a particular package to numerically solve differential equations; or a computer science professor might expect knowledge of the details of a particular programming environment. Is it realistic to meet such diverse expectations? Should there be a different introductory course for each set of students?

Colleges and universities have been wrestling with such questions since computers came into widespread use in the latter part of the 20th century. Our answer to them is found in this common introductory treatment of programming, which is analogous to commonly accepted introductory courses in mathematics, physics, biology, and chemistry. *An Introduction to Programming in Python* strives to provide the basic preparation needed by all students in science and engineering, while sending the clear message that there is much more to understand about computer science than programming. Instructors teaching students who have studied from this book can expect that they will have the knowledge and experience necessary to enable those students to adapt to new computational environments and to effectively exploit computers in diverse applications.

What can *students* who have completed a course based on this book expect to accomplish in later courses?

Our message is that programming is not difficult to learn and that harnessing the power of the computer is rewarding. Students who master the material in this book are prepared to address computational challenges wherever they might appear later in their careers. They learn that modern programming environments, such as the one provided by Python, help open the door to any computational problem they might encounter later, and they gain the confidence to learn, evaluate, and use other computational tools. Students interested in computer science will be well prepared to pursue that interest; students in science and engineering will be ready to integrate computation into their studies.

Booksite An extensive amount of information that supplements this text may be found on the web at

```
http://introcs.cs.princeton.edu/python
```

For economy, we refer to this site as the *booksite* throughout. It contains material for instructors, students, and casual readers of the book. We briefly describe this material here, though, as all web users know, it is best surveyed by browsing. With a few exceptions to support testing, the material is all publicly available.

One of the most important implications of the booksite is that it empowers instructors and students to use their own computers to teach and learn the material. Anyone with a computer and a browser can begin learning to program by following a few instructions on the booksite. The process is no more difficult than downloading a media player or a song. As with any website, our booksite is continually evolving. It is an essential resource for everyone who owns this book. In particular, the supplemental materials are critical to our goal of making computer science an integral component of the education of all scientists and engineers.

For *instructors*, the booksite contains information about teaching. This information is primarily organized around a teaching style that we have developed over the past decade, where we offer two lectures per week to a large audience, supplemented by two class sessions per week where students meet in small groups with instructors or teaching assistants. The booksite has presentation slides for the lectures, which set the tone.

For *teaching assistants*, the booksite contains detailed problem sets and programming projects, which are based on exercises from the book but contain much more detail. Each programming assignment is intended to teach a relevant concept in the context of an interesting application while presenting an inviting and engaging challenge to each student. The progression of assignments embodies our approach to teaching programming. The booksite fully specifies all the assignments and provides detailed, structured information to help students complete them in the allotted time, including descriptions of suggested approaches and outlines for what should be taught in class sessions.

For *students*, the booksite contains quick access to much of the material in the book, including source code, plus extra material to encourage self-learning. Solutions are provided for many of the book's exercises, including complete program code and test data. There is a wealth of information associated with programming assignments, including suggested approaches, checklists, FAQs, and test data.

For *casual readers* , the booksite is a resource for accessing all manner of extra information associated with the book's content. All of the booksite content provides web links and other routes to pursue more information about the topic under consideration. There is far more information accessible than any individual could fully digest, but our goal is to provide enough to whet any reader's appetite for more information about the book's content.

Acknowledgments This project has been under development since 1992, so far too many people have contributed to its success for us to acknowledge them all here. Special thanks are due to Anne Rogers, for helping to start the ball rolling; to Dave Hanson, Andrew Appel, and Chris van Wyk, for their patience in explaining data abstraction; and to Lisa Worthington, for being the first to truly relish the challenge of teaching this material to first-year students. We also gratefully acknowledge the efforts of `/dev/126` ; the faculty, graduate students, and teaching staff who have dedicated themselves to teaching this material over the past 25 years here at Princeton University; and the thousands of undergraduates who have dedicated themselves to learning it.

Robert Sedgewick
Kevin Wayne
Robert Dondero

April 2015

Chapter One

Elements of Programming

Our goal in this chapter is to convince you that composing a program is easier than writing a piece of text, such as a paragraph or essay. Writing prose is difficult: you spend many years in school to learn how to do it. By contrast, just a few building blocks suffice to enable you to compose programs that can solve all sorts of fascinating, but otherwise unapproachable, problems. In this chapter, we take you through these building blocks, get you started on programming in Python, and study a variety of interesting programs. You will be able to express yourself (by composing programs) within just a few weeks. Like the ability to write prose, the ability to program is a lifetime skill that you can continually refine well into the future.

In this book, you will learn the *Python programming language*. This task will be much easier for you than, for example, learning a foreign language. Indeed, programming languages are characterized by only a few dozen vocabulary words and rules of grammar. Much of the material that we cover in this book could also be expressed in the Java or C++ languages, or any of several other modern programming languages. We describe everything specifically in Python so that you can get started creating and running programs right away. On the one hand, we will focus on learning to program, as opposed to learning details about Python. On the other hand, part of the challenge of programming is knowing which details are relevant in a given situation. Python is widely used, so learning Python will enable you to compose programs on many computers (your own, for example). Also, learning to program in Python will make it easy for you to learn other languages, including lower-level languages such as C and specialized languages such as Matlab.

1.1 Your First Program

IN THIS SECTION, OUR PLAN IS to lead you into the world of Python programming by taking you through the basic steps required to get a simple program running. The *Python system* (hereafter abbreviated *Python*) is a collection of applications, not unlike many of the other applications that you are accustomed to using (such as your word processor, email program, and web browser). As with any application, you need to be sure that Python is properly installed on your computer. It comes preloaded on many computers, or you can download it easily. You also need a text editor and a terminal application. Your first task is to find the instructions for installing such a Python programming environment on your computer by visiting

Programs in this section

`http://introcs.cs.princeton.edu/python`

We refer to this site as the *booksite*. It contains an extensive amount of supplementary information about the material in this book for your reference and use while programming.

Programming in Python To introduce you to developing Python programs, we break the process down into two steps. To program in Python, you need to:

- *Compose* a program by typing it into a file named, say, `myprogram.py`.
- *Run* (or *execute*) it by typing `python myprogram.py` in the terminal window.

In the first step, you start with a blank screen and end with a sequence of typed characters on the screen, just as when you write an email message or an essay. Programmers use the term *code* to refer to program text and the term *coding* to refer to the act of creating and editing the code. In the second step, you transfer control of the computer from the system to your program (which returns control back to the system when finished). Many systems support several different ways to compose and execute programs. We choose the sequence given here because it is the simplest to describe and use for small programs.

Composing a program. A Python program is nothing more than a sequence of characters, like a paragraph or a poem, stored in a file whose name has a `.py` extension. To compose one, therefore, you need simply define that sequence of characters, in the same way as you do for email or any other computer application. You can use any text editor for this task, or you can use one of the more sophisticated program development environments described on the booksite. Such environments are overkill for the sorts of programs we consider in this book, but they are not difficult to use, have many useful features, and are widely used by professionals.

Executing a program. Once you compose the program, you can run (or execute) it. This is the exciting part, where your program takes control of your computer (within the constraints of what Python allows). It is perhaps more accurate to say that your computer follows your instructions. It is even more accurate to say that the Python *compiler* translates your Python program into a language that is more suitable for execution on a computer. Then, the Python *interpreter* directs your computer to follow these instructions. Throughout this book we use the term *executing* or *running* to refer to the combination of compiling and interpreting a program (as in "When Python executes this program…"). To use the Python compiler and interpreter to execute your program, type the `python` command followed by the name of the file containing the Python program in a terminal window.

Program 1.1.1 is an example of a complete Python program. Its code resides in a file named `helloworld.py`. The program's sole action is to write a message back to the terminal window. A Python program consists of *statements*. Typically you place each statement on a distinct line.

- The first line of `helloworld.py` contains an `import` statement. That statement tells Python that you intend to use the features defined in the `stdio` *module*—that is, in a file named `stdio.py`. The `stdio.py` file is one that we designed specifically for this book. It defines functions related to reading input and writing output. Having imported the `stdio` module, you can later *call a function* that is defined in that module.

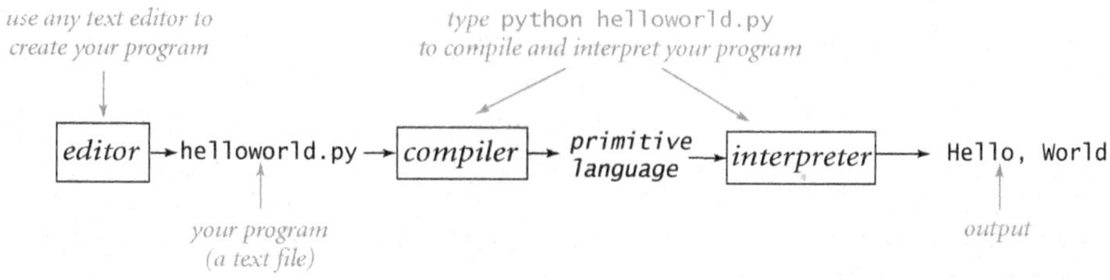

Developing a Python program

Program 1.1.1 Hello, World (helloworld.py)

```
import stdio

# Write 'Hello, World' to standard output.
stdio.writeln('Hello, World')
```

This code is a Python program that accomplishes a simple task. It is traditionally a beginner's first program. The box below shows what happens when you execute the program. The terminal application gives a command prompt (% in this book) and executes the commands that you type (in boldface in this book). The result of executing `python` *with this code is that the program writes* `Hello, World` *in the terminal window (the fourth line).*

```
% python helloworld.py
Hello, World
```

- The second line is a blank line. Python ignores blank lines; programmers use them to separate logical blocks of code.
- The third line contains a *comment*, which serves to document the program. In Python a comment begins with the '#' character and extends to the end of the line. In this book, we display comments in gray. Python ignores comments—they are present only for human readers of the program.
- The fourth line is the heart of the program. It is a statement that calls the `stdio.writeln()` function to write one line with the given text on it. Note that we call a function in another module by writing the module name, followed by a period, followed by the function name.

Python 2. *The lingua franca in this book is Python 3, because it is the future of Python programming. However, we have been very careful to ensure that the code in the book works with either Python 2 or Python 3. For example, in Python 2, PROGRAM 1.1.1 could be simply the single line* `print 'Hello, World'`*, but this is not a valid program in Python 3. To develop code for writing output that works in either version of Python, we use our* `stdio` *module. Whenever there is a significant difference between the two languages, we call attention to Python 2 users in a callout box like this one.*

Since the 1970s, it has been a tradition that a beginning programmer's first program should write `'Hello, World'`. So, you should go ahead and type the code in Program 1.1.1 into a file named `helloworld.py` and then execute it. By doing so, you will be following in the footsteps of countless others who have learned how to program. Also, you will be checking that you have a usable editor and terminal application. At first, accomplishing the task of writing something out in a terminal window might not seem very interesting; upon reflection, however, you will see that one of the most basic functions that we need from a program is its ability to tell us what it is doing.

For the time being, all our program code will be just like `helloworld.py`, except with a different file name, different comments, and a different sequence of statements following the comment. Thus, you do not need to start with a blank page to compose a program. Instead,

- Copy `helloworld.py` into a new file having a name of your choice, but make sure that the new file name ends with `.py`.
- Replace the comment and the `stdio.writeln()` statement with a different sequence of statements.

Your program is characterized by its sequence of statements and its name. By convention, each Python program resides in a file whose name has a `.py` extension.

Errors. It is easy to blur the distinction among editing, compiling, and interpreting programs. You should keep them separate in your mind when you are learning to program, to better understand the effects of the errors that inevitably arise. You can find several examples of errors in the Q&A at the end of this section.

You can fix or avoid most errors by carefully examining the program as you create it, the same way you fix spelling and grammatical errors when you compose an email message. Some errors, known as *compile-time* errors, are *raised* when Python compiles the program, because they prevent the compiler from doing the translation. Python reports a compile-time error as a `SyntaxError`. Other errors, known as *run-time* errors, are not raised until Python interprets the program. For example, if you forget the `import stdio` statement in `helloworld.py`, then Python will raise a `NameError` at run time.

In general, errors in programs, also commonly known as *bugs*, are the bane of a programmer's existence: the error messages can be confusing or misleading, and the source of the error can be very hard to find. One of the first skills that you will learn is to identify errors; you will also learn to be sufficiently careful when coding, to avoid making many of them in the first place.

Input and output Typically, we want to provide input to our programs—that is, data that they can process to produce a result. The simplest way to provide input data is illustrated in `useargument.py` (PROGRAM 1.1.2). Whenever you run the program `useargument.py`, it accepts the command-line argument that you type after the program name and writes it back out to the terminal as part of the message. The result of executing this program depends on what you type after the program name. You can run the program with different command-line arguments and get different written results.

In `useargument.py`, the statement `import sys` tells Python that you wish to use the features defined in the `sys` module. One of those features, named `argv`, is a list of command-line arguments (which appear after "`python useargument.py`" on the command line, delimited by spaces). Later in the book (SECTION 2.1) we will discuss this mechanism in more detail. For now it is sufficient to understand that `sys.argv[1]` is the first command-line argument that you type after the program name, `sys.argv[2]` is the second command-line argument that you type after the program name, and so forth. You can use `sys.argv[1]` within your program's body to represent the string that you type on the command line when you execute it, just as in `useargument.py`.

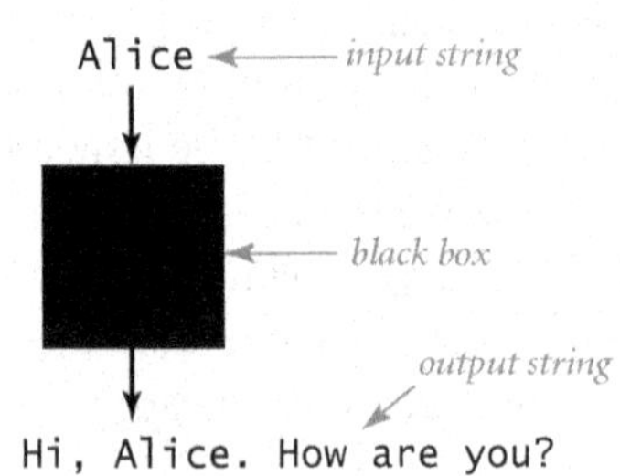

A bird's-eye view of a Python program

In addition to `writeln()`, PROGRAM 1.1.2 calls the `write()` function. This function is just like `writeln()`, but writes just the string (not a newline character).

Again, accomplishing the task of getting a program to write back out what we type in to it may not seem interesting at first, but upon reflection you will realize that another basic function of a program is its ability to respond to basic information from the user to control what the program does. The simple model that `useargument.py` represents will suffice to allow us to consider Python's basic programming mechanism and to address all sorts of interesting computational problems.

Stepping back, we can see that `useargument.py` does neither more nor less than map a string of characters (the argument) into another string of characters (the message written back to the terminal). When using it, we might think of our Python program as a black box that converts our input string to some output string.

Program 1.1.2 Using a command-line argument (useargument.py)

```
import sys
import stdio

stdio.write('Hi, ')
stdio.write(sys.argv[1])
stdio.writeln('. How are you?')
```

This program shows how we can control the actions of our programs: by providing an argument on the command line. Doing so allows us to tailor the behavior of our programs. The program accepts a command-line argument, and writes a message that uses it.

```
% python useargument.py Alice
Hi, Alice. How are you?

% python useargument.py Bob
Hi, Bob. How are you?

% python useargument.py Carol
Hi, Carol. How are you?
```

This model is attractive because it is not only simple but also sufficiently general to allow completion, in principle, of any computational task. For example, the Python compiler itself is nothing more than a program that takes one string as input (a .py file) and produces another string as output (the corresponding program in a more primitive language). Later, you will be able to compose programs that accomplish a variety of interesting tasks (though we stop short of programs as complicated as a compiler). For the moment, we live with various limitations on the size and type of the input and output to our programs; in SECTION 1.5, you will see how to incorporate more sophisticated mechanisms for program input and output. In particular, you will see that we can work with arbitrarily long input and output strings and other types of data such as sound and pictures.

Q&A

Q. Why Python?

A. The programs that we are studying are very similar to their counterparts in several other languages, so our choice of language is not crucial. We use Python because it is widely available, embraces a full set of modern abstractions, and has a variety of automatic checks for mistakes in programs, so it is suitable for learning to program. Python is evolving and comes in many versions.

Q. Which version of Python should I use?

A. We recommend Python 3, but we have been very careful to ensure that the code in the book works with either Python 2 or Python 3. All of the code has been tested with Python versions 2.7 and 3.4 (the latest major releases of Python 2 and Python 3 at the time of publication). We use the generic term Python 2 to refer to Python 2.7 and Python 3 to refer to Python 3.4.

Q. How do I install a Python programming environment?

A. The booksite provides step-by-step instructions for installing a Python programming environment on your Mac OS X, Windows, or Linux system. This includes installation of our booksite modules, such as `stdio.py`.

Q. Do I really have to type in the programs in the book to try them out? I believe that you ran them and that they produce the indicated output.

A. You should type in and run `helloworld.py`. Your understanding will be greatly magnified if you also run `useargument.py`, try it on various inputs, and modify it to test different ideas of your own. To save some typing, you can find all of the code in this book (and much more) on the booksite. This site also has information about installing Python on your computer, answers to selected exercises, web links, and other extra information that you may find useful or interesting.

Q. When I run `helloworld.py`, Python generates the message

```
ImportError: No module named stdio.
```

What does that mean?

A. That means that the booksite module `stdio` is not available to Python.

Q. How can I make the booksite module `stdio` available to Python?

A. If you followed the step-by-step instructions on the booksite for installing a Python programming environment, the `stdio` module should already be available to Python. Alternatively, you can download the file `stdio.py` from the booksite and put it in the same directory as the program that uses it.

Q. What are Python's rules regarding *whitespace* characters such as tabs, spaces, and newlines?

A. In general, Python considers most whitespace in program text to be equivalent, with two important exceptions: *string literals* and *indentation*. A string literal is a sequence of characters inside single quotes, such as `'Hello, World'`. If you put any number of spaces within the quotes, you get precisely the same number of spaces in the string literal. *Indentation* is whitespace at a beginning of a line—the number of spaces at the beginning of a line plays an important role in structuring Python programs, as we will see in SECTION 1.3. For now you should not indent any code.

Q. Why should I use comments?

A. Comments are indispensable because they help other programmers to understand your code and even can help you to understand your own code in retrospect. The constraints of the book format demand that we use comments sparingly in the programs shown in this book (instead we describe each program thoroughly in the accompanying text and figures). The programs on the booksite are commented to a more realistic degree.

Q. Can I put more than one statement on a line?

A. Yes, by separating statements with semicolons. For example, this single line of code produces the same output as `helloworld.py`:

```
import stdio; stdio.writeln('Hello, World')
```

But many programmers advise against doing this, as a matter of style.

Q. What happens when you omit a parenthesis or misspell one of the words, like `stdio` or `write` or `writeln`?

A. It depends upon precisely what you do. These so-called *syntax errors* are usually caught by the compiler. For example, if you make a program `bad.py` that is exactly the same as `helloworld.py` except that you omit the first left parenthesis, you get the following reasonably helpful message:

```
% python bad.py
  File "bad.py", line 4
    stdio.write'Hello, World')
                            ^
SyntaxError: invalid syntax
```

From this message, you might correctly surmise that you need to insert a left parenthesis. But the compiler may not be able to tell you exactly which mistake you made, so the error message may be hard to understand. For example, if you omit the first right parenthesis instead of the first left parenthesis, you get the following less helpful message, which references the line following the erroneous one:

```
% python bad.py

  File "bad.py", line 5


                                ^
SyntaxError: unexpected EOF while parsing
```

One way to get used to such messages is to intentionally introduce mistakes into a simple program and then see what happens. Whatever the error message says, you should treat the compiler as a friend, because it is just trying to tell you that something is wrong with your program.

Q. When I run `useargument.py`, I get a strange error message. Please explain.

A. Most likely, you forgot to include a command-line argument:

```
% python useargument.py
Hi, Traceback (most recent call last):
  File "useargument.py", line 5, in <module>
    stdio.write(sys.argv[1])
IndexError: list index out of range
```

The Python interpreter is complaining that you ran the program but did not type a command-line argument as promised. You will learn more details about list indices in Section 1.4. Remember this error message: you are likely to see it again. Even experienced programmers forget to type command-line arguments on occasion.

Q. Which Python modules and functions are available for me to use?

A. Many standard modules are bundled with any Python installation. Many others are available as *extension* modules that you can download and install subsequently. We composed still others (such as the `stdio` module) specifically for this book and booksite; we'll call them *booksite* modules. In short, hundreds of Python modules, each (typically) defining multiple functions, are available for you to use. This book introduces only the most fundamental modules and functions, and does so in a deliberately incremental fashion (starting in the next section) to avoid overwhelming you with information.

Exercises

1.1.1 Compose a program that writes the `Hello, World` message 10 times.

1.1.2 Describe what happens if you omit the following in `helloworld.py`:

a. `import`
b. `stdio`
c. `import stdio`

1.1.3 Describe what happens if you misspell (by, say, omitting the second letter) the following in `helloworld.py`:

a. `import`
b. `stdio`
c. `write`
d. `writeln`

1.1.4 Describe what happens if you omit the following in `helloworld.py`:

a. the first `'`
b. the second `'`
c. the `stdio.writeln()` statement

1.1.5 Describe what happens if you try to execute `useargument.py` with each of the following command lines:

a. `python useargument.py python`
b. `python useargument.py @!&^%`
c. `python useargument.py 1234`
d. `python useargument Bob`
e. `useargument.py Bob`
f. `python useargument.py Alice Bob`

1.1.6 Modify `useargument.py` to compose a program `usethree.py` that takes three names and writes a proper sentence with the names in the reverse of the order they are given, so that, for example, `python usethree.py Alice Bob Carol` writes the string `'Hi Carol, Bob, and Alice'`.

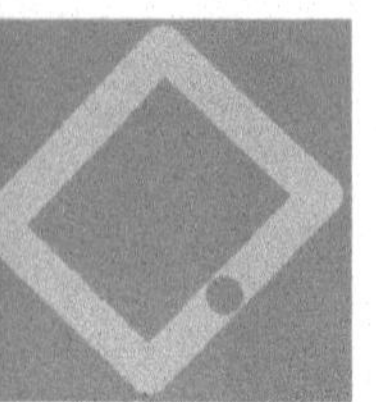

1.2 Built-in Types of Data

When programming in Python, you must always be aware of the type of data that your program is processing. The programs in Section 1.1 process strings, many of the programs in this section process numbers, and we consider numerous other types later in the book. Understanding the distinctions among them is so important that we formally define the idea: a *data type* is a *set of values* and a *set of operations* defined on those values.

Programs in this section

Several data types are built into the Python language. In this section, we consider Python's built-in data types `int` (for integers), `float` (for floating-point numbers), `str` (for sequences of characters) and `bool` (for true-false values), which are summarized in the table below.

For now, we concentrate on programs that are based on computing with these four basic built-in data types. Later, you will learn about additional data types that are available for your use, and you will learn how to compose your own data types. Indeed, programming in Python often is centered on composing data types, as you will see in Chapter 3.

After defining basic terms, we consider several sample programs and code fragments that illustrate the use of different types of data. These code fragments do not perform much real computing, but you will soon see similar code in longer programs. Understanding data types (values and operations on them) is an essential step in beginning to program. It sets the stage for you to begin working with more intricate programs in the next section. Every program that you compose will use code like the tiny fragments shown in this section.

type	*set of values*	*common operators*	*sample literals*
`int`	*integers*	`+ - * // % **`	`99 12 2147483647`
`float`	*floating-point numbers*	`+ - * / **`	`3.14 2.5 6.022e23`
`bool`	*true-false values*	`and or not`	`True False`
`str`	*sequences of characters*	`+`	`'AB' 'Hello' '2.5'`

Basic built-in data types

Definitions To talk about data types, we need to introduce some terminology. To do so, we start with the following code fragment:

```
a = 1234
b = 99
c = a + b
```

This code creates three *objects*, each of type `int`, using the *literals* `1234` and `99` and the *expression* `a + b`, and *binds* ("bind" is a technical term indicating the creation of an association) *variables* `a`, `b`, and `c` to those objects using *assignment statements*. The end result is that variable `c` is bound to an object of type `int` whose value is `1333`. Next, we define all of these italicized terms.

Literals. A *literal* is a Python-code representation of a data-type value. We use sequences of digits such as `1234` or `99` to represent values of data type `int`; we add a decimal point, as in `3.14159` or `2.71828`, to represent values of type `float`, we use `True` or `False` to represent the two values of type `bool`; and we use a sequence of characters enclosed in matching quotes, such as `'Hello, World'`, to represent values of type `str`.

Operators. An *operator* is a Python-code representation of a data-type operation. Python uses + and * to represent addition and multiplication for integers and floating-point numbers; Python uses `and`, `or`, and `not` to represent boolean operations; and so forth. We will describe in detail the most commonly used operations for each of the four basic built-in types later in this section.

Identifiers. An *identifier* is a Python-code representation of a name. Each identifier is a sequence of letters, digits, and underscores, the first of which is not a digit. The sequences of characters `abc`, `Ab_`, `abc123`, and `a_b` are all legal Python identifiers, but `Ab*`, `1abc`, and `a+b` are not. Identifiers are case-sensitive, so `Ab`, `ab`, and `AB` are all different names. Certain *keywords*—such as `and`, `import`, `in`, `def`, `while`, `from`, and `lambda`—are reserved, and you cannot use them as identifiers. Other names—such as `int`, `sum`, `min`, `max`, `len`, `id`, `file`, and `input`—have special meaning in Python, so it is best not to use them, either.

Variables. A *variable* is a name associated with a data-type value. We use variables to keep track of changing values as a computation unfolds. For example, we use a variable `total` in several programs in this book to keep the running total of a sum of a sequence of numbers. Programmers typically follow stylistic conventions when naming things. In this book our convention is to give each variable a name that consists of a lowercase letter followed by lowercase letters, uppercase letters, and digits. We use uppercase letters to mark the words of a multi-word variable name. So, for example, we use the variable names `i`, `x`, `y`, `total`, `isLeapYear`, and `outDegrees`, among many others.

Constant variables. We use the oxymoronic term *constant variable* to describe a variable whose associated a data-type value does not change during the execution of a program (or from one execution of the program to the next). In this book, our convention is to give each constant variable a name that consists of an uppercase letter followed by uppercase letters, digits, and underscores. For example, we might use the constant variable names `SPEED_OF_LIGHT` and `DARK_RED`.

Expressions. An *expression* is a combination of literals, variables, and operators that Python *evaluates* to produce a value. Many expressions look just like mathematical formulas, using operators to specify data-type operations to be performed on one or more *operands*. Most of the operators that we use are *binary operators* that take exactly two operands, such as `x - 3` or `5 * x`. Each operand can be any expression, perhaps within parentheses. For example, we can compose expressions like `4 * (x - 3)` or `5 * x - 6` and Python will understand what we mean. An expression is a directive to perform a sequence of operations; the expression is a representation of the resulting value.

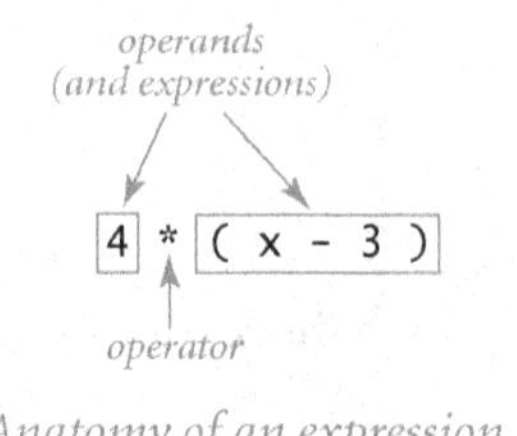

Anatomy of an expression

Operator precedence. An expression is shorthand for a sequence of operations: in which order should the operators be applied? Python has natural and well-defined *precedence* rules that fully specify this order. For arithmetic operations, multiplication and division are performed before addition and subtraction, so that `a - b * c` and `a - (b * c)` represent the same sequence of operations. When arithmetic operators have the same precedence, they are *left associative*, which means that `a - b - c` and `(a - b) - c` represent the same sequence of operations. The exponentiation operator `**` is the exception: it is *right associative*, which means that `a ** b ** c` and `a ** (b ** c)` represent the same sequence of operations. You can use parentheses to override the rules, so you can write `a - (b - c)` if that is what you want. You might encounter in the future some Python code that depends subtly on precedence rules, but we use parentheses to avoid such code in this book. If you are interested, you can find full details on the rules on the booksite.

Assignment statements. How do we define an identifier to be a variable in Python code? How do we associate a variable with a data-type value? In Python, we use an *assignment statement* for both purposes. When we write `a = 1234` in Python, we are not expressing mathematical equality, but are instead expressing an *action*, directing Python to

- define the identifier `a` to be a new variable (if no variable `a` already exists).
- associate the variable `a` with the integer data-type value `1234`.

The right side of an assignment statement can be any expression. In such cases, Python evaluates the expression and associates the variable on the left side with the value produced by the expression. For example, when we write `c = a + b`, we are expressing this action: "associate the variable `c` with the sum of the values associated with the variables `a` and `b`." The left side of an assignment statement must be a single variable. So, for example, both `1234 = a` and `a + b = b + a` are invalid statements in Python. *In short, the meaning of = in a program is decidedly not the same as in a mathematical equation.*

Informal trace. An effective way to keep track of the values associated with variables is to use a table like the one at right, with one line giving the values after each statement has been executed. Such a table is called a *trace*, and is a time-honored technique for understanding the behavior of a program. We use traces like this throughout this book.

	a	b	c
`a = 1234`	1234		
`b = 99`	1234	99	
`c = a + b`	1234	99	1333

Your first informal trace

WHILE DESCRIPTIONS OF THIS SORT ARE a valid way to understand the Python code in this section, it is worthwhile at the outset to consider in more detail how Python represents data-type values using objects and to revisit the definitions in that context. While these definitions are more complicated than the ones just considered, it is important for you to understand the underlying mechanism, as it is used consistently throughout Python and prepares you for object-oriented programming in CHAPTER 3.

Objects. All data values in a Python program are represented by *objects* and relationships among objects. An *object* is an in-computer-memory representation of a value from a particular data type. Each object is characterized by its *identity*, *type*, and *value*.

- The *identity* uniquely identifies an object. You should think of it as the location in the computer's memory (or *memory address*) where the object is stored.
- The *type* of an object completely specifies its behavior—the set of values it might represent and the set of operations that can be performed on it.
- The *value* of an object is the data-type value that it represents.

Each object stores one value; for example, an object of type `int` can store the value `1234` or the value `99` or the value `1333`. Different objects may store the same value. For example, one object of type `str` might store the value `'hello'`, and another object of type `str` also might store the same value `'hello'`. We can apply to an object any of the operations defined by its type (and only those operations). For example, we can multiply two `int` objects but not two `str` objects.

Object references. An *object reference* is nothing more than a concrete representation of the object's identity (the memory address where the object is stored). Python programs use object references either to access the object's value or to manipulate the object references themselves, as you will see.

Formal object-based definitions. Now, we consider more formal definitions for the terminology we have been using.

- A *literal* is a directive to Python to create an object having the specified value.
- A *variable* is a name for an object reference. We use diagrams like the one at right to show the *binding* of a variable to an object.
- An *expression* is a directive to Python to perform the indicated operations, producing an object having the value defined by the expression.
- An *assignment statement* is a directive to Python to bind the variable on the left side of the = operator to the object produced by evaluating the expression on the right side (regardless of the object, if any, to which the variable was previously bound).

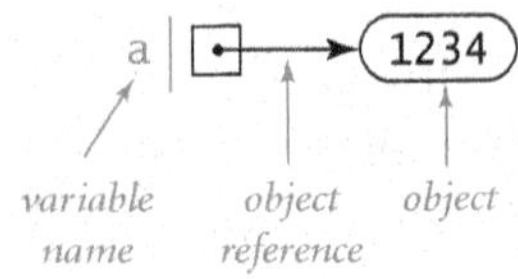

A variable refers to an object

Object-level trace. For a more complete understanding, we sometimes keep track of objects and references in traces, as in the *object-level trace* in the figure at right. For our example, the object-level trace illustrates the full effect of the three assignment statements:

- The statement `a = 1234` creates an `int` object whose value is `1234`; it then binds the variable `a` to this new `int` object.
- The statement `b = 99` creates an `int` object whose value is `99`; it then binds the variable `b` to this new `int` object.
- The statement `c = a + b` creates the `int` object whose value is `1333` as the sum of the value of the `int` object bound to `a` and the value of the `int` object bound to `b`; it then binds the variable `c` to the new `int` object.

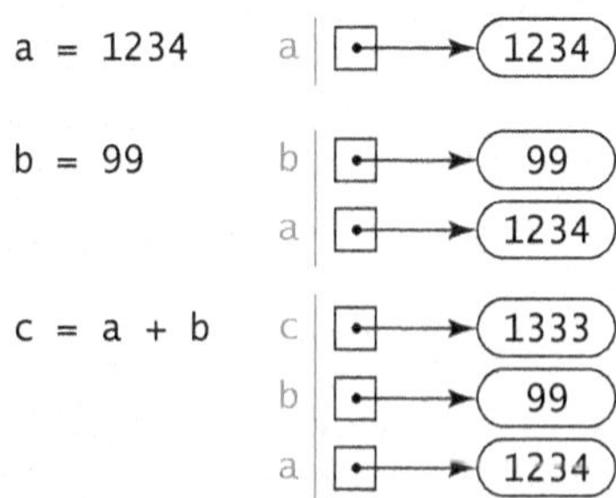

Your first object-level trace

Throughout this book, we generally use the more succinct and intuitive informal traces just discussed, reserving object-level traces for situations when they provide a more insightful view of the underlying computation.

Example: incrementing a variable. As a first check on these concepts, consider the following code, which binds the variable `i` to an `int` object whose value is `17`, and then increments it:

```
i = 17
i = i + 1
```

As we have noted, this second statement is nonsensical as a mathematical equality, but it is a very common operation in Python programming. Specifically, these two statements are a directive to Python to take the following actions:

- Create an `int` object whose value is `17` and bind the variable `i` to that object.
- Evaluate the expression `i + 1` and create a new `int` object whose value is `18`.
- Bind the variable `i` to this new object.

You can consult the traces at right to see the results after Python executes each statement.

informal trace

	i
`i = 17`	17
`i = i + 1`	18

object-level trace with new object

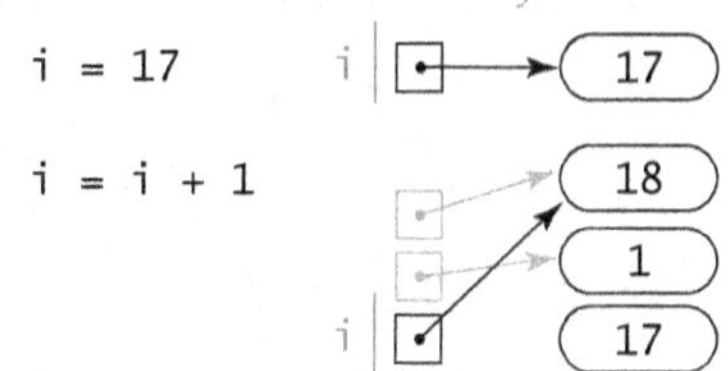

Incrementing a variable

This simple code fragment leads us to consider two aspects of the process of creating an object in a bit more detail. First, the assignment statement `i = i + 1` does not change the value of any object. Instead, it creates a new object (with the desired value) and binds the variable `i` to this new object. Second, after Python executes the assignment statement `i = i + 1`, there is no variable bound to the object whose value is `17` (or to the object whose value is `1`). Python takes responsibility for managing memory resources. When it identifies that a program can no longer access an object, it automatically reclaims the memory used to store the object.

Example: exchanging two variables. As a second check on these concepts, convince yourself that this code *exchanges* `a` and `b` (more precisely, the objects bound to `a` and `b`):

```
t = a
a = b
b = t
```

To do so, assume that `a` and `b` are bound to objects having two different values—`1234` and `99`, respectively—and consult the traces at right to convince yourself, step by step, that:

- `t = a` assigns `a` to `t`. That is, it assigns `a` (an object reference) to `t`, and thus `a` and `t` are bound to the same object—the `int` object whose value is `1234`.
- `a = b` assigns `b` to `a`. That is, it assigns `b` (an object reference) to `a`, and thus `a` and `b` are bound to the same object—the `int` object whose value is `99`.
- `b = t` assigns `t` to `b`. That is, it assigns `t` (an object reference) to `b`, and thus `t` and `b` are bound to the same object—the `int` object whose value is `1234`.

Thus, the references are exchanged: the variable `a` now is bound to the object whose value is `99` and the variable `b` now is bound to the object whose value is `1234`.

informal trace

	a	b	t
	1234	99	
`t = a`	1234	99	1234
`a = b`	99	99	1234
`b = t`	99	1234	1234

object-level trace

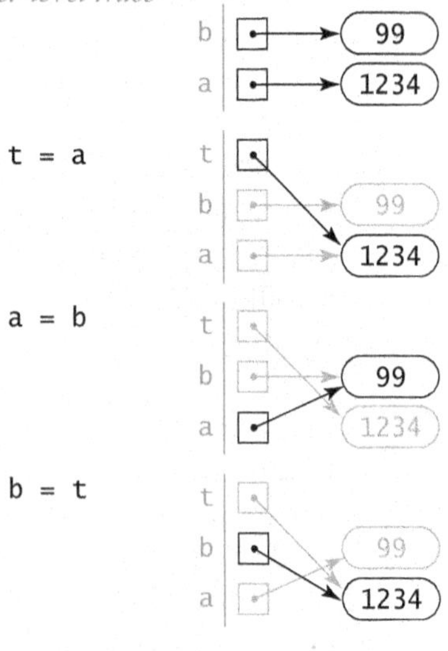

Exchanging two variables

Abbreviation alert. From this point forward we often abbreviate our descriptions of Python statements involving variables, objects, and object references. For example, we often omit some or all of the bracketed phrases in sentences like the examples here. When describing the statement `a = 1234`, we might say:

- "Bind/set `a` to [*an* `int` *object whose value is*] `1234`."
- "Assign to `a` [*a reference to*] [*an* `int` *object whose value is*] `1234`."

Similarly, after Python executes the statement `a = 1234`, we might say:

- "`a` is [*bound/set to*] [*an* `int` *object whose value is*] `1234`."
- "`a` is [*a reference to*] [*an* `int` *object whose value is*] `1234`."
- "[*The value of*] [*the* `int` *object referenced by*] `a` *is* `1234`."

So, when describing the statement `c = a + b`, we might say "`c` is the sum of `a` and `b`" instead of the more precise but untenably verbose "`c` is bound to an object whose value is the sum of the value of the object bound to `a` and the value of the object bound to `b`." We use language that is as succinct as possible, but no more precise than necessary to make the point at hand.

We refer to binding a variable to an object for the first time in a program as *defining* and *initializing* the variable. So, when describing the statement `a = 1234` in our first trace, we might say that it "defines the variable `a` and initializes it to `1234`." In Python, you cannot define a variable without simultaneously initializing it.

YOU MIGHT WONDER WHETHER THE DISTINCTION between an object and a reference to an object is purely pedantic. In fact, understanding the difference between objects and references is the key to mastering many important features of Python programming, including *functions* (in CHAPTER 2), *object-oriented programming* (in CHAPTER 3), and *data structures* (in CHAPTER 4).

Next, we consider the details for the data types that you will use most often (strings, integers, floating-point numbers, and boolean values), along with sample code illustrating their use. To use a data type, you need to know not just its set of values, but also which operations you can perform, the language mechanism for invoking the operations, and the conventions for specifying literals.

Strings The `str` data type represents strings, for use in text processing. The value of a `str` object is a sequence of *characters*. You can specify a `str` literal by enclosing a sequence of characters in matching single quotes; for example `'ab'`, represents a `str` object that stores two characters, the letter `'a'` followed by the letter `'b'`. There are many possible characters, but we usually restrict attention to the ones that represent letters, digits, symbols, and whitespace characters such as tab and newline. You can use a backslash to specify characters that otherwise would have special meaning. For example, you can specify the tab, newline, backslash, and single quote characters using the *escape sequences* `'\t'`, `'\n'`, `'\\'`, and `'\''`, respectively.

values	*sequences of characters*
typical literals	`'Hello, World'` `'Python\'s'`
operation	*concatenation*
operator	`+`

Python's `str` data type

You can *concatenate* two strings using the operator +. That is, the + operator takes two `str` objects as operands and produces a new `str` object whose value is the sequence of characters in the first `str` object followed by the sequence of characters in the second `str` object. For example, the expression `'123' + '456'` evaluates to the `str` object whose value is `'123456'`. This example illustrates that applying the + operator to two `str` objects has quite different behavior (string concatenation) than applying the + operator to two `int` objects (addition).

expression	*value*	*comment*
`'Hello, ' + 'World'`	`'Hello, World'`	*concatenation*
`'123' + '456'`	`'123456'`	*not addition*
`'1234' + ' + ' + '99'`	`'1234 + 99'`	*two concatenations*
`'123' + 456`	*run-time error*	*second operand is not a* `str`

Typical `str` expressions

Abbreviation alert. From this point forward we use the term *string* to mean *an object of type* `str` whenever the rigor of the full phrase is unnecessary. We also use `'abc'` instead of *an object of type `str` whose value is* `'abc'`.

Program 1.2.1 String concatenation example (ruler.py)

```
import stdio

ruler1 = '1'
ruler2 = ruler1 + ' 2 ' + ruler1
ruler3 = ruler2 + ' 3 ' + ruler2
ruler4 = ruler3 + ' 4 ' + ruler3
stdio.writeln(ruler1)
stdio.writeln(ruler2)
stdio.writeln(ruler3)
stdio.writeln(ruler4)
```

```
% python ruler.py
1
1 2 1
1 2 1 3 1 2 1
1 2 1 3 1 2 1 4 1 2 1 3 1 2 1
```

This program writes the relative lengths of the subdivisions on a ruler. The nth line of output is the relative lengths of the marks on a ruler subdivided in intervals of 1/2ⁿ of an inch.

String concatenation is sufficiently powerful to allow us to attack some nontrivial computing tasks. As an example, `ruler.py` (Program 1.2.1) computes a table of values of the ruler function that describes the relative lengths of the marks on a ruler. One noteworthy feature of this computation is that it illustrates how easy it is to craft short programs that produce huge amounts of output. If you extend this program in the obvious way to write five lines, six lines, seven lines, and so forth, you will see that each time you add just two statements to this program, you increase the size of its output by precisely one more than a factor of 2. Specifically, if the program writes n lines, the nth line contains $2^n - 1$ numbers. For example, if you were to add statements in this way so that the program writes 30 lines, it would attempt to write more than 1 billion numbers.

The ruler function for $n = 4$

Next we consider two convenient mechanisms in Python for converting numbers to strings and strings to numbers.

Converting numbers to strings for output. Python provides the built-in function `str()` to convert numbers to strings. For example, `str(123)` evaluates to the `str` object `'123'`, and `str(123.45)` evaluates to the `str` object `'123.45'`. If the argument to either `stdio.write()` or `stdio.writeln()` is not of type `str`, then these two functions automatically call the `str()` function on its argument to generate the string representation. For example, `stdio.write(123)`, `stdio.write(str(123))`, and `stdio.write('123')` all write `123`.

Our most frequent use of the string concatenation operator is to chain together the results of a computation for output with `stdio.write()` and `stdio.writeln()`, often in conjunction with the `str()` function, as in this example:

```
stdio.writeln(str(a) + ' + ' + str(b) + ' = ' + str(a+b))
```

If `a` and `b` are `int` objects whose values are `1234` and `99`, respectively, then that statement writes the line of output `1234 + 99 = 1333`. We consider the `str` data type first precisely because we need it to produce this sort of output in programs that process other types of data.

Converting strings to numbers for input. Python also provides built-in functions to convert strings (such as the ones we type as command-line arguments) to numeric objects. We use the Python built-in functions `int()` and `float()` for this purpose. For example, typing `int('1234')` in program text is equivalent to typing the `int` literal `1234`. If the user types `1234` as the first command-line argument, then the code `int(sys.argv[1])` also evaluates to the `int` object whose value is `1234`. You will see several examples of this usage in this section.

WITH THESE FEATURES, OUR VIEW OF each Python program as a black box that takes string arguments and produces string results is still valid, but we can now interpret those strings as numbers and use them as the basis for meaningful computation.

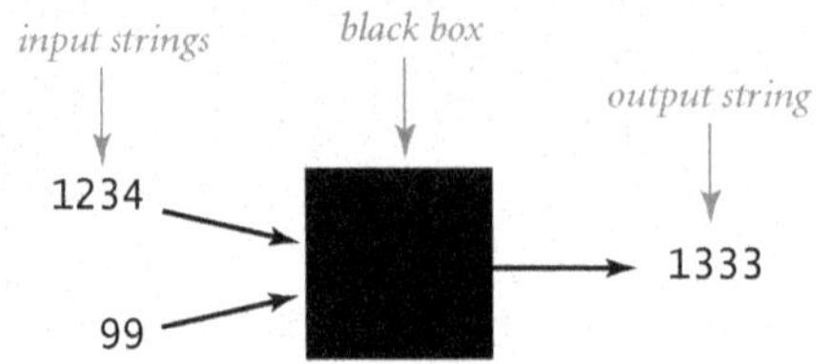

A bird's-eye view of a Python program (revised)

Integers The int data type represents integers or natural numbers. We can specify an int literal with a sequence of the digits 0 through 9. When Python encounters an int literal, it creates an int object that stores the specified value. We use int objects frequently not just because they occur frequently in the real world, but also because they arise naturally when we are composing programs.

Python includes operators for common arithmetic operations on integers, including + for addition, - for subtraction, * for multiplication, // for floored division, % for remainder, and ** for exponentiation. These binary operators take two int objects as operands and typically produce an int object as a result. Python also includes the unary operators + and - to specify the sign of an integer. All of these operators are defined just as in grade school (keeping in mind that the floored division operator results in an integer): given two int objects a and b, the expression a // b evaluates to the number of times b goes into a with the fractional part discarded, and a % b evaluates to the remainder that you get when you divide a by b. For example, 17 // 3 evaluates to 5, and 17 % 3 evaluates to 2. Floored division or remainder with a zero divisor raises a ZeroDivisionError at run time.

values	*integers*						
typical literals	1234 99 0 1000000						
operations	*sign*	*add*	*subtract*	*multiply*	*floored divide*	*remainder*	*power*
operators	+ -	+	-	*	//	%	**

Python's int data type

Program 1.2.2 (intops.py) illustrates basic operations for manipulating int objects, such as the use of expressions involving arithmetic operators. It also demonstrates the use of the built-in function int() to convert strings on the command line to int objects, as well as the use of the built-in function str() to convert int objects to strings for output.

Abbreviation alert. From this point forward we use the term *integer* to mean *an object of type* int whenever the rigor of the full phrase is unnecessary. We also use 123 instead of *an object of type* int *whose value is* 123.

Program 1.2.2 Integer operators (`intops.py`)

```
import sys
import stdio

a = int(sys.argv[1])
b = int(sys.argv[2])

total  = a +  b
diff   = a -  b
prod   = a *  b
quot   = a // b
rem    = a %  b
exp    = a ** b

stdio.writeln(str(a) + ' +  ' + str(b) + ' = ' + str(total))
stdio.writeln(str(a) + ' -  ' + str(b) + ' = ' + str(diff))
stdio.writeln(str(a) + ' *  ' + str(b) + ' = ' + str(prod))
stdio.writeln(str(a) + ' // ' + str(b) + ' = ' + str(quot))
stdio.writeln(str(a) + ' %  ' + str(b) + ' = ' + str(rem))
stdio.writeln(str(a) + ' ** ' + str(b) + ' = ' + str(exp))
```

This program accepts integer command-line arguments `a` *and* `b`*, uses them to illustrate integer operators, and writes the results. Arithmetic for integers is built into Python. Most of this code is devoted to reading input and writing output; the actual arithmetic is in the simple statements in the middle of the program that assign values to* `total`*,* `diff`*,* `prod`*,* `quot`*,* `rem`*, and* `exp`*.*

```
% python intops.py 1234 5
1234 +  5 = 1239
1234 -  5 = 1229
1234 *  5 = 6170
1234 // 5 = 246
1234 %  5 = 4
1234 ** 5 = 2861381721051424
```

In Python, the range of `int` values is arbitrarily large, constrained only by the amount of memory available on your computer system. Many other programming languages constrain the range of integers. For example, the Java programming language constrains integers to the range -2^{31} (–2147483648) to $2^{31} - 1$ (2147483647). On the one hand, Python programmers do not have to worry about integers becoming too large to fit in the allowed range; on the other hand, Python programmers *do* have to worry about a faulty program filling the memory of their computer with one or more extremely huge integers.

expression	*value*	*comment*
`99`	`99`	*integer literal*
`+99`	`99`	*positive sign*
`-99`	`-99`	*negative sign*
`5 + 3`	`8`	*addition*
`5 - 3`	`2`	*subtraction*
`5 * 3`	`15`	*multiplication*
`5 // 3`	`1`	*no fractional part*
`5 % 3`	`2`	*remainder*
`5 ** 3`	`125`	*exponentiation*
`5 // 0`	*run-time error*	*division by zero*
`3 * 5 - 2`	`13`	`*` *has precedence*
`3 + 5 // 2`	`5`	`//` *has precedence*
`3 - 5 - 2`	`-4`	*left associative*
`(3 - 5) - 2`	`-4`	*better style*
`3 - (5 - 2)`	`0`	*unambiguous*
`2 ** 2 ** 3`	`256`	*right associative*
`2 ** 1000`	`107150...376`	*arbitrarily large*

Typical `int` expressions

Python 2 alert. *In Python 3, the / operator has the same behavior as the floating-point division operator when both its operands are integers. In Python 2, the / operator has the same behavior as the floored division operator // when both its operands are integers. For example,* `17 / 2` *evaluates to* `8.5` *in Python 3 and to* `8` *in Python 2. For compatibility among Python versions, we do not use the / operator with two* `int` *operands in this book.*

Floating-point numbers The `float` data type is for representing *floating-point* numbers, for use in scientific and commercial applications. We use floating-point numbers to represent real numbers, but they are decidedly not the same as real numbers! There are infinitely many real numbers, but we can represent only a finite number of floating-point numbers in any digital computer. Floating-point numbers do approximate real numbers sufficiently well that we can use them in applications, but we often need to cope with the fact that we cannot always do exact computations.

expression	*value*	*comment*
`3.14159`	`3.14159`	*floating-point literal*
`6.02e23`	`6.02e23`	*floating-point literal*
`3.141 + 2.0`	`5.141`	*addition*
`3.141 - 2.0`	`1.141`	*subtraction*
`3.141 * 2.0`	`6.282`	*multiplication*
`3.141 / 2.0`	`1.5705`	*division*
`5.0 / 3.0`	`1.6666666666666667`	*17 digits of precision*
`3.141 ** 2.0`	`9.865881`	*exponentiation*
`1.0 / 0.0`	*run-time error*	*division by zero*
`2.0 ** 1000.0`	*run-time error*	*too large to represent*
`math.sqrt(2.0)`	`1.4142135623730951`	`math` *module function*
`math.sqrt(-1.0)`	*run-time error*	*square root of a negative*

Typical `float` *expressions*

We can specify a floating-point literal using a sequence of digits with a decimal point. For example, `3.14159` represents an approximation to π. Alternatively, we can use a notation like scientific notation: the literal `6.022e23` represents the number 6.022×10^{23}. As with integers, you can use these conventions to express floating-point literals in your programs or to provide floating-point numbers as string arguments on the command line.

Program 1.2.3 (`floatops.py`) illustrates the basic operations for manipulating `float` objects. Python includes the operators you expect for floating-point numbers, including + for addition, - for subtraction, * for multiplication, / for di-

values	*real numbers*				
typical literals	`3.14159` `6.022e23` `2.0` `1.4142135623730951`				
operations	*addition*	*subtraction*	*multiplication*	*division*	*exponentiation*
operators	`+`	`-`	`*`	`/`	`**`

Python's `float` *data type*

Program 1.2.3 Float operators (`floatops.py`)

```
import sys
import stdio

a = float(sys.argv[1])
b = float(sys.argv[2])

total  = a +  b
diff   = a -  b
prod   = a *  b
quot   = a /  b
exp    = a ** b

stdio.writeln(str(a) + ' +  ' + str(b) + ' = ' + str(total))
stdio.writeln(str(a) + ' -  ' + str(b) + ' = ' + str(diff))
stdio.writeln(str(a) + ' *  ' + str(b) + ' = ' + str(prod))
stdio.writeln(str(a) + ' /  ' + str(b) + ' = ' + str(quot))
stdio.writeln(str(a) + ' ** ' + str(b) + ' = ' + str(exp))
```

This program takes floating-point numbers `a` *and* `b` *as command-line arguments, uses them to illustrate floating-point operations, and writes the results. Arithmetic for floating-point numbers is built into Python. As with* Program 1.2.2, *most of this code is devoted to reading input and writing output; the actual arithmetic is in the simple statements in the middle of the program that assign values to* `total`, `diff`, `prod`, `quot`, *and* `exp`.

```
% python floatops.py 123.456 78.9
123.456 +  78.9 = 202.356
123.456 -  78.9 = 44.556
123.456 *  78.9 = 9740.6784
123.456 /  78.9 = 1.5647148288973383
123.456 ** 78.9 = 1.0478827916671325e+165
```

vision, and `**` for exponentiation. These operators take two `float` objects as operands and typically produce a `float` object as a result. PROGRAM 1.2.3 also illustrates the use of the `float()` function to convert a `str` object to a `float` object, and the use of the `str()` function to convert a `float` object to a `str` object.

When working with floating-point numbers, one of the first things that you will encounter is the issue of precision: `5.0/2.0` evaluates to `2.5` but `5.0/3.0` evaluates to `1.6666666666666667`. Typically, floating-point numbers have 15-17 decimal digits of precision. In SECTION 1.5, you will learn Python's mechanism for controlling the number of digits that you see in output. Until then, we will work with Python's default output format. Though there are myriad details to consider when calculations involve `float` objects, you can use them in a natural way and compose Python programs instead of using a calculator for all kinds of calculations. For example, `quadratic.py` (PROGRAM 1.2.4) shows the use of `float` objects in computing the two roots of a quadratic equation using the quadratic formula.

Note the use of the `math.sqrt()` function in this program. The standard `math` module defines trigonometric functions, logarithm/exponential functions, and other common mathematical functions. When Python calls the function, it produces a value—the value computed by the function. You can use the `math` module in the same way that we have been using `stdio` in every program since `helloworld.py`: place the statement `import math` near the beginning of the program and then call functions using syntax such as `math.sqrt(x)`. We discuss in more detail the mechanism behind this arrangement in SECTION 2.1 and provide more details about the `math` module at the end of this section.

As illustrated in the sample execution accompanying PROGRAM 1.2.4, `quadratic.py` does not check for error conditions. In particular, it assumes that the roots are real numbers. If not, it calls `math.sqrt()` with a negative number as its argument, which raises a `ValueError` at run time. Generally, it is good programming practice to check for such errors and inform the user about them. We will discuss how to do so after you learn a few more Python language mechanisms.

Abbreviation alert. From this point forward we use the term *float* to mean *an object of type* `float` whenever the rigor of the full phrase is unnecessary. We also use `123.456` instead of *an object of type* `float` *whose value is* `123.456`.

Program 1.2.4 Quadratic formula (quadratic.py)

```
import math
import sys
import stdio

b = float(sys.argv[1])
c = float(sys.argv[2])

discriminant = b*b - 4.0*c
d = math.sqrt(discriminant)
stdio.writeln((-b + d) / 2.0)
stdio.writeln((-b - d) / 2.0)
```

This program writes the roots of the polynomial $x^2 + bx + c$, using the quadratic formula. For example, the roots of $x^2 - 3x + 2$ are 1 and 2 since we can factor the equation as $(x - 1)(x - 2)$; the roots of $x^2 - x - 1$ are ϕ and $1 - \phi$, where ϕ is the golden ratio, and the roots of $x^2 + x + 1$ are not real numbers.

```
% python quadratic.py -3.0 2.0
2.0
1.0

% python quadratic.py -1.0 -1.0
1.618033988749895
-0.6180339887498949

% python quadratic.py 1.0 1.0
Traceback (most recent call last):
  File "quadratic.py", line 9, in <module>
    d = math.sqrt(discriminant)
ValueError: math domain error
```

values	true or false		
literals	True False		
operations	*and*	*or*	*not*
operators	and	or	not

Python's `bool` data type

Booleans The `bool` data type represents *truth values* (either *true* or *false*) from logic. The data type has two possible values and two corresponding literals: `True` and `False`. The `bool` operations that we use have operands that are either `True` or `False` and evaluate to a result that is also either `True` or `False`. This simplicity is deceiving—the `bool` data type lies at the foundation of computer science. The operators defined for `bool` objects (`and`, `or`, and `not`) are known as *logical operators* and have familiar definitions:

- `a and b` is `True` if both operands are `True`, and `False` if either is `False`.
- `a or b` is `False` if both operands are `False`, and `True` if either is `True`.
- `not a` is `True` if `a` is `False`, and `False` if `a` is `True`.

Despite the intuitive nature of these definitions, it is worthwhile to fully specify each possibility for each operation in *truth tables*, as shown at the bottom of this page. The `not` operator has only one operand: its result for each of the two possible values of the operand is specified in the second column. The `and` and `or` operators each have two operands: the results for each of the four possible values of these operands are specified in the right two columns.

We can use these operators with parentheses (and precedence rules) to develop arbitrarily complex expressions, each of which specifies a boolean function. The `not` operator has higher precedence than the `and` operator, which in turn has higher precedence than the `or` operator.

Often the same function appears in different guises. For example, the expressions `(a and b)` and `not (not a or not b)` are equivalent. One way to establish that this is the case is to use a *truth-table proof* like the one at the top of the next page, which checks all possibilities.

a	not a
False	True
True	False

a	b	a and b	a or b
False	False	False	False
False	True	False	True
True	False	False	True
True	True	True	True

Truth-table definitions of `bool` operations

a	b	a and b	not a	not b	not a or not b	not (not a or not b)
False	False	False	True	True	True	False
False	True	False	True	False	True	False
True	False	False	False	True	True	False
True	True	True	False	False	False	True

Truth-table proof that a and b *and* !(not a or not b) *are identical*

The study of manipulating expressions of this kind is known as *Boolean logic*. This field of mathematics is fundamental to computing: it plays an essential role in the design and operation of computer hardware itself, and it is also a starting point for the theoretical foundations of computation. In the present context, we are interested in `bool` expressions because we use them to control the behavior of our programs. Typically, a particular condition of interest is specified as a boolean expression and a piece of program code is written to execute one set of statements if the expression evaluates to `True` and a different set of statements if the expression evaluates to `False`. The mechanics of doing so are the topic of SECTION 1.3.

Abbreviation alert. From this point forward we use the term *boolean* to mean *an object of type* `bool` whenever the rigor of the full phrase is unnecessary. We also use `True` instead of *the object of type* `bool` *whose value is* `True` and `False` instead of *the object of type* `bool` *whose value is* `False`.

Comparisons Some *mixed-type* operators take operands of one type and produce a result of another type. The most important operators of this kind are the *comparison operators* ==, !=, <, <=, >, and >=, which all are defined for both integers and floats and evaluate to a boolean result. Since operations are defined only with respect to data types, each of these operators stands for many operations, one for

op	*meaning*	True	False
==	*equal*	2 == 2	2 == 3
!=	*not equal*	3 != 2	2 != 2
<	*less than*	2 < 13	2 < 2
<=	*less than or equal*	2 <= 2	3 <= 2
>	*greater than*	13 > 2	2 > 13
>=	*greater than or equal*	3 >= 2	2 >= 3

Comparisons with int *operands and a* bool *result*

each data type. Both operands must be of compatible type. The result is always a boolean.

non-negative discriminant?	`(b*b - 4.0*a*c) >= 0.0`
beginning of a century?	`(year % 100) == 0`
legal month?	`(month >= 1) and (month <= 12)`

Typical comparison expressions

Even without going into the details of number representation, it is clear that the operations for the various types are really quite different. For example, it is one thing to compare two integers to check that `(2 <= 2)` is `True`, but quite another to compare two floats to check whether `(2.0 <= 0.002e3)` is `True`. Still, these operations are well defined and useful to compose code that tests for conditions such as `(b*b - 4.0*a*c) >= 0.0`, which is frequently needed, as you will see.

Comparison operators have lower precedence than arithmetic operators and higher precedence than boolean operators, so you do not need the parentheses in an expression like `(b*b - 4.0*a*c) >= 0.0`, and you could write an expression like `month >= 1 and month <= 12` without parentheses to test whether `month` is between 1 and 12. (It is better style to use the parentheses, however.)

Comparison operations, together with boolean logic, provide the basis for decision making in Python programs. PROGRAM 1.2.5 (`leapyear.py`) shows the use of boolean expressions and comparison operations to compute whether a given year is a leap year. You can find other examples in the exercises at the end of this section. More importantly, in SECTION 1.3 we will see the role that boolean expressions play in more sophisticated programs.

PROGRAM 1.2.5 also illustrates a special and useful property of the logical operators known as *short-circuiting*: the `and` operator evaluates the second operand only if the first operand is `True`; the `or` operator evaluates the second operand only if the first operand is `False`. For example, in `leapyear.py`, Python evaluates the comparison expression `(year % 100) != 0` only if the year is divisible by 4 and the comparison expression `(year % 400) != 0` only if the year is divisible by 100.

Functions and APIs As we have seen, many programming tasks involve using not only built-in operators, but also *functions* that perform useful operations. We distinguish three kinds of functions: *built-in functions* (such as `int()`, `float()`,

Program 1.2.5 *Leap year* (leapyear.py)

```
import sys
import stdio

year = int(sys.argv[1])

isLeapYear = (year % 4 == 0)
isLeapYear = isLeapYear and ((year % 100) != 0)
isLeapYear = isLeapYear or  ((year % 400) == 0)

stdio.writeln(isLeapYear)
```

This program tests whether an integer corresponds to a leap year in the Gregorian calendar. A year is a leap year if it is divisible by 4 (2004), unless it is divisible by 100 in which case it is not (1900), unless it is divisible by 400 in which case it is (2000).

```
% python leapyear.py 2016
True
% python leapyear.py 1900
False
% python leapyear.py 2000
True
```

and `str()`) that you can use directly in any Python program, *standard functions* (such as `math.sqrt()`) that are defined in a Python standard module and are available in any program that imports the module, and *booksite functions* (such as `stdio.write()` and `stdio.writeln()`) that are defined in our booksite modules and available for you to use after you have made them available to Python and imported them. The number of built-in functions, standard functions, and booksite functions available to you is very large. As you learn to program, you will learn to use more and more of those functions, but it is best at the beginning to restrict your attention to a relatively small set. In this chapter, you have already used some functions for writing, for converting data from one type to another, and for computing mathematical functions. We will describe some more useful functions in this section. In later chapters, you will learn not just how to use other functions, but how to define and use your own functions.

For convenience, we summarize the functions that you need to know how to use in tables like the one shown on the facing page. It includes examples of built-in functions, booksite functions from our `stdio` module, and standard functions from Python's `math` and `random` modules. Such a table is known as an *application programming interface* (API). The first column specifies the information you need to use the function, including its name and its number of arguments; the second column describes its purpose.

In your code, you can call a function by typing its name followed by *arguments*, enclosed in parentheses and separated by commas. When Python executes your program, we say that it *calls* (or *evaluates*) the function with the given arguments and that the function *returns* a value. More precisely, the function returns a reference to an object, which has a value. A function call is an expression, so you can use a function call in the same way that you use variables and literals to build up more complicated expressions. For example, you can compose expressions like `math.sin(x) * math.cos(y)` and so on. You can also represent an argument using an expression—Python evaluates the expression and passes the result as an argument to the function. So, you can compose code like `math.sqrt(b*b - 4.0*a*c)` and Python knows what you mean.

In some cases, a function can have *default values* for optional arguments. The function `math.log()` is an example—it takes the base of the logarithm as an optional second argument, defaulting to the natural logarithm (base *e*) if you do not specify a second argument.

function call	*return value*	*comment*
`abs(-2.0)`	`2.0`	*built-in function*
`max(3, 1)`	`3`	*built-in function with two arguments*
`stdio.write('Hello')`		*booksite function (with side effect)*
`math.log(1000, math.e)`	`6.907755278982137`	*function in* `math` *module*
`math.log(1000)`	`6.907755278982137`	*second argument defaults to* `math.e`
`math.sqrt(-1.0)`	*run-time error*	*square root of a negative number*
`random.random()`	`0.3151503393010261`	*function in* `random` *module*

Typical function calls

function call	*description*
built-in functions	
`abs(x)`	*absolute value of* `x`
`max(a, b)`	*maximum value of* `a` *and* `b`
`min(a, b)`	*minimum value of* `a` *and* `b`
booksite functions for standard output from our `stdio` *module*	
`stdio.write(x)`	*write* `x` *to standard output*
`stdio.writeln(x)`	*write* `x` *to standard output, followed by a newline*

Note 1: Any type of data can be used (and will be automatically converted to `str`*).*
Note 2: If no argument is specified, `x` *defaults to the empty string.*

function call	*description*
standard functions from Python's `math` *module*	
`math.sin(x)`	*sine of* `x` *(expressed in radians)*
`math.cos(x)`	*cosine of* `x` *(expressed in radians)*
`math.tan(x)`	*tangent of* `x` *(expressed in radians)*
`math.atan2(y, x)`	*polar angle of the point* (`x`, `y`)
`math.hypot(x, y)`	*Euclidean distance between the origin and* (`x`, `y`)
`math.radians(x)`	*conversion of* `x` *(expressed in degrees) to radians*
`math.degrees(x)`	*conversion of* `x` *(expressed in radians) to degrees*
`math.exp(x)`	*exponential function of* `x` (e^x)
`math.log(x, b)`	*base-*`b` *logarithm of* `x` ($\log_b x$) *(the base* `b` *defaults to e—the natural logarithm)*
`math.sqrt(x)`	*square root of* `x`
`math.erf(x)`	*error function of* `x`
`math.gamma(x)`	*gamma function of* `x`

Note: The `math` *module also includes the inverse functions* `asin()`, `acos()`, *and* `atan()` *and the constant variables* `e` (`2.718281828459045`) *and* `pi` (`3.141592653589793`).

function call	*description*
standard functions from Python's `random` *module*	
`random.random()`	*a random* `float` *in the interval [0, 1)*
`random.randrange(x, y)`	*a random* `int` *in* [`x`, `y`) *where* `x` *and* `y` *are* `int`*s*

APIs for some commonly used Python functions

With three exceptions, the functions on the previous page are *pure functions*—given the same arguments, they always return the same value, without producing any observable *side effect*. The function `random.random()` is impure because it returns potentially a different value each time it is called; the functions `stdio.write()` and `stdio.writeln()` are impure because they produce side effects—writing strings to standard output. In APIs, we use a verb phrase to describe the behavior of a function that produces side effects; otherwise, we use a noun phrase to describe the return value.

The `math` module also defines the constant variables `math.pi` (for π) and `math.e` (for *e*), so that you can use those names to refer to those constants in your programs. For example, the function call `math.sin(math.pi/2)` returns `1.0` (because `math.sin()` takes its argument in radians) and the function call `math.log(math.e)` returns `1.0` (because the default base for `math.log()` is *e*).

These APIs are typical of the online documentation that is the standard in modern programming. There is extensive online documentation of the Python APIs that is used by professional programmers, and it is available to you (if you are interested) through our booksite. You do not need to consult the online documentation to understand the code in this book or to compose similar code, because we present and explain in the text all of the functions that we use in APIs like these and summarize them in the endpapers.

More important, in CHAPTERS 2 and 3 you will learn how to develop your own APIs and to implement functions for your own use.

Abbreviation alert. From this point forward we often abbreviate our descriptions of Python statements involving functions and function calls. For example, we often omit the bracketed phrases in sentences such as the following description of the function call `math.sqrt(4.0)`: "The function call `math.sqrt(4.0)` returns [*a reference to*] [*a `float` object whose value is*] `2.0`." So we might say, "The function call `sqrt(16.0)` returns `4.0`" instead of the more accurate but more verbose "When we pass to `math.sqrt()` a reference to an object of type `float` whose value is `16.0`, it returns a reference to an object of type `float` whose value is `4.0`." We also use the term *return value* to describe the object whose reference is returned by a function.

Type conversion Typical programming tasks involve processing multiple types of data. You should always be aware of the type of data that your program is processing, because only by knowing the type can you know precisely which set of values each object can have and which operations you can perform. In particular, we often need to convert data from one type to another. For example, suppose that we wish to compute the average of the four integers 1, 2, 3, and 4. Naturally, the expression `(1 + 2 + 3 + 4) / 4` comes to mind, but it does not produce the desired result in many programming languages, because of type conversion conventions. Indeed, as we have already noted, Python 3 and Python 2 produce different results for this expression, so it is a worthy example for introducing this topic.

The problem stems from the fact that the operands are integers, but it is natural to expect a float for the result, so conversion from integer to float is necessary at some point. There are two ways to do so in Python.

Explicit type conversion. One approach is to use a function that takes an argument of one type (the object to be converted) and returns an object of another type. We have already used the built-in functions `int()`, `float()`, and `str()` to convert from strings to integers or floats, and vice versa. This is by far their most common usage, but you can also use them (and the additional function `round()`) to convert between integers and floats, as shown in the API at the top of the next page. For example, you can use either `int(x)` or `int(round(x))` to convert from a float to an integer and `float(x)` to convert from an integer to a float. So, the expression `float(1 + 2 + 3 + 4) / float(4)` evaluates to `2.5` in both Python 3 and Python 2, as you would expect.

expression	*value*	*type*
explicit		
`str(2.718)`	`'2.718'`	`str`
`str(2)`	`'2'`	`str`
`int(2.718)`	`2`	`int`
`int(3.14159)`	`3`	`int`
`float(3)`	`3.0`	`float`
`int(round(2.718))`	`3`	`int`
implicit		
`3.0 * 2`	`6.0`	`float`
`10 / 4.0`	`2.5`	`float`
`math.sqrt(4)`	`2.0`	`float`

Typical type conversions

Python 2 alert. *In Python 3, `round(x)` returns an integer; in Python 2, `round(x)` returns a float. In this book, we always use the expression `int(round(x))` to round a float `x` to the nearest integer, so that the code works in both Python 3 and Python 2.*

function call	*description*
`str(x)`	*conversion of object x to a string*
`int(x)`	*conversion of string x to an integer or conversion of float x to an integer by truncation towards zero*
`float(x)`	*conversion of string or integer x to a float*
`round(x)`	*nearest integer to number x*

APIs for some built-in type conversion functions

Implicit type conversion (from integer to float). You can use an integer where a float is expected, because Python automatically converts integers to floats when appropriate. For example, `10/4.0` evaluates to `2.5` because `4.0` is a float and both operands need to be of the same type; thus, `10` is converted to a float and then the result of dividing two floats is a float. For another example, `math.sqrt(4)` evaluates to `2.0` because the `4` is converted to a float, as expected by `math.sqrt()`, which then returns a float. This kind of conversion is called *automatic promotion* or *coercion.* It is appropriate that Python implements automatic promotion because it can be done with no loss of information. But, as we have noted, there are pitfalls. For example, as we have seen, Python 3 automatically promotes each integer operand of the `/` operator to a float but Python 2 does not do so. So, `(1 + 2 + 3 + 4) / 4` evaluates to the float `2.5` in Python 3 but to the integer 2 in Python 2.

The concept of automatic promotion is irrelevant if you always use the `int()` and `float()` functions to indicate your type-conversion wishes explicitly; in turn, some programmers avoid automatic promotion whenever possible. In this book we generally do rely upon automatic promotion because it leads to compact and easy-to-read code. *However, whenever we want to divide two numbers with the / operator, we always arrange for (at least) one of the two operands to be a float.* For our examples, when Python evaluates the expression `(1 + 2 + 3 + 4) / 4.0`, it triggers automatic promotion to a float for the first operand and produces the float `2.5`, as expected. This practice ensures that our code works properly in both Python 3 and Python 2 (and many other languages). Again, in this book, we do not use the `/` operator when both operands are integers.

Beginning programmers tend to find type conversion to be an annoyance, but experienced programmers know that paying careful attention to data types is a key to success in programming. It may also be a key to avoiding failure: In a famous incident in 1985, a French rocket exploded in midair because of a type-conversion problem. While a bug in your program may not cause an explosion, it is well worth your while to take the time to understand what type conversion is all about. After you have written just a few programs, you will see that an understanding of data types will help you not only compose compact code but also make your intentions explicit and avoid subtle bugs in your programs.

Photo: ESA

Explosion of Ariane 5 rocket

Summary A *data type* is a set of values and a set of operations defined on those values. Python has built-in data types `bool`, `str`, `int`, and `float`; you will encounter others later in this book. In Python code, we use operators and expressions like those in familiar mathematical expressions to invoke the operations associated with each type. The `bool` type is for computing with true-false values; the `str` type is for sequences of characters; the `int` and `float` data types are numeric types, for computing with numbers.

The `bool` type (which includes the logical operators `and`, `or`, and `not`) is the basis for logical decision making in Python programs, when used in conjunction with the comparison operators `==`, `!=`, `<`, `<=`, `>`, and `>=`. Specifically, we use `bool` expressions to control Python's conditional (`if`) and loop (`while`) statements, which we will study in detail in the next section.

The numeric types, built-in functions, and functions defined in Python's standard and extension modules and in our booksite modules give us the ability to use Python as an extensive mathematical calculator. We compose arithmetic expressions using the built-in operators `+`, `-`, `*`, `/`, `//`, `%`, and `**` along with Python function calls.

Although the programs in this section are rudimentary by the standards of what we will be able to do after the next section, this class of programs is quite useful in its own right. You will use data types and basic mathematical functions extensively in Python programming, so the effort that you spend now in understanding them certainly will be worthwhile.

Interactive Python. Indeed, we can use Python as a calculator, directly. To do that, issue the command `python` (that is, the word `python` stand-alone, with no following file name) in your terminal window. Python identifies itself, and writes a `>>>` prompt. At that point you can type a Python statement and Python will execute it. Or, you can type a Python expression and Python will evaluate it and write the resulting value. Or, you can type `help()` to get access to Python's extensive interactive documentation. Some examples are shown below (boldface indicates what you type). This is a convenient way to test new constructs and access documentation, thereby learning about modules and functions that are of interest to you. You are encouraged to do so in several of the Q&A sections that follow.

```
% python
...
>>> 1 + 2
3
>>> a = 1
>>> b = 2
>>> a + b
3

>>> import math
>>> math.sqrt(2.0)
1.4142135623730951
>>> math.e
2.718281828459045
>>>
```

```
% python
...
>>> import math
>>> help(math)

Help on module math:

NAME
    math

DESCRIPTION
    This module is always available. It provides
    access to the mathematical functions defined
    by the C standard.

FUNCTIONS
    acos(...)
        acos(x)
        Return the arc cosine (in radians) of x.
...
    sqrt(...)
        sqrt(x)
        Return the square root of x
...
DATA
    e = 2.718281828459045
    pi = 3.141592653589793
```

Q&A (strings)

Q. How does Python store strings internally?

A. Strings are sequences of characters that are encoded with *Unicode*, a modern standard for encoding text. Unicode supports over 100,000 different characters, including more than 100 different languages plus mathematical and musical symbols.

> ***Strings in Python 2.*** *Python 2 uses ASCII instead of Unicode to encode characters. ASCII is a legacy standard that supports 128 characters, including the English alphabet, numbers, and punctuation. Python 2 offers a separate data type `unicode` for strings composed of Unicode characters, but many Python 2 libraries do not support it.*

Q. Which data type does Python provide for characters?

A. Python has no special data type for characters. A character is simply a string consisting of one element, such as `'A'`.

Q. Can I compare strings using comparison operators such as == and < or built-in functions such as `max()` and `min()`?

A. Yes. Informally, Python uses *lexicographic order* to compare two strings, like words in a book index or dictionary. For example, `'hello'` and `'hello'` are equal, `'hello'` and `'goodbye'` are unequal, and `'goodbye'` is less than `'hello'`. See the Q&A at the end of Section 4.2 for full details.

Q. Can I use matching double quotes for string literals instead of single quotes?

A. Yes. For example, `'hello'` and `"hello"` are identical literals. Double quotes are useful to specify a string that contains single quotes, so that you don't need to escape them. For example, `'Python\'s'` and `"Python's"` are identical string literals. You can also use matching triple quotes for multiline strings. For example, the following creates a two-line string and assigns it to the variable `s`:

```
s = """Python's "triple" quotes are useful to
specify string literals that span multiple lines
"""
```

In this book, we do not use double or triple quotes to delimit string literals.

Q&A (integers)

Q. How does Python store integers internally?

A. The simplest representation is for small positive integers, where the *binary number system* is used to represent each integer with a fixed amount of computer memory.

Q. What's the binary number system?

A. You probably learned it in grade school. In the binary number system, we represent an integer as a sequence of *bits*. A bit is a single binary (base 2) digit—either 0 or 1—and is the basis for representing information in computers. In this case the bits are coefficients of powers of 2. Specifically, the sequence of bits $b_n b_{n-1} \ldots b_2 b_1 b_0$ represents the integer

$$b_n 2^n \; + b_{n-1} 2^{n-1} \; + \ldots b_2 2^2 \; + b_1 2^1 \; + b_0 2^0$$

For example, 1100011 represents the integer

$$99 = 1 \cdot 64 + 1 \cdot 32 + 0 \cdot 16 + 0 \cdot 8 + 0 \cdot 4 + 1 \cdot 2 + 1 \cdot 1.$$

The more familiar *decimal number system* is the same except that the digits are between zero and 9 and we use powers of 10. Converting a number to binary is an interesting computational problem that we will consider in the next section. For small integers, Python uses a fixed number of bits, typically dictated by a basic design parameter of your computer—usually 32 or 64. For example, the integer 99 might be represented with the 32 bits 00000000000000000000000001100011.

Q. How about negative numbers?

A. Small negative numbers are handled with a convention known as *two's complement*, which we need not consider in detail. The definition of "small" depends on the underlying computer system. On older 32-bit machines, "small" typically covers the range −2147483648 (-2^{31}) to 2147483647 ($2^{31} - 1$). On newer 64-bit machines, "small" typically covers the range -2^{63} to $2^{63} - 1$, in which case "small" is not so small! If an integer is not "small," then Python automatically uses a more elaborate representation whose range is limited only by the amount of memory available on your computer system. Note that details of these internal representations are hidden from your programs, so you can use them systems with different representations without having to change them.

Q. What does the expression `1/0` evaluate to in Python?

A. It raises a `ZeroDivisionError` at run time. *Note*: The easiest way to answer such questions is to use Python's interactive mode. Try it!

Q. How do the floored division operator `//` and remainder operator `%` work on negative operands?

A. Try them and see! `-47 // 5` evaluates to `-10` and `-47 % 5` evaluates to 3. Generalizing, the floored division operator `//` yields the floored quotient; that is, the quotient is rounded toward minus infinity. The behavior of the remainder operator `%` is more complicated. In Python, if `a` and `b` are integers, then the expression `a % b` evaluates to an integer that has the same sign as `b`. This implies that `b * (a // b) + a % b == a` for any integers `a` and `b`. In some other languages (such as Java), the expression `a % b` evaluates to an integer that has the same sign as `a`.

Q. How does the exponentiation operator `**` work with negative operands?

A. Try it out and see for yourself. Note that the `**` operator has higher precedence than a unary plus/minus operator on its left but lower precedence than a unary plus/minus operator on its right. For example, `-3**4` evaluates to `-81` (and not `81`). Also, it can result in an object of a different type. For example, `10**-2` evaluates to the float `0.01` and `(-10)**(10**-2)` evaluates to a complex number in Python 3 (but raises a run-time error in Python 2).

Q. Why does `10^6` evaluate to `12` instead of `1000000`?

A. The `^` operator is not an exponentiation operator, which you must have been thinking. Instead, it is an operator that we do not use in this book. You want the literal `1000000`. You could use the expression `10**6`, but it is wasteful to use an expression (which requires evaluation at run time) when a literal would suffice.

Integers in Python 2. *Python 2 supports two separate types for integers—`int` (for small integers) and `long` (for larger integers). Python 2 automatically promotes from type `int` to `long` whenever necessary.*

Q&A (floating-point numbers)

Q. Why is the type for real numbers named `float`?

A. The decimal point can "float" across the digits that make up the real number. In contrast, with integers the (implicit) decimal point is fixed after the least significant digit.

Q. How does Python store floating-point numbers internally?

A. Generally, Python uses the representation that is natural for the underlying computer system. Most modern computer systems store floating-point numbers as defined by the IEEE 754 standard. That standard specifies that a floating-point number is stored using three fields: sign, mantissa, and exponent. If you are interested, see the booksite for more details. The IEEE 754 standard also specifies how special floating-point values—positive zero, negative zero, positive infinity, negative infinity, and `NaN` (not a number)—should be handled. For example, it specifies that `-0.0/3.0` should evaluate to `-0.0`, `1.0/0.0` should evaluate to positive infinity, and `0.0/0.0` should evaluate to `NaN`. You can use the (rather unusual) expressions `float('inf')` and `float('-inf')` for positive and negative infinity in some simple calculations, but Python does not conform to this part of the IEEE 754 standard. For example, in Python, `-0.0/3.0` correctly evaluates to `-0.0`, but both `1.0/0.0` and `0.0/0.0` raise a `ZeroDivisionError` at run time.

Q. Fifteen digits for floating-point numbers certainly seems enough to me. Do I really need to worry much about precision?

A. Yes, because you are used to mathematics based on real numbers with infinite precision, whereas the computer always deals with approximations. For example, in IEEE 754 floating point, the expression `(0.1 + 0.1 == 0.2)` evaluates to `True` but `(0.1 + 0.1 + 0.1 == 0.3)` evaluates to `False`! Pitfalls like this are not at all unusual in scientific computing. Novice programmers should avoid comparing two floating-point numbers for equality.

Q. It is annoying to see all those digits when writing a float. Is it possible to get `stdio.write()` and `stdio.writeln()` to write just two or three digits after the decimal point?

A. The booksite function `stdio.writef()` is one way to do the job—it is similar to the basic formatted writing function in the C programming language and many other modern languages, as discussed in Section 1.5. Until then, we will live with the extra digits (which is not all bad, since doing so helps us to get used to the different types of numbers).

Q. Can I apply the floored division operator `//` to two float operands?

A. Yes, it produces the floored division of its operands. That is, the result is the quotient in which digits after the decimal place are removed. We do not use the floored division operator on floats in this book.

Q. What does `round()` return if the fractional part of its argument is `0.5`?

A. In Python 3, it returns the nearest even integer, so `round(2.5)` is `2`, `round(3.5)` is `4`, and `round(-2.5)` is `-2`. But in Python 2, the `round()` function rounds away from zero (and returns a float), so `round(2.5)` is `3.0`, `round(3.5)` is `4.0`, and `round(-2.5)` is `-3.0`.

Q. Can I compare a `float` to an `int`?

A. Not without doing a type conversion, but remember that Python does the requisite type conversion automatically. For example, if `x` is the integer `3`, then the expression `(x < 3.1)` evaluates to `True` because Python promotes the integer `3` to generate the float `3.0` and then compares `3.0` with `3.1`.

Q. Are there functions in Python's `math` module for other trigonometric functions, such as arc sine, hyperbolic sine, and secant?

A. Yes, Python's `math` module includes inverse trigonometric functions and hyperbolic functions. However, there are no functions for secant, cosecant, and cotangent because you could use `math.sin()`, `math.cos()`, and `math.tan()` to compute them easily. Choosing which functions to include in an API is a tradeoff between the convenience of having every function that you need and the annoyance of having to find one of the few that you need in a long list. No choice will satisfy all users, and the Python designers have many users to satisfy. Note that there are plenty of redundancies even in the APIs that we have listed. For example, you could use `math.sin(x) / math.cos(x)` instead of `math.tan(x)`.

Q&A

Q. What happens if I access a variable that I haven't bound to an object?

A. Python will raise a `NameError` at run time.

Q. How can I determine the type of a variable?

A. That's a trick question. Unlike variables in many programming languages (such as Java), a Python variable does not have a type. Instead, it is the *object* to which a variable is bound that has a type. You can bind the same variable to objects of different types, as in this code fragment:

```
x = 'Hello, World'
x = 17
x = True
```

However, for clarity, it's usually a bad idea to do so.

Q. How can I determine the type, identity, and value of an object?

A. Python provides built-in functions for this purpose. The function `type()` returns the type of an object; the function `id()` returns the identity of an object; the function `repr()` returns an unambiguous string representation of an object.

```
>>> import math
>>> a = math.pi
>>> id(a)
140424102622928
>>> type(a)
<class 'float'>
>>> repr(a)
'3.141592653589793'
```

You will rarely use these functions in ordinary programming, but you may find them useful when debugging.

Q. Is there a difference between = and == ?

A. Yes, they are quite different! The first specifies an assignment to a variable, and the second is a comparison operator that produces a boolean result. Your ability to understand this answer is a sure test of whether you understood the material in this section. Think about how you might explain the difference to a friend.

Q. Will `a < b < c` test whether the three numbers `a`, `b`, and `c` are in order?

A. Yes, Python supports arbitrary *chaining* of comparisons such as `a < b < c` that behave according to standard mathematical conventions. However, in many programming languages (such as Java) the expression `a < b < c` is illegal because the subexpression `a < b` evaluates to a boolean and that boolean is then compared with a number, which is meaningless. We do not use chained comparisons in this book; instead we prefer expressions such as `(a < b) and (b < c)`.

Q. Will `a = b = c = 17` set the three variables to `17`?

A. Yes, even though Python assignment statements are not expressions, Python supports arbitrary *chaining* of assignment statements. We do not use chained assignments in the book because many Python programmers consider it poor style.

Q. Can I use the logical operators `and`, `or`, and `not` with operands that are not booleans?

A. Yes, but for clarity it's usually a bad idea to do so. In this context, Python considers `0`, `0.0`, and the empty string `''` to mean `False`, and any other integer, float, or string to mean `True`.

Q. Can I use arithmetic operators with boolean operands?

A. Yes, but again it's bad form to do so. When you use boolean operands with arithmetic operators, they are promoted to integers: `0` for `False` and `1` for `True`. For example, `(False - True - True) * True` evaluates to the `int` value `-2`.

Q. Can I name a variable `max`?

A. Yes, but if you do, then you won't be able to use the built-in function `max()`. The same holds for `min()`, `sum()`, `float()`, `eval()`, `open()`, `id()`, `type()`, `file()`, and other built-in functions.

Exercises

1.2.1 Suppose that a and b are integers. What does the following sequence of statements do? Draw an object-level trace of this computation.

```
t = a
b = t
a = b
```

1.2.2 Compose a program that uses `math.sin()` and `math.cos()` to check that the value of $\cos^2\theta + \sin^2\theta$ is approximately `1.0` for any θ entered as a command-line argument. Just write the value. Why are the values not always exactly `1.0`?

1.2.3 Suppose that a and b are booleans. Show that the expression

```
(not (a and b) and (a or b)) or ((a and b) or not (a or b))
```

evaluates to `True`.

1.2.4 Suppose that a and b are integers. Simplify the following expression:

```
(not (a < b) and not (a > b))
```

1.2.5 What does each of these statements write?

a. `stdio.writeln(2 + 3)`

b. `stdio.writeln(2.2 + 3.3)`

c. `stdio.writeln('2' + '3')`

d. `stdio.writeln('2.2' + '3.3')`

e. `stdio.writeln(str(2) + str(3))`

f. `stdio.writeln(str(2.2) + str(3.3))`

g. `stdio.writeln(int('2') + int('3'))`

h. `stdio.writeln(int('2' + '3'))`

i. `stdio.writeln(float('2') + float('3'))`

j. `stdio.writeln(float('2' + '3'))`

k. `stdio.writeln(int(2.6 + 2.6))`

l. `stdio.writeln(int(2.6) + int(2.6))`

Explain each outcome.

1.2.6 Explain how to use `quadratic.py` (PROGRAM 1.2.4) to find the square root of a number.

1.2.7 What does `stdio.writeln((1.0 + 2 + 3 + 4) / 4)` write?

1.2.8 Suppose that a is `3.14159`. What do each of these statements write?

a. `stdio.writeln(a)`

b. `stdio.writeln(a + 1.0)`

c. `stdio.writeln(8 // int(a))`

d. `stdio.writeln(8.0 / a)`

e. `stdio.writeln(int(8.0 / a))`

Explain each outcome.

1.2.9 Describe the effect of writing `sqrt` instead of `math.sqrt` in PROGRAM 1.2.4.

1.2.10 Does `(math.sqrt(2) * math.sqrt(2) == 2)` evaluate to `True` or `False`?

1.2.11 Compose a program that takes two positive integers as command-line arguments and writes `True` if either evenly divides the other.

1.2.12 Compose a program that takes three positive integers as command-line arguments and writes `False` if any one of them is greater than or equal to the sum of the other two and `True` otherwise. (*Note*: This computation tests whether the three numbers could be the lengths of the sides of some triangle.)

1.2.13 Give the value of a after the execution of each of the following sequences:

```
a = 1            a = True         a = 2
a = a + a        a = not a        a = a * a
a = a + a        a = not a        a = a * a
a = a + a        a = not a        a = a * a
```

1.2.14 A physics student gets unexpected results when using the code

```
force = G * mass1 * mass2 / radius * radius
```

to compute values according to the formula $F = Gm_1m_2 / r^2$. Explain the problem and correct the code.

1.2.15 Suppose that `x` and `y` are two floats that represent the Cartesian coordinates of a point (x, y) in the plane. Give an expression that evaluates to the distance of the point from the origin.

1.2.16 Compose a program that takes two integers `a` and `b` from the command line and writes a random integer between `a` and `b`.

1.2.17 Compose a program that writes the sum of two random integers between `1` and `6` (such as you might get when rolling dice).

1.2.18 Compose a program that takes a float `t` from the command line and writes the value of $\sin(2t) + \sin(3t)$.

1.2.19 Compose a program that takes three floats x_0, v_0, and t from the command line, evaluates $x_0 + v_0t - Gt^2/2$, and writes the result. (*Note*: G is the constant 9.80665. This value is the displacement in meters after t seconds when an object is thrown straight up from initial position x_0 at velocity v_0 meters per second.)

1.2.20 Compose a program that takes two integers `m` and `d` from the command line and writes `True` if day d of month m is between March 20 and June 20, and `False` otherwise. (Interpret `m` with `1` for January, `2` for February, and so forth.)

Creative Exercises

1.2.21 *Continuously compounded interest.* Compose a program that calculates and writes the amount of money you would have if you invested it at a given interest rate compounded continuously, taking the number of years t, the principal P, and the annual interest rate r as command-line arguments. The desired value is given by the formula Pe^{rt}.

1.2.22 *Wind chill.* Given the temperature T (in degrees Fahrenheit) and the wind speed v (in miles per hour), the National Weather Service defines the effective temperature (the wind chill) to be:

$$w = 35.74 + 0.6215\,T + (0.4275\,T - 35.75)\,v^{0.16}$$

Compose a program that takes two floats `t` and `v` from the command line and writes out the wind chill. *Note*: This formula is not valid if t is larger than 50 in absolute value or if v is larger than 120 or less than 3 (you may assume that the values you get are in that range).

1.2.23 *Polar coordinates.* Compose a program that converts from Cartesian to polar coordinates. Your program should accept two floats `x` and `y` from the command line and write the polar coordinates r and θ. Use the Python function `math.atan2(y, x)`, which computes the arctangent value of `y/x` that is in the range from $-\pi$ to π.

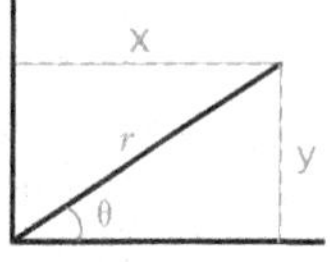

Polar coordinates

1.2.24 *Gaussian random numbers.* One way to generate a random number taken from the Gaussian distribution is to use the *Box-Muller* formula

$$w = \sin(2\,\pi\,v)\,(-2\ln u)^{1/2}$$

where u and v are real numbers between 0 and 1 generated by the `Math.random()` method. Compose a program that writes a standard Gaussian random variable.

1.2.25 *Order check.* Compose a program that accepts three floats `x`, `y`, and `z` as command-line arguments and writes `True` if the values are strictly ascending or descending ($x < y < z$ or $x > y > z$), and `False` otherwise.

1.2.26 *Day of the week.* Compose a program that accepts a date as input and writes the day of the week that date falls on. Your program should accept three command-line arguments: `m` (month), `d` (day), and `y` (year). For `m`, use `1` for January, `2` for February, and so forth. For output, write `0` for Sunday, `1` for Monday, `2` for Tuesday, and so forth. Use the following formulas for the Gregorian calendar:

$$y_0 = y - (14 - m) / 12$$
$$x = y_0 + y_0/4 - y_0/100 + y_0/400$$
$$m_0 = m + 12 \times ((14 - m) / 12) - 2$$
$$d_0 = (d + x + (31 \times m_0)/12) \% 7$$

Example: On what day of the week was February 14, 2000?

$$y_0 = 2000 - 1 = 1999$$
$$x = 1999 + 1999/4 - 1999/100 + 1999/400 = 2483$$
$$m_0 = 2 + 12 \times 1 - 2 = 12$$
$$d_0 = (14 + 2483 + (31 \times 12) / 12) \% 7 = 2500 \% 7 = 1 \text{ (Monday)}$$

1.2.27 *Uniform random numbers.* Compose a program that writes five uniform random floats between 0.0 and 1.0, their average value, and their minimum and maximum values. Use the built-in `min()` and `max()` functions.

1.2.28 *Mercator projection.* The *Mercator projection* is a conformal (angle preserving) projection that maps latitude φ and longitude λ to rectangular coordinates (x, y). It is widely used—for example, in nautical charts and in the maps that you print from the web. The projection is defined by the equations $x = \lambda - \lambda_0$ and $y = 1/2 \ln((1 + \sin\varphi) / (1 - \sin\varphi))$, where λ_0 is the longitude of the point in the center of the map. Compose a program that accepts λ_0 and the latitude and longitude of a point from the command line and writes its projection.

1.2.29 *Color conversion.* Several different formats are used to represent color. For example, the primary format for LCD displays, digital cameras, and web pages, known as the *RGB format,* specifies the level of red (R), green (G), and blue (B) on an integer scale from 0 to 255. The primary format for publishing books and magazines, known as the *CMYK format*, specifies the level of cyan (C), magenta (M), yellow (Y), and black (K) on a real scale from 0.0 to 1.0. Compose a program that converts RGB to CMYK. Accept three integers—`r`, `g`, and `b`—from the command line and write the equivalent CMYK values. If the RGB values are all 0, then the CMY values are all 0 and the K value is 1; otherwise, use these formulas:

$$
\begin{aligned}
w &= \max\,(\, r/255, g/255, b/255 \,) \\
c &= (w - (r/255)) / w \\
m &= (w - (g/255)) / w \\
y &= (w - (b/255)) / w \\
k &= 1 - w
\end{aligned}
$$

1.2.30 *Great circle.* Compose a program that accepts four floats as command-line arguments—`x1`, `y1`, `x2`, and `y2`—(the latitude and longitude, in degrees, of two points on the earth) and writes the great-circle distance between them. The great-circle distance d (in nautical miles) is given by the following equation:

$$d = 60 \arccos(\sin(x_1) \sin(x_2) + \cos(x_1) \cos(x_2) \cos(y_1 - y_2))$$

Note that this equation uses degrees, whereas Python's trigonometric functions use radians. Use `math.radians()` and `math.degrees()` to convert between the two. Use your program to compute the great-circle distance between Paris (48.87° N and −2.33° W) and San Francisco (37.8° N and 122.4° W).

1.2.31 *Three-sort.* Compose a program that takes three integers from the command line and writes them in ascending order. Use the built-in `min()` and `max()` functions.

1.2.32 *Dragon curves.* Compose a program to write the instructions for drawing the dragon curves of order 0 through 5. The instructions are strings of `F`, `L`, and `R` characters, where `F` means "draw line while moving 1 unit forward," `L` means "turn left," and `R` means "turn right." A dragon curve of order n is formed when you fold a strip of paper in half n times, then unfold it to right angles. The key to solving this problem is to note that a curve of order n is a curve of order $n-1$ followed by an `L` followed by a curve of order $n-1$ traversed in reverse order, and then to figure out a similar description for the reverse curve.

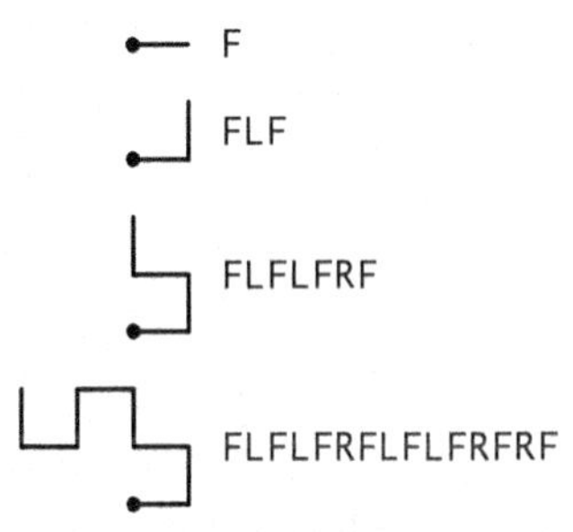

Dragon curves of order 0, 1, 2, and 3

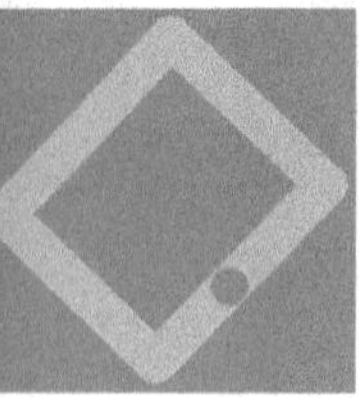

1.3 Conditionals and Loops

IN THE PROGRAMS THAT WE HAVE examined to this point, each of the statements in the program is executed once, in the order given. Most programs are more complicated because the sequence of statements and the number of times each is executed can vary. We use the term *control flow* to refer to statement sequencing in a program. In this section, we introduce statements that allow us to change the control flow, using logic about the values of program variables. This feature is an essential component of programming.

Programs in this section

Specifically, we consider Python statements that implement *conditionals*, where some other statements may or may not be executed depending on certain conditions, and *loops*, where some other statements may be executed multiple times, again depending on certain conditions. As you will see in numerous examples in this section, conditionals and loops truly harness the power of the computer and will equip you to compose programs to accomplish a broad variety of tasks that you could not contemplate attempting without a computer.

If statements Most computations require different actions for different inputs. One way to express these differences in Python is the `if` statement:

```
if <boolean expression>:
    <statement>
    <statement>
    ...
```

This description introduces a formal notation known as a *template* that we will use to specify the format of Python constructs. We put within angle brackets (< >) a construct that we have already defined, to indicate that we can use any instance of that construct where specified. In this case, `<boolean expression>` represents an expression that evaluates to a boolean, such as one involving a comparison operation, and *<statement>* represents a statement (each occurrence may represent a different statement). It is possible to make formal definitions of *<boolean expression>* and *<statement>*, but we refrain from going into that level of detail. The meaning of an `if` statement is self-explanatory: Python executes the *indented* statement(s) if and only if the boolean expression evaluates to `True`. We refer to the indented lines as a *block*. The first unindented line marks the end of the block. Most Python programmers indent by four spaces.

As a simple example, suppose that you want to compute the absolute value of an integer *x*. This code does the job:

```
if x < 0:
    x = -x
```

(Precisely, if the value of the object referenced by `x` is negative, it changes `x` to refer to a new object whose value is the absolute value of that value.)

As a second simple example, consider the following code:

```
if x > y:
    temp = x
    x = y
    y = temp
```

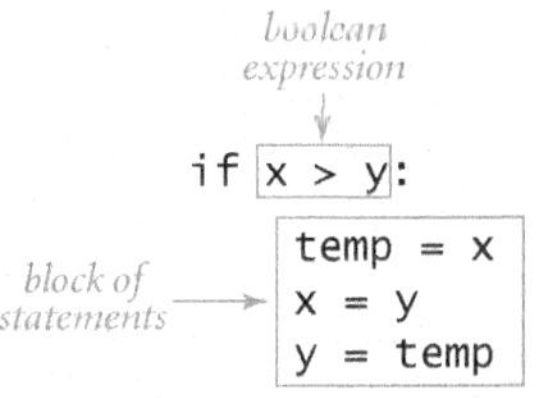

Anatomy of an `if` *statement*

This code puts `x` and `y` in ascending order, by exchanging references if necessary.

Most other modern programming languages use some different mechanism to denote statement blocks (such as enclosing statements in matching curly braces). In Python *the amount of indentation on each line is consequential*, so you need to pay attention to it. For example, contrast these two code fragments, which have slightly different indentation.

```
if x >= 0:
    stdout.write('not ')
stdout.writeln('negative')
```

```
if x >= 0:
    stdout.write('not ')
    stdout.writeln('negative')
```

The code on the left is an `if` statement with a one-statement block followed by another statement; the code on the right is an `if` statement with a two-statement block. If `x` is greater than or equal to `0`, then both fragments write `not negative`. In contrast, if `x` is less than 0, then the code on the left writes `negative` but the code on the right writes nothing at all.

Else clauses You can add an `else` clause to an `if` statement, to express the concept of executing either one statement (or block of statements) or another, depending on whether the boolean expression is `True` or `False`, as in this template:

```
if <boolean expression>:
    <block of statements>
else:
    <block of statements>
```

As a simple example of the need for an `else` clause, the following code assigns the maximum of two `int` values to the variable `maximum`. (Alternatively, you can achieve the same result by calling the built-in function `max()`.)

```
if x > y:
    maximum = x
else:
    maximum = y
```

When an `if` or `else` block contains only a single statement, for brevity, you can put that statement on the same line as the keyword `if` or `else`, as in the third and fourth rows in the table below.

absolute value	`if x < 0:` `    x = -x`

put x and y into sorted order	`if x > y:`
	`    temp = x`
	`    x = y`
	`    y = temp`

maximum of x and y	`if x > y: maximum = x` `else:      maximum = y`
error check for remainder operation	`if den == 0: stdio.writeln('Division by zero')` `else:        stdio.writeln('Remainder = ' + num % den)`

error check for quadratic formula	`discriminant = b*b - 4.0*a*c`
	`if discriminant < 0.0:`
	`    stdio.writeln('No real roots')`
	`else:`
	`    d = math.sqrt(discriminant)`
	`    stdio.writeln((-b + d)/2.0)`
	`    stdio.writeln((-b - d)/2.0)`

Typical examples of using `if` statements

Program 1.3.1 Flipping a fair coin (`flip.py`)

```
import random
import stdio

if random.randrange(0, 2) == 0:
    stdio.writeln('Heads')
else:
    stdio.writeln('Tails')
```

This program simulates a fair coin flip by writing `Heads` *or* `Tails`*, depending on the outcome of* `random.randrange()`*. A sequence of flips will have many of the same properties as a sequence that you would get by flipping a fair coin, but it is not a truly random sequence.*

```
% python flip.py
Heads
% python flip.py
Tails
% python flip.py
Tails
```

The table on the facing page summarizes these and gives two other examples of the use of `if` and `if-else` statements. These examples are typical of simple calculations you might need in programs that you compose. Conditional statements are an essential part of programming. As the *semantics* (meaning) of statements like these is similar to their meanings as natural-language phrases, you will quickly grow used to them.

Program 1.3.1 (`flip.py`) is another example of the use of the `if-else` statement, in this case for the task of simulating a fair coin flip. The body of the program is a single statement, like the other considered so far, but it is worthy of special attention because it introduces an interesting philosophical issue that is valuable to contemplate: can a computer program produce *random* values? Certainly not, but a program *can* produce values that have many of the properties of random values.

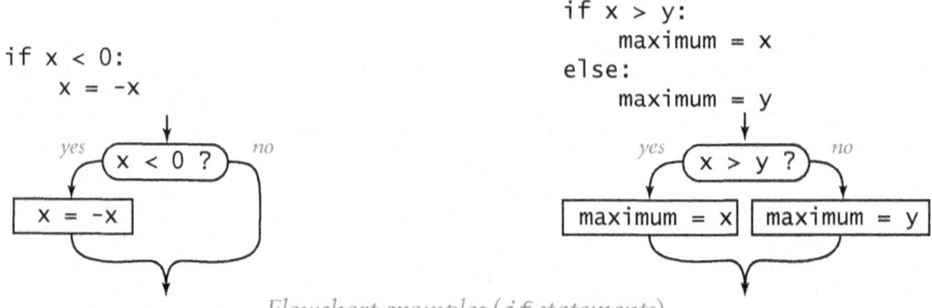

Flowchart examples (`if` statements)

One way to understand control flow is to visualize it with a diagram called a *flowchart*. Paths through the flowchart correspond to flow-of-control paths in the program. In the early days of computing, when programmers used low-level languages and difficult-to-understand flows of control, flowcharts were an essential part of programming. With modern languages, we use flowcharts just to understand basic building blocks like the `if` statement.

While statements Many computations are inherently repetitive. The basic Python construct for handling such computations has the following format:

```
while <boolean expression>:
    <statement 1>
    <statement 2>
    ...
```

The `while` statement has the same form as the `if` statement (the only difference being the use of the keyword `while` instead of `if`), but the meaning is quite different. It is an instruction to the computer to behave as follows: if the boolean expression evaluates to `False`, do nothing; if the expression evaluates to `True`, execute the block of statements in sequence (just as with `if`) but then check the expression again, execute the sequence of statements again if the expression evaluates to `True`, and continue as long as the expression

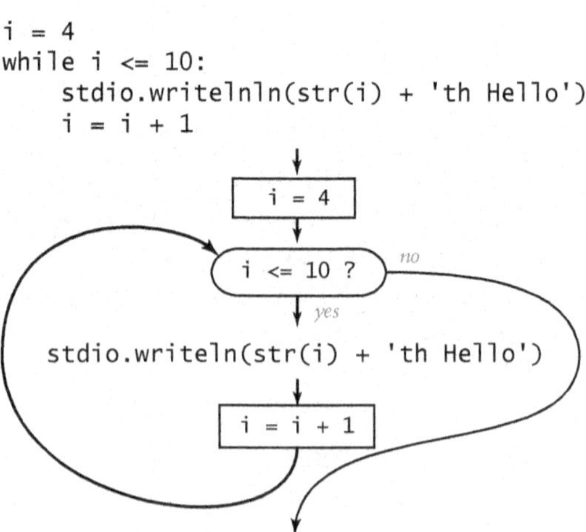

Flowchart example (`while` statement)

evaluates to `True`. Thus the flow of control "loops back" to the boolean expression repeatedly. This loop back is evident at the left of the flowchart. (The `while` statement in this diagram is taken from PROGRAM 1.3.2, which we will examine shortly.) We say that the `while` statement implements a *loop*. We refer to the indented statement block within a `while` statement as the *body of the loop* and to the boolean expression as the *loop-continuation condition*. The loop-continuation condition is typically a test about the value of some variable(s), so each `while` loop is typically preceded by *initialization* code that sets initial value(s).

The `while` statement is equivalent to a sequence of identical `if` statements:

```
if <boolean expression>:
    <statement 1>
    <statement 2>
    ...
if <boolean expression>:
    <statement 1>
    <statement 2>
    ...
if <boolean expression>:
    <statement 1>
    <statement 2>
    ...
...
```

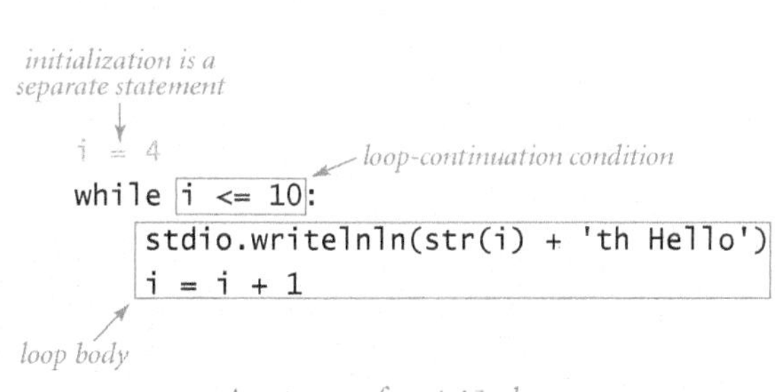

initialization is a separate statement
i = 4
loop-continuation condition
while i <= 10:
stdio.writeln(str(i) + 'th Hello')
i = i + 1
loop body

Anatomy of a while loop

The body of the loop should change one or more variables to make the loop-continuation condition eventually evaluate to `False`, so that the sequence is broken and the loop terminates.

A common programming paradigm involves maintaining an integer value that keeps track of the number of times a loop iterates. We start at some initial value, and then increment the value by 1 each time through the loop, testing whether it exceeds a predetermined maximum before deciding to continue. PROGRAM 1.3.2 (`tenhellos.py`) is a simple example of this paradigm that uses a `while` statement. The key to the computation is the statement

```
i = i + 1
```

Program 1.3.2 Your first loop (`tenhellos.py`)

```
import stdio

stdio.writeln('1st Hello')
stdio.writeln('2nd Hello')
stdio.writeln('3rd Hello')

i = 4
while i <= 10:
    stdio.writeln(str(i) + 'th Hello')
    i = i + 1
```

`i`	*loop control counter*

This program writes 10 "hellos." It accomplishes that by using a `while` loop. After the third line to be written, the lines differ only in the index counting the line written, so we define a variable `i` to contain that index. After initializing `i` to 4, we enter into a `while` loop where we use the `i` in the `stdio.writeln()` function call and increment it each time through the loop. After the program writes `10th Hello`, `i` becomes 11 and the loop terminates.

```
% python tenhellos.py
1st Hello
2nd Hello
3rd Hello
4th Hello
5th Hello
6th Hello
7th Hello
8th Hello
9th Hello
10th Hello
```

`i`	`i <= 10`	*output*
4	`true`	`4th Hello`
5	`true`	`5th Hello`
6	`true`	`6th Hello`
7	`true`	`7th Hello`
8	`true`	`8th Hello`
9	`true`	`9th Hello`
10	`true`	`10th Hello`
11	`false`	

Trace of `while` loop

As a mathematical equation, this statement is nonsense, but as a Python assignment statement it makes perfect sense: it says to compute the value `i + 1` and then assign the result to the variable `i`. If `i` is `4` before the statement executed, then it is `5` afterward; if `i` is `5` before the statement executes, then it is `6` afterward; and so forth. With the initial condition in `tenhellos.py` that `i` starts at `4`, the statement block is executed seven times until the sequence is broken, when `i` finally is greater than `10`.

Using the `while` statement is barely worthwhile for this simple task, but you will soon be addressing tasks where you will need to specify that statements be repeated far too many times to contemplate doing it without loops. There is a profound difference between programs with `while` statements and programs without them, because `while` statements allow us to specify a potentially unlimited number of statements to be executed in a program. In particular, the `while` statement allows us to specify lengthy computations in short programs. This ability opens the door to composing programs for tasks that we could not contemplate addressing without a computer. But there is also a price to pay: as your programs become more sophisticated, they become more difficult to understand.

Program 1.3.3 (`powersoftwo.py`) uses a `while` statement to write a table of the powers of 2. Beyond the loop control counter `i`, it maintains a variable `power` that holds the powers of 2 as it computes them. The loop body contains three statements: one to write the current power of 2, one to compute the next power of 2 (multiply the current one by 2), and one to increment the loop control counter.

Incidentally, there are many situations in computer science where it is useful to be familiar with powers of 2. You should know at least the first 10 values in this table and you should note that 2^{10} is about 1,000, 2^{20} is about 1 million, and 2^{30} is about 1 billion.

Program 1.3.3 is a prototype for many useful computations. By varying the computations that change the accumulated value and the way that the loop control variable is incremented, we can write tables of a variety of functions (see Exercise 1.3.10).

It is worthwhile to carefully examine the behavior of programs that use loops by studying a trace of the program. For example, a trace of the operation of `powersoftwo.py` should show the value of each variable before each iteration of the loop and the value of the conditional expression that controls the loop. Tracing the operation of a loop can be very tedious, but it is nearly always worthwhile to run a trace because it clearly exposes what a program is doing.

Program 1.3.3 Computing powers of 2 (powersoftwo.py)

```
import sys
import stdio

n = int(sys.argv[1])
power = 1
i = 0
while i <= n:
    # Write the ith power of 2.
    stdio.writeln(str(i) + ' ' + str(power))
    power = 2 * power
    i = i + 1
```

n	*loop termination value*
i	*loop control counter*
power	*current power of 2*

This program accepts an integer n *as command-line argument and writes a table containing the first* n *powers of 2. Each time through the loop, we increment* i *and double* power*. We show only the first three and the last three lines of the table; the program write* n + 1 *lines.*

```
% python powersoftwo.py 5
0 1
1 2
2 4
3 8
4 16
5 32
```

```
% python powersoftwo.py 29
0 1
1 2
2 4
...
27 134217728
28 268435456
29 536870912
```

Program 1.3.3 is nearly a self-tracing program, because it writes the values of its variables each time through the loop. You can make any program produce a trace of itself by adding appropriate `stdio.writeln()` statements. Modern programming environments provide sophisticated tools for tracing, but this tried-and-true method is simple and effective. You certainly should add `stdio.writeln()` statements to the first few loops that you compose, to be sure that they are doing precisely what you expect.

As a more complicated example, suppose that we want to compute the largest power of 2 that is less than or equal to a given positive integer `n`. If `n` is 13 we want the result 8; if `n` is 1000, we want the result 512; if `n` is 64, we want the result 64; and so forth. This computation is simple to perform with a `while` loop:

```
power = 1
while 2*power <= n:
    power = 2*power
```

It takes some thought to convince yourself that this simple piece of code produces the desired result. You can do so by making these observations:

- `power` is always a power of 2.
- `power` is never greater than `n`.
- `power` increases each time through the loop, so the loop must terminate.
- After the loop terminates, `2*power` is greater than `n`.

Reasoning of this sort is often important in understanding how `while` loops work. Even though many of the loops you will compose are much simpler than this one, you should verify for yourself that each loop you compose will behave as you expect.

The logic behind such arguments is the same whether the loop iterates just a few times, as in `tenhellos.py`; dozens of times, as in `powersoftwo.py`; or millions of times, as in several examples that we will soon consider. That leap from a few tiny cases to a huge computation is profound. When composing loops, understanding how the values of the variables change each time through the loop (and checking that understanding by adding statements to trace their values and running the program for a small number of iterations) is essential. Having done so, you can confidently remove those training wheels and truly unleash the power of the computer.

i	power	i <= n
0	1	true
1	2	true
2	4	true
3	8	true
4	16	true
5	32	true
6	64	true
7	128	true
8	256	true
9	512	true
10	1024	true
11	2048	true
12	4096	true
13	8192	true
14	16384	true
15	32768	true
16	65536	true
17	131072	true
18	262144	true
19	524288	true
20	1048576	true
21	2097152	true
22	4194304	true
23	8388608	true
24	16777216	true
25	33554432	true
26	67108864	true
27	134217728	true
28	268435456	true
29	536870912	true
30	1073741824	false

Trace of `powersoftwo.py` when n is 29

Shorthand assignment notation. Modifying a variable is something that we do so often in programming that modern programming languages like Python provide shorthand notations for the purpose. The most common practice is to abbreviate an assignment statement of the form `i = i + 1` with the shorthand notation `i += 1`. The same notation works for other binary operators, including `-`, `*`, and `/`. For example, most programmers would use `power *= 2` instead of `power = 2 * power` in PROGRAM 1.3.3. Such shortcuts came into widespread use with the C programming language in the 1970s and have become standard. They have survived the test of time because they lead to compact, elegant, and easy-to-understand programs. From this point forward, we will use such *augmented assignment statements* in our programs whenever possible.

For statements As you will see, the `while` statement allows us to compose programs for all manner of applications. Before considering more examples, we will look at an alternative Python construct—the `for` statement—that allows us even more flexibility when composing programs with loops. This alternative notation is not fundamentally different from the basic `while` statement, but it often allows us to compose more compact and more readable programs than if we used only `while` statements.

As noted previously, we often need to design a loop that uses an integer to keep track of the number of times the loop iterates. We initially assign some integer to the variable, and then each time through the loop assign to the variable the integer that is one larger than the previous integer, testing whether the integer exceeds a predetermined maximum before deciding to continue. We call such a loop a *counting* loop.

In Python, we might implement a counting loop with a `while` statement using this code pattern:

```
<variable> = <start>
while <variable> < <stop>:
    <block of statements>
    <variable> += 1
```

The `for` statement is a more succinct way to implement a counting loop. In Python, the `for` statement has several formats. For now, we consider the following template:

```
for <variable> in range(<start>, <stop>):
    <block of statements>
```

The <start> and <stop> arguments to the built-in range() function must be integers. When given a statement of this form, Python executes the indented block of statements repeatedly. The first time through the loop <variable> is <start>, the second time <variable> is <start> + 1, and so forth. The final time <variable> is <stop> - 1. In short, a for statement executes its indented statement repeatedly, with <variable> ranging from the integer <start> to the integer <stop> - 1, inclusive. For example, these lines of tenhellos.py (Program 1.3.2):

```
i = 4
while i <= 10:
    stdio.writeln(str(i) + 'th Hello')
    i = i + 1
```

can be expressed more succinctly using this for statement:

```
for i in range(4, 11):
    stdio.writeln(str(i) + 'th Hello')
```

If range() has only one argument—that is, the <stop> value—then the <start> value defaults to 0. For example, the following for loop

```
power = 1
for i in range(n+1):
    stdio.writeln(str(i) + ' ' + str(power))
    power *= 2
```

is an improvement over the while loop in powersoftwo.py (Program 1.3.3).

Choosing among different formulations of the same computation is a matter of each programmer's taste, as when a writer picks from among synonyms or chooses between using active and passive voice when composing a sentence. You will not find good hard-and-fast rules on how to compose a program any more than you will find such rules on how to compose a paragraph. Your goal should be to find a style that suits you, gets the computation done, and can be appreciated by others. Generally, in this book we use for statements for counting loops, and while statements for other kinds of loops.

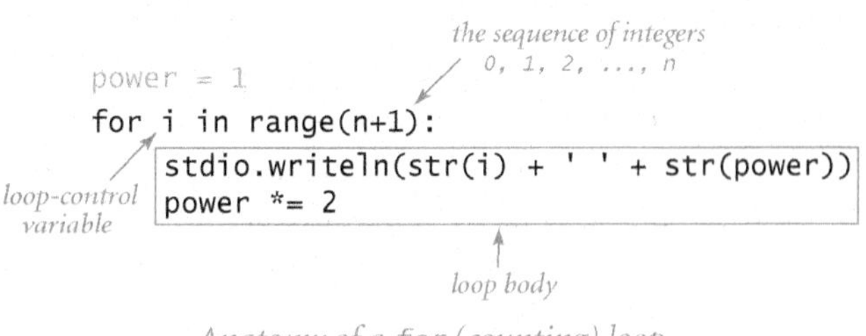

Anatomy of a for (counting) loop

write first n+1 powers of 2	`power = 1`
	`for i in range(n+1):`
	`    stdio.writeln(str(i) + ' ' + str(power))`
	`    power *= 2`

write largest power of 2 less than or equal to n	`power = 1`
	`while 2*power <= n:`
	`    power *= 2`
	`stdio.writeln(power)`

write a sum (1 + 2 + . . . + n)	`total = 0`
	`for i in range(1, n+1):`
	`    total += i`
	`stdio.writeln(total)`

write a product ($n! = 1 \times 2 \times \ldots \times n$)	`product = 1`
	`for i in range(1, n+1):`
	`    product *= i`
	`stdio.writeln(product)`

write a table of n+1 function values	`for i in range(n+1):`
	`    stdio.write(str(i) + ' ')`
	`    stdio.writeln(2.0 * math.pi * i / n)`

write the ruler function (see Program 1.2.1)	`ruler = '1'`
	`stdio.writeln(ruler)`
	`for i in range(2, n+1):`
	`    ruler = ruler + ' ' + str(i) + ' ' + ruler`
	`    stdio.writeln(ruler)`

Typical examples of using `for` *and* `while` *statements*

The preceding table includes several code fragments with typical examples of loops used in Python code. Some of these relate to code that you have already seen; others are new code for straightforward computations. To cement your understanding of loops in Python, put each of these code snippets into a program that takes an integer `n` from the command line (like `powersoftwo.py`) *and run it.* Then, compose some loops of your own to perform for similar computations of your own invention, or do some of the early exercises at the end of this section. There is no substitute for the experience gained by running code that you compose yourself, and it is imperative that you develop an understanding of how to compose code that uses loops.

Nesting The `if`, `while`, and `for` statements have the same status as assignment statements or any other statements in Python. That is, we can use them whenever a statement is called for. In particular, we can *nest* one or more of them in the body of another. As a first example, `divisorpattern.py` (PROGRAM 1.3.4) has a `for` loop whose statements are a for `loop` (whose statement is an `if` statement) and a `stdio.writeln()` statement. It writes a pattern of asterisks where the `i`th row has an asterisk in each position corresponding to divisors of `i` (the same holds true for the columns).

PROGRAM 1.3.4 has a complicated control flow, as you can see from its flowchart (shown below). To derive a flowchart like this, it is best to work with a statement-by-statement version of the computation that uses `while` loops (see EXERCISE 1.3.15), because the `for` loop version masks the details. This diagram illustrates the importance of using a limited number of simple control structures in programming. With nesting, you can compose loops and conditionals to build programs that are easy to understand even though they may have a complicated control flow. A great many useful computations can be accomplished with just one or two levels of nesting. For example, many programs in this book have the same general structure as `divisorpattern.py`.

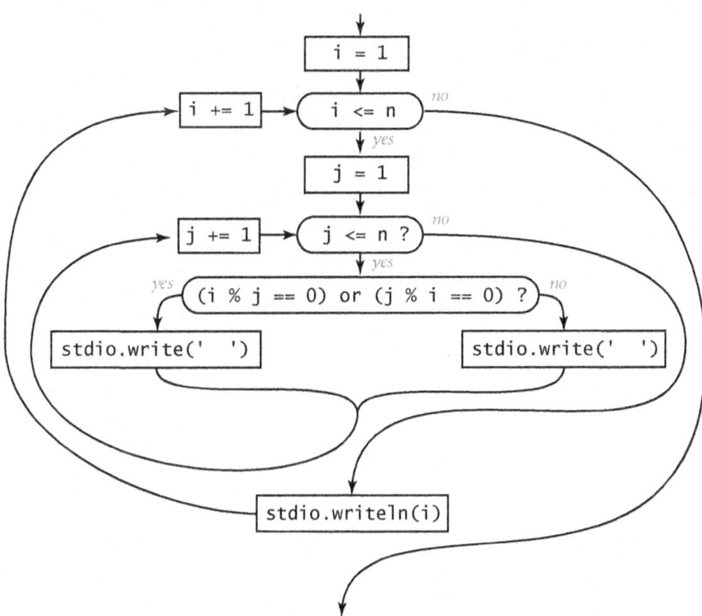

Flowchart for `divisorpattern.py`

Program 1.3.4 Your first nested loops (`divisorpattern.py`)

```
import sys
import stdio

n = int(sys.argv[1])

for i in range(1, n+1):
    # Write the ith line.
    for j in range(1, n+1):
        # Write the jth entry in the ith line.
        if (i % j == 0) or (j % i == 0):
            stdio.write('* ')
        else:
            stdio.write('  ')
    stdio.writeln(i)
```

`n`	*number of rows and columns*
`i`	*row index*
`j`	*column index*

This program accepts an integer command-line argument `n` *and writes an* `n`*-by-*`n` *table with an asterisk in row* `i` *and column* `j` *if either* `i` *divides* `j` *or* `j` *divides* `i`*. The program uses nested* `for` *loops. The loop control variables* `i` *and* `j` *control the computation.*

```
% python divisorpattern.py 3
* * * 1
* *   2
*   * 3

% python divisorpattern.py 16
* * * * * * * * * * * * * * * * 1
* *   *   *   *   *   *   *   * 2
*   *     *     *     *     *   3
* *   *       *       *       * 4
*       *         *         *   5
* * *     *           *         6
*           *             *     7
* *   *       *               * 8
*   *           *               9
* *     *         *             10
*                   *           11
* * * *   *           *         12
*                       *       13
* *         *             *     14
*   *   *                   *   15
* *   *       *               * 16
```

i	*j*	*i % j*	*j % i*	*output*
1	1	0	0	*
1	2	1	0	*
1	3	1	0	*
				1
2	1	0	1	*
2	2	0	0	*
2	3	2	1	
				2
3	1	0	1	*
3	2	1	2	
3	3	0	0	*
				3

Trace when `n` *is* 3

To indicate the nesting, we use indentation in the program code. Again, the indentation is significant in Python (many other programming languages require curly braces or some other notation to indicate nesting). In PROGRAM 1.3.4, we refer to the `i` loop as the *outer* loop and the `j` loop as the *inner* loop. The inner loop iterates all the way through for each iteration of the outer loop. As usual, the best way to understand a new programming construct like this is to study a trace.

As a second example of nesting, consider a tax preparation program that computes income tax rates. People with no income (or less) pay no income tax; people with income of \$0 or more but less than \$8,925 pay 10 percent; people with income of \$8,925 or more but less than \$36,250 pay 15 percent; and so forth. We might accomplish this by using `if` statements with `else` clauses, one nested within another:

```
if income < 0.0:
    rate = 0.00
else:
    if income < 8925:
        rate = 0.10
    else:
        if income < 36250:
            rate = 0.15
        else:
            if income < 87850:
                rate = 0.25
            ...
```

In this application, the level of nesting becomes so deep that it makes the code hard to understand. Choosing among several mutually exclusive alternatives in this way is such a common task that an alternative that avoids this deep nesting is appropriate. The Python construct for this purpose is a generalized `if` statement that allows any number of "else if" clauses of the form

```
elif <boolean expression>:
    <block of statements>
```

before the "else" clause. When an `elif` block contains only a single statement, you can put the statement on the same line as the `elif` keyword for brevity and clarity. With this construct, the code to compute a marginal tax rate is straightforward:

```
if   income <      0: rate = 0.00
elif income <   8925: rate = 0.10
elif income <  36250: rate = 0.15
elif income <  87850: rate = 0.23
elif income < 183250: rate = 0.28
elif income < 398350: rate = 0.33
elif income < 400000: rate = 0.35
else:                 rate = 0.396
```

Python evaluates the boolean expressions sequence until reaching one that is `True`, when its corresponding block of statements is executed. Note that the final `else` is for the case where none of the conditions is satisfied (the tax rate for the rich, in this case). This construct is a special one that we use often.

Applications The ability to program with conditionals and loops immediately opens up the full world of computation. To emphasize this fact, we next consider a variety of examples. These examples all involve working with the types of data that we considered in SECTION 1.2, but rest assured that the same mechanisms serve us well for any computational application. The programs are carefully crafted, and by studying and appreciating them, you will be prepared to compose your own programs containing loops.

The examples that we consider here involve computing with numbers. Several of our examples are tied to problems pondered by mathematicians and scientists over the past several centuries. While computers have existed for only 50 years or so, many of the computational methods that we use are based on a rich mathematical tradition tracing back to antiquity.

Finite sum. The computational paradigm used by `powersoftwo.py` is one that you will use frequently. It uses two variables—one as an index that controls a loop and the other to accumulate a computational result. PROGRAM 1.3.5 (`harmonic.py`) uses the same paradigm to evaluate the finite sum $H_n = 1 + 1/2 + 1/3 + \ldots + 1/n$. These numbers, which are known as the *harmonic numbers*, arise frequently in discrete mathematics. Harmonic numbers are the discrete analog of the logarithm. They also approximate the area under the curve $y = 1/x$. You can use PROGRAM 1.3.5 as a model for computing the values of other sums (see EXERCISE 1.3.16).

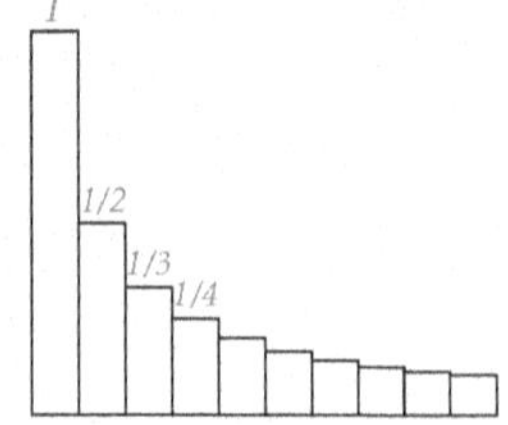

Program 1.3.5 Harmonic numbers (harmonic.py)

```
import sys
import stdio

n = int(sys.argv[1])

total = 0.0
for i in range(1, n+1):
    # Add the ith term to the sum.
    total += 1.0 / i

stdio.writeln(total)
```

n	*number of terms in sum*
i	*loop control variable*
total	*cumulated sum*

This program accepts integer n as a command-line argument and writes the nth harmonic number. The value is known from mathematical analysis to be about $\ln(n) + 0.57721$ for large n. Note that $\ln(10{,}000) \approx 9.21034$.

```
% python harmonic.py 2
1.5
% python harmonic.py 10
2.9289682539682538
% python harmonic.py 10000
9.787606036044348
```

Computing the square root. How are functions in Python's `math` module, such as `math.sqrt()`, implemented? PROGRAM 1.3.6 (`sqrt.py`) illustrates one technique. To compute the square root function, it uses an iterative computation that was known to the Babylonians over 4,000 years ago. It is also a special case of a general computational technique that was developed in the 17th century by Isaac Newton and Joseph Raphson and is widely known as *Newton's method.* Under generous conditions on a given function $f(x)$, Newton's method is an effective way to find roots (values of x for which the function is 0). Start with an initial estimate, t_0. Given the estimate t_i, compute a new estimate by drawing a line tangent to the curve $y = f(x)$ at the point $(t_i, f(t_i))$ and set t_{i+1} to the x-coordinate of the point where that line hits the x-axis. Iterating this process, we get closer to the root.

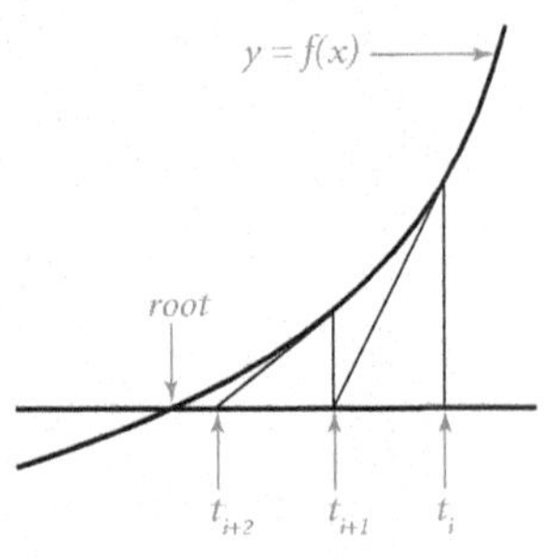

Newton's method

Computing the square root of a positive number c is equivalent to finding the positive root of the function $f(x) = x^2 - c$. For this special case, Newton's method amounts to the process implemented in `sqrt.py` (see PROGRAM 1.3.6 and EXERCISE 1.3.17). Start with the estimate $t = c$. If t is equal to c / t, then t is equal to the square root of c, so the computation is complete. If not, refine the estimate by replacing t with the average of t and c / t. With Newton's method, we get the value of the square root of 2 accurate to 15 places in just 5 iterations of the loop.

Newton's method is important in scientific computing because the same iterative approach is effective for finding the roots of a broad class of functions, including many for which analytic solutions are not known (so the Python `math` module would be no help). Nowadays, we take for granted that we can find whatever values we need of mathematical functions; before computers, scientists and engineers had to use tables or compute values by hand. Computational techniques that were developed to enable calculations by hand needed to be very efficient, so it is not surprising that many of those same techniques are effective when we use computers. Newton's method is a classic example of this phenomenon.

Another useful approach for evaluating mathematical functions is to use Taylor series expansions (see EXERCISES 1.3.37 and 1.3.38). Evaluating trigonometric functions is a typical application.

Program 1.3.6 *Newton's method* (sqrt.py)

```
import sys
import stdio

EPSILON = 1e-15

c = float(sys.argv[1])
t = c
while abs(t - c/t) > (EPSILON * t):
    # Replace t by the average of t and c/t.
    t = (c/t + t) / 2.0

stdio.writeln(t)
```

c	*argument*
EPSILON	*error tolerance*
t	*estimate of c*

This program accepts a positive float c *as a command-line argument, and writes the square root of* c *to 15 decimal places of accuracy. It uses Newton's method (see text) to compute the square root.*

```
% python sqrt.py 2.0
1.414213562373095
% python sqrt.py 2544545
1595.1630010754388
```

iteration	t	c/t
1	2.00000000000	1.0
2	1.50000000000	1.33333333333
3	1.41666666667	1.41176470588
4	1.41421568627	1.41421143847
5	1.41421356237	1.41421356237

Trace when c *is* 2.0

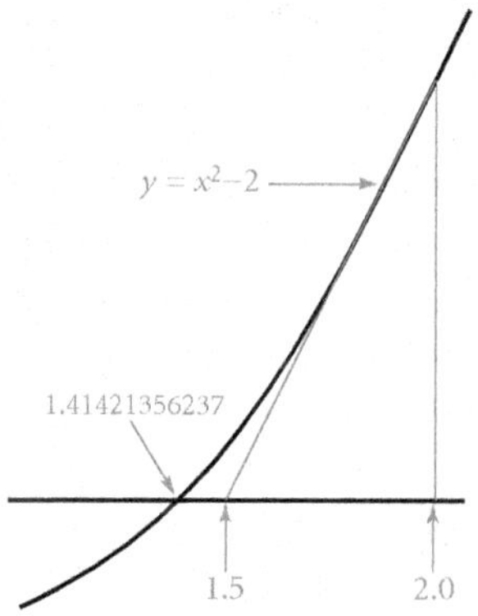

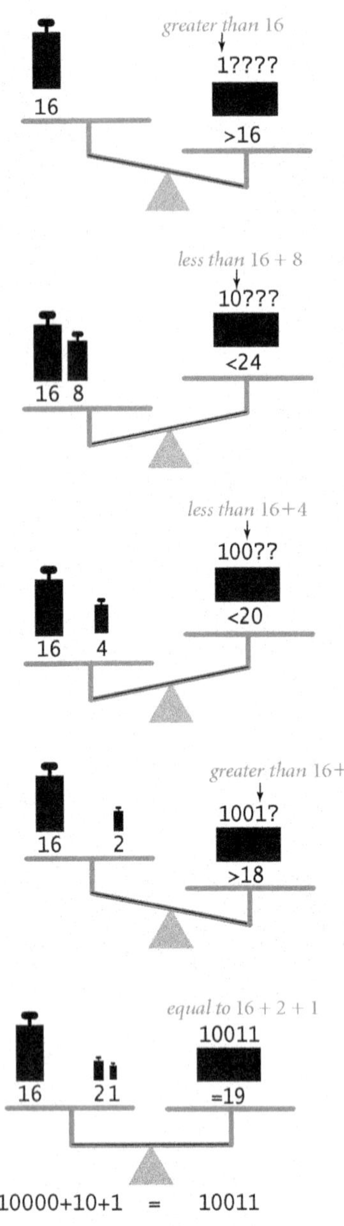

Scale metaphor for binary conversion

Number conversion. Program 1.3.7 (`binary.py`) writes the binary (base 2) representation of the decimal number typed as the command-line argument. It is based on decomposing a number into a sum of powers of 2. For example, the binary representation of 19 is 10011, which is the same as saying that 19 = 16 + 2 + 1. To compute the binary representation of `n`, we consider the powers of 2 less than or equal to `n` in decreasing order to determine which belong in the binary decomposition (and therefore correspond to a 1 bit in the binary representation). This process corresponds precisely to using a balance scale to weigh an object, using weights whose values are powers of 2. First, we find the largest weight not heavier than the object. Then, considering the weights in decreasing order, we add each weight to test whether the object is lighter. If so, we remove the weight; if not, we leave the weight and try the next one. Each weight corresponds to a bit in the binary representation of the weight of the object: leaving a weight corresponds to a 1 bit in the binary representation of the object's weight, and removing a weight corresponds to a 0 bit in the binary representation of the object's weight.

In `binary.py`, the variable `v` corresponds to the current weight being tested, and the variable `n` accounts for the excess (unknown) part of the object's weight (to simulate leaving a weight on the balance, we just subtract that weight from `n`). The value of `v` decreases through the powers of 2. When `v` is larger than `n`, `binary.py` writes `0`; otherwise, it writes `1` and subtracts `v` from `n`. As usual, a trace (of the values of `n`, `v`, `n < v`, and the output bit for each loop iteration) can be very useful in helping you to understand the program. Read from top to bottom in the rightmost column of the trace, the output is `10011`—the binary representation of 19.

Program 1.3.7 Converting to binary (binary.py)

```
import sys
import stdio

n = int(sys.argv[1])

# Compute v as the largest power of 2 <= n.
v = 1
while v <= n // 2:
    v *= 2

# Cast out powers of 2 in decreasing order.
while v > 0:
    if n < v:
        stdio.write(0)
    else:
        stdio.write(1)
        n -= v
    v //= 2

stdio.writeln()
```

v	*current power of 2*
n	*current excess*

This program writes the binary representation of a positive integer given as the command-line argument, by casting out powers of 2 in decreasing order (see text).

```
% python binary.py 19
10011
% python binary.py 255
11111111
% python binary.py 512
1000000000
% python binary.py 100000000
101111101011110000100000000
```

n	binary representation of n	v	v > 0	binary representation of v	n < v	output
19	10011	16	True	10000	False	1
3	0011	8	True	1000	True	0
3	011	4	True	100	True	0
3	01	2	True	10	False	1
1	1	1	True	1	False	1
0		0	False			

Trace of casting-out-powers-of-2 loop for **`python binary.py 19`**

Converting data from one representation to another is a frequent theme in composing computer programs. Thinking about conversion emphasizes the distinction between an abstraction (an integer like the number of hours in a day) and a representation of that abstraction (24 or 11000). The irony here is that the computer's representation of an integer is actually based on its binary representation.

Monte Carlo simulation. Our next example is different in character from the ones we have been considering, but it is representative of a common situation where we use computers to simulate what might happen in the real world so that we can make informed decisions. The specific example that we consider now is from a thoroughly studied class of problems known as *gambler's ruin.* Suppose that a gambler makes a series of fair $1 bets, starting with some given initial stake. The gambler always goes broke eventually, but when we set other limits on the game, various questions arise. For example, suppose that the gambler decides ahead of time to walk away after reaching a certain goal. What are the chances that the gambler will win? How many bets might be needed to win or lose the game? What is the maximum amount of money that the gambler will have during the course of the game?

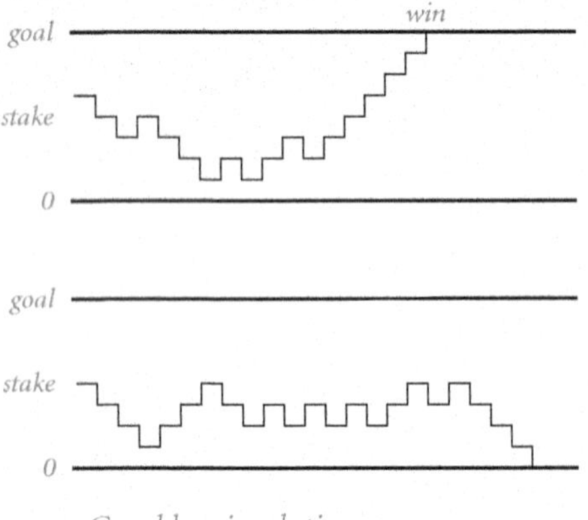

Gambler simulation sequences

Program 1.3.8 (`gambler.py`) is a simulation that can help answer these questions. It performs a sequence of trials, using `random.randrange()` to simulate the sequence of bets, continuing until the gambler is broke or the goal is reached, and keeping track of the number of wins and the number of

Program 1.3.8 Gambler's ruin simulation (gambler.py)

```
import random
import sys
import stdio

stake  = int(sys.argv[1])
goal   = int(sys.argv[2])
trials = int(sys.argv[3])

bets = 0
wins = 0
for t in range(trials):
    # Run one experiment.
    cash = stake
    while (cash > 0) and (cash < goal):
        # Simulate one bet.
        bets += 1
        if random.randrange(0, 2) == 0:
            cash += 1
        else:
            cash -= 1
    if cash == goal:
        wins += 1

stdio.writeln(str(100 * wins // trials) + '% wins')
stdio.writeln('Avg # bets: ' + str(bets // trials))
```

stake	*initial stake*
goal	*walkaway goal*
trials	*number of trials*
bets	*bet count*
wins	*win count*
cash	*cash on hand*

```
% python gambler.py 10 20 1000
50% wins
Avg # bets: 100
% python gambler.py 50 250 100
19% wins
Avg # bets: 11050
% python gambler.py 500 2500 100
21% wins
Avg # bets: 998071
```

This program accepts integer command-line arguments `stake`, `goal`, *and* `trials`. *It performs* `trials` *experiments, each of which starts with* `stake` *dollars and terminates on 0 dollars or* `goal`. *Then it writes the percentage of wins and the average number of bets per experiment. The inner* `while` *loop simulates a gambler with* `stake` *dollars who makes a series of $1 bets, continuing until going broke or reaching* `goal`. *The running time of this program is proportional to the total number of bets (*`trials` *times the average number of bets). For example, the last experiment shown causes nearly 100 million random numbers to be generated.*

bets. After running the experiment for the specified number of trials, the program averages and writes the results. You might wish to run this program for various command-line arguments—not necessarily just to plan your next trip to the casino, but to help you think about the following questions: Is the simulation an accurate reflection of what would happen in real life? How many trials are needed to get an accurate answer? What are the computational limits on performing such a simulation? Simulations are widely used in applications in economics, science, and engineering, and questions of this sort are important in any simulation.

In the case of `gambler.py`, we are verifying classical results from probability theory, which say the *probability of success is the ratio of the stake to the goal* and that the *expected number of bets is the product of the stake and the desired gain* (the difference between the goal and the stake). For example, if you want to go to Monte Carlo and try to turn $500 into $2,500, you have a reasonable (20 percent) chance of success, but you should expect to make a million $1 bets! If you try to turn $1 into $1,000, you have a 0.1 percent chance and can expect to be done (ruined, most likely) in about 999 bets (on average).

Simulation and analysis go hand-in-hand, each validating the other. In practice, the value of simulation is that it can suggest answers to questions that might be too difficult to resolve with analysis. For example, suppose that our gambler, recognizing that there will never be enough time to make a million bets, decides ahead of time to set an upper limit on the number of bets. How much money can the gambler expect to take home in that case? You can address this question with an easy change to PROGRAM 1.3.8 (see EXERCISE 1.3.24), but addressing it with mathematical analysis is not so easy.

Factoring. A *prime* is an integer greater than 1 whose only positive divisors are 1 and itself. The prime factorization of an integer is the multiset of primes whose product is the integer. For example, `3757208 = 2*2*2*7*13*13*397`. PROGRAM 1.3.9 (`factors.py`) computes the prime factorization of any given positive integer. In contrast to many of the other programs that we have seen (which we could do in a few minutes with a calculator or even a pencil and paper), this computation would not be feasible without a computer. How would you go about trying to find the factors of a number like `287994837222311`? You might find the factor `17` quickly, but even with a calculator it would take you quite a while to find `1739347`.

Although `factors.py` is compact and straightforward, it certainly will take some thought to convince yourself that it produces the desired result for any given

Program 1.3.9 Factoring integers (factors.py)

```
import sys
import stdio

n = int(sys.argv[1])

factor = 2
while factor*factor <= n:
    while (n % factor) == 0:
        # Cast out and write factor.
        n //= factor
        stdio.write(str(factor) + ' ')
    factor += 1
    # Any factors of n are greater than or equal to factor.

if n > 1:
    stdio.write(n)
stdio.writeln()
```

n	*unfactored part*
factor	*potential factor*

This program writes the prime factorization of any positive integer. The code is simple, but it takes some thought to convince oneself that it is correct (see text).

```
% python factors.py 3757208
2 2 2 7 13 13 397
% python factors.py 287994837222311
17 1739347 9739789
```

integer. As usual, following a trace that shows the values of the variables at the beginning of each iteration of the outer `for` loop is a good way to understand the computation. For the case where `n` is initially `3757208`, the inner `while` loop iterates three times when `factor` is 2, to remove the three factors of 2; then zero times when `factor` is 3, 4, 5, and 6, since none of those numbers divides `469651`; and so forth.

Tracing the program for a few example inputs clearly reveals its basic operation. To convince ourselves that the program will behave as expected for all inputs, we reason about what we expect each of the loops to do. The inner `while` loop clearly writes and removes from `n` all factors of `factor`. The key to understanding the program is to see that the following invariant holds at the beginning of each iteration of the outer `while` loop: `n` has no factors between `2` and `factor-1`. Thus, if `factor` is not prime, it will not divide `n`; if `factor` is prime, the `while` loop will do its job and the invariant will continue to hold. We can stop looking for factors when `factor*factor` is greater than `n` because if an integer `n` has a factor, it has one less than or equal to the square root of `n`.

factor	*n*	*output*
2	3757208	2 2 2
3	469651	
4	469651	
5	469651	
6	469651	
7	469651	7
8	67093	
9	67093	
10	67093	
11	67093	
12	67093	
13	67093	13 13
14	397	
15	397	
16	397	
17	397	
18	397	
19	397	
20	397	
		397

Trace when n is 3757208

In a more naïve implementation, we might simply have used the condition `(factor < n)` to terminate the outer loop. Even given the blinding speed of modern computers, such a decision would have a dramatic effect on the size of the numbers that we could factor. Exercise 1.3.26 encourages you to experiment with the program to explore the effectiveness of this simple change. On a computer that can do billions of operations per second, we could factor numbers on the order of 10^9 in a few seconds; with the `(factor*factor <= n)` test, we can factor numbers on the order of 10^{18} in a comparable amount of time. Loops give us the ability to solve difficult problems, but they also give us the ability to construct simple programs that run slowly, so we must always be cognizant of performance issues.

In modern applications such as cryptography, there are important situations where we wish to factor truly huge numbers (with, say, hundreds or thousands of digits). Even for experts, such a computation has so far turned out to be prohibitively difficult even *with* the use of a computer.

Loop and a half Sometimes the loop we need does not fit neatly into the flow-control structure of either a `for` or `while` loop. For example, suppose we want a loop that repeatedly does the following: execute some sequence of statements, exit the loop if some loop-termination condition is satisfied, and execute some other sequence of statements. That is, we want to position the loop-control condition in the middle of the loop, not at the beginning. This is known as a *loop and a half* because you must go partway through the loop before reaching the loop-termination test. Python provides the `break` statement for this purpose. When Python executes a `break` statement, it immediately exits the (innermost) loop.

For example, consider the problem of generating points that are randomly distributed in the unit disk. We can call `random.random()` to generate *x*- and *y*-coordinates to get points that are randomly distributed in the 2-by-2 square centered at the origin. Most of these points fall within the unit disk, so we just reject those that do not. Since we always want to generate at least one point, we compose a `while` loop whose loop-continuation condition is always satisfied, generate the random point (*x*, *y*) in the 2-by-2 square, and use a `break` statement to terminate the loop if (*x*, *y*) is in the unit disk.

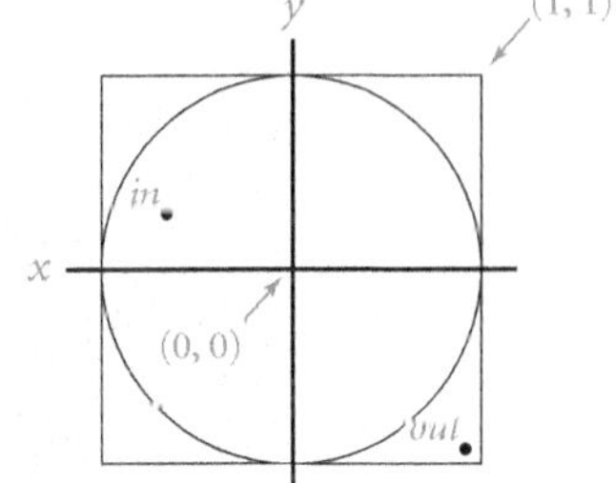

Random point in unit disk

```
while True:
    x = 1.0 + 2.0*random.random()
    y = 1.0 + 2.0*random.random()
    if x*x + y*y <= 1.0:
        break
```

Since the area of the unit disk is π and the area of the square is 4, the expected number of times the loop is iterated is $4/\pi$ (about 1.27).

Experts debate the merits of such internal exits from a loop. When misused, `break` statements can complicate the flow of control for a loop. However, in situations like this one, alternatives can be complicated (see Exercise 1.3.30). Some languages provide a "do–while" statement specifically to handle such cases. In Python, we recommend judicious use of a `break` statement, when necessary.

Infinite loops Before you compose programs that use loops, you need to think about the following issue: what if the loop-continuation condition in a `while` loop is always satisfied? With the statements that you have learned so far, one of two bad things could happen, both of which you need to learn to cope with.

First, suppose that such a loop calls `stdout.writeln()`. For example, if the loop-continuation condition in `tenhellos.py` were `i > 3` instead of `i <= 10`, it would always be `True`. What happens? Nowadays, we use *write* as an abstraction to mean *display in a terminal window*, and the result of attempting to display an unlimited number of lines in a terminal window depends on the operating system's conventions. If your system is set up to have *write* mean *print characters on a piece of paper*, you might run out of paper or have to unplug the printer. In a terminal window, you need a “stop writing” operation. Before running programs with loops on your own, you should make sure that you know how to “pull the plug” on an infinite loop of `stdout.writeln()` calls and then test out that strategy by making the change to `tenhellos.py` indicated previously and trying to stop it. On most systems, `<Ctrl-c>` means *stop the current program* and should do the job.

Second, *nothing* might happen. At least, nothing visible might happen. If your program has an infinite loop that does not produce any output, it will spin through the loop and you will see no results at all. The program will appear to stall. When you find yourself in such a situation, you can inspect the loops to make sure that the loop-termination condition always happens, but the problem may not be easy to identify. One way to locate such a bug is to insert calls to `stdout.writeln()` to produce a trace. If these calls fall within an infinite loop, this strategy reduces the problem to the case discussed in the previous paragraph, but the output might give you a clue about what to do.

You might not know (or it might not matter) whether a loop is infinite or just very long. If you run `gambler.py` with arguments such as `python gambler.py 100000 200000 100`, you may not want to wait for the answer. Later, you will learn to be aware of and to estimate the running time of your programs. Section 4.1 introduces this topic.

Why not have Python detect infinite loops and warn us about them? You might be surprised to know that it is not possible to do so, in general. This counterintuitive fact is one of the fundamental results of theoretical computer science.

An infinite loop (with output)

```
import stdio
i = 4
while i > 3:
    stdio.write(i)
    stdio.writeln('th Hello')
    i += 1
```

```
% python infiniteloop1.py
1st Hello
2nd Hello
3rd Hello
5th Hello
6th Hello
7th Hello
8th Hello
9th Hello
10th Hello
11th Hello
12th Hello
13th Hello
14th Hello
...
```

An infinite loop (with no output)

```
while True:
    x = random.random()
    y = random.random()
    if x*x + y*y >= 2.0:
        break
```

```
% python infiniteloop2.py
...
```

Summary For reference, the accompanying table lists the programs that we have considered in this section. They are representative of the kinds of tasks we can address with short programs consisting of `if`, `while`, and `for` statements that process built-in types of data. These types of computations are an appropriate way to become familiar with the basic Python flow-of-control constructs. The time that you spend now working with as many such programs as you can will certainly pay off in the future.

To learn how to use conditionals and loops, you must practice composing and debugging programs with `if`, `while`, and `for` statements. The exercises at the end of this section provide many opportunities for you to begin this process. For each exercise, you will compose a Python program, then run and test it. All programmers know that it is unusual to have a program work as planned the first time it is run, so you will want to have an understanding of your program and an expectation of what it should do, step by step. At first, use explicit traces to check your understanding and expectation. As you gain experience, you will find yourself thinking in terms of what a trace might produce as you compose your loops. Ask yourself the following kinds of questions: What will be the values of the variables after the loop iterates the first time? The second time? The final time? Is there any way this program could get stuck in an infinite loop?

program	*description*
`flip.py`	*simulate a coin flip*
`tenhellos.py`	*your first loop*
`powersoftwo.py`	*compute and write a table of values*
`divisorpattern.py`	*your first nested loop*
`harmonic.py`	*compute a finite sum*
`sqrt.py`	*classic iterative algorithm*
`binary.py`	*basic number conversion*
`gambler.py`	*simulation with nested loops*
`factors.py`	`while` *loop within a* `while` *loop*

Summary of programs in this section

Loops and conditionals are a giant step in our ability to compute: `if`, `while`, and `for` statements take us from simple straight-line programs to an arbitrarily complicated flow of control. In the next several chapters, we will take more giant steps that will allow us to process large amounts of input data and to define and process types of data other than simple numeric types. The `if`, `while`, and `for` statements of this section will play an essential role in the programs that we consider as we take these steps.

Q&A

Q. What is the difference between `=` and `==`?

A. We repeat this question here to remind you that you should not use `=` when you really mean `==` in a conditional expression. The statement `x = y` assigns `y` to `x`, whereas the expression `x == y` tests whether the two variables currently are equal. In some programming languages, this difference can wreak havoc in a program and be difficult to detect. In Python, assignment statements are not expressions. For example, if we were to make the mistake of typing `cash = goal` instead of `cash == goal` in Program 1.3.8, the compiler would find the bug for us:

```
% python gambler.py 10 20 1000
  File "gambler.py", line 21
    if cash = goal:
            ^
SyntaxError: invalid syntax
```

Q. What happens if I leave out the colon in an `if`, `while`, or `for` statement?

A. Python raises a `SyntaxError` at compile time.

Q. What are the rules for indenting statement blocks?

A. Each statement in a block must have the same indentation; if it does not, Python will raise an `IndentationError` at compile time. Python programmers commonly use a four-space indentation scheme, which we follow throughout this book.

Q. Should I use tab characters to indent my code?

A. No, you should avoid placing tab characters in your `.py` files. Many editors, however, offer the option of automatically placing a sequence of spaces into your program when you type the `<Tab>` key; it's appropriate to use that option when composing Python programs.

Q. Can I spread a long statement over multiple lines?

A. Yes, but some care is needed because of the way Python treats indentation. If the expression that spans multiple lines is enclosed inside parentheses (or square brackets or curly braces), then there is no need to do anything special. For example, this is a single statement that is spread over three lines:

```
stdio.write(a0 + a1 + a2 + a3 +
            a4 + a5 + a6 + a7 +
            a8 + a9)
```

However, if there is no implied line continuation, you must use the backslash character at the end of each line to be continued.

```
total = a0 + a1 + a2 + a3 + \
        a4 + a5 + a6 + a7 + \
        a8 + a9
```

Q. Suppose I want to skip over some of code in a loop in some cases, or suppose that I want the body of a conditional statement to be empty, so that no statement is executed. Does Python have language support for such things?

A. Yes, Python provides the `continue` and `pass` statements, respectively, for these conditions. However, situations in which they are really necessary are rare, and we do not use them in this book. Also, there is no *switch* statement in Python (for mutually exclusive alternatives), though one is commonly found in other languages, and no *goto* statement (for unstructured control flow).

Q. Can I use a non-boolean expression in an `if` or `while` statement?

A. Yes, but this is probably not a good idea. Expressions that evaluate to zero or the empty string are considered `False`; all other numeric and string expressions are considered `True`.

Q. Are there cases where I must use a `for` statement but not a `while` statement, or vice versa?

A. You can use a `while` statement to implement any kind of loop, but, as defined here, you can use a `for` statement only for the kind of loop that iterates over a finite sequence of integers. Later (Sections 1.4, 3.3, and 4.4), we will consider other ways to use the `for` statement.

Q. Can I use the built-in `range()` function to create a sequence of integers with a step size of some value other than 1?

A. Yes, `range()` supports an optional third argument `step`, which defaults to `1`. That is, `range(start, stop, step)` produces the sequence of integers `start`, `start + step`, `start + 2 * step`, and so forth. If `step` is a positive integer, the sequence continues as long as `start + i * step` is less than `stop`; if `step` is a negative integer, the sequence continues as long as `start + i * step` is greater than `stop`. For example, `range(0, -100, -1)` returns the integer sequence 0, -1, -2, ..., -99.

Q. Can I use floats as arguments to `range()`?

A. No, all arguments must be integers.

Q. Can I change the loop-index variable within a `for` loop?

A. Yes, but it will not affect the sequence of integers produced by `range()`. For example, the following loop writes the 100 integers from 0 to 99:

```
for i in range(100):
    stdio.writeln(i)
    i += 10
```

Q. In a `for` loop, what is the value of the loop-control variable after the loop terminates?

A. It is the last value of the loop-control variable during the loop. Upon termination of the `for` loop above, `i` refers to the integer `109`. Using the loop-control variable after the termination of a `for` loop is generally considered poor style, so we do not do so in any of our programs.

Exercises

1.3.1 Compose a program that takes three integer command-line arguments and writes `'equal'` if all three are equal, and `'not equal'` otherwise.

1.3.2 Compose a more general and more robust version of `quadratic.py` (PROGRAM 1.2.4) that writes the roots of the polynomial $ax^2 + bx + c$, writes an appropriate message if the discriminant is negative, and behaves appropriately (avoiding division by zero) if a is zero.

1.3.3 Compose a code fragment that takes two float command-line arguments and writes `True` if both are strictly between `0.0` and `1.0`, and `False` otherwise.

1.3.4 Improve your solution to EXERCISE 1.2.22 by adding code to check that the values of the command-line arguments fall within the ranges of validity of the wind chill formula, as well as code to write an error message if that is not the case.

1.3.5 What is `j` after each of the following code fragments is executed?

a.
```
j = 0
for i in range(j, 10):
    j += i
```

b.
```
j = 0
for i in range(10):
    j += j
```

c.
```
for j in range(10):
    j += j
```

1.3.6 Redesign `tenhellos.py` to compose a program `hellos.py` that takes the number of lines to write as a command-line argument. You may assume that the argument is less than `1000`. *Hint*: Use `i % 10` and `i % 100` to determine when to use `st`, `nd`, `rd`, or `th` for writing the `i`th `Hello`.

1.3.7 Compose a program `fiveperline.py` that, using one `for` loop and one `if` statement, writes the integers from 1,000 (inclusive) to 2,000 (exclusive) with five integers per line. *Hint*: Use the `%` operator.

1.3.8 Generalizing the "uniform random numbers" exercise from SECTION 1.2 (EXERCISE 1.2.27), compose a program `stats.py` that accepts an integer `n` as a command-line argument, uses `random.random()` to write `n` uniform random numbers between 0 and 1, and then writes their average value, their minimum value, and their maximum value.

1.3.9 In this section, we presented this code to implement the ruler function:

```
ruler = '1'
stdio.writeln(ruler)
for i in range(2, n+1):
    ruler = ruler + ' ' + str(i) + ' ' + ruler
    stdio.writeln(ruler)
```

Describe what happens when you run this code when `n` is too large—for example, when `n` is 100.

1.3.10 Compose a program `functiongrowth.py` that writes a table of the values $\log_2 n$, n, $n \log_e n$, n^2, n^3, and 2^n for $n = 2, 4, 8, 16, 32, 64, \ldots, 2048$. To line up columns, use tabs (`\t` characters).

1.3.11 What are `m` and `n` after the following code is executed?

```
n = 123456789
m = 0
while n != 0:
    m = (10 * m) + (n % 10)
    n /= 10
```

1.3.12 What does this code write?

```
f = 0
g = 1
for i in range(16):
    stdio.writeln(f)
    f = f + g
    g = f - g
```

Solution: Even an expert programmer will tell you that the only way to understand a program like this is to trace it. When you do, you will find that it writes the values 0, 1, 1, 2, 3, 5, 8, 13, 21, 34, 55, 89, 134, 233, 377, and 610. These numbers are the first 16 of the famous *Fibonacci sequence*, which are defined by the following formulas: $F_0 = 0$, $F_1 = 1$, and $F_n = F_{n-1} + F_{n-2}$ for $n > 1$. The Fibonacci sequence arises in a surprising variety of contexts; it has been studied for centuries, and many of its properties are well known. For example, the ratio of successive numbers approaches the *golden ratio* ϕ (about 1.618) as n approaches infinity.

1.3.13 Compose a program that takes a command-line argument `n` and writes all the positive powers of 2 less than or equal to `n`. Make sure that your program works properly for all values of `n`. (Your program should write nothing if `n` is negative.)

1.3.14 Expand your solution to the "Continuously compounded interest" exercise from Section 1.2 (Exercise 1.2.21) to write a table giving the total amount paid and the remaining principal after each monthly payment.

1.3.15 Compose a version of `divisorpattern.py` (Program 1.3.4) that uses `while` loops instead of `for` loops.

1.3.16 Unlike the harmonic numbers, the sum $1/1^2 + 1/2^2 + \ldots + 1/n^2$ *does* converge to a constant as n grows to infinity. (Indeed, the constant is $\pi^2/6$, so this formula can be used to estimate the value of π.) Which of the following `for` loops computes this sum? Assume that `n` is the integer `1000000` and `total` is a float initialized to `0.0`.

a.
```
for i in range(1, n+1):
    total += 1 / (i*i)
```
b.
```
for i in range(1, n+1):
    total += 1.0 / i*i
```
c.
```
for i in range(1, n+1):
    total += 1.0 / (i*i)
```
d.
```
for i in range(1, n+1):
    total += 1.0 / (1.0*i*i)
```

1.3.17 Show that `sqrt.py` (Program 1.3.6) implements Newton's method for finding the square root of *c*. *Hint*: Use the fact that the slope of the tangent to a (differentiable) function $f(x)$ at $x = t$ is $f'(t)$ to find the equation of the tangent line and then use that equation to find the point where the tangent line intersects the x-axis to show that you can use Newton's method to find a root of any function as follows: at each iteration, replace the estimate t by $t - f(t) / f'(t)$.

1.3.18 Using Newton's method, develop a program that takes integers `n` and `k` as command-line arguments and writes the `k`th root of `n` (*Hint*: See Exercise 1.3.17.)

1.3.19 Modify `binary.py` to create a program `kary.py` that takes `i` and `k` as command-line arguments and converts `i` to base `k`. Assume that `k` is an integer between 2 and 16. For bases greater than 10, use the letters `A` through `F` to represent the 11th through 16th digits, respectively.

1.3.20 Compose a code fragment that puts the binary representation of a positive integer `n` into a `String s`.

Solution: Working from Program 1.3.7, we get the solution

```
s = ''
v = 1
while v <= n//2:
    v *= 2
while v > 0:
    if n < v:
        s += '0'
    else:
        s += '1'
        n -= v
    v //= 2
```

A simpler option is to work from right to left:

```
s = ''
while n > 0:
    s = str(n % 2) + s
    n /= 2
```

Both of these methods are worthy of careful study.

1.3.21 Compose a version of `gambler.py` that uses two nested `while` loops or two nested `for` loops instead of a `while` loop inside a `for` loop.

1.3.22 Compose a program `gamblerplot.py` that traces a gambler's ruin simulation by writing a line after each bet in which one asterisk corresponds to each dollar held by the gambler.

1.3.23 Modify `gambler.py` to take an extra command-line argument that specifies the (fixed) probability that the gambler wins each bet. Use your program to try to learn how this probability affects the chance of winning and the expected number of bets. Try a value of p close to 0.5 (say, 0.48).

1.3.24 Modify `gambler.py` to take an extra command-line argument that specifies the number of bets the gambler is willing to make, so that there are three possible ways for the game to end: the gambler wins, loses, or runs out of time. Add to the output to give the expected amount of money the gambler will have when the game ends. *Extra credit*: Use your program to plan your next trip to Monte Carlo.

1.3.25 Modify `factors.py` to write just one copy each of the prime divisors.

1.3.26 Run quick experiments to determine the impact of using the termination condition `(i < n)` instead of `(i *i <= n)` in `factors.py` (Program 1.3.9). For each method, find the largest n such that when you type in an n-digit number, the program is sure to finish within 10 seconds.

1.3.27 Compose a program `checkerboard.py` that takes one command-line argument `n` and uses a loop within a loop to write a two-dimensional `n`-by-`n` checkerboard pattern with alternating spaces and asterisks, like the following 5-by-5 pattern:

```
* * * * *
 * * * *
* * * * *
 * * * *
* * * * *
```

1.3.28 Compose a program `gcd.py` that finds the greatest common divisor (gcd) of two integers using *Euclid's algorithm*, which is an iterative computation based on the following observation: if `x` is greater than `y`, then if `y` divides `x`, the gcd of `x` and `y` is `y`; otherwise, the gcd of `x` and `y` is the same as the gcd of `x % y` and `y`.

1.3.29 Compose a program `relativelyprime.py` that takes one command-line argument `n` and writes an `n`-by-`n` table such that there is an * in row `i` and column `j` if the gcd of `i` and `j` is `1` (`i` and `j` are relatively prime), and a space in that position otherwise.

1.3.30 Compose a program that generates a point that is randomly distributed in the unit disk, but without using a `break` statement. Compare your solution to the one given at the end of this section.

1.3.31 Compose a program that writes the coordinates of a random point (a, b, c) on the surface of a sphere. To generate such a point, use *Marsaglia's method*: Start by picking a random point (x, y) in the unit disk using the method described at the end of this section. Then, set a to $2\,x\,\sqrt{1 - x^2 - y^2}$, b to $2\,\sqrt{1 - x^2 - y^2}$, and c to $1 - 2\,(x^2 + y^2)$.

Creative Exercises

1.3.32 *Ramanujan's taxi.* S. Ramanujan was an Indian mathematician who became famous for his intuition about numbers. When the English mathematician G. H. Hardy came to visit him in the hospital one day, Hardy remarked that the number of his taxi was 1729, a rather dull number. To which Ramanujan replied, "No, Hardy! No, Hardy! It is a very interesting number. It is the smallest number expressible as the sum of two cubes in two different ways." Verify this claim by composing a program that takes a command-line argument `n` and writes all integers less than or equal to `n` that can be expressed as the sum of two cubes in two different ways. In other words, find distinct positive integers a, b, c, and d such that $a^3 + b^3 = c^3 + d^3$. Use four nested `for` loops.

1.3.33 *Checksums.* The International Standard Book Number (ISBN) is a 10-digit code that uniquely specifies a book. The rightmost digit is a *checksum* digit that can be uniquely determined from the other 9 digits, from the condition that $d_1 + 2d_2 + 3d_3 + \ldots + 10d_{10}$ must be a multiple of 11 (here d_i denotes the ith digit from the right). The checksum digit d_i can be any value from 0 to 10: the ISBN convention is to use the character `'X'` to denote 10. Example: The checksum digit corresponding to 020131452 is 5, because 5 is the only value of x between 0 and 10 for which

$$10 \cdot 0 + 9 \cdot 2 + 8 \cdot 0 + 7 \cdot 1 + 6 \cdot 3 + 5 \cdot 1 + 4 \cdot 4 + 3 \cdot 5 + 2 \cdot 2 + 1 \cdot x$$

is a multiple of 11. Compose a program that takes a 9-digit integer as a command-line argument, computes the checksum, and writes the ISBN number.

1.3.34 *Counting primes.* Compose a program `primecounter.py` that takes a command-line argument `n` and writes the number of primes less than or equal to `n`. Use it to write the number of primes less than or equal to 10 million. *Note*: If you are not careful to make your program efficient, it may not finish in a reasonable amount of time. Later (in Section 1.4), you will learn about a more efficient way to perform this computation called the *Sieve of Eratosthenes* (see Program 1.4.3).

1.3.35 *2D random walk.* A two-dimensional random walk simulates the behavior of a particle moving in a grid of points. At each step, the random walker moves north, south, east, or west with probability equal to 1/4, independent of previous moves. Compose a program `randomwalker.py` that takes a command-line argument `n` and estimates how long it will take a random walker to hit the boundary of a $2n$-by-$2n$ square centered at the starting point.

1.3.36 *Median-of-5.* Compose a program that takes five distinct integers from the command line and writes the median value (the value such that two of the other integers are smaller and two are larger). *Extra credit*: Solve the problem with a program that compares values fewer than seven times for any given input.

1.3.37 *Exponential function.* Assume that `x` is a float. Compose a code fragment that uses the Taylor series expansion to assign $e^x = 1 + x + x^2/2! + x^3/3! + \ldots$ to `total`.

Solution: The purpose of this exercise is to get you to think about how a library function like `math.exp()` might be implemented in terms of elementary operators. Try solving it, then compare your solution with the one developed here.

We start by considering the problem of computing one term. Suppose that `x` is a float and `n` is an integer. The following code assigns $x^n / n!$ to `term` using the direct method of having one loop for the numerator and another loop for the denominator, then dividing the results:

```
num = 1.0
den = 1.0
for i in range(1, n+1):
    num *= x
for i in range(1, n+1):
    den *= i
term = num / den
```

A better approach is to use just a single `for` loop:

```
term = 1.0
for i in range(1, n+1):
    term *= x / i
```

Besides being more compact and elegant, the latter solution is preferable because it avoids inaccuracies caused by computing with huge numbers. For example, the two-loop approach breaks down for values like $x = 10$ and $n = 100$ because 100! is too large to represent accurately as a float.

To compute e^x, we nest this `for` loop within another `for` loop:

```
term = 1.0
total = 0.0
n = 1
while total != total + term:
    total += term
    term = 1.0
    for i in range(1, n+1):
        term *= x / i
    n += 1
```

The number of times the `while` loop iterates depends on the relative values of the next term and the accumulated sum. Once `total` stops changing, we leave the loop. (This strategy is more efficient than using the termination condition `(term > 0)` because it avoids a significant number of iterations that do not change the value of the total.) This code is effective, but it is inefficient because the inner `for` loop recomputes all the values it computed on the previous iteration of the outer `for` loop. Instead, we can make use of the term that was added in on the previous loop iteration and solve the problem with a single `while` loop:

```
term = 1.0
total = 0.0
n = 1
while total != total + term:
    total += term
    term *= x/n
    n += 1
```

1.3.38 *Trigonometric functions.* Compose programs `sine.py` and `cosine.py` that compute the sine and cosine functions using their Taylor series expansions $\sin x = x - x^3/3! + x^5/5! - \ldots$ and $\cos x = 1 - x^2/2! + x^4/4! - \ldots$

1.3.39 *Experimental analysis.* Run experiments to determine the relative costs of `math.exp()` and the three approaches from EXERCISE 1.3.37 for computing e^x: the direct method with nested `for` loops, the improvement with a single `while` loop, and the latter with the termination condition `(term > 0)`. Use trial-and-error with a command-line argument to determine how many times your computer can perform each computation in 10 seconds.

1.3.40 *Pepys's problem.* In 1693 Samuel Pepys asked Isaac Newton which is more likely: getting 1 at least once when rolling a fair die six times or getting 1 at least twice when rolling it 12 times. Compose a program that could have provided Newton with a quick answer.

1.3.41 *Game simulation.* In the 1970s game show *Let's Make a Deal*, a contestant is presented with three doors. Behind one of them is a valuable prize. After the contestant chooses a door, the host opens one of the other two doors (never revealing the prize, of course). The contestant is then given the opportunity to switch to the other unopened door. Should the contestant do so? Intuitively, it might seem that the contestant's initial choice door and the other unopened door are equally likely to contain the prize, so there would be no incentive to switch. Compose a program `montehall.py` to test this intuition by simulation. Your program should take a command-line argument `n`, play the game `n` times using each of the two strategies (switch or do not switch), and write the chance of success for each of the two strategies.

1.3.42 *Chaos.* Compose a program to study the following simple model for population growth, which might be applied to study fish in a pond, bacteria in a test tube, or any of a host of similar situations. We suppose that the population ranges from 0 (extinct) to 1 (maximum population that can be sustained). If the population at time t is x, then we suppose the population at time $t + 1$ to be $rx(1-x)$, where the parameter r, known as the *fecundity parameter*, controls the rate of growth. Start with a small population—say, $x = 0.01$—and study the result of iterating the model, for various values of r. For which values of r does the population stabilize at $x = 1 - 1/r$? Can you say anything about the population when r is 3.5? 3.8? 5?

1.3.43 *Euler's sum-of-powers conjecture.* In 1769 Leonhard Euler formulated a generalized version of Fermat's Last Theorem, conjecturing that at least n nth powers are needed to obtain a sum that is itself an nth power, for $n > 2$. Compose a program to disprove Euler's conjecture (which stood until 1967), using a quintuply nested loop to find four positive integers whose 5th power sums to the 5th power of another positive integer. That is, find five integers a, b, c, d, and e such that $a^5 + b^5 + c^5 + d^5 = e^5$.

1.4 Arrays

In this section, we introduce you to the idea of a *data structure* and to your first data structure, the *array*. The primary purpose of an array is to facilitate storing and manipulating large quantities of data. Arrays play an essential role in many data processing tasks. They also correspond to vectors and matrices, which are widely used in science and in scientific programming. We will consider basic properties of array processing in Python, with many examples illustrating why arrays are useful.

Programs in this section

A *data structure* is a way to organize data that we wish to process with a computer program. Data structures play an essential role in computer programming—indeed, Chapter 4 of this book is devoted to the study of classic data structures of all sorts.

A *one-dimensional array* (or *array*) is a data structure that stores a *sequence* of (references to) objects. We refer to the objects within an array as its *elements*. The method that we use to refer to elements in an array is *numbering* and then *indexing* them. If we have n elements in the sequence, we think of them as being numbered from 0 to $n - 1$. Then, we can unambiguously specify one of them by referring to the ith element for any integer i in this range.

A *two-dimensional array* is an array of (references to) one-dimensional arrays. Whereas the elements of a one-dimensional array are indexed by a single integer, the elements of a two-dimensional array are indexed by a pair of integers: the first specifying a row, and the second specifying a column.

Often, when we have a large amount of data to process, we first put all of the data into one or more arrays. Then we use indexing to refer to individual elements and to process the data. We might have exam scores, stock prices, nucleotides in a DNA strand, or characters in a book. Each of these examples involves a large number of objects that are all of the same type. We consider such applications when we discuss data input in Section 1.5 and in the case study that is the subject of Section 1.6. In this section, we expose the basic properties of arrays by considering examples where our programs first populate arrays with objects having computed values from experimental studies and then process them.

Arrays in Python The simplest way to create an array in Python is to place comma-separated literals between matching square brackets. For example, the code

```
suits = ['Clubs', 'Diamonds', 'Hearts', 'Spades']
```

creates an array `suits[]` with four strings, and the code

```
x = [0.30, 0.60, 0.10]
y = [0.40, 0.10, 0.50]
```

creates two arrays `x[]` and `y[]`, each with three floats. Each array is an object that contains data (references to objects) structured for efficient access. While the truth is a bit complicated (and explained in detail in SECTION 4.1), it is useful to think of references to the elements in an array as stored contiguously, one after the other, in your computer's memory, as shown in the diagram at right for the `suits[]` array defined above.

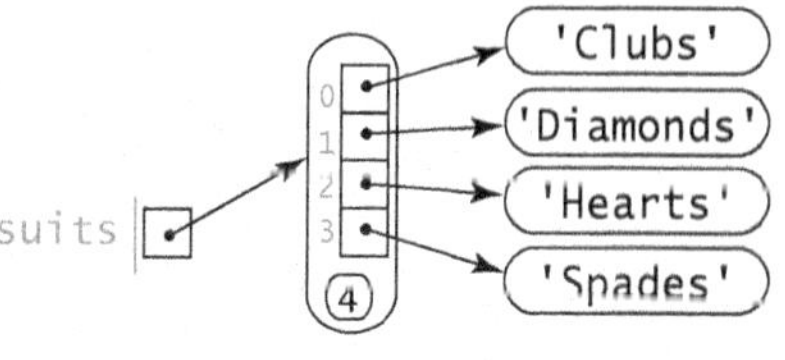

Array data structure

After creating an array, you can refer to any individual object anywhere you would use a variable name in a program by specifying the array name followed by an integer index within square brackets. In the preceding examples, `suits[1]` refers to `'Diamonds'`, `x[0]` refers to `.30`, `y[2]` refers to `.50`, and so forth. Note that `x` is a reference to the whole array, as opposed to `x[i]`, which is a reference to the `i`th element. In the text, we use the notation `x[]` to indicate that variable `x` is an array (but we do not use `x[]` in Python code).

The obvious advantage of using an array is to avoid explicitly naming each variable individually. Using an array index is virtually the same as appending the index to the array name. For example, if we wanted to process eight floats, we could refer to them each individually with variable names like `a0`, `a1`, `a2`, `a3`, `a4`, `a5`, `a6`, and `a7`. Naming dozens of individual variables in this way would be cumbersome, however, and naming millions is untenable.

As an example of code that uses arrays, consider using arrays to represent *vectors*. We consider vectors in detail in SECTION 3.3; for the moment, think of a vector as a sequence of real numbers. The *dot product* of two vectors (of the same length) is the sum of the products of their corresponding components. For example, if our two example arrays `x[]` and `y[]` represent vectors, their dot product is the expression `x[0]*y[0] + x[1]*y[1] + x[2]*y[2]`. More generally, if we have two one-dimensional arrays of floats x[] and y[] whose length is given by a variable n, we can use a for loop to computer their dot product:

```
total = 0.0
for i in range(n)
    total += x[i]*y[i]
```

The simplicity of coding such computations makes the use of arrays the natural choice for all kinds of applications. Before considering more examples, we describe a number of important characteristics of programming with arrays.

i	x[i]	y[i]	x[i]*y[i]	total
				0.00
0	0.30	0.50	0.15	0.15
1	0.60	0.10	0.06	0.21
2	0.10	0.40	0.04	0.25

Trace of dot product computation

Zero-based indexing. We always refer to the first element of an array a[] as a[0], the second as a[1], and so forth. It might seem more natural to refer to the first element as a[1], the second element as a[2], and so forth, but starting the indexing with 0 has some advantages and has emerged as the convention used in most modern programming languages. Misunderstanding this convention often leads to *off-by one errors* that are notoriously difficult to avoid and debug, so be careful!

Array length. You can access the length of an array using Python's built-in len() function: len(a) is the number of elements in a[]. Note that the last element of an array a[] is always a[len(a)-1].

Increasing the length of an array at run time. In Python, we can use the += operator to append elements to an array. For example, if a[] is the array [1, 2, 3], then the statement a += [4] extends it to [1, 2, 3, 4]. More generally, we can make an array of n floats, with each element initialized to 0.0, with the code

```
a = []
for i in range(n)
    a += [0.0]
```

The statement a = [] creates an empty array (of length 0, with no elements) and the statement a += [0.0] appends one extra element to the end. We note that, in Python, the time required to create an array in this manner is proportional to its length (for details, see SECTION 4.1).

Memory representation. Arrays are fundamental data structures in that they have a direct correspondence with memory systems on virtually all computers. References to the elements of an array are stored contiguously in memory, so that accessing any array element is easy and efficient. Indeed, we can view memory itself as a giant array. On modern computers, memory is implemented in hardware as a sequence of indexed memory locations, each of which can be quickly accessed with an appropriate index. When referring to computer memory, we normally refer to a location's index as its *address*. It is convenient to think of the name of the array—say, x—as storing the memory address of a contiguous block of memory containing the length of the array and references to its elements. For the purposes of illustration, suppose that the computer's memory is organized as 1,000 values, with addresses from 000 to 999. Now, suppose that an array x[] of three elements is stored in memory locations 523 through 526, with the length stored in 523 and references to the array elements stored in 524 through 526. When we specify x[i], Python generates code that adds the index i to the memory address of the first element of the array. In the example pictured here, the Python code x[2] would generate machine code that finds the reference at memory location 524 + 2 = 526. The same simple method is effective even when the memory and the array (and i) are huge. Accessing a reference to element i of an array is an efficient operation because it simply requires adding two integers and then referencing memory—just two elementary operations.

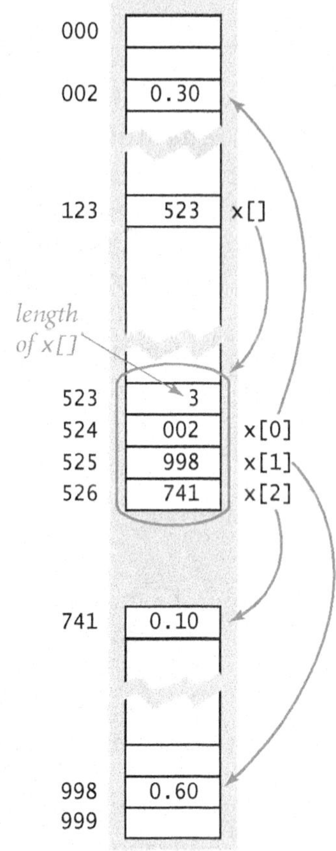

Memory representation (idealized) of x = [0.30, 0.60, 0.10]

Bounds checking. As already indicated, you must be careful when programming with arrays. It is your responsibility to use legal indices when accessing an array element. If you have created an array of size n and use an index whose value is greater than n-1, your program will raise an IndexError at run time. (In many programming languages, such *buffer overflow* conditions are not checked by the system. These kinds of unchecked errors can and do lead to debugging nightmares, but it is also not uncommon for such an error to go unnoticed and remain in a finished program. You might be surprised to know that such a mistake can be exploited by a hacker to take control of a system—even your personal computer—to spread viruses, steal personal information, or wreak other malicious havoc.) The error messages provided by Python may seem annoying to you at first, but they are small price to pay to have a more secure program.

Mutability. An object is *mutable* if its value can change. Arrays are mutable objects because we can change their elements. For example, if we create an array with the code `x = [.30, .60, .10]`, then the assignment statement `x[1] = .99` changes it to the array `[.30, .99, .10]`. An object-level trace of this operation is shown at right.

x = [.30, .60, .10]

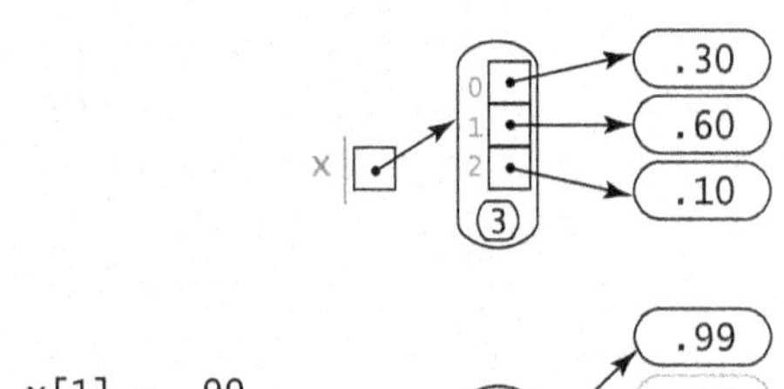

x[1] = .99

Reassigning an array element

Often the point of a piece of code is to rearrange the elements in an array. For example, the following code reverses the order of the elements in an array `a[]`:

```
n = len(a)
for i in range(n // 2):
    temp = a[i]
    a[i] = a[n-1-i]
    a[n-1-i] = temp
```

The three statements in the `for` loop implement the exchange operation that we studied when first learning about assignment statements in SECTION 1.2. You might wish to check your understanding of arrays by studying the informal trace of this code for a seven-element array `[3, 1, 4, 1, 5, 9, 2]`, shown at the right. This table keeps track of `i` and all seven array elements at the end of each iteration of the `for` loop.

i	*a[]*						
	0	*1*	*2*	*3*	*4*	*5*	*6*
	3	1	4	1	5	9	2
0	2	1	4	1	5	9	3
1	2	9	4	1	5	1	3
2	2	9	5	3	4	1	3
	2	9	5	1	4	1	3

Informal trace for reversing an array

It is natural to expect mutability in arrays, but, as you will see, mutability is a key issue in data type design and has a number of interesting implications. We will discuss some of these implications later in this section, but defer most of the discussion to SECTION 3.3.

Iteration. One of the most basic operations on an array is to *iterate* over all its elements. For example, the following code computes the average of an array of floats:

```
total = 0.0
for i in range(len(a))
    total += a[i]
average = total / len(a)
```

Python also supports iterating over the elements in an array in `a[]` without referring to the indices explicitly. To do so, put the array name after the `in` keyword in a `for` statement, as follows:

```
total = 0.0
for v in a:
    total += v
average = total / len(a)
```

Python successively assigns each element in the array to the loop-control variable `v`, so this code is essentially equivalent to the code given earlier. In this book, we iterate over the indices when we need to refer to the array elements by their indices (as in the dot-product and array-reversal examples just considered). We iterate over the elements when only the sequence of elements matters, and not the indices (as in this compute-the-average example).

Built-in functions. Python has several built-in functions that can take arrays as arguments. We have already discussed the `len()` function. As another example, if the elements of `a[]` are numeric, then `sum(a)` computes their sum, so that we can compute their average with `float(sum(a)) / len(a)` instead of using either of the loops just described. Other useful built-in functions that can take arrays as arguments are `min()` for computing the minimum and `max()` for computing the maximum.

Writing an array. You can write an array by passing it as an argument to `stdio.write()` or `stdio.writeln()`. The array is written with a leading open square bracket, followed by the array's objects separated with commas and spaces, followed by a trailing close square bracket, all on a single line. Each object in the array is converted to a string. If this format is not suited to your needs, you can use a `for` statement to write each array element individually.

Array aliases and copies Before looking at programs that use arrays, it is worthwhile to examine two fundamental array-processing operations in more detail. The points that we discuss are subtle, but they are more important than they might seem at first glance. If you find yourself becoming a bit overwhelmed by technical details, you might prefer to return to these two pages after studying the applications programs that use arrays later in this section. Rereading this material to cement your understanding of these concepts is certain to pay dividends.

Aliasing. We can use variables that reference arrays in much the same way in our code that we can use variables that reference other types of objects, but it is very important to take the time to understand the effects of such usage. If you reflect on the situation, perhaps the first question that arises is this: What happens when you use an array variable name on the left side of an assignment statement? In other words, if x[] and y[] are arrays, what is the effect of the statement x = y? The answer is simple and consistent with Python usage for other data types: x and y *reference the same array*. But this result has an effect that is perhaps unexpected, at first, because it is natural to think of x and y as references to two independent arrays, which is not the case. For example, *after the assignment statements*

```
x = [.30, .60, .10]
y = x
x[1] = .99
```

y[1] is also .99, even though the code does not refer directly to y[1]. This situation—whenever two variables refer to the same object—is known as *aliasing*, and is illustrated in the object-level trace at right. We avoid aliasing arrays (and other mutable objects) because it makes it more difficult to find errors in our programs. Still, as you will see in CHAPTER 2, there are natural situations where aliasing two arrays is helpful, so it is worthwhile for you to be aware of this concept at the outset.

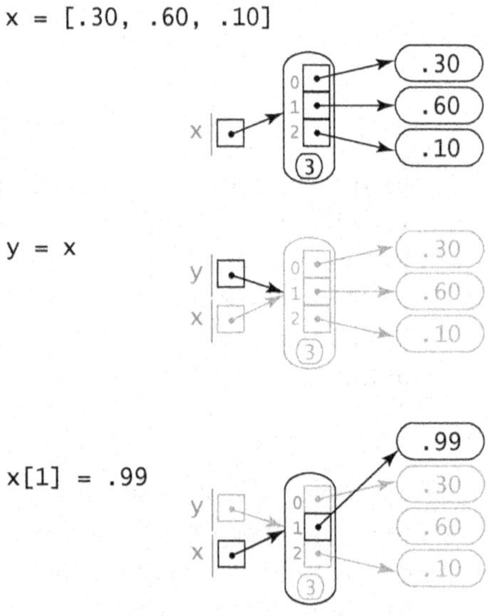

Aliasing an array

Copying and slicing. The next natural question you might ask is the following: How *do* we arrange to make a copy `y[]` of a given array `x[]`? One answer to this question is to iterate through `x[]` to build `y[]`, as in the following code:

```
y = []
for v in x:
    y += [v]
```

```
x = [.30, .60, .10]
```

After the copy operation, `x` and `y` refer to two different arrays. If we change the object that `x[1]` references, that change has no effect on `y[1]`. This situation is illustrated in the object-level trace at right.

Actually, copying an array is such a useful operation that Python provides language support for a more general operation known as *slicing*, where we can copy any contiguous sequence of elements within an array to another array. The expression `a[i:j]` evaluates to a new array whose elements are `a[i]`, ..., `a[j-1]`. Moreover, the default value for `i` is `0` and the default value for `j` is `len(a)`, so

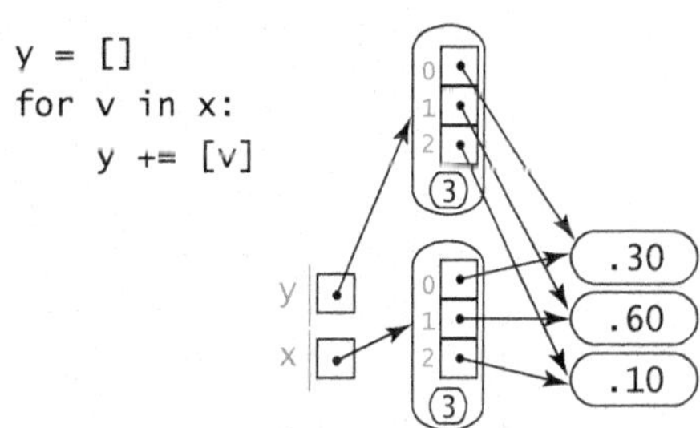


```
y = x[:]
```

is equivalent to the code given earlier. This compact notation is convenient, but it is important for you to remember that it masks a potentially expensive operation—it takes time proportional to the length of `x[]`.

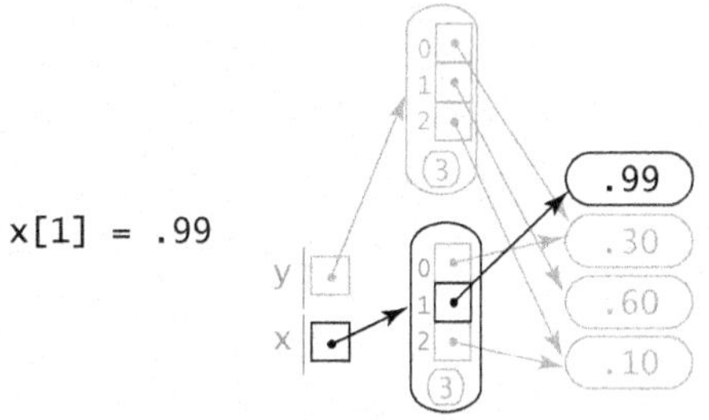

Copying an array

System support for arrays Python code for processing arrays can take many forms. We describe each briefly for context, but our emphasis for most of this book is on the few operations that you need to know to write meaningful and effective code. After you have some experience reading and composing code using these basic operations, you will better be able to understand the differences among the various approaches that are available for processing arrays in Python, so we revisit this topic in CHAPTER 4.

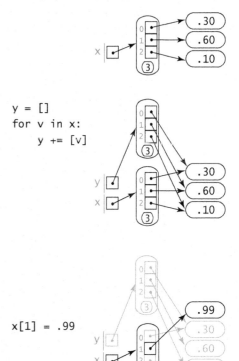

Python's built-in `list` data type. In its most basic form, an array supports four core operations: creation, indexed access, indexed assignment, and iteration. In this book, we use Python's built-in `list` data type for arrays because it supports these basic operations. We consider more elaborate operations supported by Python's `list` data type in CHAPTER 4, including array-resizing operations that change the length of the array. Arrays, as defined here, are sufficiently powerful that you will be able to learn a great deal about programming and approach a number of interesting applications in the meantime. Python programmers typically do not make a distinction between arrays and Python lists. We make this distinction here because many other programming languages (such as Java and C) provide built-in support for *fixed-length arrays* and the four core operations (but not for the more elaborate array-resizing operations).

Python's `numpy` module. The essence of programming language design is a tradeoff between simplicity and efficiency. Even though computers might seem to have the capability to perform huge numbers of elementary operations per second, you know that they can seem slow sometimes. In the case of Python, its built-in `list` data type can have severe performance problems, even for simple programs that use arrays to solve real-world problems. For that reason, scientists and engineers often use a Python extension module called `numpy` for processing huge arrays of numbers, because that module uses a lower-level representation that avoids many of the inefficiencies in the standard Python representation. Again we will delve deeply into understanding performance in CHAPTER 4, so that you may have a better understanding of how to approach such situations. In that context, we describe the use of `numpy` on the booksite.

Our `stdarray` module. Earlier in this chapter, we introduced our `stdio` module, which defines functions related to writing and reading integers, floats, strings, and booleans, and you have used the `stdio.write()` and `stdio.writeln()` functions extensively. The `stdio` module is a *booksite* module; that is, it is a nonstandard module that we composed specifically to support this book and its booksite. Now, we introduce another booksite module: the `stdarray` module. Its primary purpose is to define functions for processing arrays that we use throughout the book.

A fundamental operation that is found in nearly every array-processing program is to *create an array of n elements, each initialized to a given value.* As we have seen, you can do this in Python with code like the following:

```
a = []
for i in range(n):
    a += [0.0]
```

Creating an array of a given length and initializing all of its elements to a given value is so common that Python even has a special shorthand notation for it: the code `a = [0.0]*n` is equivalent to the code just given. Rather than repeat such code throughout the book, we will use code like this:

```
a = stdarray.create1D(n, 0.0)
```

For consistency, `stdarray` also includes a `create2D()` function, which we will examine later in this section. We use these functions because they make our code "self-documenting" in the sense that the code itself precisely indicates our intent and does not depend on idioms specific to Python. We will delve deeply into issues surrounding library design in SECTION 2.2 (and show you how to create modules like `stdarray` yourself), again so that you may have a better understanding of how to approach such situations.

function call	*description*
`stdarray.create1D(n, val)`	*array of length* n*, each element initialized to* `val`
`stdarray.create2D(m, n, val)`	m*-by-*n *array, each element initialized to* `val`

API for booksite functions in `stdarray` *module related to creating arrays*

YOU NOW KNOW HOW TO CREATE arrays in Python and access individual elements, and you have a basic understanding of Python's built-in `list` data type. The table at the top of the next page describes the array operations that we have discussed. With this conceptual foundation complete, we can now move to applications. As you will see, this foundation leads to applications code that is not only easy to compose and understand, but also makes efficient use of computational resources.

Abbreviation alert. Throughout this book, we refer to Python lists as *arrays* because Python lists support the fundamental operations that characterize arrays—creation, indexed access, indexed assignment, and iteration.

operation	*operator*	*description*
indexed access	`a[i]`	*ith element in* `a[]`
indexed assignment	`a[i] = x`	*replace ith element in* `a[]` *with* `x`
iteration	`for v in a:`	*assign* `v` *to each of the elements in* `a[]`
slicing	`a[i:j]`	*a new array* `[a[i], a[i+1],..., a[j-1]]` *(*`i` *defaults to 0 and* `j` *defaults to* `len(a)`*)*

operation	*function call*	*description*
length	`len(a)`	*number of elements in* `a[]`
sum	`sum(a)`	*sum of elements in* `a[]`
minimum	`min(a)`	*a minimum element in* `a[]`
maximum	`max(a)`	*a maximum element in* `a[]`

Note: Array elements must be numeric for `sum()` *and comparable for* `min()` *and* `max()`.

Array operations and built-in functions

Sample applications of arrays Next, we consider a number of applications that illustrate the utility of arrays and also are interesting in their own right.

Representing playing cards. Suppose that we want to compose programs that process playing cards. We might start with the following code:

```
SUITS = ['Clubs', 'Diamonds', 'Hearts', 'Spades']
RANKS = ['2', '3', '4', '5', '6', '7', '8', '9', '10',
         'Jack', 'Queen', 'King', 'Ace']
```

For example, we might use these two arrays to write a random card name, such as `Queen of Clubs`, as follows:

```
rank = random.randrange(0, len(RANKS))
suit = random.randrange(0, len(SUITS))
stdio.writeln(RANKS[rank] + ' of ' + SUITS[suit])
```

A more typical situation is when we compute the values to be stored in an array. For example, we might use the following code to initialize an array of length 52 that represents a deck of playing cards, using the two arrays just defined:

```
deck = []
for rank in RANKS:
    for suit in SUITS:
        card = rank + ' of ' + suit
        deck += [card]
```

After this code has been executed, writing the elements of `deck[]` in order from `deck[0]` through `deck[51]` with one element per line gives the sequence

```
2 of Clubs
2 of Diamonds
2 of Hearts
2 of Spades
3 of Clubs
3 of Diamonds
...
Ace of Hearts
Ace of Spades
```

Exchange. Frequently, we wish to exchange two elements in an array. Continuing our example with playing cards, the following code exchanges the cards at indices `i` and `j` using the same idiom that we used previously in this section to reverse an array:

```
temp = deck[i]
deck[i] = deck[j]
deck[j] = temp
```

When we use this code, we are assured that we are perhaps changing the *order* of the elements in the array but not the *set* of elements in the array. When `i` and `j` are equal, the array is unchanged. When `i` and `j` are not equal, the values `a[i]` and `a[j]` are found in different places in the array. For example, if we were to use this code with `i` equal to `1` and `j` equal to `4` in the `deck[]` of the previous example, it would leave the string `'3 of Clubs'` in `deck[1]` and the string `'2 of Diamonds'` in `deck[4]`.

Shuffle. The following code shuffles our deck of cards:

```
n = len(deck)
for i in range(n):
    r = random.randrange(i, n)
    temp = deck[r]
    deck[r] = deck[i]
    deck[i] = temp
```

Proceeding from left to right, we pick a random card from `deck[i]` through `deck[n-1]` (each card equally likely) and exchange it with `deck[i]`. This code is more sophisticated than it might seem. First, we ensure that the cards in the deck after the shuffle are the same as the cards in the deck before the shuffle by using the exchange idiom. Second, we ensure that the shuffle is random by choosing uniformly from the cards not yet chosen. Incidentally, Python includes a standard function named `shuffle()` in the `random` module that uniformly shuffles a given array, so the function call `random.shuffle(deck)` does the same job as this code.

Sampling without replacement. In many situations, we want to draw a random sample from a set such that each element in set appears at most once in the sample. Drawing numbered ping-pong balls from a basket for a lottery is an example of this kind of sample, as is dealing a hand from a deck of cards. PROGRAM 1.4.1 (`sample.py`) illustrates how to sample, using the basic operation underlying shuffling. It takes command-line arguments `m` and `n` and creates a *permutation* of size `n` (a rearrangement of the integers from `0` to `n-1`) whose first `m` elements constitute a random sample.

The accompanying trace of the contents of the `perm[]` array at the end of each iteration of the main loop (for a run where the values of `m` and `n` are `6` and `16`, respectively) illustrates the process. If the values of `r` are chosen such that each value in the given range is equally likely, then `perm[0]` through `perm[m-1]` are a random sample at the end of the process (even though some elements might move multiple times) because each element in the sample is chosen by taking each item not yet sampled, with each choice having equal probability of being selected.

One important reason to explicitly compute the permutation is that we can use it to write a random sample of *any* array by using the elements of the permutation as indices into the array. Doing so is often an attractive alternative to actually rearranging the array, because it may need to be in order for some other reason

Program 1.4.1 Sampling without replacement (sample.py)

```
import random
import sys
import stdarray
import stdio

m = int(sys.argv[1])   # Choose this many elements
n = int(sys.argv[2])   # from 0, 1, ..., n-1.

# Initialize array perm = [0, 1, ..., n-1].
perm = stdarray.create1D(n, 0)
for i in range(n):
    perm[i] = i

# Create a random sample of size m in perm[0..m).
for i in range(m):
    r = random.randrange(i, n)

    # Exchange perm[i] and perm[r].
    temp    = perm[r]
    perm[r] = perm[i]
    perm[i] = temp

# Write the results.
for i in range(m):
    stdio.write(str(perm[i]) + ' ')
stdio.writeln()
```

m	*sample size*
n	*range*
perm[]	*permutation of 0 to n-1*

This program accepts integers m and n as command-line arguments, and writes a random sample of m integers in the range 0 to n-1 (no duplicates). This process is useful not just in state and local lotteries, but in scientific applications of all sorts. If the first argument is less than or equal to the second, the result is a random permutation of the integers from 0 to n-1. If the first argument is greater than the second, the program raises a ValueError at run time.

```
% python sample.py 6 16
9 5 13 1 11 8

% python sample.py 10 1000
656 488 298 534 811 97 813 156 424 109

% python sample.py 20 20
6 12 9 8 13 19 0 2 4 5 18 1 14 16 17 3 7 11 10 15
```

i	*r*	perm[]															
		0	*1*	*2*	*3*	*4*	*5*	*6*	*7*	*8*	*9*	*10*	*11*	*12*	*13*	*14*	*15*
		0	1	2	3	4	5	6	7	8	9	10	11	12	13	14	15
0	9	9	1	2	3	4	5	6	7	8	0	10	11	12	13	14	15
1	5	9	5	2	3	4	1	6	7	8	0	10	11	12	13	14	15
2	13	9	5	13	3	4	1	6	7	8	0	10	11	12	2	14	15
3	5	9	5	13	1	4	3	6	7	8	0	10	11	12	2	14	15
4	11	9	5	13	1	11	3	6	7	8	0	10	4	12	2	14	15
5	8	9	5	13	1	11	8	6	7	3	0	10	4	12	2	14	15
		9	5	13	1	11	8	6	7	3	0	10	4	12	2	14	15

Trace of **python sample.py 6 16**

(for instance, a company might wish to draw a random sample from a list of customers that is kept in alphabetical order). To see how this trick works, suppose that we wish to draw a random poker hand from our `deck[]` array, constructed as just described. We use the code in `sample.py` with `m = 5` and `n = 52` and replace `perm[i]` with `deck[perm[i]]` in the `stdio.write()` statement (and change it to `writeln()`), resulting in output such as the following:

```
3 of Clubs
Jack of Hearts
6 of Spades
Ace of Clubs
10 of Diamonds
```

Sampling like this is widely used as the basis for statistical studies in polling, scientific research, and many other applications, whenever we want to draw conclusions about a large population by analyzing a small random sample. Python includes a standard function in the `random` module for sampling: given an array `a[]` and an integer `k`, the function call `random.sample(a, k)` returns a new array containing a sample of size `k`, chosen uniformly at random among the elements in `a[]`.

Precomputed values. Another application of arrays is to save values that you have computed for later use. As an example, suppose that you are composing a program that performs calculations using small values of the harmonic numbers (see PROGRAM 1.3.5). An efficient approach is to save the values in an array, as follows:

```
harmonic = stdarray.create1D(n+1, 0.0)
for i in range(1, n+1):
    harmonic[i] = harmonic[i-1] + 1.0/i
```

Note that we waste one slot in the array (element 0) to make `harmonic[1]` correspond to the first harmonic number `1.0` and `harmonic[i]` correspond to the `i`th harmonic number. Precomputing values in this way is an example of a *space–time tradeoff*: by investing in space (to save the values), we save time (since we do not need to recompute them). This method is not effective if we need values for huge `n`, but it is very effective if we need values for small `n` many different times.

Simplifying repetitive code. As an example of another simple application of arrays, consider the following code fragment, which writes the name of a month given its number (1 for January, 2 for February, and so forth):

```
if   m ==  1: stdio.writeln('Jan')
elif m ==  2: stdio.writeln('Feb')
elif m ==  3: stdio.writeln('Mar')
elif m ==  4: stdio.writeln('Apr')
...
elif m == 11: stdio.writeln('Nov')
elif m == 12: stdio.writeln('Dec')
```

A more compact alternative is to use an array of strings holding the month names:

```
MONTHS = ['', 'Jan', 'Feb', 'Mar', 'Apr', 'May', 'Jun',
              'Jul', 'Aug', 'Sep', 'Oct', 'Nov', 'Dec']
...
stdio.writeln(MONTHS[m])
```

This technique would be especially useful if you needed to access the name of a month by its number in several different places in your program. Note that, again, we intentionally waste one slot in the array (element `0`) to make `MONTHS[1]` correspond to January, as required.

WITH THESE BASIC DEFINITIONS AND EXAMPLES out of the way, we can now consider two applications that both address interesting classical problems and illustrate the fundamental importance of arrays in efficient computation. In both cases, the idea of using data to efficiently index into an array plays a central role and enables a computation that would not otherwise be feasible.

Coupon collector Suppose that you have a deck of cards and you pick cards at random (with replacement) one by one. How many cards do you need to turn up before you have seen one of each suit? How many cards do you need to turn up before seeing one of each rank? These are examples of the famous *coupon collector* problem. In general, suppose that a trading card company issues trading cards with n different possible cards: how many do you have to collect before you have all n possibilities, assuming that each possibility is equally likely for each card that you collect?

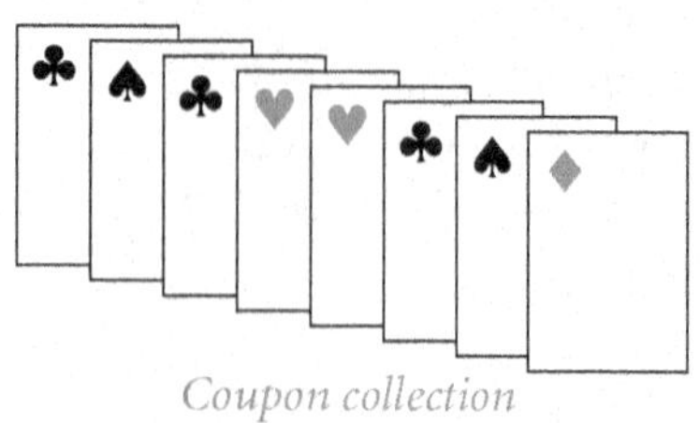
Coupon collection

Program 1.4.2 (`couponcollector.py`) is an example program that simulates this process and illustrates the utility of arrays. It takes the integer `n` from the command line and generates a sequence of random integer values between 0 and `n-1` using the function call `random.randrange(0, n)` (see Program 1.3.8). Each value represents a card; for each card, we want to know if we have seen that value before. To maintain that knowledge, we use an array `isCollected[]`, which uses the card value as an index: `isCollected[i]` is `True` if we have seen a card with value `i` and `False` if we have not. When we get a new card that is represented by the integer `value`, we check whether we have seen its value before simply by accessing `isCollected[value]`. The computation consists of keeping count of the number of distinct values seen and the number of cards generated and writing the latter when the former reaches `n`.

As usual, the best way to understand a program is to consider a trace of the values of its variables for a typical run. It is easy to add code to `couponcollector.py` that produces a trace that gives the values of the variables at the end of the `while` loop. In the table at right, we use `F` for `False` and `T` for `True` to make the trace easier to follow. Tracing programs that use large arrays can be a challenge: when you have an array of length n in your program, it represents n variables, so

`val`	`isCollected[]` 0	1	2	3	4	5	`count`	`collectedCount`
	F	F	F	F	F	F	0	0
2	F	F	T	F	F	F	1	1
0	T	F	T	F	F	F	2	2
4	T	F	T	F	T	F	3	3
0	T	F	T	F	T	F	3	4
1	T	T	T	F	T	F	4	5
2	T	T	T	F	T	F	4	6
5	T	T	T	F	T	T	5	7
0	T	T	T	F	T	T	5	8
1	T	T	T	F	T	T	5	9
3	T	T	T	T	T	T	6	10

Trace for a typical run of **`python couponcollector.py 6`**

Program 1.4.2 *Coupon collector simulation* (couponcollector.py)

```
import random
import sys
import stdarray
import stdio

n = int(sys.argv[1])

count = 0
collectedCount = 0
isCollected = stdarray.create1D(n, False)

while collectedCount < n:
    # Generate another coupon.
    value = random.randrange(0, n)
    count += 1
    if not isCollected[value]:
        collectedCount += 1
        isCollected[value] = True

stdio.writeln(count)
```

n	*# of coupon values (0 to n-1)*
count	*# of coupons collected*
collectedCount	*# of distinct coupons collected*
isCollected[i]	*has coupon i been collected?*
value	*value of current coupon*

This program accepts an integer n as a command-line argument, and writes the number of coupons collected before obtaining one of each of n types. Thus it simulates a coupon collector.

```
% python couponcollector.py 1000
6583

% python couponcollector.py 1000
6477

% python couponcollector.py 1000000
12782673
```

you have to list them all. Tracing programs that use `random.randrange()` also can be a challenge because you get a different trace every time you run the program. Accordingly, we check relationships among variables carefully. Here, note that `collectedCount` always is equal to the number of `True` values in `isCollected[]`.

Coupon collecting is no trivial problem. For example, it is very often the case that scientists want to know whether a sequence that arises in nature has the same characteristics as a random sequence. If so, that fact might be of interest; if not, further investigation may be warranted to look for patterns that might be of importance. For example, such tests are used by scientists to decide which parts of a genome are worth studying. One effective test of whether a sequence is truly random is the *coupon collector test*: compare the number of elements that need to be examined before all values are found against the corresponding number for a uniformly random sequence.

Without arrays, we could not contemplate simulating the coupon collector process for huge n; with arrays, it is easy to do so. We will see many examples of such processes throughout the book.

Sieve of Eratosthenes Prime numbers play an important role in mathematics and computation, including cryptography. A *prime number* is an integer greater than 1 whose only positive divisors are 1 and itself. The prime counting function $\pi(n)$ is the number of primes less than or equal to n. For example, $\pi(25) = 9$ because the first nine primes are 2, 3, 5, 7, 11, 13, 17, 19, and 23. This function plays a central role in number theory.

We might use a program like `factors.py` (Program 1.3.9) to count primes. Specifically, we could modify the code in `factors.py` to set a boolean variable to `True` if a given number is prime and `False` otherwise (instead of writing out factors), then enclose that code in a loop that increments a counter for each prime number. This approach is effective for small n, but becomes too slow as n grows.

Program 1.4.3 (`primesieve.py`) is an alternative that computes $\pi(n)$ using a technique known as the *sieve of Eratosthenes*. The program uses an array `isPrime[]` of `n` booleans to record which of the integers less than or equal to `n` are prime. The goal is to set `isPrime[i]` to `True` if `i` is prime, and to `False` otherwise. The sieve works as follows: Initially, the program assigns `True` to all elements of the array, indicating that no factors of any integer have yet been found. Then, it repeats the following steps as long as `i < n`:

- Find the next smallest `i` for which no factors have been found.
- Leave `isPrime[i]` as `True` since `i` has no smaller factors.
- Assign `False` to all `isPrime[]` elements whose indices are multiples of `i`.

Program 1.4.3 Sieve of Eratosthenes (primesieve.py)

```
import sys
import stdarray
import stdio

n = int(sys.argv[1])

isPrime = stdarray.create1D(n+1, True)

for i in range(2, n):
    if (isPrime[i]):
        # Mark multiples of i as nonprime.
        for j in range(2, n//i + 1):
            isPrime[i*j] = False

# Count the primes.
count = 0
for i in range(2, n+1):
    if (isPrime[i]):
        count += 1
stdio.writeln(count)
```

n	*argument*
isPrime[i]	*is i prime?*
count	*prime counter*

This program takes a command-line argument n and computes the number of primes less than or equal to n. To do so, it computes an array of booleans with isPrime[i] *set to True if i is prime, and to* False *otherwise.*

```
% python primesieve.py 25
9

% python primesieve.py 100
25

% python primesieve.py 10000
1229

% python primesieve.py 1000000
78498

% python primesieve.py 100000000
5761455
```

i	isPrime[]																						
	2	3	4	5	6	7	8	9	10	11	12	13	14	15	16	17	18	19	20	21	22	23	24	25
	T	T	T	T	T	T	T	T	T	T	T	T	T	T	T	T	T	T	T	T	T	T	T	T
2	T	T	F	T	F	T	F	T	F	T	F	T	F	T	F	T	F	T	F	T	F	T	F	T
3	T	T	F	T	F	T	F	F	F	T	F	T	F	F	F	T	F	T	F	F	F	T	F	T
5	T	T	F	T	F	T	F	F	F	T	F	T	F	F	F	T	F	T	F	F	F	T	F	F
	T	T	F	T	F	T	F	F	F	T	F	T	F	F	F	T	F	T	F	F	F	T	F	F

Trace of `python primesieve.py 25`

When the nested `for` loop ends, we have set the `isPrime[]` elements for all nonprimes to be `False` and have left the `isPrime[]` elements for all primes as `True`. Note that we might stop when `i*i >= n`, just as we did for `factors.py`, but the savings in this case would be marginal at best, since the inner `for` loop does not iterate at all for large `i`. With one more pass through the array, we can count the number of primes less than or equal to `n`.

As usual, it is easy to add code to write a trace. For programs such as `primesieve.py`, you have to be a bit careful—it contains a nested `for-if-for`, so you have to pay attention to the indentation to put the tracing code in the correct place.

With `primesieve.py`, we can compute $\pi(n)$ for large n, limited primarily by the maximum array size allowed by Python. This is another example of a space–time tradeoff. Programs like `primesieve.py` play an important role in helping mathematicians to develop the theory of numbers, which has many important applications.

Two-dimensional arrays In many applications, a convenient way to store information is to use a table of numbers organized in a rectangular table and refer to *rows* and *columns* in the table. For example, a teacher might need to maintain a table with a row corresponding to each student and a column corresponding to each assignment, a scientist might need to maintain a table of experimental data with rows corresponding to experiments and columns corresponding to various outcomes, or a programmer might want to prepare an image for display by setting a table of pixels to various grayscale values or colors.

	99	85	98
row →	98	57	78
	92	77	76
	94	32	11
	99	34	22
	90	46	54
	76	59	88
	92	66	89
	97	71	24
	89	29	38
			↑ *column*

A table of numbers

The mathematical abstraction corresponding to such tables is a *matrix*; the corresponding data structure is a *two-dimensional array*. You are likely to have already encountered many applications of matrices and two-dimensional arrays, and you will certainly encounter many others in science, in engineering, and in commercial applications, as we will demonstrate with examples throughout this book. As with vectors and one-dimensional arrays, many of the most important applications involve processing large amounts of data, and we defer considering those applications until we consider input and output, in Section 1.5.

Extending the one-dimensional array data structure that we have discussed to two-dimensional arrays is straightforward, once you realize that since an array can contain any type of data, its elements can also be arrays! That is, a two-dimensional array is implemented as an array of one-dimensional arrays, as detailed next.

Initialization. The simplest way to create a two-dimensional array in Python is to place comma-separated one-dimensional arrays between matching square brackets. For example, this matrix of integers having two rows and three columns

```
18 19 20
21 22 23
```

could be represented in Python using this array of arrays:

```
a = [[18, 19, 20], [21, 22, 23]]
```

We call such an array a *2-by-3 array*. By convention, the first dimension is the number of rows and the second dimension is the number of columns. Python represents a 2-by-3 array as an array that contains two objects, each of which is an array that contains three objects.

```
a = [[99, 85, 98],
     [98, 57, 78],
     [92, 77, 76],
     [94, 32, 11],
     [99, 34, 22],
     [90, 46, 54],
     [76, 59, 88],
     [92, 66, 89],
     [97, 71, 24],
     [89, 29, 38]]
```

Creating a 10-by-3 array

More generally, Python represents an *m*-by-*n* array as an array that contains *m* objects, each of which is an array that contains *n* objects. For example, this Python code creates an `m`-by-`n` array `a[][]` of floats, with all elements initialized to `0.0`:

```
a = []
for i in range(m):
    row = [0.0] * n
    a += [row]
```

As for one-dimensional arrays, we use the self-descriptive alternative

```
stdarray.create2D(m, n, 0.0)
```

from our booksite module `stdarray` throughout this book.

Indexing. When `a[][]` is a two-dimensional array, the syntax `a[i]` denotes a reference to its `i`th row. For example, if `a[][]` is the array `[[18, 19, 20], [21 22, 23]]`, then `a[1]` is the array `[21, 22, 23]`. It is more common to refer to a particular element in a two-dimensional array. The syntax `a[i][j]` refers to the object at row `i` and column `j` of the two-dimensional array `a[][]`. In our example, `a[1][0]` is `21`. To access each of the elements in a two-dimensional array, we use two nested `for` loops. For example, this code writes each object of the `m`-by-`n` array `a[][]`, one row per line.

```
for i in range(m):
    for j in range(n):
        stdio.write(a[i][j])
        stdio.write(' ')
    stdio.writeln()
```

This code achieves the same effect without using indices:

```
for row in a:
    for v in row:
        stdio.write(v)
        stdio.write(' ')
    stdio.writeln()
```

Spreadsheets. One familiar use of arrays is a *spreadsheet* for maintaining a table of numbers. For example, a teacher with m students and n test grades for each student might maintain an $(m+1)$-by-$(n+1)$ array, reserving the last column for each student's average grade and the last row for the average test grades. Even though we typically do such computations within specialized applications, it is worthwhile to study the underlying code as an introduction to array processing. To compute the average grade for each student (average values for each row), sum the elements for each row and divide by n. The row-by-row order in which this code processes the matrix elements is known as *row-major* order. Similarly, to compute the average test grade (average values for each column), sum the elements for each column and

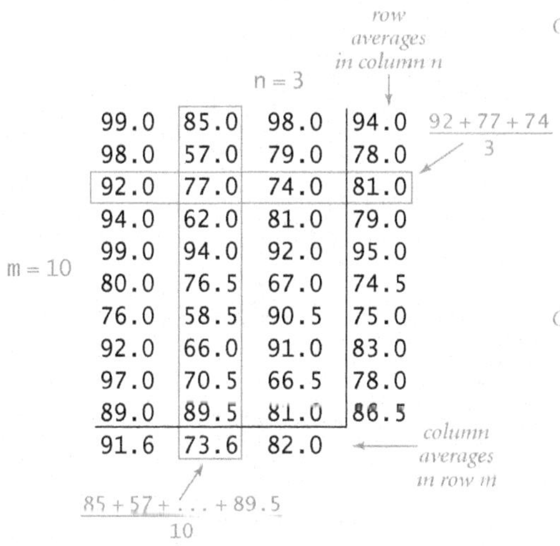

		n = 3		row averages in column n	
	99.0	85.0	98.0	94.0	$\frac{92 + 77 + 74}{3}$
	98.0	57.0	79.0	78.0	
	92.0	77.0	74.0	81.0	
	94.0	62.0	81.0	79.0	
	99.0	94.0	92.0	95.0	
m = 10	80.0	76.5	67.0	74.5	
	76.0	58.5	90.5	75.0	
	92.0	66.0	91.0	83.0	
	97.0	70.5	66.5	78.0	
	89.0	89.5	81.0	86.5	
	91.6	73.6	82.0		column averages in row m

$\frac{85 + 57 + \ldots + 89.5}{10}$

Compute row averages (row-major order)

```
for i in range(m):
    # Average for row i
    total = 0.0
    for j in range(n):
        total += a[i][j]
    a[i][n] = total / m
```

Compute column averages (column-major order)

```
for j in range(n):
    # Average for column j
    total = 0.0
    for i in range(m):
        total += a[i][j]
    a[m][j] = total / n
```

Typical spreadsheet calculations

divide by *n*. The column-by-column order in which this code processes the matrix elements is known as *column-major* order. These operations are all illustrated in the figure at the top of the this page. To allow for half points, our teacher records all grades as floats.

Matrix operations. Typical applications in science and engineering involve representing matrices as two-dimensional arrays and then implementing various mathematical operations with matrix operands. Again, even though such processing is often done within specialized applications and libraries, it is worthwhile for you to understand the underlying computation.

For example, we can *add* two n-by-n matrices a[][] and b[][] as follows:

```
c = stdarray.create2D(n, n, 0.0)
for i in range(n):
    for j in range(n):
        c[i][j] = a[i][j] + b[i][j]
```

Similarly, we can *multiply* two matrices. You may have learned matrix multiplication, but if you do not recall or are not familiar with it, the following Python code for square matrices is essentially the same as the mathematical definition. Each

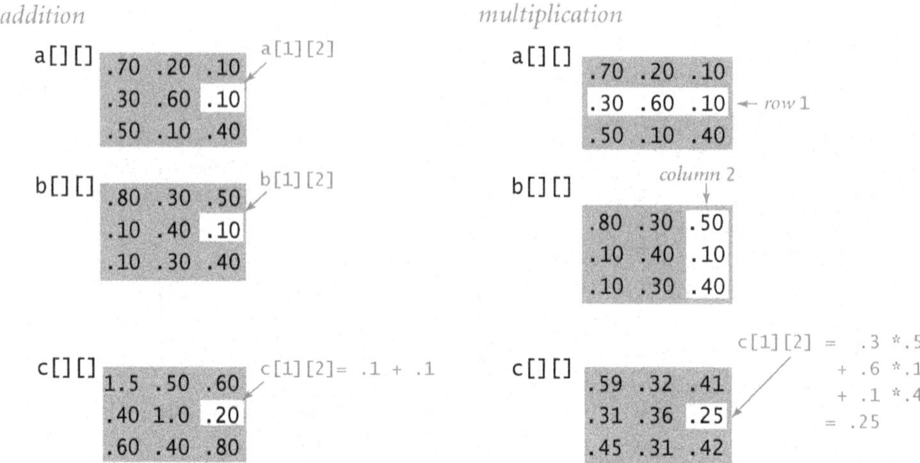

Typical matrix operations

element c[i][j] in the product of a[][] and b[][] is computed by taking the dot product of row i of a[][] with column j of b[][].

```
c = stdarray.create2D(n, n, 0.0)
for i in range(n):
    for j in range(n):
        # Compute the dot product of row i and column j
        for k in range(n):
            c[i][j] += a[i][k] * b[k][j]
```

The definition extends to matrices that may not be square (see Exercise 1.4.17).

Special cases of matrix multiplication. Two special cases of matrix multiplication are important. These special cases occur when one of the dimensions of one of the matrices is 1, so we can view it as a vector. In *matrix–vector multiplication*, we multiply an m-by-n matrix by a *column vector* (an n-by-1 matrix) to get an m-by-1 column vector result (each element in the result is the dot product of the corresponding row in the matrix with the operand vector). In *vector–matrix multiplication*, we multiply a *row vector* (a 1-by-m matrix) by an m-by-n matrix to get a 1-by-n row vector result (each element in the result is the dot product of the operand vector with the corresponding column in the matrix).

*Matrix–vector multiplication b[] = a[][]*x[]*

```
b = stdarray.create1D(m, 0.0)
for i in range(m):
   for j in range(n):
      b[i] += a[i][j]*x[j]
```

dot product of row i of a[][] and x[]

a[][]

99.0	85.0	98.0
98.0	57.0	79.0
92.0	77.0	74.0
94.0	62.0	81.0
99.0	94.0	92.0
80.0	76.5	67.0
76.0	58.5	90.5
92.0	66.0	91.0
97.0	70.5	66.5
89.0	89.5	81.0

x[]

0.33333
0.33333
0.33333

b[] (*row averages*)

94.0
78.0
81.0
79.0
95.0
74.5
75.0
83.0
78.0
86.5

*Vector–matrix multiplication c[] = y[]*a[][]*

```
c = stdarray.create1D(n, 0.0)
for j in range(n):
   for i in range(m):
      c[j] += y[i]*a[i][j]
```

dot product of column j of a[][] and y[]

y[] [.1 .1 .1 .1 .1 .1 .1 .1 .1 .1]

a[][]

99.0	85.0	98.0
98.0	57.0	79.0
92.0	77.0	74.0
94.0	62.0	81.0
99.0	94.0	92.0
80.0	76.5	67.0
76.0	58.5	90.5
92.0	66.0	91.0
97.0	70.5	66.5
89.0	89.5	81.0

c[] [91.6 73.6 82.0] ← *column averages*

Special cases of matrix operations (when one of the arguments is a vector)

These operations provide a succinct way to express numerous matrix calculations. For example, the row-average computation for such a spreadsheet with `m` rows and `n` columns is equivalent to a matrix–vector multiplication where the row vector has `n` elements all equal to `1.0 / n`. Similarly, the column-average computation in such a spreadsheet is equivalent to a vector-matrix multiplication where the column vector has `m` elements all equal to `1.0 / m`. We return to vector–matrix multiplication in the context of an important application at the end of this chapter.

Ragged arrays. There is actually no requirement that all rows in a two-dimensional array have the same length. An array with rows of nonuniform length is known as a *ragged array* (see Exercise 1.4.32 for an example application). The possibility of ragged arrays creates the need for taking more care in crafting array-processing code. For example, this code writes the contents of a ragged array:

```
for i in range(len(a)):
    for j in range(len(a[i])):
        stdio.write(a[i][j])
        stdio.write(' ')
    stdio.writeln()
```

This code tests your understanding of Python arrays, so you should take the time to study it. In this book, we normally use square or rectangular arrays, whose dimensions are given by the variable `m` and `n`. Code that uses `len(a[i])` in this way is a clear signal to you that an array is ragged.

Note that the equivalent code that does not use indices works equally well with both rectangular and ragged arrays:

```
for row in a:
    for v in row:
        stdio.write(v)
        stdio.write(' ')
    stdio.writeln()
```

Multidimensional arrays. The same notation extends to allow us to compose code using arrays that have any number of dimensions. Using arrays of arrays of arrays..., we can create three-dimensional arrays, four-dimensional arrays, and so forth, and then refer to an individual element with code like `a[i][j][k]`.

Two-dimensional arrays provide a natural representation for matrices, which are omnipresent in science, mathematics, and engineering. They also provide a natural way to organize large amounts of data—a key factor in spreadsheets and many other computing applications. Through Cartesian coordinates, two- and three-dimensional arrays provide the basis for a models of the physical world. With all of these natural applications, arrays will provide fertile ground for interesting examples throughout this book as you learn to program.

Example: self-avoiding random walks Suppose that you leave your dog in the middle of a large city whose streets form a familiar grid pattern. We assume that there are n north–south streets and n east–west streets, all regularly spaced and fully intersecting in a pattern known as a *lattice.* Trying to escape the city, the dog makes a random choice of which way to go at each intersection, but knows by scent to avoid visiting any place previously visited. But it is possible for the dog to get stuck in a dead end where there is no choice but to revisit some intersection. What is the chance that this will happen? This amusing problem is a simple example of a famous model known as the *self-avoiding random walk,* which has important scientific applications in the study of polymers and in statistical mechanics, among many others. For example, you can see that this process models a chain of material growing a bit at a time, until no growth is possible. To better understand such processes, scientists seek to understand the properties of self-avoiding walks.

The dog's escape probability is certainly dependent on the size of the city. In a tiny 5-by-5 city, it is easy to convince yourself that the dog is certain to escape. But what are the chances of escape when the city is large? We are also interested in other parameters. For example, how long is the dog's path, on average? How often does the dog come within one block of a previous position other than the one just left, on average? How often does the dog come within one block of escaping? These sorts of properties are important in the various applications just mentioned.

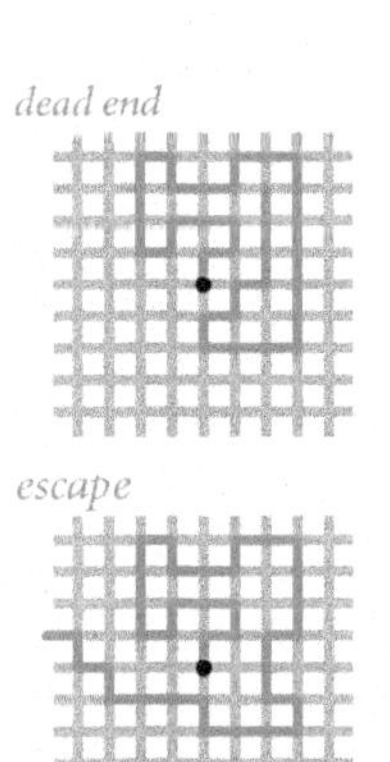

Self-avoiding walks

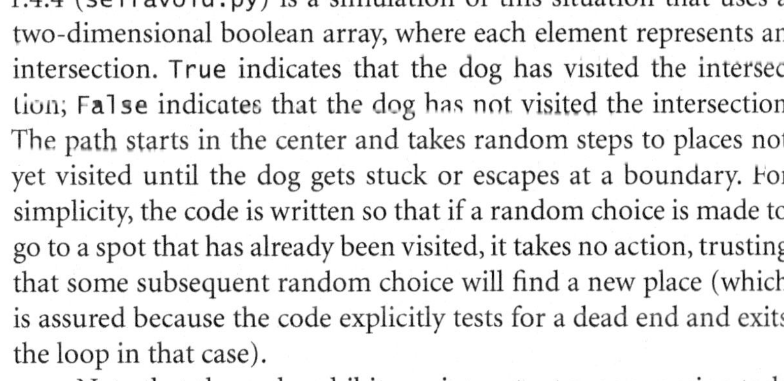

PROGRAM 1.4.4 (`selfavoid.py`) is a simulation of this situation that uses a two-dimensional boolean array, where each element represents an intersection. `True` indicates that the dog has visited the intersection; `False` indicates that the dog has not visited the intersection. The path starts in the center and takes random steps to places not yet visited until the dog gets stuck or escapes at a boundary. For simplicity, the code is written so that if a random choice is made to go to a spot that has already been visited, it takes no action, trusting that some subsequent random choice will find a new place (which is assured because the code explicitly tests for a dead end and exits the loop in that case).

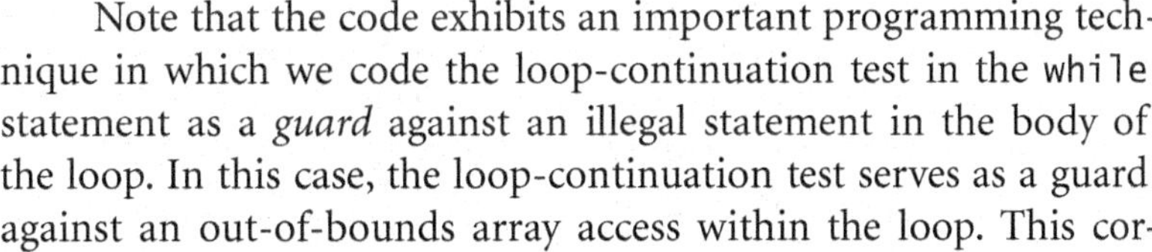

Note that the code exhibits an important programming technique in which we code the loop-continuation test in the `while` statement as a *guard* against an illegal statement in the body of the loop. In this case, the loop-continuation test serves as a guard against an out-of-bounds array access within the loop. This corresponds to checking whether the dog has escaped. Within the loop, a successful dead-end test results in a `break` out of the loop.

As you can see from the sample runs, the unfortunate truth is that your dog is nearly certain to get trapped in a dead end in a large city. If you are interested in learning more about self-avoiding walks, you can find several suggestions in the exercises. For example, the dog is almost certain to escape in the three-dimensional version of the problem. While this is an intuitive result that is confirmed by our simulations, the development of a mathematical model that explains the behavior of self-avoiding walks is a famous open problem: despite extensive research, no one knows a succinct mathematical expression for the escape probability, the average length of the path, or any other important parameter.

Program 1.4.4 Self-avoiding random walks (selfavoid.py)

n	*lattice size*
trials	*# of trials*
deadEnds	*# of trials with a dead end*
a[][]	*intersections*
x, y	*current position*
r	*random number in [1, 5)*

```
import random
import sys
import stdarray
import stdio

n      = int(sys.argv[1])
trials = int(sys.argv[2])
deadEnds = 0
for t in range(trials):
    a = stdarray.create2D(n, n, False)
    x = n // 2
    y = n // 2
    while (x > 0) and (x < n-1) and (y > 0) and (y < n-1):
        # Check for dead end and make a random move.
        a[x][y] = True
        if a[x-1][y] and a[x+1][y] and a[x][y-1] and a[x][y+1]:
            deadEnds += 1
            break
        r = random.randrange(1, 5)
        if   (r == 1) and (not a[x+1][y]): x += 1
        elif (r == 2) and (not a[x-1][y]): x -= 1
        elif (r == 3) and (not a[x][y+1]): y += 1
        elif (r == 4) and (not a[x][y-1]): y -= 1

stdio.writeln(str(100*deadEnds//trials) + '% dead ends')
```

This program accepts integers n and `trials` as command-line arguments. It performs `trials` experiments, each a random self-avoiding walk in an n-by-n lattice, and then writes the percentage of dead ends encountered. For each walk, it creates an array of booleans, starts the walk in the center, and continues until reaching either a dead end or a boundary.

```
% python selfavoid.py 5 100
0% dead ends
% python selfavoid.py 20 100
35% dead ends
% python selfavoid.py 40 100
80% dead ends
% python selfavoid.py 80 100
98% dead ends
```

```
% python selfavoid.py 5 1000
0% dead ends
% python selfavoid.py 20 1000
32% dead ends
% python selfavoid.py 40 1000
76% dead ends
% python selfavoid.py 80 1000
98% dead ends
```

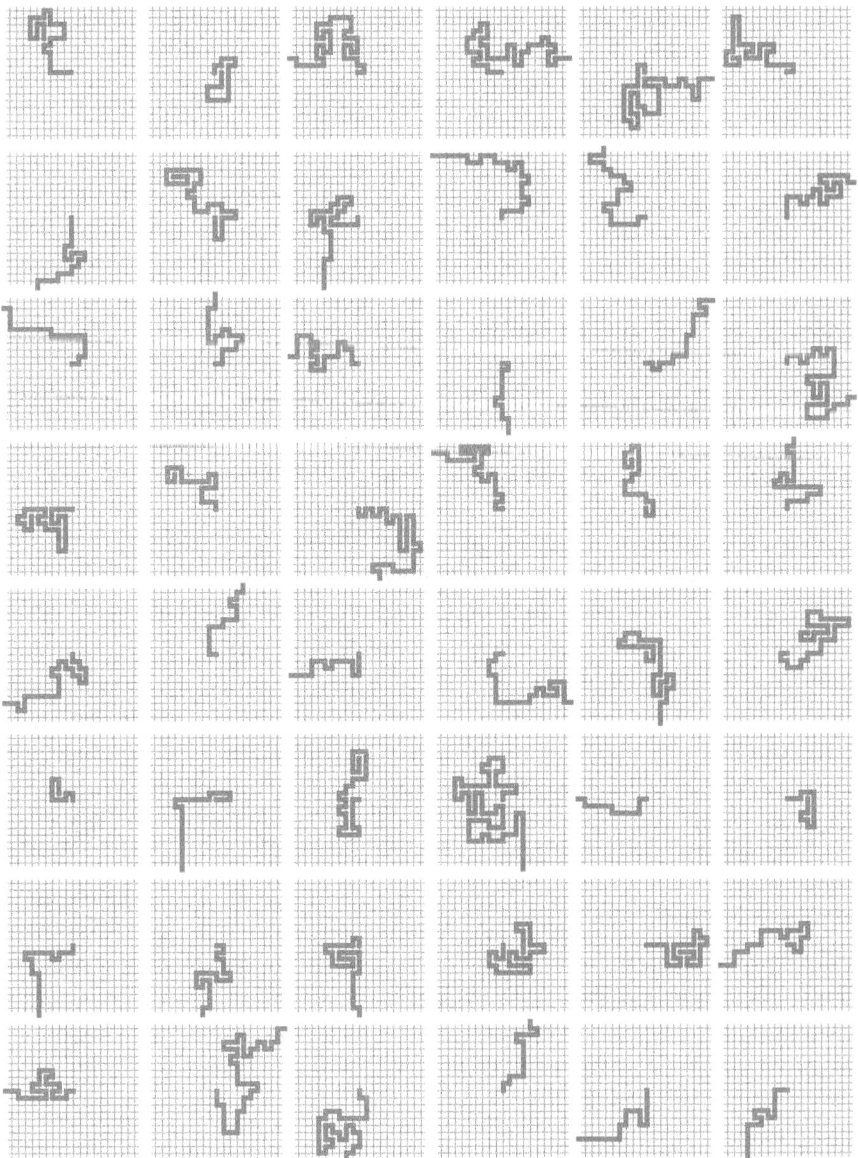

Self-avoiding random walks in a 21-by-21 grid

Summary Arrays are the fourth basic construct (the first three are assignments, conditionals, and loops) found in almost every programming language. As you have seen with the sample programs presented in this section, you can compose programs that can solve all sorts of problems using just these constructs. In the next section, we consider mechanisms for communicating with our programs, which will complete our coverage of elementary programming mechanisms.

Arrays are prominent in many of the programs that we consider, and the basic operations that we have discussed here will serve you well in addressing many programming tasks. When you are not using arrays explicitly (and you are sure to be doing so frequently), you will be using them implicitly, because all computers have a memory that is conceptually equivalent to an array.

The fundamental ingredient that arrays add to our programs is a potentially huge increase in the size of a program's *state*. The state of a program can be defined as the information you need to know to understand what a program is doing. In a program without arrays, if you know the values of the variables and which statement is the next to be executed, you can normally determine what the program will do next. When we trace a program, we are essentially tracking its state. When a program uses arrays, however, there can be too huge a number of values (each of which might be changed in each statement) for us to effectively track them all. This difference makes composing programs with arrays more of a challenge than composing programs without them.

Arrays directly represent vectors and matrices, so they are of direct use in computations associated with many basic problems in science and engineering. Arrays also provide a succinct notation for manipulating a potentially huge amount of data in a uniform way, so they play a critical role in any application that involves processing large amounts of data, as you will see throughout this book.

More importantly, arrays represent the tip of an iceberg. They are your first example of a *data structure*, where we organize data to enable us to conveniently and efficiently process it. We will consider more examples of data structures in CHAPTER 4, including *resizing arrays*, *linked lists*, and *binary search trees*, and *hash tables*. Arrays are also your first example of a *collection*, which groups many elements into a single unit. We will consider many more example of collections in CHAPTER 4, including Python *lists*, *tuples*, *dictionaries*, and *sets*, along with two classic examples, *stacks* and *queues*.

Q&A

Q. Why do Python array indices start at 0 instead of 1?

A. That convention originated with machine-language programming, where the address of an array element would be computed by adding the index to the address of the beginning of an array. Starting indices at 1 would entail either a waste of space at the beginning of the array or string, or a waste of time to subtract the 1.

Q. What happens if I use a negative integer to index an array?

A. The answer may surprise you. Given an array `a[]`, you can use the index `-i` as shorthand for `len(a) - i`. For example, you can refer to the last element in the array with `a[-1]` or `a[len(a) - 1]` and the first element with `a[-len(a)]` or `a[0]`. Python raises an `IndexError` at run time if you use an index outside of the range `-len(a)` through `len(a) - 1`.

Q. Why does the slice `a[i:j]` include `a[i]` but exclude `a[j]`?

A. The notation is consistent with ranges defined with `range()`, which includes the left endpoint but excludes the right endpoint. It leads to some appealing properties: `j - i` is the length of the subarray (assuming no truncation); `a[0:len(a)]` is the entire array; `a[i:i]` is the empty array; and `a[i:j] + a[j:k]` is the subarray `a[i:k]`.

Q. What happens when I compare two arrays `a[]` and `b[]` with `(a == b)`?

A. It depends. For arrays (or multidimensional arrays) of numbers, it works as you might expect: the arrays are equal if each has the same length and the corresponding elements are equal.

Q. What happens when a random walk does not avoid itself?

A. This case is well understood. It is a two-dimensional version of the gambler's ruin problem, as described in Section 1.3.

Q. Which pitfalls should I watch out for when using arrays?

A. Remember that *creating an array takes time proportional to the length of the array*. You need to be particularly careful about creating arrays within loops.

Exercises

1.4.1 Compose a program that creates a one-dimensional array a containing exactly 1,000 integers and then attempts to access a[1000]. What happens when you run the program?

1.4.2 Given two vectors of length n that are represented with one-dimensional arrays, compose a code fragment that computes the *Euclidean distance* between them (the square root of the sums of the squares of the differences between corresponding elements).

1.4.3 Compose a code fragment that reverses the order of the elements in a one-dimensional array of floats. Do not create another array to hold the result. *Hint*: Use the code in the text for exchanging two elements.

1.4.4 What is wrong with the following code fragment?

```
a = []
for i in range(10):
    a[i] = i * i
```

Solution: Initially a is the empty array. Subsequently no elements are appended to the array. Thus a[0], a[1], and so forth do not exist. The attempts to use them in an assignment statement will raise an IndexError at run time.

1.4.5 Compose a code fragment that writes the contents of a two-dimensional array of booleans, using * to represent True and a space to represent False. Include row and column numbers.

1.4.6 What does the following code fragment write?

```
a = stdarray.create1D(10, 0)
for i in range(10):
    a[i] = 9 - i
for i in range(10):
    a[i] = a[a[i]]
for v in a:
    stdio.writeln(v)
```

1.4.7 What is a[] after executing the following code fragment?

```
n = 10
a = [0, 1]
for i in range(2, n):
    a += [a[i-1] + a[i-2]]
```

1.4.8 Compose a program deal.py that takes a command-line argument n and writes n poker hands (five cards each) from a shuffled deck, separated by blank lines.

1.4.9 Compose code fragments to create a two-dimensional array b[][] that is a copy of an existing two-dimensional array a[][], under each of the following assumptions:

a. a is square

b. a is rectangular

c. a may be ragged

Your solution to *b* should work for *a*, and your solution to *c* should work for both *b* and *a*.

1.4.10 Compose a code fragment to write the *transposition* (rows and columns changed) of a two-dimensional array. For the example spreadsheet array in the text, your code would write the following:

```
99  98  92  94  99  90  76  92  97  89
85  57  77  32  34  46  59  66  71  29
98  78  76  11  22  54  88  89  24  38
```

1.4.11 Compose a code fragment to transpose a square two-dimensional array *in place* without creating a second array.

1.4.12 Compose a code fragment to create a two-dimensional array b[][] that is the transpose of an existing *m*-by-*n* array a[][].

1.4.13 Compose a program that computes the product of two square matrices of booleans, using the or operator instead of + and the and operator instead of *.

1.4.14 Compose a program that accepts an integer n from the command line and creates an n-by-n boolean array `a` such that `a[i][j]` is `True` if `i` and `j` are relatively prime (have no common factors), and `False` otherwise. Then write the array (see Exercise 1.4.5) using * to represent `True` and a space to represent `False`. Include row and column numbers. *Hint*: Use sieving.

1.4.15 Modify the spreadsheet code fragment in the text to compute a *weighted* average of the rows, where the weights of each test score are in a one-dimensional array `weights[]`. For example, to assign the last of the three tests in our example to be twice the weight of the others, you would use

```
weights = [.25, .25, .50]
```

Note that the weights should sum to `1.0`.

1.4.16 Compose a code fragment to multiply two rectangular matrices that are not necessarily square. *Note*: For the dot product to be well defined, the number of columns in the first matrix must be equal to the number of rows in the second matrix. Write an error message if the dimensions do not satisfy this condition.

1.4.17 Modify `selfavoid.py` (Program 1.4.4) to calculate and write the average length of the paths as well as the dead-end probability. Keep separate the average lengths of escape paths and dead-end paths.

1.4.18 Modify `selfavoid.py` to calculate and write the average area of the smallest axis-oriented rectangle that encloses the path. Keep separate statistics for escape paths and dead-end paths.

1.4.19 Compose a code fragment that creates a three-dimensional n-by-n-by-n array of booleans, with each element initialized to `False`.

Creative Exercises

1.4.20 *Dice simulation.* The following code computes the exact probability distribution for the sum of two dice:

```
probabilities = stdarray.create1D(13, 0.0)
for i in range(1, 7):
    for j in range(1, 7):
        probabilities[i+j] += 1.0
for k in range(2, 13):
    probabilities[k] /= 36.0
```

After this code completes, `probabilities[k]` is the probability that the dice sum to `k`. Run experiments to validate this calculation simulating n dice throws, keeping track of the frequencies of occurrence of each value when you compute the sum of two random integers between 1 and 6. How large does n have to be before your empirical results match the exact results to three decimal places?

1.4.21 *Longest plateau.* Given an array of integers, compose a program that finds the length and location of the longest contiguous sequence of equal values where the values of the elements just before and just after this sequence are smaller.

1.4.22 *Empirical shuffle check.* Run computational experiments to check that our shuffling code works as advertised. Compose a program `shuffletest.py` that takes command-line arguments m and n, does n shuffles of an array of size m that is initialized with `a[i] = i` before each shuffle, and writes an m-by-m table such that row `i` gives the number of times `i` wound up in position `j` for all `j`. All elements in the array should be close to n/m.

1.4.23 *Bad shuffling.* Suppose that you choose a random integer between `0` and `n-1` in our shuffling code instead of one between `i` and `n-1`. Show that the resulting order is *not* equally likely to be one of the $n!$ possibilities. Run the test of the previous exercise for this version.

1.4.24 *Music shuffling.* You set your music player to shuffle mode. It plays each of the m songs before repeating any. Compose a program to estimate the likelihood that you will not hear any sequential pair of songs (that is, song 3 does not follow song 2, song 10 does not follow song 9, and so on).

1.4.25 *Minima in permutations.* Compose a program that takes an integer n from the command line, generates a random permutation, writes the permutation, and writes the number of left-to-right minima in the permutation (the number of times an element is the smallest seen so far). Then compose a program that takes integers m and n from the command line, generates m random permutations of size n, and writes the average number of left-to-right minima in the permutations generated. *Extra credit*: Formulate a hypothesis about the number of left-to-right minima in a permutation of size n, as a function of n.

1.4.26 *Inverse permutation.* Compose a program that reads in a permutation of the integers `0` to `n-1` from `n` command-line arguments and writes its inverse. (If the permutation is an array `a[]`, its inverse is the array `b[]` such that `a[b[i]] = b[a[i]] = i`.) Be sure to check that the input is a valid permutation.

1.4.27 *Hadamard matrix.* The n-by-n Hadamard matrix H_n is a boolean matrix with the remarkable property that any two rows differ in exactly $n/2$ elements. (This property makes it useful for designing error-correcting codes.) H_1 is a 1-by-1 matrix with the single element `True`, and for $n > 1$, H_{2n} is obtained by aligning four copies of H_n in a large square, and then inverting all of the elements in the lower right n-by-n copy, as shown in the following examples (with `T` representing `True` and `F` representing `False`, as usual).

H_1	H_2	H_4
T	T T	T T T T
	T F	T F T F
		T T F F
		T F F T

Compose a program that takes one command-line argument n and writes H_n. Assume that n is a power of 2.

1.4.28 *Rumors.* Alice is throwing a party with n other guests, including Bob. Bob starts a rumor about Alice by telling it to one of the other guests. A person hearing this rumor for the first time will immediately tell it to one other guest, chosen at random from all the people at the party except Alice and the person from whom they heard it. If a person (including Bob) hears the rumor for a second time, he or she will not propagate it further. Compose a program to estimate the probability that everyone at the party (except Alice) will hear the rumor before it stops propagating. Also calculate an estimate of the expected number of people to hear the rumor.

1.4.29 *Find a duplicate.* Given an array of n elements with each element between 1 and n, compose a code fragment to determine whether there are any duplicates. You do not need to preserve the contents of the given array, but do not use an extra array.

1.4.30 *Counting primes.* Compare `primesieve.py` with the alternative approach described in the text. This is an example of a space–time tradeoff: `primesieve.py` is fast, but requires a boolean array of length n; the alternative approach uses only two integer variables, but is substantially slower. Estimate the magnitude of this difference by finding the value of n for which this second approach can complete the computation in about the same time as `python primesieve.py 1000000`.

1.4.31 *Minesweeper.* Compose a program that takes three command-line arguments m, n, and p and produces an m-by-n boolean array where each element is occupied with probability p. In the minesweeper game, occupied cells represent bombs and empty cells represent safe cells. Write the array using an asterisk for bombs and a period for safe cells. Then, replace each safe square with the number of neighboring bombs (above, below, left, right, or diagonal) and write the result, as in this example.

```
* * . . .        * * 1 0 0
. . . . .        3 3 2 0 0
. * . . .        1 * 1 0 0
```

Try to express your code so that you have as few special cases as possible to deal with, by using an $(m+2)$-by-$(n+2)$ boolean array.

1.4.32 *Self-avoiding walk length.* Suppose that there is no limit on the size of the grid. Run experiments to estimate the average walk length.

1.4.33 *Three-dimensional self-avoiding walks.* Run experiments to verify that the dead-end probability is 0 for a three-dimensional self-avoiding walk and to compute the average walk length for various values of n.

1.4.34 *Random walkers.* Suppose that n random walkers, starting in the center of an n-by-n grid, move one step at a time, choosing to go left, right, up, or down with equal probability at each step. Compose a program to help formulate and test a hypothesis about the number of steps taken before all cells are touched.

1.4.35 *Bridge hands.* In the game of bridge, four players are dealt hands of 13 cards each. An important statistic is the distribution of the number of cards in each suit in a hand. Which is the most likely, 5-3-3-2, 4-4-3-2, or 4-3-3-3? Compose a program to help you answer this question.

1.4.36 *Birthday problem.* Suppose that people continue to enter an empty room until a pair of people share a birthday. On average, how many people will have to enter before there is a match? Run experiments to estimate the value of this quantity. Assume birthdays to be uniform random integers between 0 and 364.

1.4.37 *Coupon collector.* Run experiments to validate the classical mathematical result that the expected number of coupons needed to collect n values is about nH_n. For example, if you are observing the cards carefully at the blackjack table (and the dealer has enough decks randomly shuffled together), you will wait until about 235 cards are dealt, on average, before seeing every card value.

1.4.38 *Riffle shuffle.* Compose a program to rearrange a deck of n cards using the Gilbert–Shannon–Reeds model of a riffle shuffle. First, generate a random integer r according to a *binomial distribution*: flip a fair coin n times and let r be the number of heads. Now, divide the deck into two piles: the first r cards and the remaining $n - r$ cards. To complete the shuffle, repeatedly take the top card from one of the two piles and put it on the bottom of a new pile. If there are n_1 cards remaining in the first pile and n_2 cards remaining in the second pile, choose the next card from the first pile with probability $n_1 / (n_1 + n_2)$ and from the second pile with probability $n_2 / (n_1 + n_2)$. Investigate how many riffle shuffles you need to apply to a deck of 52 cards to produce a (nearly) uniformly shuffled deck.

1.4.39 *Binomial coefficients.* Compose a program that builds and writes a two-dimensional ragged array a such that `a[n][k]` contains the probability that you get exactly `k` heads when you toss a fair coin `n` times. Take a command-line argument to specify the maximum value of `n`. These numbers are known as the *binomial distribution*: if you multiply each element in row k by 2^n, you get the *binomial coefficients* (the coefficients of x^k in $(x+1)^n$) arranged in *Pascal's triangle*. To compute them, start with `a[n][0] = 0.0` for all `n` and `a[1][1] = 1.0`, then compute values in successive rows, left to right, with `a[n][k] = (a[n-1][k] + a[n-1][k-1])/2.0`.

Pascal's triangle	*binomial distribution*
1	1
1 1	1/2 1/2
1 2 1	1/4 1/2 1/4
1 3 3 1	1/8 3/8 3/8 1/8
1 4 6 4 1	1/16 1/4 3/8 1/4 1/16

1.5 Input and Output

IN THIS SECTION WE EXTEND THE set of simple abstractions (command-line arguments and standard output) that we have been using as the interface between our Python programs and the outside world to include *standard input*, *standard drawing*, and *standard audio*. Standard input makes it convenient for us to compose programs that process arbitrary amounts of input and to interact with our programs; standard drawing makes it possible for us to work with graphical representations of images, freeing us from having to encode everything as text; and standard audio adds sound. These extensions are easy to use, and will bring you to yet another new world of programming.

Programs in this section

The abbreviation *I/O* is universally understood to mean *input/output*, a collective term that refers to the mechanisms by which programs communicate with the outside world. Your computer's operating system controls the physical devices that are connected to your computer. To implement our "standard I/O" abstractions, we use modules containing functions that interface to the operating system.

You have already been accepting arguments from the command line and writing strings in a terminal window; the purpose of this section is to provide you with a much richer set of tools for processing and presenting data. Like the `stdio.write()` and `stdio.writeln()` functions that you have been using, these functions do not implement pure mathematical functions—their purpose is to produce some *side effect*, either on an input device or on an output device. Our prime concern is using such devices to get information into and out of our programs.

An essential feature of standard I/O mechanisms is that there is no limit on the amount of input or output data, from the point of view of the program. Your programs can consume input or produce output indefinitely.

One use of standard I/O mechanisms is to connect your programs to *files* on your computer's external storage. It is easy to connect standard input, standard output, standard drawing, and standard audio to files. Such connections make it easy to have your Python programs save or load results to files for archival purposes or for later reference by other programs or other applications.

Bird's-eye view The conventional model that we have been using for Python programming has served us since Section 1.1. To build context, we begin by briefly reviewing the model.

A Python program takes input values from the command line and writes a string of characters as output. By default, both *command-line arguments* and *standard output* are associated with the application that takes commands (the one in which you have been typing the `python` command). We use the generic term *terminal window* to refer to this application. This model has proved to be a convenient and direct way for us to interact with our programs and data.

Command-line arguments. This mechanism, which we have been using to provide input to our programs, is a standard part of Python programming. The operating system presents the command-line arguments that we type to Python programs in an array named `sys.argv[]`. By convention, both Python and the operating system process the arguments as strings, so if we intend for an argument to be a number, we use a conversion function such as `int()` or `float()` to convert it from a string to the appropriate type.

Standard output. To write output values in our programs, we have been using the booksite functions `stdio.write()` and `stdio.writeln()`. Python puts the results of a program's sequence of calls on these functions into the form of an abstract stream of characters known as *standard output*. By default, the operating system connects standard output to the terminal window. All of the output in our programs so far has been appearing in the terminal window.

For reference, and as a starting point, `randomseq.py` (Program 1.5.1) is a program that uses this model. It takes a command-line argument `n` and produces an output sequence of `n` random numbers between 0 and 1.

Now we will complement command-line arguments and standard output with three additional mechanisms that address their limitations and provide us with a far more useful programming model. These mechanisms give us a new bird's-eye view of a Python program in which the program converts a standard input stream and a sequence of command-line arguments into a standard output stream, a standard drawing, and a standard audio stream.

Program 1.5.1 Generating a random sequence (`randomseq.py`)

```
import random
import sys
import stdio

n = int(sys.argv[1])
for i in range(n):
    stdio.writeln(random.random())
```

This program accepts an integer command-line argument n, and writes to standard output a random sequence of n floats in the range [0, 1). The program illustrates the conventional model that we have been using so far for Python programming. From the program's point of view, there is no limit on the length of the output sequence.

```
% python randomseq.py 1000000
0.879948024484513
0.8698170909139995
0.6358055797752076
0.9546013485661425
...
```

Standard input. The booksite `stdio` module defines several functions in addition to `stdio.write()` and `stdio.writeln()`. These additional functions implement a standard input abstraction to complement the standard output abstraction. That is, the `stdio` module contains functions that allow your programs to *read* from *standard input*. Just as you can write to standard output at any time during the execution of your program, so you can read from a standard input stream at any time.

Standard drawing. The booksite `stddraw` module allows you to create drawings with your programs. It uses a simple graphics model that allows you to create drawings consisting of points, lines, and geometric figures in a window on your computer. The `stddraw` module also includes facilities for text, color, and animation.

Standard audio. The booksite `stdaudio` module allows you to create and manipulate sound with your programs. It uses a standard format to convert arrays of floats into sound.

To use these modules, you must make the files `stdio.py`, `stddraw.py`, and `stdaudio.py` available to Python (see the Q&A at the end of this section).

The standard input and standard output abstractions date back to the development of the Unix operating system in the 1970s and are found in some form on all modern systems. Although they are primitive by comparison to various mechanisms developed since, modern programmers still depend on them as a reliable way to connect data to programs. We have developed for this book `stddraw` and `stdaudio` in the same spirit as these earlier abstractions to provide you with an easy way to produce visual and aural output.

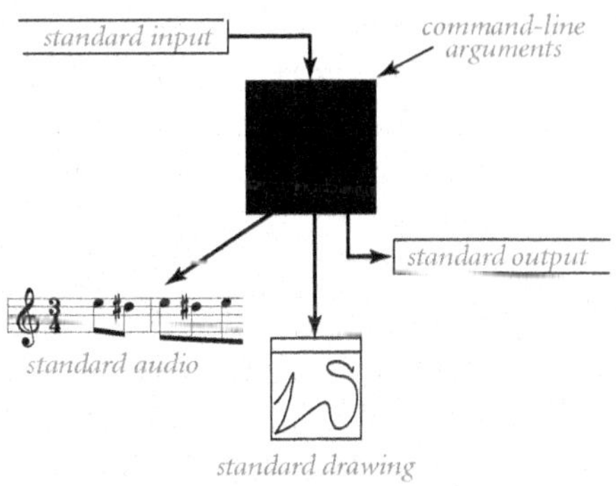

A bird's-eye view of a Python program (revisited)

Standard output As noted in Section 1.2, an *application programming interface (API)* is a description of the features that a module offers to its clients. At the bottom of this page is the API of the part of the `stdio` module that is relevant to standard output. The `stdio.write()` and `stdio.writeln()` functions are the ones that you have been using. The `stdio.writef()` function is a main topic of this section and will be of interest to you now because it gives you more control over the appearance of the output. It was a feature of the C language of the early 1970s and continues to survive in modern languages because it is so useful.

function call	*description*
`stdio.write(x)`	*write* `x` *to standard output*
`stdio.writeln(x)`	*write* `x` *and a newline to standard output (write only a newline if no argument)*
`stdio.writef(fmt, arg1, ...)`	*write the arguments* `arg1`, ... *to standard output as specified by the format string* `fmt`

API for booksite functions related to standard output

Since the first time that we wrote `float` objects, we have been distracted by excessive precision in the output. For example, when we call `stdio.write(math.pi)`, we get the output `3.141592653589793`, even though we might prefer to see `3.14` or `3.14159`. The `stdio.write()` and `stdio.writeln()` functions present each number to up to 16 decimal digits of precision even when we would be happy with just a few digits of precision. The `stdio.writef()` function is more flexible: it allows us to specify the number of digits and the precision when converting numeric objects to strings for output. With `stdio.writef()`, we can write `stdio.writef('%7.5f', math.pi)` to get `3.14159`.

Next, we describe the meaning and operation of these statements, along with extensions to handle the other built-in types of data.

Formatted writing basics. The simplest kind of call of `stdio.writef()` passes only one argument, a string. In that case, `stdio.writef()` simply writes the string to standard output, so it is equivalent to `stdio.write()`. A more commonly used call of `stdio.writef()` passes two arguments. In that context the first argument is called the *format string*. It contains a *conversion specification* that describes how the second argument is to be converted to a string for output. A conversion specification has the form `%w.pc`, where `w` and `p` are small integers and `c` is a character, to be interpreted as follows:

- `w` is the *field width*, the number of characters that should be written. If the number of characters to be written exceeds (or equals) the field width, then the field width is ignored; otherwise, the output is padded with spaces on the left. A negative field width indicates that the output instead should be padded with spaces on the right.
- `p` is the *precision*. For floats, the precision is the number of digits that should be written after the decimal point; for strings, it is the number of characters of the string that should be written. The precision is not used with integers.
- `c` is the *conversion code*. It should be `d` when writing an integer, `f` when writing a float, `e` when writing a float using scientific notation, and `s` when writing a string.

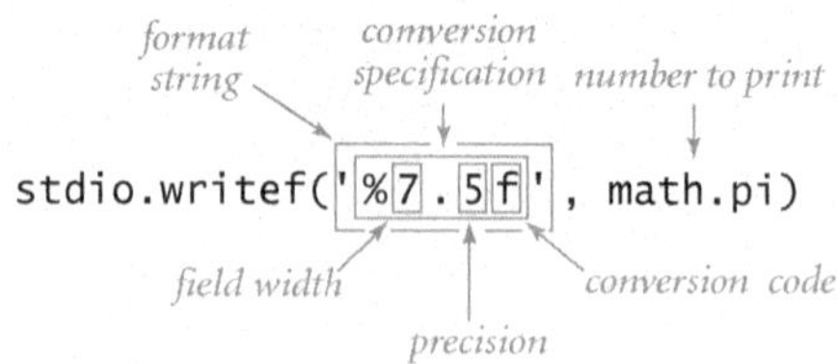

Anatomy of a formatted print statement

The field width and precision can be omitted , but every specification must have a conversion code.

Python must be able to convert the second argument to the type required by the specification. For `s`, there is no restriction, because every type of data can be converted to a string (via a call to the `str()` function). In contrast, a statement such as `stdio.writef('%12d', 'Hello')`—which asks Python to convert a string to an integer—causes Python to raise a `TypeError` at run time. The table at the bottom of this page shows format strings containing some common conversion specifications.

Any part of the format string that is not a conversion specification is simply passed through to standard output. For example, the statement

```
stdio.writef('pi is approximately %.2f\n', math.pi)
```

writes the line

```
pi is approximately 3.14
```

Note that we need to explicitly include the newline character `\n` in the argument to write a new line with `stdio.writef()`.

Multiple arguments. The `stdio.writef()` function can take more than two arguments. In this case, the format string must have a format specifier for each additional argument, perhaps separated by other characters to pass through to the output. For example, we could replace `stdio.write(t)` in `sqrt.py` (Program 1.3.6) with

```
stdio.writef('The square root of %.1f is %.6f', c, t)
```

type	*code*	*typical literal*	*sample format strings*	*converted string values for output*
`int`	`d`	`512`	`'%14d'` `'%-14d'`	`'           512'` `'512           '`

`float`	`f`
	`e`
		`1595.1680010754388`	`'%14.2f'`
			`'%.7f'`
			`'%14.4e'`
				`'       1595.17'`
				`'1595.1680011'`
				`'    1.5952e+03'`

`String`	`s`	`'Hello, World'`	`'%14s'`
			`'%-14s'`
			`'%-14.5s'`
				`'  Hello, World'`
				`'Hello, World  '`
				`'Hello         '`

Format conventions for `stdio.writef()` (see the booksite for many other options)

to get output like

```
The square root of 2.0 is 1.414214
```

As a more detailed example, if you were making payments on a loan, you might use code whose inner loop contains the statements

```
format = '%3s  $%6.2f   $%7.2f   $%5.2f\n'
stdio.writef(format, month[i], pay, balance, interest)
```

to write the second and subsequent lines in a table like this (see EXERCISE 1.5.14):

```
     payment    balance  interest
Jan  $299.00   $9742.67   $41.67
Feb  $299.00   $9484.26   $40.59
Mar  $299.00   $9224.78   $39.52
 ...
```

Formatted writing is convenient because this sort of code is much more compact than the string-concatenation approach that we have been using to create output strings. We have described only the basic options; see the booksite for many details.

Standard input Several functions in the booksite `stdio` module take data from a *standard input stream* that may be empty or may contain a sequence of values separated by whitespace (spaces, tabs, newline characters, and the like). Each value represents an integer, a float, a boolean, or a string. One of the key features of the standard input stream is that your program consumes values when it reads them. Once your program has read a value, it cannot back up and read it again. This assumption is restrictive, but it reflects physical characteristics of some input devices and simplifies implementing the abstraction. The `stdio` module offers 13 functions that are related to reading from standard input, as shown in the API on the next page. These functions fall into one of three categories: those for reading individual tokens, one at a time, and converting each to an integer, float, boolean or string; those for reading lines from standard input, one at a time; and those for reading a sequence of values of the same type (returning the values in an array). Generally, it is best not to mix functions from the different categories in the same program. Within the input stream model, those functions are largely self-documenting (the names describe their effect), but their precise operation is worthy of careful consideration, so we will consider several examples in detail.

function call	description
functions that read individual tokens from standard input	
`stdio.isEmpty()`	*is standard input empty (or only whitespace)?*
`stdio.readInt()`	*read a token, convert it to an integer, and return it*
`stdio.readFloat()`	*read a token, convert it to a float, and return it*
`stdio.readBool()`	*read a token, convert it to a boolean, and return it*
`stdio.readString()`	*read a token and return it as a string*
functions that read lines from standard input	
`stdio.hasNextLine()`	*does standard input have a next line?*
`stdio.readLine()`	*read the next line and return it as a string*
functions that read a sequence of values of the same type until standard input is empty	
`stdio.readAll()`	*read all remaining input and return it as a string*
`stdio.readAllInts()`	*read all remaining tokens and return them as an array of integers*
`stdio.readAllFloats()`	*read all remaining tokens and return them as an array of floats*
`stdio.readAllBools()`	*read all remaining tokens and return them as an array of booleans*
`stdio.readAllStrings()`	*read all remaining tokens and return them as an array of strings*
`stdio.readAllLines()`	*read all remaining lines and return them as an array of strings.*

Note 1: A token is a maximal sequence of non-whitespace characters.
Note 2: Before reading a token, any leading whitespace is discarded.
Note 3: Each function that reads input raises a run-time error if it cannot read in the next value, either because there is no more input or because the input does not match the expected type.

API for booksite functions related to standard input

Typing input. When you use the `python` command to invoke a Python program from the command line, you actually are doing three things: (1) issuing a command to start executing your program, (2) specifying the values of the command line arguments, and (3) beginning to define the standard input stream. The string of characters that you type in the terminal window after the command line *is* the standard input stream. When you type characters, you are interacting with your program. The program *waits* for you to create the standard input stream. For example, consider the following program `addints.py`, which takes a integer `n` from the command line and then reads `n` integers from standard input, adds them, and writes the sum to standard output:

```
import sys
import stdio
n = int(sys.argv[1])
total = 0
for i in range(n):
    total += stdio.readInt()
stdio.writeln('Sum is ' + str(total))
```

When you type `python addints.py 4`, the program starts execution. It takes the command-line argument, initializes `total` to `0`, enters the `for` loop, eventually calls `stdio.readInt()`, and *waits* for you to type an integer. Suppose that you want `144` to be the first value. As you type `1`, then `4`, and then `4`, nothing happens, because `stdio` does not know that you are done typing the integer. But when you finally type `<return>` to signify the end of your integer, `stdio.readInt()` immediately returns the value `144`, which your program adds to `total` and then calls `stdio.readInt()` again. Again, nothing happens until you type the second value: if you type `2`, then `3`, then `3`, and then `<return>` to end the number, `stdio.readInt()` returns the value `233`, which your program again adds to `total`. After you have typed four numbers in this way, the program expects no more input and writes the sum, as desired. In the command-line traces, we use boldface to highlight the text that you type and differentiate it from the output of the program.

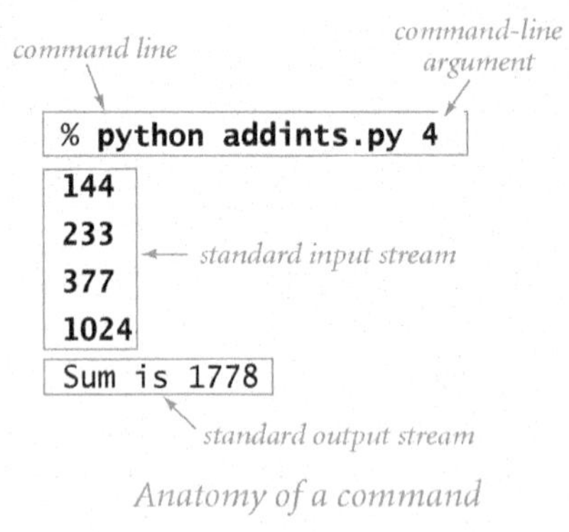

Anatomy of a command

Input format. The `stdio.readInt()` function expects an integer. If you type `abc` or `12.2` or `True`, Python raises a `ValueError` at run time. The format for each type is the same as you have been using to specify literals within Python programs. For convenience, `stdio` treats strings of consecutive whitespace characters as identical to one space and allows you to delimit your numbers with such strings. It does not matter how many spaces you put between numbers, or whether you enter numbers on one line or separate them with tab characters or spread them out over several lines (except that your terminal application processes standard input one line at a time, so it will wait until you type `<return>` before sending all of the numbers on that line to standard input). You can mix values of different types in an input stream, but whenever the program expects a value of a particular type, the input stream must have a value of that type.

Interactive user input. Program 1.5.2 (`twentyquestions.py`) is a simple example of a program that interacts with its user. The program generates a random integer and then gives clues to a user trying to guess the number. (*Note*: By using *binary search*, you can always get to the answer in at most 20 questions. See Section 4.2.) The fundamental difference between this program and others that we have composed is that the user has the ability to change the control flow *while* the program is executing. This capability was very important in early applications of computing, but we rarely compose such programs nowadays because modern applications typically take such input through a graphical user interface, as discussed in Chapter 3. Even a simple program like `twentyquestions.py` illustrates that composing programs that support user interaction is potentially very difficult because you have to plan for all possible user inputs.

Processing an arbitrary-size input stream. Typically, input streams are finite: your program marches through the input stream, consuming values until the stream is empty. But there is no restriction on the size of the input stream, and some programs simply process all the input presented to them. Our next example, `average.py` (Program 1.5.3), reads in a sequence of real numbers from standard input and writes their average. It illustrates a key property of using an input stream: the length of the stream is not known to the program. We type all the numbers that we have, and then the program averages them. Before reading each number, the program calls the function `stdio.isEmpty()` to check whether there are any more numbers in the input stream.

Program 1.5.2 Interactive user input (`twentyquestions.py`)

```
import random
import stdio

RANGE = 1000000

secret = random.randrange(1, RANGE+1)
stdio.write('I am thinking of a secret number between 1 and ')
stdio.writeln(RANGE)

guess = 0
while guess != secret:
    # Solicit one guess and provide one answer.
    stdio.write('What is your guess? ')
    guess = stdio.readInt()

    if   (guess < secret): stdio.writeln('Too low')
    elif (guess > secret): stdio.writeln('Too high')
    else:                  stdio.writeln('You win!')
```

`secret`	*secret value*
`guess`	*user's guess*

This program generates a random integer between 1 and 1 million. Then it repeatedly reads user guesses from standard input. It writes `Too low` *or* `Too high` *to standard output, as appropriate, in response to each guess. It writes* `You win!` *to standard output and exits when the user's guess is correct. You always can get the program to write* `You win!` *with fewer than 20 questions.*

```
% python twentyquestions.py
I am thinking of a secret number between 1 and 1000000
What is your guess? 500000
Too high
What is your guess? 250000
Too low
What is your guess? 375000
Too high
What is your guess? 312500
Too high
What is your guess? 300500
Too low
...
```

How do we signal that we have no more data to type? By convention, we type a special sequence of characters known as the *end-of-file* sequence. Sadly, the terminal applications that we typically encounter on modern operating systems use different conventions for this critically important sequence. In this book, we use <Ctrl-d> (many systems require <Ctrl-d> to appear on a line by itself); the other widely used convention is <Ctrl-z> on a line by itself.

Actually, we rarely type numbers one by one on standard input. Instead, we keep our input data in files, as illustrated in the example accompanying PROGRAM 1.5.3 and explained in detail in the text.

Certainly `average.py` is a simple program, but it represents a profound new capability in programming: with standard input, we can compose programs that process an unlimited amount of data. As you will see, composing such programs is an effective approach for numerous data-processing applications.

STANDARD INPUT IS A SUBSTANTIAL STEP up from the command-line argument model that we have been using, for two reasons, as illustrated by `twentyquestions.py` and `average.py`. First, we can interact with our program—with command-line arguments, we can provide data to the program only *before* it begins execution. Second, we can read in large amounts of data—with command-line arguments, we can enter only values that fit on the command line. Indeed, as illustrated by `average.py`, the amount of data processed by a program can be potentially unlimited, and many programs are made simpler by that assumption. A third reason for standard input is that your operating system makes it possible to change the source of standard input, so that you do not have to type all the input. Next, we consider the mechanisms that enable this possibility.

Redirection and piping For many applications, typing input data as a standard input stream from the terminal window is untenable because our program's processing power is then limited by the amount of data that we can type (and our typing speed). Similarly, we often want to save the information written on the standard output stream for later use. To address such limitations, we next focus on the idea that standard input is an *abstraction*—the program just expects its input and has no dependence on the source of the input stream. Standard output is a similar abstraction. The power of these abstractions derives from our ability (through the operating system) to specify various other sources for standard input and standard output, such as a file, the network, or another program. All modern operating systems implement these mechanisms.

Program 1.5.3 Averaging a stream of numbers (average.py)

```
import stdio

total = 0.0
count = 0
while not stdio.isEmpty():
    value = stdio.readFloat()
    total += value
    count += 1
avg = total / count

stdio.writeln('Average is ' + str(avg))
```

count	*count of numbers read*
total	*cumulated sum*

This program reads floats from the standard input stream until it reaches the end-of-file. Then it writes to standard output the average of those floats. From its point of view, there is no limit on the size of the input stream. The commands shown below after the first one use redirection and piping (discussed in the next subsection) to provide 100,000 numbers to average.py.

```
% python average.py
10.0 5.0 6.0
3.0
7.0 32.0
<Ctrl-d>
Average is 10.5
```

```
% python ramdomseq.py 1000 > data.txt
% python average.py < data.txt
Average is 0.510473676174824

% python randomseq.py 1000 | python average.py
Average is 0.50499417963857
```

Redirecting standard output to a file. By adding a simple directive to the command that executes a program, we can *redirect* its standard output to a file, either for permanent storage or for input to another program at a later time. For example,

```
% python randomseq.py 1000 > data.txt
```

specifies that the standard output stream is not to be written in the terminal window, but instead is to be written to a text file named `data.txt`. Each call to `stdio.write()`, `stdio.writeln()`, or `stdio.writef()` appends text at the end of that file. In this example, the end result is a file that contains 1,000 random values. No output appears in the terminal window: it goes directly into the file named after the > symbol. Thus, we can save information for later retrieval. Note that we do not have to change `randomseq.py` (PROGRAM 1.5.1) in any way for this mechanism to work—it relies on using the standard output abstraction and is unaffected by our use of a different implementation of that abstraction. You can use this mechanism to save output from any program that you compose. Once we have expended a significant amount of effort to obtain a result, we often want to save the result for later reference. In a modern system, you can save some information by using cut-and-paste or some similar mechanism that is provided by the operating system, but cut-and-paste is inconvenient for large amounts of data. By contrast, redirection is specifically designed to make it easy to handle large amounts of data.

```
% python randomseq.py 1000 > data.txt
```

randomseq.py

standard output

data.txt

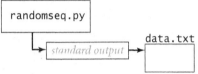

Redirecting standard output to a file

Redirecting from a file to standard input. We can redirect standard input so that our program reads data from a file instead of the terminal application:

```
% python average.py < data.txt
```

This command reads a sequence of numbers from the file `data.txt` and computes their average value. Specifically, the < symbol is a directive that tells the operating system to implement the standard input stream by reading from the text file `data.txt` instead of waiting for the user to type something into the terminal window. When the program calls `stdio.readFloat()`, the operating system reads the value from the file. The file `data.txt` could have been created by any application, not just a Python program—almost every application on your computer can create text files. This facility to redirect from a file to standard input enables us to create *data-driven code*, in which we can change the data processed by a

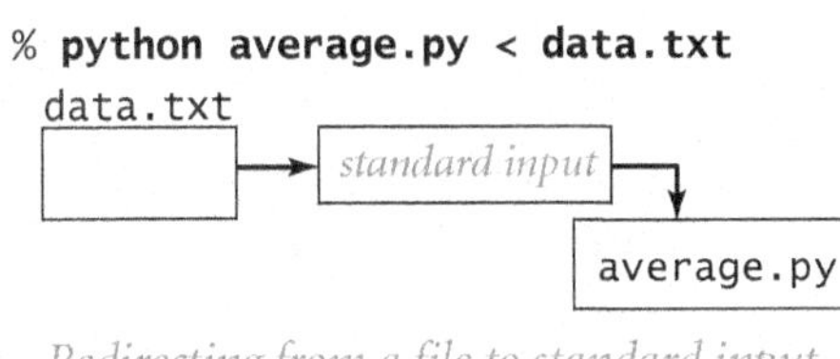

Redirecting from a file to standard input

program without having to change the program at all. Instead, we keep data in files and compose programs that read from standard input.

Connecting two programs. The most flexible way to implement the standard input and standard output abstractions is to specify that they are implemented by our own programs! This mechanism is called *piping*. For example, the command

```
% python randomseq.py 1000 | python average.py
```

specifies that the standard output for `randomseq.py` and the standard input stream for `average.py` are the *same* stream. The effect is as if `randomseq.py` were typing the numbers it generates into the terminal window while `average.py` is running. This example also has the same effect as the following sequence of commands:

```
% python randomseq.py 1000 > data.txt
% python average.py < data.txt
```

With piping, however, the file `data.txt` is not created. This difference is profound, because it removes another limitation on the size of the input and output streams that we can process. For example, we could replace `1000` in our example with `1000000000`, even though we might not have the space to save a billion numbers on our computer (we do need the *time* to process them, however). When `randomseq.py` calls `stdio.writeln()`, a string is added to the end of the stream; when `average.py` calls `stdio.readFloat()`, a string is removed from the beginning of the stream. The timing of precisely what happens is up to the operating system: it might run `randomseq.py` until it produces some output, and then run `average.py` to consume that output, or it might run `average.py` until it needs some output, and then run `randomseq.py` until it produces the needed output. The end result is the same, but our programs are freed from worrying about such details because they work solely with the standard input and standard output abstractions.

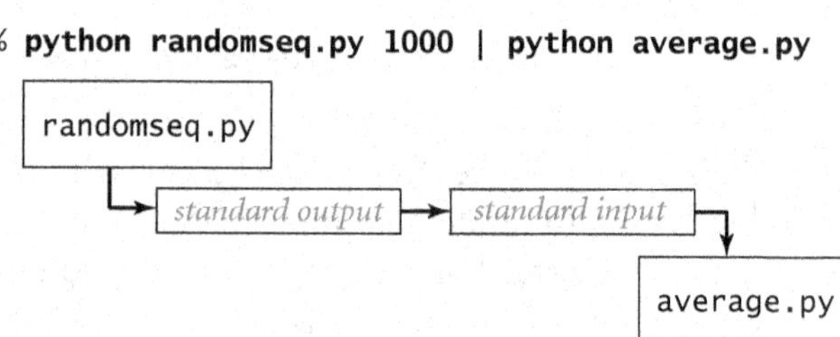

Piping the output of one program to the input of another

Filters. Piping, a core feature of the original Unix system of the early 1970s, still survives in modern systems because it is a simple abstraction for communicating among disparate programs. Testimony to the power of this abstraction is the fact that many Unix programs are still being used today to process files that are thousands or millions of times larger than imagined by the programs' authors. We can communicate with other Python programs via calls on functions, but standard input and standard output allow us to communicate with programs that were written at another time and, perhaps, in another language. When we use standard input and standard output, we are agreeing on a simple interface to the outside world.

For many common tasks, it is convenient to think of each program as a *filter* that converts a standard input stream to a standard output stream in some way, with piping as the command mechanism to connect programs together. For example, `rangefilter.py` (PROGRAM 1.5.4) takes two command line arguments and writes to standard output those numbers from standard input that fall within the specified range. You might imagine standard input to be measurement data from some instrument, with the filter being used to throw away data outside the range of interest for the experiment at hand.

Several standard filters that were designed for Unix still survive (sometimes with different names) as commands in modern operating systems. For example, the `sort` filter reads the lines from standard input and writes them to standard output in sorted order:

```
% python randomseq.py 9 | sort
0.0472650078535
0.0681950168757
0.0967410236589
0.0974385525393
0.118855769243
0.46604926859
0.522853708616
0.599692836211
0.685576779833
```

We discuss sorting in SECTION 4.2. A second useful filter is `grep`, which writes the lines from standard input that match a given pattern. For example, if you type

```
% grep lo < rangefilter.py
```

Program 1.5.4 A simple filter (rangefilter.py)

```
import sys
import stdio

lo = int(sys.argv[1])
hi = int(sys.argv[2])

while not stdio.isEmpty():
    # Process one integer.
    value = stdio.readInt()
    if (value >= lo) and (value <= hi):
        stdio.write(str(value) + ' ')
stdio.writeln()
```

lo	*lower bound of range*
hi	*upper bound of range*
value	*current number*

This program accepts integer command-line arguments lo *and* hi *and then reads integers from standard input until it reaches end-of-file, writing to standard output each of those integers that is in the range* lo *to* hi*, inclusive. Thus the program is a filter (see text). There is no limit on the length of the streams.*

```
% more rangedata.txt
3 1 4 1 5 9 2 6 5 3 5 8 9 7 9 3 2 3 8 4 6 2 6 4 3 3 8 3 2 7 9

% python rangefilter.py 5 9 < rangedata.txt
5 9 6 5 5 8 9 7 9 8 6 6 8 7 9

% python rangefilter.py 100 400
358 1330 55 165 689 1014 3066 387 575 843 203 48 292 877 65 998
358 165 387 203 292
<Ctrl-d>
```

you get all the lines in `rangefilter.py` that contain `'lo'`:

```
lo = int(sys.argv[1])
    if (value >= lo) and (value <= hi):
```

Programmers often use tools such as `grep` to get a quick reminder of variable names or language usage details. A third useful filter is `more`, which reads data from standard input (or from a file specified as a command-line argument) and displays it in your terminal window one screenful at a time. For example, if you type

```
% python randomseq.py 1000 | more
```

you will see as many numbers as fit in your terminal window, but `more` will wait for you to hit the space bar before displaying each succeeding screenful. The term *filter* is perhaps misleading: it was meant to describe programs like `rangefilter.py` that write some subsequence of standard input to standard output, but it is now often used to describe any program that reads from standard input and writes to standard output.

Multiple streams. For many common tasks, we want to compose programs that take input from multiple sources and/or produce output intended for multiple destinations. In SECTION 3.1 we discuss our `instream.py` and `outstream.py` modules, which generalize `stdio.py` to allow for multiple input and output streams. These modules include provisions for redirecting these streams, not just to and from files, but also from arbitrary web pages.

PROCESSING LARGE AMOUNTS OF INFORMATION PLAYS an essential role in many applications of computing. A scientist may need to analyze data collected from a series of experiments, a stock trader may wish to analyze information about recent financial transactions, or a student may wish to maintain collections of music and movies. In these and countless other applications, data-driven programs are the norm. Standard output, standard input, redirection, and piping provide us with the capability to address such applications with our Python programs. We can collect data into files on our computer through the web or any of the standard devices and use redirection and piping to connect data to our programs.

Standard drawing Up to this point, our input/output abstractions have focused exclusively on text input and output. Now we introduce an abstraction for producing drawings as output. This module is easy to use and allows us to take advantage of a visual medium to cope with far more information than is possible with just text.

Standard drawing is very simple: we imagine an abstract drawing device capable of drawing lines and points on a two-dimensional canvas and then displaying that "canvas" on your screen in the standard drawing window. The device is capable of responding to the commands that our programs issue in the form of calls to functions in the `stddraw` module.

The module's API consists of two kinds of functions: *drawing* functions that cause the device to take an action (such as drawing a line or drawing a point) and *control functions* that control how the drawing is shown and set parameters such as the pen size or the coordinate scales.

Creating drawings. The basic functions for drawing are described in the API at the bottom of this page. Like the functions for standard input and standard output, the drawing functions are nearly self-documenting: `stddraw.line()` draws a straight line segment connecting two points whose coordinates are given as arguments and `stddraw.point()` draws a dot centered at the given coordinates. The default coordinate scale is the unit square (all coordinates between 0 and 1). The point (0.0, 0.0) is at the lower left, and the point (1.0, 1.0) is at the upper right—thus corresponding to the first quadrant of the familiar Cartesian coordinate system. The default settings draw black lines and black points on a white background.

The control function `stddraw.show()` needs a bit more explanation. When your program calls any drawing function such as `stddraw.line()` or `stddraw.point()`, `stddraw` uses an abstraction known as the *background canvas.* The background canvas is not displayed; it exists only in computer memory. All points, lines, and so forth are drawn on the background canvas, not directly in the

function call	*description*
`stddraw.line(x0, y0, x1, y1)`	*draw a line from* `(x0, y0)` *to* `(x1, y1)`
`stddraw.point(x, y)`	*draw a point at* `(x, y)`
`stddraw.show()`	*show the drawing in the standard drawing window (and wait until it is closed by the user)*

API for basic booksite functions for drawings

standard drawing window. Only when you call `stddraw.show()` does your drawing get copied from the background canvas to the standard drawing window, where it is displayed until the user closes the standard drawing window—typically by clicking on the *Close* button in the window's title bar.

Why does `stddraw` need to use a background canvas? The main reason is that use of two canvases instead of one makes the `stddraw` module more efficient. Incrementally displaying a complex drawing as it is being created can be intolerably inefficient on many computer systems. In computer graphics, this technique is known as *double buffering*.

To summarize the information that you need to know, a typical program using the `stddraw` module has this structure:

- Import the `stddraw` module.
- Call drawing functions such as `stddraw.line()` and `stddraw.point()` to create a drawing on the background canvas.
- Call `stddraw.show()` to show the background canvas in the standard drawing window and wait until the window is closed.

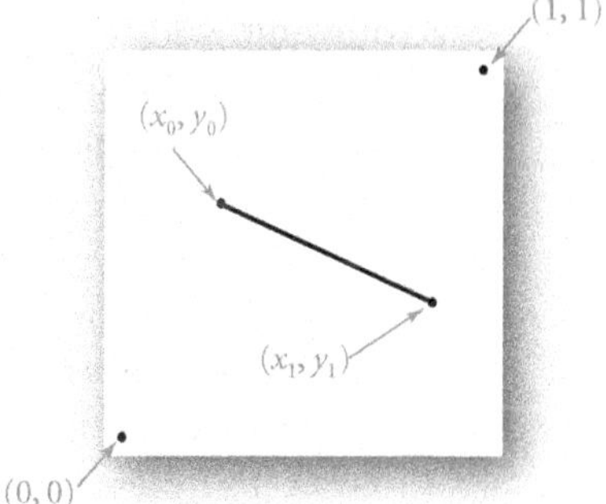


```
import stddraw
stddraw.line(x0, y0, x1, y1)
stddraw.show()
```

It is important to remember that *all drawing goes to the background canvas.* Typically, a program that creates a drawing finishes with a call to `stddraw.show()`, because only when `stddraw.show()` is called will you see your picture.

Next, we will consider several examples that will open up a whole new world of programming by freeing you from the restriction of communicating with your program just through text.

Your first drawing. The "Hello, World" equivalent for graphics programming with `stddraw` is to draw a triangle with a point inside. To form the triangle, we draw three lines: one from the point (0, 0) at the lower-left corner to the point (1, 0), one from that point to the third point at $(1/2, \sqrt{3}/2)$, and one from that point back to (0, 0). As a final flourish, we draw a spot in the middle of the triangle. Once you have successfully downloaded and run `triangle.py`, you are ready to compose your own programs that draw figures consisting of lines and points. This ability literally adds a new dimension to the output that you can produce.

When you use a computer to create drawings, you get immediate feedback (the drawing) so that you can refine and improve your program quickly. With a computer program, you can create drawings that you could not contemplate making by hand. In particular, instead of viewing our data as just numbers, we can use pictures, which are far more expressive. We will consider other graphics examples after we discuss a few other drawing commands.

```
import math
import stddraw

t = math.sqrt(3.0) / 2.0
stddraw.line(0.0, 0.0, 1.0, 0.0)
stddraw.line(1.0, 0.0, 0.5, t)
stddraw.line(0.5, t, 0.0, 0.0)
stddraw.point(0.5, t/3.0)
stddraw.show()
```

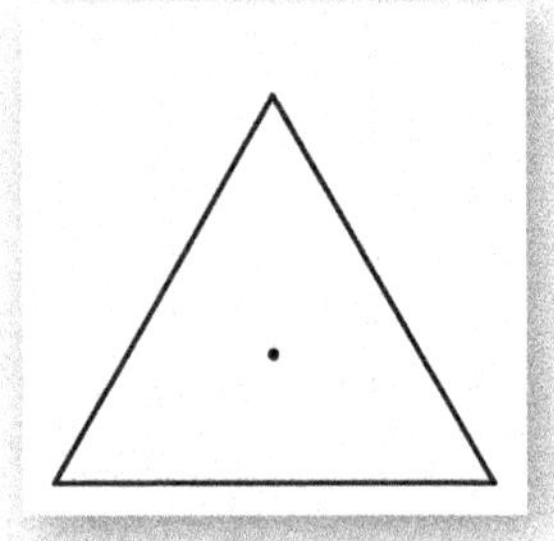

Your first drawing

Saving a drawing. You can save the standard drawing window canvas to a file, thus giving you the ability to print a drawing or to share a drawing with other people. To do so, right-click anywhere on the window canvas (usually while `stddraw` is waiting forever because your program called its `stddraw.show()` function). After you do that, `stddraw` displays a file dialog box which allows you to specify a file name. Then, after you type a file name into the dialog box and click the *Save* button, `stddraw` saves the window canvas to a file with the specified name. The file name must end with either `.jpg` (to save the window canvas in JPEG format) or `.png` (to save the window canvas in "Portable Network Graphics" format). The drawings generated by the graphics programs shown in this chapter were saved to files using this mechanism.

Control commands. The default coordinate system for standard drawing is the unit square, but we often want to draw plots at different scales. For example, a typical situation is to use coordinates in some range for the x-coordinate, or the y-coordinate, or both. Also, we often want to draw lines of different thickness and points of different size from the standard. To accommodate these needs, `stddraw` has the functions shown at the top of the next page.

For example, when you call the function `stddraw.setXscale(0, n)`, you are telling the drawing device that you will be using x-coordinates between `0` and `n`. Note that the two-call sequence

```
stddraw.setXscale(x0, x1)
stddraw.setYscale(y0, y1)
```

function call	*description*
`stddraw.setCanvasSize(w, h)`	*set the size of the canvas to* `w`*-by-*`h` *pixels (*`w` *and* `h` *default to* `512`*)*
`stddraw.setXscale(x0, x1)`	*set the x-range of the canvas to* `(x0, x1)` *(*`x0` *defaults to* `0` *and* `x1` *defaults to* `1`*)*
`stddraw.setYscale(y0, y1)`	*set the y-range of the canvas to* `(y0, y1)` *(*`y0` *defaults to* `0` *and* `y1` *defaults to* `1`*)*
`stddraw.setPenRadius(r)`	*set the pen radius to* `r` *(*`r` *defaults to* `0.005`*)*

Note: If the pen radius is 0*, then points and line widths will be the minimum possible size.*

API for booksite control functions for setting drawing parameters

sets the drawing coordinates to be within a *bounding box* whose lower left corner is at (x_0, y_0) and whose upper-right corner is at (x_1, y_1). If you use integer coordinates, Python promotes them to floats, as expected. The figure at right is a simple example that demonstrates the utility of scaling. Scaling is the simplest of the transformations commonly used in graphics. Several of the applications that we consider in this chapter are typical—we use scaling in a straightforward way to match our drawings to our data.

The pen is circular, so that when you set the pen radius to *r* and draw a point, you get a circle of radius *r*. Also, lines are of thickness 2*r* and have rounded ends. The default pen radius is 0.005 and is not affected by coordinate scaling. This default pen radius is about 1/200 the width of the default window, so that if you draw 100 points equally spaced along a horizontal or vertical line, you will be able to see individual circles, but if you draw 200 such points, the result will look like a line. When you make the function call `stddraw.setPenRadius(.025)`, you are saying that you want the thickness of the lines and the size of the points to be five times the 0.005 standard. To draw points with the minimum possible radius (one pixel on typical displays), set the pen radius to 0.0.

```
import stddraw
n = 50
stddraw.setXscale(0, n)
stddraw.setYscale(0, n)
for i in range(n+1):
    stddraw.line(0, n-i, i, 0)
stddraw.show()
```

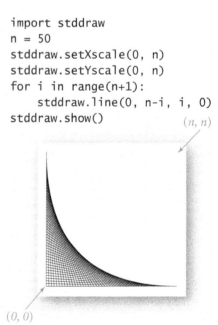

(*n*, *n*)

(0, 0)

Scaling to integer coordinates

Program 1.5.5 Standard input to drawing filter (plotfilter.py)

```
import stddraw
import stdio

# Read and set the x- and y-scales.
x0 = stdio.readFloat()
y0 = stdio.readFloat()
x1 = stdio.readFloat()
y1 = stdio.readFloat()
stddraw.setXscale(x0, x1)
stddraw.setYscale(y0, y1)

# Read and plot the points.
stddraw.setPenRadius(0.0)
while not stdio.isEmpty():
    x = stdio.readFloat()
    y = stdio.readFloat()
    stddraw.point(x, y)

stddraw.show()
```

`x0`	*left bound*
`y0`	*bottom bound*
`x1`	*right bound*
`y1`	*top bound*
`x, y`	*current point*

This program reads x- and y-scales from standard input, and configures the `stddraw` *canvas accordingly. Then it reads points from standard input until it reaches end-of-file, and plots them to standard drawing. The file* `usa.txt` *on the booksite has the coordinates of the U.S. cities with populations over 500. Some data, such as the data in* `usa.txt`*, is inherently visual.*

```
% python plotfilter.py < usa.txt
```

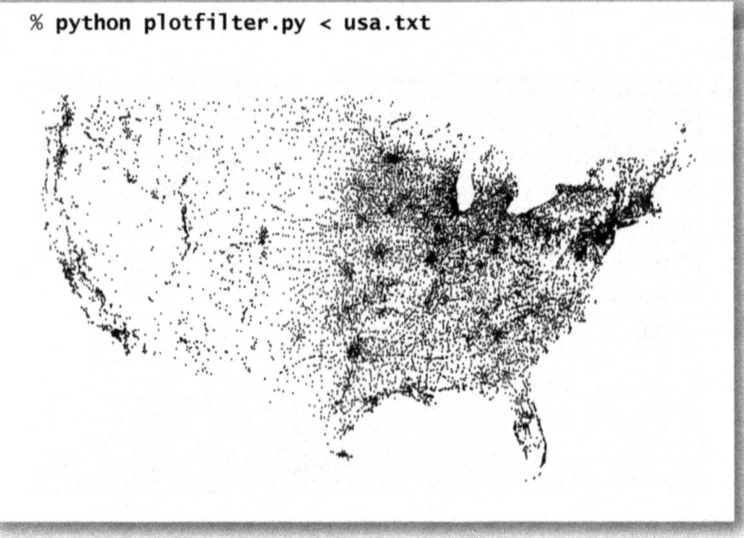

Filtering data to a standard drawing. One of the simplest applications of standard drawing is to plot data, by filtering it from standard input to the drawing. PROGRAM 1.5.5 (`plotfilter.py`) is such a filter: it reads a sequence of points defined by (x, y) coordinates and draws a spot at each point. It adopts the convention that the first four numbers read from standard input specify the bounding box, so that it can scale the plot without having to make an extra pass through all the points to determine the scale (this kind of convention is typical with such data files).

The graphical representation of points plotted in this way is far more expressive (and far more compact) than the numbers themselves or anything that we could create with the standard output representation that our programs have been limited to until now. The plotted image that is produced by `plotfilter.py` makes it far easier for us to infer properties of the cities (such as, for example, clustering of population centers) than does a list of the coordinates. Whenever we are processing data that represents the physical world, a visual image is likely to be one of the most meaningful ways in which we can use to display output. PROGRAM 1.5.5 illustrates just how easily you can create such an image.

Plotting a function graph. Another important use of `stddraw` is to plot experimental data or the values of a mathematical function. For example, suppose that we want to plot values of the function $y = \sin(4x) + \sin(20x)$ in the interval $[0, \pi]$. Accomplishing this task is a prototypical example of *sampling*: there are an infinite number of points in the interval, so we have to make do with evaluating the function at a finite number of points within the interval. We sample the function by choosing a set of x-values, then computing y-values by evaluating the function at each x-value. Plotting the function by connecting successive points with lines produces a *piecewise linear approximation*. The simplest way to proceed is to regularly space the x values: we decide ahead of time on a sample size, then space the x-coordinates by the interval size divided by the sample size. To make sure that the values we plot fall in the visible canvas, we scale the x-axis corresponding to the interval and the y-axis corresponding to the maximum and minimum values of the function within the interval. PROGRAM 1.5.6 (`functiongraph.py`) gives the Python code for this process.

The smoothness of the curve depends on properties of the function and the size of the sample. If the sample size is too small, the rendition of the function may not be at all accurate (it might not be very smooth, and it might miss major fluctuations, as shown in the example on the next page); if the sample is too large, pro-

Program 1.5.6 Function graph (functiongraph.py)

```
import math
import sys
import stdarray
import stddraw

n = int(sys.argv[1])

x = stdarray.create1D(n+1, 0.0)
y = stdarray.create1D(n+1, 0.0)
for i in range(n+1):
    x[i] = math.pi * i / n
    y[i] = math.sin(4.0*x[i]) + math.sin(20.0*x[i])
stddraw.setXscale(0, math.pi)
stddraw.setYscale(-2.0, +2.0)
for i in range(n):
    stddraw.line(x[i], y[i], x[i+1], y[i+1])

stddraw.show()
```

n	*# of samples*
x[]	*x-coordinates*
y[]	*y-coordinates*

This program accepts integer command-line argument n *and then plots a piecewise linear approximation to the function $y = \sin(4x) + \sin(20x)$ by sampling the function at* n+1 *points between $x = 0$ and $x = \pi$ and drawing* n *line segments. This example illustrates the need for choosing the number of samples carefully—on the left, with only 20 samples, we miss most of the fluctuations in the curve.*

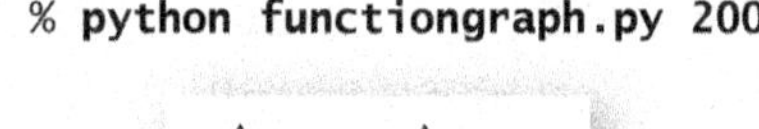
% python functiongraph.py 20
% python functiongraph.py 200

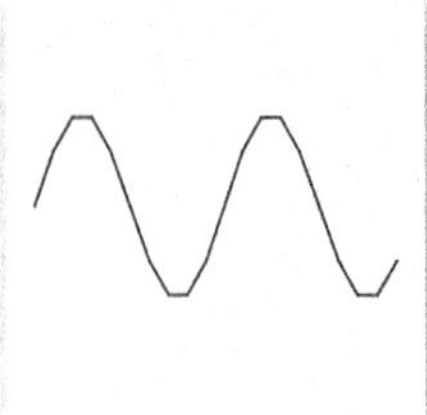

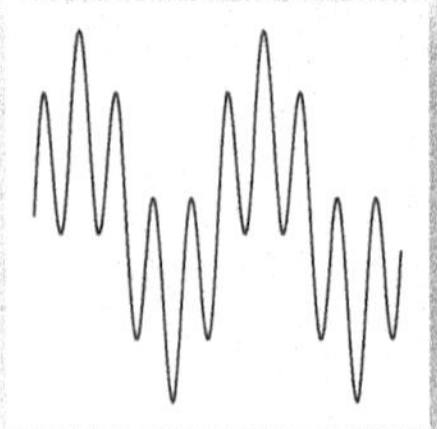

ducing the plot may be time-consuming, since some functions are time-consuming to compute. (In Section 2.4, we will look at an efficient method for accurately plotting a smooth curve.) You can use this same technique to plot the function graph of any function you choose: identify an x-interval where you want to plot the function, compute function values evenly spaced in that interval and store them in an array, determine and set the y-scale, and draw the line segments.

Outline and filled shapes. The booskite's `stddraw` module also includes functions to draw circles, rectangles, and arbitrary polygons. Each shape defines an outline. When the function name is just the shape name, that outline is traced by the drawing pen. When the name begins with `filled`, the named shape is instead filled solid, not traced. As usual, we summarize the available functions in an API, shown at the bottom of this page.

The arguments for `stddraw.circle()` and `stddraw.filledCircle()` define a circle of radius r centered at (x, y); the arguments for `stddraw.square()` and `stddraw.filledSquare()` define a square of side length $2r$ centered at (x, y); and the arguments for `stddraw.polygon()` and `stddraw.filledPolygon()` define a sequence of points that we connect by lines, including one from the last point to the first point. If you want to define shapes other than squares or circles, use one of these functions. To check your understanding, try to figure out what this code draws, before reading the answer:

```
xd = [x-r, x, x+r, x]
yd = [y, y+r, y, y-r]
stddraw.polygon(xd, yd)
```

function call	*description*
`stddraw.circle(x, y, r)`	*draw a circle of radius* `r` *centered at* `(x, y)`
`stddraw.square(x, y, r)`	*draw a 2*`r`*-by-2*`r` *square centered at* `(x, y)`
`stddraw.rectangle(x, y, w, h)`	*draw a* `w`*-by-*`h` *rectangle with lower-left endpoint* `(x, y)`
`stddraw.polygon(x, y)`	*draw a polygon that connects* `(x[i], y[i])`

Note: `filledCircle()`, `filledSquare()`, `filledRectangle()`, *and* `filledPolygon()` *correspond to these and draw filled shapes, not just outlines.*

API for booksite functions for drawing shapes

The answer is that you would never know, because it draws on the background canvas and there is no call to `stddraw.show()`. If there were such a call, it would draw a diamond (a rotated square) centered at the point (x, y). Several other examples of code that draws shapes and filled shapes are shown on the facing page.

Text and color. Occasionally, you may wish to annotate or highlight various elements in your drawings. The `stddraw` module has a function for drawing text, two other functions for setting parameters associated with text, and another for changing the color of the ink in the pen. We make scant use of these features in this book, but they can be very useful, particularly for drawings on your computer screen. You will find many examples of their use on the booksite.

In this code, color and fonts use types that you will learn about in SECTION 3.1. Until then, we leave the details to `stddraw`. The available pen colors are `BLACK`, `BLUE`, `CYAN`, `DARK_GRAY`, `GRAY`, `GREEN`, `LIGHT_GRAY`, `MAGENTA`, `ORANGE`, `PINK`, `RED`, `WHITE`, and `YELLOW`, defined as constants within `stddraw`. For example, the call `stddraw.setPenColor(stddraw.GRAY)` changes to gray ink. The default ink color is `stddraw.BLACK`. The default font in `stddraw` suffices for most of the drawings that you need (and you can find information on using other fonts on the booksite). For example, you might wish to call these functions to annotate function plots to highlight relevant values, and you might find it useful to compose similar functions to annotate other parts of your drawings.

Shapes, color, and text are basic tools that you can use to produce a dizzying variety of images, but you should use them judiciously. Use of such artifacts usually presents a design challenge, and our `stddraw` commands are crude by the standards of modern graphics libraries, so that you are likely to need more code than you might expect to produce the beautiful images that you may imagine.

function call	*description*
`stddraw.text(x, y, s)`	*draw string* `s`*, centered at* `(x, y)`
`stddraw.setPenColor(color)`	*set the pen color to* `color` (`color` *defaults to* `stddraw.BLACK`)
`stddraw.setFontFamily(font)`	*set the font family to* `font` (`font` *defaults to* `'Helvetica'`)
`stddraw.setFontSize(size)`	*set the font size to* `size` (`size` *defaults to* 12)

API for booksite functions for text and color in drawings

```
import stddraw
stddraw.circle(x, y, r)
stddraw.show()
```

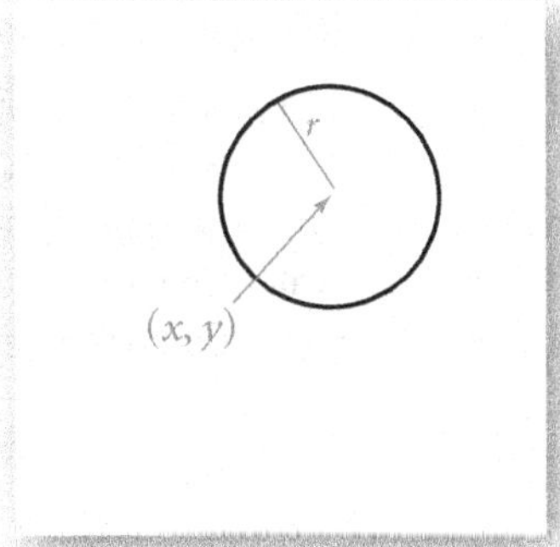


```
import stddraw
stddraw.square(x, y, r)
stddraw.show()
```

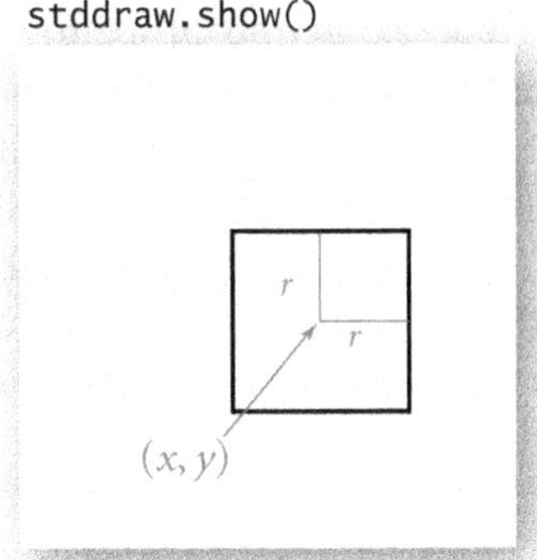


```
import stddraw
x = [x0, x1, x2, x3]
y = [y0, y1, y2, y3]
stddraw.polygon(x, y)
stddraw.show()
```

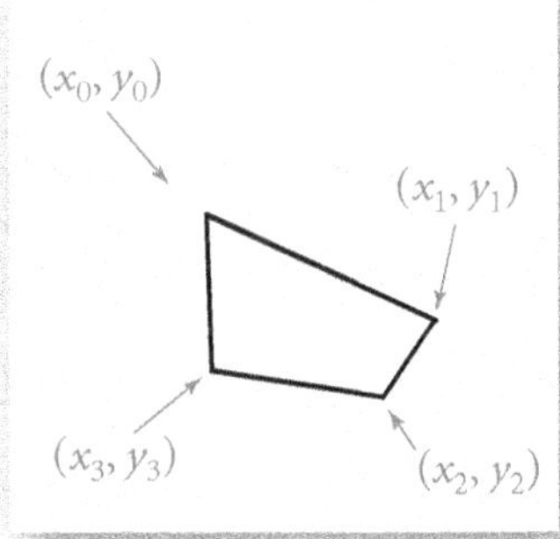


```
import stddraw
stddraw.square(.2, .8, .1)
stddraw.filledSquare(.8, .8, .2)
stddraw.circle(.8, .2, .2)
xd = [.1, .2, .3, .2]
yd = [.2, .3, .2, .1]
stddraw.filledPolygon(xd, yd)
stddraw.text(.2, .5, 'black text')
stddraw.setPenColor(stddraw.WHITE)
stddraw.text(.8, .8, 'white text')
stddraw.show()
```

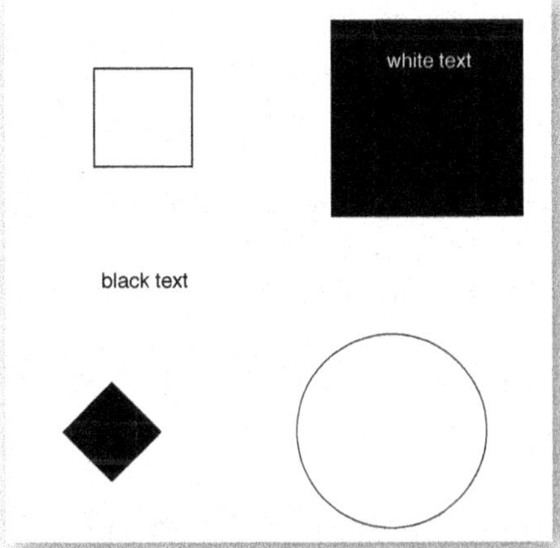

Examples of standard drawings with shapes and colors

Animation If we provide an argument to `stddraw.show()`, then that call need not be the last action of a program: it will copy the background canvas to the standard drawing window and then wait for the specified number of milliseconds. As you will soon see, this capability (coupled with the ability to erase, or *clear* the background canvas) provides limitless opportunities for creating interesting effects involving dynamic changes in the images in the standard drawing window. Such effects can provide compelling visualizations. We give an example next that also works for the printed page. The booksite offers even more examples that are likely to capture your imagination.

function call	*description*
`stddraw.clear(color)`	*clear the background canvas by coloring every pixel with color* `color`
`stddraw.show(t)`	*show the drawing in the standard drawing window and wait for* `t` *milliseconds*

API for booksite functions for animation

Bouncing ball. The "Hello, World" program for animation is to produce a black ball that appears to move around on the canvas. Suppose that the ball is at position (r_x, r_y) and we want to create the impression of moving it to a new position nearby, such as, for example, $(r_x + 0.01, r_y + 0.02)$. We do so in three steps:

- Clear the background canvas.
- Draw a black ball at the new position.
- Show the drawing and wait for a short while.

To create the illusion of movement, we iterate these steps for a whole sequence of positions (one that will form a straight line, in this case). The argument to `stddraw.show()` quantifies "a short while" and controls the apparent speed.

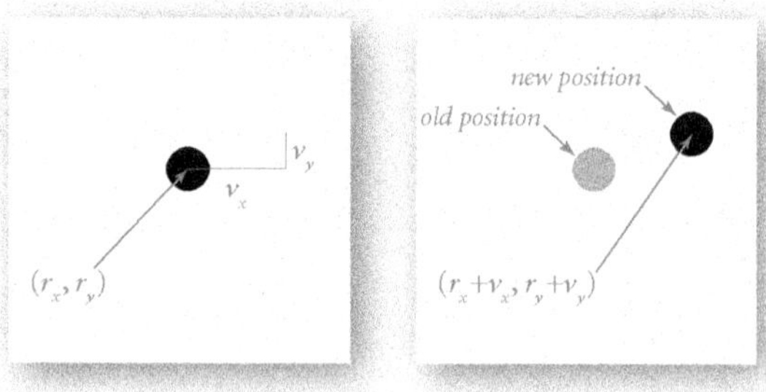

Simulating a moving ball

Program 1.5.7 **Bouncing ball** (`bouncingball.py`)

```
import stddraw

stddraw.setXscale(-1.0, 1.0)
stddraw.setYscale(-1.0, 1.0)

DT = 20.0
RADIUS = 0.05
rx = 0.480
ry = 0.860
vx = 0.015
vy = 0.023

while Truc:
    # Update ball position and draw it there.
    if abs(rx + vx) + RADIUS > 1.0: vx = -vx
    if abs(ry + vy) + RADIUS > 1.0: vy = -vy
    rx = rx + vx
    ry = ry + vy

    stddraw.clear(stddraw.GRAY)
    stddraw.filledCircle(rx, ry, RADIUS)
    stddraw.show(DT)
```

`DT`	*wait time*
`RADIUS`	*ball radius*
`rx, ry`	*position*
`vx, vy`	*velocity*

This program draws a bouncing ball to standard drawing. That is, it simulates the movement of a bouncing ball in the unit box. The ball bounces off the boundary according to the laws of elastic collision. The 20-millisecond wait period keeps the black image of the ball persistent on the screen, even though most of the ball's pixels alternate between black and white. If you modify this code to take the wait time `dt` *as a command-line argument, you can control the speed of the ball. The images below, which show the track of the ball, are produced by a modified version of this code where the call to* `stddraw.clear()` *is outside the loop (see Exercise 1.5.34).*

100 steps

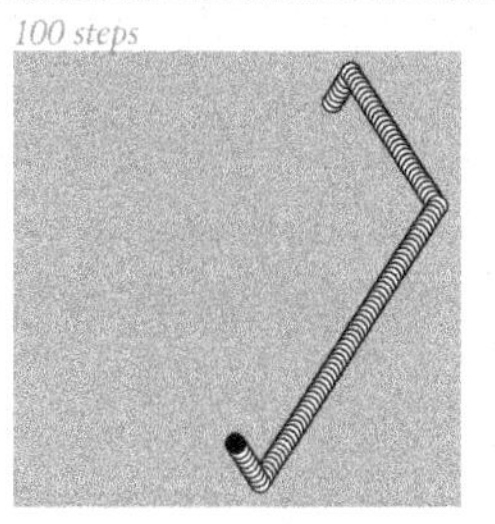

200 steps

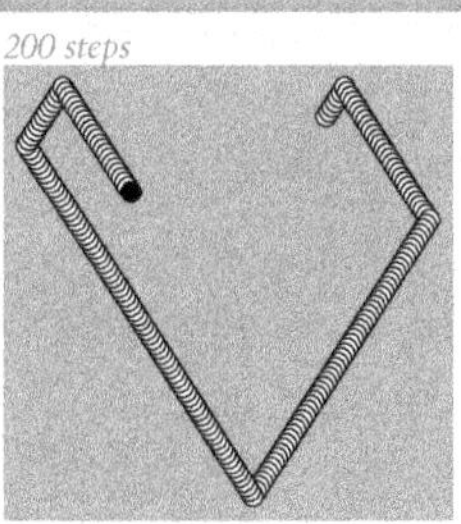

500 steps

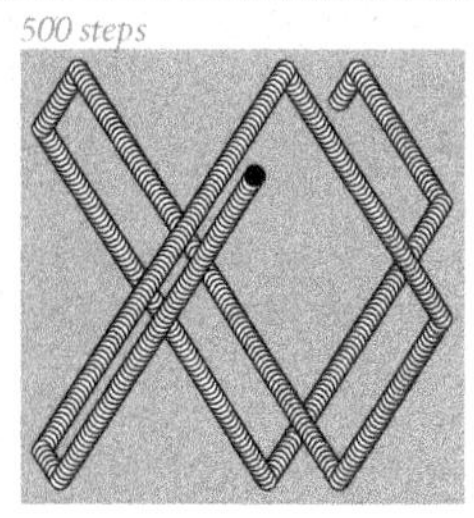

PROGRAM 1.5.7 (`bouncingball.py`) implements these steps to create the illusion of a ball moving in the 2-by-2 box centered at the origin. The current position of the ball is (r_x, r_y), and we compute the new position at each step by adding v_x to r_x and v_y to r_y. Since (v_x, v_y) is the fixed distance that the ball moves in each time unit, it represents the *velocity*. To keep the ball in the drawing, we simulate the effect of the ball bouncing off the walls according to the laws of elastic collision. This effect is easy to implement: when the ball hits a vertical wall, we just change the velocity in the *x*-direction from v_x to $-v_x$, and when the ball hits a horizontal wall, we change the velocity in the *y*-direction from v_y to $-v_y$. Of course, you have to download the code from the booksite and run it on your computer to see motion.

Since we cannot show a moving image on the printed page, we slightly modified `bouncingball.py` to show the track of the ball as it moves (see EXERCISE 1.5.34) in the examples shown below the code.

To familiarize yourself with animation on your computer, you are encouraged to modify the various parameters in `bouncingball.py` to draw a bigger ball, make it move faster or slower, and experiment with the distinction between the velocity in the simulation and the apparent speed on your display. For maximum flexibility, you might wish to modify `bouncingball.py` to take all these parameters as command-line arguments.

STANDARD DRAWING SUBSTANTIALLY IMPROVES OUR PROGRAMMING model by adding a "picture is worth a thousand words" component. It is a natural abstraction that you can use to better open up your programs to the outside world. With it, you can easily produce the function plots and visual representations of data that are commonly used in science and engineering. We will put it to such uses frequently throughout this book. Any time that you spend now working with the sample programs on the last few pages will be well worth the investment. You can find many useful examples on the booksite and in the exercises, and you are certain to find some outlet for your creativity by using `stddraw` to meet various challenges. Can you draw an *n*-pointed star? Can you make our bouncing ball actually bounce (add gravity)? You may be surprised at how easily you can accomplish these and other tasks.

Standard audio As a final example of a basic abstraction for output, we consider `stdaudio`, a module that you can use to play, manipulate, and synthesize sound. You probably have used your computer to process music; now you can compose programs to do so. At the same time, you will learn some concepts behind a venerable and important area of computer science and scientific computing: *digital signal processing*. We will merely scratch the surface of this fascinating subject, but you may be surprised at the simplicity of the underlying concepts.

Concert A. Sound is the perception of the vibration of molecules—in particular, the vibration of our eardrums. Therefore, oscillation is the key to understanding sound. Perhaps the simplest place to start is to consider the musical note *A* above middle *C*, which is known as *concert A*. This note is nothing more than a sine wave, scaled to oscillate at a frequency of 440 times per second. The function $\sin(t)$ repeats itself once every 2π units, so if we measure t in seconds and plot the function $\sin(2\pi t \times 440)$, we get a curve that oscillates 440 times per second. When you play an *A* by plucking a guitar string, pushing air through a trumpet, or causing a small cone to vibrate in a speaker, this sine wave is the prominent part of the sound that you hear and recognize as concert *A*. We measure frequency in *hertz* (cycles per second). When you double or halve the frequency, you move up or down one octave on the scale. For example, 880 hertz is one octave above concert *A* and 110 hertz is two octaves below concert *A*. For reference, the frequency range of human hearing is about 20 to 20,000 hertz. The amplitude (y-value) of a sound corresponds to the volume. We plot our curves between -1 and $+1$ and assume that any devices that record and play sound will scale as appropriate, with further scaling controlled by you when you turn the volume knob.

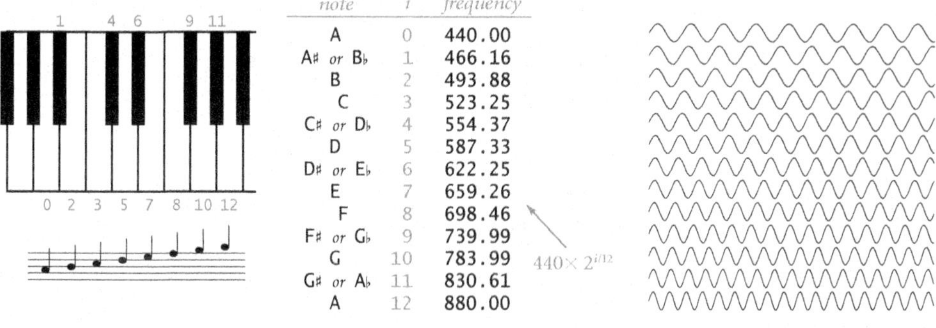

note	i	frequency
A	0	440.00
A♯ *or* B♭	1	466.16
B	2	493.88
C	3	523.25
C♯ *or* D♭	4	554.37
D	5	587.33
D♯ *or* E♭	6	622.25
E	7	659.26
F	8	698.46
F♯ *or* G♭	9	739.99
G	10	783.99
G♯ *or* A♭	11	830.61
A	12	880.00

Notes, numbers, and waves

Other notes. A simple mathematical formula characterizes the other notes on the chromatic scale. There are 12 notes on the chromatic scale, divided equally on a logarithmic (base 2) scale. We get the ith note above a given note by multiplying its frequency by the $(i/12)$th power of 2. In other words, the frequency of each note in the chromatic scale is precisely the frequency of the previous note in the scale multiplied by the twelfth root of 2 (about 1.06). This information suffices to create music! For example, to play the tune *Frère Jacques,* we just need to play each of the notes *A B C# A* by producing sine waves of the appropriate frequency for about half a second and then repeat the pattern.

Sampling. For digital sound, we represent a curve by sampling it at regular intervals, in precisely the same manner as when we plot function graphs. We sample sufficiently often that we have an accurate representation of the curve—a widely used sampling rate for digital sound is 44,100 samples per second. For concert *A,* that rate corresponds to plotting each cycle of the sine wave by sampling it at about 100 points. Since we sample at regular intervals, we need to compute only the y-coordinates of the sample points. It is that simple: *we represent sound as an array of numbers* (`float` values that are between -1 and $+1$). Our booksite sound module function `stdaudio.playSamples()` takes an array of floats as its argument and plays the sound represented by that array on your computer.

For example, suppose that you want to play concert *A* for 10 seconds. At 44,100 samples per second, you need an array of 441,001 `float` values. To fill in the array, use a `for` loop that samples the function $\sin(2\pi t \times 440)$ at $t = 0 / 44100$, $1 / 44100$, $2 / 44100$, $3 / 44100$, …, $441000 / 44100$. Once we fill the array with these values, we are ready for `stdaudio.playSamples()`, as in the following code:

```
SPS = 44100                     # samples per second
hz = 440.0                      # concert A
duration = 10.0                 # ten seconds
n = int(SPS * duration)

a = stdarray.create1D(n+1)
for i in range(n+1):
    a[i] = math.sin(2.0 * math.pi * i * hz / SPS)
stdaudio.playSamples(a)
stdaudio.wait()
```

This code is the "Hello, World" of digital audio. Once you use it to get your computer to play this note, you can compose code to play other notes and make music!

The difference between creating sound and plotting an oscillating curve is nothing more than the output device. Indeed, it is instructive and entertaining to send the same numbers to both standard drawing and standard audio (see EXERCISE 1.5.27).

Saving to a file. Music can take up a lot of space on your computer. At 44,100 samples per second, a four-minute song corresponds to 4 × 60 × 44100=10,584,000 numbers. Therefore, it is common to represent the numbers corresponding to a song in a binary format that uses less space than the string-of-digits representation that we use for standard input and output. Many such formats have been developed in recent years—`stdaudio` uses the `.wav` format. You can find some information about the `.wav` format on the booksite, but you do not need to know the details, because `stdaudio` takes care of the conversions for you. The `stdaudio` module allows you to play `.wav` files, to compose programs to create and manipulate arrays of floats, and to read and write them as `.wav` files.

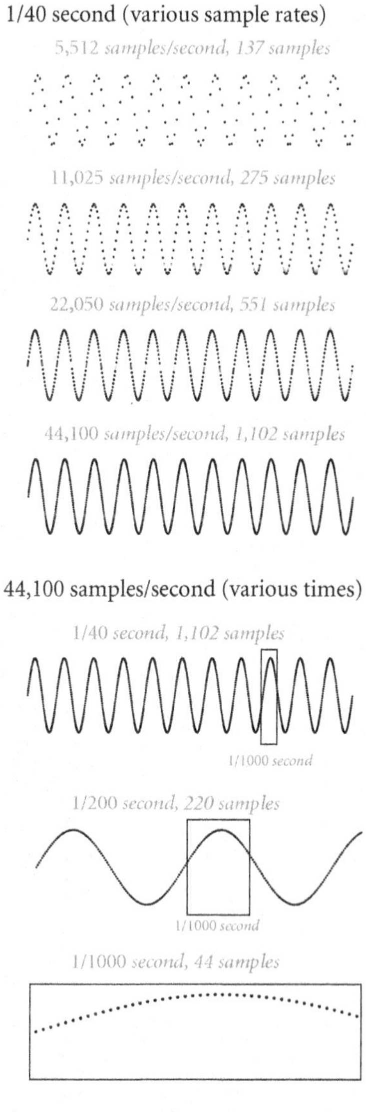

Sampling a sine wave

TO SEE HOW EASILY WE CAN create music with the functions in the `stdaudio` module (detailed at the top of page 175), consider PROGRAM 1.5.8 (`playthattune.py`). It takes notes from standard input, indexed on the chromatic scale from concert *A*, and plays them to standard audio. You can imagine all sorts of extensions on this basic scheme, some of which are addressed in the exercises.

We include `stdaudio` in our basic arsenal of programming tools because sound processing is one important application of scientific computing that is certainly familiar to you. Not only has the commercial application of digital signal processing had a phenomenal impact on modern society, but the science and engineering behind it combine physics and computer science in interesting ways. We will study more components of digital signal processing in some detail later in the book. (For example, you will learn in SECTION 2.1 how to create sounds that are more musical than the pure sounds produced by `playthattune.py`.)

Program 1.5.8 Digital signal processing (`playthattune.py`)

```
import math
import stdarray
import stdaudio
import stdio

SPS = 44100
CONCERT_A = 440.0

while not stdio.isEmpty():
    pitch = stdio.readInt()
    duration = stdio.readFloat()
    hz = CONCERT_A * (2 ** (pitch / 12.0))
    n = int(SPS * duration)
    samples = stdarray.create1D(n+1, 0.0)
    for i in range(n+1):
        samples[i] = math.sin(2.0 * math.pi * i * hz / SPS)
    stdaudio.playSamples(samples)
stdaudio.wait()
```

`pitch`	*distance from A*
`duration`	*note play time*
`hz`	*frequency*
`n`	*number of samples*
`samples[]`	*sampled sine wave*

This program reads sound samples from standard input, and plays the sound to standard audio. This data-driven program plays pure tones from the notes on the chromatic scale, specified on standard input as a pitch (distance from concert A) and a duration (in seconds). The test client reads the notes from standard input, creates an array by sampling a sine wave of the specified frequency and duration at 44,100 samples per second, and then plays each note by calling `stdaudio.playSamples()`.

```
% more elise.txt
7 .25
6 .25
7 .25
6 .25
7 .25
2 .25
5 .25
3 .25
0 .50
```

```
% python playthattune.py < elise.txt
```

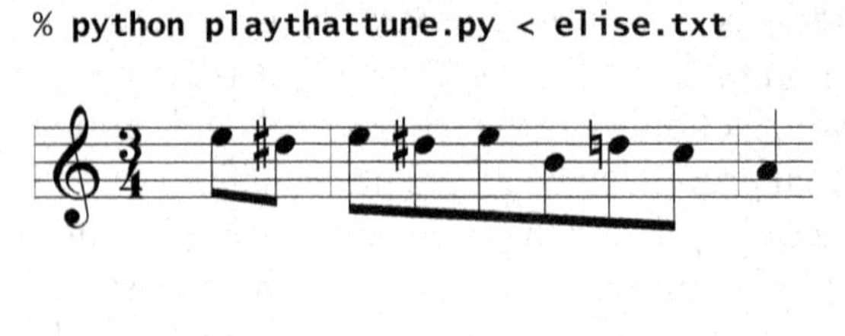

function call	*description*
`stdaudio.playFile(filename)`	*play all sound samples in the file* `filename.wav`
`stdaudio.playSamples(a)`	*play all sound samples in the float array* `a[]`
`stdaudio.playSample(x)`	*play the sound sample in the float* `x`
`stdaudio.save(filename, a)`	*save all sound samples in the float array* `a[]` *to the file* `filename.wav`
`stdaudio.read(filename)`	*read all sound samples from the file* `filename.wav` *and return as a float array*
`stdaudio.wait()`	*wait for the currently playing sound to finish (must be the last call to* `stdaudio` *in each program)*

API for booksite functions for producing sound

Summary I/O is a particularly convincing example of the power of abstraction because standard input, standard output, standard drawing, and standard audio can be tied to different physical devices at different times without making any changes to programs. Although devices may differ dramatically, we can compose programs that can do I/O without depending on the properties of specific devices. From this point forward, we will call functions from `stdio`, `stddraw`, and/or `stdaudio` in nearly every program in this book, and you will use them in nearly all of your programs. One important advantage of using such modules is that you can switch to new devices that are faster or cheaper, or hold more data, without changing your program at all. In such a situation, the details of the connection are a matter to be resolved between your operating system and the booksite module implementations. On modern systems, new devices are typically supplied with software that resolves such details automatically for both the operating system and for Python.

Conceptually, one of the most significant features of the standard input, standard output, standard drawing, and standard audio data streams is that they are *infinite*: from the point of view of your program, there is no limit on their length. This point of view leads to more than just programs that have a long useful life (because they are less sensitive to changes in technology than programs with built-in limits). It also is related to the *Turing machine*, an abstract device used by theoretical computer scientists to help us understand fundamental limitations on the capabilities of real computers. One of the essential properties of the model is the idea of a finite discrete device that works with an unlimited amount of input and output.

Q&A

Q. How can I make the booksite modules `stdio`, `stddraw`, and `stdaudio` available to Python?

A. If you followed the step-by-step instructions on the booksite for installing Python, these module should already be available to Python. Note that copying the files `stddraw.py` and `stdaudio.py` from the booksite and putting them in the same directory as the programs that use them is insufficient because they rely upon a library (set of modules) named *Pygame* for graphics and audio.

Q. Are there standard Python modules for handling standard output?

A. Actually, such features are built into Python. In Python 2, you can use the `print` statement to write data to `stdout`. In Python 3, there is no `print` statement; instead, there is a `print()` function, which is similar.

Q. Why, then, are we using the booksite `stdio` module for writing to standard output instead of using the features already provided by Python?

A. Our intention is to compose code that works (as much as possible) with all versions of Python. For example, using the `print` statement in all our programs would mean they would work with Python 2, but not with Python 3. Since we use `stdio` functions, we just need to make sure that we have the proper library.

Q. How about standard input?

A. There are (different) capabilities in Python 2 and Python 3 that correspond to `stdio.readLine()`, but nothing corresponding to `stdio.readInt()` and similar functions. Again, by using `stdio`, we can compose programs that not just take advantage of these additional capabilities, but also work in both versions of Python.

Q. How about drawing and sound?

A. Python does not come with an audio library. Python comes with a graphics library named *Tkinter* for producing drawings, but it is too slow for some of the graphics applications in the book. Our `stddraw` and `stdaudio` modules provide easy-to-use APIs, based on the *Pygame* library.

Q. So, let me get this straight; if I use the format `%2.4f` with `stdio.writef()` to write a float, I get two digits before the decimal point and four digits after the decimal point, right?

A. No, that specifies just four digits after the decimal point. The number preceding the decimal point is the width of the whole field. You want to use the format `%7.2f` to specify seven characters in total—four before the decimal point, the decimal point itself, and two digits after the decimal point.

Q. Which other conversion codes are there for `stdio.writef()`?

A. For integers, there is `o` for octal and `x` for hexadecimal. There are also numerous formats for dates and times. See the booksite for more information.

Q. Can my program reread data from standard input?

A. No. You get only one shot at it, in the same way that you cannot undo a call of `stdio.writeln()`.

Q. What happens if my program attempts to read data from standard input after it is exhausted?

A. Python will raise an `EOFError` at run time. The functions `stdio.isEmpty()` and `stdio.hasNextLine()` allow you to avoid such an error by checking whether more input is available.

Q. Why does `stddraw.square(x, y, r)` draw a square of width `2r` instead of `r`?

A. This makes it consistent with the function `stddraw.circle(x, y, r)`, where the third argument is the radius of the circle, not the diameter. In this context, `r` is the radius of the biggest circle that can fit inside the square.

Q. What happens if my program calls `stddraw.show(0)`?

A. That function call tells `stddraw` to copy the background canvas to the standard drawing window, and then wait 0 milliseconds (that is, do not wait at all) before proceeding. That function call is appropriate if, for example, you want to run an animation at the fastest rate supported by your computer.

Q. Can I draw curves other than circles with `stddraw`?

A. We had to draw the line somewhere (pun intended), so we support only the basic shapes discussed in the text. You can draw other shapes one point at a time, as explored in several exercises in the text, but filling them is not directly supported.

Q. So I use negative integers to go below concert *A* when making input files for `playthattune.py`?

A. Right. Actually, our choice to put concert *A* at 0 is arbitrary. A popular standard, known as the *MIDI Tuning Standard*, starts numbering at the *C* five octaves below concert *A*. By that convention, concert *A* is 69 and you do not need to use negative numbers.

Q. Why do I hear weird results from standard audio when I try to sonify a sine wave with a frequency of 30,000 hertz (or more)?

A. The *Nyquist frequency*, defined as one-half the sampling frequency, represents the highest frequency that can be reproduced. For standard audio, the sampling frequency is 44,100, so the Nyquist frequency is 22,050.

Exercises

1.5.1 Compose a program that reads in integers (as many as the user enters) from standard input and writes the maximum and minimum values to standard output.

1.5.2 Modify your program from the previous exercise to insist that the integers must be positive (by prompting the user to enter positive integers whenever the value entered is not positive).

1.5.3 Compose a program that accepts an integer n from the command line, reads n floats from standard input, and writes their *mean* (average value) and *standard deviation* (square root of the sum of the squares of their differences from the average, divided by n) to standard output.

1.5.4 Extend your program from the previous exercise to create a filter that writes all the floats in standard input that are more than 1.5 standard deviations from the mean.

1.5.5 Compose a program that reads in a sequence of integers and writes both the integer that appears in a longest consecutive run and the length of the run. For example, if the input is `1 2 2 1 5 1 1 7 7 7 7 1 1`, then your program should write `Longest run: 4 consecutive 7s`.

1.5.6 Compose a filter that reads in a sequence of integers and writes the integers, removing repeated values that appear consecutively. For example, if the input is `1 2 2 1 5 1 1 7 7 7 7 1 1 1 1 1 1 1 1`, your program should write `1 2 1 5 1 7 1`.

1.5.7 Compose a program that takes a command-line argument `n`, reads from standard input `N-1` distinct integers between `1` and `n`, and determines the missing integer.

1.5.8 Compose a program that reads in positive real numbers from standard input and writes their geometric and harmonic means. The *geometric mean* of n positive numbers $x_1, x_2, \ldots, x_n$ is $(x_1 \times x_2 \times \ldots \times x_n)^{1/n}$. The *harmonic mean* is $(1/x_1 + 1/x_2 + \ldots + 1/x_n) / (1/n)$. *Hint*: For the geometric mean, consider taking logarithms to avoid overflow.

1.5.9 Suppose that the file `in.txt` contains the two strings `F` and `F`, and consider the following program (`dragon.py`):

```
import stdio
dragon = stdio.readString()
nogard = stdio.readString()
stdio.write(dragon + 'L' + nogard)
stdio.write(' ')
stdio.write(dragon + 'R' + nogard)
stdio.writeln()
```

What does the following command do (see Exercise 1.2.35)?

```
python dragon.py < in.txt | python dragon.py | python dragon.py
```

1.5.10 Compose a filter `tenperline.py` that reads a sequence of integers between 0 and 99 and writes 10 integers per line, with columns aligned. Then compose a program `randomintseq.py` that takes two command-line arguments `m` and `n` and outputs `n` random integers between `0` and `m-1`. Test your programs with the command `python randomintseq.py 200 100 | python tenperline.py`.

1.5.11 Compose a program that reads in text from standard input and writes the number of words in the text. For the purpose of this exercise, a word is a sequence of non-whitespace characters that is surrounded by whitespace.

1.5.12 Compose a program that reads in lines from standard input with each line containing a name and two integers and then uses `writef()` to write a table with a column of the names, the integers, and the result of dividing the first by the second, accurate to three decimal places. You could use a program like this to tabulate batting averages for baseball players or grades for students.

1.5.13 Which of the following *require* saving all the values from standard input (in an array, say), and which could be implemented as a filter using only a fixed number of variables? For each, the input comes from standard input and consists of n floats between 0 and 1.

- Write the maximum and minimum float.
- Write the kth smallest float.

- Write the sum of the squares of the floats.
- Write the average of the n floats.
- Write the percentage of floats greater than the average.
- Write the n floats in increasing order.
- Write the n floats in random order.

1.5.14 Compose a program that writes a table of the monthly payments, remaining principal, and interest paid for a loan, taking three numbers as command-line arguments: the number of years, the principal, and the interest rate (see EXERCISE 1.2.21).

1.5.15 Compose a program that takes three command-line arguments x, y, and z, reads from standard input a sequence of point coordinates (x_i, y_i, z_i), and writes the coordinates of the point closest to (x, y, z). Recall that the square of the distance between (x, y, z) and (x_i, y_i, z_i) is $(x - x_i)^2 + (y - y_i)^2 + (z - z_i)^2$. For efficiency, do not use either `math.sqrt()` or the `**` operator.

1.5.16 Compose a program that, given the positions and masses of a sequence of objects, computes their center-of-mass, or *centroid*. The centroid is the average position of the n objects, weighted by mass. If the positions and masses are given by (x_i, y_i, m_i), then the centroid (x, y, m) is given by

$$m = m_1 + m_2 + \dots + m_n$$
$$x = (m_1 x_1 + \dots + m_n x_n) / m$$
$$y = (m_1 y_1 + \dots + m_n y_n) / m$$

1.5.17 Compose a program that reads in a sequence of real numbers between -1 and $+1$ and writes their average magnitude, average power, and the number of zero crossings. The *average magnitude* is the average of the absolute values of the data values. The *average power* is the average of the squares of the data values. The number of *zero crossings* is the number of times a data value transitions from a strictly negative number to a strictly positive number, or vice versa. These three statistics are widely used to analyze digital signals.

1.5.18 Compose a program that takes a command-line argument `n` and plots an `n`-by-`n` checkerboard with red and black squares. Color the lower-left square red.

1.5.19 Compose a program that takes as command-line arguments an integer `n` and a float `p` (between 0 and 1), plots `n` equally spaced points of size on the circumference of a circle, and then, with probability `p` for each pair of points, draws a gray line connecting them.

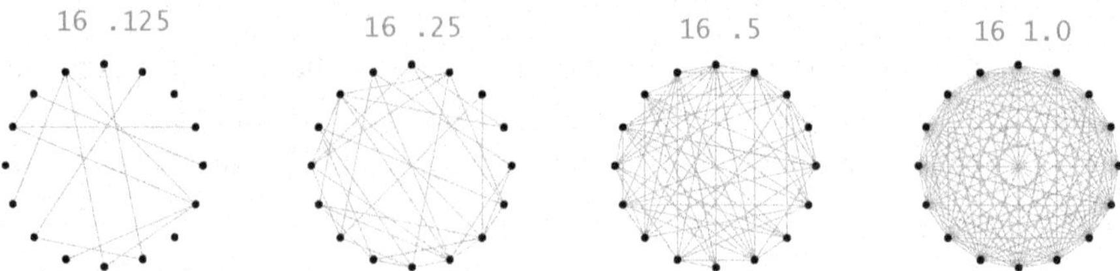

1.5.20 Compose code to draw hearts, spades, clubs, and diamonds. To draw a heart, draw a diamond, then attach two semicircles to the upper-left and upper-right sides.

1.5.21 Compose a program that takes a command-line argument `n` and plots a "flower" with `n` petals (if `n` is odd) or 2`n` petals (if `n` is even), by plotting the polar coordinates (r, θ) of the function $r = \sin(n\,\theta)$ for θ ranging from 0 to 2π radians.

1.5.22 Compose a program that takes a string `s` from the command line and displays it in banner style on the screen, moving from left to right and wrapping back to the beginning of the string as the end is reached. Add a second command-line argument to control the speed.

1.5.23 Modify `playthattune.py` to take additional command-line arguments that control the volume (multiply each sample value by the volume) and the tempo (multiply each note's duration by the tempo).

1.5.24 Compose a program that takes the name of a `.wav` file and a playback rate r as command-line arguments and plays the file at the given rate. First, use `stdaudio.read()` to read the file into an array `a[]`. If $r = 1$, just play `a[]`; otherwise, create a new array `b[]` of approximate size r times `a.length`. If $r < 1$, populate `b[]` by *sampling* from the original; if $r > 1$, populate `b[]` by *interpolating* from the original. Then play `b[]`.

1.5.25 Compose programs that use `stddraw` to create each of these designs.

1.5.26 Compose a program `circles.py` that draws filled circles of random size at random positions in the unit square, producing images like those below. Your program should take four command-line arguments: the number of circles, the probability that each circle is black, the minimum radius, and the maximum radius.

`200 1 .01 .01`

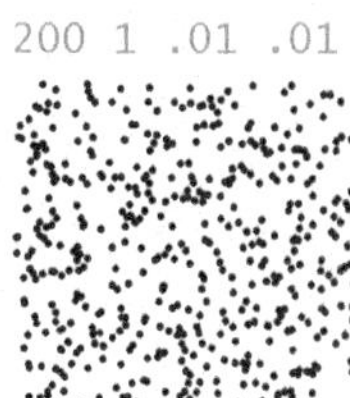

`100 1 .01 .05`

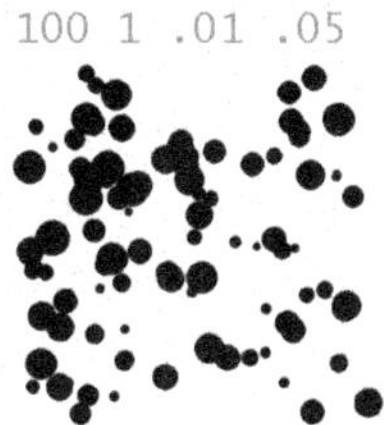

`500 .5 .01 .05`

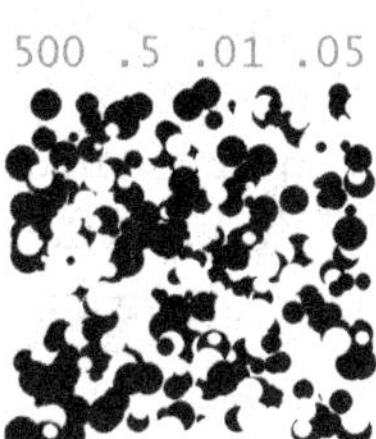

`50 .75 .1 .2`

Creative Exercises

1.5.27 *Visualizing audio.* Modify `playthattune.py` (Program 1.5.8) to send the values played to standard drawing, so that you can watch the sound waves as they are played. You will have to experiment with plotting multiple curves in the drawing canvas to synchronize the sound and the picture.

1.5.28 *Statistical polling.* When collecting statistical data for certain political polls, it is very important to obtain an unbiased sample of registered voters. Assume that you have a file with `n` registered voters, one per line. Compose a filter that writes a random sample of size `m` (see `sample.py`, Program 1.4.1).

1.5.29 *Terrain analysis.* Suppose that a terrain is represented by a two-dimensional grid of elevation values (in meters). A *peak* is a grid point whose four neighboring cells (left, right, up, and down) have strictly lower elevation values. Compose a program `peaks.py` that reads a terrain from standard input and then computes and writes the number of peaks in the terrain.

1.5.30 *Histogram.* Suppose that the standard input stream is a sequence of floats. Compose a program that takes an integer `n` and two floats `lo` and `hi` from the command line and uses `stddraw` to plot a histogram of the count of the numbers in the standard input stream that fall into each of the `n` intervals defined by dividing the interval `(lo, hi)` into `n` equal-sized intervals.

1.5.31 *Spirographs.* Compose a program that takes three parameters R, r, and a from the command line and draws the resulting *spirograph*. A spirograph (technically, an epicycloid) is a curve formed by rolling a circle of radius r around a larger fixed circle of radius R. If the pen offset from the center of the rolling circle is $(r+a)$, then the equation of the resulting curve at time t is given by

$$x(t) = (R + r)\cos(t) - (r + a)\cos((R + r)t/r)$$
$$y(t) = (R + r)\sin(t) - (r + a)\sin((R + r)t/r)$$

Such curves were popularized by a best-selling toy that contains discs with gear teeth on the edges and small holes that you could put a pen in to trace spirographs.

1.5.32 *Clock.* Compose a program that displays an animation of the second, minute, and hour hands of an analog clock. Use the call `stddraw.show(1000)` to update the display roughly once per second.

1.5.33 *Oscilloscope.* Compose a program to simulate the output of an oscilloscope and produce Lissajous patterns. These patterns are named after the French physicist, Jules A. Lissajous, who studied the patterns that arise when two mutually perpendicular periodic disturbances occur simultaneously. Assume that the inputs are sinusoidal, so that the following parametric equations describe the curve:

$$x(t) = A_x \sin (w_x t + \theta_x)$$
$$y(t) = A_y \sin (w_y t + \theta_y)$$

Take the six parameters A_x and A_y (amplitudes); w_x and w_y (angular velocity); and θ_x and θ_y (phase factors) from the command line.

1.5.34 *Bouncing ball with tracks.* Modify `bouncingball.py` to produce images like the ones shown in the text, which show the track of the ball on a gray background.

1.5.35 *Bouncing ball with gravity.* Modify `bouncingball.py` to incorporate gravity in the vertical direction. Add calls to `stdaudio.playFile()` to add one sound effect when the ball hits a wall and a different one when it hits the floor.

1.5.36 *Random tunes.* Compose a program that uses `stdaudio` to play random tunes. Experiment with keeping in key, assigning high probabilities to whole steps, repetition, and other rules to produce reasonable melodies.

1.5.37 *Tile patterns.* Using your solution to Exercise 1.5.25, compose a program `tilepattern.py` that takes a command-line argument `n` and draws an `n`-by-`n` pattern, using the tile of your choice. Add a second command-line argument that adds a checkerboard option. Add a third command-line argument for color selection. Using the patterns on the facing page as a starting point, design a tile floor. Be creative! *Note*: These are all designs from antiquity that you can find in many ancient (and modern) buildings.

1.6 Case Study: Random Web Surfer

Communicating across the web has become an integral part of everyday life. This communication is enabled in part by scientific studies of the structure of the web, a subject of active research since its inception. We next consider a simple model of the web that has proved to be a particularly successful approach to understanding some of its properties. Variants of this model are widely used and have been a key factor in the explosive growth of search applications on the web.

Programs in this section

The model, which is known as the *random surfer* model, is simple to describe. We consider the web to be a fixed set of *pages*, with each page containing a fixed set of *links*, and each link a reference to some other page. We study what happens to a person (the random surfer) who randomly moves from page to page, either by typing a page name into the address bar or by clicking a link on the current page.

The underlying mathematical model behind the web model is known as the *graph*, which we will consider in detail at the end of the book (in Section 4.5). We defer discussion of the details of processing graphs until then. Instead, we concentrate on calculations associated with a natural and well-studied probabilistic model that accurately describes the behavior of the random surfer.

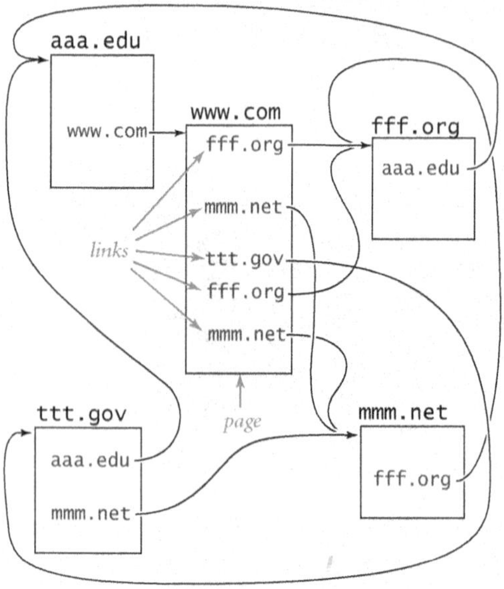

Pages and links

The first step in studying the random surfer model is to formulate it more precisely. The crux of the matter is to specify what it means to randomly move from page to page. The following intuitive *90-10 rule* captures both methods of moving to a new page: *Assume that 90 percent of the time the random surfer clicks a random link on the current page (each link chosen with equal probability) and that 10 percent of the time the random surfer goes directly to a random page (all pages on the web chosen with equal probability).*

You can immediately see that this model has flaws, because you know from your own experience that the behavior of a real web surfer is not quite so simple:

- No one chooses links or pages with equal probability.
- There is no real potential to surf directly to each page on the web.
- The 90-10 (or any fixed) breakdown is just a guess.
- It does not take the "back" button or bookmarks into account.
- We can afford to work with only a small sample of the web.

Despite these flaws, the model is sufficiently rich that computer scientists have learned a great deal about properties of the web by studying it. To appreciate the model, consider the small example on the previous page. Which page do you think the random surfer is most likely to visit?

Each person using the web behaves a bit like the random surfer, so understanding the fate of the random surfer is of intense interest to people building web infrastructure and web applications. The model is a tool for understanding the experience of each of the billions of web users. In this section, you will use the basic programming tools from this chapter to study the model and its implications.

Input format We want to be able to study the behavior of the random surfer on various web models, not just one example. Consequently, we want to compose *data-driven code*, where we keep data in files and compose programs that read the data from standard input. The first step in this approach is to define an input format that we can use to structure the information in the input files. We are free to define any convenient input format.

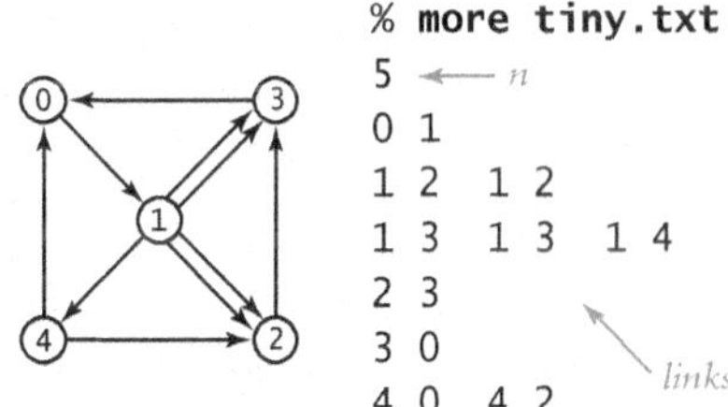

Random surfer input format

Later in the book, you will learn how to read web pages in Python programs (Section 3.1) and to convert from names to numbers (Section 4.4) as well as other techniques for efficient graph processing. For now, we assume that there are n web pages, numbered from 0 to $n - 1$, and we represent links with ordered pairs of such numbers, the first specifying the page containing the link and the second specifying the page to which it refers. Given these conventions, a straightforward input format for the random surfer problem is an input stream consisting of an integer (the value of n) followed by a sequence of pairs of integers (the representations of all the links). Because of the way `stdio` reading functions treat whitespace characters, we are free to either put one link per line or arrange them several to a line.

Transition matrix We use a two-dimensional matrix, which we refer to as the *transition matrix*, to completely specify the behavior of the random surfer. With n web pages, we define an n-by-n matrix such that the element in row `i` and column `j` is the probability that the random surfer moves to page `j` when on page `i`. Our first task is to compose code that can create such a matrix for any given input. When we apply the 90-10 rule, this computation is not difficult. We do so in three steps:

- Read n, and then create arrays `linkCounts[][]` and `outDegrees[]`.
- Read the links and accumulate counts so that `linkCounts[i][j]` counts links from `i` to `j` and `outDegrees[i]` counts links from `i` to anywhere.
- Use the 90-10 rule to compute the probabilities.

The first two steps are elementary, and the third is not much more difficult: multiply `linkCounts[i][j]` by `0.90/outDegrees[i]` if there is a link from `i` to `j` (take a random link with probability 0.9), and then add `0.10/n` to each element (go to a random page with probability 0.1). PROGRAM 1.6.1 (`transition.py`) performs this calculation: it is a filter that converts the list-of-links representation of a web model into a transition-matrix representation.

The transition matrix is significant because each row represents a *discrete probability distribution*—the elements fully specify the behavior of the random surfer's next move, giving the probability of surfing to each page. Note in particular that the elements sum to 1 (the surfer always goes somewhere).

The output of `transition.py` defines another file format, one for matrices of `float` values: the numbers of rows and columns followed by the values for matrix elements. Now, we can compose code that reads and processes transition matrices.

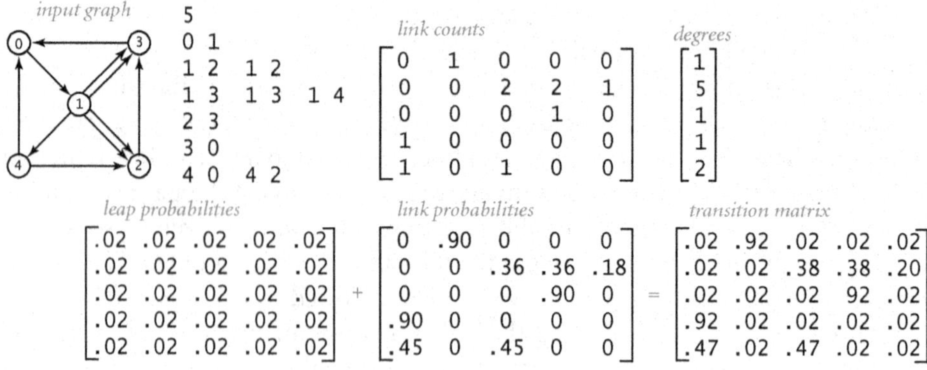

Transition matrix computation

Program 1.6.1 Computing the transition matrix (transition.py)

```
import stdarray
import stdio

n = stdio.readInt()

linkCounts = stdarray.create2D(n, n, 0)
outDegrees = stdarray.create1D(n, 0)

while not stdio.isEmpty():
    # Accumulate link counts.
    i = stdio.readInt()
    j = stdio.readInt()
    outDegrees[i] += 1
    linkCounts[i][j] += 1

stdio.writeln(str(n) + ' ' + str(n))

for i in range(n):
    # Write probability distribution for row i.
    for j in range(n):
        # Write probability for column j.
        p = (0.90 * linkCounts[i][j] / outDegrees[i]) + (0.10 / n)
        stdio.writef('%8.5f', p)
    stdio.writeln()
```

n	*# pages*
linkCounts[i][j]	*# links from page i to page j*
outDegrees[i]	*# links out of page i*
p	*transition probability*

This program is a filter that reads links from standard input and writes the corresponding transition matrix to standard output. First, it processes the input to count the links from each page. Then it applies the 90-10 rule to compute the transition matrix (see text). It assumes that there are no pages in the input that have zero outdegrees (see Exercise *1.6.3).*

```
% more tiny.txt
5
0 1
1 2  1 2
1 3  1 3  1 4
2 3
3 0
4 0  4 2
```

```
% python transition.py < tiny.txt
5 5
 0.02000 0.92000 0.02000 0.02000 0.02000
 0.02000 0.02000 0.38000 0.38000 0.20000
 0.02000 0.02000 0.02000 0.92000 0.02000
 0.92000 0.02000 0.02000 0.02000 0.02000
 0.47000 0.02000 0.47000 0.02000 0.02000
```

Simulation Given the transition matrix, simulating the behavior of the random surfer involves surprisingly little code, as you can see in `randomsurfer.py` (Program 1.6.2). This program reads a transition matrix and surfs according to the rules, starting at page 0 and taking the number of moves as a command-line argument. It counts the number of times that the surfer visits each page. Dividing that count by the number of moves yields an estimate of the probability that a random surfer winds up on the page. This probability is known as the page's *rank*. In other words, `randomsurfer.py` computes an estimate of all page ranks.

One random move. The key to the computation is the random move, which is specified by the transition matrix. We maintain a variable `page` whose value is the current location of the surfer. Row `page` of the matrix `p[][]` gives, for each `j`, the probability that the surfer next goes to `j`. In other words, when the surfer is at `page`, our task is to generate a random integer between 0 and `n-1` according to the distribution given by row `page` in the transition matrix (the one-dimensional array `p[page]`). How can we accomplish this task? We can use `random.random()` to generate a random float `r` between 0 and 1, but how does that help us get to a random page? One way to answer this question is to think of the probabilities in row `page` as defining a set of n intervals in (0, 1), with each probability corresponding to an interval length. Then our random variable `r` falls into one of the intervals, with probability precisely specified by the interval length. This reasoning leads to the following code:

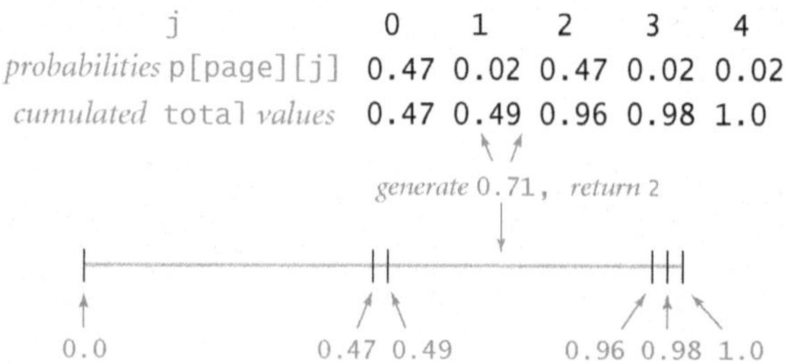

Generating a random integer from a discrete distribution

```
total = 0.0
for j in range(0, n)
    total += p[page][j]
    if r < total:
        page = j
        break
```

The variable `total` tracks the endpoints of the intervals defined in row `p[page]`, and the `for` loop finds the interval containing the random value `r`. For example,

Program 1.6.2 Simulating a random surfer (`randomsurfer.py`)

```
import random
import sys
import stdarray
import stdio

moves = int(sys.argv[1])

n = stdio.readInt()
stdio.readInt()  # Not needed (another n).
p = stdarray.create2D(n, n, 0.0)
for i in range(n):
    for j in range(n):
        p[i][j] = stdio.readFloat()

hits = stdarray.create1D(n, 0)
page = 0  # Start at page 0.
for i in range(moves):
    r = random.random()        # Compute a random page
    total = 0.0                # according to distribution
    for j in range(0, n):      # in row p[page] (see text).
        total += p[page][j]    #
        if r < total:          #
            page = j           #
            break              #
    hits[page] += 1

for v in hits:
    stdio.writef('%8.5f', 1.0 * v / moves)
stdio.writeln()
```

`moves`	*# moves*
`n`	*# pages*
`page`	*current page*
`p[i][j]`	*probability that the surfer moves from page i to page j*
`hits[i]`	*# times the surfer hits page i*

This program uses a transition matrix to simulate the behavior of a random surfer. It accepts the number of moves as a command-line argument, reads the transition matrix, performs the indicated number of moves as prescribed by the matrix, and writes the relative frequency of hitting each page. The key to the computation is the random move to the next page (see text).

```
% python transition.py < tiny.txt | python randomsurfer.py 100
 0.24000 0.23000 0.16000 0.25000 0.12000
% python transition.py < tiny.txt | python randomsurfer.py 10000
 0.27280 0.26530 0.14820 0.24830 0.06540
% python transition.py < tiny.txt | python randomsurfer.py 1000000
0.27324 0.26568 0.14581 0.24737 0.06790
```

suppose that the surfer is at page `4` in our example. The transition probabilities are 0.47, 0.02, 0.47, 0.02, and 0.02, and `total` takes on the values `0.0`, `0.47`, `0.49`, `0.96`, `0.98`, and `1.0`. These values indicate that the probabilities define the five intervals (0, 0.47), (0.47, 0.49), (0.49, 0.96), (0.96, 0.98), and (0.98, 1), one for each page. Now, suppose that `random.random()` returns the value `0.71` . We increment `j` from 0 to 1 to 2 and stop there, which indicates that `0.71` is in the interval (0.49, 0.96), so we send the surfer to the third page (page `2`). Then, we perform the same computation for `p[2]`, and the random surfer is off and surfing. For large n, we can use *binary search* to substantially speed up this computation (see EXERCISE 4.2.35). Typically, we are interested in speeding up the search in this situation because we are likely to need a huge number of random moves, as you will see.

Markov chains. The random process that describes the surfer's behavior is known as a *Markov chain*, named after the Russian mathematician Andrey Markov, who developed the concept in the early 20th century. Markov chains are widely applicable, are well studied, and have many remarkable and useful properties. For example, you might have wondered why `randomsurfer.py` starts the random surfer at page 0, whereas you might have expected a random choice. A basic limit theorem for Markov chains says that the surfer could start *anywhere*, because the probability that a random surfer eventually winds up on any particular page is the same for all starting pages! No matter where the surfer starts, the process eventually stabilizes to a point where further surfing provides no further information. This phenomenon is known as *mixing*. Although this phenomenon might seem counterintuitive at first, it explains coherent behavior in a situation that might seem chaotic. In the present context, it captures the idea that the web looks pretty much the same to everyone after surfing for a sufficiently long time.

Not all Markov chains have this mixing property. For example, if we eliminate the random leap from our model, certain configurations of web pages can present problems for the surfer. Indeed, there exist on the web sets of pages known as *spider traps*, which are designed to attract incoming links but have no outgoing links. Without the random leap, the surfer could get stuck in a spider trap. The primary purpose of the 90-10 rule is to guarantee mixing and eliminate such anomalies.

Page ranks. The `randomsurfer.py` simulation is straightforward: it loops for the indicated number of moves, randomly surfing through the graph. Because of the mixing phenomenon, increasing the number of iterations gives increasingly accurate estimates of the probability that the surfer lands on each page (the page ranks). How do the results compare with your intuition when you first thought about the question? You might have guessed that page 4 was the lowest-ranked page, but did you think that pages 0 and 1 would rank higher than page 3? If we want to know which page is the highest rank, we need more precision and more accuracy. The `randomsurfer.py` program needs 10^d moves to get answers precise to d decimal places and many more moves for those answers to stabilize to an accurate value. For our example, it takes tens of thousands of iterations to get answers accurate to two decimal places and millions of iterations to get answers accurate to three places (see EXERCISE 1.6.5). The end result is that page 0 beats page 1 by 27.3 percent to 26.6 percent. That such a tiny difference would appear in such a small problem is quite surprising: if you guessed that page 0 is the most likely spot for the surfer to end up, you were lucky!

Accurate page rank estimates for the web are valuable in practice for many reasons. First, using them to put in order the pages that match the search criteria for web searches proved to be vastly more in line with people's expectations than previous methods. Next, this measure of confidence and reliability led to the investment of huge amounts of money in web advertising based on page ranks. Even in our tiny example, page ranks might be used to convince advertisers to pay up to four times as much to place an ad on page 0 as on page 4. Computing page ranks is mathematically sound, an interesting computer science problem, and big business, all rolled into one.

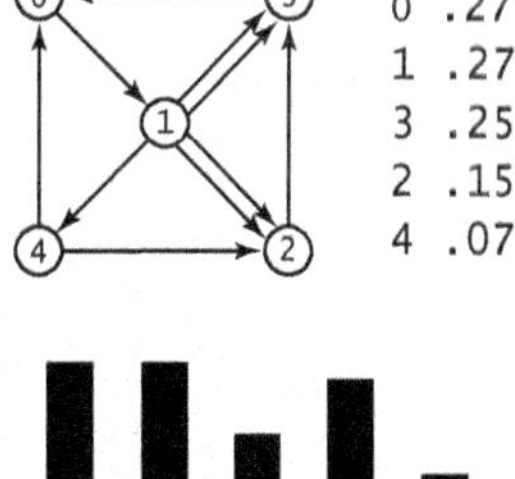

Page ranks with histogram

Visualizing the histogram. With `stddraw`, it is easy to create a visual representation that can give you a feeling for how the random surfer visit frequencies converge to the page ranks. If you scale the x- and y-coordinates in the standard drawing window appropriately and add this code

```
if i % 1000 == 0:
    stddraw.clear()
    for k in range(n):
        stddraw.filledRectangle(k - 0.25, 0.0, 0.5, hits[k])
    stddraw.show(10)
```

to the random move loop in `randomsurfer.py` and run the code for, say, millions of moves, you will see a drawing of the frequency histogram that eventually stabilizes to the page ranks. (The constants `1000` and `10` in this code are a bit arbitrary; you might wish to change them when you run the code.) After you have used this tool once, you are likely to find yourself using it *every* time you want to study a new model (perhaps with some minor adjustments to handle larger models).

Studying other models. Our programs `randomsurfer.py` and `transition.py` are excellent examples of data-driven programs. You can easily create a data model just by creating a file like `tiny.txt` that starts with an integer `n` and then specifies pairs of integers between `0` and `n-1` that represent links connecting pages. You are encouraged to run it for various data models as suggested in the exercises, or make up some models of your own to study. If you have ever wondered how web page ranking works, this calculation is your chance to develop better intuition about what causes one page to be ranked more highly than another. Which kind of page is likely to be rated highly? One that has many links to other pages, or one that has just a few links to other pages? The exercises in this section present many opportunities to study the behavior of the random surfer. Since `randomsurfer.py` uses standard input, you can compose simple programs that generate large input models, pipe their output to `randomsurfer.py`, and thereby study the random surfer on large models. Such flexibility is an important reason to use standard input and standard output.

Directly simulating the behavior of a random surfer to understand the structure of the web is appealing, but it has limitations. Think about the following question: Could you use it to compute page ranks for a web model with millions (or billions!) of web pages and links? The quick answer to this question is *no*, because you cannot even afford to store the transition matrix for such a large number of pages. A matrix for millions of pages would have *trillions* of elements. Do you have that much space on your computer? Could you use `randomsurfer.py` to find page ranks for a smaller model with, say, thousands of pages? To answer this question, you might run multiple simulations, record the results for a large number of trials, and then interpret those experimental results. We do use this approach for many scientific problems (the gambler's ruin problem is one example; Section 2.4 is devoted to another), but it can be very time-consuming, as a huge number of trials may be necessary to get the desired accuracy. Even for our tiny example, we saw that it takes millions of iterations to get the page ranks accurate to three or four decimal places. For larger models, the required number of iterations to obtain accurate estimates becomes truly huge.

Mixing a Markov chain It is important to remember that the page ranks are a property of the web model, not any particular approach for computing it. That is, `randomsurfer.py` is just *one* way to compute page ranks. Fortunately, a simple computational model based on a well-studied area of mathematics provides a far more efficient approach than simulation to the problem of computing page ranks. That model makes use of the basic arithmetic operations on two-dimensional matrices that we considered in SECTION 1.4.

Squaring a Markov chain. What is the probability that the random surfer will move from page `i` to page `j` in *two* moves? The first move goes to an intermediate page `k`, so we calculate the probability of moving from `i` to `k` and then from `k` to `j` for all possible `k` and add up the results. For our example, the probability of moving from 1 to 2 in two moves is the probability of moving from 1 to 0 to 2 (0.02 × 0.02), plus the probability of moving from 1 to 1 to 2 (0.02 × 0.38), plus the probability of moving from 1 to 2 to 2 (0.38 × 0.02), plus the probability of moving from 1 to 3 to 2 (0.38 × 0.02), plus the probability of moving from 1 to 4 to 2 (0.20 × 0.47), which adds up to a grand total of 0.1172. The same process works for each pair of pages. *This calculation is one that we have seen before*, in the definition of matrix multiplication: the element in row `i` and column `j` in the result is the dot product of row `i` and column `j` in the original. In other words, the result of multiplying `p[][]` by itself is a matrix where the element in row `i` and column `j` is the probability that the random surfer moves from page `i` to page `j` in two moves. Studying the elements of the two-move transition matrix for our example is well worth your time and will help you better understand the movement of the random surfer.

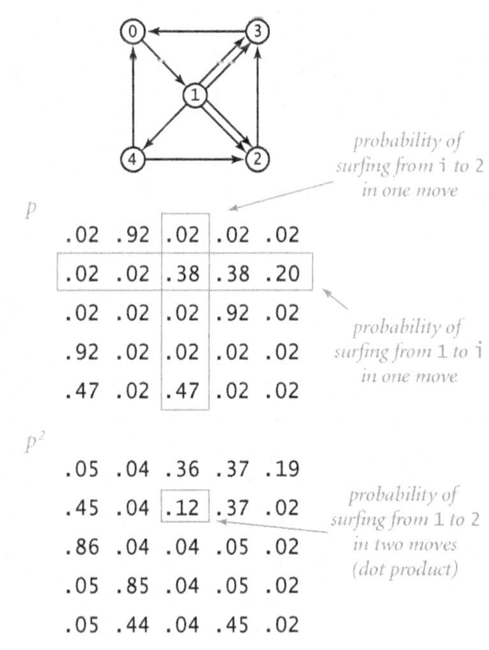

Squaring a Markov chain

For instance, the largest element in the square is the one in row 2 and column 0, reflecting the fact that a surfer starting on page 2 has only one link out, to page 3, where there is also only one link out, to page 0. Therefore, by far the most likely outcome for a surfer starting on page 2 is to end up in page 0 after two moves. All of the other two-move routes involve more choices and are less probable. It is important to note that this is an exact computation (up to the limitations of Python's floating-point precision), in contrast to `randomsurfer.py`, which produces an estimate and needs more iterations to get a more accurate estimate.

The power method. We might then calculate the probabilities for three moves by multiplying by `p[][]` again, and for four moves by multiplying by `p[][]` yet again, and so forth. However, matrix–matrix multiplication is expensive, and we are actually interested in a *vector*–matrix calculation. For our example, we start with the vector

```
[1.0 0.0 0.0 0.0 0.0]
```

which specifies that the random surfer starts on page 0. Multiplying this vector by the transition matrix gives the vector

```
[.02 .92 .02 .02 .02]
```

which is the probabilities that the surfer winds up on each of the pages after one step. Now, multiplying *this* vector by the transition matrix gives the vector

```
[.05 .04 .36 .37 .19]
```

which contains the probabilities that the surfer winds up on each of the pages after *two* steps. For example, the probability of moving from 0 to 2 in two moves is the probability of moving from 0 to 0 to 2 (0.02×0.02), plus the probability of moving from 0 to 1 to 2 (0.92×0.38), plus the probability of moving from 0 to 2 to 2 (0.02×0.02), plus the probability of moving from 0 to 3 to 2 (0.02×0.02), plus the probability of moving from 0 to 4 to 2 (0.02×0.47), which adds up to a grand total of 0.36. From these initial calculations, the pattern is clear: *the vector giving the probabilities that the random surfer is at each page after t steps is precisely the product of the corresponding vector for $t-1$ steps and the transition matrix.* By the basic limit theorem for Markov chains, this process converges to the same vector no matter where we start; in other words, after a sufficient number of moves, the probability that the surfer ends up on any given page is independent of the starting point.

PROGRAM 1.6.3 (`markov.py`) is an implementation that you can use to check convergence for our example. For instance, it gets the same results (the page ranks accurate to two decimal places) as `randomsurfer.py`, but with just 20 matrix–vector

```
            ranks[]                       p[][]                    newRanks[]
first move
                                   .02 .92 .02 .02 .02
                                   .02 .02 .38 .38 .20
 [ 1.0 0.0 0.0 0.0 0.0 ] *         .02 .02 .02 .92 .02   = [ .02 .92 .02 .02 .02 ]
                                   .92 .02 .02 .02 .02
                                   .47 .02 .47 .02 .02     probabilities of surfing
                                                           from 0 to i in one move

second move                        probabilities of surfing
                                   from i to 2 in one move
  probabilities of surfing                                 probability of surfing from 0 to 2
  from 0 to i in one move          .02 .92 .02 .02 .02     in two moves (dot product)
                                   .02 .02 .38 .38 .20
 [ .02 .92 .02 .02 .02 ] *         .02 .02 .02 .92 .02   = [ .05 .04 .36 .37 .19 ]
                                   .92 .02 .02 .02 .02
                                   .47 .02 .47 .02 .02     probabilities of surfing
                                                           from 0 to i in two moves
third move

  probabilities of surfing         .02 .92 .02 .02 .02
  from 0 to i in two moves         .02 .02 .38 .38 .20
 [ .05 .04 .36 .37 .19 ] *         .02 .02 .02 .92 .02   = [ .44 .06 .12 .36 .03 ]
                                   .92 .02 .02 .02 .02     probabilities of surfing
                                   .47 .02 .47 .02 .02     from 0 to i in three moves

                                          .
                                          .
                                          .
20th move

  probabilities of surfing         .02 .92 .02 .02 .02
  from 0 to i in 19 moves          .02 .02 .38 .38 .20
 [ .27 .26 .15 .25 .07 ] *         .02 .02 .02 .92 .02   = [ .27 .26 .15 .25 .07 ]
                                   .92 .02 .02 .02 .02     probabilities of surfing
                                   .47 .02 .47 .02 .02     from 0 to i in 20 moves
                                                           (steady state)
```

The power method for computing page ranks (limit values of transition probabilities)

Program 1.6.3 Mixing a Markov chain (markov.py)

```
import sys
import stdarray
import stdio

moves = int(sys.argv[1])
n = stdio.readInt()
stdio.readInt()

p = stdarray.create2D(n, n, 0.0)
for i in range(n):
    for j in range(n):
        p[i][j] = stdio.readFloat()

ranks = stdarray.create1D(n, 0.0)
ranks[0] = 1.0
for i in range(moves):
    newRanks = stdarray.create1D(n, 0.0)
    for j in range(n):
        for k in range(n):
            newRanks[j] += ranks[k] * p[k][j]
    ranks = newRanks

for i in range(n):
    stdio.writef('%8.5f', ranks[i])
stdio.writeln()
```

moves	*number of iterations*
n	*number of pages*
p[][]	*transition matrix*
ranks[]	*page ranks*
newRanks[]	*new page ranks*

This program takes a command-line integer moves*, reads a transition matrix from standard input, computes the probabilities that a random surfer lands on each page (page ranks) after* moves *matrix–vector multiplications, and writes the page ranks to standard output.*

```
% python transition.py < tiny.txt | python markov.py 20
 0.27245 0.26515 0.14669 0.24764 0.06806

% python transition.py < tiny.txt | python markov.py 40
 0.27303 0.26573 0.14618 0.24723 0.06783
```

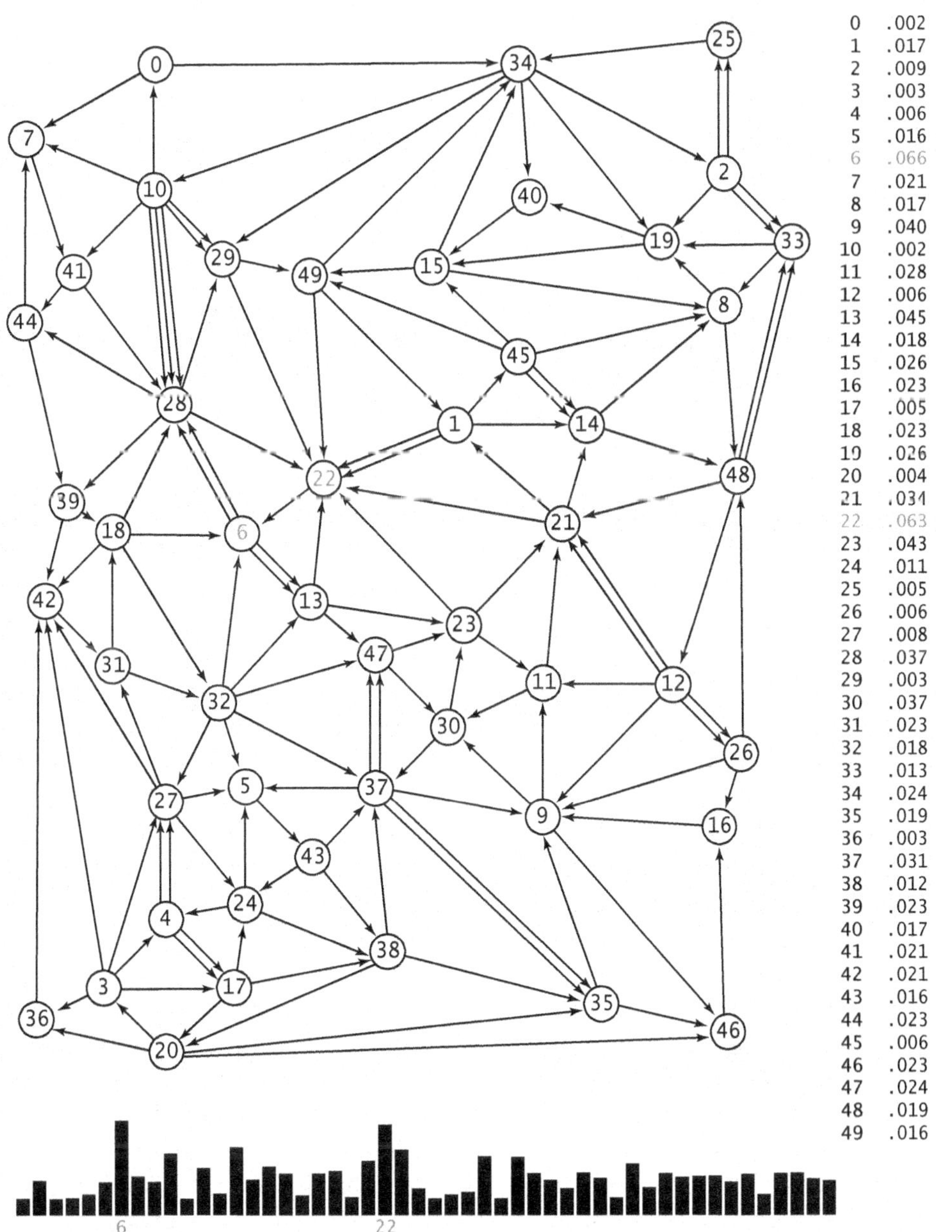

0	.002
1	.017
2	.009
3	.003
4	.006
5	.016
6	.066
7	.021
8	.017
9	.040
10	.002
11	.028
12	.006
13	.045
14	.018
15	.026
16	.023
17	.005
18	.023
19	.026
20	.004
21	.034
22	.063
23	.043
24	.011
25	.005
26	.006
27	.008
28	.037
29	.003
30	.037
31	.023
32	.018
33	.013
34	.024
35	.019
36	.003
37	.031
38	.012
39	.023
40	.017
41	.021
42	.021
43	.016
44	.023
45	.006
46	.023
47	.024
48	.019
49	.016

Page ranks with histogram for a larger example

multiplications instead of the tens of thousands of iterations needed by `randomsurfer.py`. Another 20 multiplications gives the results accurate to three decimal places, as compared with millions of iterations for `randomsurfer.py`, and just a few more multiplications give the results to full precision (see Exercise 1.6.6).

Markov chains are well studied, but their impact on the web was not truly felt until 1998, when two graduate students, Sergey Brin and Lawrence Page, had the audacity to build a Markov chain and compute the probabilities that a random surfer hits each page for *the whole web*. Their work revolutionized web search and is the basis for the page ranking method used by Google, the highly successful web search company that they founded. Specifically, the company periodically recomputes the random surfer's probability for each page. Then, when you do a search, it lists the pages related to your search keywords in order of these ranks. Such page ranks now predominate because they somehow correspond to the expectations of typical web users, reliably providing them with *relevant* web pages for typical searches. The computation that is involved is enormously time-consuming, due to the huge number of pages on the web, but the result has turned out to be enormously profitable and well worth the expense. The method used in `markov.py` is far more efficient than simulating the behavior of a random surfer, but it is still too slow to actually compute the probabilities for a huge matrix corresponding to all the pages on the web. That computation is enabled by better data structures for graphs (see Chapter 4).

Lessons Developing a full understanding of the random surfer model is beyond the scope of this book. Instead, our purpose is to show you an application that involves composing a bit more code than the short programs that we have been using to teach specific concepts. Which specific lessons can we learn from this case study?

We already have a full computational model. Built-in data types, combined with conditionals and loops, arrays, and standard input/output, enable you to address interesting problems of all sorts. Indeed, it is a basic precept of theoretical computer science that this model suffices to specify any computation that can be performed on any reasonable computing device. In the next two chapters, we discuss two critical ways in which the model has been extended to drastically reduce the amount of time and effort required to develop large and complex programs.

Data-driven code is prevalent. The concept of using standard input and output streams and saving data in files is a powerful one. We compose filters to convert from one kind of input to another, generators that can produce huge input files for study, and programs that can handle a wide variety of models. We can save data for archiving or later use. We can also process data derived from some other source and then save it in a file, whether it is from a scientific instrument or a distant website. The concept of data-driven code is an easy and flexible way to support this suite of activities.

Accuracy can be elusive. It is a mistake to assume that a program produces accurate answers simply because it can write numbers to many decimal places of precision. Often, the most difficult challenge that we face is ensuring that we have accurate answers.

Uniform random numbers are just a start. When we speak informally about random behavior, we often are thinking of something more complicated than the "every value equally likely" model that `random.random()` gives us. Many of the problems that we consider involve working with random numbers from other distributions, such as `randomsurfer.py`.

Efficiency matters. It is also a mistake to assume that your computer is so fast that it can do *any* computation. Some problems require much more computational effort than others. CHAPTER 4 is devoted to a thorough discussion of evaluating the performance of the programs that you compose. We defer detailed consideration of such issues until then, but remember that you always need to have some general idea of the performance requirements of your programs.

PERHAPS THE MOST IMPORTANT LESSON TO learn from composing programs for complicated problems like the example in this section is that *debugging is difficult.* The polished programs in the book mask that lesson, but you can rest assured that each one is the product of a long bout of testing, fixing bugs, and running the program on numerous inputs. Generally we avoid describing bugs and the process of fixing them in the text because that makes for a boring account and overly focuses attention on bad code, but you can find some examples and descriptions in the exercises and on the booksite.

Exercises

1.6.1 Modify `transition.py` to take the leap probability from the command line and use your modified version to examine the effect on page ranks of switching to an 80-20 rule or a 95-5 rule.

1.6.2 Modify `transition.py` to ignore the effect of multiple links. That is, if there are multiple links from one page to another, count them as one link. Create an example that shows how this modification can change the order of page ranks.

1.6.3 Modify `transition.py` to handle pages with no outgoing links, by filling rows corresponding to such pages with the value $1/n$.

1.6.4 The code fragment in `randomsurfer.py` that generates the random move fails if the probabilities in the row `p[page]` do not add up to 1. Explain what happens in that case, and suggest a way to fix the problem.

1.6.5 Determine, to within a factor of 10, the number of iterations required by `randomsurfer.py` to compute page ranks to four decimal places and to five decimal places for `tiny.txt`.

1.6.6 Determine the number of iterations required by `markov.py` to compute page ranks to three decimal places, to four decimal places, and to ten decimal places for `tiny.txt`.

1.6.7 Download the file `medium.txt` from the booksite (which reflects the 50-page example depicted in this section) and add to it links *from* page 23 *to* every other page. Observe the effect on the page ranks, and discuss the result.

1.6.8 Add to `medium.txt` (see the previous exercise) links *to* page 23 *from* every other page, observe the effect on the page ranks, and discuss the result.

1.6.9 Suppose that your page is page 23 in `medium.txt`. Is there a link that you could add from your page to some other page that would *raise* the rank of *your* page?

1.6.10 Suppose that your page is page 23 in `medium.txt`. Is there a link that you could add from your page to some other page that would *lower* the rank of *that* page?

1.6.11 Use `transition.py` and `randomsurfer.py` to determine the transition probabilities for the eight-page example shown below.

1.6.12 Use `transition.py` and `markov.py` to determine the transition probabilities for the eight-page example shown below.

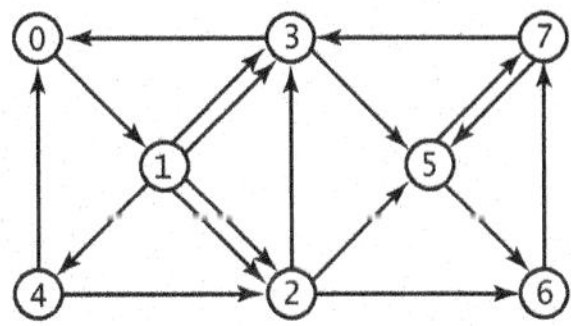

Eight-page example

Creative Exercises

1.6.13 *Matrix squaring.* Compose a program like `markov.py` that computes page ranks by repeatedly squaring the matrix, thus computing the sequence p, p^2, p^4, p^8, p^{16}, and so forth. Verify that all of the rows in the matrix converge to the same values.

1.6.14 *Random web.* Compose a generator for `transition.py` that takes as input a page count `n` and a link count `m` and writes to standard output `n` followed by `m` random pairs of integers between `0` and `n-1`. (See SECTION 4.5 for a discussion of more realistic web models.)

1.6.15 *Hubs and authorities.* Add to your generator from the previous exercise a fixed number of *hubs*, which have links pointing to them from 10 percent of the pages, chosen at random, and *authorities*, which have links pointing from them to 10 percent of the pages. Compute page ranks. Which rank higher, hubs or authorities?

1.6.16 *Page ranks.* Design an array of pages and links where the highest-ranking page has fewer links pointing to it than some other page.

1.6.17 *Hitting time.* The hitting time for a page is the expected number of moves between times the random surfer visits the page. Run experiments to estimate page hitting times for `tiny.txt`, compare the results with page ranks, formulate a hypothesis about the relationship, and test your hypothesis on `medium.txt`.

1.6.18 *Cover time.* Compose a program that estimates the time required for the random surfer to visit every page at least once, starting from a random page.

1.6.19 *Graphical simulation.* Create a graphical simulation where the size of the dot representing each page is proportional to its rank. To make your program data-driven, design a file format that includes coordinates specifying where each page should be drawn. Test your program on `medium.txt`.

Chapter Two

Functions and Modules

THIS CHAPTER IS CENTERED ON A construct that has as profound an impact on control flow as do conditionals and loops: the *function*, which allows us to transfer control back and forth between different pieces of code. Functions are important because they allow us to clearly separate tasks within a program and because they provide a general mechanism that enables us to reuse code. Using and defining functions is a central component of Python programming.

When we have a number of functions to work with, we group them together in *modules*. With the use of modules, we can break a computational task into subtasks of a reasonable size. You will learn in this chapter how to build modules of your own and how to use them in a style of programming known as *modular programming*. In particular, we consider in this chapter modules for generating random numbers, analyzing data, and input/output for arrays. Modules vastly extend the set of operations that we can use in our programs.

We pay special attention to functions that transfer control to themselves. This process is known as *recursion*. At first, recursion may seem counterintuitive, but it allows us to develop simple programs that can address complex tasks that would otherwise be much more difficult to carry out.

Whenever you can clearly separate tasks within a computation, you should do so. We repeat this mantra throughout this chapter, and end the chapter with an example showing how a complex programming task can be handled by breaking it into smaller subtasks, then independently developing modules that interact with one another to address the subtasks. Throughout the chapter, we make use of functions and modules developed earlier in the chapter, to emphasize the utility of modular programming.

2.1 Defining Functions

YOU HAVE BEEN COMPOSING CODE THAT calls Python functions since the beginning of this book, from writing strings with `stdio.writeln()` to using type conversion functions such as `str()` and `int()` to computing mathematical functions such as `math.sqrt()` to using all of the functions in `stdio`, `stddraw`, and `stdaudio`. In this section, you will learn how to define and call your own functions.

Programs in this section

In mathematics, a function maps an input value of one type (the domain) to an output value of another type (the range). For example, the square function $f(x) = x^2$ maps 2 to 4, 3 to 9, 4 to 16, and so forth. At first, we work with Python functions that implement mathematical functions, because they are so familiar. Many standard mathematical functions are implemented in Python's `math` module, but scientists and engineers work with a broad variety of mathematical functions, which cannot all be included in the module. At the beginning of this section, you will learn how to implement and use such functions on your own.

Later, you will learn that we can do more with Python functions than implement mathematical functions: Python functions can have strings and other types as their domain or range, and they can have side effects such as writing output. We also consider in this section how to use Python functions to organize programs and thereby simplify complicated programming tasks.

From this point forward, we use the generic term *function* to mean either *Python function* or *mathematical function* depending on the context. We use the more specific terminology only when the context requires that we do so.

Functions support a key concept that will pervade your approach to programming from this point forward: *Whenever you can clearly separate tasks within a computation, you should do so.* We will be overemphasizing this point throughout this section and reinforcing it throughout the rest of the chapter (and the rest of the book). When you write an essay, you break it up into paragraphs; when you compose a program, you break it up into functions. Separating a larger task into smaller ones is much more important when programming than when writing an essay, because it greatly facilitates debugging, maintenance, and reuse, which are all critical in developing good software.

Using and defining functions As you know from the functions you have been using, the effect of calling a Python function is easy to understand. For example, when you place `math.sqrt(a-b)` in a program, the effect is as if you had replaced that code with the *return value* that is produced by Python's `math.sqrt()` function when passed the expression `a-b` as an *argument*. This usage is so intuitive that we have hardly needed to comment on it. If you think about what the system has to do to create this effect, however, you will see that it involves changing a program's *control flow*. The implications of being able to change the control flow in this way are as profound as doing so for conditionals and loops.

You can define functions in any Python program, using the `def` statement that specifies the function signature, followed by a sequence of statements that constitute the function. We will consider the details shortly, but begin with a simple example that illustrates how functions affect control flow. Our first example, PROGRAM 2.1.1 (`harmonicf.py`), includes a function named `harmonic()` that takes an argument `n` and computes the `n`th harmonic number (see PROGRAM 1.3.5). It also illustrates the typical structure of a Python program, having three components:

- A sequence of `import` statements
- A sequence of *function definitions*
- Arbitrary *global code*, or the body of the program

PROGRAM 2.1.1 has two `import` statements, one function definition, and four lines of arbitrary global code. Python executes the global code when we invoke the program by typing **`python harmonicf.py`** on the command line; that global code calls the `harmonic()` function defined earlier.

The implementation in `harmonicf.py` is preferable to our original implementation for computing harmonic numbers (PROGRAM 1.3.5) because it clearly separates the two primary tasks performed by the program: calculating harmonic numbers and interacting with the user. (For purposes of illustration, we have made the user-interaction part of the program a bit more complicated than in PROGRAM 1.3.5.) *Whenever you can clearly separate tasks within a computation, you should do so*. Next, we carefully examine precisely how `harmonicf.py` achieves this goal.

Control flow. The diagram on the next page illustrates the flow of control for the command **`python harmonicf.py 1 2 3`**. First, Python processes the `import` statements, thus making all of the features defined in the `sys` and `stdio` modules available to the program. Next, Python processes the definition of the `harmonic()` function at lines 4 through 8, but *does not execute the function*—Python executes a function only when it is called. Then, Python executes the first statement in the global code after the function definition, the `for` statement, which proceeds normally until Python begins to execute the statement `value = harmonic(arg)`, starting by evaluating the expression `harmonic(arg)` when `arg` is 1. To do so it transfers control to the `harmonic()` function—the flow of control passes to the code in the function definition. Python initializes the "parameter" variable `n` to `1` and the "local" variable `total` to `0.0` and then executes the `for` loop within `harmonic()`, which terminates after one iteration with `total` equal to `1.0`. Then, Python executes the `return` statement at the end of the definition of `harmonic()`, causing the flow of control to jump back to the calling statement `value = harmonic(arg)`, continuing from where it left off, but now with the expression `harmonic(arg)` replaced by `1.0`. Thus, Python assigns `1.0` to `value` and writes it to standard output. Then, Python iterates the loop once more, and calls the `harmonic()` function a second time with `n` initialized to `2`, which results in `1.5` being written. The process is then repeated a third time with `arg` (and then `n`) equal to `4`, which results in `2.083333333333333` being written. Finally, the `for` loop terminates and the whole process is complete. As the diagram indicates, the simple code masks a rather intricate flow of control.

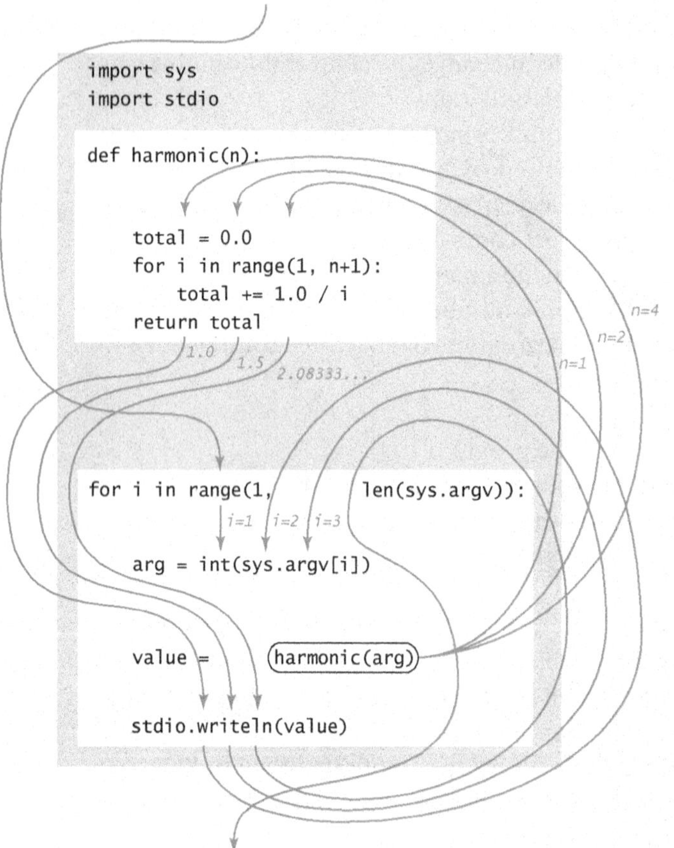

Flow of control for **`python harmonicf.py 1 2 4`**

Program 2.1.1 **Harmonic numbers (revisited)** (harmonicf.py)

```
import sys
import stdio

def harmonic(n):
    total = 0.0
    for i in range(1, n+1):
        total += 1.0 / i
    return total

for i in range(1, len(sys.argv)):
    arg = int(sys.argv[i])
    value = harmonic(arg)
    stdio.writeln(value)
```

n	*parameter variable*
i	*loop index*
total	*return value*

i	*argument index*
arg	*argument*
value	*Harmonic number*

This program writes to standard output the harmonic numbers specified as command-line arguments. The program defines a function harmonic() *that, given an* int *argument n, computes the nth harmonic number* $1 + 1/2 + 1/3 + \ldots + 1/n$.

```
% python harmonicf.py 1 2 4
1.0
1.5
2.083333333333333
```

```
% python harmonicf.py 10 100 1000 10000
2.9289682539682538
5.187377517639621
7.485470860550343
9.787606036044348
```

Abbreviation alert. We continue to use the abbreviations that we introduced in SECTION 1.2 for functions and function calls. For example, we might say, "The function call `harmonic(2)` returns the value `1.5`," instead of the more accurate but verbose "When we pass to `harmonic()` a reference to an object of type `int` whose value is 2, it returns a reference to an object of type `float` whose value is `1.5`." We strive to use language that is succinct and only as precise as necessary in a given context.

Informal function call/return trace. One simple approach to following the control flow through function calls is to imagine that each function writes its name and argument(s) when it is called and its return value just before returning, with indentation added on calls and subtracted on returns. The result enhances the process of tracing a program by writing the values of its variables, which we have been using since SECTION 1.2. An informal trace for our example is shown at right. The added indentation exposes the flow of the control, and helps us check that each function has the effect that we expect. Generally, adding calls on `stdio.writef()` to trace *any* program's control flow in this way is a fine approach to begin to understand what it is doing. If the return values match our expectations, we need not trace the function code in detail, saving us a substantial amount of work.

```
i = 1
arg = 1
harmonic(1)
    total = 0.0
    total = 1.0
    return 1.0
value = 1.0
i = 2
arg = 2
harmonic(2)
    total = 0.0
    total = 1.0
    total = 1.5
    return 1.5
value = 1.5
i = 3
arg = 4
harmonic(4)
    total = 0.0
    total = 1.0
    total = 1.5
    total = 1.8333333333333333
    total = 2.083333333333333
    return 2.083333333333333
value = 2.083333333333333
```

Informal trace with function call/return for **`python harmonicf.py 1 2 4`**

FOR THE REST OF THIS CHAPTER, your programming will be centered on creating and using functions, so it is worthwhile to consider in more detail their basic properties and, in particular, the terminology surrounding functions. Following that, we will study several examples of function implementations and applications.

Basic terminology. As we have been doing throughout, it is useful to draw a distinction between abstract concepts and Python mechanisms to implement them (the Python `if` statement implements the conditional, the `while` statement implements the loop, and so forth). There are several concepts rolled up in the idea of a mathematical function and there are Python constructs corresponding to each, as summarized in the table at the top of the following page. While you can rest assured that these formalisms have served mathematicians well for centuries (and have served programmers well for decades), we will refrain from considering in detail all of the implications of this correspondence and focus on those that will help you learn to program.

When we use a symbolic name in a formula that defines a mathematical function (such as $f(x) = 1 + x + x^2$), the symbol x is a placeholder for some input value

concept	*Python construct*	*description*
function	function	mapping
input value	argument	input to function
output value	return value	output of function
formula	function body	function definition
independent variable	parameter variable	symbolic placeholder for input value

that will be substituted into the formula to determine the output value. In Python, we use a *parameter variable* as a symbolic placeholder and we refer to a particular input value where the function is to be evaluated as an *argument*.

Function definition. The first line of a function definition, known as its *signature*, gives a name to the function and to each parameter variable. The signature consists of the keyword `def`; the *function name*; a sequence of zero or more parameter variable names separated by commas and enclosed in parentheses; and a colon. The indented statements following the signature define the *function body*. The function body can consist of the kinds of statements that we discussed in Chapter 1. It also can contain a *return statement*, which transfers control back to the point where the function was called and returns the result of the computation or *return value*. The body may also define *local variables*, which are variables that are available only inside the function in which they are defined.

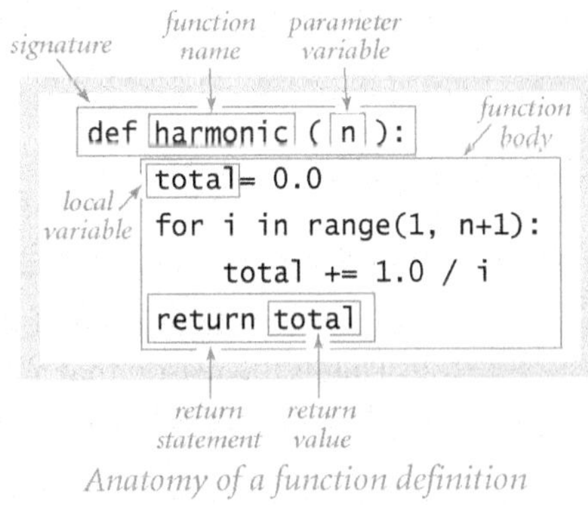

Anatomy of a function definition

Function calls. As we have seen throughout, a Python function call is nothing more than the function name followed by its arguments, separated by commas and enclosed in parentheses, in precisely the same form as is customary for mathematical functions. As noted in Section 1.2, each argument can be an expression, which is evaluated and the resulting value passed as input to the function. When the function finishes, the return value takes the place of the function call as if it were the value of a variable (perhaps within an expression).

```
for i in range(1, len(sys.argv)):
    arg = int(sys.argv[i])
    value = harmonic( arg )
    stdio.writeln(value)
```
(labels: *function call*, *argument*)

Anatomy of a function call

Multiple arguments. Like a mathematical function, a Python function can have more than one parameter variable, so it can be called with more than one argument. The function signature lists the name of each parameter variable, separated by commas. For example, the following function computes the length of the hypotenuse of a right triangle with sides of length a and b:

```
def hypot(a, b)
    return math.sqrt(a*a + b*b)
```

Multiple functions. You can define as many functions as you want in a .py file. The functions are independent, except that they may refer to each other through calls. They can appear in any order in the file:

```
def square(x):
    return x*x

def hypot(a, b):
    return math.sqrt(square(a) + square(b))
```

However, the definition of a function must appear before any global code that calls it. That is the reason that a typical Python program contains (1) `import` statements, (2) function definitions, and (3) arbitrary global code, in that order.

Multiple return statements. You can put `return` statements in a function wherever you need them: control goes back to the calling program as soon as the first `return` statement is reached. This *primality-testing* function is an example of a function that is natural to define using multiple `return` statements:

```
def isPrime(n):
    if n < 2: return False
    i = 2
    while i*i <= n:
        if n % i == 0: return False
        i += 1
    return True
```

Single return value. A Python function provides only one return value to the caller (or, more precisely, it returns a reference to one object). This policy is not as restrictive as it might seem, because Python data types can contain more information than a single number, boolean, or string. For example, you will see later in this section that you can use arrays as return values.

Scope. The *scope* of a variable is the set of statements that can refer to that variable directly. The scope of a function's local and parameter variables is limited to that function; the scope of a variable defined in global code—known as a *global variable*—is limited to the `.py` file containing that variable. Therefore, global code cannot refer to either a function's local or parameter variables. Nor can one function refer to either the local or parameter variables that are defined in another function. When a function defines a local (or parameter) variable with the same name as a global variable (such as `i` in PROGRAM 2.1.1), the variable name in the function refers to the local (or parameter) variable, not the global variable.

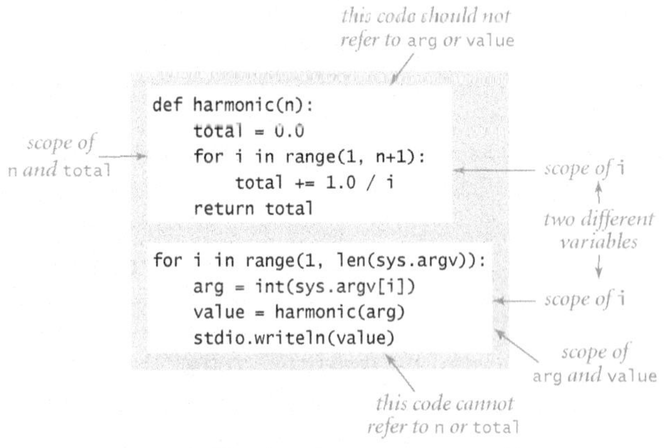

Scope of local and parameter variables

A guiding principle when designing software is to define each variable so that its scope is as small as possible. One of the important reasons that we use functions is so that changes made to one part of a program will not affect an unrelated part of the program. So, while code in a function *can* refer to global variables, it *should not* do so: all communication from a caller to a function should take place via the function's parameter variables, and all communication from a function to its caller should take place via the function's return value. In SECTION 2.2, we consider a technique for removing most global code, thereby limiting scope and the potential for unexpected interactions.

Default arguments. A Python function may designate an argument to be *optional* by specifying a *default value* for that argument. If you omit an optional argument in a function call, then Python substitutes the default value for that argument. We have already encountered a few examples of this feature. For example, `math.log(x, b)` returns the base-`b` logarithm of `x`. If you omit the second argument, then `b` defaults to `math.e`—that is, `math.log(x)` returns the natural logarithm of `x`. It might appear that the `math` module has two different logarithm functions, but it actually has just one, with an optional argument and a default value.

You can specify an optional argument with a default value in a user-defined function by putting an equals sign followed by the default value after the parameter variable in the function signature. You can specify more than one optional argument in a function signature, but all of the optional arguments must follow all of the mandatory arguments.

For example, consider the problem of computing the *n*th *generalized harmonic number of order r*: $H_{n,r} = 1 + 1/2^r + 1/3^r + \ldots + 1/n^r$. For example, $H_{1,2} = 1$, $H_{2,2} = 5/4$, and $H_{2,2} = 49/36$. The generalized harmonic numbers are closely related to the Riemann zeta function from number theory. Note that the *n*th generalized harmonic number of order $r = 1$ is equal to the *n*th harmonic number. Therefore it is appropriate to use `1` as the default value for `r` if the caller omits the second argument. We specify by writing `r=1` in the signature:

```
def harmonic(n, r=1):
    total = 0.0
    for i in range(1, n+1):
        total += 1.0 / (i ** r)
    return total
```

With this definition, `harmonic(2, 2)` returns `1.25`, while both `harmonic(2, 1)` and `harmonic(2)` return `1.5`. To the client, it appears that we have two different functions, one with a single argument and one with two arguments, but we achieve this effect with a single implementation.

Side effects. In mathematics, a function maps one or more input values to some output value. In computer programming, many functions fit that same model: they accept one or more arguments, and their only purpose is to return a value. A *pure function* is a function that, given the same arguments, always return the same value, without producing any observable *side effects*, such as consuming input, producing output, or otherwise changing the state of the system. So far, in this section we have considered only pure functions.

However, in computer programming it is also useful to define functions that do produce side effects. In fact, we often define functions whose only purpose is to produce side effects. An explicit `return` statement is optional in such a function: control returns to the caller after Python executes the function's last statement. Functions with no specified return value actually return the special value `None`, which is usually ignored.

For example, the `stdio.write()` function has the side effect of writing the given argument to standard output (and has no specified return value). Similarly, the following function has the side effect of drawing a triangle to standard drawing (and has no specified return value):

```
def drawTriangle(x0, y0, x1, y1, x2, y2):
    stddraw.line(x0, y0, x1, y1)
    stddraw.line(x1, y1, x2, y2)
    stddraw.line(x2, y2, x0, y0)
```

It is generally poor style to compose a function that both produces side effects and returns a value. One notable exception arises in functions that read input. For example, the `stdio.readInt()` function both returns a value (an integer) and produces a side effect (consuming one integer from standard input).

Type checking. In mathematics, the definition of a function specifies both the domain and the range. For example, for the harmonic numbers, the domain is the positive integers and the range is the positive real numbers. In Python, we do not specify the types of the parameter variables or the type of the return value. As long as Python can apply all of the operations within a function, Python executes the function and returns a value.

If Python cannot apply an operation to a given object because it is of the wrong type, it raises a run-time error to indicate the invalid type. For example, if you call the `square()` function defined earlier with an `int` argument, the result is an `int`; if you call it with a `float` argument, the result is a `float`. However, if you call it with a string argument, then Python raises a `TypeError` at run time.

This flexibility is a popular feature of Python (known as *polymorphism*) because it allows us to define a single function for use with objects of different types. It can also lead to unexpected errors when we call a function with arguments of unanticipated types. In principle, we could include code to check for such errors, and we could carefully specify which types of data each function is supposed to work with. Like most Python programmers, we refrain from doing so. However, in this book, our message is that *you should always be aware of the type of your data*, and the functions that we consider in this book are built in line with this philosophy, which admittedly clashes with Python's tendency toward polymorphism. We will discuss this issue in some detail in SECTION 3.3.

THE TABLE BELOW SUMMARIZES OUR DISCUSSION by collecting together the function definitions that we have examined so far. To check your understanding, take the time to reread these examples carefully.

primality test	`def isPrime(n):`
	`    if n < 2: return False`
	`    i = 2`
	`    while i*i <= n:`
	`        if n % i == 0: return False`
	`        i += 1`
	`    return True`

hypotenuse of a right triangle	`def hypot(a, b)` `    return math.sqrt(a*a + b*b)`

generalized harmonic number	`def harmonic(n, r=1):`
	`    total = 0.0`
	`    for i in range(1, n+1):`
	`        total += 1.0 / (i ** r)`
	`    return total`

draw a triangle	`def drawTriangle(x0, y0, x1, y1, x2, y2):`
	`    stddraw.line(x0, y0, x1, y1)`
	`    stddraw.line(x1, y1, x2, y2)`
	`    stddraw.line(x2, y2, x0, y0)`

Typical code for implementing functions

Implementing mathematical functions Why not just use the Python built-in functions and those that are defined in the standard or extension Python modules? For example, why not use the `math.hypot()` function instead of defining our own `hypot()` function? The answer to this question is that we *do* use such functions when they are present (because they are likely to be faster and more accurate). However, there is an unlimited number of functions that we may wish to use and only a finite number of functions is defined in the Python standard and extension modules. When you need a function that is not defined in the Python standard or extension modules, you need to define the function yourself.

As an example, we consider the kind of code required for a familiar and important application that is of interest to many potential college students in the United States. In a recent year, over 1 million students took the Scholastic Aptitude Test (SAT). The test consists of two major sections: critical reading and mathematics. Scores range from 200 (lowest) to 800 (highest) on each section, so overall test scores range from 400 to 1600. Many universities consider these scores when making important decisions. For example, student athletes are required by the National Collegiate Athletic Association (NCAA), and thus by many universities, to have a combined score of at least 820 (out of 1600), and the minimum eligibility requirement for certain academic scholarships is 1500 (out of 1600). What percentage of test takers is ineligible for athletics? What percentage is eligible for the scholarships?

Two functions from statistics enable us to compute accurate answers to these questions. The *standard normal (Gaussian) probability density function* is characterized by the familiar bell-shaped curve and defined by the formula $\phi(x) = e^{-x^2/2}/\sqrt{2\pi}$. The standard normal (Gaussian) *cumulative distribution function* $\Phi(z)$ is defined to be the area under the curve defined by $\phi(x)$ above the x-axis and to the left of the vertical line $x=z$. These functions play an important role in science, engineering, and finance because they arise as accurate models throughout the natural world and because they are essential in understanding experimental error. In particular, these functions are known to accurately describe the distribution of test scores in our example, as a function of the mean (average value of the scores) and the standard deviation (square root of the average of the squares of the differences between each score and the mean), which are published each year. Given the mean μ and the standard deviation σ of the test scores, the percentage of students with scores less than a given value z is closely approximated by the function $\Phi(z, \mu, \sigma) = \Phi((z-\mu)/\sigma)$. Functions to calculate ϕ and Φ are not available in Python's `math` module, so we develop our own implementations.

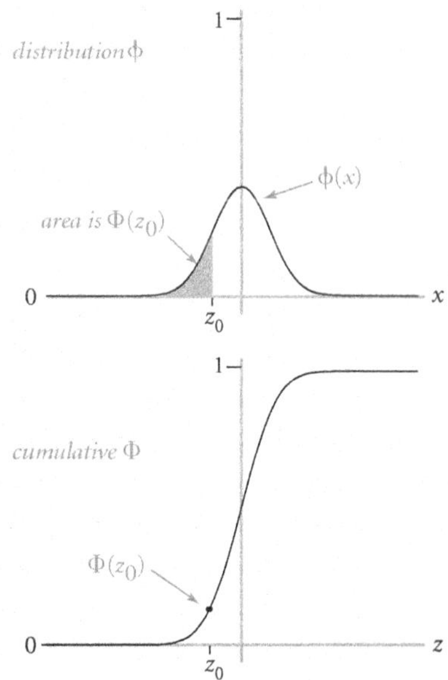

Gaussian probability functions

Closed form. In the simplest situation, we have a closed-form mathematical formula defining our function in terms of functions that are implemented in Python's `math` module. This situation is the case for ϕ—the `math` module includes functions to compute the exponential and the square root functions (and a constant value for π), so a function `pdf()` corresponding to the mathematical definition is easy to implement. For convenience, `gauss.py` (PROGRAM 2.1.2) uses the default arguments $\mu = 0$ and $\sigma = 1$ and actually computes $\phi(x, \mu, \sigma) = \phi((x-\mu) / \sigma) / \sigma$.

No closed form. If no formula is known, we may need a more complicated algorithm to compute function values. This situation is the case for Φ—no closed-form expression exists for this function. Algorithms to compute function values sometimes follow immediately from Taylor series approximations, but developing reliably accurate implementations of mathematical functions is an art and a science that needs to be addressed carefully, taking advantage of the knowledge built up in mathematics over the past several centuries. Many different approaches have been studied for evaluating Φ. For example, a Taylor series approximation to the ratio of Φ and ϕ turns out to be an effective basis for evaluating the function:

$$\Phi(z) = 1/2 + \phi(z)\,(\,z + z^3/3 + z^5/(3\cdot5) + z^7/(3\cdot5\cdot7) + \ldots\,).$$

This formula readily translates to the Python code for the function `cdf()` in PROGRAM 2.1.2. For small (respectively large) z, the value is extremely close to 0 (respectively 1), so the code directly returns 0 (respectively 1); otherwise, it uses the Taylor series to add terms until the sum converges. Again, for convenience, PROGRAM 2.1.2 actually computes $\Phi(z, \mu, \sigma) = \Phi((z-\mu) / \sigma)$, using the defaults $\mu = 0$ and $\sigma = 1$.

Running `gauss.py` with the appropriate arguments on the command line tells us that about 17% of the test takers were ineligible for athletics in a year when the mean was 1019 and the standard deviation was 209. In the same year, about 1% percent qualified for academic scholarships.

COMPUTING WITH MATHEMATICAL FUNCTIONS OF ALL sorts plays a central role in science and engineering. In a great many applications, the functions that you need are expressed in terms of the functions in Python's `math` module, as we have just seen with `pdf()`, or in terms of a Taylor series approximation or some other formulation that is easy to compute, as we have just seen with `cdf()`. Indeed, support for such computations has played a central role throughout the evolution of computing systems and programming languages.

Program 2.1.2 Gaussian functions (gauss.py)

```
import math
import sys
import stdio

def pdf(x, mu=0.0, sigma=1.0):
    x = float(x - mu) / sigma
    return math.exp(-x*x/2.0) / math.sqrt(2.0*math.pi) / sigma

def cdf(z, mu=0.0, sigma=1.0):
    z = float(z - mu) / sigma
    if z < -8.0: return 0.0
    if z > +8.0: return 1.0
    total = 0.0
    term = z
    i = 3
    while total != total + term:
        total += term
        term *= z * z / i
        i += 2
    return 0.5 + total * pdf(z)

z     = float(sys.argv[1])
mu    = float(sys.argv[2])
sigma = float(sys.argv[3])
stdio.writeln(cdf(z, mu, sigma))
```

total	*cumulated sum*
term	*current term*

This code implements the Gaussian (normal) probability density (pdf) and cumulative distribution (cdf) functions, which are not implemented in Python's math *library. The* pdf() *implementation follows directly from its definition, and the* cdf() *implementation uses a Taylor series and also calls* pdf() *(see accompanying text at left and* Exercise *1.3.36). Note: If you are referring to this code for use in another program, please see* gaussian.py *(*Program *2.2.1), which is designed for reuse.*

```
% python gauss.py  820 1019 209
0.17050966869132106
% python gauss.py 1500 1019 209
0.9893164837383885
```

Using functions to organize code Beyond evaluating mathematical functions, the process of calculating an output value as a function of input values is important as a general technique for organizing control flow in *any* computation. Doing so is a simple example of an extremely important principle that is a prime guiding force for any good programmer: *Whenever you can clearly separate tasks within a computation, you should do so.*

Functions are natural and universal mechanism for expressing computational tasks. Indeed, the "bird's-eye view" of a Python program that we began with in Section 1.1 was equivalent to a function: we began by thinking of a Python program as a function that transforms command-line arguments into an output string. This view expresses itself at many different levels of computation. In particular, it is generally the case that you can express a long program more naturally in terms of functions instead of as a sequence of Python assignment, conditional, and loop statements. With the ability to define functions, you can better organize your programs by defining functions within them when appropriate.

For example, `coupon.py` (Program 2.1.3) on the facing page is an improved version of `couponcollector.py` (Program 1.4.2) that better separates the individual components of the computation. If you study Program 1.4.2, you will identify three separate tasks:

- Given the number of coupon values n, compute a random coupon value.
- Given n, do the coupon collection experiment.
- Get n from the command line, then compute and write the result.

Program 2.1.3 rearranges the code to reflect the reality that these three activities underlie the computation. The first two are implemented as functions, the third as global code.

With this organization, we could change `getCoupon()` (for example, we might want to draw the random numbers from a different distribution) or the global code (for example, we might want to take multiple inputs or run multiple experiments) without worrying about the effect of any of these changes on `collect()`.

Using functions isolates the implementation of each component of the collection experiment from others, or *encapsulates* them. Typically, programs have many independent components, which magnifies the benefits of separating them into different functions. We will discuss these benefits in further detail after we have seen several other examples, but you certainly can appreciate that it is better to express a computation in a program by breaking it up into functions, just as it is better to express an idea in an essay by breaking it up into paragraphs. *Whenever you can clearly separate tasks within a computation, you should do so.*

Program 2.1.3 Coupon collector (revisited) (coupon.py)

```
import random
import sys
import stdarray
import stdio

def getCoupon(n):
    return random.randrange(0, n)

def collect(n):
    isCollected = stdarray.create1D(n, False)
    count = 0
    collectedCount = 0
    while collectedCount < n:
        value = getCoupon(n)
        count += 1
        if not isCollected[value]:
            collectedCount += 1
            isCollected[value] = True
    return count

n = int(sys.argv[1])
result = collect(n)
stdio.writeln(result)
```

`n`	*# of coupon values (0 to n-1)*
`isCollected[i]`	*has coupon i been collected?*
`count`	*# of coupons collected*
`collectedCount`	*# of distinct coupons collected*
`value`	*value of current coupon*

This version of PROGRAM *1.4.2 illustrates the style of encapsulating computations in functions. This code has the same effect as* `couponcollector.py`*, but better separates the code into its three constituent pieces: generating a random integer between 0 and n-1, running a collection experiment, and managing the I/O.*

```
% python coupon.py 1000
6522
% python coupon.py 1000
6481
% python coupon.py 1000000
12783771
```

Passing arguments and returning values Next, we examine the specifics of Python's mechanisms for passing arguments to and returning values from functions. These mechanisms are conceptually very simple, but it is worthwhile to take the time to understand them fully, as the effects are actually profound. Understanding argument-passing and return-value mechanisms is key to learning *any* new programming language. In the case of Python, the concepts of *immutability* and *aliasing* play a central role.

Call by object reference. You can use parameter variables anywhere in the body of the function in the same way as you use local variables. The only difference between a parameter variable and a local variable is that Python initializes the parameter variable with the corresponding argument provided by the calling code. We refer to this approach as *call by object reference.* (It is more commonly known as *call by value,* where the value is always an object reference—not the object's value.) One consequence of this approach is that if a parameter variable refers to a mutable object and you change that object's value within a function, then this also changes the object's value in the calling code (because it is the same object). Next, we explore the ramifications of this approach.

Immutability and aliasing. As discussed in SECTION 1.4, arrays are *mutable* data types, because we can change array elements. By contrast, a data type is *immutable* if it is not possible to change the value of an object of that type. The other data types that we have been using (`int`, `float`, `str`, and `bool`) are all immutable. In an immutable data type, operations that might seem to change a value actually result in the creation of a new object, as illustrated in the simple example at right. First, the statement `i = 99` creates an integer 99, and assigns to `i` a reference to that integer. Then `j = i` assigns `i` (an object reference) to `j`, so both `i` and `j` reference the same object—the integer 99. Two variables that reference the same objects are said to be *aliases.* Next, `j += 1` results in `j` referencing an object with value 100, but *it does not do so by changing the value of the existing integer* from 99 to 100! Indeed, since `int` objects are immutable, *no* statement

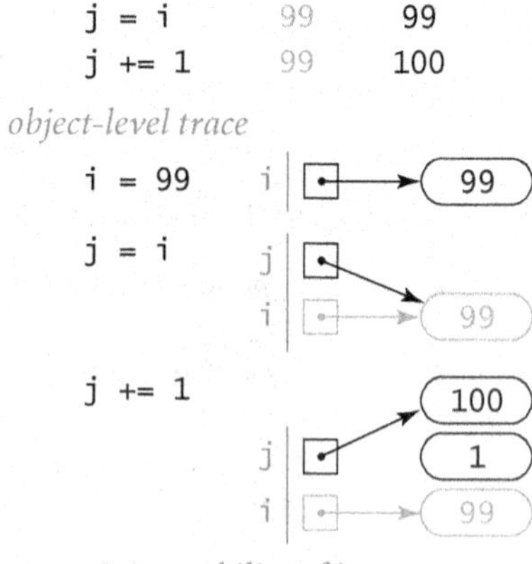

Immutability of integers

can change the value of that existing integer. Instead, that statement creates a new integer `1`, adds it to the integer `99` to create another new integer `100`, and assigns to `j` a reference to that integer. But `i` still references the original `99`. Note that the new integer `1` has no reference to it in the end—that is the system's concern, not ours. The immutability of integers, floats, strings, and booleans is a fundamental aspect of Python. We will consider the advantages and disadvantages of this approach in more detail in Section 3.3.

Integers, floats, booleans, and strings as arguments. The key point to remember about passing arguments to functions in Python is that *whenever you pass arguments to a function, the arguments and the function's parameter variables become aliases.* In practice, this is the predominant use of aliasing in Python, and it is important to understand its effects. For purposes of illustration, suppose that we need a function that increments an integer (our discussion applies to any more complicated function as well). A programmer new to Python might try this definition:

```
def inc(j):
    j += 1
```

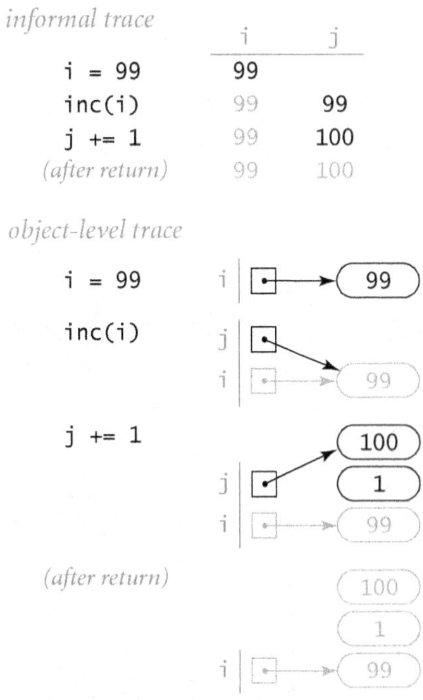

Aliasing in a function call

and then expect to increment an integer `i` with the call `inc(i)`. Code like this would work in some programming languages, but it has no effect in Python, as shown in the figure at right. First, the statement `i = 99` assigns to global variable `i` a reference to the integer `99`. Then, the statement `inc(i)` passes `i`, an object reference, to the `inc()` function. That object reference is assigned to the parameter variable `j`. At this point `i` and `j` are aliases. As before, the `inc()` function's `j += 1` statement does not change the integer `99`, but rather creates a new integer `100` and assigns a reference to that integer to `j`. But when the `inc()` function returns to its caller, its parameter variable `j` goes out of scope, and the variable `i` still references the integer `99`.

This example illustrates that, in Python, *a function cannot produce the side effect of changing the value of an integer object* (nothing can do so). To increment variable `i`, we could use the definition

```
def inc(j):
    j += 1
    return j
```

and call the function with the assignment statement `i = inc(i)`.

The same holds true for any immutable type. A function cannot change the value of an integer, a float, a boolean, or a string.

Arrays as arguments. When a function takes an array as an argument, it implements a function that operates on an arbitrary number of objects. For example, the following function computes the mean (average) of an array of floats or integers:

```
def mean(a):
    total = 0.0
    for v in a:
        total += v
    return total / len(a)
```

We have been using arrays as arguments from the beginning of the book. For example, by convention, Python collects the strings that you type after the program name in the `python` command into an array `sys.argv[]` and implicitly calls your global code with that array of strings as the argument.

Side effects with arrays. Since arrays *are* mutable, it is often the case that the purpose of a function that takes an array as argument is to produce a side effect (such as changing the order of array elements). A prototypical example of such a function is one that exchanges the elements at two given indices in a given array. We can adapt the code that we examined at the beginning of Section 1.4:

```
def exchange(a, i, j):
   temp = a[i]
   a[i] = a[j]
   a[j] = temp
```

This implementation stems naturally from the Python array representation. The first parameter variable in `exchange()` is a reference to the array, not to all of the array's elements: when you pass an array as an argument to a function, you are giving it the opportunity to operate on that array (not a copy of it). A formal trace of a call on this function is shown on the facing page. This diagram is worthy of careful study to check your understanding of Python's function-call mechanism.

A second prototypical example of a function that takes an array argument and produces side effects is one that randomly shuffles the elements in the array, using this version of the algorithm that we examined in SECTION 1.4 (and the exchange() function just defined):

```
def shuffle(a):
    n = len(a)
    for i in range(n):
        r = random.randrange(i, n)
        exchange(a, i, r)
```

Incidentally, Python's standard function random.shuffle() does the same task. As another example, we will consider in SECTION 4.2 functions that sort an array (rearrange its elements so that they are in order).

Arrays as return values. A function that sorts, shuffles, or otherwise modifies an array taken as argument does not have to return a reference to that array, because it is changing the contents of a client array, not a copy. But there are many situations where it is useful for a function to provide an array as a return value. Chief among these are functions that create arrays for the purpose of returning multiple objects of the same type to a client.

As an example, consider the following function, which returns an array of random floats:

```
def randomarray(n):
    a = stdarray.create1D(n)
    for i in range(n):
        a[i] = random.random()
    return a
```

Later in this chapter, we will be developing numerous functions that return huge amounts of data in this way.

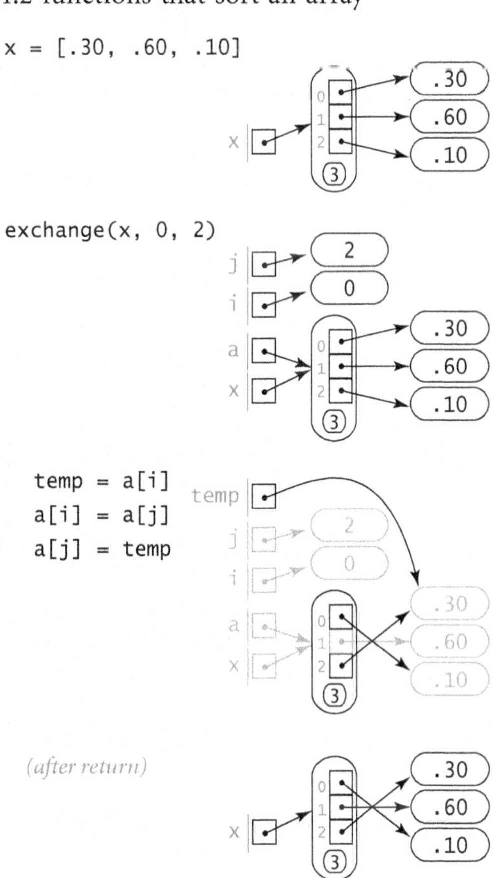

Exchanging two elements in an array

The table below concludes our discussion of arrays as function arguments by highlighting some typical array-procession functions.

mean of an array	`def mean(a):`
	`    total = 0.0`
	`    for v in a:`
	`        total += v`
	`    return total / len(a)`

dot product of two vectors of the same length	`def dot(a, b):`
	`    total = 0`
	`    for i in range(len(a)):`
	`        total += a[i] * b[i]`
	`    return total`

exchange two elements in an array	`def exchange(a, i, j):`
	`    temp = a[i]`
	`    a[i] = a[j]`
	`    a[j] = temp`

write a one-dimensional array (and its length)	`def write1D(a):`
	`    stdio.writeln(len(a))`
	`    for v in a:`
	`        stdio.writeln(v)`

read a two-dimensional array of floats (with dimensions)	`def readFloat2D():`
	`    m = stdio.readInt()`
	`    n = stdio.readInt()`
	`    a = stdarray.create2D(m, n, 0.0)`
	`    for i in range(m):`
	`        for j in range(n):`
	`            a[i][j] = stdio.readFloat()`
	`    return a`

Typical code for implementing functions with arrays

Example: superposition of sound waves As discussed in Section 1.5, the simple audio model that we studied there needs to be embellished to create sound that resembles the sound produced by a musical instrument. Many different embellishments are possible; with functions, we can systematically apply them to produce sound waves that are far more complicated than the simple sine waves that we produced in Section 1.5. As an illustration of the effective use of functions to solve an interesting computational problem, we consider a program that has essentially the same functionality as `playthattune.py` (Program 1.5.8), but adds harmonic tones one octave above and one octave below each note to produce a more realistic sound.

Chords and harmonics. Notes like concert *A* have a pure sound that is not very musical, because the sounds that you are accustomed to hearing have many other components. The sound from a guitar string echoes off the wooden part of the instrument, the walls of the room that you are in, and so forth. You may think of such effects as modifying the basic sine wave. For example, most musical instruments produce *harmonics* (the same note in different octaves and not as loud), or you might play *chords* (multiple notes at the same time). To combine multiple sounds, we use *superposition*: simply add their waves together and rescale to make sure that all values stay between -1 and $+1$. As it turns out, when we superpose sine waves of different frequencies in this way, we can get arbitrarily complicated waves. Indeed, one of the triumphs of 19th-century mathematics was the development of the idea that any smooth periodic function can be expressed as a sum of sine and cosine waves, known as a *Fourier series*. This mathematical idea corresponds to the notion that we can create a large range of sounds with musical instruments or our vocal cords and that all sound consists of a composition of various oscillating curves. Any sound corresponds to a curve and any curve corresponds to a sound, so we can create arbitrarily complex curves with superposition.

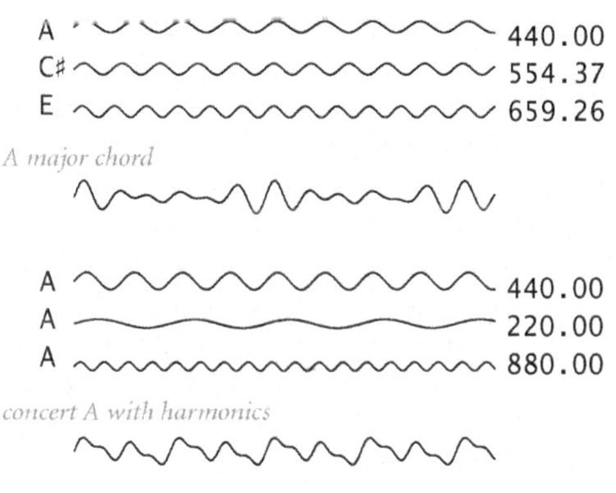

Superposing waves to make composite sounds

Computing with sound waves. In SECTION 1.5, we saw how to represent sound waves by arrays of numbers that represent their values at the same sample points. Now, we will use such arrays as return values and arguments to functions to process such data. For example, the following function takes a frequency (in hertz) and a duration (in seconds) as arguments and returns a representation of a sound wave (more precisely, an array that contains values sampled from the specified wave at the standard 44,100 samples per second).

```
def tone(hz, duration, sps=44100):
    n = int(sps * duration)
    a = stdarray.create1D(n+1, 0.0)
    for i in range(n+1):
        a[i] = math.sin(2.0 * math.pi * i * hz / sps)
    return a
```

The size of the array returned depends on the duration: it contains about `sps*duration` floats (nearly half a million floats for 10 seconds). But we can now treat that array (the value returned from tone) as a single entity and compose code that processes sound waves, as we will soon see in PROGRAM 2.1.4.

Weighted superposition. Since we represent sound waves by arrays of numbers that represent their values at the same sample points, superposition is simple to implement: we add together their sample values at each sample point to produce the combined result. For greater control, we also specify a relative weight for each of the two waves to be superposed, with the following function:

```
def superpose(a, b, aWeight, bWeight):
    c = stdarray.create1D(len(a), 0.0)
    for i in range(len(a)):
        c[i] = aWeight*a[i] + bWeight*b[i]
    return c
```

(This code assumes that `a[]` and `b[]` are of the same length.) For example, if we have a sound represented by an array `a[]` that we want to have three times the effect of the sound represented by an array `b[]`, we would call `superpose(a, b, 0.75, 0.25)`. The figure at the top of the next page shows the use of two calls on this function to add harmonics to a tone (we superpose the harmonics, then superpose the result with the original tone, which has the effect of giving the original tone twice

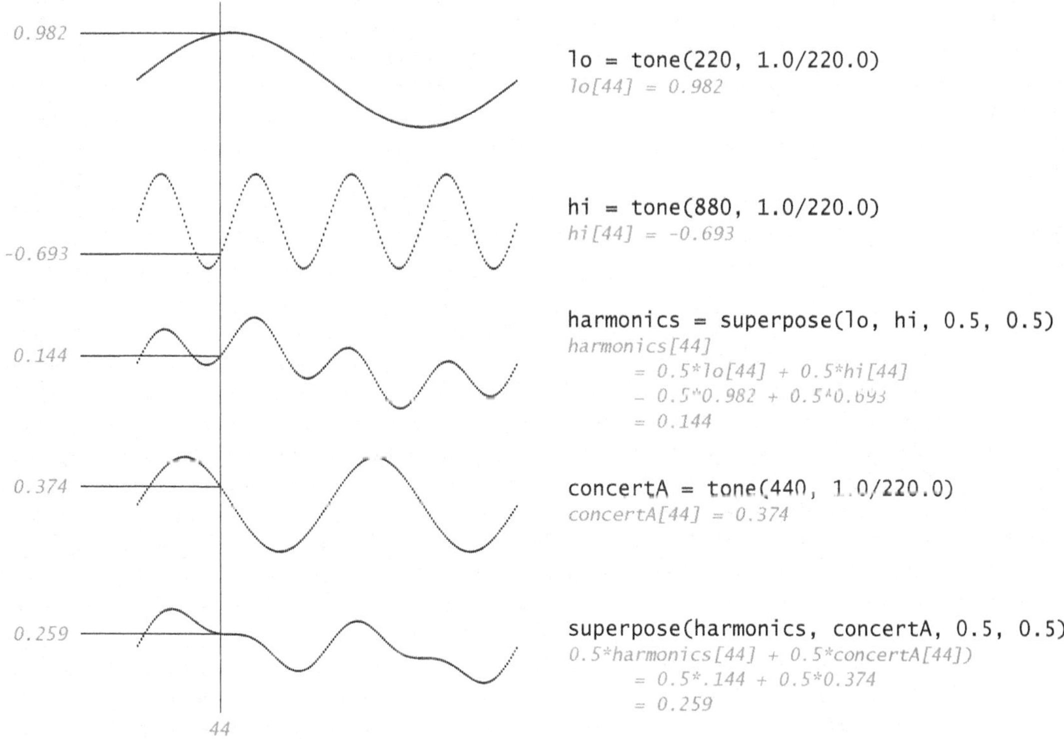
0.982
lo = tone(220, 1.0/220.0)
lo[44] = 0.982
hi = tone(880, 1.0/220.0)
-0.693
hi[44] = -0.693
harmonics = superpose(lo, hi, 0.5, 0.5)
0.144
harmonics[44]
= 0.5*lo[44] + 0.5*hi[44]
= 0.5*0.982 + 0.5*0.693
= 0.144
0.374
concertA = tone(440, 1.0/220.0)
concertA[44] = 0.374
0.259
superpose(harmonics, concertA, 0.5, 0.5)
0.5*harmonics[44] + 0.5*concertA[44])
= 0.5*.144 + 0.5*0.374
= 0.259
44

Adding harmonics to concert A (1/220 second at 44,100 samples/second)

the weight of each harmonic). As long as the weights are positive and sum to 1, `superpose()` preserves our convention of keeping the values of all waves between −1 and +1.

Program 2.1.4 (`playthattunedeluxe.py`) is an implementation that applies these concepts to produce a more realistic sound than that produced by Program 1.5.8. To do so, it makes use of functions to divide the computation into four parts:

- Given a frequency and duration, create a pure tone.
- Given two sound waves and relative weights, superpose them.
- Given a pitch and duration, create a note with harmonics.
- Read and play a sequence of pitch/duration pairs from standard input.

Program 2.1.4 Play that tune (revisited) (playthattunedeluxe.py)

```
import math
import stdarray
import stdaudio
import stdio

def superpose(a, b, aWeight, bWeight):
    c = stdarray.create1D(len(a), 0.0)
    for i in range(len(a)):
        c[i] = aWeight*a[i] + bWeight*b[i]
    return c

def tone(hz, duration, sps=44100):
    n = int(sps * duration)
    a = stdarray.create1D(n+1, 0.0)
    for i in range(n+1):
        a[i] = math.sin(2.0 * math.pi * i * hz / sps)
    return a

def note(pitch, duration):
    hz = 440.0 * (2.0 ** (pitch / 12.0))
    lo = tone(hz/2, duration)
    hi = tone(2*hz, duration)
    harmonics = superpose(lo, hi, 0.5, 0.5)
    a = tone(hz, duration)
    return superpose(harmonics, a, 0.5, 0.5)

while not stdio.isEmpty():
    pitch = stdio.readInt()
    duration = stdio.readFloat()
    a = note(pitch, duration)
    stdaudio.playSamples(a)
stdaudio.wait()
```

hz	*frequency*
lo[]	*lower harmonic*
hi[]	*upper harmonic*
h[]	*combined harmonics*
a[]	*pure tone*

This program reads sound samples, embellishes the sounds by adding harmonics to create a more realistic tone than Program *1.5.8, and plays the resulting sound to standard audio.*

```
% python playthattunedeluxe.py < elise.txt
```

```
% more elise.txt
7 .125  6 .125
7 .125  6 .125  7 .125
2 .125  5 .125  3 .125
0 .25
```

These tasks are all amenable to implementation as functions, which depend on one another. Each function is well defined and straightforward to implement. All of them (and `stdaudio`) represent sound as a series of discrete values kept in an array, corresponding to sampling a sound wave at 44,100 samples per second.

Up to this point, our use of functions has been somewhat of a notational convenience. For example, the control flow in Program 2.1.1, Program 2.1.2, and Program 2.1.3 is simple—each function is called in just one place in the code. By contrast, Program 2.1.4 is a convincing example of the effectiveness of defining functions to organize a computation because each function is called multiple times. For example, as illustrated in the figure below, the function `note()` calls the function `tone()` three times and the function `superpose()` twice. Without functions, we would need multiple copies of the code in `tone()` and `superpose()`; with functions, we can deal directly with concepts close to the application. Like loops, functions have a simple but profound effect: one sequence of statements (those in the function definition) is executed multiple times during the execution of our program—once for each time the function is called in the control flow in the global code.

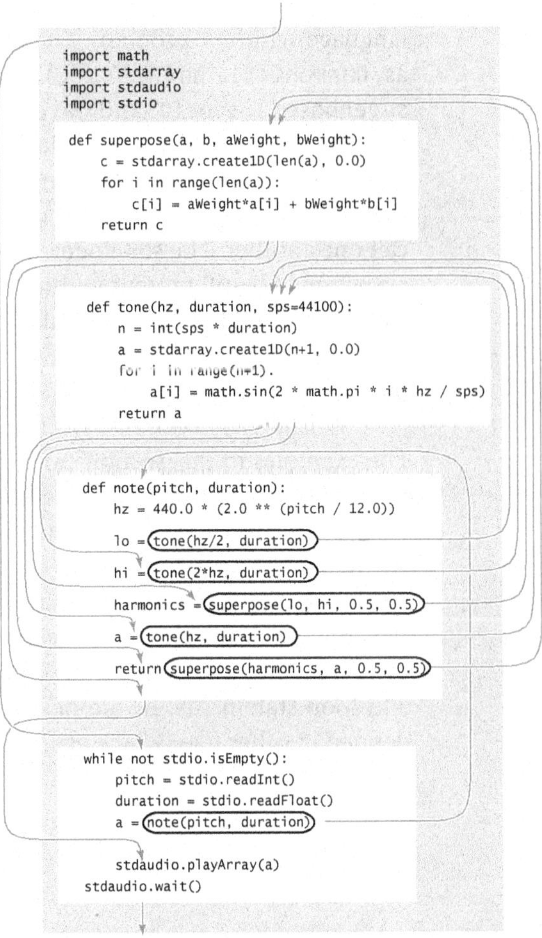

Flow of control among several functions

FUNCTIONS ARE IMPORTANT BECAUSE THEY GIVE us the ability to *extend* the Python language within a program. Having implemented and debugged functions such as `harmonic()`, `pdf()`, `cdf()`, `mean()`, `exchange()`, `shuffle()`, `isPrime()`, `superpose()`, `tone()`, and `note()`, we can use them almost as if they were built into Python. The flexibility to do so opens up a whole new world of programming. Before, you were safe in thinking about a Python program as a sequence of statements. Now you need to think of a Python program as a *set of functions* that can call one another. The statement-to-statement control flow to which you have been accustomed is still present within functions, but programs have a higher-level control flow defined by function calls and returns. This ability enables you to think in terms of operations called for by the application, not just the operations that are built into Python.

Whenever you can clearly separate tasks within a computation, you should do so. The examples in this section (and the programs throughout the rest of the book) clearly illustrate the benefits of adhering to this maxim. With functions, we can

- Divide a long sequence of statements into independent parts.
- Reuse code without having to copy it.
- Work with higher-level concepts (such as sound waves).

This point of view leads to code that is easier to understand, maintain, and debug compared to a long program composed solely of Python assignment, conditional, and loop statements. In the next section, we discuss the idea of using functions defined in other files, which again takes us to another level of programming.

Q&A

Q. Can I use the statement `return` in a function without specifying a value?

A. Yes. Technically, it returns the `None` object, which is the sole value of the type `NoneType`.

Q. What happens if a function has one control flow that leads to a `return` statement that returns a value but another control flow that reaches the end of the function body?

A. It would be poor style to define such a function, because doing so would place a severe burden on the function's callers: the callers would need to know under which circumstances the function returns a value, and under which circumstances it returns `None`.

Q. What happens if I compose code in the body of a function that appears after the `return` statement?

A. Once a `return` statement is reached, control returns to the caller. So any code in the body of a function that appears after a `return` statement is useless; it is never executed. In Python, it is poor style, but not illegal to define such a function.

Q. What happens if I define two functions with the same name (but possibly a different number of arguments) in the same `.py` file?

A. This is known as *function overloading*, which is embraced by many programming languages. Python, however, is not one of those languages: the second function definition will overwrite the first one. You can often achieve the same effect by using default arguments.

Q. What happens if I define two functions with the same name in different files?

A. That is fine. For example, it would be good design to have a function named `pdf()` in `gauss.py` that computes the Gaussian probability density function and another function named `pdf()` in `cauchy.py` that computes the Cauchy probability density function. In Section 2.2 you will learn how to call functions defined in different `.py` files.

Q. Can a function change the object to which a parameter variable is bound?

A. Yes, you can use a parameter variable on the left side of an assignment statement. However, many Python programmers consider it poor style to do so. Note that such an assignment statement has no effect in the client.

Q. The issue with side effects and mutable objects is complicated. Is it really all that important?

A. Yes. Properly controlling side effects is one of a programmer's most important tasks in large systems. Taking the time to be sure that you understand the difference between passing arrays (which are mutable) and passing integers, floats, booleans, and strings (which are immutable) will certainly be worthwhile. The very same mechanisms are used for all other types of data, as you will learn in CHAPTER 3.

Q. How can I arrange to pass an array to a function in such a way that the function cannot change the elements in the array?

A. There is no direct way to do so. In SECTION 3.3 you will see how to achieve the same effect by building a *wrapper* data type and passing an object of that type instead. You will also see how to use Python's built-in `tuple` data type, which represents an immutable sequence of objects.

Q. Can I use a mutable object as a default value for an optional argument?

A. Yes, but it may lead to unexpected behavior. Python evaluates a default value only once, when the function is defined (not each time the function is called). So, if the body of a function modifies a default value, subsequent function calls will use the modified value. Similar difficulties arise if you initialize the default value by calling an impure function. For example, after Python executes the code fragment

```
def append(a=[], x=random.random()):
    a += [x]
    return a

b = append()
c = append()
```

`b[]` and `c[]` are aliases for the same array of length 2 (not 1), which contains one float repeated twice (instead of two different floats).

Exercises

2.1.1 Compose a function `max3()` that takes three `int` or `float` arguments and returns the largest one.

2.1.2 Compose a function `odd()` that takes three `bool` arguments and returns `True` if an odd number of arguments are `True`, and `False` otherwise.

2.1.3 Compose a function `majority()` that takes three `bool` arguments and returns `True` if at least two of the arguments are `True`, and `False` otherwise. Do not use an `if` statement.

2.1.4 Compose a function `areTriangular()` that takes three numbers as arguments and returns `True` if they could be lengths of the sides of a triangle (none of them is greater than or equal to the sum of the other two), and `False` otherwise.

2.1.5 Compose a function `sigmoid()` that takes a `float` argument `x` and returns the `float` obtained from the formula $1 / (1+e^{-x})$.

2.1.6 Compose a function `lg()` that takes an integer `n` as an argument and returns the base-2 logarithm of `n`. You may use Python's `math` module.

2.1.7 Compose a function `lg()` that takes an integer `n` as an argument and returns the largest integer not larger than the base-2 logarithm of `n`. Do *not* use the `math` module.

2.1.8 Compose a function `signum()` that takes a `float` argument `n` and returns `-1` if `n` is less than `0`, `0` if `n` is equal to `0`, and `+1` if `n` is greater than `0`.

2.1.9 Consider this function `duplicate()`:

```
def duplicate(s):
    t = s + s
```

What does the following code fragment write?

```
s = 'Hello'
s = duplicate(s)
t = 'Bye'
t = duplicate(duplicate(duplicate(t)))
stdio.writeln(s + t)
```

2.1.10 Consider this function cube():

```
def cube(i):
    i = i * i * i
```

How many times is the following while loop iterated?

```
i = 0
while i < 1000:
    cube(i)
    i += 1
```

Solution: Just 1,000 times. A call to cube() has no effect on the client code. It changes the parameter variable i, but that change has no effect on the variable i in the while loop, which is a different variable. If you replace the call to cube(i) with the statement i = i * i * i (maybe that was what you were thinking), then the loop is iterated five times, with i taking on the values 0, 1, 2, 9, and 730 at the beginning of the five iterations.

2.1.11 What does the following code fragment write?

```
for i in range(5):
    stdio.write(i)
for j in range(5):
    stdio.write(i)
```

Solution: 0123444444. Note that the second call to stdio.write() uses i, not j. Unlike analogous loops in many other programming languages, when the first for loop terminates, the variable i is 4 and it remains in scope.

2.1.12 The following *checksum* formula is widely used by banks and credit card companies to validate legal account numbers:

$$d_0 + f(d_1) + d_2 + f(d_3) + d_4 + f(d_5) + \ldots = 0 \pmod{10}$$

The d_i are the decimal digits of the account number and $f(d)$ is the sum of the decimal digits of $2d$ (for example, $f(7) = 5$ because $2 \times 7 = 14$ and $1 + 4 = 5$). For example 17327 is valid because $1 + 5 + 3 + 4 + 7 = 20$, which is a multiple of 10.

Implement the function f and compose a program to take a 10-digit integer as a command-line argument and write a valid 11-digit number with the given integer as its first 10 digits and the checksum as the last digit.

2.1.13 Given two stars with angles of declination and right ascension (d_1, a_1) and (d_2, a_2), respectively, the angle they subtend is given by the formula

$$2 \arcsin((\sin^2(d/2) + \cos(d_1)\cos(d_2)\sin^2(a/2))^{1/2}),$$

where a_1 and a_2 are angles between -180 and 180 degrees, d_1 and d_2 are angles between -90 and 90 degrees, $a = a_2 - a_1$, and $d = d_2 - d_1$. Compose a program to take the declination and right ascension of two stars as command-line arguments and write the angle they subtend. *Hint*: Be careful about converting from degrees to radians.

2.1.14 Compose a `readBool2D()` function that reads a two-dimensional matrix of 0 and 1 values (with dimensions) into an array of booleans.

Solution: The body of the function is virtually the same as for the corresponding function given in the table in the text for two-dimensional arrays of floats:

```
def readBool2D():
    m = stdio.readInt()
    n = stdio.readInt()
    a = stdarray.create2D(m, n, False)
    for i in range(m):
        for j in range(n):
            a[i][j] = stdio.readBool()
    return a
```

2.1.15 Compose a function that takes an array `a[]` of strictly positive floats as its argument and rescales the array so that each element is between 0 and 1 (by subtracting the minimum value from each element and then dividing each element by the difference between the minimum and maximum values). Use the built-in `max()` and `min()` functions.

2.1.16 Compose a function `histogram()` that takes an array `a[]` of integers and an integer `m` as arguments and returns an array of length `m` whose `i`th element is the number of times the integer `i` appears in the argument array. Assume that the values in `a[]` are all between `0` and `m-1`, so that the sum of the values in the returned array should be equal to `len(a)`.

2.1.17 Assemble code fragments in this section and in Section 1.4 to develop a program that takes an integer `n` from the command line and writes `n` five-card hands, separated by blank lines, drawn from a randomly shuffled card deck, one card per line using card names like `Ace of Clubs`.

2.1.18 Compose a function `multiply()` that takes two square matrices of the same dimension as arguments and returns their product (another square matrix of that same dimension). *Extra credit*: Make your program work whenever the number of columns in the first matrix is equal to the number of rows in the second matrix.

2.1.19 Compose a function `any()` that takes an array of booleans as an argument and returns `True` if *any* of the elements in the array is `True`, and `False` otherwise. Compose a function `all()` that takes an array of booleans as an argument and returns `True` if *all* of the elements in the array are `True`, and `False` otherwise. Note that `all()` and `any()` are built-in Python functions; the goal of this exercise is to understand them better by creating your own versions.

2.1.20 Develop a version of `getCoupon()` that better models the situation when one of the n coupons is rare: choose one value at random, return that value with probability $1/(1000n)$, and return all other values with equal probability. *Extra credit*: How does this change affect the average value of the coupon collector function?

2.1.21 Modify `playthattune.py` to add harmonics two octaves away from each note, with half the weight of the one-octave harmonics.

Creative Exercises

2.1.22 *Birthday problem.* Compose a program with appropriate functions for studying the birthday problem (see Exercise 1.4.35).

2.1.23 *Euler's totient function.* Euler's totient function is an important function in number theory: $\varphi(n)$ is defined as the number of positive integers less than or equal to n that are relatively prime with n (no factors in common with n other than 1). Compose a function that takes an integer argument n and returns $\varphi(n)$. Include global code that takes an integer from the command line, calls the function, and writes the result.

2.1.24 *Harmonic numbers.* Create a program `harmonic.py` that defines three functions `harmonic()`, `harmonicSmall()`, and `harmonicLarge()` for computing the harmonic numbers. The `harmonicSmall()` function should just compute the sum (as in Program 2.1.1), the `harmonicLarge()` function should use the approximation $H_n = \log_e(n) + \gamma + 1/(2n) - 1/(12n^2) + 1/(120n^4)$ (the number $\gamma = 0.577215664901532...$ is known as *Euler's constant*), and the `harmonic()` function should call `harmonicSmall()` for $n < 100$ and `harmonicLarge()` otherwise.

2.1.25 *Gaussian random values.* Experiment with the following function for generating random variables from the Gaussian distribution, which is based on generating a random point in the unit circle and using a form of the Box-Muller formula (see Exercise 1.2.24).

```
def gaussian():
    r = 0.0
    while (r >= 1.0) or (r == 0.0):
        x = -1.0  + 2.0 * random.random()
        y = -1.0  + 2.0 * random.random()
        r = x*x + y*y
    return x * math.sqrt(-2.0 * math.log(r) / r)
```

Take a command-line argument `n` and generate `n` random numbers, using an array `a[]` of 20 integers to count the numbers generated that fall between `i*.05` and `(i+1)*.05` for `i` from 0 to 19. Then use `stddraw` to plot the values and to compare your result with the normal bell curve. *Remark*: This approach is faster and more accurate than the one described in Exercise 1.2.24. Although it involves a loop, the loop is executed only 4 / π (about 1.273) times on average. This reduces the overall expected number of calls to transcendental functions.

2.1.26 *Binary search.* A general function that we study in detail in Section 4.2 is effective for computing the inverse of a cumulative distribution function like `cdf()`. Such functions are continuous and nondecreasing from (0,0) to (1,1). To find the value x_0 for which $f(x_0) = y_0$, check the value of $f(0.5)$. If it is greater than y_0, then x_0 must be between 0 and 0.5; otherwise, it must be between 0.5 and 1. Either way, we halve the length of the interval known to contain x_0. Iterating, we can compute x_0 to within a given tolerance. Add a function `cdfInverse()` to `gauss.py` that uses binary search to compute the inverse. Change the global code to take a number p between 0 and 100 as a third command-line argument and write the minimum score that a student would need to be in the top p percent of students taking the SAT in a year when the mean and standard deviation were the first two command-line arguments.

2.1.27 *Black-Scholes option valuation.* The Black-Scholes formula supplies the theoretical value of a European call option on a stock that pays no dividends, given the current stock price s, the exercise price x, the continuously compounded risk-free interest rate r, the standard deviation σ of the stock's return (volatility), and the time (in years) to maturity t. The value is given by the formula $s\,\Phi(a) - x e^{-rt}\Phi(b)$, where $\Phi(z)$ is the Gaussian cumulative distribution function, $a = (\ln(s/x) + (r + \sigma^2/2)\,t) / (\sigma\sqrt{t})$, and $b = a - \sigma\sqrt{t}$. Compose a program that takes `s`, `x`, `r`, `sigma`, and `t` from the command line and writes the Black-Scholes value.

2.1.28 *Implied volatility.* Typically the volatility is the unknown value in the Black-Scholes formula. Compose a program that reads `s`, `x`, `r`, `t`, and the current price of the European call option from the command line and uses binary search (see Exercise 2.1.26) to compute σ.

2.1.29 *Horner's method.* Compose a program `horner.py` with a function `evaluate(x, a)` that evaluates the polynomial $a(x)$ whose coefficients are the elements in the array `a[]`:

$$a_0 + a_1x^1 + a_2x^2 + \ldots + a_{n-2}x^{n-2} + a_{n-1}x^{n-1}$$

Use *Horner's method*, an efficient way to perform the computations that is suggested by the following parenthesization:

$$a_0 + x\,(a_1 + x\,(a_2 + \ldots + x\,(a_{n-2} + x a_{n-1}) \ldots))$$

Then compose a function `exp()` that calls `evaluate()` to compute an approximation to e^x, using the first n terms of the Taylor series expansion $e^x = 1 + x + x^2/2! + x^3/3! + \ldots$. Take an argument `x` from the command line, and compare your result against that computed by `math.exp(x)`.

2.1.30 *Benford's law.* The American astronomer Simon Newcomb observed a quirk in a book that compiled logarithm tables: the beginning pages were much grubbier than the ending pages. He suspected that scientists performed more computations with numbers starting with 1 than with 8 or 9, and postulated the first digit law, which says that under general circumstances, the leading digit is much more likely to be 1 (roughly 30%) than 9 (less than 4%). This phenomenon is known as *Benford's law* and is now often used as a statistical test. For example, IRS forensic accountants rely on it to discover tax fraud. Compose a program that reads in a sequence of integers from standard input and tabulates the number of times each of the digits 1–9 is the leading digit, breaking the computation into a set of appropriate functions. Use your program to test the law on some tables of information from your computer or from the web. Then, compose a program to foil the IRS by generating random amounts from $1.00 to $1,000.00 with the same distribution that you observed.

2.1.31 *Binomial distribution.* Compose a function `binomial()` that accepts an integer `n`, an integer `k`, and a float `p`, and computes the probability of obtaining exactly `k` heads in `n` biased coin flips (heads with probability `p`) using the formula

$$f(k, n, p) = p^k(1-p)^{n-k}\, n!/(k!(n-k)!)$$

Hint: To avoid computing with huge integers, compute $x = \ln f(k, n, p)$ and then return e^x. In the global code, take `n` and `p` from the command line and check that the sum over all values of `k` between 0 and `n` is (approximately) 1. Also, compare every value computed with the normal approximation

$$f(k, n, p) \;\approx\; \Phi(k + 1/2, np, \sqrt{np(1-p)}) \;-\; \Phi(k - 1/2, np, \sqrt{np(1-p)})$$

2.1.32 *Coupon collecting from a binomial distribution.* Compose a version of `getCoupon()` that uses `binomial()` from the previous exercise to return coupon values according to the binomial distribution with $p = 1/2$. *Hint*: Generate a uniformly distributed random number x between 0 and 1, then return the smallest value of k for which the sum of $f(j, n, p)$ for all $j < k$ exceeds x. *Extra credit*: Develop a hypothesis for describing the behavior of the coupon collector function under this assumption.

2.1.33 *Chords.* Compose a version of `playthattunedeluxe.py` that can handle songs with chords (three or more different notes, including harmonics). Develop an input format that allows you to specify different durations for each chord and different amplitude weights for each note within a chord. Create test files that exercise your program with various chords and harmonics, and create a version of *Für Elise* that uses them.

0
1
2
3
4
5
6
7
8
9

2.1.34 *Postal barcodes.* The barcode used by the U.S. Postal System to route mail is defined as follows: Each decimal digit in the ZIP code is encoded using a sequence of three half-height and two full-height bars. The barcode starts and ends with a full-height bar (the guard rail) and includes a checksum digit (after the five-digit ZIP code or ZIP+4), computed by summing up the original digits modulo 10. Define the following functions:

- Draw a half-height or full-height bar on `stddraw`.
- Given a digit, draw its sequence of bars.
- Compute the checksum digit.

Also define global code that reads in a five- (or nine-) digit ZIP code as the command-line argument and draws the corresponding postal barcode.

2.1.35 *Calendar.* Compose a program `cal.py` that takes two command-line arguments `m` and `y` and writes the monthly calendar for the `m`th month of year `y`, as in this example:

```
% python cal.py 2 2015
February 2015
 S  M Tu  W Th  F  S
 1  2  3  4  5  6  7
 8  9 10 11 12 13 14
15 16 17 18 19 20 21
22 23 24 25 26 27 28
```

Hint: See `leapyear.py` (PROGRAM 1.2.5) and EXERCISE 1.2.26.

2.1.36 *Fourier spikes.* Compose a program that takes a command-line argument n and plots the function

$$(\cos(t) + \cos(2t) + \cos(3t) + \ldots + \cos(Nt)) / N$$

for 500 equally spaced samples of t from -10 to 10 (in radians). Run your program for $n = 5$ and $n = 500$. *Note*: You will observe that the sum converges to a spike (0 everywhere except a single value). This property is the basis for a proof that *any* smooth function can be expressed as a sum of sinusoids.

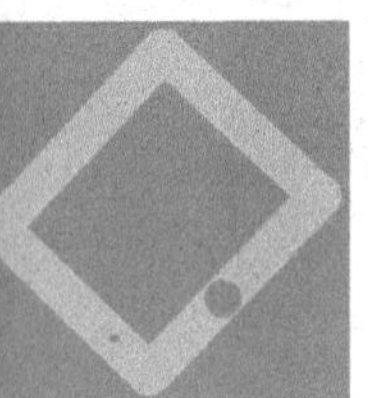

2.2 Modules and Clients

EACH PROGRAM THAT YOU HAVE WRITTEN so far consists of Python code that resides in a single .py file. For large programs, keeping all the code in a single file is restrictive and unnecessary. Fortunately, it is easy in Python to call a function that is defined in another file. This ability has two important consequences.

Programs in this section

First, it enables *code reuse*. One program can use code that is already written and debugged, not by copying the code, but just by calling it. This ability to define code that can be reused is an essential part of modern programming. It amounts to extending Python—you can define and use your own set of operations on data.

Second, it enables *modular programming*. You can not only divide a program into functions, as just described in SECTION 2.1, but also keep them in different files, grouped together according to the needs of the application. Modular programming is important because it allows us to independently compose and debug parts of big programs one piece at a time, leaving each finished piece in its own file for later use without having to worry about its details again. We compose modules of functions for use by any other program, keeping each module in its own file and using its functions in any other program. Python's math module and the booksite std* modules for input/output are examples that you have already used. More important, you will soon see that it is very easy to define modules of your own. The ability to define modules and then use them in multiple programs is a critical ingredient in our ability to build programs to address complex tasks.

Having just moved in SECTION 2.1 from thinking of a Python program as a sequence of statements to thinking of a Python program as a set of *functions* (and global code), you will be ready after this section to think of a Python program as a set of *files*, each of which is an independent module consisting of a set of functions. Since each function can call a function in another module, all of your code can interact as a network of functions that call one another, grouped together in modules. With this capability, you can start to think about managing complexity when programming by breaking up programming tasks into modules that can be implemented and tested independently.

Using functions in other programs To refer to a function in one Python program that is defined in another, we use the same mechanism that we have been using to call functions in our `std*` modules and Python's `math` and `random` modules. In this section, we describe this basic Python language mechanism. To do so, we distinguish two types of Python programs:

- A *module* contains functions that are available for use by other programs.
- A *client* is a program that makes use of a function in a module.

A program can be both a module and a client: the terminology is just with respect to any particular function.

There are five (simple) steps that you need to take to create and use a module: import the module in the client, qualify function calls in the client, compose a test client for the module, eliminate global code in the module, and make the module accessible to the client. Next, we discuss each of these steps in turn. In this discussion, we use the notation *`module.py`* to refer to the name of the module and *`client.py`* to refer to the name of the client. In the following discussion, we illustrate the complete process with the module `gaussian.py` (Program 2.2.1), which is a modularized version of `gauss.py` (Program 2.1.2) for computing the Gaussian distribution functions, and the client `gaussiantable.py` (Program 2.2.2), which uses the module to compute and write a table of values.

In the client: import the module. To use a module, place the statement `import` *`module`* (note the absence of the `.py` extension) in *`client`*`.py`. The purpose of the `import` statement is to inform Python that the code in the client might call one or more of the functions defined in *`module`*`.py`. In our example, the client `gaussiantable.py` contains the statement `import gaussian`; now it can call any function defined in the module `gaussian.py`. In most Python code (including all the programs in the book), `import` statements appear at the beginning of a program, with all standard Python modules appearing before all user-defined modules.

In the client: qualify function calls to the module. To call a function that is defined in a module *`module`*`.py` in any other Python (client) program, type the module name *`module`* followed by the dot operator (`.`) and the function name. You are already accustomed to doing this with function calls such as `stdio.writeln()` and `math.sqrt()`. In our example, the client `gaussiantable.py` uses the function call `gaussian.cdf(score, mu, sigma)` to call the `cdf()` function that is defined in the module `gaussian.py`.

Program 2.2.1 Gaussian functions module (gaussian.py)

```
import math
import sys
import stdio

def pdf(x, mu=0.0, sigma=1.0):
    x = float(x - mu) / sigma
    return math.exp(-x*x/2.0) / math.sqrt(2.0*math.pi) / sigma

def cdf(z, mu=0.0, sigma=1.0):
    z = float(z - mu) / sigma
    if z < -8.0: return 0.0
    if z > +8.0: return 1.0
    total = 0.0
    term = z
    i = 3
    while total != total + term:
        total += term
        term *= z * z / i
        i += 2
    return 0.5 + total * pdf(z)

def main():
    z     = float(sys.argv[1])
    mu    = float(sys.argv[2])
    sigma = float(sys.argv[3])
    stdio.writeln(cdf(z, mu, sigma))

if __name__ == '__main__': main()
```

```
% python gaussian.py  820 1019 209
0.17050966869132106
% python gaussian.py 1500 1019 209
0.9893164837383885
% python gaussian.py 1500 1025 231
0.9801220907365491
```

This program repackages the pdf() *and* cdf() *functions from* gauss.py *(Program 2.1.2) into a module that is usable by client code that resides in another file, such as* gaussiantable.py *(Program 2.2.2). It also defines a* main() *test client that accepts floats* z*,* mu*, and* sigma *as command-line arguments and uses them to test the* pdf() *and* cdf() *functions.*

Program 2.2.2 Sample Gaussian client (gaussiantable.py)

```
import sys
import stdio
import gaussian

mu       = float(sys.argv[1])
sigma    = float(sys.argv[2])

for score in range(400, 1600+1, 100):
    percent = gaussian.cdf(score, mu, sigma)
    stdio.writef('%4d  %.4f\n', score, percent)
```

This client of `gaussian` (and `sys` and `stdio`) writes a table of the percentage of students scoring below certain scores on the SAT, assuming the test scores obey a Gaussian distribution with a given mean and standard deviation. It illustrates how to call functions in other modules: `import` the module and then call any functions within the module by prepending the module name and a period before the function name. In particular, this code calls the `cdf()` function in `gaussian.py` (Program 2.2.1).

```
% python gaussiantable.py 1019 209
 400  0.0015
 500  0.0065
 600  0.0225
 700  0.0635
 800  0.1474
 900  0.2845
1000  0.4638
1100  0.6508
1200  0.8068
1300  0.9106
1400  0.9658
1500  0.9893
1600  0.9973
```

In the module: compose a test client. An excellent programming practice that good programmers have adhered to for decades is to compose code to test the functions in a module and to *include that code within that module.* A long-standing tradition is to put this code in a function named `main()`. In our example, the module `gaussian.py` contains a `main()` function that takes three command-line arguments, calls the functions in the module, and writes the results to standard output.

In the module: eliminate arbitrary global code. Python's `import` statement executes all global code that appears in the imported module (including function definitions and arbitrary global code). So, we cannot leave arbitrary global code in a module (such as test code that writes output) because Python will execute it every time the module is imported. Instead, we put our test code in a `main()` function, as just described. Now, we can arrange for Python to call `main()` when we execute the program from the command line (and only then), using the following incantation:

```
if __name__ == '__main__': main()
```

Informally, this code tells Python that if this `.py` file is being executed directly by the `python` command (and not via an `import` statement), then call `main()`. The effect is that the `main()` function defined in *`module`*`.py` is executed when you are debugging the module by issuing the command `python` *`module`*`.py`, but it is *not* executed during the `import` process when you are using the module in a client.

Make the module accessible to the client. Python needs to be able to find the file *`module`*`.py` when it processes the `import` *`module`* statement in *`client`*`.py`. When a module is not a built-in or a standard Python module, the first place it looks is in the same directory as *`client`*`.py`. So, the simplest way for you to proceed is to place the client and the module in the same directory. The Q&A at the end of this section describes an alternative approach.

IN SUMMARY, THE FUNCTIONS IN THE module `gaussian.py` are available for use by any other program via an `import gaussian` statement. In contrast, the client `gaussiantable.py` contains arbitrary global code and is not intended for use by other programs—it is code that might be typed in interactive mode. We use the term *script* to refer to such code. There is not much difference between a module and a script: Python programmers often begin by composing a script and ultimately *modularize* it by removing arbitrary global code.

Abbreviation alert. From this point forward we reserve the term *module* to refer to a `.py` file structured so that its features can be reused in other Python programs (so it does not contain any arbitrary global code) and the term *script* to refer to a `.py` file not intended for reuse (because it contains arbitrary global code), although we most often refer to either as a *program*.

Modular programming. The potential effect of programming by defining multiple files, each an independent module with multiple functions, is another profound change in our programming style. Generally, we refer to this approach as *modular programming*. We independently develop and debug functions for an application and then utilize them at any later time. In this section, we will consider numerous illustrative examples to help you get used to the idea.

If you think of each program that you compose as something that you might want to make use of later, you will soon find yourself with all sorts of useful tools. Modular programming allows us to view every solution to a computational problem that we may develop as adding value to our computational environment.

For example, suppose that you need to evaluate the Gaussian cumulative distribution function for some future application. Why not just cut and paste the code that implements `cdf()` from our original `gauss.py`? That would work, but would leave you with two copies of the code, making it more difficult to maintain. If you later want to fix or improve the code, you would need to do so in both copies. Instead, you can modularize your code, as we just did to turn `gauss.py` (Program 2.1.2) into `gaussian.py` (Program 2.2.1). Then you can use any function in your module by adding an `import` *`module`* statement at the beginning and prepending "*`module.`*" to any function call.

The impact of modular programming on the flow of control of Python program is profound, and worth reflecting upon. Even for our simple example (illustrated on the next page), the flow of control moves from our `gaussiantable.py` script to `cdf()` and then `pdf()` in `gaussian.py` to `exp()` and then to `sqrt()` in Python's `math` module and then back to `pdf()` and then to `cdf()` in `gaussian.py` and finally back to `gaussiantable.py` again. In a typical modular programming application, the flow of control meanders among several modules, as you will see in examples later in this section. Each module is useful for and is used by many other modules and scripts.

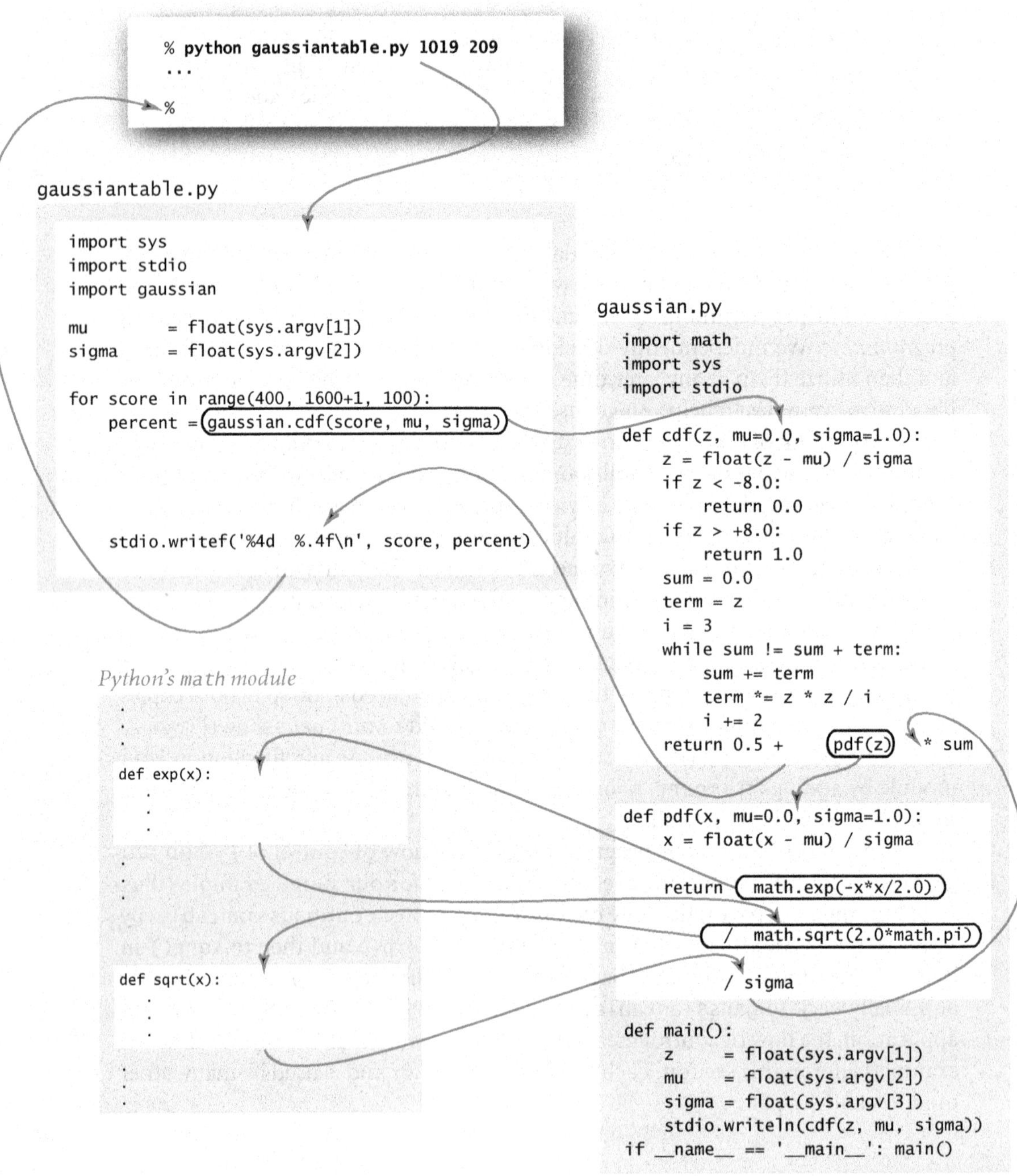

% python gaussiantable.py 1019 209
...
%
gaussiantable.py
import sys
import stdio
import gaussian
mu = float(sys.argv[1])
sigma = float(sys.argv[2])
for score in range(400, 1600+1, 100):
percent = gaussian.cdf(score, mu, sigma)
stdio.writef('%4d %.4f\n', score, percent)
gaussian.py
import math
import sys
import stdio
def cdf(z, mu=0.0, sigma=1.0):
z = float(z - mu) / sigma
if z < -8.0:
return 0.0
if z > +8.0:
return 1.0
sum = 0.0
term = z
i = 3
while sum != sum + term:
sum += term
term *= z * z / i
i += 2
return 0.5 + pdf(z) * sum
def pdf(x, mu=0.0, sigma=1.0):
x = float(x - mu) / sigma
return math.exp(-x*x/2.0)
/ math.sqrt(2.0*math.pi)
/ sigma
def main():
z = float(sys.argv[1])
mu = float(sys.argv[2])
sigma = float(sys.argv[3])
stdio.writeln(cdf(z, mu, sigma))
if __name__ == '__main__': main()
Python's math module
def exp(x):
def sqrt(x):

Flow of control in a modular program

THE KEY BENEFIT OF MODULAR PROGRAMMING, and the reason that every programmer should practice it, is that encourages us to break a computation up into smaller parts that can be individually debugged and tested. Generally, you should compose *every* program by identifying a reasonable way to divide the computation into separate parts of a manageable size and implement each part as if someone will want to use it later. This mindset yields important and fruitful benefits, even for small programs. Most frequently, that someone will be you, and you will have yourself to thank for saving the effort of re-composing and re-debugging code.

In this book, we modularize any program containing a function that we want to reuse. Our implementations and uses of them will soon proliferate, so having them properly packaged for later use is a worthy goal.

Modular programming abstractions One of the most important characteristics of programming in Python is that many, many functions have been predefined for you, in literally thousands of Python modules that are available for your use. In this section, however, we focus on the even more important idea that we can build *user-defined modules*, which are nothing more than files that each contain a set of related functions for use by other programs. No Python module (or library of modules) can contain all the functions that we might need for a given computation, so this ability is a crucial step in addressing complex programming applications. To manage the process, we work with a time-honored approach that gives us some flexibility during development. Next, we describe three abstractions that serve as the basis of that approach.

Implementations. We use the generic term *implementation* to describe code that implements a set of functions that are intended for reuse. A Python module is an implementation: we refer to the set of functions collectively with a name `module` and keep them in a file `module.py`. For example, as you have seen, `gaussian.py` is an implementation. Choosing an appropriate set of functions to group together and implement is a design art and one of the key challenges in developing a large program. The guiding principle in module design is to *provide to clients the functions that they need and no others.* A module with a huge number of functions may be a burden to implement; a module that is lacking important functions may be unnecessarily inconvenient for clients. We have already seen examples of this principle. For example, Python's `math` module does not contain functions for secant, cosecant, and cotangent because it is so easy to use `math.sin()`, `math.cos()`, and `math.tan()` to compute them.

Clients. We use the generic term *client* to refer to a program that makes use of an implementation. We say that a Python program (a script or a module) that calls a function that is defined in a file named *module*.py is a client of *module*. For example, as you have seen, gaussiantable.py is a client of gaussian.py. Typically, a module will have multiple clients—the programs that you have composed that call math.sqrt() all are clients of Python's math module. When you implement a new module, you need to have a very clear of idea of what it is going to do for its clients.

Application programming interfaces (APIs). Programmers normally think in terms of a *contract* between the client and the implementation that is a clear specification of what the implementation is to do. This approach enables code reuse. You have been able to compose programs that are clients of math and random and other standard Python modules because of an informal contract (an English-language description of what they are supposed to do) along with a precise specification of the signatures of the functions that are available for use. Collectively, this information is known as an *application programming interface (API)*. The same mechanism is effective for user-defined modules. The API allows any client to use the module without having to examine the code that defines the module, just as you have been doing with math and random. When we compose a new module, we always provide an API. For example, the API for our gaussian.py module is shown at the top of the next page.

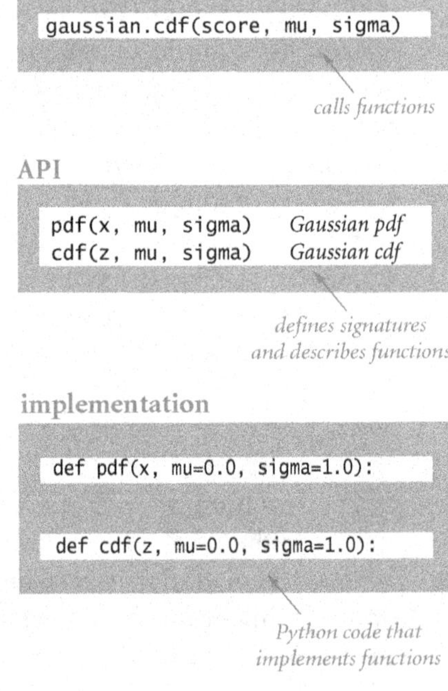

Modular programming abstractions

How much information should an API contain? This is a gray area and a hotly debated issue among programmers and computer-science educators. We might try to put as much information as possible in the API, but (as with any contract!) there are limits to the amount of information that we can productively include. In this book, we stick to a principle that parallels our guiding design principle: *provide to client programmers the information they need and no more.* Doing so gives us

function call	*description*
`gaussian.pdf(x, mu, sigma)`	*Gaussian probability density function* $\phi(x, \mu, \sigma)$
`gaussian.cdf(z, mu, sigma)`	*Gaussian cumulative distribution function* $\Phi(x, \mu, \sigma)$

Note: The default value for `mu` *is* `0.0` *and for* `sigma` *is* `1.0`.

API for our `gaussian` *module*

vastly more flexibility than the alternative of providing detailed information about implementations. Indeed, any extra information amounts to implicitly extending the contract, which is undesirable.

Private functions. Sometimes we wish to define in a module a helper function that is not intended to be called directly by clients. We refer to such a function as a *private function.* By convention, Python programmers use an underscore as the first character in the name of a private function. For example, the following is an alternative implementation of the `pdf()` function from `gaussian.py` that calls the private function `_phi()`:

```
def _phi(x):
    return math.exp(-x*x/2.0) / math.sqrt(2*math.pi)

def pdf(x, mu=0.0, sigma=1.0):
    return _phi(float((x - mu) / sigma)) / sigma
```

We do not include private functions in APIs because they are not part of the contract between clients and implementations. Indeed, a leading underscore in the name of a function signals clients *not* to call the function explicitly. (Regrettably, Python has no mechanism for enforcing this convention.)

Libraries. A *library* is a collection of related modules. For example, Python has a standard library (which includes the modules `random` and `math`) and many extension libraries (such as *NumPy* for scientific computing and *Pygame* for graphics and sound). Also, for this book, we provide a booksite library (which includes the modules `stdio` and `stddraw`).We reveal information about modules and libraries that might be of interest to you throughout the book. After you gain more experience with Python programming, you will be better prepared to cope with the range and scope of libraries available to you.

Documentation. The APIs of all standard, extension, and booksite modules are available through the built-in `help()` function in interactive Python. As illustrated below, all you need to do is type `python` (to enter interactive Python), then enter the statement `import module` (to load the module), then type `help(module)` to see the API for `module`. The APIs of the standard and extension Python modules also are available in another form through the online Python documentation; see the booksite for details. The APIs of some standard Python modules and some of our booksite modules were discussed in previous sections of this book. Specifically, Section 1.5 provides the APIs of the `stdio`, `stddraw`, and `stdaudio` modules, and Section 1.4 provides part of the API of the `stdarray` module.

```
% python
...
>>> import stddraw
>>> help(stddraw)

Help on module stddraw:

NAME
    stddraw - stddraw.py

FILE
    .../stddraw.py

DESCRIPTION
    The stddraw module defines functions that allow the user
    to create a drawing. A drawing appears on the canvas.
    The canvas appears in the window.

FUNCTIONS
    circle(x, y, r)
        Draw a circle of radius r centered at (x, y).

    filledCircle(x, y, r)
        Draw a filled circle of radius r centered at (x, y).

    filledPolygon(x, y)
        Draw a filled polygon with coordinates (x[i], y[i]).
...
```

Accessing an API in interactive Python

Every Python module and every module that we compose is an implementation of some API, but no API is of any use without some implementation, and no implementation is of any use without a client. Our goal when developing an implementation is to honor the terms of the contract. Often, there are many ways to do so. The idea of separating client code from implementation code through the API gives us the freedom to substitute new and improved implementations. This is a powerful idea that has served programmers well for decades.

Next, we present the APIs for our `stdrandom` module (for generating random numbers), our `stdarray` module (for one- and two-dimensional arrays), and our `stdstats` module (for statistical calculations). We discuss implementations of some of the functions in the modules to illustrate how you might implement your own module. However, we stop short of exhibiting all of the implementations because there is no reason to do so, just as there is no reason to show you the implementations of all the functions in Python's `math` module. We also describe some interesting clients of these modules. Our purpose in considering all of these modules is twofold. First, they provide an enriched programming environment for your use as you develop increasingly sophisticated client programs of your own. Second, they serve as examples for you to study as you begin to develop modules for your own use and build your own modular programs.

Random numbers We have composed several programs that use Python's `random` module, but our code often uses particular idioms to provide the type of randomness that we need for particular applications. For example, we studied code to randomly shuffle an array in Section 1.4 and code to draw randomly from a discrete distribution in Section 1.6.

To effectively reuse our code that implements these idioms, we will, from now on, use the `stdrandom` module (Program 2.2.3), which includes functions that generate random numbers from various distributions and an array-shuffling function. We summarize these functions in the API at the top of the next page. These functions are familiar, so the short descriptions in the API suffice to specify what they do. As usual, to use these functions, the client must include an `import` statement and you must make `stdrandom.py` available to Python, either by putting it in the same directory as your client code or by using your operating system's path mechanism (see the Q&A at the end of this section).

By collecting all of these functions that use `random` to generate random numbers of various types in one file (`stdrandom.py`), we concentrate our attention on

function call	*description*
`uniformInt(lo, hi)`	*uniformly random integer in the range [`lo`, `hi`)*
`uniformFloat(lo, hi)`	*uniformly random float in the range [`lo`, `hi`)*
`bernoulli(p)`	*`True` with probability `p` (`p` defaults to `0.5`)*
`binomial(n, p)`	*number of heads in `n` coin flips, each of which is heads with probability `p` (`p` defaults to `0.5`)*
`gaussian(mu, sigma)`	*normal, mean `mu`, standard deviation `sigma` (`mu` defaults to `0.0`, `sigma` defaults to `1.0`)*
`discrete(a)`	*`i` with probability proportional to `a[i]`*
`shuffle(a)`	*randomly shuffle the array `a[]`*

API for our `stdrandom` module

generating random numbers on this one file (and reuse the code in that file) instead of spreading it through every program that uses these functions. Each program that uses one of these functions is clearer than code that calls `random.random()` directly, because its purpose is clearly articulated by the choice of function from `stdrandom`. In some cases, implementations are available or might become available in other Python libraries. In practice, we might make use of these implementations (indeed, our booksite code might differ from Program 2.2.3). Articulating our own API gives us the freedom to do so without having to change any client code.

API design. We make certain assumptions about the objects passed to each function in `stdrandom`. For example, we assume that clients will pass to `stdrandom.bernoulli()` a float between `0.0` and `1.0`, and to `stdrandom.discrete()` an array of nonnegative numbers (not all of which are zero). Such assumptions are part of the contract between the client and the implementation. We strive to design modules such that the contract is clear and unambiguous and to avoid getting bogged down with details. As with many tasks in programming, a good API design is often the result of several iterations of trying out and living with various possibilities. We always take special care in designing APIs, because when we change an API we might have to change all clients and all implementations. *Our goal is to articulate what clients are to expect in the API, separate from the code.* This practice frees us to change the code, and perhaps to change to an implementation that achieves the desired effect more efficiently or with more accuracy.

Program 2.2.3 Random number module (stdrandom.py)

```
import math
import random

def uniformInt(lo, hi):
    return random.randrange(lo, hi)

def uniformFloat(lo, hi):
    return random.uniform(lo, hi)

def bernoulli(p=0.5):
    return random.random() < p

def binomial(n, p=0.5):
    heads = 0
    for i in range(n):
        if bernoulli(p): heads += 1
    return heads

def gaussian(mu=0.0, sigma=1.0):
    # See Exercise 2.1.25.

def discrete(a):
    r = uniformFloat(0.0, sum(a))
    subtotal = 0.0
    for i in range(len(a)):
        subtotal += a[i]
        if subtotal > r: return i

def shuffle(a):
    # See Exercise 2.2.13.
```

```
% python stdrandom.py 5
90 26.36076 False 47 8.79269 0
13 18.02210 False 55 9.03992 1
58 56.41176 True  51 8.80501 0
29 16.68454 False 58 8.90827 0
85 86.24712 True  47 8.95228 0
```

This module defines functions that implement various types of randomness: random integers or floats uniformly distributed in a given range, a random boolean (Bernoulli), random integers drawn from a binomial distribution, random floats drawn from a Gaussian distribution, random integers drawn from a given discrete distribution, and randomly shuffling an array. The test client appears on the next page.

Unit testing. We implement `stdrandom` without reference to any particular client, but it is good programming practice to include a basic *test client* `main()` that, at a minimum,

- Exercises all the code.
- Provides some assurance that the code is working.
- Takes an argument from the command line to allow flexibility in testing.

Although it is not intended for clients, we use `main()` when debugging, testing, and improving the functions in a module. This practice is call *unit testing*. For example, a test client for `stdrandom` is shown below (we omit testing of the `shuffle()` function—see Exercise 1.4.22). As shown with Program 2.2.1, when we invoke this function by typing `python stdrandom.py 10`, the output brings no surprises: the numbers in the first column might be equally likely to be any integer from `0` to `99`; the numbers in the second column might be uniformly spread between `10.0` and `99.0`; about half of the values in the third column are `True`; the numbers in the fourth column are close to `50`; the numbers in the fifth column seem to average about `9.0`, and seem unlikely to be too far from `9.0`; and the last column seems to be not far from 50% `0`s, 30% `1`s, 10% `2`s, and 10% `3`s. If something seems amiss, we can see many more results by typing `python stdrandom.py 100`. Typically, it is good practice to refine the `main()` function to do more exhaustive testing as you use the library more extensively.

Proper unit testing can be a significant programming challenge in itself. In this particular case, it is appropriate to do more extensive testing in a separate cli-

```
def main():
    trials = int(sys.argv[1])
    for i in range(trials):
        stdio.writef('%2d '  , uniformInt(10, 100))
        stdio.writef('%8.5f ', uniformFloat(10.0, 99.0))
        stdio.writef('%5s '  , bernoulli(0.5))
        stdio.writef('%2d '  , binomial(100, 0.5))
        stdio.writef('%7.5f ', gaussian(9.0, 0.2))
        stdio.writef('%1d '  , discrete([5, 3, 1, 1]))
        stdio.writeln()

if __name__ == '__main__': main()
```

Basic test client for `stdrandom`

ent to check that the numbers have many of the same properties as truly random numbers drawn from the cited distributions (see Exercise 2.2.2). *Note*: Experts still debate the best way of testing whether the functions in `stdrandom` produce numbers that have the same characteristics as truly random numbers.

One effective approach is to compose test clients that use `stddraw`, as data visualization can be a quick indication that a program is behaving as intended. In the present context, a plot of a large number of points whose x- and y-coordinates are both drawn from various distributions often produces a pattern that gives direct insight into the important properties of the distribution. More important, a bug in the random number generation code is likely to show up immediately in such a plot. An example script that tests `stdrandom.gaussian()` is shown at right.

```
import sys
import stddraw
import stdrandom

trials = int(sys.argv[1])
stddraw.setPenRadius(0.0)
for i in range(trials):
    x = stdrandom.gaussian(0.5, 0.2)
    y = stdrandom.gaussian(0.5, 0.2)
    stddraw.point(x, y)
stddraw.show()
```

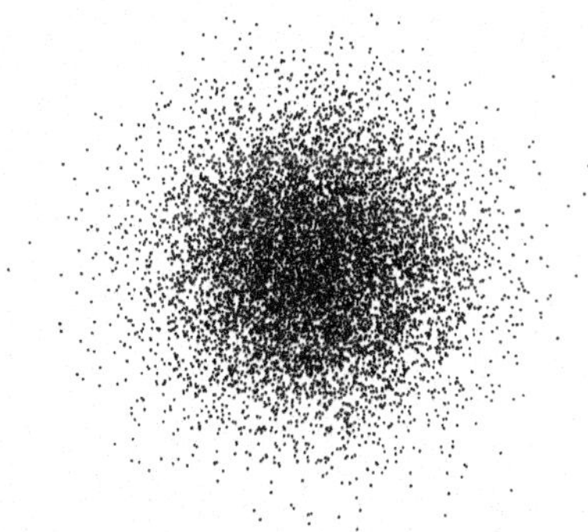

A `stdrandom.gaussian()` *test client*

Stress testing. An extensively used module such as `stdrandom` should also be subject to *stress testing*, where we make sure that it does not fail unexpectedly, even when the client does not follow the contract or makes some assumption that is not explicitly covered. Python's standard modules have all been subject to such testing, which requires carefully examining each line of code and questioning whether some condition might cause a problem. What should `stdrandom.discrete()` do if some array elements are negative? What if the argument is an array of length 0? What should `stdrandom.uniform()` do if the second argument is less than (or equal to) the first argument? Any question that you can think of is fair game. Such cases are sometimes referred to as *corner cases*. You are certain to encounter a teacher or a supervisor who is a stickler about corner cases. With experience, most programmers learn to address them early, to avoid an unpleasant bout of debugging later. Again, a reasonable approach is to implement a stress test as a separate client.

Array-processing API In SECTION 1.4 we saw the utility of functions that create one-dimensional arrays of a specified length and two-dimensional arrays with a specified number of rows and columns. Thus, we introduced the `stdarray` module from the booksite library, and specifically its functions for creating and initializing arrays `stdarray.create1D()` and `stdarray.create2D()`.

Moreover, we have seen and will continue to see many examples where we wish to read values from standard input into an array and write values from an array to standard output. Accordingly, we have included in the `stdarray` module functions for reading arrays of integers, floats, and booleans from standard input and for writing them to standard output—thus complementing the `stdio` module. Here is the full API for `stdarray`:

function call	*description*
`create1D(n, val)`	*array of length* `n`*, each element initialized to* `val`
`create2D(m, n, val)`	`m`*-by-*`n` *array, each element initialized to* `val`
`readInt1D()`	*array of integers, read from standard input*
`readInt2D()`	*two-dimensional array of integers, read from standard input*
`readFloat1D()`	*array of floats, read from standard input*
`readFloat2D()`	*two-dimensional array of floats, read from standard input*
`readBool1D()`	*array of booleans, read from standard input*
`readBool2D()`	*two-dimensional array of booleans, read from standard input*
`write1D(a)`	*write array* `a[]` *to standard output*
`write2D(a)`	*write two-dimensional array* `a[]` *to standard output*

Note 1: 1D format is an integer `n` *followed by* `n` *elements.*
2D format is two integers `m` *and* `n` *followed by* `m × n` *elements in row-major order.*
Note 2: Booleans are written as `0` *and* `1` *instead of* `False` *and* `True`.

API for our `stdarray` *module*

As usual, you can also find this information when working online, with interactive Python: first type **`import stdarray`**, then type **`help(stdarray)`** to see the API.

The array writing and reading functions must agree on a *file format*. For simplicity and harmony, we have adopted the convention that arrays appearing on standard input include the dimension(s) and appear in the order indicated, as illustrated in the diagram at the bottom of this page. The `read*()` functions expect this format, the `write*()` functions produce output in this format, and we can easily create files in this format for data from some other source.

For arrays of booleans, our file format uses `0` and `1` values instead of `False` and `True`. This convention is much more economical for large arrays. More important, patterns in the data are much easier to spot with this file format, as you will see in SECTION 2.4.

Implementing these functions is straightforward with the array-processing code that we have considered in SECTION 1.4 and in SECTION 2.1. We omit the module implementation because we have already studied the basic code. If you are interested, you can find the full implementation in the `stdarray.py` file on the booksite.

Packaging up all of these functions into one file—`stdarray.py`—allows us to easily reuse the code and saves us from having to worry about the details of creating, writing, and reading arrays when composing client programs later on. Moreover, these client programs, having calls to these functions instead of code that implements them, are more compact and easier to understand.

		Python array initializer	*file*
floats	*one-dimensional*	`[0.01, 0.85, 0.07, 0.07]`	`4` `.01 .85 .07 .07`

	two-dimensional	`[[ 0.00,  0.00,  0.500],`
		` [ 0.85,  0.04, -0.075],`
		` [ 0.20, -0.26,  0.400],`
		` [-0.15,  0.28,  0.575]]`
			`4 3`
			`.00  .00  .500`
			`.85  .04 -.075`
			`.20 -.26  .400`
			`-.15  .28  .575`

booleans	*one-dimensional*	`[False, True, True]`	`3` `0 1 1`

	two-dimensional	`[[False, True,  False],`
		` [ True, False, True ],`
		` [ True, False, True ],`
		` [False, True,  False]]`
			`4 3`
			`0 1 0`
			`1 0 1`
			`1 0 1`
			`0 1 0`

File formats for arrays

Iterated function systems Scientists have discovered that complex visual images can arise unexpectedly from simple computational processes. With `stdrandom`, `stddraw`, and `stdarray`, we can easily study the behavior of such systems.

Sierpinski triangle. As a first example, consider the following simple process: Start by plotting a point at one of the vertices of a given equilateral triangle. Then pick one of the three vertices at random and plot a new point halfway between the point just plotted and that vertex. Continue performing this same operation. Each time, we are picking a random vertex from the triangle to establish the line whose midpoint will be the next point plotted. Since we are making a random choice, the set of points should have some of the characteristics of random points, and that does seem to be the case after the first few iterations:

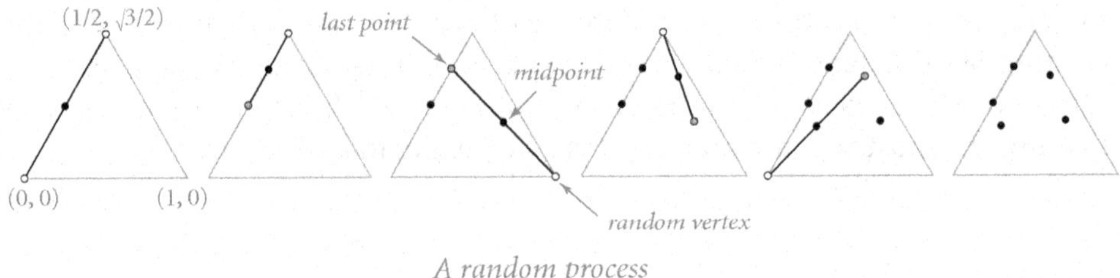

A random process

But we can study the process for a large number of iterations by composing a script to plot `n` points according to the rules:

```
cx = [0.000, 1.000, 0.500]
cy = [0.000, 0.000, 0.866]
x = 0.0
y = 0.0
for i in range(n):
    r = stdrandom.uniformInt(0, 3)
    x = (x + cx[r]) / 2.0
    y = (y + cy[r]) / 2.0
    stddraw.point(x, y)
stddraw.show()
```

We keep the x- and y-coordinates of the triangle vertices in the arrays `cx[]` and `cy[]`, respectively. We use `stdrandom.uniformInt()` to choose a random index `r` into these arrays—the coordinates of the chosen vertex are (`cx[r], cy[r]`). The x-coordinate of the midpoint of the line from (`x, y`) to that vertex is given by the expression `(x + cx[r]) / 2.0`, and a similar calculation gives the y-coordinate. Adding a call to `stddraw.point()` and putting this code in a loop completes the implementation. Remarkably, despite the randomness, the same figure always emerges after a large number of iterations! This figure is known as the *Sierpinski triangle* (see Exercise 2.3.27). Understanding why such a regular figure should arise from such a random process is a fascinating question.

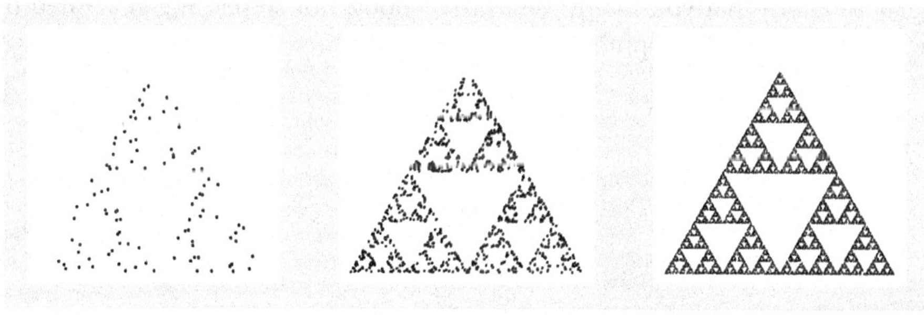

A random process?

Barnsley fern. To add to the mystery, we can produce pictures of remarkable diversity by playing the same game with different rules. One striking example is known as the *Barnsley fern*. To generate it, we use the same process, but this time driven by the following table of formulas. At each step, we choose the formulas to use to update x and y with the indicated probability (1% of the time we use the first pair of formulas, 85% of the time we use the second pair of formulas, and so forth).

probability	*x-update*	*y-update*
1%	$x = 0.500$	$x = 0.16y$
85%	$x = 0.85x + 0.04y + 0.075$	$y = -0.04x + 0.85y + 0.180$
7%	$x = 0.20x - 0.26y + 0.400$	$y = 0.23x + 0.22y + 0.045$
7%	$x = -0.15x + 0.28y + 0.575$	$y = 0.26x + 0.24y - 0.086$

We could compose code just like the code we just wrote for the Sierpinski triangle to iterate these rules, but matrix processing provides a uniform way to generalize that code to handle any set of rules. We have m different transformations, chosen from a 1-by-m vector with `stdrandom.discrete()`. For each transformation, we have an equation for updating x and an equation for updating y, so we use two m-by-3 matrices for the equation coefficients—one for x and one for y. PROGRAM 2.2.4 (`ifs.py`) implements this data-driven version of the computation. This program enables limitless exploration: it performs the iteration for any input containing a vector that defines the probability distribution and the two matrices that define the coefficients, one for updating x and the other for updating y. For the coefficients just given, even though we choose a random equation at each step, the same figure emerges every time that we do this computation: an image that looks remarkably similar to a fern that you might see in the woods, not something generated by a random process on a computer.

Generating a Barnsley fern

That the same short program that takes a few numbers from standard input and plots points to standard drawing can (given different data) produce both the Sierpinski triangle and the Barnsley fern (and many, many other images) is truly remarkable. Because of its simplicity and the appeal of the results, this sort of calculation is useful in making synthetic images that have a realistic appearance in computer-generated movies and games.

Perhaps more significantly, the ability to produce such realistic diagrams so easily suggests intriguing scientific questions: What does computation tell us about nature? What does nature tell us about computation?

Program 2.2.4 Iterated function systems (ifs.py)

```
import sys
import stdarray
import stddraw
import stdrandom

n = int(sys.argv[1])
probabilities = stdarray.readFloat1D()
cx = stdarray.readFloat2D()
cy = stdarray.readFloat2D()
x = 0.0
y = 0.0
stddraw.setPenRadius(0.0)
for i in range(n):
    r = stdrandom.discrete(probabilities)
    x0 = cx[r][0]*x + cx[r][1]*y + cx[r][2]
    y0 = cy[r][0]*x + cy[r][1]*y + cy[r][2]
    x = x0
    y = y0
    stddraw.point(x, y)
stddraw.show()
```

`n`	*iterations*
`probabilities[]`	*probabilities*
`cx[][]`	*x coefficients*
`cy[][]`	*y coefficients*
`x, y`	*current point*

This data-driven script is a client of `stdarray`, `stdrandom`, and `stddraw`. It iterates the function system defined by a 1-by-m vector (probabilities) and two m-by-3 matrices (coefficients for updating x and y, respectively) on standard input, plotting the result as a set of points on standard drawing. Curiously, this code does not need to refer to m.

```
% more sierpinski.txt
3
  .33 .33 .34
3 3
  .50 .00 .00
  .50 .00 .50
  .50 .00 .25
3 3
  .00 .50 .00
  .00 .50 .00
  .00 .50 .433
```

```
% python ifs.py 100000 < sierpinski.txt
```

```
% more barnsley.txt
4
  .01 .85 .07 .07
4 3
  .00  .00  .500
  .85  .04  .075
  .20 -.26  .400
 -.15  .28  .575
4 3
  .00  .16  .000
 -.04  .85  .180
  .23  .22  .045
  .26  .24 -.086
```

```
% python ifs.py 100000 < barnsley.txt
```

```
% more tree.txt
6
  .1 .1 .2 .2 .2 .2
6 3
  .00  .00  .550
 -.05  .00  .525
  .46 -.15  .270
  .47 -.15  .265
  .43  .26  .290
  .42  .26  .290
6 3
  .00  .60  .000
 -.50  .00  .750
  .39  .38  .105
  .17  .42  .465
 -.25  .45  .625
 -.35  .31  .525
```

```
% python ifs.py 100000 < tree.txt
```

```
% more coral.txt
3
  .40 .15 .45
3 3
  .3077 -.5315  .8863
  .3077 -.0769  .2166
  .0000  .5455  .0106
3 3
 -.4615 -.2937 1.0962
  .1538 -.4476  .3384
  .6923 -.1958  .3808
```

```
% python ifs.py 100000 < coral.txt
```

Examples of iterated function systems

Standard statistics Next, we consider a module for a set of mathematical calculations and basic visualization tools that arise in all sorts of applications in science and engineering (and are not all implemented in standard Python modules). These calculations relate to the task of understanding the statistical properties of a sequence of numbers. Such a module is useful, for example, when we perform a series of scientific experiments that yield measurements of a quantity. One of the most important challenges facing modern scientists is proper analysis of such data, and computation is playing an increasingly important role in such analysis. These basic data analysis functions are not difficult to implement and are summarized in the API shown at the bottom of this page.

Basic statistics. Suppose that we have n measurements $x_0, x_1, \ldots, x_{n-1}$. The average value of these measurements, otherwise known as the *mean*, is given by the formula $\mu = (x_0 + x_1 + \ldots + x_{n-1}) / n$ and is an estimate of the value of the quantity. The minimum and maximum values are also of interest, as is the median (the middle value if the measurements are sorted and n is odd, or the average of the two middle values if n is even). Also of interest is the *sample variance*, which is given by the formula

$$\sigma^2 = ((x_0 - \mu)^2 + (x_1 - \mu)^2 + \ldots + (x_{n-1} - \mu)^2) / (n-1)$$

and the *sample standard deviation*, the square root of the sample variance. PROGRAM 2.2.5 (`stdstats.py`) is a module for computing these basic statistics (the median is

function call	*description*
`mean(a)`	*average of the values in the numeric array* `a[]`
`var(a)`	*sample variance of the values in the numeric array* `a[]`
`stddev(a)`	*sample standard deviation of the values in the numeric array* `a[]`
`median(a)`	*median of the values in the numeric array* `a[]`
`plotPoints(a)`	*point plot of the values in the numeric array* `a[]`
`plotLines(a)`	*line plot of the values in the numeric array* `a[]`
`plotBars(a)`	*bar plot of the values in the numeric array* `a[]`

API for our `stdstats` *module*

Program 2.2.5 Data analysis module (stdstats.py)

```
import math
import stdarray
import stddraw
import stdio

def mean(a):
    return sum(a) / float(len(a))

def var(a):
    mu = mean(a)
    total = 0.0
    for x in a:
        total += (x - mu) * (x - mu)
    return total / (len(a) - 1)

def stddev(a):
    return math.sqrt(var(a))

def median(a):
    # See Exercise 4.2.16.

# See Program 2.2.6 for plotting functions.

def main():
    a = stdarray.readFloat1D()
    stdio.writef('   mean %7.3f\n', mean(a))
    stdio.writef('std dev %7.3f\n', stddev(a))
    stdio.writef(' median %7.3f\n', median(a))

if __name__ == '__main__':  main()
```

This module implements functions to compute the minimum, maximum, mean, variance, and standard deviation of numbers in a client array. Plotting functions are in PROGRAM *2.2.6.*

```
% more tiny1D.txt
7
3.0 1.0 4.0 7.0 8.0 9.0 6.0
```

```
% python stdstats.py < tiny1D.txt
   mean   5.429
std dev   2.878
 median   6.000
```

more difficult to compute efficiently than the others—we will consider the implementation of `median()` in SECTION 4.2). The `main()` test client for `stdstats` reads numbers from standard input into an array and calls each of the functions. As with `stdrandom`, a more extensive test of the calculations is called for. Typically, as we debug or test new functions in the module, we adjust the unit testing code accordingly, testing the functions one at a time. A mature and widely used module like `stdstats` also deserves a stress-testing client for extensively testing everything after any change. If you are interested in seeing what such a client might look like, you can find one for `stdstats` on the booksite (also see EXERCISE 2.2.2). Most experienced programmers will advise you that any time spent doing unit testing and stress testing will more than pay for itself later.

Plotting. One important use of `stddraw` is to help us visualize data rather than relying on tables of numbers. In a typical situation, we perform experiments, save the experimental data in an array, and then compare the results against a model, perhaps a mathematical function that describes the data. To expedite this process for the typical case where values of one variable are equally spaced, our `stdstats` module defines functions that you can use for plotting data in an array. PROGRAM 2.2.6 is an implementation of the `plotPoints()`, `plotLines()`, and `plotBars()` functions for `stdstats`. These functions display the values in the argument array at regularly spaced intervals in the drawing window, either connected together by line segments (`lines`), filled circles at each value (`points`), or bars from the x-axis to the value (`bars`). They all plot the points with x-coordinate `i` and y-coordinate `a[i]` using filled circles, lines through the points, and bars, respectively. They all rescale x to fill the drawing window (so that the points are evenly spaced along the x-coordinate) and leave to the client scaling the y-coordinates.

These functions are not intended to form a general-purpose plotting module. Indeed, you can certainly think of all sorts of things that you might want to add: different types of spots, labeled axes, color, and many other artifacts are commonly found in modern systems that can plot data. Some situations might call for more complicated functions than these. Our intent with `stdstats` is to introduce you to data analysis while showing you how easy it is to define a module to take care of useful tasks. In fact, this module has already proved useful—we used these plotting functions to produce the figures in this book that depict function graphs, sound waves, and experimental results. Next, we consider several examples of their use.

Plotting function graphs. You can use the `stdstats.plot*()` functions to draw a plot of the function graph for any function at all: choose an x-interval where you want to plot the function, compute function values evenly spaced through that interval and store them in an array, determine and set the y-scale, and then call `stdstats.plotLines()` or another `plot*()` function, as shown in the example plot at right. The smoothness of the curve is determined by properties of the function and by the number of points plotted. As we discussed when first considering `stddraw`, you have to be careful to sample enough points to catch fluctuations in the function. We will consider another approach to plotting functions based on sampling values that are not equally spaced in SECTION 2.4. Often, rescaling the y-axis is necessary (scaling the x-axis is automatically handled by the `stdstats` functions). For example, to plot a sine function, rescale the y-axis to cover values between -1 and $+1$. Generally, to rescale the y-axis, you can call `stddraw.setYscale(min(a), max(a))`.

```
n = int(sys.argv[1])
a = stdarray.create1D(n+1, 0.0)
for i in range(n+1):
    a[i] = gaussian.pdf(-4.0 + 8.0 * i / n)
stdstats.plotPoints(a)
stdstats.plotLines(a)
stddraw.show()
```

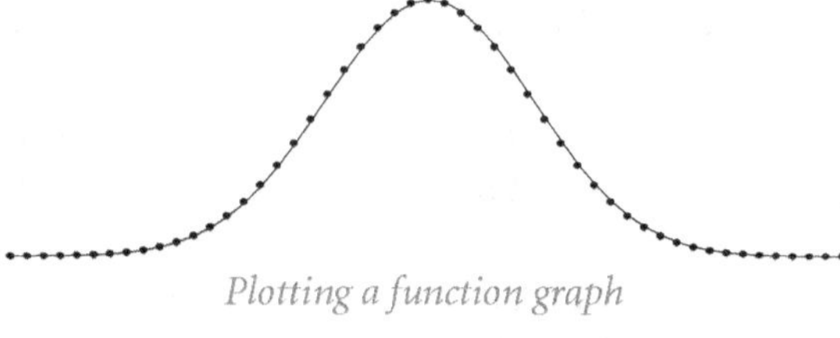

Plotting a function graph

Plotting sound waves. Both the `stdaudio` module and the `stdstats` plot functions work with arrays that contain sampled values at regular intervals, so it is easy to plot sound waves. The diagrams of sound waves in SECTION 1.5 and at the beginning of this section were each produced by first scaling the y-axis so as to give the curve a reasonable appearance, then plotting the points with `stdstats.plotPoints()`. As you have seen, such plots give direct insight into processing audio. You can also produce interesting effects by plotting sound waves as you play them with `stdaudio`, although this task is a bit challenging because of the huge amount of data involved (see EXERCISE 1.5.27).

```
def tone(hz, t):
    # See Program 2.4.7
stddraw.setYscale(-6.0, 6.0)
hi = tone(440, 0.01)
stdstats.plotPoints(hi)
stddraw.show()
```

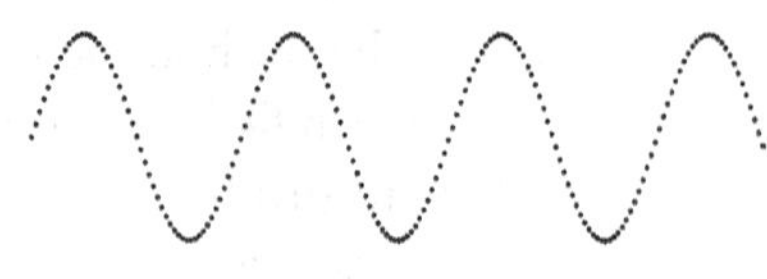

Plotting a sound wave

Program 2.2.6 Plotting data values (`stdstats.py`, *continued*)

```
def plotPoints(a):
    n = len(a)
    stddraw.setXscale(0, n-1)
    stddraw.setPenRadius(1.0 / (3.0 * n))
    for i in range(n):
        stddraw.point(i, a[i])

def plotLines(a):
    n = len(a)
    stddraw.setXscale(0, n-1)
    stddraw.setPenRadius(0.0)
    for i in range(1, n):
        stddraw.line(i-1, a[i-1], i, a[i])

def plotBars(a):
    n = len(a)
    stddraw.setXscale(0, n-1)
    for i in range(n):
        stddraw.filledRectangle(i-0.25, 0.0, 0.5, a[i])
```

This code implements the three functions in `stdstats.py` *(Program 2.2.5) for plotting data. Given an array a[], they plot the points (i, a[i]) with filled circles, connecting line segments, and bars, respectively. Clients are responsible for calling* `stddraw.show()`.

```
n = 20
a = stdarray.create1D(n, 0.0)
for i in range(n):
    a[i] = 1.0 / (i + 1)
```

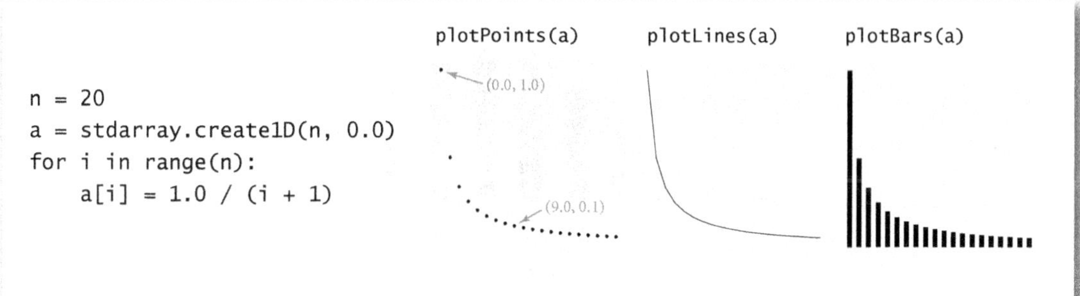

Plotting experimental results. You can put multiple plots on the same drawing. One typical reason to do so is to compare experimental results with a theoretical model. For example, `bernoulli.py` (PROGRAM 2.2.7) counts the number of heads found when a fair coin is flipped n times and compares the result with the predicted Gaussian (normal) distribution function. A famous result from probability theory is that the distribution of this quantity is the binomial distribution, which is extremely well approximated by the Gaussian probability density function ϕ with mean $n / 2$ and standard deviation $\sqrt{n} / 2$. The more trials we perform, the more accurate the approximation. The drawing produced by `bernoulli.py`, shown at the bottom of this page, is a succinct summary of the results of the experiment and a convincing validation of the theory. This example is prototypical of a scientific approach to applications programming that we use often throughout this book and that you should use whenever you run an experiment. If a theoretical model that can explain your results is available, a visual plot comparing the experiment to the theory can validate both.

THESE FEW EXAMPLES ARE INTENDED TO indicate to you what is possible with a well-designed module of functions for data analysis. Several extensions and other ideas are explored in the exercises. You may find `stdstats` to be useful for basic plots, and you are encouraged to experiment with these implementations and modify them or to add functions to make your own module that can draw plots of your own design. As you continue to address an ever-widening circle of programming tasks, you will naturally be drawn to the idea of developing tools like these for your own use.

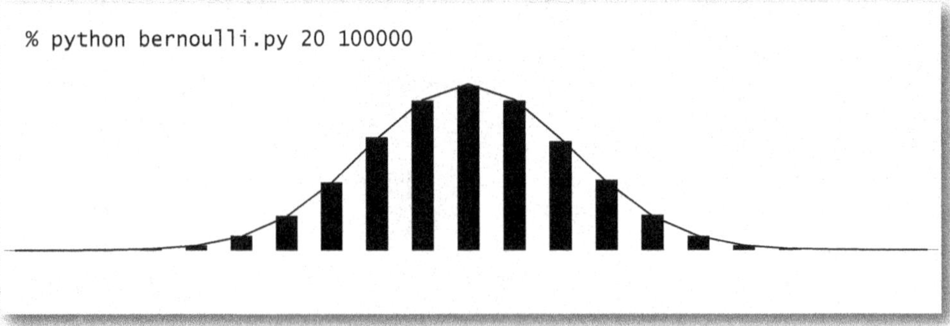
% python bernoulli.py 20 100000

Program 2.2.7 Bernoulli trials (bernoulli.py)

```
import sys
import math
import stdarray
import stddraw
import stdrandom
import stdstats
import gaussian

n      = int(sys.argv[1])
trials = int(sys.argv[2])

freq = stdarray.create1D(n+1, 0)
for t in range(trials):
    heads = stdrandom.binomial(n, 0.5)
    freq[heads] += 1

norm = stdarray.create1D(n+1, 0.0)
for i in range(n+1):
    norm[i] = 1.0 * freq[i] / trials

phi = stdarray.create1D(n+1, 0.0)
stddev = math.sqrt(n)/2.0
for i in range(n+1):
    phi[i] = gaussian.pdf(i, n/2.0, stddev)

stddraw.setCanvasSize(1000, 400)
stddraw.setYscale(0, 1.1 * max(max(norm), max(phi)))
stdstats.plotBars(norm)
stdstats.plotLines(phi)
stddraw.show()
```

`n`	*number of flips per trial*
`trials`	*number of trials*
`freq[]`	*experimental results*
`norm[]`	*normalized results*
`phi[]`	*Gaussian model*

This script provides convincing visual evidence that the number of heads observed when a fair coin is flipped n times obeys a Gaussian distribution (see output on facing page).

Modular programming The modules that we have developed illustrate a programming style known as *modular programming*. Instead of composing a new program that is self-contained in its own file to address a new problem, we break up each large task into smaller, more manageable subtasks, then implement and independently debug code that addresses each subtask. *Whenever you can clearly separate tasks within a computation, you should do so.* Python supports such separation by allowing us to independently develop functions in *modules*, which can then be used by clients. Thus, Python facilitates modular programming by allowing us to define modules of important subtasks for use by clients.

Our iterated function system script `ifs.py` (PROGRAM 2.2.4) exemplifies modular programming because it is a relatively sophisticated computation that is implemented with several relatively small interacting modules, each developed independently. It makes use of `stdrandom` and `stdarray`, as well as the functions from `sys` and `stddraw` that we are accustomed to using. If we were to put all of the code required for `ifs.py` in a single file, we would have a large amount of code to maintain and debug; with modular programming, we can study iterated function systems with some confidence that the arrays are read properly and that the random number generator will produce properly distributed values, because we have already implemented and tested the code for these tasks in separate modules.

module/script	*description*
`gaussian`	Gaussian distribution functions
`stdrandom`	functions for random numbers
`stdarray`	input and output for arrays
`ifs`	client for iterated function systems
`stdstats`	functions for data analysis
`bernoulli`	client for Bernoulli trials experiments

Summary of modules and scripts in this section

Similarly, `bernoulli.py` (PROGRAM 2.2.7) exemplifies modular programming. It is a client of `gaussian`, `sys`, `math`, `stdrandom`, `stdarray`, `stddraw`, and `stdstats`. Again, we can have some confidence that the functions in these modules produce the expected results because they are system modules or modules that we have tested, debugged, and used before.

To describe the relationships among modules in a modular program, we can draw a *dependency graph*, where we connect two module names with an arrow if the first module uses features defined in the second module. Such diagrams play an important role because understanding the relationships among modules is necessary for proper development and maintenance. A dependency graph for `ifs.py` and `bernoulli.py` and the modules they use appears at the top of the next page.

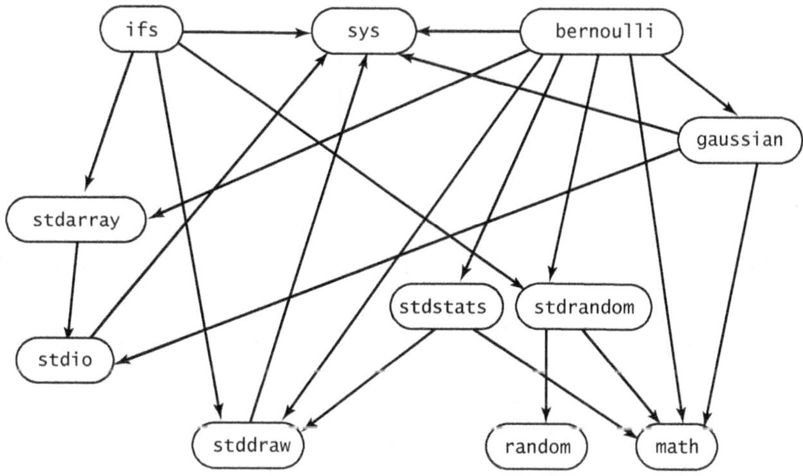

Dependency graph for the clients and modules in this section

We emphasize modular programming throughout this book because it has many important advantages that have come to be accepted as essential in modern programming, including the following:

- We can compose programs of a reasonable size, even in large systems.
- Debugging is restricted to small pieces of code.
- We can reuse code without having to reimplement it.
- Maintaining (and improving) code is much simpler.

The importance of these advantages is difficult to overstate, so we will expand upon each of them.

Programs of a reasonable size. No large task is so complex that it cannot be divided into smaller subtasks. If you find yourself with a program that stretches to more than a few pages of code, you must ask yourself the following questions: Are there subtasks that could be implemented separately? Can some of these subtasks logically be grouped together in a separate module? Could other clients use this code in the future? At the other end of the range, if you find yourself with a huge number of tiny modules, you must ask yourself questions such as these: Is there some group of subtasks that logically belong in the same module? Is each module likely to be used by multiple clients? There is no hard-and-fast rule on module size:

one implementation of a critically important abstraction might properly be a few lines of code, whereas another module with a large number of functions might properly extend to hundreds of lines of code.

Debugging. Tracing a program rapidly becomes more difficult as the number of statements and interacting variables increases. Tracing a program with hundreds of variables requires keeping track of hundreds of objects, as any statement might affect or be affected by any variable. To do so for hundreds or thousands of statements or more is untenable. With modular programming and our guiding principle of keeping the scope of variables local to the extent possible, we severely restrict the number of possibilities that we have to consider when debugging. Equally important is the idea of a contract between the client and the implementation. Once we are satisfied that an implementation is meeting its end of the bargain, we can debug all its clients under that assumption.

Code reuse. Once we have implemented modules such as `stdrandom` and `stdstats`, we do not have to worry about composing code to compute means or standard deviations or to generate random numbers again—we can simply reuse the code that we have composed. Moreover, we do not need to make copies of the code—any module can refer to any function in any other module.

Maintenance. Like a good essay, a good program can always be improved, and modular programming facilitates the process of continually improving your Python programs because improving a module improves all of its clients. Normally there are several different approaches to solving a particular problem. With modular programming, you can implement more than one and try them independently. As long as client code relies only on behavior documented in the APIs, it should continue to work without modification with new implementations. More important, suppose that while developing a new client, you find a bug in some module. With modular programming, fixing that bug essentially fixes the same bugs in all of the module's clients.

If you encounter an old program (or a new program composed by an old programmer!), you are likely to find one huge module—a long sequence of statements, stretching to several pages or more, where any statement can refer to any variable in the program. Huge modules of this sort are extremely difficult to understand, maintain, and debug. Old programs of this kind are found in critical parts of our computational infrastructure (for example, some nuclear power plants and some banks) precisely because the programmers charged with maintaining them cannot even understand them well enough to reimplement them in a modern language! With support for modular programming, modern languages like Python help us avoid such situations by separately developing sets of functions in independent files.

The ability to share functions among different files fundamentally extends our programming model in two different ways. First, it allows us to reuse code without having to maintain multiple copies of it. Second, by allowing us to organize a program into files of manageable size that can be independently tested and debugged, it strongly supports our basic message: *whenever you can clearly separate tasks within a computation, you should do so.*

In this section, we have supplemented the `std*` libraries of Section 1.5 with several other libraries that you can use: `gaussian`, `stdarray`, `stdrandom`, and `stdstats`. Furthermore, we have illustrated their use with several client programs. These tools are centered on basic mathematical concepts that may arise in any scientific project or engineering task. Our intent is not just to provide tools, but also to illustrate that it is easy for you to create your own tools. The first question that most modern programmers ask when addressing a complex task is "Which tools do I need?" When the needed tools are not conveniently available, the second question is "How difficult would it be to implement them?" To be a good programmer, you must have the confidence to build a software tool when you need it and the wisdom to know when it might be better to seek a solution in an existing module.

After modules and modular programming, you have one more step to learn to have a complete modern programming model: *object-oriented programming*, the topic of Chapter 3. With object-oriented programming, you can build modules of functions that use side effects (in a tightly controlled manner) to vastly extend the Python programming model. Before moving to object-oriented programming, we consider in this chapter the profound ramifications of the idea that any function can call itself (in Section 2.3) and a more extensive case study (in Section 2.4) of modular programming than the small clients in this section.

Q&A

Q. How can I make a module such as `gaussian` or `stdrandom` available to my Python programs?

A. The easiest way is to download `gaussian.py` from the booksite and put it in the same directory as the client. However, if you do this, you might end up with several copies of `gaussian.py` in different directories, which makes the code harder to maintain. Instead, you can put `gaussian.py` in a single directory and configure the `PYTHONPATH` environment variable to include this directory. The booksite contains instructions for setting the `PYTHONPATH` variable on your operating system. If you followed the step-by-step instructions on the booksite for installing Python, all of our standard modules (including `stdio`, `stddraw`, `stdarray`, `stdrandom`, and `stdstats`) should already be available for use in your Python programs.

Q. I tried to import the `gaussian` module, but got the following error message. What's wrong?

```
ImportError: No module named gaussian
```

A. You did not make `gaussian` available to Python, as described above.

Q. I tried to call `gaussian.pdf()` but I got the following error. What's wrong?

```
NameError: name 'gaussian' is not defined
```

A. You left out the `import gaussian` statement.

Q. Is there a keyword that identifies a `.py` file as a module (and not a script)?

A. No. Technically, the key point is to avoid arbitrary global code using the patterns described earlier in this section. If you avoid arbitrary global code in a `.py` file, so that the `.py` file can be imported into some other `.py` file, then we call it a module. Pragmatically, however, there is a bit of a conceptual leap in this viewpoint, because it is one thing to sit down to create a `.py` file that you will run (and perhaps run again sometime later with different data), but quite another thing to create a `.py` file that you will rely on much later in the future, and still another thing to create a `.py` file for someone else to use in the future.

Q. How do I develop a new version of a module that I have been using for a while?

A. With care. Any change to the API might break any client program, so it is best to work in a separate directory. Of course, with this approach you are working with a copy of the code. If you are changing a module that has a lot of clients, you can appreciate the problems faced by companies putting out new versions of their software. If you just want to add a few functions to a module, go ahead: that is usually not too dangerous.

Q. How do I know that an implementation behaves properly? Why not automatically check that it satisfies the API?

A. We use informal specifications because composing a detailed specification is not much different from composing a program. Moreover, a fundamental tenet of theoretical computer science says that doing so does not even solve the basic problem because there is no way in general to check that two different programs perform the same computation.

Q. I notice that files whose names are suffixed with `.pyc` are appearing when I run the programs from this section. For example, when I issue the command `python gaussiantable.py`, I notice that Python automatically creates a file named `gaussian.pyc`. What are these `.pyc` files?

A. As noted in Section 1.1, whenever Python executes a program, it compiles the program into an internal (not human-readable) form that is more amenable to execution, known as *bytecode*. When you `import` a module for the first time, Python compiles the code and stores the resulting bytecode in a `.pyc` file. This makes the module load faster because Python does not need to recompile it each time (but it does not make running the program any faster). It's fine to delete `.pyc` files at any time; Python will regenerate them when appropriate. It's also fine *not* to delete `.pyc` files because if you edit a `.py` file after Python has generated the corresponding `.pyc` file, Python will regenerate the `.pyc` file automatically.

Exercises

2.2.1 Compose a module that implements the hyperbolic trigonometric functions based on the definitions sinh(x) = ($e^x - e^{-x}$) / 2 and cosh(x) = ($e^x + e^{-x}$) / 2, with tanh(x), coth(x), sech(x), and csch(x) defined in a manner analogous to the standard trigonometric functions.

2.2.2 Compose a test client for both `stdstats` and `stdrandom` that checks that all of the functions in both modules (with the exception of `shuffle()`—see Exercise 1.4.22) operate as expected. Take a command-line argument `n`, generate `n` random numbers using each of the functions in `stdrandom`, and write their statistics. *Extra credit*: Defend the results that you get by comparing them to the results expected from mathematical analysis.

2.2.3 Develop a client that does stress testing for `stdrandom`. Pay particular attention to `discrete()`. For example, are the probabilities nonnegative? Are they all zero?

2.2.4 Compose a function that takes floats `ymin` and `ymax` (with `ymin` strictly less than `ymax`) and a float array `a[]` as arguments and linearly scales the elements in `a[]` so that they are all between `ymin` and `ymax`.

2.2.5 Compose a `gaussian` and `stdstats` client that explores the effects of changing the mean and standard deviation of the Gaussian distribution curve. Create one plot with curves having a fixed mean and various standard deviations and another with curves having a fixed standard deviation and various means.

2.2.6 Add to `stdrandom` a function `maxwellBoltzmann()` that returns a random value drawn from a Maxwell-Boltzmann distribution with parameter σ. To produce such a value, return the square root of the sum of the squares of three Gaussian random variables with mean 0 and standard deviation σ. (The speeds of molecules in an ideal gas have a Maxwell-Boltzmann distribution.)

2.2.7 Modify `bernoulli.py` to animate the bar graph, replotting it after each experiment, so that you can watch it converge to the normal distribution.

2.2.8 Modify `bernoulli.py` to take an extra command-line argument p that specifies the probability p that a biased coin comes up heads. Run experiments to get a feeling for the distribution corresponding to a biased coin. Be sure to try values of p that are close to 0 and close to 1.

2.2.9 Compose a module `matrix.py` that implements the following API for vectors and matrices (see Section 1.4):

function call	*description*
`rand(m, n)`	*an* m*-by-*n *matrix containing random floats between 0 and 1*
`identity(n)`	*an* n*-by-*n *identity matrix*
`dot(v1, v2)`	*the dot product of vectors* v1 *and* v2
`transpose(m)`	*the transpose of the matrix* m
`add(m1, m2)`	*the sum of the matrices* m1 *and* m2
`subtract(m1, m2)`	*the difference of the matrices* m1 *and* m2
`multiplyMM(m1, m2)`	*the product of the matrices* m1 *and* m2
`multiplyMV(m, v)`	*the matrix–vector product of matrix* m *and vector* v *(a vector)*
`multiplyVM(v, m)`	*the vector–matrix product of vector* v *and matrix* m *(a vector)*

API for a `matrix` *module*

As a test client, use the following code, which performs the same calculation as `markov.py` (Program 1.6.3):

```
moves = int(sys.argv[1])
p = stdarray.readFloat2D()
ranks = stdarray.create1D(len(p), 0.0)
ranks[0] = 1.0
for i in range(moves):
    ranks = matrix.multiplyVM(ranks, p)
stdarray.write1D(ranks)
```

In practice, mathematicians and scientists use mature libraries such as *NumPy* (or special-purpose matrix-processing languages such as Matlab) for such tasks because they are likely to be more efficient, accurate, and robust than anything you could compose yourself. See the booksite for information on using *NumPy*.

2.2.10 Compose a `matrix.py` client that implements the version of `markov.py` described in Section 1.6 but is based on squaring the matrix, instead of iterating the vector–matrix multiplication.

2.2.11 Redesign `randomsurfer.py` (Program 1.6.2) using the `stdarray` and `stdrandom` modules.

Partial solution:

```
...
p = stdarray.readFloat2D()
page = 0   # Start at page 0.
hits = stdarray.create1D(n, 0)
for i in range(moves):
    page = stdrandom.discrete(p[page])
    hits[page] += 1
...
```

2.2.12 Add a function `exp()` to `stdrandom.py` that takes an argument λ and returns a random number from the *exponential distribution* with rate λ: if x is a random number uniformly distributed between 0 and 1, then $-\ln x / \lambda$ is a random number from the exponential distribution with rate λ.

2.2.13 Implement the function `shuffle()` in `stdrandom.py` that takes an array as an argument and shuffles the elements in the array. Use the shuffling algorithm described in Section 1.4.

Creative Exercises

2.2.14 *Sicherman dice.* Suppose that you have two six-sided dice, one with faces labeled 1, 3, 4, 5, 6, and 8 and the other with faces labeled 1, 2, 2, 3, 3, and 4. Compare the probabilities of occurrence of each of the values of the sum of the dice with those for a standard pair of dice. Use `stdrandom` and `stdstats`.

2.2.15 *Craps.* The following are the rules for a *pass bet* in the game of *craps*. Roll two six-sided dice, and let x be their sum.

- If x is 7 or 11, you win.
- If x is 2, 3, or 12, you lose.

Otherwise, repeatedly roll the two dice until their sum is either x or 7.

- If their sum is x, you win.
- If their sum is 7, you lose.

Compose a modular program to estimate the probability of winning a pass bet. Modify your program to handle loaded dice, where the probability of a die landing on 1 is taken from the command line, the probability of landing on 6 is 1/6 minus that probability, and 2–5 are assumed equally likely. *Hint*: Use `stdrandom.discrete()`.

2.2.16 *Dynamic histogram.* Suppose that the standard input stream is a sequence of floats. Compose a program that takes an integer `n` and two floats `l` and `r` from the command line and uses `stdstats` to plot a histogram of the count of the numbers in the standard input stream that fall in each of the `n` intervals defined by dividing `(l, r)` into `n` equal-sized intervals. Use your program to add code to your solution to Exercise 2.2.2 to plot a histogram of the distribution of the numbers produced by each function, taking `n` from the command line.

2.2.17 *Tukey plot.* A Tukey plot is a data visualization that generalizes a histogram; it is appropriate for use when each integer in a given range is associated with a set of y-values. For each integer i in the range, we compute the mean, standard deviation, 10th percentile, and 90th percentile of all the associated y-values; draw a vertical line with x-coordinate i running from the 10th percentile y-value to the 90th percentile y-value; and then draw a thin rectangle centered on the line that runs from one standard deviation below the mean to one standard deviation above the mean. Suppose that the standard input stream is a sequence of pairs of numbers where the first number in each pair is an integer and the second a float. Compose a `stdstats` and `stddraw` client that takes an integer `n` from the command line and, assuming that all the integers on the input stream are between `0` and `n-1`, uses standard drawing to make a Tukey plot of the data.

2.2.18 *IFS.* Experiment with various inputs to `ifs.py` to create patterns of your own design like the Sierpinski triangle, the Barnsley fern, or the other examples in the text. You might begin by experimenting with minor modifications to the given inputs.

2.2.19 *IFS matrix implementation.* Compose a version of `ifs.py` that uses `matrix.multiplyMV()` (see EXERCISE 2.2.9) instead of the equations that compute the new values of `x` and `y`.

2.2.20 *Stress test.* Compose a client that does stress testing for `stdstats`. Work with a classmate, with one person composing code and the other testing it.

2.2.21 *Gambler's ruin.* Compose a `stdrandom` client to study the gambler's ruin problem (see PROGRAM 1.3.8 and EXERCISE 1.3.23).

2.2.22 *Module for properties of integers.* Compose a module based on the functions that we have considered in this book for computing properties of integers. Include functions for determining whether a given integer is prime; whether two integers are relatively prime; all the factors of a given integer; the greatest common divisor and least common multiple of two integers; Euler's totient function (see EXERCISE 2.1.23); and any other functions that you think might be useful. Create an API, a client that performs stress testing, and clients that solve several of the exercises earlier in this book.

2.2.23 *Voting machines.* Compose a `stdrandom` client (with appropriate functions of its own) to study the following problem: Suppose that in a population of 100 million voters, 51% vote for candidate *A* and 49% vote for candidate *B*. However, the voting machines are prone to make mistakes, and 5% of the time they produce the wrong answer. Assuming the errors are made independently and at random, is a 5% error rate enough to invalidate the results of a close election? Which error rate can be tolerated?

2.2.24 *Poker analysis.* Compose a `stdrandom` and `stdstats` client (with appropriate functions of its own) to estimate the probabilities of getting one pair, two pair, three of a kind, a full house, and a flush in a five-card poker hand via simulation. Divide your program into appropriate functions and defend your design decisions. *Extra credit*: Add straight and straight flush to the list of possibilities.

2.2.25 *Music module.* Develop a module based on the functions in `playthattunedeluxe.py` (PROGRAM 2.1.4) that you can use to compose client programs to create and manipulate songs.

2.2.26 *Animated plots.* Compose a program that takes a command-line argument `m` and produces a bar graph of the `m` most recent floats on standard input. Use the same animation technique that we used for `bouncingball.py` (PROGRAM 1.5.7): repeatedly call `clear()`, draw the graph, and call `show()`. Each time your program reads a new number, it should redraw the whole graph. Since most of the picture does not change as it is redrawn slightly to the left, your program will produce the effect of a fixed-size window dynamically sliding over the input values. Use your program to plot a huge time-variant data file, such as stock prices.

2.2.27 *Array plot module.* Develop your own plot functions that improve upon those in `stdstats`. Be creative! Try to make a plotting module that you think will be useful for some application in the future.

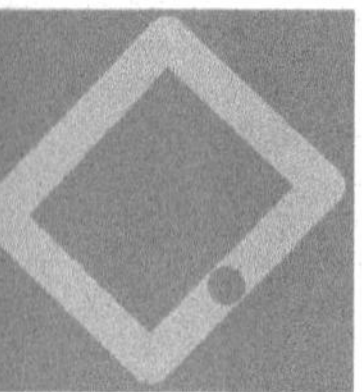

2.3 Recursion

The idea of calling one function from another immediately suggests the possibility of a function calling *itself*. The function-call mechanism in Python and in most modern programming languages supports this possibility, which is known as *recursion*. In this section, we will study examples of elegant and efficient recursive solutions to a variety of problems. Once you get used to the idea, you will see that recursion is a powerful general-purpose programming technique with many attractive properties. It is a fundamental tool that we use often in this book. Recursive programs are often more compact and easier to understand than their nonrecursive counterparts. Few programmers become sufficiently comfortable with recursion to use it in everyday code, but solving a problem with an elegantly crafted recursive program is a satisfying experience that is certainly accessible to every programmer (even you!).

Programs in this section

A recursive model of the natural world

Recursion is much more than a programming technique. In many settings, it is a useful way to describe the natural world. For example, the recursive tree (to the left) resembles a real tree, and has a natural recursive description. Many, many phenomena are well explained by recursive models. In particular, recursion plays a central role in computer science. It provides a simple computational model that embraces everything that can be computed with any computer; it helps us to organize and to analyze programs; and it is the key to numerous critically important computational applications, ranging from combinatorial search to tree data structures that support information processing to the fast Fourier transform for signal processing.

One important reason to embrace recursion is that it provides a straightforward way to build simple mathematical models that we can use to prove important facts about our programs. The proof technique that we use to do so is known as *mathematical induction*. Generally, we avoid going into the details of mathematical proofs in this book, but you will see in this section that it is worthwhile to understand that point of view and to make the effort to convince yourself that recursive programs have the intended effect.

Functions and Modules

2.3 Recursion

The idea of calling one function from another immediately suggests the possibility of a function calling *itself*. The function-call mechanism in Python and in most modern programming languages supports this possibility, which is known as *recursion*. In this section, we will study examples of elegant and efficient recursive solutions to a variety of problems. Once you get used to the idea, you will see that recursion is a powerful general-purpose programming technique with many attractive properties. It is a fundamental tool that we use often in this book. Recursive programs are often more compact and easier to understand than their nonrecursive counterparts. Few programmers become sufficiently comfortable with recursion to use it in everyday code, but solving a problem with an elegantly crafted recursive program is a satisfying experience that is certainly accessible to every programmer (even you!).

Programs in this section

A recursive model of the natural world

Recursion is much more than a programming technique. In many settings, it is a useful way to describe the natural world. For example, the recursive tree (to the left) resembles a real tree, and has a natural recursive description. Many, many phenomena are well explained by recursive models. In particular, recursion plays a central role in computer science. It provides a simple computational model that embraces everything that can be computed with any computer; it helps us to organize and to analyze programs; and it is the key to numerous critically important computational applications, ranging from combinatorial search to tree data structures that support information processing to the fast Fourier transform for signal processing.

One important reason to embrace recursion is that it provides a straightforward way to build simple mathematical models that we can use to prove important facts about our programs. The proof technique that we use to do so is known as *mathematical induction*. Generally, we avoid going into the details of mathematical proofs in this book, but you will see in this section that it is worthwhile to understand that point of view and to make the effort to convince yourself that recursive programs have the intended effect.

A recursive image

Your first recursive program The "Hello, World" for recursion (the first recursive program that most programmers implement) is the *factorial* function, defined for positive integers n by the equation

$$n! = n \times (n-1) \times (n-2) \times \ldots \times 2 \times 1$$

In other words, $n!$ is the product of the positive integers less than or equal to n. Now, $n!$ is easy to compute with a `for` loop, but an even easier approach is to use the following recursive function:

```
def factorial(n)
    if n == 1: return 1
    return n * factorial(n-1)
```

This function calls itself to produce the desired effect. You can persuade yourself that it does so by noting that `factorial()` returns $1 = 1!$ when n is 1 and that if it properly computes the value

$$(n-1)! = (n-1) \times (n-2) \times \ldots \times 2 \times 1$$

then it properly computes the value

$$\begin{aligned} n! &= n \times (n-1)! \\ &= n \times (n-1) \times (n-2) \times \ldots \times 2 \times 1 \end{aligned}$$

```
 1 1
 2 2
 3 6
 4 24
 5 120
 6 720
 7 5040
 8 40320
 9 362880
10 3628800
11 39916800
12 479001600
13 6227020800
14 87178291200
15 1307674368000
16 20922789888000
17 355687428096000
18 6402373705728000
19 121645100408832000
20 2432902008176640000
```

Values of n!

To compute `factorial(5)`, the recursive function needs to compute `factorial(4)`; to compute `factorial(4)`, it needs to compute `factorial(3)`; and so forth. This process is repeated until `factorial(1)`, which directly returns the value 1. Then `factorial(2)` multiplies that return value by 2 and returns 2; `factorial(3)` multiplies that return value by 3 and returns 6, and so forth. We can trace this computation in precisely the same way that we trace any sequence of function calls. Since we

```
factorial(5)
   factorial(4)
      factorial(3)
         factorial(2)
            factorial(1)
               return 1
            return 2*1 = 2
         return 3*2 = 6
      return 4*6 = 24
   return 5*24 = 120
```

Function call trace for `factorial()`

view all of the calls as invoking independent copies of the code, the fact that they are recursive is immaterial.

Our `factorial()` implementation exhibits the two main components that are required for every recursive function. The *base case* returns a value without making any subsequent recursive calls. It does this for one or more special arguments for which the function can be evaluated without recursion. For `factorial()`, the base case is when `n` is `1`. The *reduction step* is the central part of a recursive function. It relates the function at one (or more) arguments to the function evaluated at one (or more) other arguments. For `factorial()`, the reduction step is `n * factorial(n-1)`. All recursive functions must have these two components. Furthermore, the sequence of argument values must converge to the base case. For `factorial()`, the value of `n` decreases by 1 for each call, so the sequence of argument values converges to the base case.

Tiny functions such as `factorial()` are slightly clearer if we put the reduction step in an `else` clause. However, adopting this convention for every recursive function would unnecessarily complicate larger functions because it would involve putting most of the code (for the reduction step) in an indented block after the `else`. Instead, we adopt the convention of putting the base case as the first statement, ending with a `return`, and then devoting the rest of the code to the reduction step.

The same technique is effective for defining all sorts of functions. For example, the recursive function

```
def harmonic(n):
    if n == 1: return 1.0
    return harmonic(n-1) + 1.0/n
```

is an effective function for computing the harmonic numbers (see PROGRAM 1.3.5) when n is small, based on the following equations:

$$\begin{aligned} H_n &= 1 + 1/2 + \ldots + 1/n \\ &= \big(1 + 1/2 + \ldots + 1/(n-1)\big) + 1/n \;=\; H_{n-1} + 1/n \end{aligned}$$

Indeed, this same approach is effective for computing, with only a few lines of code, the value of *any* discrete sum for which you have a compact formula. Recursive programs like these are just loops in disguise, but recursion can help us better understand this sort of computation.

Mathematical induction Recursive programming is directly related to *mathematical induction*, a technique for proving facts about discrete functions.

Proving that a statement involving an integer n is true for infinitely many values of n by mathematical induction involves the following two steps:

- The *base case*: prove the statement true for some specific value or values of n (usually 1).
- The *induction step* (the central part of the proof): assume the statement to be true for all positive integers less than n, then use that fact to prove it true for n.

Such a proof suffices to show that the statement is true for *all* positive integers n: we can start at the base case, and use our proof to establish that the statement is true for each larger value of n, one by one.

Everyone's first induction proof is to demonstrate that the sum of the positive integers less than or equal to n is given by the formula $n\ (n+1)/\ 2$. That is, we wish to prove that the following equation is valid for all $n \geq 1$:

$$1 + 2 + 3\ \ldots + (n-1) + n \;=\; n\ (n+1)\,/\,2$$

The equation is certainly true for $n = 1$ (base case) because $1 = 1$. If we assume it to be true for all integers less than n, then, in particular, it is true for $n-1$, so

$$1 + 2 + 3\ \ldots + (n-1) \;=\; (n-1)\ n\,/\,2$$

and we can add n to both sides of this equation and simplify to get the desired equation (induction step).

Every time we compose a recursive function, we need mathematical induction to be convinced that the function has the desired effect. The correspondence between induction and recursion is self-evident. The difference in nomenclature indicates a difference in outlook: in a recursive function, our outlook is to get a computation done by reducing to a smaller problem, so we use the term *reduction step*; in an induction proof, our outlook is to establish the truth of the statement for larger problems, so we use the term *induction step*.

When we compose recursive functions, we usually do not write down a full formal proof that they produce the desired result, but we always depend on the existence of such a proof. We do often appeal to an informal induction proof to convince ourselves that a recursive function operates as expected. For example, we just discussed an informal proof that `factorial(n)` computes the product of the positive integers less than or equal to `n`.

Program 2.3.1 Euclid's algorithm (euclid.py)

```
import sys
import stdio

def gcd(p, q):
    if q == 0: return p
    return gcd(q, p % q)

def main():
    p = int(sys.argv[1])
    q = int(sys.argv[2])
    stdio.writeln(gcd(p, q))

if __name__ == '__main__': main()
```

```
% python euclid.py 1440 408
24
% python euclid.py 314159 271828
1
```

This script takes two positive integers from the command line and computes their greatest common divisor, using a recursive implementation of Euclid's algorithm.

Euclid's algorithm The *greatest common divisor* (gcd) of two positive integers is the largest integer that divides evenly into both of them. For example, the greatest common divisor of 102 and 68 is 34 since both 102 and 68 are multiples of 34, but no integer larger than 34 divides evenly into 102 and 68. You may recall learning about the greatest common divisor when you learned to reduce fractions. For example, we can simplify 68/102 to 2/3 by dividing both numerator and denominator by 34, their gcd. Finding the gcd of huge integers is an important problem that arises in many commercial applications, including the famous RSA cryptosystem.

We can efficiently compute the gcd using the following property, which holds for positive integers p and q:

If p > q, the gcd of p and q is the same as the gcd of q and p % q.

To convince yourself of this fact, first note that the gcd of p and q is the same as the gcd of q and $p-q$, because a number divides both p and q if and only if it divides both q and $p-q$. By the same argument, q and $p-2q$, q and $p-3q$, and so forth have the same gcd, and one way to compute $p \% q$ is to subtract q from p until we get a number less than q.

The function `gcd()` in `euclid.py` (PROGRAM 2.3.1) is a compact recursive function whose reduction step is based on this property. The base case is when `q` is 0, with `gcd(p, 0) = p`. To see that the reduction step converges to the base case, observe that the value of the second argument strictly decreases in each recursive call since `p % q < q`. If `p < q`, then the first recursive call switches the two arguments. In fact, the value of the second argument decreases by at least a factor of 2 for every second recursive call, so the sequence of argument values quickly converges to the base case (see EXERCISE 2.3.13). This recursive solution to the problem of computing the greatest common divisor is known as *Euclid's algorithm* and is one of the oldest known algorithms—it is over 2,000 years old.

```
gcd(1440, 408)
   gcd(408, 216)
      gcd(216, 24)
         gcd(192, 24)
            gcd(24, 0)
               return 24
            return 24
         return 24
      return 24
   return 24
```

Function call trace for gcd()

Towers of Hanoi No discussion of recursion would be complete without the famous *towers of Hanoi* problem. In this problem, we have three poles and n discs that fit onto the poles. The discs differ in size and are initially stacked on one of the poles, in order from largest (disc n) at the bottom to smallest (disc 1) at the top. The task is to move all n discs to another pole, while obeying the following rules:

- Move only one disc at a time.
- Never place a larger disc on a smaller one.

One legend says that the world will end when a certain group of monks accomplishes this task in a temple with 64 golden discs on three diamond needles. But how can the monks accomplish the task at all, playing by the rules?

To solve the problem, our goal is to issue a sequence of instructions for moving the discs. We assume that the poles are arranged in a row, and that each instruction to move a disc specifies its number and whether to move it left or right. If a disc is on the left pole, an instruction to move left means to wrap

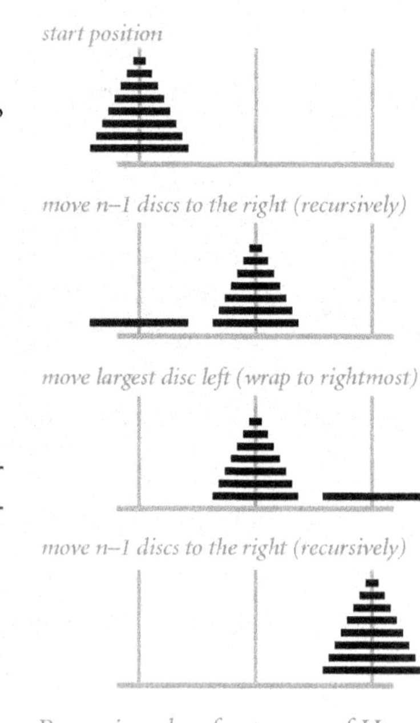

Recursive plan for towers of Hanoi

to the right pole; if a disc is on the right pole, an instruction to move right means to wrap to the left pole. When the discs are all on one pole, there are two possible moves (move the smallest disc left or right); otherwise, there are three possible moves (move the smallest disc left or right, or make the one legal move involving the other two poles). Choosing among these possibilities on each move to achieve the goal is a challenge that requires a plan. Recursion provides just the plan that we need, based on the following idea: first we move the top $n-1$ discs to an empty pole, then we move the largest disc to the other empty pole (where it does not interfere with the smaller ones), and then we complete the job by moving the $n-1$ discs onto the largest disc. To simplify the instructions, we move discs either left or right, with *wraparound*: moving left from the leftmost pole means to move to the rightmost pole and moving right from the rightmost pole means move to the leftmost pole.

PROGRAM 2.3.2 (`towersofhanoi.py`) is a direct implementation of this strategy. It reads in a command-line argument `n` and writes the solution to the towers of Hanoi problem on `n` discs. The recursive function `moves()` writes the sequence of moves to move the stack of discs to the left (if the argument `left` is `True`) or to the right (if `left` is `False`), with wraparound. It does so exactly according to the plan just described.

Function-call trees To better understand the behavior of modular programs that have multiple recursive calls (such as `towersofhanoi.py`), we use a visual representation known as a *function-call tree*. Specifically, we represent each function call as a *tree node*, depicted as a circle labeled with the values of the arguments for that call. Below each tree node, we draw the tree nodes corresponding to each call in that use of the function (in order from left to right) and lines connecting to them. This diagram contains all the information we need to understand the behavior of the program. It contains a tree node for each function call.

We can use function-call trees to understand the behavior of any modular program, but they are particularly useful in exposing the behavior of recursive programs. For example, the tree corresponding to a call to `move()` in `towersofhanoi.py` is easy to construct. Start by drawing a tree node labeled with the values of the command-line arguments. The first argument is the number of discs in the pile to be

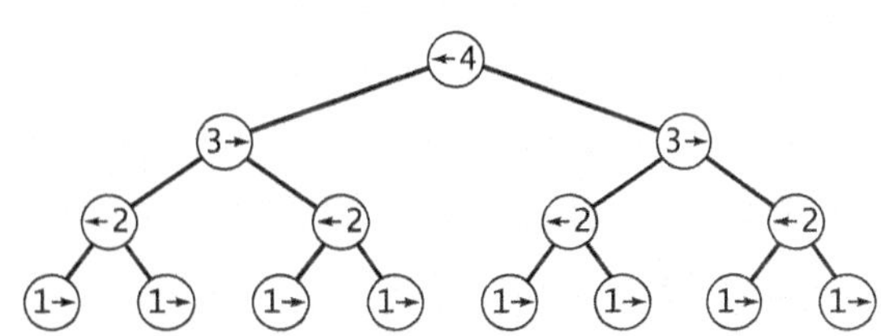

Function-call tree for `moves(4, true)` *in* `towersofhanoi.py`

Program 2.3.2 Towers of Hanoi (towersofhanoi.py)

```
import sys
import stdio

def moves(n, left):
    if n == 0: return
    moves(n-1, not left)
    if left:
        stdio.writeln(str(n) + ' left')
    else:
        stdio.writeln(str(n) + ' right')
    moves(n-1, not left)

n = int(sys.argv[1])
moves(n, True)
```

n	*number of discs*
left	*direction to move pile*

This script writes the instructions for the towers of Hanoi problem. The recursive function moves() *writes the moves needed to move* n *discs to the left (if* left *is* True*) or to the right (if* left *is* False*).*

```
% python towersofhanoi.py 1
1 left

% python towersofhanoi.py 2
1 right
2 left
1 right

% python towersofhanoi.py 3
1 left
2 right
1 left
3 left
1 left
2 right
1 left
```

```
% python towersofhanoi.py 4
1 right
2 left
1 right
3 right
1 right
2 left
1 right
4 left
1 right
2 left
1 right
3 right
1 right
2 left
1 right
```

moved (and the label of the disc to actually be moved); the second is the direction to move the pile. For clarity, we depict the direction (a boolean value) as an arrow that points left or right, since that is our interpretation of the value—the direction to move the disc. Then draw two tree nodes below with the number of discs decremented by 1 and the direction switched, and continue doing so until only nodes with labels corresponding to a first argument value 1 have no nodes below them. These nodes correspond to calls on `moves()` that do not lead to further recursive calls.

Take a moment to study the function-call tree depicted earlier in this section and to compare it with the corresponding function-call trace depicted at right. When you do so, you will see that the function-call tree is just a compact representation of the trace. In particular, reading the node labels from left to right gives the moves needed to solve the problem.

Moreover, when you study the tree, you may notice several patterns, including the following two:

- Alternate moves involve the smallest disc.
- That disc always moves in the same direction.

These observations are relevant because they give a solution to the problem that does not require recursion (or even a computer): every other move involves the smallest disc (including the first and last), and each intervening move is the only legal move at the time not involving the smallest disc. We can *prove* that this strategy produces the same outcome as the recursive program, using induction. Having started centuries ago without the benefit of a computer, perhaps our monks are using this strategy.

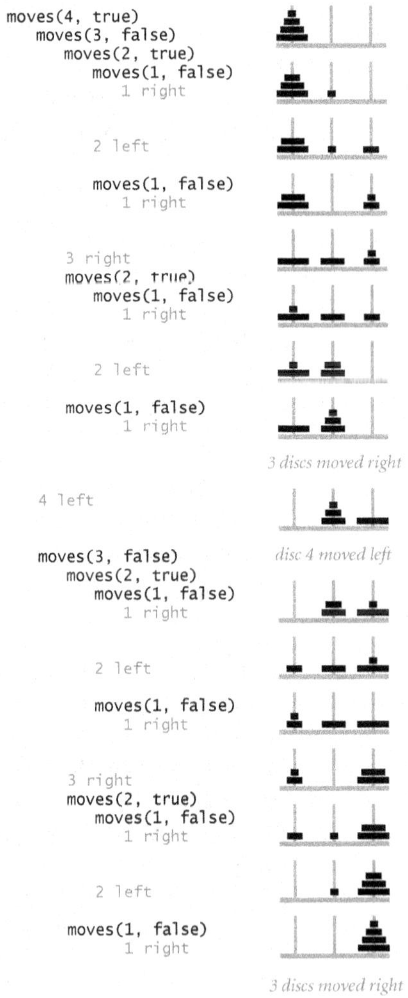

Trees are relevant and important in understanding recursion because the tree is the quintessential recursive object. As an abstract mathematical model, trees play an essential role in many applications, and in Chapter 4, we will consider the use of trees as a computational model to structure data for efficient processing.

```
moves(4, true)
   moves(3, false)
      moves(2, true)
         moves(1, false)
            1 right
         2 left
         moves(1, false)
            1 right
      3 right
      moves(2, true)
         moves(1, false)
            1 right
         2 left
         moves(1, false)
            1 right
   4 left
   moves(3, false)
      moves(2, true)
         moves(1, false)
            1 right
         2 left
         moves(1, false)
            1 right
      3 right
      moves(2, true)
         moves(1, false)
            1 right
         2 left
         moves(1, false)
            1 right
```

3 discs moved right

disc 4 moved left

3 discs moved right

Function-call trace for `moves(4, true)`

Exponential time One advantage of using recursion is that often we can develop mathematical models that allow us to prove important facts about the behavior of recursive programs. For the towers of Hanoi, we can estimate the amount of time until the end of the world (assuming that the legend is true). This exercise is important not just because it tells us that the end of the world is quite far off (even if the legend is true), but also because it provides insight that can help us avoid composing programs that will not finish until then.

For the towers of Hanoi problem, the mathematical model is simple: if we define the function $T(n)$ to be the number of move directives issued by `towersofhanoi.py` to move n discs from one pole to another, then the recursive code immediately implies that $T(n)$ must satisfy the following equation:

$$T(n) = 2\ T(n-1) + 1 \text{ for } n > 1, \text{with } T(1) = 1$$

Such an equation is known in discrete mathematics as a *recurrence relation*. Recurrence relations naturally arise in the study of recursive programs. We can often use them to derive a closed-form expression for the quantity of interest. For $T(n)$, you may have already guessed from the initial values $T(1) = 1$, $T(2) = 3$, $T(3) = 7$, and $T(4) = 15$ that $T(n) = 2^n - 1$. The recurrence relation provides a way to *prove* this to be true, by mathematical induction:

- *Base case*: $T(1) = 2^n - 1 = 1$
- *Induction step*: if $T(n-1)= 2^{n-1} - 1$, $T(n) = 2\ (2^{n-1} - 1) + 1 = 2^n - 1$

Therefore, by induction, $T(n) = 2^n - 1$ for all $n > 0$. The minimum possible number of moves also satisfies the same recurrence (see Exercise 2.3.11).

Knowing the value of $T(n)$, we can estimate the amount of time required to perform all the moves. If the monks move discs at the rate of one per second, it would take more than one week for them to finish a 20-disc problem, more than 34 years to finish a 30-disc problem, and more than 348 *centuries* for them to finish a 40-disc problem (assuming that they do not make a mistake). The 64-disc problem would take more than 5.8 *billion* centuries. The end of the world is likely to be even further off than that because those monks presumably never have had the benefit of using Program 2.3.2, and might not be able to move the discs so rapidly or to figure out so quickly which disc to move next.

Even computers are no match for exponential growth. A computer that can do a billion operations per second will still take centuries to do 2^{64} operations, and no computer will ever do $2^{1,000}$ operations, say. The lesson is profound: with recursion, you can easily compose simple short programs that take exponential time, but they simply will not run to completion when you try to run them for large n.

Novices are often skeptical of this basic fact, so it is worth your while to pause now to think about it. To convince yourself that it is true, take calls on `stdio.writeln()` out of `towersofhanoi.py` and run it for increasing values of n starting at 20. You can easily verify that each time you increase the value of n by 1, the running time doubles, and you will quickly lose patience waiting for it to finish. If you wait for an hour for some value of n, you will wait more than a day for n+5, more than a month for n+10, and more than a century for n+20 (no one has *that* much patience). Your computer is just not fast enough to run every short Python program that you compose, no matter how simple the program might seem! *Beware of programs that might require exponential time.*

We are often interested in predicting the running time of our programs. In SECTION 4.1, we will discuss the use of the same process that we just used to help estimate the running time of other programs.

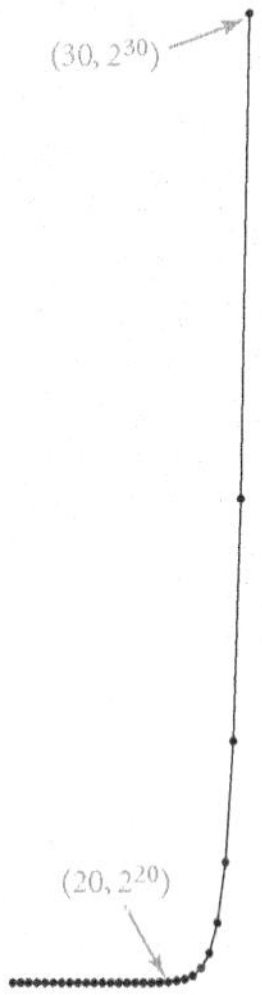

Exponential growth

Gray codes The towers of Hanoi problem is no toy. It is intimately related to basic algorithms for manipulating numbers and discrete objects. As an example, we consider *Gray codes*, a mathematical abstraction with numerous applications.

The playwright Samuel Beckett, perhaps best known for *Waiting for Godot*, wrote a play called *Quad* that had the following property: starting with an empty stage, characters enter and exit one at a time so that each subset of characters on the stage appears exactly once. How did Beckett generate the stage directions for this play?

code	subset	move
0 0 0 0	*empty*	
0 0 0 1	1	enter 1
0 0 1 1	2 1	enter 2
0 0 1 0	2	exit 1
0 1 1 0	3 2	enter 3
0 1 1 1	3 2 1	enter 1
0 1 0 1	3 1	exit 2
0 1 0 0	3	exit 1
1 1 0 0	4 3	enter 4
1 1 0 1	4 3 1	enter 1
1 1 1 1	4 3 2 1	enter 2
1 1 1 0	4 3 2	exit 1
1 0 1 0	4 2	exit 3
1 0 1 1	4 2 1	enter 1
1 0 0 1	4 1	exit 2
1 0 0 0	4	exit 1

Gray code representations

One way to represent a subset of n discrete objects is to use a string of n bits. For Beckett's problem, we use a 4-bit string, with bits numbered 1 to n from right to left and a bit value of `1` indicating the character onstage. For example, the string `0 1 0 1` corresponds to the scene with characters 3 and 1 onstage. This representation gives a quick proof of a basic fact: *the number of different subsets of n objects is exactly* 2^n. *Quad* has four characters, so there are $2^4 = 16$ different scenes. Our task is to generate the stage directions.

An n-bit *Gray code* is a list of the 2^n different n-bit binary numbers such that each entry in the list differs in precisely one bit from its predecessor. Gray codes directly apply to Beckett's problem because changing the value of a bit from 0 to 1 corresponds to a character entering the subset onstage; changing a bit from 1 to 0 corresponds to a character exiting the subset.

How do we generate a Gray code? A recursive plan that is very similar to the one that we used for the towers of Hanoi problem is effective. The n-bit *binary-reflected Gray code* is defined recursively as follows:

- The $(n-1)$ bit code, with 0 prepended to each codeword, followed by
- The $(n-1)$ bit code *in reverse order*, with 1 prepended to each codeword

The 0-bit code is defined to be null, so the 1-bit code is 0 followed by 1. From this recursive definition, we can verify by induction that the n-bit binary reflected Gray code has the required property: adjacent codewords differ in one bit position. It is true by the inductive hypothesis, except possibly for the last codeword in the first half and the first codeword in the second half: this pair differs only in their first bit.

The recursive definition leads, after some careful thought, to the implementation in `beckett.py` (PROGRAM 2.3.3) for writing Beckett's stage directions. This program is remarkably similar to `towersofhanoi.py`. Indeed, except for nomenclature, the only difference is in the values of the second arguments in the recursive calls!

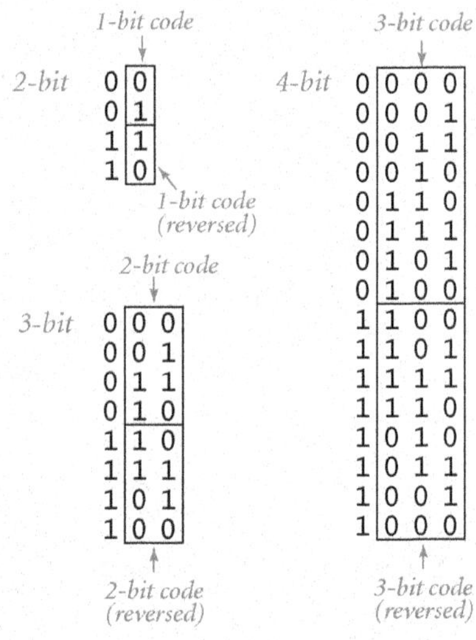

2-, 3-, and 4-bit Gray codes

As with the directions of the disc moves in `towersofhanoi.py`, the enter and exit directions are redundant in `beckett.py`, since `exit` is issued only when an actor is onstage, and `enter` is issued only when an actor is not onstage. Indeed, both `beckett.py` and `towersofhanoi.py` directly involve the ruler function that we considered in one of our first programs, `ruler.py` (PROGRAM 1.2.1). Without the redundant instructions, they both implement a simple recursive function that could be used to write the values of the ruler function for any value given as a command-line argument.

Gray codes have many applications, ranging from analog-to-digital converters to experimental design. They have been used in pulse code communication, the minimization of logic circuits, and hypercube architectures, and were even proposed to organize books on library shelves.

Program 2.3.3 Gray code (beckett.py)

```
import sys
import stdio

def moves(n, enter):
    if n == 0: return
    moves(n-1, True)
    if enter:
        stdio.writeln('enter ' + str(n))
    else:
        stdio.writeln('exit  ' + str(n))
    moves(n-1, False)

n = int(sys.argv[1])
moves(n, True)
```

n	*number of characters*
enter	*stage direction*

This script reads an integer n from the command line and uses a recursive function to write Beckett's stage instructions (the bit positions that change in a binary-reflected Gray code) for an n-character play. The bit position that changes is precisely described by the ruler function, and (of course) each character alternately enters and exits.

```
% python beckett.py 1
enter 1

% python beckett.py 2
enter 1
enter 2
exit  1

% python beckett.py 3
enter 1
enter 2
exit  1
enter 3
enter 1
exit  2
exit  1
```

```
% python beckett.py 4
enter 1
enter 2
exit  1
enter 3
enter 1
exit  2
exit  1
enter 4
enter 1
enter 2
exit  1
enter 3
enter 1
exit  2
exit  1
```

Recursive graphics Simple recursive drawing schemes can lead to pictures that are remarkably intricate. Recursive drawings not only relate to numerous applications, but also provide an appealing platform for developing a better understanding of properties of recursive programs, because we can watch the process of a recursive figure taking shape.

As a first simple example, we define an *H-tree of order n*, as follows: The base case is to draw nothing for $n = 0$. The reduction step is to draw, within the unit square

- Three lines in the shape of the letter H
- Four H-trees of order $n-1$, one connected to each tip of the H

with the additional provisos that the H-trees of order $n-1$ are halved in size and centered on the four tips of the square. PROGRAM 2.3.4 (`htree.py`) takes a command-line argument n, and draws an H-tree of order n.

Drawings like these have many practical applications. For example, consider a cable company that needs to run cable to all of the homes distributed throughout its region. A reasonable strategy is to use an H-tree to get the signal to a suitable number of centers distributed throughout the region, then run cables connecting each home to the nearest center. The same problem is faced by computer designers who want to distribute power or signal throughout an integrated circuit chip.

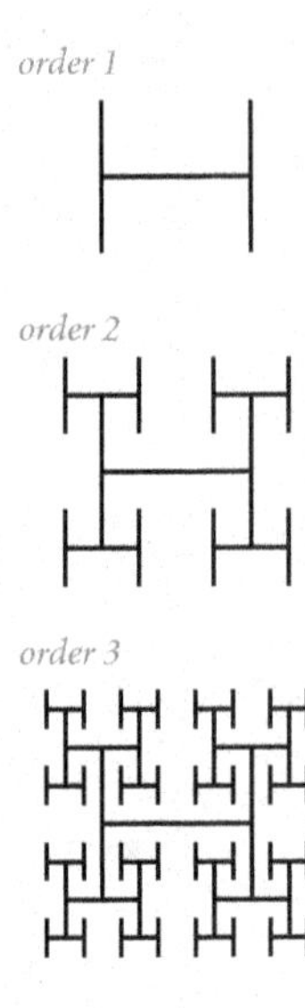

H-trees

H-trees exhibit exponential growth. An H-tree of order n connects 4^n centers, so you would be trying to plot more than 1 million lines with $n = 10$ and more than 1 billion with $n = 15$. The program will certainly not finish the drawing with $n = 30$.

EXERCISE 2.3.14 asks you to modify `htree.py` to animate the drawing of the H-tree. If you run the resulting program on your computer for a drawing that takes a minute or so to complete, you will, just by watching the drawing progress, have the opportunity to gain substantial insight into the nature of recursive functions, because you can see the order in which the H figures appear and how they form into H-trees. An even more instructive exercise, which derives from the fact that the same drawing results no matter in which order the recursive `draw()` calls and the `stddraw.line()` calls appear, is to observe the effect of rearranging the order of these calls on the order in which the lines appear in the emerging drawing (see EXERCISE 2.3.14).

Program 2.3.4 Recursive graphics (htree.py)

```
import sys
import stddraw

def draw(n, size, x, y):
    if n == 0: return
    x0 = x - size/2.0
    x1 = x + size/2.0
    y0 = y - size/2.0
    y1 = y + size/2.0

    stddraw.line(x0, y, x1, y)
    stddraw.line(x0, y0, x0, y1)
    stddraw.line(x1, y0, x1, y1)

    draw(n-1, size/2.0, x0, y0)
    draw(n-1, size/2.0, x0, y1)
    draw(n-1, size/2.0, x1, y0)
    draw(n-1, size/2.0, x1, y1)

n = int(sys.argv[1])
stddraw.setPenRadius(0.0)
draw(n, 0.5, 0.5, 0.5)
stddraw.show()
```

`n`	*depth*
`size`	*line length*
`x, y`	*center*

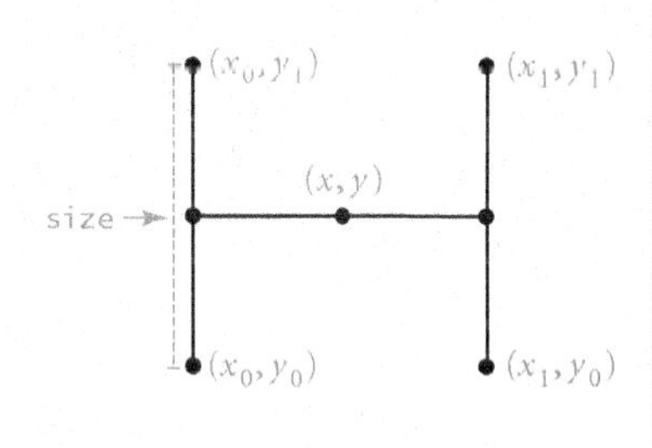

This script accepts a command-line argument n and uses a recursive function to draw an H-tree of order n: it draws three lines in the shape of the letter H that connect the center (x, y) of the square with the centers of the four tips, then calls itself for each of the tips. The integer argument controls the depth of the recursion and the float argument is the size of the initial H.

% python htree.py 3

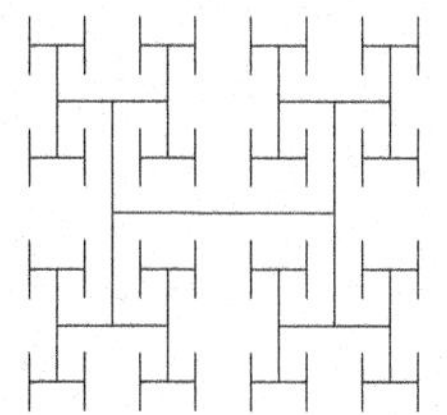

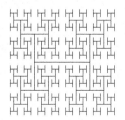

% python htree.py 4

% python htree.py 5

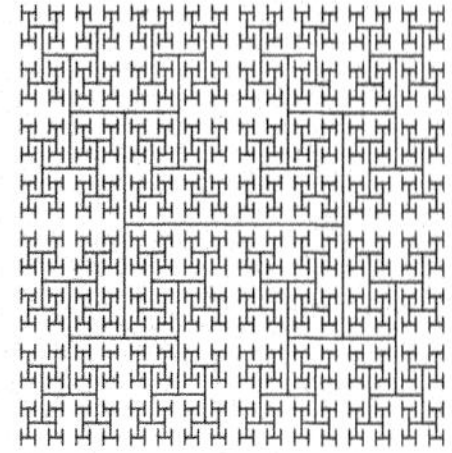

Brownian bridge An H-tree is a simple example of a *fractal*: a geometric shape that can be divided into parts, each of which is (approximately) a reduced-size copy of the original. Fractals are easy to produce with recursive functions, although scientists, mathematicians, and programmers study them from many different points of view. We have already encountered fractals several times in this book—for example, `ifs.py` (PROGRAM 2.2.4).

The study of fractals plays an important and lasting role in artistic expression, economic analysis, and scientific discovery. Artists and scientists use them to build compact models of complex shapes that arise in nature and resist description using conventional geometry, such as clouds, plants, mountains, riverbeds, human skin, and many others. Economists also use fractals to model function graphs of economic indicators.

Fractional Brownian motion is a mathematical model for creating realistic fractal models for many naturally rugged shapes. It is used in computational finance and in the study of many natural phenomena, including ocean flows and nerve membranes. Computing the exact fractals specified by the model can be a difficult challenge, but it is not difficult to compute approximations with recursive functions. We consider one simple example here; you can find much more information about the model on the booksite.

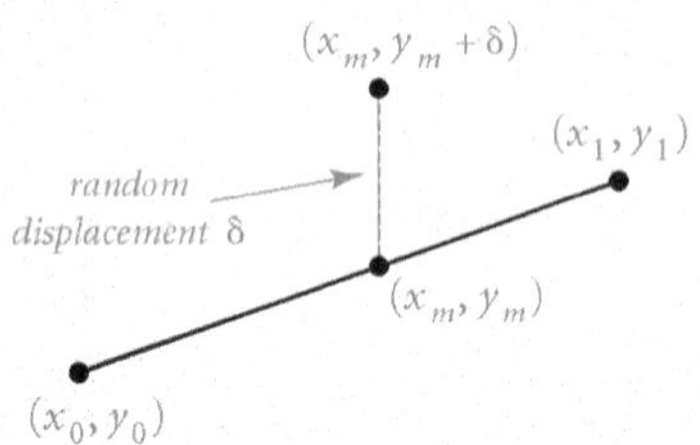

Brownian bridge calculation

PROGRAM 2.3.5 (`brownian.py`) plots a function graph that approximates a simple example of fractional Brownian motion known as a *Brownian bridge* and closely related functions. You can think of this graph as a random walk that connects two points, from (x_0, y_0) to (x_1, y_1), controlled by a few parameters. The implementation is based on the *midpoint displacement method*, which is a recursive plan for drawing the plot within the interval $[x_0, x_1]$. The base case is to draw a straight line connecting the two endpoints. The reduction case is to divide the interval into two halves, proceeding as follows:

- Compute the midpoint (x_m, y_m) of the interval.
- Add to the y-coordinate y_m of the midpoint a random value δ, drawn from the Gaussian distribution with mean 0 and a given variance.
- Recur on the subintervals, dividing the variance by a given scaling factor β.

The shape of the curve is controlled by two parameters: the *volatility* (the initial value of the variance) controls the distance the graph strays from the straight line connecting the points, and *the Hurst exponent* controls the smoothness of the

Program 2.3.5 **Brownian bridge** (brownian.py)

```
import math
import sys
import stddraw
import stdrandom

def curve(x0, y0, x1, y1, var, beta, n=7):
    if n == 0:
        stddraw.line(x0, y0, x1, y1)
        return

    xm = (x0 + x1) / 2.0
    ym = (y0 + y1) / 2.0
    delta = stdrandom.gaussian(0.0, math.sqrt(var))
    curve(x0, y0, xm, ym+delta, var/beta, beta, n-1)
    curve(xm, ym+delta, x1, y1, var/beta, beta, n-1)

hurstExponent = float(sys.argv[1])
stddraw.setPenRadius(0.0)
beta = 2.0 ** (2.0 * hurstExponent)
curve(0.0, 0.5, 1.0, 0.5, 0.01, beta)
stddraw.show()
```

n	*recursion depth*
x0, y0	*left endpoint*
x1, y1	*right endpoint*
xm, ym	*middle*
delta	*displacement*
var	*variance*
beta	*smoothness*

This script draws a Brownian bridge across the middle of the window, by adding a small random number (drawn from the Gaussian distribution) to a recursive function that would otherwise plot a straight line. The command-line argument, known as the Hurst exponent, controls the smoothness of the curves—the recursive function uses it to compute a factor beta *that adjusts the variance of the Gaussian distribution.*

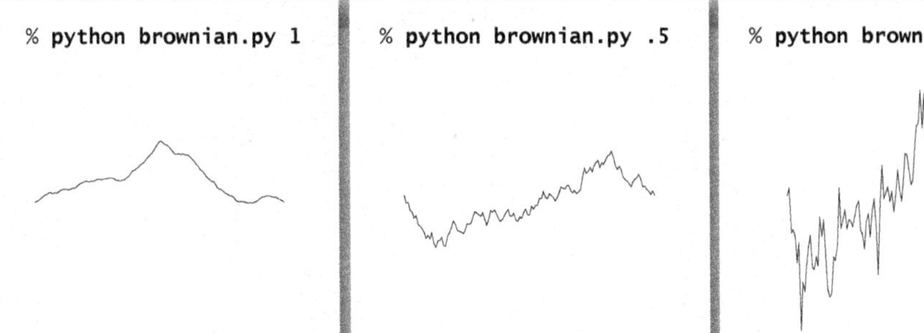
% python brownian.py 1
% python brownian.py .5
% python brownian.py .05

curve. We denote the Hurst exponent by H and divide the variance by $\beta = 2^{2H}$ at each recursive level. When H is 1/2 (divide by 2 at each level), the curve is a Brownian bridge: a continuous version of the gambler's ruin problem (see PROGRAM 1.3.8). When $0 < H < 1/2$, the displacements tend to increase, resulting in a rougher curve; and when $1/2 < H < 2$, the displacements tend to decrease, resulting in a smoother curve. The value $2 - H$ is known as the *fractal dimension* of the curve.

The volatility and initial endpoints of the interval have to do with scale and positioning. The global code in `brownian.py` allows you to experiment with the smoothness parameter H. With values larger than 1/2, you get plots that look something like the horizon in a mountainous landscape; with values smaller than 1/2, you get plots similar to those you might see for the value of a stock index.

Extending the midpoint displacement method to two dimensions produces fractals known as *plasma clouds*. To draw a rectangular plasma cloud, we use a recursive plan where the base case is to draw a rectangle of a given color and the reduction step is to draw a plasma cloud in each quadrant with colors that are

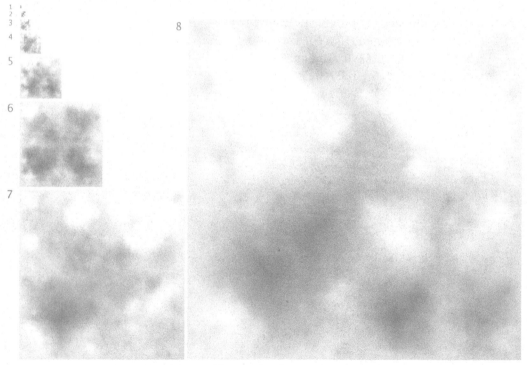

Plasma clouds

perturbed from the average with a random number drawn from the Gaussian distribution. Using the same volatility and smoothness controls as in `brownian.py`, we can produce synthetic clouds that are remarkably realistic. We can use the same code to produce synthetic terrain, by interpreting the color value as the altitude. Variants of this scheme are widely used in the entertainment industry to generate background scenery for movies and computer games.

Pitfalls of recursion By now, you are perhaps persuaded that recursion can help you compose compact and elegant programs. As you begin to craft your own recursive programs, you need to be aware of several common pitfalls that can arise. We have already discussed one of them in some detail (the running time of your program might grow exponentially). Once identified, these problems are generally not difficult to overcome, but you must be very careful to avoid them when composing recursive functions.

Missing base case. Consider the following recursive function, which is supposed to compute harmonic numbers, but is missing a base case:

```
def harmonic(n):
    return harmonic(n-1) + 1.0/n
```

If you run a client that calls this function, it will repeatedly call itself and never return, so your program will never terminate. You probably already have encountered infinite loops, where you run your program and nothing happens (or perhaps you get an unending sequence of lines of output). With infinite recursion, however, the result is different because the system keeps track of each recursive call (using a mechanism that we will discuss in SECTION 4.3, based on a data structure known as a stack) and eventually runs out of memory trying to do so. Eventually, Python raises a `RuntimeError` and reports `maximum recursion depth exceeded`. When you run a recursive program, you should always try to convince yourself that it has the desired effect by making an informal argument based on mathematical induction. Doing so might uncover a missing base case.

No guarantee of convergence. Another common problem is to include within a recursive function a recursive call to solve a subproblem that is not smaller than the original problem. For example, the following function goes into an infinite recursive loop for any value of its argument `n` except `1`:

```
def harmonic(n):
    if n = 1: return 1.0
    return harmonic(n) + 1.0/n
```

Bugs like this one are easy to spot, but subtle versions of the same problem can be harder to identify.

Excessive memory requirements. If a function calls itself recursively an excessive number of times before returning, the memory required by Python to keep track of the recursive calls may be prohibitive, resulting in a "maximum depth exceeded" run-time error. To get an idea of how much memory is involved, run a small set of experiments using this recursive function for computing the harmonic numbers for increasing values of n (say, by starting at 1,000 and increasing by factors of 10):

```
def harmonic(n):
    if n == 1: return 1.0
    return harmonic(n-1) + 1.0/n
```

The point at which you get the "maximum recursion depth exceeded" run-time error will give you some idea of how much memory Python uses to implement recursion. By contrast, you can run Program 1.3.5 to compute H_n for huge n using only a tiny bit of space.

Excessive recomputation. The temptation to compose a simple recursive function to solve a problem must always be tempered by the understanding that a simple function might take exponential time (unnecessarily) due to excessive recomputation. This effect is possible even in the simplest recursive functions, and you certainly need to learn to avoid it. For example, the *Fibonacci sequence*

$$0, 1, 1, 2, 3, 5, 8, 13, 21, 34, 55, 89, 144, 233, 377, \ldots$$

is defined by the recurrence $F_n = F_{n-1} + F_{n-2}$ for $n \geq 2$ with $F_0 = 0$ and $F_1 = 1$. The Fibonacci sequence has many interesting properties and arises in numerous applications. A novice programmer might implement this recursive function to compute numbers in the Fibonacci sequence:

```
def fib(n):
    if n == 0: return 0
    if n == 1: return 1
    return fib(n-1) + fib(n-2)
```

This function is spectacularly inefficient—do not use it! Novice programmers often refuse to believe this fact, and run code like this expecting that the computer is certainly fast enough to crank out an answer. Go ahead; see if your computer is fast enough to compute `fib(50)`. To see why it is futile to do so, consider what the function does to compute `fib(7)` = 13. It first computes `fib(6)` = 8 and `fib(5)` = 5. To compute `fib(6)`, it recursively computes `fib(5)` = 5 *again* and `fib(4)` = 3. Things rapidly get worse because both times it computes `fib(5)`, it ignores the fact that it already computed `fib(4)`, and so forth. In fact, you can prove by induction that the number of times this program computes `fib(1)` when computing `fib(n)` is precisely F_n (see EXERCISE 2.3.12). The mistake of recomputation is compounded exponentially. As an example, to compute `fib(200)`, the number of times the naive recursive function needs to compute `fib(1)` is $F_{200} > 10^{43}$! No imaginable computer will ever be able to do this many calculations. *Beware of programs that might require exponential time.* Many calculations that arise and find natural expression as recursive functions fall into this category. Do not fall into the trap of implementing and trying to run them.

The following is one caveat: a systematic technique known as *memoization* allows us to avoid this pitfall while still taking advantage of the compact recursive description of a computation. In memoization, we maintain an array that keeps track of the values we have computed so that we can return those values and make recursive calls only for new values. This technique is a form of *dynamic programming*, a well-studied technique for organizing computations that you will learn if you take courses in algorithms or in operations research.

```
fib(7)
  fib(6)
    fib(5)
      fib(4)
        fib(3)
          fib(2)
            fib(1)
              return 1
            fib(0)
              return 0
            return 1
          fib(1)
            return 1
          return 2
        fib(2)
          fib(1)
            return 1
          fib(0)
            return 0
          return 1
        return 3
      fib(3)
        fib(2)
          fib(1)
            return 1
          fib(0)
            return 0
          return 1
        fib(1)
          return 1
        return 2
      return 5
    fib(4)
      fib(3)
        fib(2)
          .
          .
          .
```

Wrong way to compute Fibonacci numbers

Perspective Programmers who do not use recursion are missing two opportunities. First, recursion leads to compact solutions to complex problems. Second, recursive solutions embody an argument that the program operates as anticipated. In the early days of computing, the overhead associated with recursive functions was prohibitive in some systems, and many people avoided recursion. In modern systems like Python, recursion is often the method of choice.

If you are intrigued by the mystery of how Python manages to implement the illusion of independently operating copies of the same piece of code, be assured that we will consider this issue in CHAPTER 4. You may be surprised at the simplicity of the solution. It is so easy to implement that programmers were using recursion well before the advent of high-level programming languages like Python. Indeed, you might be surprised to learn that you could compose programs equivalent to the ones considered in this chapter with just the basic loops, conditionals, and arrays programming model discussed in CHAPTER 1.

Recursion has reinforced for us the idea of proving that a program operates as intended. The natural connection between recursion and mathematical induction is essential. For everyday programming, our interest in correctness is to save time and energy tracking down bugs. In modern applications, security and privacy concerns make correctness an *essential* part of programming. If the programmer cannot be convinced that an application works as intended, how can a user who wants to keep personal data private and secure be so convinced?

Recursive functions truly illustrate the power of a carefully articulated abstraction. While the concept of a function having the ability to call itself seems absurd to many people at first, the many examples that we have considered are certainly evidence that mastering recursion is essential to understanding and exploiting computation and in understanding the role of computational models in studying natural phenomena.

Recursion is the last piece in a programming model that served to build much of the computational infrastructure that was developed as computers emerged to take a central role in daily life in the latter part of the 20th century. Programs built from modules of functions consisting of statements that operate on built-in types of data, conditionals, loops, and function calls (including recursive ones) can solve important applications of all sorts. In the next section, we emphasize this point and review these concepts in the context of a large application. In CHAPTER 3 and CHAPTER 4, we will examine extensions to these basic ideas that embrace the more expansive style of programming that now dominates the computing landscape.

Q&A

Q. Are there situations when iteration is the only option available to address a problem?

A. No, any loop can be replaced by a recursive function, though the recursive version might require excessive memory.

Q. Are there situations when recursion is the only option available to address a problem?

A. No, any recursive function can be replaced by an iterative counterpart. In SECTION 4.3, we will see how compilers produce code for function calls by using a data structure called a *stack*.

Q. Which should I prefer, recursion or iteration?

A. Whichever leads to the simpler, more easily understood, or more efficient code.

Q. I get the concern about excessive space and excessive recomputation in recursive code. Anything else to be concerned about?

A. Be extremely wary of creating arrays in recursive code. The amount of space used can pile up very quickly, as can the amount of time required for memory management.

Exercises

2.3.1 What happens if you call `factorial()` with a negative value of `n`? With a large value, say, 35?

2.3.2 Write a recursive function that computes the value of $\ln(n!)$

2.3.3 Give the sequence of integers written by a call to `ex233(6)`:

```
def ex233(n):
    if n <= 0: return
    stdio.writeln(n)
    ex233(n-2)
    ex233(n-3)
    stdio.writeln(n)
```

2.3.4 Give the value of `ex234(6)`:

```
def ex234(n):
    if n <= 0: return ''
    return ex234(n-3) + str(n) + ex234(n-2) + str(n)
```

2.3.5 Criticize the following recursive function:

```
def ex235(n):
    s = ex233(n-3) + str(n) + ex235(n-2) + str(n)
    if n <= 0: return ''
    return s
```

Solution: The base case will never be reached. A call to `ex235(3)` will result in calls to `ex235(0)`, `ex235(-3)`, `ex235(-6)`, and so forth until the "maximum depth exceeded" run-time error occurs.

2.3.6 Given four positive integers `a`, `b`, `c`, and `d`, explain the value computed by `gcd(gcd(a, b), gcd(c, d))`.

2.3.7 Explain in terms of integers and divisors the effect of the following Euclid-like function:

```
def gcdlike(p, q):
    if q == 0: return p == 1
    return gcdlike(q, p % q)
```

2.3.8 Consider the following recursive function:

```
def mystery(a, b):
    if b == 0:
        return 0
    if b % 2 == 0:
        return mystery(a+a, b/2)
    return mystery(a+a, b/2) + a
```

What are the values of `mystery(2, 25)` and `mystery(3, 11)`? Given positive integers `a` and `b`, describe the value that `mystery(a, b)` computes. Answer the same question, but replace `+` with `*` and `return 0` with `return 1`.

2.3.9 Write a recursive program `rules.py` to plot the subdivisions of a ruler using `stddraw` (see PROGRAM 1.2.1).

2.3.10 Solve the following recurrence relations, all with $T(1) = 1$. Assume n is a power of 2.

- $T(n) = T(n/2) + 1$
- $T(n) = 2T(n/2) + 1$
- $T(n) = 2T(n/2) + n$
- $T(n) = 4T(n/2) + 3$

2.3.11 Prove by induction that the minimum possible number of moves needed to solve the towers of Hanoi problem satisfies the same recurrence as the number of moves used by our recursive solution.

2.3.12 Prove by induction that the recursive program given in the text makes exactly F_n recursive calls to `fib(1)` when computing `fib(n)`.

2.3.13 Prove that the second argument to `gcd()` decreases by at least a factor of 2 for every second recursive call, and then prove that `gcd(p, q)` uses at most $2 \log_2 n + 1$ recursive calls where n is the larger of `p` and `q`.

2.3.14 Modify `htree.py` (PROGRAM 2.3.4) to animate the drawing of the H-tree:

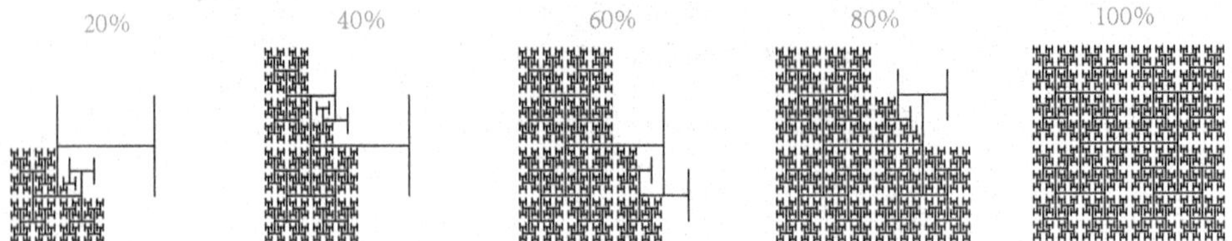

Next, rearrange the order of the recursive calls (and the base case), view the resulting animation, and explain each outcome.

Creative Exercises

2.3.15 *Binary representation.* Compose a program that takes a positive integer n (in decimal) from the command line and writes its binary representation. Recall that in `binary.py` (Program 1.3.7, we used the method of subtracting out powers of 2. Instead, use the following simpler method: repeatedly divide 2 into n and read the remainders backward. First, compose a `while` loop to carry out this computation and write the bits in the wrong order. Then, use recursion to write the bits in the correct order.

2.3.16 *A4 paper.* The width-to-height ratio of paper in the ISO format is the square root of 2 to 1. Format A0 has an area of 1 square meter. Format A1 is A0 cut with a vertical line into two equal halves, A2 is A1 cut with a horizontal line into in two halves, and so on. Compose a program that takes a command-line integer n and uses `stddraw` to show how to cut a sheet of A0 paper into 2^n pieces.

2.3.17 *Permutations.* Compose a program `permutations.py` that takes a command-line argument n and writes all $n!$ permutations of the n letters starting at a (assuming that n is no greater than 26). A permutation of n elements is one of the $n!$ possible orderings of the elements. As an example, when $n = 3$ you should get the following output. Do not worry about in which order you write the permutations.

```
bca cba cab acb bac abc
```

2.3.18 *Permutations of size k.* Modify your solution to the previous exercise so that it takes two command-line arguments n and k, and writes all of the permutations that contain exactly k of the n elements. The number of such permutations is $P(n, k) = n! / (n-k)!$. Below is the desired output when $k = 2$ and $n = 4$. Do not worry about in which order you enumerate the permutations.

```
ab ac ad ba bc bd ca cb cd da db dc
```

2.3.19 *Combinations.* Compose a program `combinations.py` that takes one command-line argument n and writes all 2^n combinations of any size. A combination is a subset of the n elements, independent of order. As an example, when $n = 3$ you should get the following output:

```
 a ab abc ac b bc c
```

Note that your program needs to write the empty string (subset of size 0).

2.3.20 *Combinations of size k.* Modify your solution to the previous exercise so that it takes two command-line arguments n and k and writes all of the combinations of size k. The number of such combinations is $C(n, k) = n! / (k!(n-k)!)$. For example, when $n = 5$ and $k = 3$, you should get the following output:

```
abc abd abe acd ace ade bcd bce bde cde
```

2.3.21 *Hamming distance.* The Hamming distance between two bit strings of length `n` is equal to the number of bits in which the two strings differ. Compose a program that takes an integer `k` and a bitstring `s` from the command line and writes all bitstrings that have Hamming distance at most `k` from `s`. For example, if `k` is `2` and `s` is `0000`, then your program should write

```
0011 0101 0110 1001 1010 1100
```

Hint: Choose `k` of the `n` bits in `s` to flip.

2.3.22 *Recursive squares.* Compose programs to produce each of the following recursive patterns. The ratio of the sizes of the squares is 2.2:1. To draw a shaded square, draw a filled gray square, then an unfilled black square.

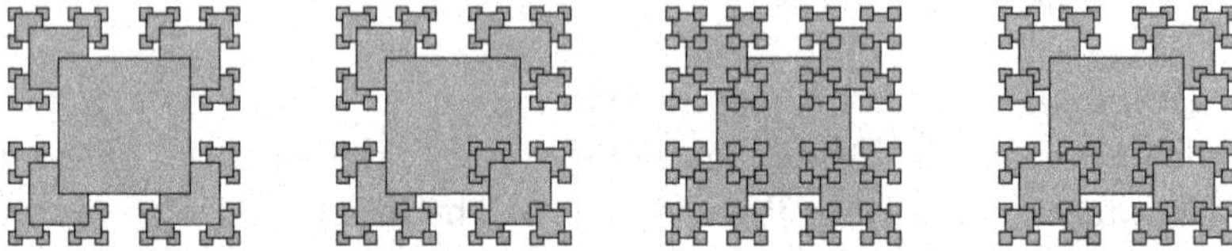

2.3.23 *Pancake flipping.* You have a stack of n pancakes of varying sizes on a griddle. Your goal is to rearrange the stack in descending order so that the largest pancake is on the bottom and the smallest one is on top. You are only permitted to flip the top k pancakes, thereby reversing their order. Devise a recursive scheme to arrange the pancakes in the proper order that uses at most $2n - 3$ flips.

2.3.24 *Gray code.* Modify `beckett.py` (PROGRAM 2.3.3) to write the Gray code (not just the sequence of bit positions that change).

2.3.25 *Towers of Hanoi variant.* Consider the following variant of the towers of Hanoi problem. There are 2n discs of increasing size stored on three poles. Initially all of the discs with odd size (1, 3, …, 2n-1) are piled on the left pole from top to bottom in increasing order of size; all of the discs with even size (2, 4, …, 2n) are piled on the right pole. Compose a program to provide instructions for moving the odd discs to the right pole and the even discs to the left pole, obeying the same rules as for towers of Hanoi.

2.3.26 *Animated towers of Hanoi.* Use stddraw to animate a solution to the towers of Hanoi problem, moving the discs at a rate of approximately 1 per second.

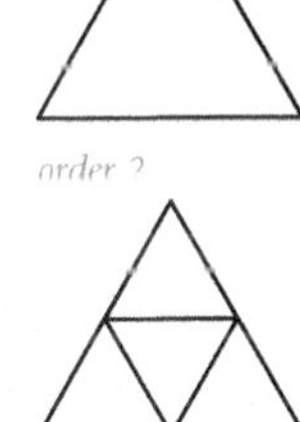

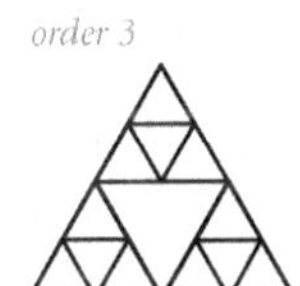

Sierpinski triangles

2.3.27 *Sierpinski triangles.* Compose a recursive program to draw Sierpinski triangles (see PROGRAM 2.2.4). As with htree.py, use a command-line argument to control the depth of the recursion.

2.3.28 *Binomial distribution.* Estimate the number of recursive calls that would be used by the code

```
def binomial(n, k):
    if (n == 0) or (k == 0): return 1.0
    if (n < 0) or (k < 0): return 0.0
    return (binomial(n-1, k) + binomial(n-1, k-1)) / 2.0
```

to compute binomial(100, 50). Develop a better implementation that is based on memoization. *Hint*: See EXERCISE 1.4.39.

2.3.29 *A strange function.* Consider McCarthy's 91 function:

```
def mcCarthy(n):
    if n > 100: return n - 10
    return mcCarthy(mcCarthy(n+11))
```

Determine the value of mcCarthy(50) without using a computer. Give the number of recursive calls used by mcCarthy() to compute this result. Either prove that the base case is reached for all positive integers n or give a value of n for which this function goes into an infinite recursive loop.

2.3.30 *Collatz function.* Consider the following recursive function, which is related to a famous unsolved problem in number theory, known as the *Collatz problem*, or the *3n+1 problem*:

```
def collatz(n):
    stdio.write(str(n) + ' ')
    if n == 1: return
    if n % 2 == 0:
        collatz(n // 2)
    else:
        collatz(3*n + 1)
```

For example, a call to `collatz(7)` writes this sequence of 17 integers

```
7 22 11 34 17 52 26 13 40 20 10 5 16 8 4 2 1
```

after 17 function calls. Compose a program that takes a command-line argument m and returns the value of $n < m$ for which the number of recursive calls for `collatz(n)` is maximized. The unsolved problem is that no one knows whether the function terminates for all positive values of n (mathematical induction is no help, because one of the recursive calls is for a larger value of the argument). Develop a better implementation that is based on memoization.

2.3.31 *Plasma clouds.* Compose a program that uses recursion to draw plasma clouds, using the approach suggested in the text.

2.3.32 *Recursive tree.* Compose a program `tree.py` that takes a command-line argument n and produces tree-like recursive patterns like these for n equal to 1, 2, 3, 4, and 8:

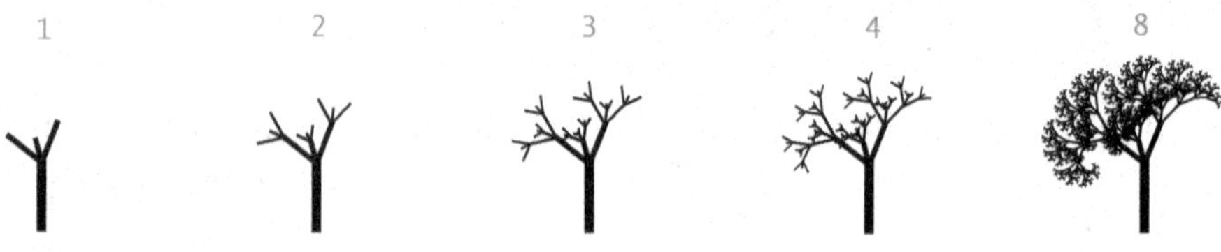

2.3.33 *Brownian island.* B. Mandelbrot asked the famous question *How long is the coast of Britain?* Modify `brownian.py` (PROGRAM 2.3.5) to get a program `brownianisland.py` that plots *Brownian islands,* whose coastlines resemble that of Great Britain. The modifications are simple: first, change `curve()` to add a Gaussian random variable to the *x*-coordinate as well as to the *y*-coordinate; second, change the global code to draw a curve from the point at the center of the canvas back to itself. Experiment with various values of the parameters to get your program to produce islands with a realistic look.

Brownian islands with Hurst exponent of 0.76

2.4 Case Study: Percolation

The programming tools that we have considered to this point allow us to attack all manner of important problems. We conclude our study of functions and modules by considering a case study of developing a program to solve an interesting scientific problem. Our purpose in doing so is to review the basic elements that we have covered, in the context of the various challenges that you might face in solving a specific problem, and to illustrate a programming style that you can apply broadly.

Programs in this section

Our example applies a computing technique to a simple model that has been extremely useful in helping scientists and engineers in numerous contexts. We consider a widely applicable technique known as Monte Carlo simulation to study a natural model known as *percolation*. This is not just of direct importance in materials science and geology, but also explains many other natural phenomena.

The term *Monte Carlo simulation* is broadly used to encompass any computational technique that employs randomness to estimate an unknown quantity by performing multiple trials (known as *simulations*). We have used Monte Carlo simulation in several other contexts already—for example, in the gambler's ruin and coupon collector problems. Rather than develop a complete mathematical model or measure all possible outcomes of an experiment, we rely on the laws of probability and statistics.

You will learn quite a bit about percolation in this case study, but our focus is on the process of developing modular programs to address computational tasks. We identify subtasks that can be addressed independently, striving to identify the key underlying abstractions and asking ourselves questions such as the following: Is there some specific subtask that would help solve this problem? What are the essential characteristics of this specific subtask? Might a solution that addresses these essential characteristics be useful in solving other problems? Asking such questions pays significant dividends, because they lead us to develop software that is easier to create, debug, and reuse, so that we can more quickly address the main problem of interest.

Percolation It is not unusual for local interactions in a system to imply global properties. For example, an electrical engineer might be interested in composite systems consisting of randomly distributed insulating and metallic materials: which fraction of the materials needs to be metallic so that the composite system is an electrical conductor? As another example, a geologist might be interested in a porous landscape with water on the surface (or oil below); under which conditions will the water be able to drain through to the bottom (or the oil to gush through to the surface)? Scientists have defined an abstract process known as *percolation* to model such situations. It has been studied widely and shown to be an accurate model in a dizzying variety of applications, beyond insulating materials and porous substances to the spread of forest fires and disease epidemics to evolution to the study of the Internet.

For simplicity, we begin by working in two dimensions and model the system as an n-by-n grid of *sites*. Each site is either *blocked* or *open;* open sites are initially *empty*. A *full* site is an open site that can be connected to an open site in the top row via a chain of neighboring (left, right, up, down) open sites. If there is a full site in the bottom row, then we say that the system *percolates*. In other words, a system percolates if we fill all open sites connected to the top row and that process fills some open site on the bottom row. For the insulating/metallic materials example, the open sites correspond to metallic materials, so that a system that percolates has a metallic path from top to bottom, with full sites conducting. For the porous substance example, the open sites correspond to empty space through which water might flow, so that a system that percolates lets water fill open sites, flowing from top to bottom.

In a famous scientific problem, researchers are interested in the following question: if sites are independently set to be open with *vacancy probability* p (and therefore blocked with probability $1-p$), what is the probability that the system percolates? Despite decades of scientific research, no mathematical solution to this problem has yet been derived. Our task is to compose computer programs to help study the problem.

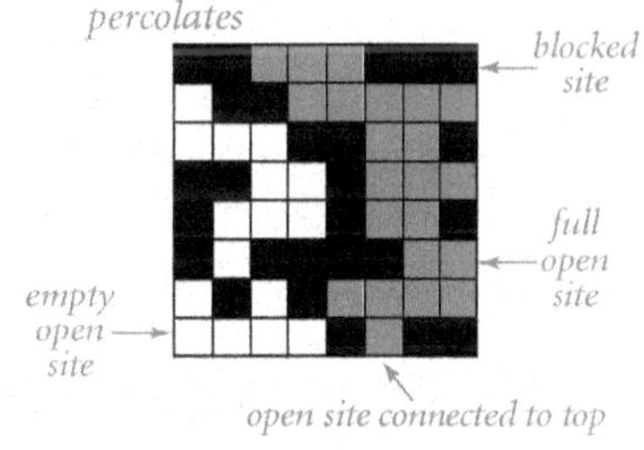

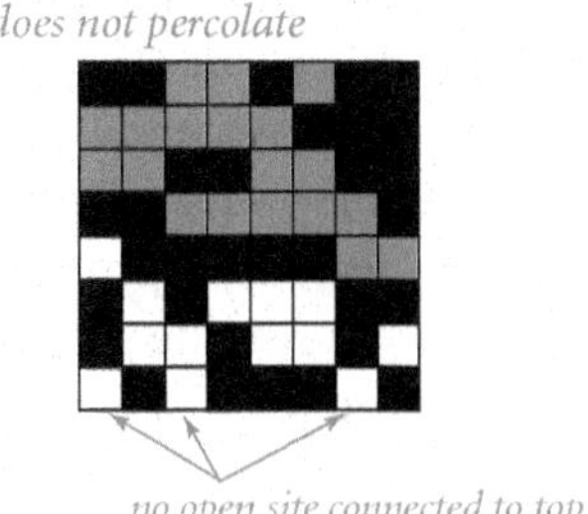

Percolation in an 8-by-8 grid of sites

Basic scaffolding To address percolation with a Python program, we face numerous decisions and challenges, and we certainly will end up with much more code than in the short programs that we have considered so far in this book. Our goal is to illustrate an incremental style of programming where we independently develop modules that address parts of the problem, building confidence with a small computational infrastructure of our own design and construction as we proceed.

The first step is to pick a representation of the data. This decision will have substantial impact on the kind of code that we compose later, so it is not to be taken lightly. Indeed, it is often the case that we learn something while working with a chosen representation that causes us to scrap it and start all over using a new one.

For percolation, the path to an effective representation is clear: use an n-by-n array. One possibility is to use a code such as 0 to indicate an empty site, 1 to indicate a blocked site, and 2 to indicate a full site. Alternatively, note that we typically describe sites in terms of questions: Is the site open or blocked? Is the site full or empty? This characteristic of the elements suggests that we might use an n-by-n array in which each element is either `True` or `False`. In computer science, we refer to such two-dimensional arrays as *boolean matrices*.

Boolean matrices are fundamental mathematical objects with many applications. Python does not provide direct support for operations on boolean matrices, but we can use the functions in `stdarray` to read and write boolean matrices. This choice illustrates a basic principle that often comes up in programming: the effort required to build a more general tool usually pays dividends. Using a natural abstraction such as boolean matrices is preferable to using a specialized representation. In the present context, it turns out that using boolean matrices instead of integer matrices leads to code that is easier to understand.

Eventually, we will want to work with random data, but we also want to be able to read and write files because debugging programs with random inputs can be counterproductive. With random data, you get a different input each time that you run the program; after fixing a bug, what you want to see is the same input that you just used, to check that the fix was effective. Accordingly, it is best to start with some specific cases that we understand, kept in files formatted to be read by `stdarray.readBool2D()` (dimensions followed by `0` and `1` values in row-major order).

When you start working on a new problem that involves several files, it is usually worthwhile to create a new folder (directory) to isolate those files from others that you may be working on. For example, we might create a folder named `percolation` to store the code we compose in this section. We can then implement and debug the basic code for reading and writing percolation systems, create test files, check that the files are compatible with the code, and so forth, before really worrying about percolation at all. This type of code, sometimes called *scaffolding*, is straightforward to implement, but making sure that it is solid at the outset will save us from distraction when approaching the main problem.

Now we can turn to the code for testing whether a boolean matrix represents a system that percolates. Referring to the helpful interpretation in which we can think of the task as simulating what would happen if the top were flooded with water (does it flow to the bottom or not?), our first design decision is that we will want to have a `flow()` function that takes as an argument a boolean matrix `isOpen[][]` that specifies which sites are open and returns another boolean matrix `isFull[][]` that specifies which sites are full. For the moment, we will not worry at all about how to implement this function; we are just deciding how to organize the computation. It is also clear that we will want client code to be able to use a `percolates()` function that checks whether the boolean matrix returned by `flow()` has any full sites on the bottom.

Program 2.4.1 (`percolation0.py`) summarizes these decisions. It does not perform any interesting computation, but, after running and debugging this code we can start thinking about actually solving the problem. A function that performs no computation, such as `flow()`, is sometimes called a *stub*. Having this stub allows us to test and debug `percolates()` and `main()` in the context in which we will need them. We refer to code like Program 2.4.1 as *scaffolding*. As with the scaffolding that construction workers use when erecting a building, this kind of code provides the support that we need to develop a program. By fully implementing and debugging this code (much, if not all, of which we need, anyway) at the outset, we provide a sound basis for building code to solve the problem at hand. Often, we carry the analogy one step further and remove the scaffolding (or replace it with something better) after the implementation is complete.

Vertical percolation Given a boolean matrix that represents the open sites, how do we figure out whether it represents a system that percolates? As we will see at the end of this section, this computation turns out to be directly related to a fundamental question in computer science. For the moment, we will consider a much simpler version of the problem that we call *vertical percolation*.

Program 2.4.1 Percolation scaffolding (percolation0.py)

```
import stdarray
import stdio

def flow(isOpen):
    n = len(isOpen)
    isFull = stdarray.create2D(n, n, False)
    # Percolation flow computation goes here.
    # See Program 2.4.2 and Program 2.4.6.
    return isFull

def percolates(isOpen):
    isFull = flow(isOpen)
    n = len(isFull)
    for j in range(n):
        if isFull[n-1][j]: return True
    return False

def main():
    isOpen = stdarray.readBool2D()
    stdarray.write2D(flow(isOpen))
    stdio.writeln(percolates(isOpen))

if __name__ == '__main__': main()
```

`n`	*system size (n-by-n)*
`isFull[][]`	*full sites*
`isOpen[][]`	*open sites*

To get started with percolation, we compose this code, which handles all the straightforward tasks surrounding the computation. The primary function `flow()` returns a two-dimensional array giving the full sites (none, in the placeholder code here). The helper function `percolates()` checks the bottom row of the returned array to decide whether the system percolates. The test client reads a boolean two-dimensional array from standard input and then writes the result of calling `flow()` and `percolates()` for that array.

```
% more test5.txt
5 5
0 1 1 0 1
0 0 1 1 1
1 1 0 1 1
1 0 0 0 1
0 1 1 1 1
```

```
% python percolation0.py < test5.txt
5 5
0 0 0 0 0
0 0 0 0 0
0 0 0 0 0
0 0 0 0 0
0 0 0 0 0
False
```

The simplification is to restrict attention to *vertical* connection paths. If such a path connects top to bottom in a system, we say that the system *vertically percolates* along the path (and that the system itself vertically percolates). This restriction is perhaps intuitive if we are talking about sand traveling through cement, but not if we are talking about water traveling through cement or about electrical conductivity. Simple as it is, vertical percolation is a problem that is interesting in its own right because it suggests various mathematical questions. Does the restriction make a significant difference? How many vertical percolation paths do we expect?

vertically percolates

site connected to top with a vertical path

does not vertically percolate

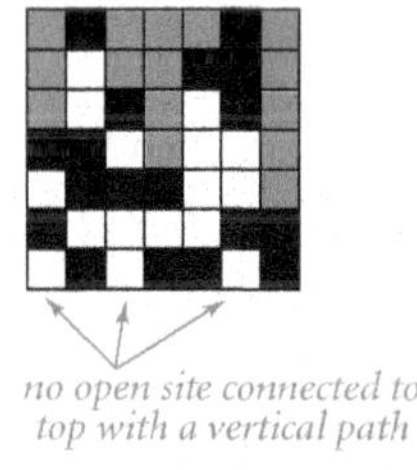

Vertical percolation

Determining the sites that are filled by some path that is connected vertically to the top is a simple calculation. We initialize the top row of our result array from the top row of the percolation system, with full sites corresponding to open ones. Then, moving from top to bottom, we fill in each row of the array by checking the corresponding row of the percolation system. Proceeding from top to bottom, we fill in the rows of `isFull[][]` to mark as `True` all elements that correspond to sites in `isOpen[][]` that are vertically connected to a full site on the previous row. Program 2.4.2 (`percolationv.py`) is the same as `percolation0.py` except for an implementation of `flow()` that returns a boolean matrix of full sites (`True` if connected to the top via a vertical path, `False` otherwise).

connected to top via a vertical path of filled sites

not connected to top via such a path

connected to top via such a path

Vertical percolation calculation

Testing After we become convinced that our code is behaving as planned, we want to run it on a broader variety of test cases and address some of our scientific questions. At this point, our initial scaffolding becomes less useful, as representing large boolean matrices with 0s and 1s on standard input and standard output and maintaining large numbers of test cases quickly becomes uninformative and unwieldy. Instead, we want to automatically generate test cases and observe the operation of our code on them, to be sure that it is operating as expected. Specifically, to

Program 2.4.2 Vertical percolation detection (percolationv.py)

```
# Same as percolation0.py except replace flow() with this:

def flow(isOpen):
    n = len(isOpen)
    isFull = stdarray.create2D(n, n, False)
    for j in range(n):
        isFull[0][j] = isOpen[0][j]
    for i in range(1, n):
        for j in range(n):
            if isOpen[i][j] and isFull[i-1][j]:
                isFull[i][j] = True
    return isFull
```

n	*system size (n-by-n)*
isFull[][]	*full sites*
isOpen[][]	*open sites*

Substituting this function for the stub in Program *2.4.2 gives a solution to the vertical-only percolation problem that solves our test case as expected (see text).*

```
% more test5.txt
5 5
0 1 1 0 1
0 0 1 1 1
1 1 0 1 1
1 0 0 0 1
0 1 1 1 1
```

```
% python percolationv.py < test5.txt
5 5
0 1 1 0 1
0 0 1 0 1
0 0 0 0 1
0 0 0 0 1
0 0 0 0 1
True
```

gain confidence in our code and to develop a better understanding of percolation, our next goals are to:

- Test our code for large random boolean matrices.
- Given a vacancy probability p, estimate the system percolation probability.

To accomplish these goals, we need new clients that are slightly more sophisticated than the scaffolding we used to get the program up and running. Our modular programming style is to develop such clients in independent modules *without modifying our percolation code at all.*

Monte Carlo simulation. We want our code to work properly for *any* boolean matrix. Moreover, the scientific question of interest involves random boolean matrices. To this end, we compose a function `random()` that takes two arguments `n` and `p` and generates a random `n`-by-`n` boolean array in which the probability that each element is `True` is `p`. Having debugged our code on a few specific test cases, we can use this function to test it on larger random systems. It is possible that such cases may uncover a few more bugs, so some care is in order to check results. However, having debugged our code for a small system, we can proceed with some confidence. It is easier to focus on new bugs after eliminating the obvious bugs.

Data visualization. We can work more easily with bigger problem instances if we use `stddraw` for output. Accordingly, we develop a function `draw()` to visualize the contents of a boolean matrix as a subdivision of the standard drawing window into squares, one for each site. For flexibility, we include a second argument that specifies which squares we want to fill—those corresponding to `True` elements or those corresponding to `False` elements. As you will see, this function pays dividends in its ability to help us visualize large problem instances. Using `draw()` to draw our arrays representing blocked and full sites in different colors gives a compelling visual representation of percolation.

With these tools, testing our percolation code for larger boolean matrices on a larger set of trials is straightforward. Program 2.4.3 (`percolationio.py`) is a small module that contains the two functions just described, for use as input and output for testing our percolation code; Program 2.4.4 (`visualizev.py`) is a client script that takes a percolation system size, a probability, and a number of trials from the command line and then runs the specified number of trials, creating a new random boolean matrix, and displaying the result of the percolation flow calculation for each, pausing for a brief time between trials.

Our eventual goal is to compute an accurate estimate of percolation probabilities, perhaps by running a large number of trials. Nevertheless, these tools helps us gain more familiarity with the problem by studying some large cases (while at the same time gaining confidence that our code is working properly). When you run `visualizev.py` for moderate-size n (50 to 100, say) and various values of p, you will immediately be drawn into using this program to try to answer some questions about percolation. Clearly, the system never percolates when p is low and always percolates when p is very high. How does it behave for intermediate values of p? How does the behavior change as n increases?

Program 2.4.3 Percolation input/output (percolationio.py)

```
import sys
import stdarray
import stddraw
import stdio
import stdrandom

def random(n, p):
    a = stdarray.create2D(n, n, False)
    for i in range(n):
        for j in range(n):
            a[i][j] = stdrandom.bernoulli(p)
    return a

def draw(a, which):
    n = len(a)
    stddraw.setXscale(-1, n)
    stddraw.setYscale(-1, n)
    for i in range(n):
        for j in range(n):
            if a[i][j] == which:
                stddraw.filledSquare(j, n-i-1, 0.5)

def main():
    n = int(sys.argv[1])
    p = float(sys.argv[2])
    test = random(n, p)
    draw(test, False)
    stddraw.show()

if __name__ == '__main__': main()
```

```
% python percolationio.py 10 0.8
```

These helper functions are useful for testing when we are studying percolation. The call `random(n, p)` *creates a random n-by-n boolean array, where the probability that each element is* `True` *is p, and the call* `draw(test, False)` *produces a visualization of the given two-dimensional array in the standard drawing window, with filled squares corresponding to* `False` *elements.*

Program 2.4.4 Visualization client (`visualizev.py`)

```
import sys
import stddraw
import percolationv
import percolationio

n = int(sys.argv[1])
p = float(sys.argv[2])
trials = int(sys.argv[3])

for i in range(trials):
    isOpen = percolationio.random(n, p)
    stddraw.clear()
    stddraw.setPenColor(stddraw.BLACK)
    percolationio.draw(isOpen, False)
    stddraw.setPenColor(stddraw.BLUE)
    isFull = percolationv.flow(isOpen)
    percolationio.draw(isFull, True)
    stddraw.show(1000.0)
stddraw.show()
```

`n`	*system size (n-by-n)*
`p`	*site vacancy probability*
`trials`	*number of trials*
`isOpen[][]`	*open sites*
`isFull[][]`	*full sites*

This client takes command-line arguments n, p, and `trials`, then generates random n-by-n boolean arrays with site vacancy probability p, computes the directed percolation flow, and draws the result in the stanard drawing window. Such drawings increase confidence that our code is operating properly and help develop an intuitive understanding of percolation.

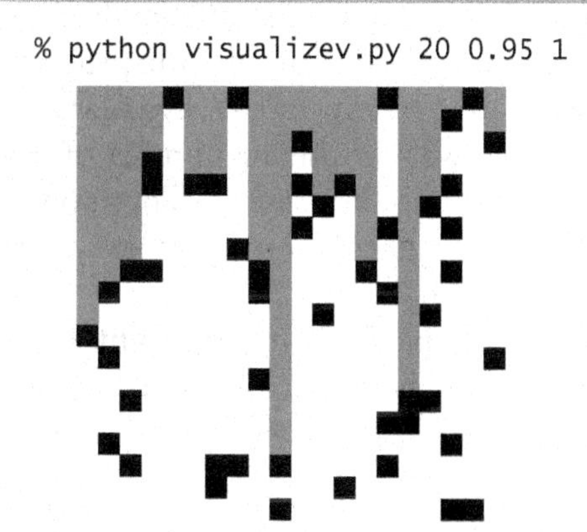

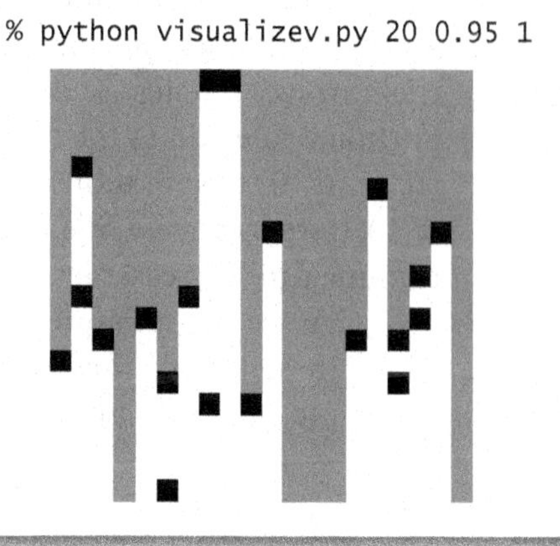

Estimating probabilities The next step in our program development process is to compose code to estimate the probability that a random system percolates. We refer to this quantity as the *percolation probability*. To estimate its value, we simply run a number of experiments. The situation is no different from our study of coin flipping (see PROGRAM 2.2.7), but instead of flipping a coin, we generate a random system and check whether it percolates.

PROGRAM 2.4.5 (`estimatev.py`) encapsulates this computation in a function `evaluate()` that returns an estimate of the probability that an n-by-n system with site vacancy probability p percolates, obtained by generating a given number of random systems and calculating the fraction of them that percolate. The function takes three arguments: `n`, `p`, and `trials`.

How many trials do we need to obtain an accurate estimate of the percolation probability? This question is addressed by basic methods in probability and statistics, which are beyond the scope of this book, but we can get a feeling for the problem with computational experience. With just a few runs of `estimatev.py`, you can learn that if the site vacancy probability is close to 0 or very close to 1, then we do not need many trials, but that there are values for which we need as many as 10,000 trials to be able to estimate the percolation probability within two decimal places. To study the situation in more detail, we might modify `estimatev.py` to produce output like `bernoulli.py` (PROGRAM 2.2.7), plotting a histogram of the data points so that we can see the distribution of values (see EXERCISE 2.4.11).

Using `estimatev.evaluate()` represents a giant leap in the amount of computation that we are doing. All of a sudden, it makes sense to run thousands of trials. It would be unwise to try to do so without first having thoroughly debugged our percolation functions. Also, we need to begin to take the time required to complete the computation into account. The basic methodology for doing so is the topic of SECTION 4.1, but the structure of these programs is sufficiently simple that we can do a quick calculation, which we can verify by running the program. Each trial involves n^2 sites, so the total running time of `estimatev.evaluate()` is proportional to n^2 times the number of trials. If we increase the number of trials by a factor of 10 (to gain more precision), the running time increases by about a factor of 10. If we increase n by a factor of 10 (to study percolation for larger systems), the running time increases by about a factor of 100.

Can we run this program to determine percolation probabilities for a system with billions of sites with several digits of precision? No. No computer is fast enough to use `estimatev.evaluate()` for this purpose. Moreover, in a scientific

Program 2.4.5 Percolation probability estimate (estimatev.py)

```
import sys
import stdio
import percolationv
import percolationio

def evaluate(n, p, trials):
    count = 0
    for i in range(trials):
        isOpen = percolationio.random(n, p)
        if (percolationv.percolates(isOpen)):
            count += 1
    return 1.0 * count / trials

def main():
    n = int(sys.argv[1])
    p = float(sys.argv[2])
    trials = int(sys.argv[3])
    q = evaluate(n, p, trials)
    stdio.writeln(q)

if __name__ == '__main__': main()
```

n	*system size (n-by-n)*
p	*site vacancy probability*
trials	*number of trials*
isOpen[][]	*open sites*
q	*percolation probability*

To estimate the probability that a system percolates, we generate random n-by-n systems with site vacancy probability p and compute the fraction of them that percolate. This is a Bernoulli process, no different from coin flipping (see *Program 2.2.6**). Increasing the number of trials increases the accuracy of the estimate. If the site vacancy probability is close to 0 or to 1, not many* `trials` *are needed.*

```
% python estimatev.py 20 .75 10
0.0
% python estimatev.py 20 .95 10
1.0
% python estimatev.py 20 .85 10
0.7
```

```
% python estimatev.py 20 .85 1000
0.564
% python estimatev.py 20 .85 1000
0.561
% python estimatev.py 40 .85 100
0.11
```

experiment on percolation, the value of n is likely to be much higher. We can hope to formulate a hypothesis from our simulation that can be tested experimentally on a much larger system, but not to precisely simulate a system that corresponds atom-for-atom with the real world. Simplification of this sort is essential in science.

You are encouraged to download `estimatev.py` from the booksite to get a feel for both the percolation probabilities and the amount of time required to compute them. When you do so, you are not just learning more about percolation, but also testing the hypothesis that the models we have described apply to the running times of our simulations of the percolation process.

What is the probability that a system with site vacancy probability p vertically percolates? Vertical percolation is sufficiently simple that elementary probabilistic models can yield an exact formula for this quantity, which we can validate experimentally with `estimatev.py`. Since our only reason for studying vertical percolation was that it represented an easy starting point around which we could develop supporting software for studying percolation methods, we leave further study of vertical percolation for an exercise (see Exercise 2.4.13) and turn to the main problem.

Recursive solution for percolation How do we test whether a system percolates in the general case when *any* path starting at the top and ending at the bottom (not just a vertical one) will do the job?

Remarkably, we can solve this problem with a compact program, based on a classic recursive scheme known as *depth-first search*. Program 2.4.6 (`percolation.py`) is an implementation of `flow()` that computes the flow matrix `isFull[][]`, based on a recursive four-argument function `_flow()`. The recursive function takes as arguments the site vacancy matrix `isOpen[][]`, the flow matrix `isFull[][]`, and a site position specified by a row index `i` and a column index `j`. The base case is a recursive call that just returns (we refer to such a call as a *null call*), for one of the following reasons:

- Either `i` or `j` is outside the two-dimensional array bounds.
- The site is blocked (`isOpen[i][j]` is `False`).
- We have already marked the site as full (`isFull[i][j]` is `True`).

The reduction case is to mark the site as filled and issue recursive calls for the site's four neighbors: `isOpen[i+1][j]`, `isOpen[i][j+1]`, `isOpen[i][j-1]`, and `isOpen[i-1][j]`. To implement `flow()`, we call the recursive `_flow()` function for every site on the top row. The recursion always terminates because each recursive call either is null or marks a new site as full. We can show by an induction-

Program 2.4.6 Percolation detection (`percolation.py`)

```
# Same as percolation0.py except replace flow() with this code:

def _flow(isOpen, isFull, i, j):
    n = len(isFull)
    if (i < 0) or (i >= n): return
    if (j < 0) or (j >= n): return
    if not isOpen[i][j]:    return
    if isFull[i][j]:        return

    isFull[i][j] = True
    _flow(isOpen, isFull, i+1, j  )  # Down.
    _flow(isOpen, isFull, i  , j+1)  # Right.
    _flow(isOpen, isFull, i  , j-1)  # Left.
    _flow(isOpen, isFull, i-1, j  )  # Up.

def flow(isOpen):
    n = len(isOpen)
    isFull = stdarray.create2D(n, n, False)
    for j in range(n):
        _flow(isOpen, isFull, 0, j)
    return isFull
```

`n`	*system size (n-by-n)*
`isOpen[][]`	*open sites*
`isFull[][]`	*full sites*
`i, j`	*current site row, column*

Substituting these functions for the `flow()` stub in Program 2.4.1 gives a depth-first-search-based solution to the percolation problem. The call `_flow(isOpen, isFull, i, j)` fills sites by setting to `True` the element in `isFull[][]` corresponding to any site that can be reached from `isOpen[i][j]` via a path of open sites. The one-argument `flow()` calls the recursive function for every site on the top row.

```
% more test8.txt
8 8
0 0 1 1 1 0 0 0
1 0 0 1 1 1 1 1
1 1 1 0 0 1 1 0
0 0 1 1 0 1 1 1
0 1 1 1 0 1 1 0
0 1 0 0 0 0 1 1
1 0 1 0 1 1 1 1
1 1 1 1 0 1 0 0
```

```
% python percolation.py < test8.txt
8 8
0 0 1 1 1 0 0 0
0 0 0 1 1 1 1 1
0 0 0 0 0 1 1 0
0 0 0 0 0 1 1 1
0 0 0 0 0 1 1 0
0 0 0 0 0 0 1 1
0 0 0 0 1 1 1 1
0 0 0 0 0 1 0 0
True
```

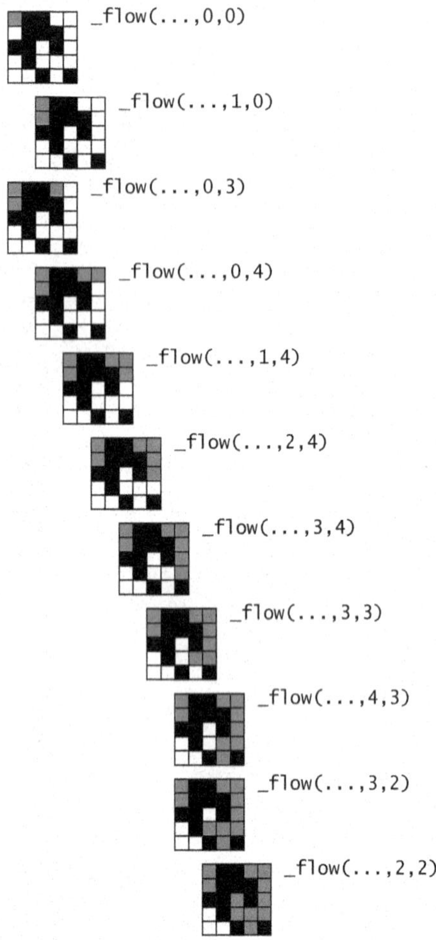

Recursive percolation (null calls omitted)

based argument (as usual for recursive programs) that a site is marked as full if and only if it is open and connected to one of the sites on the top row via a chain of neighboring open sites.

Tracing the operation of `_flow()` on a tiny test case is an instructive exercise in examining the dynamics of the process, as shown in the diagram at left. The function calls itself for every site that can be reached via a path of open sites from the top. This example illustrates that simple recursive programs can mask computations that otherwise are quite sophisticated. This function is a special case of the classic depth-first search algorithm, which has many important applications.

We can visualize and perform experiments with this algorithm using scripts like the `visualizev.py` and `estimatev.py` tools that we have developed. To do so, we can create the file `visualize.py` as a copy of `visualizev.py`, and then edit `visualize.py` by replacing the two instances of `percolationv` with `percolation`. Similarly, we can create the file `estimate.py` as an edited copy of `estimatev.py`. (To save space, we do not show `visualize.py` and `estimate.py` in the book; they are available through the booksite.) If you do so, and try various values for n and p, you will quickly get a feeling for the situation: the systems always percolate when p is high and never percolate when p is low, and (particularly as n increases) there is a value of p above which the systems (almost) always percolate and below which they (almost) never percolate (see examples at the top of the next page).

Having debugged `visualizev.py` and `estimatev.py` on the simple vertical percolation process, we can use them with more confidence to study percolation, and turn quickly to study the real scientific problem of interest. Note that if we want to study both versions of percolation, we could compose clients of both `percolationv` and `percolation` that call both `flow()` functions to compare them.

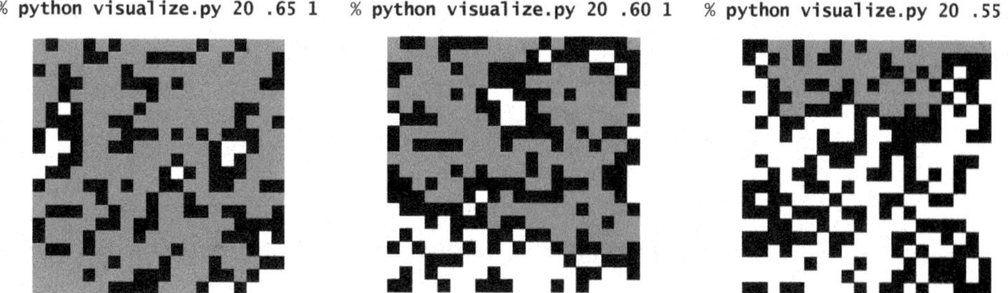

Percolation is less probable as the site vacancy probability decreases

Adaptive plot To gain more insight into percolation, our next step in program development might be to compose a program that plots the percolation probability q as a function of the site vacancy probability p for a given value of n. Perhaps the best way to produce such a plot is to first derive a mathematical equation for the function, and then use that equation to make the plot. For percolation, however, no one has been able to derive such an equation, so the next option is to use the Monte Carlo method: run simulations and plot the results.

Immediately, we are faced with numerous decisions. For how many values of p should we compute an estimate of the percolation probability? Which values of p should we choose? How much precision should we aim for in these calculations? These decisions constitute an experimental design problem. Much as we might like to instantly produce an accurate rendition of the curve for any given n, the computation cost can be prohibitive. For example, the first thing that comes to mind is to plot, say, 100 to 1,000 equally spaced points, using `stdstats.py` (Program 2.2.5). But, as you learned from using `estimate.py`, computing a sufficiently precise value of the percolation probability for each point might take several seconds or longer, so the whole plot might take minutes or hours or even longer. Moreover, it is clear that a lot of this computation time is completely wasted, because we know that values for small p are 0 and values for large p are 1. We might prefer to spend that time on more precise computations for intermediate p. How should we proceed?

Program 2.4.7 (`percplot.py`) implements a recursive approach that is widely applicable to similar problems. The basic idea is simple: we choose the minimum distance that we want between values of the x-coordinate (which we refer to as the *gap* tolerance), the minimum known error that we wish to tolerate in the y-coordinate (which we refer to as the *error* tolerance), and the number of

Program 2.4.7 Adaptive plot client (percplot.py)

```
import sys
import stddraw
import estimate

def curve(n, x0, y0, x1, y1, trials=10000, gap=0.01, err=0.0025):
    xm = (x0 + x1) / 2.0
    ym = (y0 + y1) / 2.0
    fxm = estimate.evaluate(n, xm, trials)
    if (x1 - x0 < gap) or (abs(ym - fxm) < err):
        stddraw.line(x0, y0, x1, y1)
        stddraw.show(0.0)
        return
    curve(n, x0, y0, xm, fxm)
    stddraw.filledCircle(xm, fxm, 0.005)
    stddraw.show(0.0)
    curve(n, xm, fxm, x1, y1)

n = int(sys.argv[1])
stddraw.setPenRadius(0.0)
curve(n, 0.0, 0.0, 1.0, 1.0)
stddraw.show()
```

n	*system size (n-by-n)*
x0, y0	*left endpoint*
x1, y1	*right endpoint*
xm, ym	*midpoint*
fxm	*value at midpoint*
trials	*number of trials*
gap	*gap tolerance*
err	*error tolerance*

This program accepts an integer n as a command-line argument and then runs experiments to build an adaptive plot that relates site vacancy probability (the control variable) to percolation probability (the experimental observations) for n-by-n systems.

% python percplot.py 20

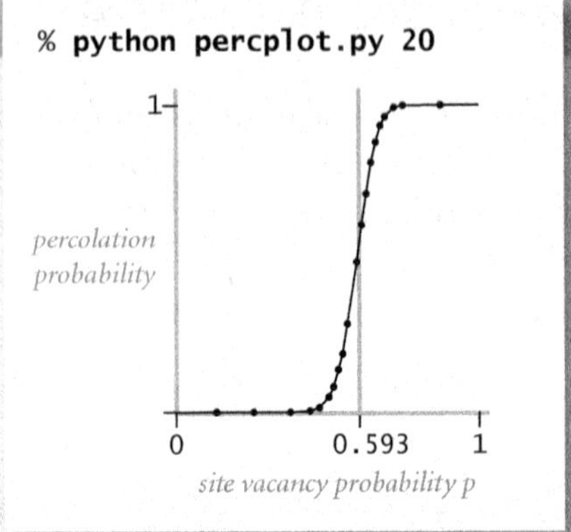

% python percplot.py 100

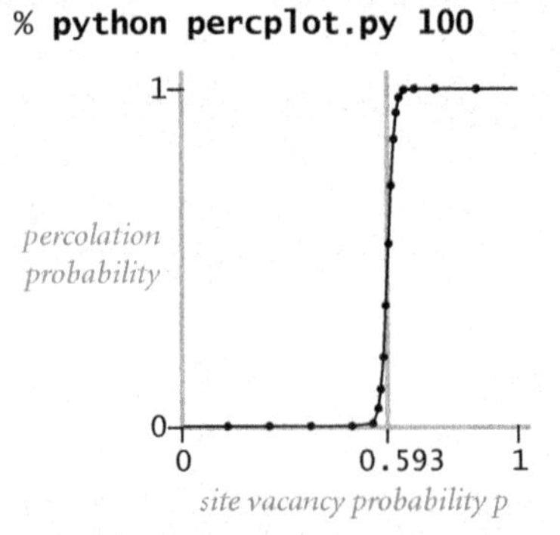

trials per point that we wish to perform. The recursive function draws the plot within a given x-interval $[x_0, x_1]$, from (x_0, y_0) to (x_1, y_1). For our problem, the plot is from (0, 0) to (1, 1). The base case (if the distance between x_0 and x_1 is less than the gap tolerance, or the distance between the line connecting the two endpoints and the value of the function at the midpoint is less than the error tolerance) is to simply draw a line from (x_0, y_0) to (x_1, y_1). The reduction step is to (recursively) plot the two halves of the curve, from (x_0, y_0) to (x_m, y_m) and from (x_m, y_m) to (x_1, y_1).

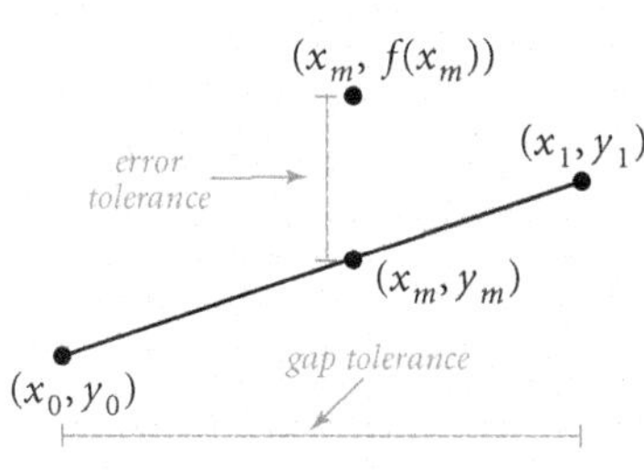

Adaptive plot tolerances

The code in `percplot.py` is relatively simple and produces a good-looking curve at relatively low cost. We can use it to study the shape of the curve for various values of n, or we can choose smaller tolerances to be more confident that the curve is close to the actual values. Precise mathematical statements about quality of approximation can, in principle, be derived, but it is perhaps not appropriate to go into too much detail while exploring and experimenting, since our goal is simply to develop a hypothesis about percolation that can be tested by scientific experimentation.

Indeed, the curves produced by `percplot.py` immediately confirm the hypothesis that there is a *threshold* value (about 0.593): if p is greater than the threshold, then the system almost certainly percolates; if p is less than the threshold, then the system almost certainly does not percolate. As n increases, the curve approaches a step function that changes value from 0 to 1 at the threshold. This phenomenon, known as a *phase transition*, is found in many physical systems.

```
percplot.curve()
   estimate.evaluate()
      percolation.random()
         stdrandom.bernoulli()
            ⋮ n² times
         stdrandom.bernoulli()
      percolation.percolates()
         flow()
            _flow()
               ⋮ between n and n² times
            _flow()
         ⋮ trials times
      percolation.random()
         stdrandom.bernoulli()
            ⋮ n² times
         stdrandom.bernoulli()
      percolation.percolates()
         flow()
            _flow()
               ⋮ between n and n² times
            _flow()
      ⋮ trials times
   ⋮ once for each point
   estimate.evaluate()
      percolation.random()
         stdrandom.bernoulli()
            ⋮ n² times
         stdrandom.bernoulli()
      percolation.percolates()
         flow()
            _flow()
               ⋮ between n and n² times
            _flow()
      ⋮ trials times
      percolation.random()
         stdrandom.bernoulli()
            ⋮ n² times
         stdrandom.bernoulli()
      percolation.percolates()
         flow()
            _flow()
               ⋮ between n and n² times
            _flow()
```

Call trace for `python percplot.py`

The simple form of the output of `percplot.py` masks the huge amount of computation behind it. For example, the curve drawn for $n = 100$ has 18 points, each the result of 10,000 trials, each trial involving n^2 sites. Generating and testing each site involves a few lines of code, so this plot comes at the cost of executing *billions* of statements. There are two lessons to be learned from this observation. First, we need to have confidence in any line of code that might be executed billions of times, so our care in developing and debugging code incrementally is justified. Second, although we might be interested in systems that are much larger, we need further study in computer science to be able to handle larger cases—that is, to develop faster algorithms and a framework for knowing their performance characteristics.

With this reuse of all of our software, we can study all sorts of variants on the percolation problem, just by implementing different `flow()` functions. For example, if you leave out the last recursive call in the recursive `_flow()` function in Program 2.4.6, it tests for a type of percolation known as *directed percolation*, where paths that go up are not considered. This model might be important for a situation like a liquid percolating through porous rock, where gravity might play a role, but not for a situation like electrical connectivity. If you run `percplot.py` for both functions, will you be able to discern the difference (see Exercise 2.4.5)?

percolates (path never goes up)

does not percolate

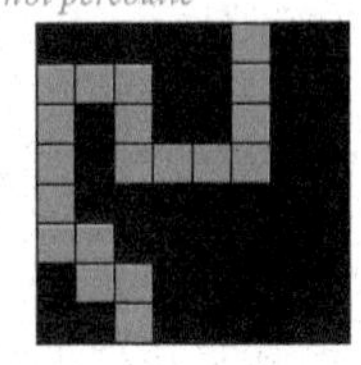

Directed percolation

To model physical situations such as water flowing through porous substances, we need to use three-dimensional arrays. Is there a similar threshold in the three-dimensional problem? If so, what is its value? Depth-first search is effective for studying this question, though the addition of another dimension requires that we pay even more attention to the computational cost of determining whether a system percolates (see Exercise 2.4.21). Scientists also study more complex lattice structures that are not well modeled by multidimensional arrays—we will see how to model such structures in Section 4.5.

Percolation is interesting to study via *in silico* experimentation because no one has been able to derive the threshold value mathematically for several natural models. The only way that scientists know the value is by using Monte Carlo simulations like those we have studied in this section. A scientist needs to do experiments to see whether the percolation model reflects what is observed in nature, perhaps through refining the model (for example, using a different lattice structure). Percolation is an example of an increasing number of problems where computer science of the kind described here is an essential part of the scientific process.

Lessons We might have approached the problem of studying percolation by sitting down to design and implement a single program, which probably would run to hundreds of lines, to produce the kind of plots that are drawn by PROGRAM 2.4.7. In the early days of computing, programmers had little choice but to work with such programs, and would spend enormous amounts of time isolating bugs and correcting design decisions. With modern programming tools like Python, we can do better, using the incremental modular style of programming presented in this chapter and keeping in mind some of the lessons that we have learned.

Expect bugs. Every interesting piece of code that you compose will have at least one or two bugs, if not many more. By running small pieces of code on small test cases that you understand, you can more easily isolate any bugs and then more easily fix them when you find them. Once the code is debugged, you can depend on using a module as a building block for any client.

Keep modules small. You can focus attention on at most a few dozen lines of code at a time, so you may as well break your code into small modules as you compose it. Some modules that contain collections of related functions may eventually grow to contain hundreds of lines of code; otherwise, we should work with small files.

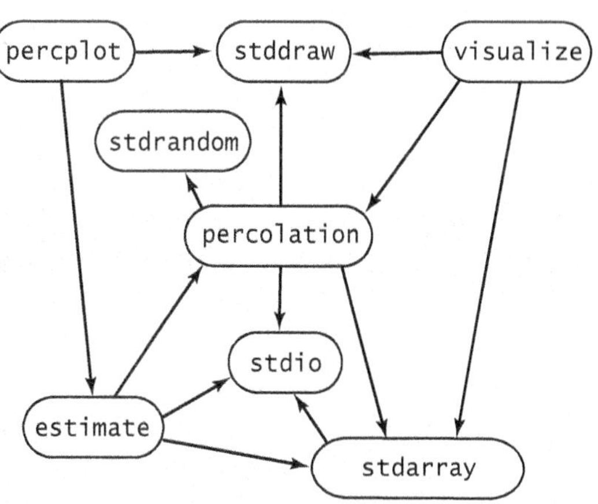

Case study dependencies (not including system calls)

Limit interactions. In a well-designed modular program, most modules should depend on just a few others. In particular, a module that *calls* a large number of other modules needs to be divided into smaller pieces. Modules that *are called by* a large number of other modules (you should have only a few) need special attention, because if you do need to make changes in a module's API, you have to reflect those changes in all its clients.

Develop code incrementally. You should run and debug each small module as you implement it. That way, you are never working with more than a few dozen lines of unreliable code at any given time. If you put all your code in one big module, it is difficult to be confident that *any* of it is safe from bugs. Running code early also forces you to think sooner rather than later about I/O formats, the nature of problem instances, and other issues. Experience gained when thinking about such issues and debugging related code makes the code that you develop later in the process more effective.

Solve an easier problem. Some working solution is better than no solution, so it is typical to begin by putting together the simplest code that you can craft that solves a given problem, as we did with vertical-only percolation. This implementation is the first step in a process of continual refinements and improvements as we develop a more complete understanding of the problem by examining a broader variety of test cases and developing support software such as our `visualize.py` and `estimate.py` programs.

Consider a recursive solution. Recursion is an indispensable tool in modern programming that you should learn to trust. If you are not already convinced of this fact by the simplicity and elegance of `percplot.py` and `percolation.py`, you might wish to try to develop a nonrecursive program for testing whether a system percolates and then reconsider the issue.

Build tools when appropriate. Our visualization function `draw()` and random boolean matrix generation function `random()` of `percolationio.py` are certainly useful for many other applications, as is the adaptive plotting function `curve()` of `percplot.py`. Incorporating these functions into appropriate modules would be simple. It is no more difficult (indeed, perhaps easier) to implement general-purpose functions like these than it would be to implement special-purpose functions for percolation.

Reuse software when possible. Our `stdio`, `stdrandom`, and `stddraw` modules all simplified the process of developing the code in this section, and we were also immediately able to reuse programs such as `estimate.py`, and `visualize.py` for percolation after developing them for vertical percolation. After you have composed a few programs of this kind, you might find yourself developing versions of these programs that you can reuse for other Monte Carlo simulations or other experimental data analysis problems.

THE PRIMARY PURPOSE OF THIS CASE study is to convince you that modular programming will take you much further than you could get without it. Although no approach to programming is a panacea for all problems, the tools and approach that we have discussed in this section will allow you to attack complex programming tasks that might otherwise be far beyond your reach.

The success of modular programming is only a start. Modern programming systems rely on a vastly more flexible programming model than the module-as-a-collection-of-functions model that we have been considering. In the next two chapters, we develop this model, along with many examples that illustrate its utility.

Q&A

Q. Editing `visualize.py` and `estimate.py` to rename every occurrence of `percolation` to `percolationv` (or whatever module we want to study) seems to be a bother. Is there a way to avoid doing so?

A. Yes. The most straightforward approach is to keep multiple files named `percolation.py` in separate subdirectories. Then copy the desired `percolation.py` file from one of the subdirectories to your working directory, thereby selecting one particular implementation. An alternative approach is to use Python's `import as` statement to define an identifier to refer to the module:

```
import percolationv as percolation
```

Now, any call to `percolation.percolates()` uses the function defined in `percolationv.py` instead of the one defined in `percolation.py`. In this situation, changing implementations involves editing only one line of source code.

Q. That recursive `flow()` function makes me nervous. How can I better understand what it's doing?

A. Run it for small examples of your own making, instrumented with instructions to write a function-call trace. After a few runs, you will gain confidence that it always fills the sites connected to the start point.

Q. Is there a simple nonrecursive approach?

A. There are several known approaches that perform the same basic computation. We will revisit the problem at the end of the book, in Section 4.5. In the meantime, working on developing a nonrecursive implementation of `flow()` is certain to be an instructive exercise, if you are interested.

Q. Program 2.4.7 (`percplot.py`) seems to involve a huge amount of calculation to get a simple function graph. Is there some better way?

A. The best strategy would be a mathematical proof of the threshold value, but that derivation has eluded scientists.

Exercises

2.4.1 Compose a program that takes a command-line argument n and creates an n-by-n boolean array with the element in row i and column j set to `True` if i and j are relatively prime, then shows the n-by-n boolean array on standard drawing (see Exercise 1.4.14). Then, compose a similar program to draw the Hadamard matrix of order n (see Exercise 1.4.27) and another program to draw the matrix with the element in row n and column j set to `True` if the coefficient of x^j in $(1+x)^i$ (binomial coefficient) is odd (see Exercise 1.4.39). You may be surprised at the pattern formed by the latter.

2.4.2 Compose a `write()` function for `percolationIO.py` that writes `1` for blocked sites, `0` for open sites, and `*` for full sites.

2.4.3 Give the recursive calls for `percolation.py` given the following input:

```
3 3
1 0 1
0 0 0
1 1 0
```

2.4.4 Compose a client of `percolation.py` like `visualize.py` that does a series of experiments for a command-line argument n where the site vacancy probability p increases from 0 to 1 by a given increment (also taken from the command line).

2.4.5 Compose a program `percolationd.py` that tests for *directed* percolation (by leaving off the last recursive call in the recursive `_flow()` function in Program 2.4.6, as described in the text), then use `percplot.py` (suitably modified) to draw a plot of the directed percolation probability as a function of the site vacancy probability.

2.4.6 Compose a client of `percolation.py` and `percolationd.py` that takes a site vacancy probability p from the command line and writes an estimate of the probability that a system percolates but does not percolate down. Perform enough experiments to get an estimate that is accurate to three decimal places.

2.4.7 Describe the order in which the sites are marked when `percolation.py` is used on a system with no blocked sites. Which is the last site marked? What is the depth of the recursion?

2.4.8 Modify `percolation.py` to animate the flow computation, showing the sites filling one by one. Check your answer to the previous exercise.

2.4.9 Experiment with using `percplot.py` to plot various mathematical functions (just by replacing the call on `estimate.evaluate()` with an expression that evaluates the function). Try the function `sin(x) + cos(10*x)` to see how the plot adapts to an oscillating curve, and come up with interesting plots for three or four functions of your own choosing.

2.4.10 Modify `percolation.py` to compute the maximum depth of the recursion used in the flow calculation. Plot the expected value of that quantity as a function of the site vacancy probability p. How does your answer change if the order of the recursive calls is reversed?

2.4.11 Modify `estimate.py` to produce output like that produced by `bernoulli.py` (PROGRAM 2.2.7). *Extra credit*: Use your program to validate the hypothesis that the data obeys the Gaussian (normal) distribution.

2.4.12 Modify `percolationio.py`, `estimate.py`, `percolation.py`, and `visualize.py` to handle m-by-n grids and m-by-n boolean matrices. Use an optional argument so that m defaults to n if only one of the two dimensions is specified.

Creative Exercises

2.4.13 *Vertical percolation.* Show that an n-by-n percolation system with site vacancy probability p vertically percolates with probability $1 - (1 - p^n)^n$, and use `estimate.py` to validate your analysis for various values of n.

2.4.14 *Rectangular percolation systems.* Modify the code in this section to allow you to study percolation in rectangular systems. Compare the percolation probability plots of systems whose ratio of width to height is 2:1 with those whose ratio is 1:2.

2.4.15 *Adaptive plotting.* Modify `percplot.py` to take its control parameters (gap tolerance, error tolerance, and number of trials) from the command line. Experiment with various values of the parameters to learn their effect on the quality of the curve and the cost of computing it. Briefly describe your findings.

2.4.16 *Percolation threshold.* Compose a `percolation.py` client that uses binary search to estimate the threshold value (see Exercise 2.1.26).

2.4.17 *Nonrecursive directed percolation.* Compose a nonrecursive program that tests for directed percolation by moving from top to bottom as in our vertical percolation code. Base your solution on the following computation: if any site in a contiguous subrow of open sites in the current row is connected to some full site on the previous row, then all of the sites in the subrow become full.

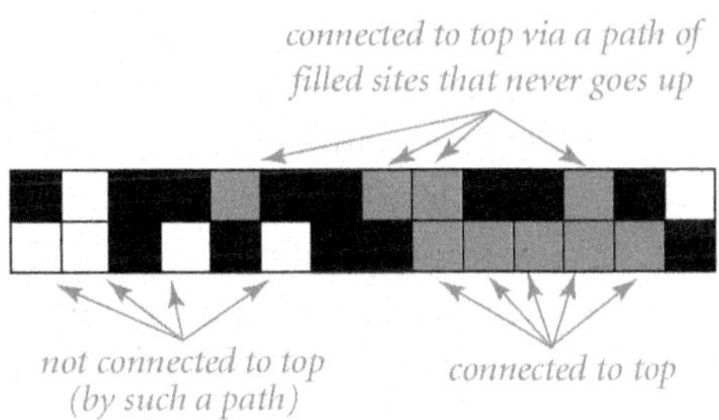

Directed percolation calculation

2.4.18 *Fast percolation test.* Modify the recursive `_flow()` function in Program 2.4.6 so that it returns as soon as it finds a site on the bottom row (and fills no more sites). *Hint*: Use an argument `done` that is `True` if the bottom has been hit, `False` otherwise. Give a rough estimate of the performance improvement factor for this change when running `percplot.py`. Use values of n for which the programs run at least a few seconds but not more than a few minutes. Note that the improvement is ineffective unless the first recursive call in `_flow()` is for the site below the current site.

2.4.19 *Bond percolation.* Compose a modular program for studying percolation under the assumption that the *edges* of the grid provide the connectivity. That is, an edge can be either empty or full, and a system percolates if there is a path consisting of full edges that goes from top to bottom. *Note*: This problem *has* been solved analytically, so your simulations should validate the hypothesis that the percolation threshold approaches 1/2 as n gets large.

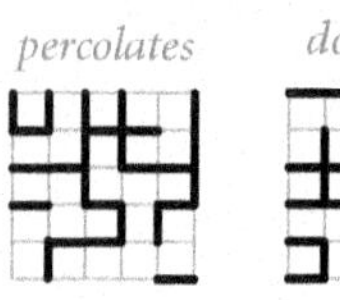

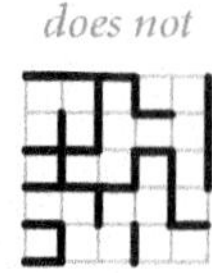

2.4.20 *Bond percolation on a triangular grid.* Compose a modular program for studying bond percolation on a *triangular grid*, where the system is composed of $2n^2$ equilateral triangles packed together in an n-by-n grid of rhombus shapes and, as in the previous exercise, the edges of the grid provide the connectivity. Each interior point has six bonds; each point on the edge has four; and each corner point has two.

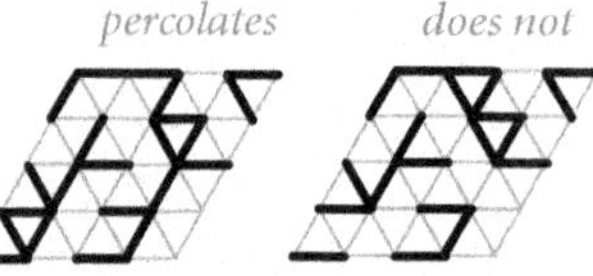

2.4.21 *Percolation in three dimensions.* Implement modules `percolation3d.py` and `percolation3dio.py` (for I/O and random generation) to study percolation in three-dimensional cubes, generalizing the two-dimensional case studied in this chapter. A percolation system is an n-by-n-by-n cube of sites that are unit cubes, with probability of being open p and probability of being blocked $1-p$. Paths can connect an open cube with any open cube that shares a common face (one of six neighbors, except on the boundary). The system percolates if there exists a path connecting any open site on the bottom plane to any open site on the top plane. Use a recursive version of `_flow()` like the one in PROGRAM 2.4.6, but with eight recursive calls instead of four. Plot percolation probability versus site vacancy probability for as large a value of n as you can. Be sure to develop your solution incrementally, as emphasized throughout this section.

2.4.22 *Game of life.* Implement a module `life.py` that simulates Conway's *game of life*. Consider a boolean matrix corresponding to a system of cells that we refer to as being either live or dead. The game consists of checking and perhaps updating the value of each cell, depending on the values of its neighbors (the adjacent cells in every direction, including diagonals). Live cells remain live and dead cells remain dead, with the following exceptions:

- A dead cell with exactly three live neighbors becomes live.
- A live cell with exactly one live neighbor becomes dead.
- A live cell with more than three live neighbors becomes dead.

Test your program with a *glider*, a famous pattern that moves down and to the right every four generations, as shown in the diagram below. Then try two gliders that collide. Then try a random boolean matrix, or use one of the starting patterns on the booksite. This game has been heavily studied, and relates to foundations of computer science (see the booksite for more information)

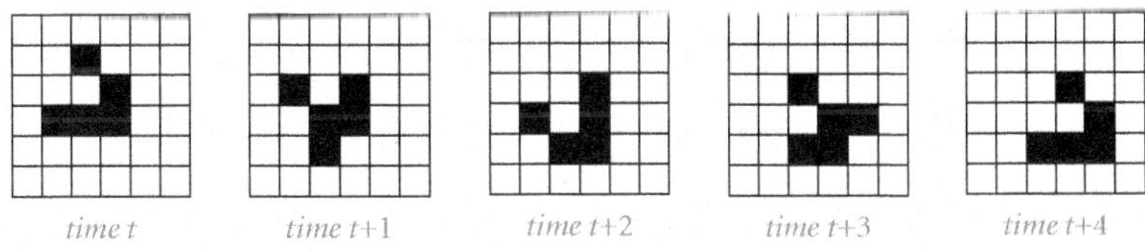

Five generations of a glider

Chapter Three

Object-Oriented Programming

YOUR NEXT STEP TO PROGRAMMING EFFECTIVELY is conceptually simple. Now that you know how to use built-in data types, you will learn in this chapter how to *use*, *create*, and *design* higher-level data types.

An *abstraction* is a simplified description of something that captures its essential elements while suppressing all other details. In science, engineering, and programming, we are always striving to understand complex systems through abstraction. In Python programming, we do so with *object-oriented programming*, where we break a large and potentially complex program into a set of interacting elements, or *objects*. The idea originates from modeling (in software) real-world entities such as electrons, people, buildings, or solar systems and readily extends to modeling abstract entities such as bits, numbers, colors, images, or programs.

As discussed in SECTION 1.2, a data type is a set of values and a set of operations defined on those values. In Python, the values and operations for many data types such as `int` and `float` are predefined. In object-oriented programming, we compose code to create *new* data types.

This ability to define new data types and to manipulate objects holding data-type values is also known as *data abstraction*, and leads us to a style of modular programming that naturally extends the *function abstraction* style that was the basis for CHAPTER 2. A data type allows us to isolate *data* as well as functions. Our mantra for this chapter is this: *Whenever you can clearly separate data and associated tasks within a computation, you should do so.*

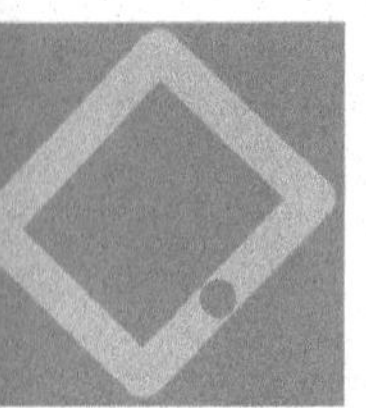

3.1 Using Data Types

ORGANIZING DATA FOR PROCESSING IS AN essential step in the development of a computer program. Programming in Python is largely based on doing so with data types that are designed to support *object-oriented programming*, a style of programming that integrates code and data.

You certainly noticed in the first two chapters of this book that our programs were confined to operations on numbers, booleans, and strings. Of course, the reason is that the Python data types that we've encountered so far—`int`, `float`, `bool`, and `str`—manipulate numbers, booleans, and strings, using familiar operations. In this chapter, we begin to consider other data types.

Programs in this section

We first examine a host of new operations on objects of type `str`, which will introduce you to object-oriented programming because most of these operations are implemented as *methods* that manipulate objects. Methods are very similar to functions, except that each method call is explicitly associated with a specified object. To illustrate the natural style of programming induced by the use of methods, we consider a string-processing application from genomics.

Even more significantly, you will learn in SECTION 3.2 to define your own data types to implement any abstraction whatsoever. This ability is crucial in modern programming. No library of modules can meet the needs of all possible applications, so programmers routinely create data types to meet their own needs.

In this section, we focus on client programs that *use* existing data types, to give you some concrete reference points for understanding these new concepts and to illustrate their broad reach. We introduce *constructors* to create objects from a data type and *methods* to operate on their values. We consider programs that manipulate electrical charges, colors, images, files, and web pages—quite a leap from the built-in data types that we used in previous chapters.

Methods In SECTION 1.2, you learned that a data type is a set of values and a set of operations defined on those values, and you learned details of Python's built-in data types `int`, `bool`, `float`, and `str`. You also learned that all data in a Python program are represented by *objects* and relationships among objects. Since then, we have focused on composing programs that use the operations associated with the built-in types to manipulate objects of those types. To do so, we have used conditionals, loops, and functions, which enable us to build large programs where the flow of control from operation to operation is well understood. In this section, we put these concepts together.

In the programs that we have encountered so far, we apply data-type operations using built-in operators such as +, -, *, /, and `[]`. Now, we are going to introduce a new way to apply data-type operations that is more general. A *method* is a function associated with a specified object (and, by extension, with the type of that object). That is, a method corresponds to a data-type operation.

We can *call* (or *invoke*) a method by using a variable name, followed by the *dot operator* (`.`), followed by the method name, followed by a list of arguments delimited by commas and enclosed in parentheses. As a simple example, Python's built-in `int` type has a method named `bit_length()`, so you can determine the number of bits in the binary representation of an `int` value as follows:

```
x = 3 ** 100
bits = x.bit_length()
stdio.writeln(bits)
```

This code writes `159` to standard output, telling you that 3^{100} (a huge integer) has 159 bits when expressed in binary.

The syntax and behavior of method calls is nearly the same as the syntax and behavior of function calls. For example, a method can take any number of arguments, those arguments are passed by object reference, and the method returns a value to its caller. Similarly, like a function call, a method call is an expression, so you can use it anywhere in your program where you would use an expression. The main difference in syntactic: you invoke a method using a specified object and the dot operator.

In "object-oriented programming," we usually prefer method-call syntax to function-call syntax because it emphasizes the role of the object. This approach has proved for decades to be a fruitful way to develop programs, particularly those that are developed to build and understand models of the real world.

Distinction between methods and functions. The key difference between a function and a method is that a method is *associated with a specified object*. You can think of this specified object as an extra argument that gets passed to a function, in addition to the ordinary methods argument. You can distinguish between method calls and function calls in client code by looking to the left of the dot operator: a function call typically uses a *module name* and a method call typically uses a *variable name*. These differences are illustrated at left and summarized in the table at the bottom of this page.

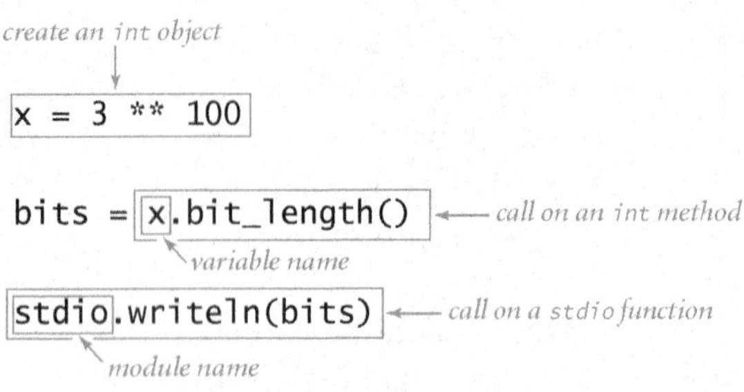

Calling a method and then a function

String processing Out of necessity, we have been using the `str` data type from the beginning of this book, to create human-readable output for our programs. Your experience with using `str` demonstrates that *you do not need to know how a data type is implemented to be able to use it* (one of several mantras we repeat in this book because of its importance). You know that `str` values are sequences of characters and that you can perform the operation of concatenating two `str` values to produce a `str` result.

Python's `str` data type includes many other operations, as documented in the API on the facing page. It is one of Python's most important data types because string processing is critical to many computational applications. Strings lie at the heart of our ability to compile and execute Python programs and to perform many other core computations; they are the basis of the information-processing systems that are critical to most business systems; people use them every day when typing into email, blog, or chat applications or preparing documents for publication; and they are critical ingredients in scientific progress in several fields, particularly molecular biology.

	method	*function*
sample call	`x.bit_length()`	`stdio.writeln(bits)`
typically invoked with	variable name	module name
parameters	object reference and argument(s)	argument(s)
primary purpose	manipulate object value	compute return value

Methods versus functions

operation	description
`len(s)`	*length of* `s`
`s + t`	*a new string that is the concatenation of* `s` *and* `t`
`s += t`	*assign to* `s` *a new string that is the concatenation of* `s` *and* `t`
`s[i]`	*the* `i`*th character of* `s` *(a string)*
`s[i:j]`	*the* `i`*th through* `(j-1)`*st characters of* `s` *(*`i` *defaults to* `0`*;* `j` *defaults to* `len(s)`*)*
`s[i:j:k]`	*slice from* `i` *to* `j` *with step size* `k`
`s < t`	*is* `s` *less than* `t`*?*
`s <= t`	*is* `s` *less than or equal to* `t`*?*
`s == t`	*is* `s` *equal to* `t`*?*
`s != t`	*is* `s` *not equal to* `t`*?*
`s >= t`	*is* `s` *greater than or equal to* `t`*?*
`s > t`	*is* `s` *greater than* `t`*?*
`s in t`	*does* `s` *appear as a substring in* `t`*?*
`s not in t`	*does* `s` *not appear as a substring in* `t`*?*
`s.count(t)`	*number of occurrences of substring* `t` *in* `s`
`s.find(t, start)`	*the first index in* `s` *where* `t` *appears (*`-1` *if not found) starting at* `start` *(default* `0`*)*
`s.upper()`	*a copy of* `s` *with lowercase letters replaced with uppercase ones*
`s.lower()`	*a copy of* `s` *with uppercase letters replaced with lowercase ones*
`s.startswith(t)`	*does* `s` *start with* `t`*?*
`s.endswith(t)`	*does* `s` *end with* `t`*?*
`s.strip()`	*a copy of* `s` *with leading and trailing whitespace removed*
`s.replace(old, new)`	*a copy of* `s` *with all occurrences of* `old` *replaced by* `new`
`s.split(delimiter)`	*an array of substrings of* `s`*, separated by* `delimiter` *(default whitespace)*
`delimiter.join(a)`	*concatenation of strings in* `a[]`*, separated by* `delimiter`

Partial API for Python's built-in `str` *data type*

On closer examination , you will see that the operations in the `str` API can be divided into three categories:

- *Built-in operators* +, +=, `[]`, `[:]`, `in`, `not in`, and the comparison operators, which are characterized by special symbols and syntax
- A *built-in function* `len()` with standard function-call syntax
- *Methods* `upper()`, `startswith()`, `find()`, and so forth, which are distinguished in the API with a variable name followed by the dot operator

From this point forward, any API that we might consider will have these kinds of operations. Next, we consider each of them in turn.

```
a = 'now is '
b = 'the time '
c = 'to'
```

call	return value
`len(a)`	`7`
`a[4]`	`'i'`
`a[2:5]`	`'w i'`
`c.upper()`	`'TO'`
`b.startswith('the')`	`True`
`a.find('is')`	`4`
`a + c`	`'now is to'`
`b.replace('t','T')`	`'The Time '`
`a.split()`	`['now','is']`
`b == c`	`False`
`a.strip()`	`'now is'`

Examples of string operations

Built-in operators. An operator (or function) that you can apply to more than one type of data is said to be *polymorphic*. Polymorphism is an important feature of Python programming, and several built-in operators allow you to compose compact code using familiar operators for processing any type of data. You have already been using the + operator, familiar for numbers, for string concatenation. The API tells you that you can use the `[]` operator, familiar for arrays, to extract a single character from a string and the `[:]` operator to extract a substring from a string. Not all data types provide implementations for all operators—for example, the operator / is not defined for strings because it makes no sense to divide two strings.

Built-in functions. Python also builds in a number of polymorphic functions, such as the `len()` function, that are likely to make sense for numerous data types. When a data type implements such a function, Python automatically calls that implementation, based on the type of the argument. Polymorphic functions are like polymorphic operators, but without the special syntax.

Methods. We include built-in operators and built-in functions for convenience (and to conform to Python norms), but most of our effort in creating data types goes into developing methods that operate on object values, such as `upper()`, `startswith()`, `find()`, and the other methods in the `str` API.

In point of fact, these three kinds of operations end up being the *same* in implementations, as you will see in Section 3.2. Python automatically maps built-in operators and functions to *special* methods, using the convention that such special methods have double underscores before and after their names. For example, s + t is equivalent to the method call `s.__add__(t)` and `len(s)` is equivalent to the method call `s.__len__()`. We never use the double underscore form in client code, but we do use it to implement special methods, as you will see in Section 3.2.

The table below gives several examples of simple string-processing applications that illustrate the utility of the various operations in Python's `str` data type. The examples are just an introduction; we examine a more sophisticated client next.

translate from DNA to mRNA (replace 'T' with 'U')	`def translate(dna):`
	`    dna = dna.upper()`
	`    rna = dna.replace('T', 'U')`
	`    return rna`

is the string s a palindrome?	`def isPalindrome(s):`
	`    n = len(s)`
	`    for i in range(n // 2):`
	`        if s[i] != s[n-1-i]:`
	`            return False`
	`    return True`

extract file name and extension from a command-line argument	`s = sys.argv[1]`
	`dot = s.find('.')`
	`base      = s[:dot]`
	`extension = s[dot+1:]`

write all lines on standard input that contain a string specified as a command-line argument	`query = sys.argv[1]`
	`while stdio.hasNextLine():`
	`    s = stdio.readLine()`
	`    if query in s:`
	`        stdio.writeln(s)`

is an array of strings in ascending order?	`def isSorted(a):`
	`    for i in range(1, len(a)):`
	`        if a[i] < a[i-1]:`
	`            return False`
	`    return True`

Typical string-processing code

String-processing application: genomics To give you more experience with string processing, we will give a very brief overview of the field of *genomics* and consider a program that a bioinformatician might use to identify potential genes. Biologists use a simple model to represent the building blocks of life, in which the letters `A`, `C`, `T`, and `G` represent the four bases in the DNA of living organisms. In each living organism, these basic building blocks appear in a set of long sequences (one for each chromosome) known as a *genome*. Understanding properties of the genome is a key to understanding the processes that manifest themselves in living organisms. The genomic sequences for many living things are known, including the human genome, which is a sequence of about 3 billion bases. Since the sequences have been identified, scientists have begun composing computer programs to study their structure. String processing is now one of the most important methodologies—experimental or computational—in molecular biology.

Gene prediction. A *gene* is a substring of a genome that represents a functional unit of critical importance in understanding life processes. A gene consists of a sequence of *codons*, each of which is a sequence of three bases that represents one amino acid. The *start codon* `ATG` marks the beginning of a gene, and any of the *stop codons* `TAG`, `TAA`, or `TGA` marks the end of a gene (and no other occurrences of any of these stop codons can appear within the gene). One of the first steps in analyzing a genome is to identify its potential genes, which is a string-processing problem that Python's `str` data type equips us to solve.

Program 3.1.1 (`potentialgene.py`) is a program that serves as a first step. It takes a DNA sequence as a command-line argument and determines whether it corresponds to a potential gene based on the following criteria: length is a multiple of 3, starts with the start codon, ends with the stop codon, and has no intervening stop codons. To make the determination, the program uses a mixture of string methods, built-in operators, and built-in functions.

Although the rules that define genes are a bit more complicated than those we have sketched here, `potentialgene.py` exemplifies how a basic knowledge of programming can enable a scientist to study genomic sequences more effectively.

In the present context, our interest in `str` is that it illustrates what a data type can be—a well-developed encapsulation of an important abstraction that is useful to clients. Python's language mechanisms, from polymorphic functions and operators to methods that operate on object values, help us achieve that goal. Next, we proceed to numerous other examples.

Program 3.1.1 *Identifying a potential gene* (potentialgene.py)

```
import sys
import stdio

def isPotentialGene(dna):
    # number of bases is a multiple of 3
    if (len(dna) % 3) != 0: return False

    # starts with start codon
    if not dna.startswith('ATG'): return False

    # no intervening stop codons
    for i in range(len(dna) - 3):
        if i % 3 == 0:
            if dna[i:i+3] == 'TAA': return False
            if dna[i:i+3] == 'TAG': return False
            if dna[i:i+3] == 'TGA': return False

    # ends with a stop codon
    if dna.endswith('TAA'): return True
    if dna.endswith('TAG'): return True
    if dna.endswith('TGA'): return True

    return False


dna = sys.argv[1]
stdio.writeln(isPotentialGene(dna))
```

This program takes a DNA sequence as a command-line argument and determines whether it corresponds to a potential gene: length is a multiple of 3, starts with the start codon (ATG), ends with a stop codon (TAA or TAG or TGA), and has no intervening stop codons.

```
% python potentialgene.py ATGCGCCTGCGTCTGTACTAG
True

% python potentialgene.py ATGCGCTGCGTCTGTACTAG
False
```

A user-defined data type As a running example of a user-defined data type, we will consider a data type `Charge` for charged particles. In particular, we are interested in a two-dimensional model that uses *Coulomb's law,* which tells us that the *electric potential* at a point due to a given charged particle is represented by $V = kq/r$, where q is the charge value, r is the distance from the point to the charge, and k=8.99×10^9 N m^2/C^2 is a constant known as the electrostatic constant, or *Coulomb's constant.* For consistency, we use SI (Système International d'Unités): in this formula, N designates newtons (force), m designates meters (distance), and C represent coulombs (electric charge). When there are multiple charged particles, the electric potential at any point is the sum of the potentials due to each charge. Our interest is computing the potential at various points in the plane due to a given set of charged particles. To do so, we will compose programs that create and manipulate `Charge` objects.

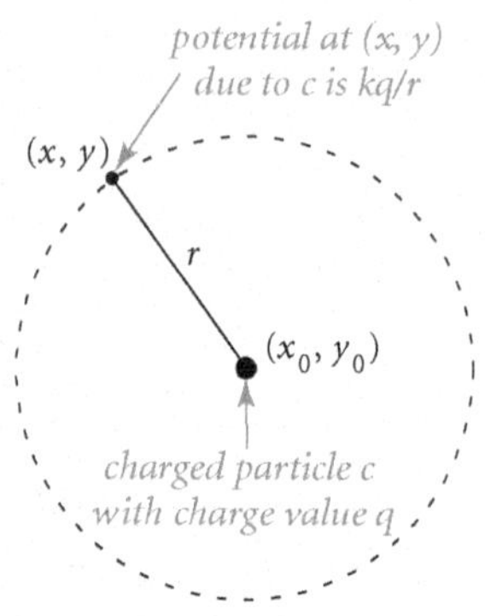

Coulomb's law for a charged particle in the plane

Application programming interface. To fulfill our mantra promise that *you do not need to know how a data type is implemented to use it,* we specify the behavior of the `Charge` data type by listing its operations in an API, deferring the discussion of the implementation until Section 3.2.

operation	*description*
`Charge(x0, y0, q0)`	*a new charge centered at* `(x0, y0)` *with charge value* `q0`
`c.potentialAt(x, y)`	*electric potential of charge* `c` *at point* `(x, y)`
`str(c)`	`'q0 at (x0, y0)'` *(string representation of charge* `c`*)*

API for our user-defined `Charge` *data type*

The first entry in the API, which has the same name as the data type, is known as a *constructor.* Clients call the constructor to create new objects; each call to the `Charge` constructor creates exactly one new `Charge` object. The other two entries define the data-type operations. The first is a method `potentialAt()`, which computes and returns the potential due to the charge at the given point `(x, y)`. The second is the built-in function `str()`, which returns a string representation of the charged particle. Next, we discuss how to make use of this data type in client code.

File conventions. The code that defines a user-defined data type resides in a `.py` file. By convention, we define each data type in a distinct `.py` file, with the same name as the data type (but not capitalized). Thus, the `Charge` data type is found in a file named `charge.py`. To compose a client program that uses the `Charge` data type, we put the following `import` statement at the top of the client `.py` file:

```
from charge import Charge
```

Note that the format of the `import` statement that we use with user-defined data types differs from the format we use with functions. As usual, you must make `charge.py` available to Python, either by putting it in the same directory as your client code or by using your operating system's path mechanism (see the Q&A at the end of Section 2.2).

Creating objects. To create an object from a user-defined data type, you call its constructor, which directs Python to create a new individual object. You call a constructor just as if it were a function, using the name of the data type, followed by the constructor's arguments enclosed in parentheses and separated by commas. For example, `Charge(x0, y0, q0)` creates a new `Charge` object with position `(x0, y0)` and charge value `q0` and returns a reference to the new object. Typically, you call a constructor to create a new object and set a variable to reference that object in the same line of code, as in the example shown in the diagram at right. Once you have created the object, the values `x0`, `y0`, and `q0` belong to the *object*. As usual, it is helpful to picture the newly created variable and object as in the memory diagram at right.

```
c1 = Charge(.51, .63, 21.3)
```

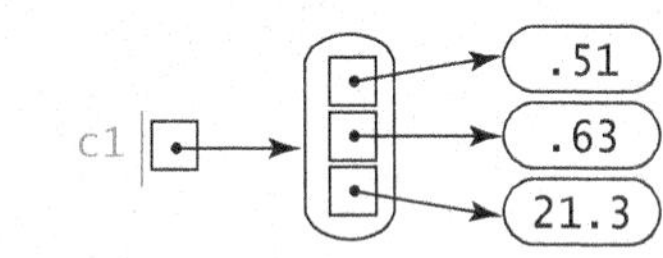

Creating a Charge object

You can create any number of objects of the same data type. Recall from Section 1.2 that each object has its own identity, type, and value. So, while any two objects reside at distinct places in computer memory, they may be of the same type and store the same value. For example, the code in the diagram at the top of the next page creates three distinct `Charge` objects. The variables `c1` and `c3` reference distinct objects, even though the two objects store the same value. In other words, the objects referenced by `c1` and `c3` are *equal* (that is, they are objects of the same data type and they happen to store the same value), but they are not *identical* (that is, they have distinct identities because they reside in different places in computer memory). In contrast, `c2` and `c4` refer to the *same* object—they are aliases.

Calling a method. As discussed at the beginning of this section, we typically use a variable name to identify the object to be associated with the method we intend to call. For our example, the method call `c1.potentialAt(.20, .50)` returns a float that represents the potential at the query point (0.20, 0.50) due to the `Charge` object referenced by `c1`. The distance between the query point and the charge location is 0.34, so this potential is $8.99 \times 10^9 \times 0.51 / 0.34 = 1.35 \times 10^{10}$.

```
c1 = Charge(.51, .63, 21.3)
c2 = Charge(.13, .94, 85.9)
c3 = Charge(.51, .63, 21.3)
c4 = c2
```

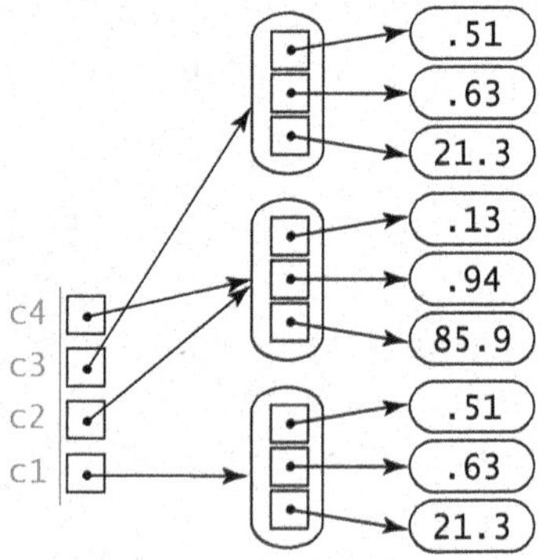

Four variables referring to three `Charge` objects

String representation. In any data-type implementation, it is typically worthwhile to include an operation that converts an object's value to a string. Python has a built-in function `str()` for this purpose, which you been using from the beginning to convert integers and floats to strings for output. Since our `Charge` API has a `str()` implementation, any client can call `str()` to get a string representation of a `Charge` object. For our example, the call `str(c1)` returns the string `'21.3 at (0.51, 0.63)'`. The nature of the conversion is completely up to the implementation, but usually the string encodes the object's value in a human-readable format. We will examine the exact mechanism behind this convention when we discuss the implementation, in SECTION 3.2.

THESE MECHANISMS ARE SUMMARIZED IN THE client `chargeclient.py` (PROGRAM 3.1.2), which creates two `Charge` objects and computes the total potential due to the two charges at a query point taken from the command line. This code illustrates the idea of developing an abstract model (for a charged particle) and separating the code that implements the abstraction (which you haven't even seen yet) from the code that uses it. This is a turning point in this book: we have not yet seen any code of this nature, but virtually all of the code that we compose from this point forward will be based on defining and invoking methods that implement data-type operations.

Program 3.1.2 ***Charged-particle client*** (`chargeclient.py`)

```
import sys
import stdio
from charge import Charge

x = float(sys.argv[1])
y = float(sys.argv[2])
c1 = Charge(.51, .63, 21.3)
c2 = Charge(.13, .94, 81.9)
v1 = c1.potentialAt(x, y)
v2 = c2.potentialAt(x, y)
stdio.writef('potential at (%.2f, %.2f) due to\n', x, y)
stdio.writeln('  ' + str(c1) + ' and')
stdio.writeln('  ' + str(c2))
stdio.writef('is %.2e\n', v1+v2)
```

`x, y`	*query point*
`c1`	*first charge*
`c2`	*second charge*
`v1`	*potential due to* `c1`
`v2`	*potential due to* `c2`

This object-oriented client takes a query point (x, y) as command-line argument, creates two charges `c1` *and* `c2` *with fixed position and charge values, and writes to standard output the two charges and the potential at (x, y) due to the two charges. The potential at (x, y) is the sum of the potential at (x, y) due to charges* `c1` *and* `c2`.

```
% python chargeclient.py .2 .5
potential at (0.20, 0.50) due to
  21.3 at (0.51, 0.63) and
  81.9 at (0.13, 0.94)
is 2.22e+12
% python chargeclient.py .51 .94
potential at (0.51, 0.94) due to
  21.3 at (0.51, 0.63) and
  81.9 at (0.13, 0.94)
is 2.56+12
```

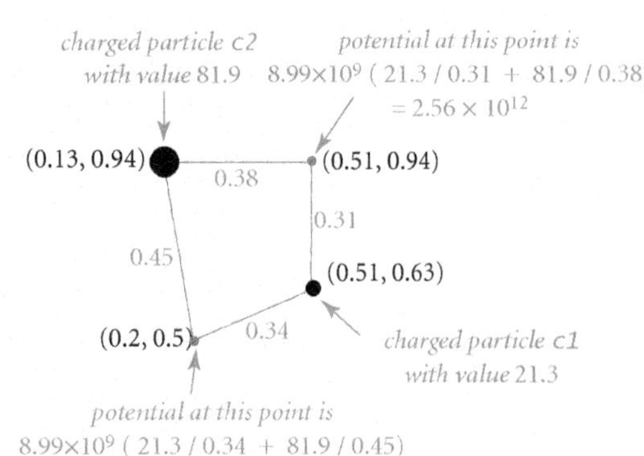

The basic concepts that we have just covered are the starting point for object-oriented programming, so it is worthwhile to review them here. At the conceptual level, a *data type* is a set of values and a set of operations defined on those values. At the concrete level, we use a data type to create *objects*. An object is characterized by three essential properties: *identity*, *type*, and *value*.

- The *identity* of an object is the location in the computer's memory where the object is stored. It uniquely identifies the object.
- The *type* of an object completely specifies the *behavior* of the object—the set of operations that the object supports.
- The *value* (or *state*) of an object is the data-type value that it currently represents.

In object-oriented programming, we call *constructors* to create objects and then manipulate their values by calling their *methods*. In Python, we access objects through references. A *reference* is a name that refers to the location in memory (identity) of an object.

This is a picture of a pipe

The famous Belgian artist René Magritte captured the concept of a reference in the painting *The Treachery of Images*, where he created an image of a pipe along with the caption *ceci n'est pas une pipe* (*this is not a pipe*) below it. We might interpret the caption as saying that the image is not actually a pipe, just an image of a pipe. Or perhaps Magritte meant that the caption is neither a pipe nor an image of a pipe, just a caption! In the present context, this image reinforces the idea that a reference to an object is nothing more than a reference; it is not the object itself.

Similarities between user-defined and built-in data types. In most ways, user-defined data types (that is, the standard, extension, and booksite data types, as well as data types that you might define) are no different from built-in data types such as `int`, `float`, `bool`, and `str`. You can use objects of any type

- In assignment statements
- As elements in arrays
- As arguments or return values in methods or functions
- As operands with built-in operators such as `+`, `-`, `*`, `/`, `+=`, `<`, `<=`, `>`, `>=`, `==`, `!=`, `[]`, and `[:]`
- As arguments to built-in functions such as `str()` and `len()`

These capabilities enable us to create elegant and understandable client code that directly manipulates our data in a natural manner, as you saw in our `str` client `potentialgene.py` and will see in many other examples later in this section.

Differences between user-defined and built-in data types. The built-in types do have special status in Python, notably evidenced by the following considerations:

- You do not need an `import` statement to use the built-in data types.
- Python provides special syntax for creating objects of built-in data types. For example, the literal `123` creates an `int` object and the expression `['Hello', 'World']` creates an array whose elements are `str` objects. In contrast, to create an object of a user-defined data type, we must call a constructor.
- By convention, built-in types begin with lowercase letters while user-defined types begin with uppercase letters.
- Python provides automatic type promotion for built-in arithmetic types, such as from `int` to `float`.
- Python provides built-in functions for type conversion *to* built-in types, including `int()`, `float()`, `bool()`, and `str()`.

To demonstrate the power of object orientation, we next consider several more examples. Our primary purpose in presenting these examples is to get you used to the idea of defining and computing with abstractions, but we also will develop data types that are generally useful and that we use throughout the rest of the book. First, we consider the familiar world of image processing, where we process `Color` and `Picture` objects. These are both quintessential abstractions, and we can reduce them to simple data types that allow us to compose programs that process images like the ones that you capture with a camera and view on a display. They are also very useful for scientific visualization, as you will see. Then, we revisit the subject of input/output, moving substantially beyond the features offered by the booksite `stdio` module. Specifically, we consider abstractions that will allow you to compose Python programs that directly process web pages and files on your computer.

Color *Color* is a sensation in the eye attributable to electromagnetic radiation. Since we often want to view and manipulate color images on our computers, color is a widely used abstraction in computer graphics. In professional publishing, in print, and on the web, working with color is a complex task. For example, the appearance of a color image depends in a significant way on the medium used to present it. Our `Color` data type, defined in the module `color.py`, separates the creative designer's problem of specifying a desired color from the system's problem of faithfully reproducing it. Its API is shown at the bottom of this page.

To represent color values, `Color` uses the *RGB color model*, in which a color is defined by three integers, each between 0 and 255, that represent the intensity of the red, green, and blue (respectively) components of the color. Other color values are obtained by mixing the red, green, and blue components. Using this model, we can represent 256^3 (that is, approximately 16.7 million) distinct colors. Scientists estimate that the human eye can distinguish only about 10 million distinct colors.

red	*green*	*blue*	
255	0	0	*red*
0	255	0	*green*
0	0	255	*blue*
0	0	0	*black*
100	100	100	*dark gray*
255	255	255	*white*
255	255	0	*yellow*
255	0	255	*magenta*
9	90	166	*this color*

Some color values

Color has a constructor that takes three integer arguments, so that you can compose the code

```
red  = color.Color(255,   0,   0)
blue = color.Color(  0,   0, 255)
```

to create objects whose values represent pure red and pure blue, respectively. We have been using colors in `stddraw` since Section 1.5, but have been limited to a set of predefined colors, such as `stddraw.BLACK`, `stddraw.RED`, and `stddraw.PINK`. Now you have millions of colors available for your use.

operation	*description*
`Color(r, g, b)`	*a new color with red, green, and blue components* `r`, `g`, *and* `b`, *all integers between 0 and 255*
`c.getRed()`	*the red component of* `c`
`c.getGreen()`	*the green component of* `c`
`c.getBlue()`	*the blue component of* `c`
`str(c)`	`'(R, G, B)'` *(string representation of* `c`*)*

API for our `Color` data type (`color.py`)

PROGRAM 3.1.3 (`alberssquares.py`) is a `Color` and `stddraw` client that allows you to experiment with colors. The program accepts two colors from the command line, and displays the colors in the format developed in the 1960s by the color theorist Josef Albers, who revolutionized the way that people think about color.

Our primary purpose is to use `Color` as an example to illustrate object-oriented programming. If you try it for a variety of arguments, you will see that even a simple program like `alberssquares.py` is a useful and interesting way to study interactions among colors. At the same time, we may as well develop a few useful tools that we can use to compose programs that process colors. Next, we choose one color property as an example to help convince you that composing object-oriented code to process abstract concepts like color is a convenient and useful approach.

Luminance. The quality of the images on modern displays such as LCD monitors, LED TVs, and cellphone screens depends on an understanding of a color property known as *monochrome luminance*, or effective brightness. A standard formula for luminance is derived from the eye's sensitivity to red, green, and blue. It is a linear combination of the three intensities: if a color's red, green, and blue values are r, g, and b, respectively, then its luminance is defined by this formula:

$$Y = 0.299\,r + 0.587g + 0.114b$$

Since the coefficients are positive and sum to 1 and the intensities are all integers between 0 and 255, the luminance is a real number between 0 and 255.

Grayscale. The RGB color model has the property that when all three color intensities are the same, the resulting color is on a grayscale that ranges from black (all 0s) to white (all 255s). To print a color photograph in a black-and-white newspaper (or a book), we need a function to convert from color to grayscale. A simple way to convert a color to grayscale is to replace the color with a new one whose red, green, and blue values equal its monochrome luminance.

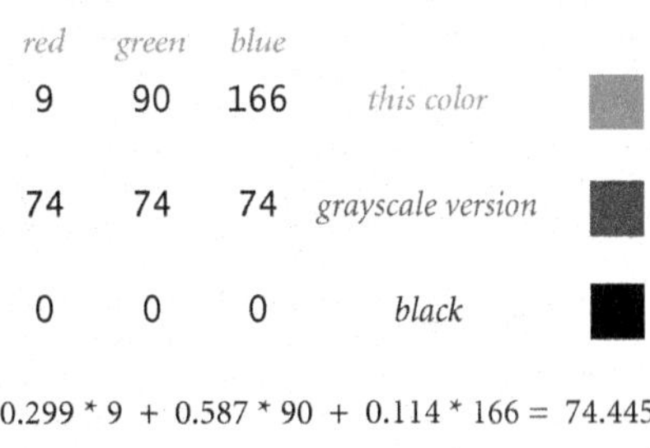

red green blue
9 90 166 this color
74 74 74 grayscale version
0 0 0 black
0.299 * 9 + 0.587 * 90 + 0.114 * 166 = 74.445

Grayscale example

Program 3.1.3 Albers squares (alberssquares.py)

```
import sys
import stddraw
from color import Color

r1 = int(sys.argv[1])
g1 = int(sys.argv[2])
b1 = int(sys.argv[3])
c1 = Color(r1, g1, b1)

r2 = int(sys.argv[4])
g2 = int(sys.argv[5])
b2 = int(sys.argv[6])
c2 = Color(r2, g2, b2)

stddraw.setPenColor(c1)
stddraw.filledSquare(.25, .5, .2)
stddraw.setPenColor(c2)
stddraw.filledSquare(.25, .5, .1)

stddraw.setPenColor(c2)
stddraw.filledSquare(.75, .5, .2)
stddraw.setPenColor(c1)
stddraw.filledSquare(.75, .5, .1)

stddraw.show()
```

r1, g1, b1	*RGB values*
c1	*first color*
r2, g2, b2	*RGB values*
c2	*second color*

This program displays the two colors entered in RGB representation on the command line in the familiar format developed in the 1960s by the color theorist Josef Albers.

```
% python alberssquares.py 9 90 166  100 100 100
```

Color compatibility. The luminance value is also crucial in determining whether two colors are *compatible*, in the sense that printing text in one of the colors on a background in the other color will be readable. A widely used rule of thumb is that the difference between the luminance of the foreground and background colors should be at least 128. For example, black text on a white background has a luminance difference of 255, but black text on a (book) blue background has a luminance difference of only 74. This rule is important in the design of advertising, road signs, websites, and many other applications. PROGRAM 3.1.4 (`luminance.py`) is a module that we can use to convert a color to grayscale and to test whether two colors are compatible, for example, when we use colors in `stddraw` applications. The `luminance()`, `toGray()`, and `areCompatible()` functions in `luminance.py` illustrate the utility of using data types to organize information. Using the `Color` data type and passing objects as arguments makes these implementations substantially simpler than the alternative of having to pass around the three intensity values. Returning multiple values from a function also would be awkward and more error prone without the `Color` data type.

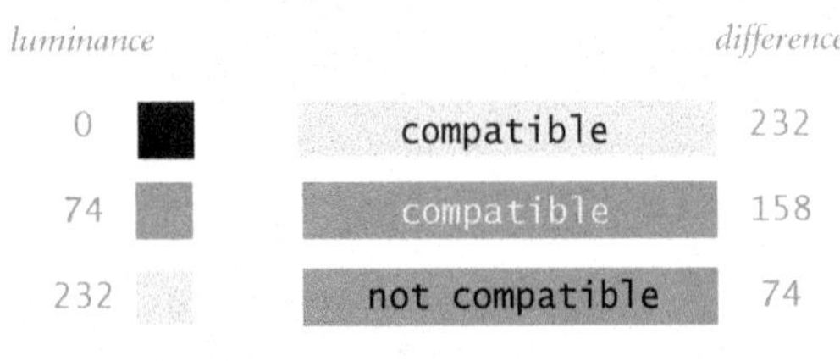

Compatibility example

HAVING AN ABSTRACTION FOR COLOR IS important not just for direct use, but also in building higher-level data types that have `Color` values. Next, we illustrate this point by building on the color abstraction to develop a data type that allows us to compose programs to process digital images.

Program 3.1.4 Luminance module (`luminance.py`)

```
import sys
import stdio
from color import Color

def luminance(c):
    red   = c.getRed()
    green = c.getGreen()
    blue  = c.getBlue()
    return .299*red + .587*green + .114*blue

def toGray(c):
    y = int(round(luminance(c)))
    return Color(y, y, y)

def areCompatible(c1, c2):
    return abs(luminance(c1) - luminance(c2)) >= 128.0

def main():
    r1 = int(sys.argv[1])
    g1 = int(sys.argv[2])
    b1 = int(sys.argv[3])
    r2 = int(sys.argv[4])
    g2 = int(sys.argv[5])
    b2 = int(sys.argv[6])
    c1 = Color(r1, g1, b1)
    c2 = Color(r2, g2, b2)
    stdio.writeln(areCompatible(c1, c2))

if __name__ == '__main__': main()
```

y	*luminance of c*

c1	*first color*
c2	*second color*

This module comprises three important functions for manipulating color: luminance, conversion to gray, and background/foreground compatibility.

```
% python luminance.py 232 232 232    0   0   0
True
% python luminance.py   9  90 166  232 232 232
True
% python luminance.py   9  90 166    0   0   0
False
```

Digital image processing You are, of course, familiar with the concept of a *photograph*. Technically, we might define a photograph as a two-dimensional image created by collecting and focusing visible wavelengths of electromagnetic radiation that constitutes a representation of a scene at a point in time. That technical definition is beyond our scope, except to note that the history of photography is a history of technological development. During the last century, photography was based on chemical processes, but its future is now based in computation. Your mobile device is a computer with lenses and light-sensitive devices capable of capturing images in digital form, and your computer has photo-editing software that allows you to process those images. You can crop them, enlarge and reduce them, adjust the contrast, brighten or darken the images, remove red eye, and perform scores of other operations. Many such operations are remarkably easy to implement, given a simple basic data type that captures the idea of a digital image.

Digital images. We have been using `stddraw` to plot geometric objects (points, lines, circles, squares) in a window on the computer screen. Which set of values do we need to process digital images, and which operations do we need to perform on those values? The basic abstraction for computer displays is the same one that is used for digital photographs and is very simple: A *digital image* is a rectangular grid of *pixels* (picture elements), where the color of each pixel is individually defined. Digital images are sometimes referred to as *raster* or *bit-mapped images*, in contrast to the types of images we produce with `stddraw`, which are referred to as *vector graphics*.

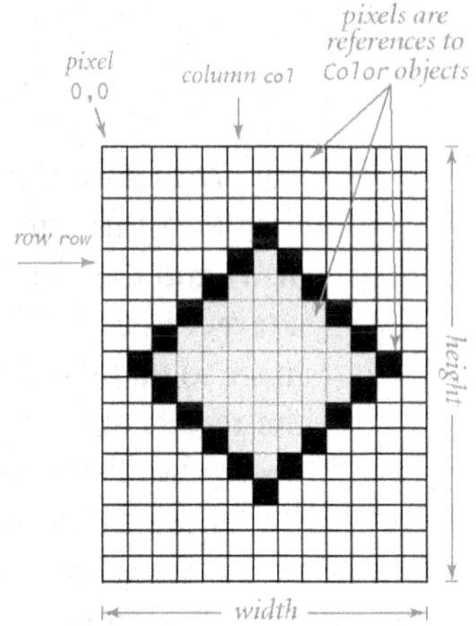

Anatomy of a digital image

Our `Picture` data type, defined in the module `picture.py`, implements the digital image abstraction. The set of values is nothing more than a two-dimensional array of `Color` values, and the operations are what you might expect: create an image (either a blank one with a given width and height or one initialized from a picture file), set a pixel to a given color, return the color of a given pixel, return the width or the height of the image, show the image in a window on your computer screen, and save the image to a file, as detailed in the API at the top of the next page.

operation	*description*
`Picture(w, h)`	*a new* `w`*-by-*`h` *array of pixels, initially all black*
`Picture(filename)`	*a new picture, initialized from* `filename`
`pic.save(filename)`	*save* `pic` *to* `filename`
`pic.width()`	*the width of the* `pic`
`pic.height()`	*the height of the* `pic`
`pic.get(col, row)`	*the* `Color` *of pixel* `(col, row)` *in* `pic`
`pic.set(col, row, c)`	*set the* `Color` *of pixel* `(col, row)` *in* `pic` *to* `c`

Note: The file name must end in `.png` *or* `.jpg`*, which denotes the file format.*

API for our `Picture` data type (`picture.py`)

By convention, (0, 0) is the upper leftmost pixel, so the image is laid out as in the customary order for arrays (by contrast, the convention for `stddraw` is to have the point (0,0) at the lower-left corner, so that drawings are oriented as in the customary manner for Cartesian coordinates). Most image-processing programs are filters that scan through the pixels in a source image as they would a two-dimensional array and then perform some computation to determine the color of each pixel in a target image. The supported file formats are the widely used `.png` and `.jpg` formats, so that you can compose programs to process your own photographs and add the results to an album or a website. The `Picture` data type, together with `Color`, opens the door to image processing.

Because of the `save()` method, you can view the images that you create in the same way that you view photographs or other images. In addition, the `stddraw` module supports a `picture()` function that allows you to draw a given `Picture` object in the standard drawing window along with lines, rectangles, circles, and so forth (details in the API below).

operation	*description*
`stddraw.picture(pic, x, y)`	*display* `pic` *in* `stddraw`*, centered at* `(x, y)`

Note: Both `x` *and* `y` *default to the center of the standard drawing canvas.*

API for displaying a `Picture` object

Grayscale. You will find many examples of color images on the booksite, and all of the methods that we describe are effective for full-color images, but all our example images in the text will be grayscale. Accordingly, our first task is to compose a program that can convert images from color to grayscale. This task is a prototypical image-processing task. For each pixel in the source, we have a pixel in the target with a different color. PROGRAM 3.1.5 (`grayscale.py`) is a filter that takes a file name from the command line and produces a grayscale version of that image. It creates a new `Picture` object initialized with the color image, then sets the color of each pixel to a new `Color` having a grayscale value computed by applying the `toGray()` function in `luminance.py` (PROGRAM 3.1.4) to the color of the corresponding pixel in the source.

Scaling. One of the most common image-processing tasks is to make an image smaller or larger. Examples of this basic operation, known as *scaling*, include making small thumbnail photos for use in a chat room or a cellphone, changing the size of a high-resolution photo to make it fit into a specific space in a printed publication or on a web page, or zooming in on a satellite photograph or an image produced by a microscope. In optical systems, we can just move a lens to achieve a desired scale, but in digital imagery, we have to do more work.

In some cases, the strategy is clear. For example, if the target image is to be half the size (in each dimension) of the source image, we simply choose half the pixels—say, by deleting half the rows and half the columns. This technique is known as *sampling*. If the target image is to be double the size (in each dimension) of the source image, we can replace each source pixel by four target pixels of the same color. Note that we can lose information when we downscale, so halving an image and then doubling it generally does not give back the same image.

A single strategy is effective for both downscaling and upscaling. Our goal is to produce the target image, so we proceed through the pixels in the target, one by one, scaling each pixel's coordinates to identify a pixel in the source whose color can be assigned to the target. If the width and height of the source are w_s and h_s, respectively, and the width and height of the target are w_t and h_t, respectively, then

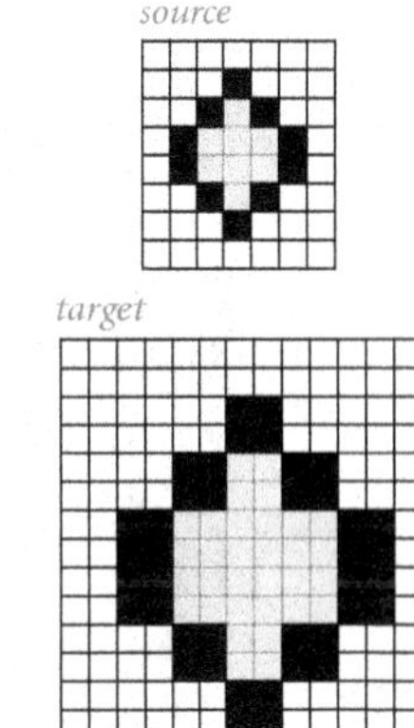

Scaling a digital image

Program 3.1.5 Converting color to grayscale (grayscale.py)

```
import sys
import stddraw
import luminance
from picture import Picture

pic = Picture(sys.argv[1])

for col in range(pic.width()):
    for row in range(pic.height()):
        pixel = pic.get(col, row)
        gray = luminance.toGray(pixel)
        pic.set(col, row, gray)

stddraw.setCanvasSize(pic.width(), pic.height())
stddraw.picture(pic)
stddraw.show()
```

pic	*image from file*
col, row	*pixel coordinates*
pixel	*pixel color*
gray	*pixel grayscale*

This program illustrates a simple image-processing client. First, it creates a `Picture` *object initialized with an image file named by the command-line argument. Then it converts each pixel in the image to grayscale by creating a grayscale version of each pixel's color and resetting the pixel to that color. Finally, it shows the image. You can perceive individual pixels in the image on the right, which was upscaled from a low-resolution image (see the discussion of scaling starting on the previous page).*

```
% python grayscale.py mandrill.jpg
```

```
% python grayscale.py darwin.jpg
```

we scale the column index by w_s/w_t and the row index by h_s/h_t. That is, we get the color of the pixel in column c and row r of the target from column $c \times w_s/w_t$ and row $r \times h_s/h_t$ in the source. For example, if we are halving the size of a picture, the scale factors are 2, so the pixel in column 4 and row 6 of the target gets the color of the pixel in column 8 and row 12 of the source; if we are doubling the size of the picture, the scale factors are 1/2, so the pixel in column 4 and column 6 of the target gets the color of the pixel in column 2 and row 3 of the source. PROGRAM 3.1.6 (`scale.py`) is an implementation of this strategy. More sophisticated strategies can be effective for low-resolution images of the sort that you might find on old web pages or from old cameras. For example, we might downscale to half size by averaging the values of four pixels in the source to make one pixel in the target. For the high-resolution images that are common in most applications today, the simple approach used in `scale.py` is effective.

The same basic idea of computing the color value of each target pixel as a function of the color values of specific source pixels is effective for all sorts of image-processing tasks. Next, we consider two more examples, and you will find numerous other examples in the exercises and on the booksite.

Fade effect. Our next image-processing example is an entertaining computation where we transform one image to another in a series of discrete steps. Such a transformation is sometimes known as a *fade effect*. PROGRAM 3.1.7 (`fade.py`) is a `Picture`, `Color`, and `stddraw` client that uses a linear interpolation strategy to implement this effect. It computes $n-1$ intermediate images, with each pixel in the tth image being a weighted average of the corresponding pixels in the source and target. The function `blend()` implements the interpolation: the source color is weighted by a factor of $1 - t / n$ and the target color by a factor of t / n (when t is 0, we have the source color; when t is n, we have the target color). This simple computation can produce striking results. When you run `fade.py` on your computer, the change appears to happen dynamically. Try running it on some images from your photo library. Note that `fade.py` assumes that the images have the same width and height; if you have images for which this is not the case, you can use `scale.py` to create a scaled version of one or both of them for `fade.py`.

Program 3.1.6 Image scaling (scale.py)

```
import sys
import stddraw
from picture import Picture

file = sys.argv[1]
wT = int(sys.argv[2])
hT = int(sys.argv[3])

source = Picture(file)
target = Picture(wT, hT)

for colT in range(wT):
    for rowT in range(hT):
        colS = colT * source.width()  // wT
        rowS = rowT * source.height() // hT
        target.set(colT, rowT, source.get(colS, rowS))

stddraw.setCanvasSize(wT, hT)
stddraw.picture(target)
stddraw.show()
```

wT, hT	*target dimensions*
source	*source image*
target	*target image*
colT, rowT	*target pixel coords*
colS, rowS	*source pixel coords*

This program accepts the name of either a .jpg *or* .png *image file and two integers* wT *and* hT *as command-line arguments and displays the image, scaled to width* wT *and height* hT.

% python scale.py mandrill.jpg 800 800

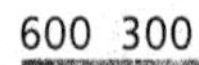

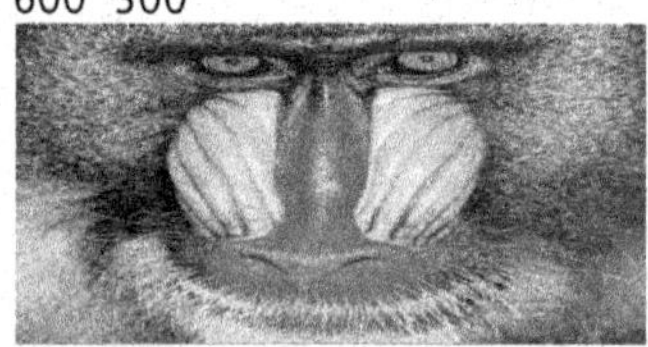

200 400

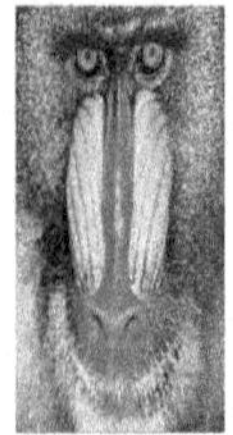

200 200

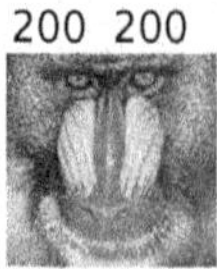

Program 3.1.7 Fade effect (`fade.py`)

```
import sys
import stddraw
from color import Color
from picture import Picture

def blend(c1, c2, alpha):
    r = (1-alpha)*c1.getRed()   + alpha*c2.getRed()
    g = (1-alpha)*c1.getGreen() + alpha*c2.getGreen()
    b = (1-alpha)*c1.getBlue()  + alpha*c2.getBlue()
    return Color(int(r), int(g), int(b))

sourceFile = sys.argv[1]
targetFile = sys.argv[2]
n = int(sys.argv[3])

source = Picture(sourceFile)
target = Picture(targetFile)

width = source.width()
height = source.height()

stddraw.setCanvasSize(width, height)
pic = Picture(width, height)
for t in range(n+1):
    for col in range(width):
        for row in range(height):
            c0 = source.get(col, row)
            cn = target.get(col, row)
            alpha = 1.0 * t / n
            pic.set(col, row, blend(c0, cn, alpha))
    stddraw.picture(pic)
    stddraw.show(1000.0)

stddraw.show()
```

To fade from one image into another in `n-1` *intermediate steps, we set each pixel in the* `t`*th image to a weighted average of the corresponding pixel in the source and the destination, with the source getting weight* `1-t/n` *and the destination getting weight* `t/n`*. The example transformation shown at right is produced by* `python fade.py mandrill.jpg darwin.jpg 9`*.*

Potential value visualization. Image processing is also helpful in scientific visualization. As an example, we consider a `Picture` client for visualizing properties of a `Charge` object—that is, an object of data type `Charge` as defined at the beginning of this section. PROGRAM 3.1.8 (`potential.py`) visualizes the potential values created by a set of charged particles. First, `potential.py` creates an array of particles, with values taken from standard input. Next, it creates a `Picture` object and sets each pixel in the picture to a shade of gray that is proportional to the potential value at the corresponding point. The calculation at the heart of the approach is very simple: for each pixel, we compute corresponding (x, y) values in the unit square, then call `potentialAt()` for each charge to find the potential at that point due to all of the charges, summing the values returned. With appropriate assignment of potential values to grayscale values (scaling them to fall between 0 and 255), we get a striking visual representation of the electric potential that is an excellent aid to understanding interactions among such particles. We could produce a similar image using `filledSquare()` in the `stddraw` module, but the `Picture` data type provides us with more accurate control over the color of each pixel on the screen. The same basic approach is useful in many other settings—you can find several examples on the booksite.

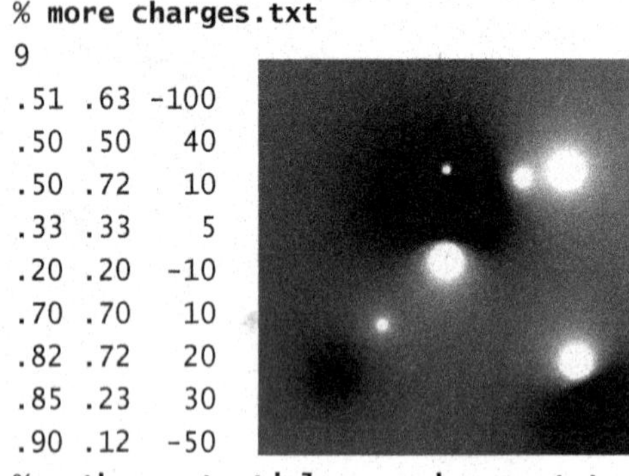

```
% more charges.txt
9
.51 .63 -100
.50 .50   40
.50 .72   10
.33 .33    5
.20 .20  -10
.70 .70   10
.82 .72   20
.85 .23   30
.90 .12  -50
% python potential.py < charges.txt
```

Potential value visualization for a set of charges

IT IS WORTHWHILE TO REFLECT BRIEFLY on the code in `potential.py`, because it exemplifies data abstraction and object-oriented programming. We want to produce an image that shows interactions among charged particles, and our code reflects precisely the process of creating that image, using a `Picture` object for the image (which is manipulated via `Color` objects) and `Charge` objects for the particles. When we want information about a `Charge`, we invoke the appropriate method directly for that `Charge`; when we want to create a `Color`, we use a `Color` constructor; when we want to set a pixel, we directly involve the appropriate method for the `Picture`. These data types are independently developed, but their use together in a single client is easy and natural. We next consider several more examples, to illustrate the broad reach of data abstraction while at the same time adding a number of useful data types to our basic programming model.

Program 3.1.8 Visualizing electric potential (potential.py)

```
import stddraw
import stdio
import stdarray
from charge import Charge
from color import Color
from picture import Picture

n = stdio.readInt()
charges = stdarray.create1D(n)
for i in range(n):
    x0 = stdio.readFloat()
    y0 = stdio.readFloat()
    q0 = stdio.readFloat()
    charges[i] = Charge(x0, y0, q0)

pic = Picture()
for col in range(pic.width()):
    for row in range(pic.height()):
        x = 1.0 * col / pic.width()
        y = 1.0 * row / pic.height()
        v = 0.0
        for i in range(n):
            v += charges[i].potentialAt(x, y)
        v = (255 / 2.0) + (v / 2.0e10)
        if   v < 0:    gray = 0
        elif v > 255:  gray = 255
        else:          gray = int(v)
        color = Color(gray, gray, gray)
        pic.set(col, pic.height()-1-row, color)

stddraw.setCanvasSize(pic.width(), pic.height())
stddraw.picture(pic)
stddraw.show()
```

n	*number of charges*
charges[]	*array of charges*
x0, y0	*charge position*
q0	*charge value*

col, row	*pixel position*
x, y	*point in unit square*
gray	*scaled potential value*
color	*pixel color*

This program reads values from standard input to create an array of charged particles, sets each pixel color in an image to a grayscale value proportional to the total of the potentials due to the particles at corresponding points, and shows the resulting image.

Input and output revisited In SECTION 1.5, you learned how to read and write numbers and text using our `stdio` module. You have certainly come to appreciate the utility of these mechanisms in getting information into and out of your programs. One reason that they are convenient is that the "standard" conventions make them accessible from anywhere within a program. One disadvantage of these conventions is that they leave us dependent upon the operating system's piping and redirection mechanism for access to files, and they restrict us to working with just one input file and one output file for any given program. With object-oriented programming, we can define mechanisms that are similar to `stdio` but allow us to work with multiple input streams and output streams within one program.

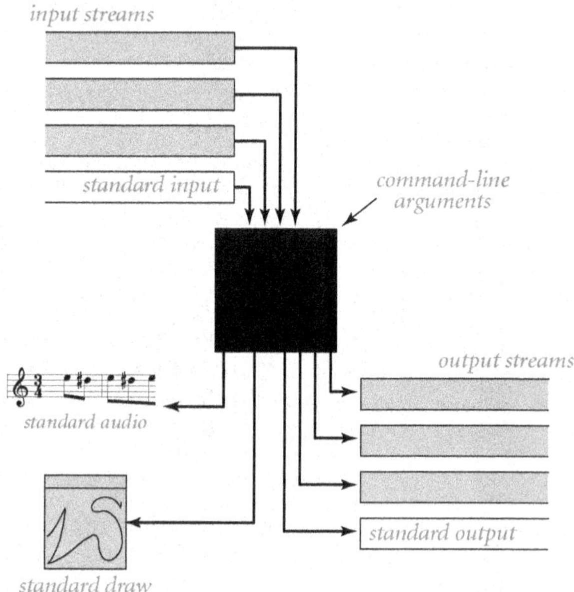

A bird's-eye view of a Python program (revisited again)

Specifically, we define in this section the data types `InStream` and `OutStream` for input streams and output streams, respectively. As usual, you must make `instream.py` and `outstream.py` available to Python, either by putting them in the same directory as your client code or by using your operating system's path mechanism (see the Q&A at the end of SECTION 2.2).

The purpose of `InStream` and `OutStream` is to provide the flexibility that we need to address many common data-processing tasks within our Python programs. Rather than being restricted to just one input stream and one output stream, we can readily create multiple objects of each data type, connecting the streams to various sources and destinations. We also get the flexibility to set variables to reference such objects, pass them as arguments to or return values from functions or methods, and create arrays of them, manipulating them just as we manipulate objects of any data type. We will consider several examples of their use after we have presented the APIs.

Input stream data type. Our data type `InStream`, defined in the module `instream.py`, is a more general version of the reading aspects of `stdio` that supports reading numbers and text from files and websites as well as the standard input stream. The API is shown at the bottom of this page.

Instead of being restricted to one abstract input stream (standard input), this data type gives you the ability to specify directly the source of an input stream. Moreover, that source can be either a file or a website. When you call the `InStream` constructor with a string argument, the constructor first tries to find a file on your local computer with that name. If it cannot do so, it assumes the argument is a website name and tries to connect to that website. (If no such website exists, it raises an `IOError` at run time.) In either case, the specified file or website becomes the source of the input for the `InStream` object thus created, and the `read*()` methods will read input from that stream.

operation	*description*
`InStream(filename)`	*a new input stream, initialized from* `filename` *(defaults to standard input if no argument)*
methods that read tokens from standard input	
`s.isEmpty()`	*is* `s` *empty? (does it consist solely of whitespace?)*
`s.readInt()`	*read a token from* `s`*, convert it to an integer, and return it*
`s.readFloat()`	*read a token from* `s`*, convert it to a float, and return it*
`s.readBool()`	*read a token from* `s`*, convert it to a boolean, and return it*
`s.readString()`	*read a token from* `s`*, convert it to a string, and return it*
methods that read lines from standard input	
`s.hasNextLine()`	*does* `s` *have another line?*
`s.readLine()`	*read the next line from* `s` *and return it as a string*

Note 1: A token is a maximal sequence of non-whitespace characters.
Note 2: Behaves like standard input; `readAll()` *methods are also supported (see SECTION 1.5).*

API for our `InStream` *data type (*`instream.py`*)*

This arrangement makes it possible to process multiple files within the same program. Moreover, the ability to directly access the web opens up the whole web as potential input for your programs. For example, it allows you to process data that is provided and maintained by someone else. You can find such files all over the web. Scientists now regularly post data files with measurements or results of experiments, ranging from genome and protein sequences to satellite photographs to astronomical observations; financial services companies, such as stock exchanges, regularly publish on the web detailed information about the performance of stock and other financial instruments; governments publish election results; and so forth. Now you can compose Python programs that read these kinds of files directly. The `InStream` data type gives you a great deal of flexibility to take advantage of the multitude of data sources that are now available.

Output stream data type. Similarly, our data type `OutStream`, defined in the module `outstream.py`, is a more general version of the writing aspect of `stdio` that supports writing strings to a variety of output streams, including standard output and files. Again, the API specifies the same methods as its `stdio` counterpart. You specify the file that you want to use for output by using the one-argument constructor with the file's name as argument. `OutStream` interprets this string as the name of a new file on your local computer, and sends its output there. If you provide no argument to the constructor, then you obtain standard output.

operation	*description*
`OutStream(filename)`	*a new output stream that will write to* `filename` *(defaults to standard output if no argument)*
`out.write(x)`	*write* `x` *to* `out`
`out.writeln(x)`	*write* `x` *to* `out`*, followed by a newline* *(*`x` *default to empty string)*
`out.writef(fmt, arg1, ...)`	*write the arguments* `arg1, ...` *to* `out` *as specified by the format string* `fmt`

API for our `OutStream` *data type (*`outstream.py`*)*

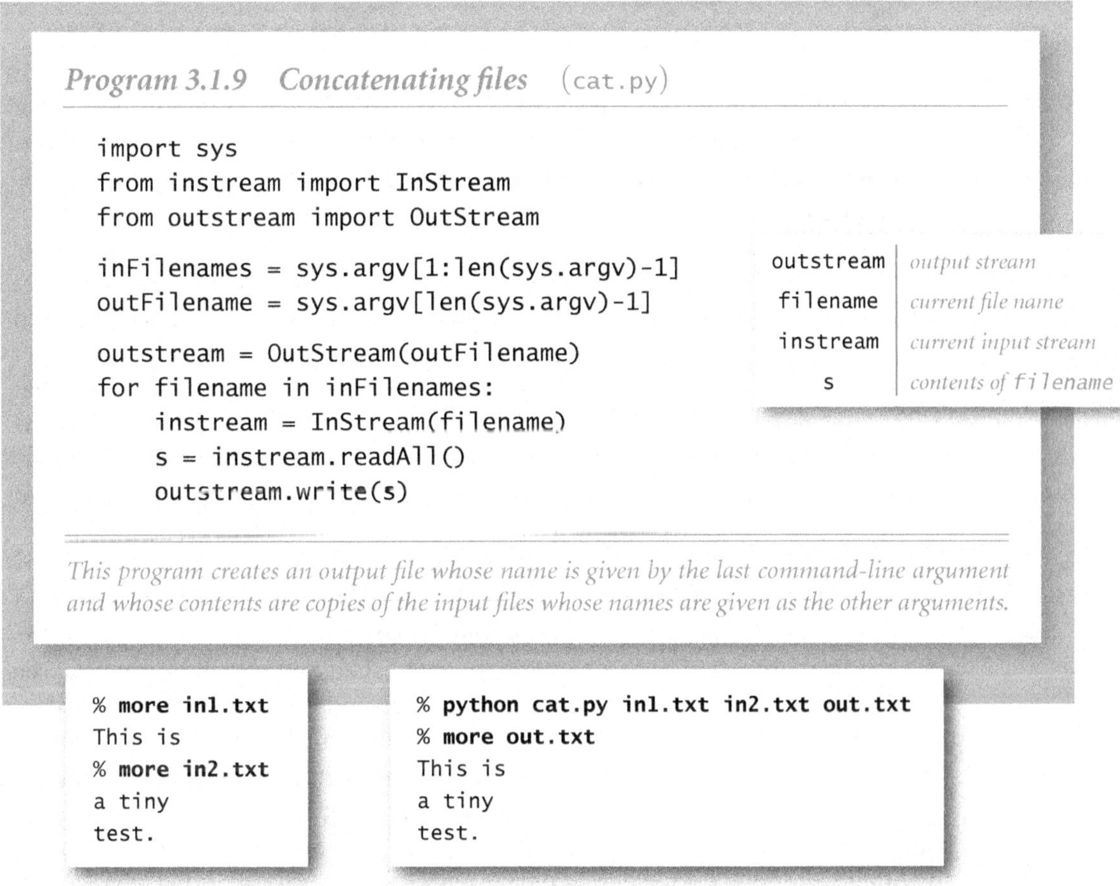

Program 3.1.9 Concatenating files (`cat.py`)

```
import sys
from instream import InStream
from outstream import OutStream

inFilenames = sys.argv[1:len(sys.argv)-1]
outFilename = sys.argv[len(sys.argv)-1]

outstream = OutStream(outFilename)
for filename in inFilenames:
    instream = InStream(filename)
    s = instream.readAll()
    outstream.write(s)
```

`outstream`	*output stream*
`filename`	*current file name*
`instream`	*current input stream*
`s`	*contents of* `filename`

This program creates an output file whose name is given by the last command-line argument and whose contents are copies of the input files whose names are given as the other arguments.

```
% more in1.txt
This is
% more in2.txt
a tiny
test.
```

```
% python cat.py in1.txt in2.txt out.txt
% more out.txt
This is
a tiny
test.
```

File concatenation and filtering. Program 3.1.9 (`cat.py`) is a sample client of `InStream` and `OutStream` that uses multiple input streams to concatenate several input files into a single output file. Some operating systems have a command known as `cat` that implements this function. However, a Python program that does the same thing is perhaps more useful, because we can tailor it to *filter* the input files in various ways: we might wish to ignore irrelevant information, change the format, or select only some of the data, to name just a few examples. We now consider one example of such processing, and you can find several others in the exercises.

Screen scraping. The combination of `InStream` (which allows us to create an input stream from any page on the web) and `str` (which provides powerful tools for processing text strings) opens up the entire web to direct access by our Python programs, without any direct dependence on the operating system or the browser. One paradigm is known as *screen scraping*: the goal is to extract some information from a web page with a program rather than having to browse to find it. To do so, we take advantage of the fact that many web pages are defined with text files in a highly structured format (because they are created by computer programs!). Your browser has a mechanism that allows you to examine the source code that produces the web page that you are viewing, and by examining that source you can often figure out what to do.

```
...
(GOOG)</h2> <span class="rtq_
exch"><span class="rtq_dash">-</span>
NMS  </span><span class="wl_sign">
</span></div></div>
<div class="yfi_rt_quote_summary_rt_top
sigfig_promo_1"><div>
<span class="time_rtq_ticker">
<span id="yfs_l84goog">1,100.62</span>
</span> <span class="down_r time_rtq_
content"><span id="yfs_c63_goog">
...
```

HTML code from the web

Suppose that we want to take a stock trading symbol as a command-line argument and write out its current trading price. Such information is published on the web by financial service companies and internet service providers. For example, you can find the stock price of a company whose symbol is goog by browsing to `http://finance.yahoo.com/q?s=goog`. Like many web pages, the name encodes an argument (goog), and we could substitute any other ticker symbol to get a web page with financial information for any other company. Also, like many other files on the web, the referenced file is a text file, written in a formatting language known as HTML. From the point of view of a Python program, it is just a `str` value accessible through an `InStream` object. You can use your browser to download the source of that file, or you could use

```
python cat.py "http://finance.yahoo.com/q?s=goog" mycopy.txt
```

to put the source into a local file `mycopy.txt` on your computer (though there is no real need to do so). Now, suppose that goog is trading at $1,100.62 at the moment. If you search for the string `'1,100.62'` in the source of that page, you will find the stock price buried within some HTML code. Without having to know details of HTML, you can figure out something about the context in which the price appears. In this case, you can see that the stock price is enclosed between the substrings `<span id="yfs_l84goog">` and `</span>`.

Program 3.1.10 Screen scraping for stock quotes (stockquote.py)

```
import sys
import stdio
from instream import InStream

def _readHTML(stockSymbol):
    WEBSITE = 'http://finance.yahoo.com/q?s='
    page = InStream(WEBSITE + stockSymbol)
    html = page.readAll()
    return html

def priceOf(stockSymbol):
    html  = _readHTML(stockSymbol)
    trade = html.find('yfs_l84', 0)
    beg   = html.find('>', trade)
    end   = html.find('</span>', beg)
    price = html[beg+1:end]
    price = price.replace(',', '')
    return float(price)

def main():
    stockSymbol = sys.argv[1]
    price = priceOf(stockSymbol)
    stdio.writef('%.2f\n', price)

if __name__ == '__main__': main()
```

page	*input stream*
html	*contents of page*
trade	*yfs_l84 index*
beg	*> after trade index*
end	*</span> after to index*
price	*current price*

This program accepts a stock ticker symbol as a command-line argument and writes to standard output the current stock price for that stock, as reported by the website `http://finance.yahoo.com`. *It uses string slicing and the* `find()` *and* `replace()` *methods from* `str`.

```
% python stockquote.py goog
1100.62
% python stockquote.py adbe
70.51
```

With the `str` data type's `find()` method and string slicing, you easily can grab this information, as illustrated in `stockquote.py` (PROGRAM 3.1.10). This program depends on the web page format used by `http://finance.yahoo.com`; if this format changes, `stockquote.py` will not work. Indeed, by the time you read this page, the format may have changed. Still, making appropriate changes is not likely to be difficult. You can entertain yourself by embellishing `stockquote.py` in all kinds of interesting ways. For example, you could grab the stock price on a periodic basis and plot it, compute a moving average, or save the results to a file for later analysis. Of course, the same technique works for sources of data found all over the web, as you can see in examples in the exercises at the end of this section and on the booksite.

Extracting data. The ability to maintain multiple input and output streams gives us a great deal of flexibility in meeting the challenges of processing large amounts of data coming from a variety of sources. We now consider one more example. Suppose that a scientist or a financial analyst has a large amount of data within a spreadsheet program. Typically such spreadsheets are tables with a relatively large number of rows and a relatively small number of columns. You are not likely to be interested in all the data in the spreadsheet, but you may be interested in a few of the columns. You can do some calculations within the spreadsheet program (this is its purpose, after all), but you certainly do not have the flexibility that you can realize with Python programming. One way to address this situation is to have the spreadsheet export the data to a text file, using some special character to delimit the columns, and then compose a Python program that reads the file from an input stream. One standard practice is to use commas as delimiters: write one line per row, with commas separating column entries. Such files are known as *comma-separated-value* or `.csv` files. With the `split()` method in Python's `str` data type, we can read the file line-by-line and isolate the data that we want. We will see several examples of this approach later in the book. PROGRAM 3.1.11 (`split.py`) is an `InStream` and `OutStream` client that goes one step further: it creates multiple output streams and makes one file for each column.

THESE EXAMPLES ARE CONVINCING ILLUSTRATIONS OF the utility of working with text files, with multiple input and output streams, and with direct access to web pages. Web pages are written in HTML precisely so that they will be accessible to any program that can read strings. People use text formats such as `.csv` files rather than data formats that are beholden to particular applications precisely to allow as many people as possible to access the data with simple programs like `split.py`.

Program 3.1.11 Splitting a file (split.py)

```
import sys
import stdarray
from instream import InStream
from outstream import OutStream

basename = sys.argv[1]
n = int(sys.argv[2])

instream = InStream(basename + '.csv')
out = stdarray.create1D(n)

for i in range(n):
    out[i] = OutStream(basename + str(i) + '.txt')

while instream.hasNextLine():
    line = instream.readLine()
    fields = line.split(',')
    for i in range(n):
        out[i].writeln(fields[i])
```

basename	*base file name*
n	*number of fields*
instream	*input stream*
out[]	*output streams*
line	*current line*
fields[]	*values in current line*

This program uses multiple output streams to split a `.csv` *file into separate files, one for each comma-delimited field. It accepts a string* `basename` *and an integer* n *as command-line arguments and splits the file whose name is* `basename.csv`*, by field (comma-separated), into* n *files named* `basename0.txt`*,* `basename1.txt`*, and so forth.*

```
% more djia.csv
...
31-Oct-29,264.97,7150000,273.51
30-Oct-29,230.98,10730000,258.47
29-Oct-29,252.38,16410000,230.07
28-Oct-29,295.18,9210000,260.64
25-Oct-29,299.47,5920000,301.22
24-Oct-29,305.85,12900000,299.47
23-Oct-29,326.51,6370000,305.85
22-Oct-29,322.03,4130000,326.51
21-Oct-29,323.87,6090000,320.91
...
```

```
% python split.py djia 4

% more djia2.txt
...
7150000
10730000
16410000
9210000
5920000
12900000
6370000
4130000
6090000
...
```

Memory management Now that you have seen several examples of object-oriented data types (`str`, `Charge`, `Color`, `Picture`, `InStream`, and `Outstream`) and client programs that use them, we can discuss in more detail the challenges Python faces in providing support for such programs. To a large extent, Python protects novice programmers from having to know these details, but having some idea of what is going on inside the system is sometimes helpful in writing correct, effective, and efficient object-oriented programs.

In Python, we create objects by calling a *constructor*. Each time we create an object, Python reserves computer memory for that object. But when and how do we destroy objects so that the memory in which they reside can be freed for reuse? We will briefly address this question.

Orphaned objects. The ability to bind a variable to a different object creates the possibility that a program may have created an object that it can no longer reference. For example, consider the three assignment statements in the figure at right. After the third assignment statement, not only do `c1` and `c2` refer to the same `Charge` object (the one at (.51, .63) with potential 21.3), but there is also no longer a reference to the `Charge` object that was created and used to initialize `c2`. The *only* reference to that object was in the variable `c2`, and this reference was overwritten by the assignment, so there is no way to refer to the object again. Such an object is said to be an *orphan*. Objects can also become orphans when variables go out of scope. Python programmers pay little attention to orphaned objects because the system automatically reuses the memory that they occupy, as we discuss next.

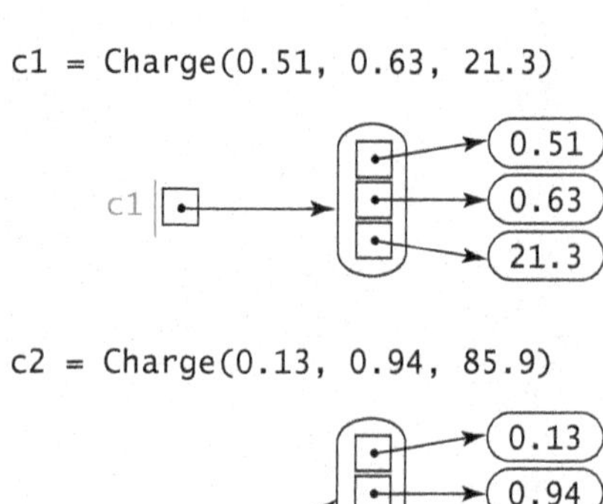

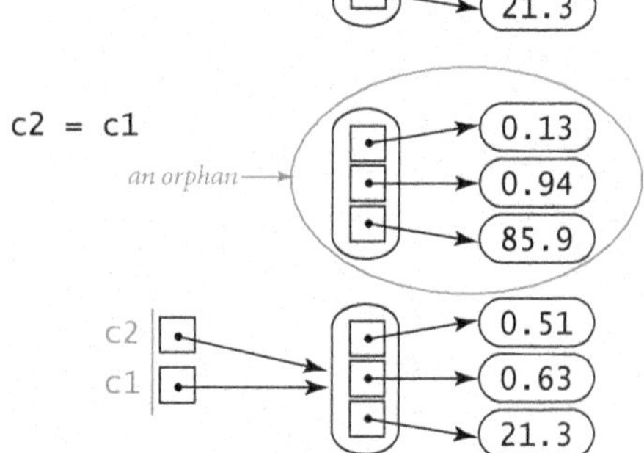

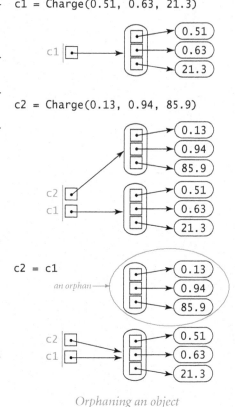

Orphaning an object

Memory management. Programs tend to create huge numbers of objects but have a need for only a small number of them at any given time. Accordingly, programming languages and systems need mechanisms to create objects (and allocate memory), and mechanisms to destroy objects (and free memory) when the objects become orphans. Most programming systems take care of allocating memory for variables when they come into existence and freeing that memory when they go out of scope. Memory management for *objects* is more complicated: Python knows to allocate memory for an object when it is created, but cannot know precisely when to free the memory associated with an object, because the dynamics of a program in execution determine when an object becomes an orphan and so should be destroyed. There is no way for the system to predict what a program will do, so it has to monitor what a program is doing and take action accordingly.

Memory leaks. In many languages (such as C and C++), the programmer is responsible for both allocating and deallocating memory. Doing so is tedious and notoriously error-prone. For example, suppose that a program deallocates the memory for an object, but then continues to refer to it (perhaps much later in the program). In the meantime, the system may have reallocated the same memory for another use, so all kinds of havoc can result. Another insidious problem occurs when a programmer neglects to ensure that the memory for an orphaned object is deallocated. This bug is known as a *memory leak* because it can result in a steadily increasing amount of memory devoted to orphaned objects (and therefore not available for use). The effect is that performance degrades, just as if memory were leaking out of your computer. Have you ever had to reboot your computer because it was gradually getting less and less responsive? A common cause of such behavior is a memory leak in one of your applications.

Garbage collection. One of Python's most significant features is its ability to automatically manage memory. The idea is to free the programmers from the responsibility of managing memory by keeping track of orphaned objects and returning the memory they use to a pool of free memory. Reclaiming memory in this way is known as *garbage collection*, and Python's type system enables it to perform this operation this efficiently and automatically. Garbage collection is an old idea, and some people still debate whether the overhead of automatic garbage collection justifies the convenience of not having to worry about memory management. But many other people (including Python and Java programmers, for example) very much enjoy the benefits of not having to worry about memory management and memory leaks.

For reference, we summarize the data types that we have considered in this section in the table at right. We chose these examples to help you understand the essential properties of data types and object-oriented programming.

A data type is a set of values and a set of operations defined on those values. With built-in numeric types, we worked with a small and simple set of values. Colors, pictures, strings, and input/output streams are high-level data types that indicate the breadth of applicability of data abstraction. *You do not need to know how a data type is implemented to be able to use it.* Each data type (there are hundreds in Python's standard and extension modules, and you will soon learn to create your own) is characterized by an API (application programming interface) that provides the information that you need to use it. A client program creates objects that hold data-type values and calls methods to manipulate those values. We compose client programs with the basic statements and control structures that you learned in Chapters 1 and 2, but now have the capability to work with a vast variety of data types, not just the built-in ones to which you have grown accustomed. With experience, you will find that this ability opens up new horizons in programming.

data type	*description*
`str`	sequence of characters
`Charge`	electrical charge
`Color`	color
`Picture`	digital image
`InStream`	input stream
`OutStream`	output stream

Summary of data types in this section

Our `Charge` example demonstrated that you can tailor one or more data types to the needs of your application. The ability to do so is a profound benefit, and also is the subject of the next section. When properly designed and implemented, data types lead to client programs that are clearer, easier to develop, and easier to maintain than equivalent programs that do not take advantage of data abstraction. The client programs in this section are testimony to this claim. Moreover, as you will see in the next section, implementing a data type is a straightforward application of the basic programming skills that you have already learned. In particular, addressing a large and complex application becomes a process of understanding its data and the operations to be performed on it, then composing programs that directly reflect this understanding. Once you have learned to do so, you might wonder how programmers ever developed large programs without using data abstraction.

Q&A

Q. What happens if I call a method that is not defined for a given object?

A. Python raises an `AttributeError` at run time.

Q. Why can we use `stdio.writeln(x)` instead of `stdio.writeln(str(x))` to write an object `x` that is not a string?

A. For convenience, the `stdio.writeln()` function calls the built-in `str()` function automatically whenever a string object is needed.

Q. I noticed that `potential.py` (Program 3.1.8) calls `stdarray.create1D()` to create an array of `Charge` objects, but provides only one argument (the desired number of elements). Doesn't `stdarray.create1D()` require that I provide two arguments: the desired number of elements and the initial value of the elements?

A. If no initial value is specified, both `stddarray.create1D()` and `stdarray.create2D()` use the special value `None`, which refers to no object. Immediately after calling `stdarray.create1D()`, `potential.py` changes each array element so it refers to a new `Charge` object.

Q. Can I call a method with a literal or other expression?

A. Yes, from the client's point of view, you can use any expression to invoke a method. When Python executes the method call, it evaluates the expression and calls the method on the resulting object. For example, `'python'.upper()` returns `'Python'` and `(3 ** 100).bit_length()` returns `159`. However, you need to be careful with integer literals—for example, `1023.bit_length()` raises a `SyntaxError` because Python interprets `1023.` as a floating-point literal; instead, you can use `(1023).bit_length()`.

Q. Can I chain together several string method calls in one expression?

A. Yes. For example, the expression `s.strip().lower()` works as expected. That is, it evaluates to a new string that is a copy of `s` with leading and trailing whitespace removed, and with all remaining characters converted to lowercase. It works because (1) each of the methods returns its result as a string and (2) the dot operator is left associative, so Python calls the methods from left to right.

Q. Why red, green, and blue instead of red, yellow, and blue?

A. In theory, any three colors that contain some amount of each primary color would work, but two different color models have evolved: RGB produces good colors on television screens, computer monitors, and digital cameras, and CMYK is typically used for the printed page (see Exercise 1.2.28). CMYK does include yellow (cyan, magenta, yellow, and black). Two different schemes are appropriate because printed inks absorb color; thus, where there are two different inks, there are more colors absorbed and fewer reflected. In contrast, video displays emit color; thus, where there are two different colored pixels, there are more colors emitted.

Q. Is there any problem with creating thousands of `Color` objects, as in `grayscale.py` (Program 3.1.5)? It seems wasteful.

A. All programming-language constructs come at some cost. In this case the cost is reasonable, since the time required to create the `Color` objects is tiny compared to the time required to actually draw the picture.

Q. Can a data type have two methods (or constructors) with the same name but with a different number of arguments?

A. No, just as with functions, you cannot have two methods (or constructors) with the same name. As with functions, methods (and constructors) can use optional arguments with default values. This is how the `Picture` data type creates the illusion of having two constructors.

Exercises

3.1.1 Compose a program that takes a float command-line argument `w`, creates four `Charge` objects that are each distance `w` in each of the four cardinal directions from (0.5, 0.5), and writes the potential at (0.25, 0.5).

3.1.2 Compose a program that takes from the command line three integers between 0 and 255 that represent red, green, and blue values of a color and then creates and shows a 256-by-256 `Picture` of that color.

3.1.3 Modify `alberssquares.py` (PROGRAM 3.1.3) to take nine command-line arguments that specify three colors and then draw the six squares showing all the Albers squares with the large square in each color and the small square in each different color.

3.1.4 Compose a program that takes the name of a grayscale picture file as a command-line argument and uses `stddraw` to plot a histogram of the frequency of occurrence of each of the 256 grayscale intensities.

3.1.5 Compose a program that takes the name of a picture file as a command-line argument and flips the image horizontally.

3.1.6 Compose a program that takes the name of a picture file as a command-line input, and creates three images—one with only the red components, one with only the green components, and one with only the blue components.

3.1.7 Compose a program that takes the name of a picture file as a command-line argument and writes the pixel coordinates of the lower-left corner and the upper-right corner of the smallest bounding box (rectangle parallel to the x- and y-axes) that contains all of the non-white pixels.

3.1.8 Compose a program that takes as command-line arguments the name of a picture file and the pixel coordinates of a rectangle within the image; reads from standard input a list of `Color` values (represented as triples of integers); and serves as a filter, writing those `Color` values for which all pixels in the rectangle are background/foreground compatible. (Such a filter can be used to pick a color for text to label an image.)

3.1.9 Compose a function `isValidDNA()` that takes a string as its argument and returns `True` if and only if it consists entirely of the characters `A`, `C`, `T`, and `G`.

3.1.10 Compose a function `complementWC()` that takes a DNA string as its argument and returns its *Watson–Crick complement*: replace `A` with `T`, and `C` with `G`, and vice versa.

3.1.11 Compose a function `palindromeWC()` that takes a DNA string as its argument and returns `True` if the string is a Watson–Crick complemented palindrome, and `False` otherwise. A *Watson–Crick complemented palindrome* is a DNA string that is equal to the reverse of its Watson–Crick complement.

3.1.12 Compose a program to check whether an ISBN number is valid (see Exercise 1.3.33), taking into account that an ISBN number can have hyphens inserted at arbitrary places.

3.1.13 What does the following code fragment write?

```
s = 'Hello World'
s.upper()
s[6:11]
stdio.writeln(s)
```

Solution: `'Hello World'`. String objects are immutable—a string method returns a new `str` object with the appropriate value, but does not change the value of the string that was used to invoke it. Therefore, this code ignores the objects returned and just writes the original string. To update `s`, write `s = s.upper()` and `s = s[6:11]`.

3.1.14 A string `s` is a *circular shift* of a string `t` if it matches when the characters are circularly shifted by any number of positions. For example, `ACTGACG` is a circular shift of `TGACGAC`, and vice versa. Detecting this condition is important in the study of genomic sequences. Compose a function that checks whether two given strings `s` and `t` are circular shifts of one another. *Hint*: The solution is a one-liner with the `in` operator and string concatenation.

3.1.15 Given a string that represents a website URL, compose a code fragment that determines its domain type. For example, the domain type for our booksite URL `http://introcs.cs.princeton.edu/python` is `edu`.

3.1.16 Compose a function that takes a domain name as an argument and returns the reverse domain (reverse the order of the strings between periods). For example, the reverse domain of `introcs.cs.princeton.edu` is `edu.princeton.cs.introcs`. This computation is useful for web log analysis. (See Exercise 4.2.33.)

3.1.17 What does the following recursive function return?

```
def mystery(s):
    n = len(s)
    if (n <= 1): return s
    a = s[0 : n//2]
    b = s[n//2 : n]
    return mystery(b) + mystery(a)
```

3.1.18 Compose a version of `potentialgene.py` (Program 3.1.1) that finds all potential genes contained in a long DNA string. Add a command-line argument to allow the user to specify a minimum length of a potential gene.

3.1.19 Compose a program that takes a start string and a stop string as command-line arguments and writes all substrings of a given string that start with the first, end with the second, and otherwise contain neither. *Note*: Be especially careful of overlaps!

3.1.20 Compose a filter that reads text from an input stream and writes it to an output stream, removing any lines that consist only of whitespace.

3.1.21 Modify `potential.py` (Program 3.1.8) to take an integer n from the command line and generate n random `Charge` objects in the unit square, with potential values drawn randomly from a Gaussian distribution with mean 50 and standard deviation 10.

3.1.22 Modify `stockquote.py` (Program 3.1.10) to take multiple symbols on the command line.

3.1.23 The example file `djia.csv` used for `split.py` (PROGRAM 3.1.11) lists the date, high price, volume, and low price of the Dow Jones stock market average for every day since records have been kept. Download this file from the booksite and compose a program that plots the prices and volumes, at a rate taken from the command line.

3.1.24 Compose a program `merge.py` that takes a delimiter string followed by an arbitrary number of file names as command-line arguments; concatenates the corresponding lines of each file, separated by the delimiter; and then writes the result to standard output, thus performing the opposite operation from `split.py` (PROGRAM 3.1.11).

3.1.25 Find a website that publishes the current temperature in your area, and write a screen-scraper program `weather.py` so that typing `python weather.py` followed by your ZIP code will give you a weather forecast.

Creative Exercises

3.1.26 *Picture filtering.* Compose a module `rawpicture.py` with `read()` and `write()` functions for use with standard input and standard output. The `write()` function takes a `Picture` as argument and writes the picture to standard output, using the following format: if the picture is w-by-h, write w, then h, then $w*h$ triples of integers representing the pixel color values, in row-major order. The `read()` function takes no arguments and returns a `Picture`, which it creates by reading a picture from standard input, in the format just described. *Note*: The picture filtering will use up much more disk space than the picture the standard formats compress this information so that it will not take up so much space.

3.1.27 *Kama Sutra cipher.* Compose a filter `KamaSutra` that takes two strings as command-line argument (the *key* strings), then reads standard input, substitutes for each letter as specified by the key strings, and writes the result to standard output. This operation is the basis for one of the earliest known cryptographic systems. The condition on the key strings is that they must be of equal length and that any letter in standard input must be in one of them. For example, if input is all capitals and the keys are `THEQUICKBROWN` and `FXJMPSVRLZYDG`, then we make this table:

```
T H E Q U I C K B R O W N
F X J M P S V L A Z Y D G
```

That is, we should substitute `F` for `T`, `T` for `F`, `H` for `X`, `X` for `H`, and so forth when copying the input to the output. The message is encoded by replacing each letter with its pair. For example, the message `MEET AT ELEVEN` is encoded as `QJJF BF JKJCJG`. Someone receiving the message can use the same keys to get the message back.

3.1.28 *Safe password verification.* Compose a function that takes a string as an argument and returns `True` if it meets the following conditions, `False` otherwise:

- At least eight characters long
- Contains at least one digit (0–9)
- Contains at least one uppercase letter
- Contains at least one lowercase letter
- Contains at least one character that is neither a letter nor a number

Such checks are commonly used for passwords on the web.

3.1.29 *Sound visualization.* Compose a program that uses `stdaudio` and `Picture` to create an interesting two-dimensional color visualization of a sound file while it is playing. Be creative!

3.1.30 *Color study.* Compose a program that displays the color study shown at right, which gives Albers squares corresponding to each of the 256 levels of blue (blue-to-white in row-major order) and gray (black-to-white in column-major order) that were used to print this book.

A color study

3.1.31 *Entropy.* The *Shannon entropy* measures the information content of an input string and plays a cornerstone role in information theory and data compression. Given a string of n characters, let f_c be the frequency of occurrence of character c. The quantity $p_c = f_c / n$ is an estimate of the probability that c would be in the string if it were a random string, and the entropy is defined to be the sum of the quantity $-p_c \log_2 p_c$, over all characters that appear in the string. The entropy is said to measure the *information content* of a string: if each character appears the same number of times, the entropy is at its minimum value. Compose a program that computes and writes to standard output the entropy of the string read from standard input. Run your program on a web page that you read regularly, on a recent paper that you wrote, and on the fruit fly genome found on the website.

3.1.32 *Minimize potential.* Compose a function that takes an array of `Charge` objects with positive potential as its argument and finds a point such that the potential at that point is within 1% of the minimum potential anywhere in the unit square. Compose a test client that calls your function to write the point coordinates and charge value for the data given in the text and for the random charges described in EXERCISE 3.1.21.

3.1.33 *Slide show.* Compose a program that takes the names of several image files as command-line arguments and displays them in a slide show (one every two seconds), using a fade effect to black and a fade from black between pictures.

3.1.34 *Tile.* Compose a program that takes the name of an image file and two integers `m` and `n` as command-line arguments and creates an `m`-by-`n` tiling of the picture.

3.1.35 *Rotation filter.* Compose a program that takes two command-line arguments (the name of an image file and a real number theta) and rotates the image θ degrees counterclockwise. To rotate, copy the color of each pixel (s_i, s_j) in the source image to a target pixel (t_i, t_j) whose coordinates are given by the following formulas:

$$t_i = (s_i - c_i)\cos\theta - (s_j - c_j)\sin\theta + c_i$$
$$t_j = (s_i - c_i)\sin\theta + (s_j - c_j)\cos\theta + c_j$$

where (c_i, c_j) is the center of the image.

3.1.36 *Swirl filter.* Creating a swirl effect is similar to rotation, except that the angle changes as a function of distance to the center. Use the same formulas as in the previous exercise, but compute θ as a function of (s_i, s_j)—specifically, π / 256 times the distance to the center.

3.1.37 *Wave filter.* Compose a filter like those in the previous two exercises that creates a wave effect, by copying the color of each pixel (s_i, s_j) in the source image to a target pixel (t_i, t_j), where $t_i = s_i$ and $t_j = s_j + 20\sin(2\pi s_i/64)$. Add code to take the amplitude (20 in the accompanying figure) and the frequency (64 in the accompanying figure) as command-line arguments. Experiment with various values of these parameters.

3.1.38 *Glass filter.* Compose a program that takes the name of an image file as a command-line argument and applies a *glass filter*: set each pixel *p* to the color of a random neighboring pixel (whose pixel coordinates are each within 5 pixels of *p*'s coordinates).

rotate 30 degrees

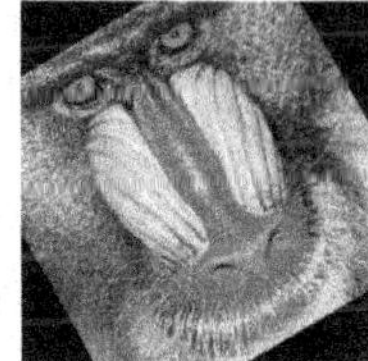

swirl filter

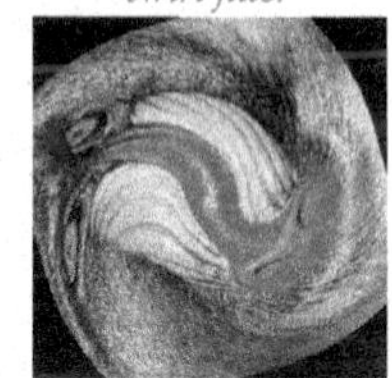

wave filter

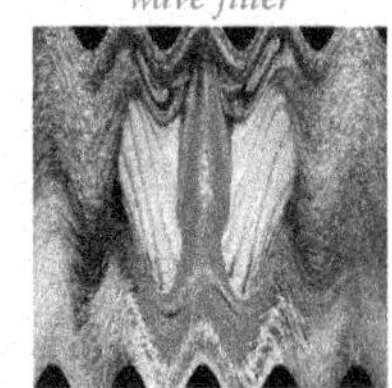

glass filter

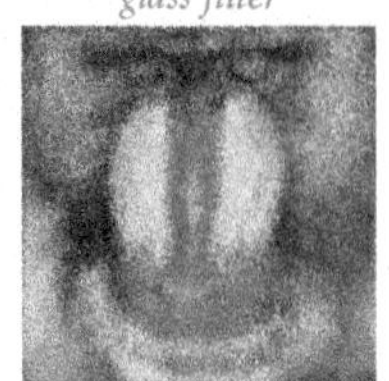

Exercises in filtering

3.1.39 *Morph.* The example images in the text for `fade.py` do not quite line up in the vertical direction (the mandrill's mouth is much lower than Darwin's mouth). Modify `fade.py` to add a transformation in the vertical dimension that makes a smoother transition.

3.1.40 *Clusters.* Compose a program that takes the name of a picture file from the command line and produces and displays to `stddraw` a picture with filled circles that cover compatible areas. First, scan the image to determine the background color (a dominant color that is found in more than half the pixels). Use a depth-first search (see PROGRAM 2.4.6) to find contiguous sets of pixels that are foreground-compatible with the background. A scientist might use a program to study natural scenarios such as birds in flight or particles in motion. Take a photo of balls on a billiards table and try to get your program to identify the balls and positions.

3.1.41 *Digital zoom.* Compose a program `zoom.py` that takes the name of a picture file and three floats *s*, *x*, and *y* as command-line arguments and displays a picture that zooms in on a portion of the input picture. The numbers should all be between 0 and 1, with *s* to be interpreted as a scale factor and (*x*, *y*) as the relative coordinates of the point that is to be at the center of the output image. Use this program to zoom in on your pet, friend, or relative in some digital image on your computer.

```
% python zoom.py boy.jpg 1 0.5 0.5
```

```
% python zoom.py boy.jpg 0.5 0.5 0.5
```

```
% python zoom.py boy.jpg 0.2 0.48 0.5
```

Digital zoom

3.2 Creating Data Types

In principle, we could compose all of our programs using only built-in data types. However, as we saw in the last section, it is much more convenient to compose programs at a higher level of abstraction. Thus, many other data types are defined in Python's standard and extension modules. Still, we certainly cannot expect those modules to define every conceivable data type that we might ever wish to use, so we need to be able to *define* our own. The purpose of this section is to explain how to build our own data types in Python.

Programs in this section

A data type is a set of values and a set of operations defined on those values. In Python, we implement a data type using a *class*. The API specifies the operations that we need to implement, but we are free to choose any convenient representation for the values. Implementing a data type as a Python class is not very different from implementing a function module as a set of functions. The primary differences are that we associate values (in the form of instance variables) with methods and that each method call is associated with the object used to invoke it.

To cement the basic concepts, we begin by defining a class that implements the data type for charged particles that we introduced in Section 3.1. Then, we illustrate the process of defining classes by considering a range of examples, from complex numbers to stock accounts, including a number of software tools that we will use later in the book. Useful client code is testimony to the value of any data type, so we also consider a number of clients, including one that depicts the famous and fascinating Mandelbrot set.

The process of defining a data type is known as *data abstraction* (as opposed to the *function abstraction* style that is the basis of Chapter 2). We focus on the data and implement operations on that data. *Whenever you can clearly separate data and associated operations within a computation, you should do so.* Modeling physical objects or mathematical abstractions is straightforward and useful, but the true power of data abstraction is that it allows us to model anything that we can precisely specify. Once you gain experience with this style of programming, you will see that it naturally helps address programming challenges of arbitrary complexity.

Basic elements of a data type To illustrate the process of implementing a data type as a Python class, we now consider an implementation of the `Charge` data type of SECTION 3.1 in full detail. We have already considered *client* programs that demonstrate the utility of having such a data type (in PROGRAM 3.1.2 and PROGRAM 3.1.8); now we focus on the *implementation* details. Every data-type implementation that you will develop has the same basic ingredients as this example.

API. The application programming interface is the contract with all clients and, therefore, the starting point for any implementation. To emphasize that APIs are critical for implementations, we repeat below the `Charge` API. To implement the `Charge` data type as a Python class, we need to define the data-type values, compose code to initialize new `Charge` objects with specified data-type values, and implement two methods that manipulate those values. When faced with the problem of creating a completely new data type for some application, the first step is to develop an API. This step is a *design* activity that we will address in SECTION 3.3. We have already looked at APIs as specifications of how to *use* data types in client code; now look at them as specifications of how to *implement* data types.

Class. In Python, we implement a data type as a *class*. As we have seen, Python's convention is to put the code for a data type in a file with the same name as the class, but in lowercase and followed by the `.py` extension. Thus, we keep the code for `Charge` in a file named `charge.py`. To define a class, you use the keyword `class`, followed by the class name, followed by a colon, and then a list of method definitions. Our class adheres to conventions that define three key features of a data type: *a constructor, instance variables*, and *methods*, which we will address in detail next. Since these features are intertwined, the discussion is a bit circular at points, so a good strategy is to read all three descriptions, then reread them.

operation	*description*
`Charge(x0, y0, q0)`	*a new charge centered at* (x_0, y_0) *with charge value* q_0
`c.potentialAt(x, y)`	*electric potential of charge* `c` *at point* `(x, y)`
`str(c)`	`'q0 at (x0, y0)'` *(string representation of charge* `c`*)*

API for our user-defined `Charge` *data type*

Constructor. A constructor creates an object of the specified type and returns a reference to that object. For our example, the client code

```
c = Charge(x0, y0, q0)
```

returns a new `Charge` object, suitably initialized. Python provides a flexible and general mechanism for object creation, but we adopt a simple subset that well serves our style of programming. Specifically, in this book, each data type defines a special method `__init__()` whose purpose is to define and initialize the *instance variables*, as described below. The double underscores before and after the name are your clue that it is "special"—we will be encountering other *special methods* soon.

When a client calls a constructor, Python's default construction process creates a new object of the specified type, calls the `__init__()` method to define and initialize the instance variables, and returns a reference to the new object. In this book, we refer to `__init__()` as the *constructor* for the data type, even though it is technically only the pertinent part of the object-creation process.

The code at right is the `__init__()` implementation for `Charge`. It is a method, so its first line is a signature consisting of the keyword `def`, its name (`__init__`), a list of parameter variables, and a colon. By convention, the first parameter variable is named `self`. *As part of Python's default object creation process, the value of the* `self` *parameter variable when* `__init()__` *is invoked is a reference to the newly created object.* The ordinary parameter variables from the client follow the special parameter variable `self`. The remaining lines make up the body of the constructor. Our convention throughout this book is for `__init()__` to consist of code that initializes the newly created object by defining and initializing the instance variables.

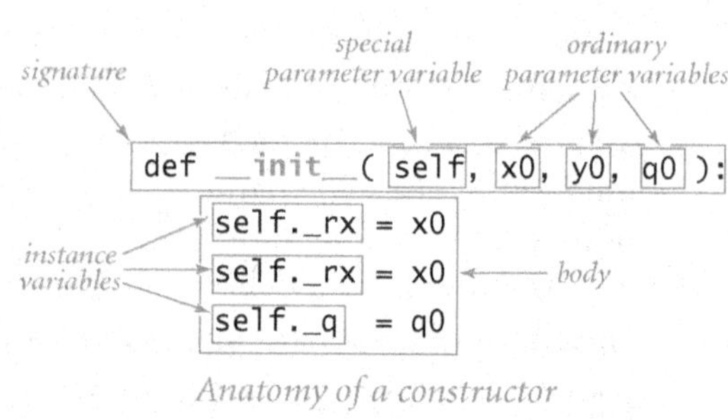

Anatomy of a constructor

Instance variables. A data type is a set of values and a set of operations defined on those values. In Python, *instance variables* implement the values. An instance variable belongs to a particular *instance* of a class—that is, to a particular object. In this book, our convention is to define and initialize each instance variable of the newly created object *in the constructor and only in the constructor.* The standard convention in Python programs is that instance variable names begin with an underscore. In our implementations, you can inspect the constructor to see the entire set of instance variables. For example, the `__init__()` implementation on the previous page tells us that `Charge` has three instance variables `_rx`, `_ry`, and `_q`. When an object is created, the value of the `self` parameter variable of the `__init__()` method is a reference to that object. Just as we can call a method for a charge `c` with the syntax `c.potentialAt()`, so we can refer to an instance variable for a charge `self` with the syntax `self._rx`. Therefore the three lines within the `__init__()` constructor for `Charge` define and initialize `_rx`, `_ry`, and `_q` for the new object.

Details of object creation. The memory diagrams at right detail the precise sequence of events when a client creates a new `Charge` object with the code

```
c1 = Charge(0.51, 0.63, 21.3)
```

- Python creates the object and calls the `__init__()` constructor, initializing the constructor's `self` parameter variable to reference the newly created object, its `x0` parameter variable to reference `0.51`, its `y0` parameter variable to reference `0.63`, and its `q0` parameter variable to reference `21.3`.
- The constructor defines and initializes the `_rx`, `_ry`, and `_q` instance variables within the newly created object referenced by `self`.
- After the constructor finishes, Python automatically returns to the client the `self` reference to the newly created object.
- The client assigns that reference to `c1`.

The parameter variables `x0` , `y0`, and `q0` go out of scope when `__init__()` is finished, but the objects they reference are still accessible via the new object's instance variables.

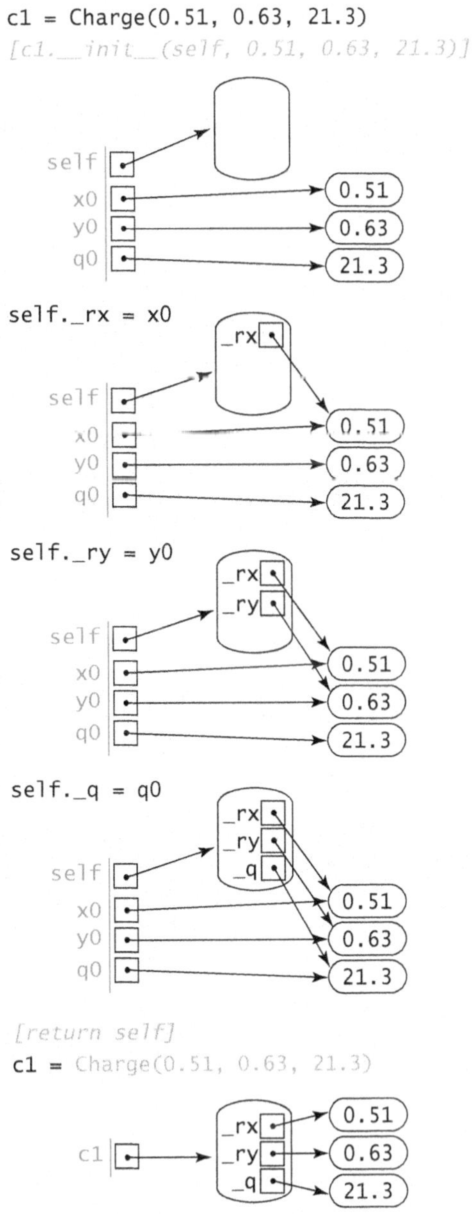

```
c1 = Charge(0.51, 0.63, 21.3)
[c1.__init__(self, 0.51, 0.63, 21.3)]
```



```
self._rx = x0
```



```
self._ry = y0
```



```
self._q = q0
```



```
[return self]
c1 = Charge(0.51, 0.63, 21.3)
```


Creating and initializing an object

Methods. A data type is a set of values and a set of operations defined on those values. In Python, *methods* (or *instance methods*) implement data-type operations, which are associated with a specified object. To define methods, we compose code that is precisely like the code that we learned in Chapter 2 to define functions, with the (significant) exception that methods can also access instance variables. For example, the code of the `potentialAt()` method for our `Charge` data type is shown below. The first line is the method's signature: the keyword `def`, the name of the method, parameter variables names in parentheses, and a colon. The first parameter variable of every method is named `self`. When a client calls a method, Python automatically sets that `self` parameter variable to reference the object to be manipulated—*the object that was used to invoke the method.* For example, when a client calls our method with `c.potentialAt(x, y)`, the value of the `self` parameter variable of the __potentialAt__() method is set to `c`. The ordinary parameter variables from the client (`x` and `y`, in this case) follow the special parameter variable `self`. The remaining lines make up the *body* of the `potentialAt()` method.

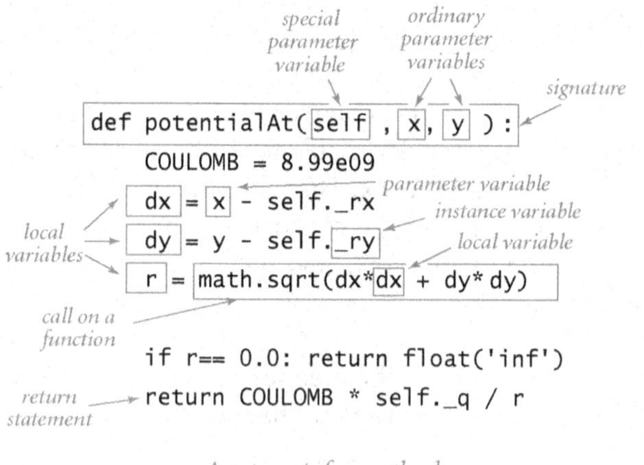

Anatomy of a method

Variables within methods. To understand method implementations, it is very important to know that a method typically uses three kinds of variables:

- The `self` object's instance variables
- The method's parameter variables
- Local variables

There is a critical distinction between instance variables and the parameter and local variables that you are accustomed to: there is just one value corresponding to each local or parameter variable at a given time, but there can be many values corresponding to each instance variable—one for each object that is an instance of the data type. There is no ambiguity with this arrangement, because each time that you call a method, you use an object to do so, and the implementation code

variable	*purpose*	*example*	*scope*
parameter	pass argument from client to method	`self, x, y`	method
instance	data-type value	`_rx, _ry`	class
local	temporary use within method	`dx, dy`	method

Variables within methods

can directly refer to that object's instance variables using the `self` parameter variable. *Be sure that you understand the distinctions among these three kinds of variables.* The differences are summarized in table above, and are a key to object-oriented programming. In our example, `potentialAt()` uses the `_rx`, `_ry`, and `_q` instance variables of the object referenced by `self`, the parameter variables `x` and `y`, and the local variables `COULOMB`, `dx`, `dy`, and `r` to compute and return a value. As an example, note that the statement

```
dx = x - self._rx
```

uses all three kinds of variables. With these distinctions in mind, check that you understand how `potentialAt()` gets its job done.

Methods are functions. A method is a special kind of function that is defined in a class and associated with an object. Since methods are functions, a method can take any number of arguments, specify optional arguments with default values, and return a value to its caller. In our example, `potentialAt()` takes two ordinary arguments and returns a float to the client. The key difference between functions and methods is that a method is associated with a specified object, with direct access to its instance variables. Indeed, we will see examples later in this section where the *purpose* of a method is to have the side effect of changing an instance variable, rather than returning a value to the client.

Built-in functions. The third operation in the `Charge` API is a built-in function `str(c)`. Python's convention is to automatically translate this function call to a standard method call `c.__str__()`. Thus, to support this operation, we implement the *special method* `__str__()`, which uses the instance variables associated with the invoking object to string together the desired result. Recall that Python knows the type of each object at run time, so Python can infer which `__str__()` method to call—the one defined in the class corresponding to the invoking object.

Privacy. A client should access a data type only through the methods in its API. Sometimes it is convenient to define helper methods in the implementation that are not intended to be called directly by the client. The special method `__str__()` is a prototypical example. As we saw in Section 2.2 with *private functions*, the standard Python convention is to name such methods with a leading underscore. The leading underscore is a strong signal to the client not to call that *private method* directly. Similarly, naming instance variables with a leading underscore signals to the client not to access such *private instance variables* directly. Even though Python has no language support for enforcing these conventions, most Python programmers treat them as sacrosanct.

These are the basic components that you must understand to implement data types as classes in Python. Every data-type implementation (Python class) that we will consider has instance variables, constructors, and methods. In each data type that we develop, we go through the same steps. Rather than thinking about which action we need to take next to accomplish a computational goal (as we did when first learning to program), we think about the needs of a client, then accommodate them in a data type. Program 3.2.1 is a full implementation of our `Charge` data type; it illustrates all of the features we have just discussed. Note that `charge.py` also has a test client. As with modules, it is good style to include a test client with every data-type implementation.

Summary. At the risk of being repetitive, we summarize the basic steps that we have described in the process of creating a new data type.

The first step in creating a data type is to specify an API. The purpose of the API is to separate clients from implementations, thereby facilitating modular programming. We have two goals when specifying an API. First, we want to enable clear and correct client code. Indeed, it is a good idea to compose some client code before finalizing the API to gain confidence that the specified data-type operations are the ones that clients need. Second, we need to be able to implement the operations. There is no point in specifying operations that we have no idea how to implement.

The second step in creating a data type is to implement a Python class that meets the API specifications. First, we compose the constructor to define and initialize the instance variables; then, we compose the methods that manipulate the instance variables to implement the desired functionality. In Python, we normally need to implement three kinds of methods:

Program 3.2.1 Charged particle (charge.py)

```
import math
import sys
import stdio

class Charge:
    def __init__(self, x0, y0, q0):
        self._rx = x0
        self._ry = y0
        self._q = q0

    def potentialAt(self, x, y):
        COULOMB = 8.99e09
        dx = x - self._rx
        dy = y - self._ry
        r = math.sqrt(dx*dx + dy*dy)
        if r == 0.0: return float('inf')
        return COULOMB * self._q / r

    def __str__(self):
        result = str(self._q) + ' at ('
        result += str(self._rx) + ', ' + str(self._ry) + ')'
        return result

def main():
    x = float(sys.argv[1])
    y = float(sys.argv[2])
    c = Charge(.51, .63, 21.3)
    stdio.writeln(c)
    stdio.writeln(c.potentialAt(x, y))

if __name__ == '__main__': main()
```

instance variables

`_rx`	*x-coordinate*
`_ry`	*y-coordinate*
`_q`	*charge value*

`COULOMB`	*Coulomb's constant*
`dx, dy`	*delta distances to query point*
`r`	*distance to query point*

`x, y`	*query point*
`c`	*charge*

This implementation of our data type for charged particles contains the basic ingredients found in every data type: instance variables `_rx`, `_ry`, and `_q`; a constructor `__init__()`; the methods `potentialAt()` and `__str__()`; and a test client `main()` (see also Program *3.1.1).*

```
% python charge.py .5 .5
21.3 at (0.51, 0.63)
1468638248194.164
```

- To implement a *constructor*, we implement a special method `__init__()` with `self` as its first parameter variable, followed by the constructor's ordinary parameter variables.
- To implement a *method*, we implement a function of the desired name, with `self` as its first parameter variable, followed by the method's ordinary parameter variables.
- To implement a *built-in function*, we implement a special method with the same name enclosed in double underscores and with `self` as its first parameter variable.

Examples from `Charge` are shown in the table at the bottom of this page. In all three cases, we use `self` to access the instance variables of the invoking object and otherwise use parameter and local variables to compute a result and return a value to the caller.

The third step in creating a data type is to compose a *test client*, to validate and test the design decisions made in the first two steps.

The diagram on the facing page summarizes the terminology that we have discussed. It is well worth careful study, as we will be using this terminology extensively for the rest of the book.

For the rest of this section, we apply these basic steps to create a number of interesting data types and clients. We start each example with an API, and then consider implementations, followed by clients. You will find many exercises at the end of this section intended to give you experience with data-type creation. Section 3.3 provides an overview of the design process and related language mechanisms.

What are the values that define the data type, and which operations do clients need to perform on those values? With these basic decisions made, you can create new data types and compose clients that use them in the same way as you have been using built-in data types.

operation	*call (in client code)*	*signature (in implementation code)*
constructor	`c = Charge(x0, y0, q0)`	`__init__(self, x0, y0, q0)`
method	`c.potentialAt(x, y)`	`potentialAt(self, x, y)`
built-in function	`str(c)`	`__str__(self)`

Summary of methods in Python data-type implementations

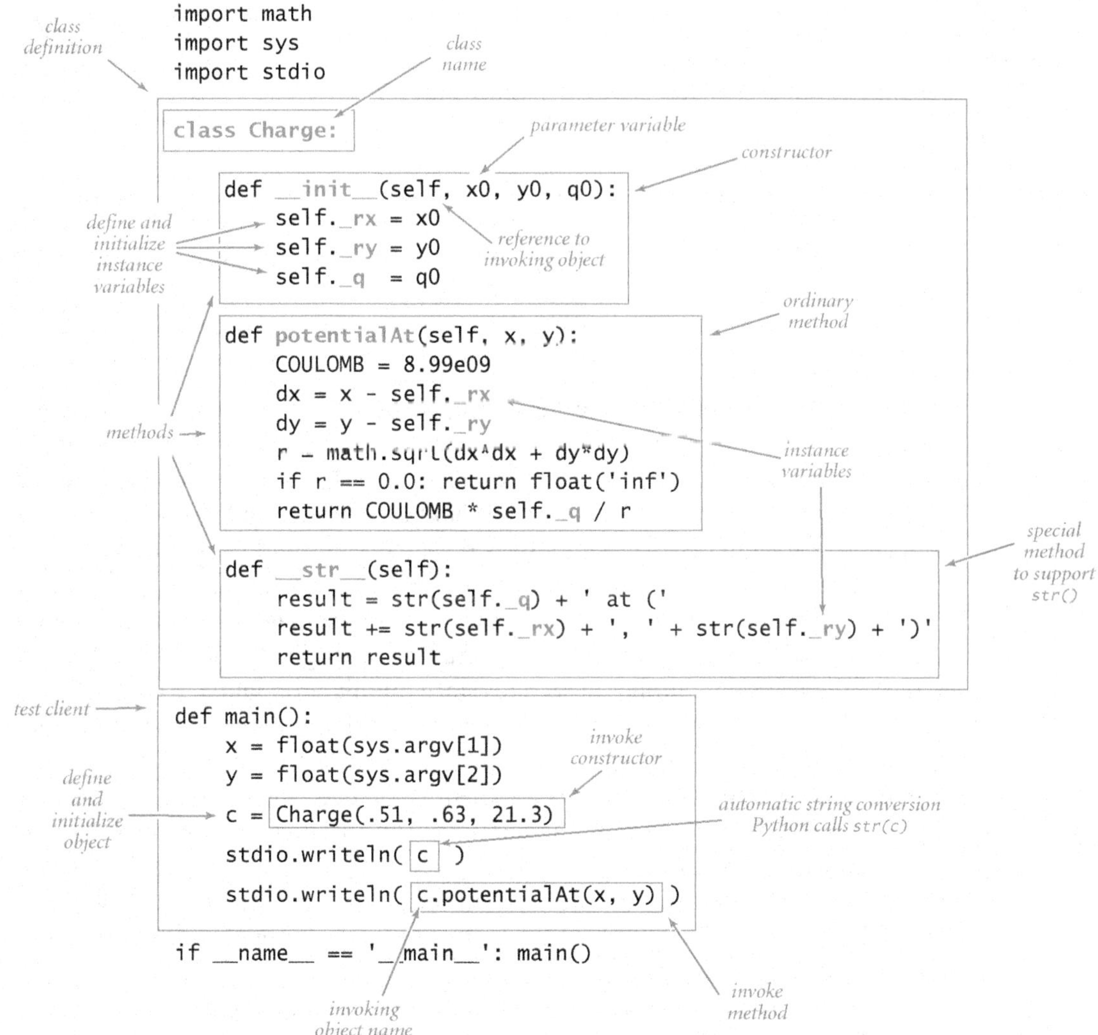

Anatomy of a class (data-type) definition

Stopwatch One of the hallmarks of object-oriented programming is the idea of easily modeling real-world objects by creating abstract programming objects. As a simple example, consider `stopwatch.py` (Program 3.2.2), which implements our `Stopwatch` data type, defined by the following API:

operation	*description*
`Stopwatch()`	*a new stopwatch (running at the start)*
`watch.elapsedTime()`	*elapsed time since* `watch` *was created, in seconds*

API for our user-defined `Stopwatch` *data type*

In other words, a `Stopwatch` object is a stripped-down version of an old-fashioned stopwatch. When you create one, it starts running, and you can ask it how long it has been running by invoking the method `elapsedTime()`. You might imagine adding all sorts of bells and whistles to `Stopwatch`, limited only by your imagination. Do you want to be able to reset the stopwatch? Start and stop it? Include a lap timer? These sorts of things are easy to add (see Exercise 3.2.11).

The implementation in `stopwatch.py` takes advantage of the Python function `time()` in the `time` module, which returns a float giving the current time in seconds (typically, the number of seconds since midnight on January 1, 1970 UTC). The data-type implementation could hardly be simpler. A `Stopwatch` object saves its creation time in an instance variable, then returns the difference between that time and the current time whenever a client calls its `elapsedTime()` method. A `Stopwatch` object itself does not actually tick (an internal system clock on your computer does all the ticking for all `Stopwatch` objects); it just creates the illusion that it does for clients. Why not just use `time.time()` in clients? We could do so, but using the higher-level `Stopwatch` abstraction leads to client code that is easier to understand and maintain.

The test client is typical. It creates two `Stopwatch` objects, uses them to measure the running time of two different computations and then writes the ratio of the running times.

The question of whether one approach to solving a problem is better than another has been lurking since the first few programs that you have run, and plays an essential role in program development. In Section 4.1, we will develop a scientific approach to understanding the cost of computation. `Stopwatch` is a useful tool in that approach.

Program 3.2.2 Stopwatch (stopwatch.py)

```
import math
import sys
import time
import stdio

class Stopwatch:
    def __init__(self):
        self._start = time.time()
    def elapsedTime(self):
        return time.time() - self._start

def main():
    n = int(sys.argv[1])

    total1 = 0.0
    watch1 = Stopwatch()
    for i in range(1, n+1):
        total1 += i**2
    time1 = watch1.elapsedTime()

    total2 = 0.0
    watch2 = Stopwatch()
    for i in range(1, n+1):
        total2 += i*i
    time2 = watch2.elapsedTime()

    stdio.writeln(total1/total2)
    stdio.writeln(time1/time2)

if __name__ == '__main__': main()
```

instance variable

`_start`	*creation time*

This module defines a class `Stopwatch` *that implements a data type that we can use to compare running times of performance-critical methods (see* Section *4.1). The test client accepts an integer* n *from the command line and compares the cost for squaring a number using either* `i**2` *or* `i*i` *for the task of computing the sum of the squares of the numbers from 1 to* n*. This quick test indicates that* `i*i` *is about three times faster than* `i**2`*.*

```
% python stopwatch.py 1000000
1.0
3.179422835633626
```

Histogram PROGRAM 3.2.3 (`histogram.py`) defines a data type `Histogram` for graphically representing the distribution of data using bars of different heights in a chart known as a *histogram*. A `Histogram` object maintains an *array* of the frequency of occurrence of integer values in a given interval. It uses `stdstats.plotBars()` to display a histogram of the values, controlled by this API:

operation	*description*
`Histogram(n)`	*a new histogram from the integer values in* `0, 1, ..., n-1`
`h.addDataPoint(i)`	*add an occurrence of integer* `i` *to the histogram* `h`
`h.draw()`	*draw* `h` *to standard drawing*

API for our user-defined `Histogram` *data type*

With this simple data type, we reap the benefits of modular programming (reusable code, independent development of small programs, and so forth) that we discussed in CHAPTER 2, with the additional benefit that we also separate the *data*. A histogram client need not maintain the data (or know anything about its representation); it just creates a histogram and calls `addDataPoint()`.

When studying this code and the next several examples, it is best to carefully consider the client code. Each class that we implement essentially extends the Python language, allowing us to create objects of the new data type and perform operations on them. All client programs are conceptually the same as the first programs that you learned that use built-in data types. Now you have the ability to define whatever types and operations you need in your client code!

In this case, using `Histogram` actually *enhances* the readability of the client code, as the `addDataPoint()` call focuses attention on the data being studied. Without `Histogram`, we would have to mix the code for creating the histogram with the code for the computation of interest, resulting in a program that is much more difficult to understand and maintain than the two separate programs. *Whenever you can clearly separate data and associated operations within a computation, you should do so.*

Once you understand how a data type will be used in client code, you can consider the implementation. An implementation is characterized by its instance variables (data-type values). `Histogram` maintains an array with the frequency of each point. Its `draw()` method scales the drawing (so that the tallest bar fits snugly in the canvas) and then plots the frequencies.

Program 3.2.3 Histogram (histogram.py)

```
import sys
import stdarray
import stddraw
import stdrandom
import stdstats

class Histogram:
    def __init__(self, n):
        self._freq = stdarray.create1D(n, 0)

    def addDataPoint(self, i):
        self._freq[i] += 1

    def draw(self):
        stddraw.setYscale(0, max(self._freq))
        stdstats.plotBars(self._freq)


def main():
    n      = int(sys.argv[1])
    p      = float(sys.argv[2])
    trials = int(sys.argv[3])
    histogram = Histogram(n+1)
    for t in range(trials):
        heads = bernoulli.binomial(n, p)
        histogram.addDataPoint(heads)
    stddraw.setCanvasSize(500, 200)
    histogram.draw()
    stddraw.show()

if __name__ == '__main__': main()
```

instance variables

`_freq[]`	*frequency counts*

```
% python histogram.py 50 .5 100000
```

This module defines a `Histogram` *class that implements a data type for creating dynamic histograms. The frequency counts are kept in an instance-variable array* `_freq`*. The test client accepts integer* n*, float* p*, and integer* `trials` *as command-line arguments. It performs* `trials` *experiments, each of which counts the number of heads found when a biased coin (heads with probability* p *and tails with probability* `1 - p`*) is flipped* n *times. Then, it draws the results to standard drawing.*

Turtle graphics *Whenever you can clearly separate tasks within a computation, you should do so.* In object-oriented programming, we extend that mantra to include *state* with the tasks. A small amount of state can be immensely valuable in simplifying a computation. Next, we consider *turtle graphics*, which is based on the data type defined by this API:

operation	*description*
`Turtle(x0, y0, a0)`	*a new turtle at (*`x0`*,* `y0`*) facing* `a0` *degrees from the x-axis*
`t.turnLeft(delta)`	*instruct* `t` *to turn left (counterclockwise) by* `delta` *degrees*
`t.goForward(step)`	*instruct* `t` *to move forward distance* `step`*, drawing a line*

API for our user-defined `Turtle` *data type*

Imagine a turtle that lives in the unit square and draws lines as it moves. It can move a specified distance in a straight line, or it can rotate left (counterclockwise) a specified number of degrees. According to the API, when we create a turtle, we place it at a specified point, facing a specified direction. Then, we create drawings by giving the turtle a sequence of `goForward()` and `turnLeft()` commands.

```
x0 = 0.5
y0 = 0.0
a0 = 60.0
step = math.sqrt(3)/2
turtle = Turtle(x0, y0, a0)
turtle.goForward(step)
```

For example, to draw a triangle we create a turtle at (0, 0.5) facing at an angle of 60 degrees counterclockwise from the x-axis, then direct it to take a step forward, then rotate 120 degrees counterclockwise, then take another step forward, then rotate another 120 degrees counterclockwise, and then take a third step forward to complete the triangle. Indeed, all of the turtle clients that we will examine simply create a turtle, then give it an alternating series of step and rotate commands, varying the step size and the amount of rotation. As you will see in the next several pages, this simple model allows us to create arbitrarily complex drawings, with many important applications.

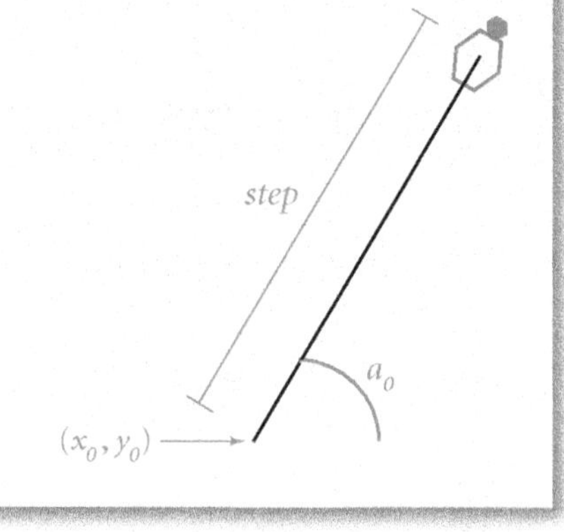

A turtle's first step

The `Turtle` class defined in PROGRAM 3.2.4 (`turtle.py`) is an implementation of this API that uses `stddraw`. It maintains three instance variables: the coordinates of the turtle's position and the current direction it is facing, measured in degrees counterclockwise from the *x*-axis (*polar angle*). Implementing the two methods requires *updating* the values of these variables, so `Turtle` objects are mutable. The necessary updates are straightforward: `turnLeft(delta)` adds `delta` to the current angle, and `goForward(step)` adds the step size times the cosine of its argument to the current *x*-coordinate and the step size times the sine of its argument to the current *y*-coordinate.

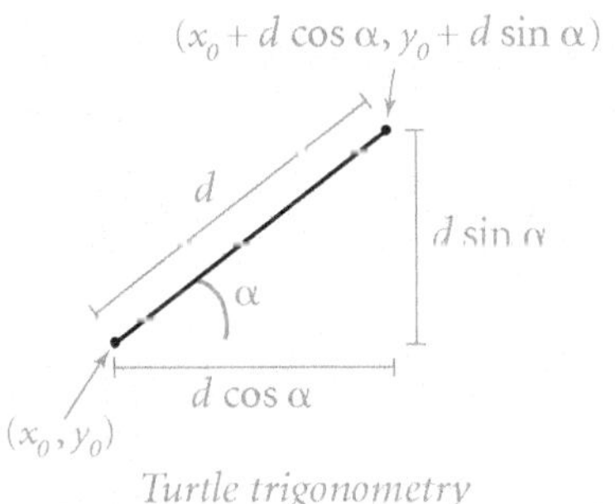

Turtle trigonometry

The test client in `Turtle` takes an integer `n` as a command-line argument and draws a regular polygon with `n` sides. If you are interested in elementary analytic geometry, you might enjoy verifying that fact. Whether or not you choose to do so, think about what you would need to do to compute the coordinates of all the points in the polygon. The simplicity of the turtle's approach is very appealing. In short, turtle graphics serves as a useful abstraction for describing geometric shapes of all sorts. For example, we obtain a good approximation to a circle by taking `n` to a sufficiently large value.

You can use a `Turtle` as you use any other object. Programs can create arrays of `Turtle` objects, pass them as arguments to functions, and so forth. Our examples will illustrate these capabilities and convince you that creating a data type like `Turtle` is both very easy and very useful. For each of them, as with regular polygons, it is *possible* to compute the coordinates of all the points and draw straight lines to get the drawings, but it is *easier* to do so with a `Turtle`. Turtle graphics exemplifies the value of data abstraction.

`t.goForward(step)`

`t.turnLeft(120.0)`

`t.goForward(step)`

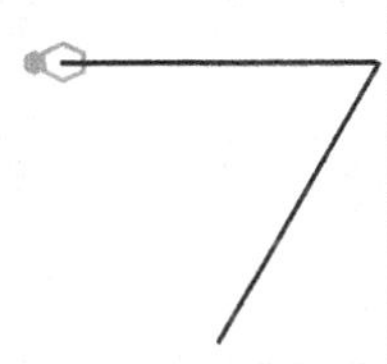

`t.turnLeft(120.0)`

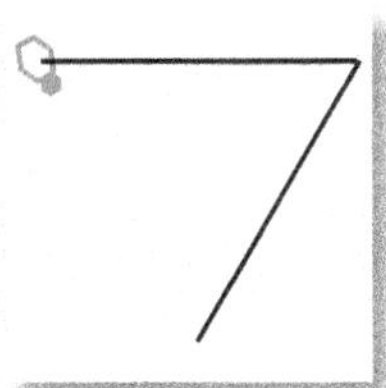

`t.goForward(step)`

Your first turtle graphics drawing

Program 3.2.4 Turtle graphics (turtle.py)

```
import math
import sys
import stddraw

class Turtle:
    def __init__(self, x0, y0, a0):
        self._x = x0
        self._y = y0
        self._angle = a0

    def turnLeft(self, delta):
        self._angle += delta

    def goForward(self, step):
        oldx = self._x
        oldy = self._y
        self._x += step * math.cos(math.radians(self._angle))
        self._y += step * math.sin(math.radians(self._angle))
        stddraw.line(oldx, oldy, self._x, self._y)

def main():
    n = int(sys.argv[1])
    step = math.sin(math.radians(180.0/n))
    turtle = Turtle(.5, .0, 180.0/n)
    for i in range(n):
        turtle.goForward(step)
        turtle.turnLeft(360.0/n)
    stddraw.show()

if __name__ == '__main__': main()
```

instance variables

`_x, _y`	*position (in unit square)*
`_angle`	*polar angle (in degrees)*

This data type supports turtle graphics, which often simplifies the creation of drawings.

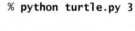

% python turtle.py 3

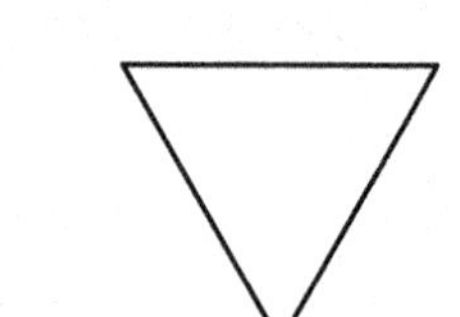

% python turtle.py 7

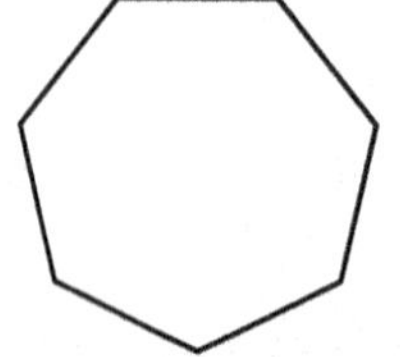

% python turtle.py 1000

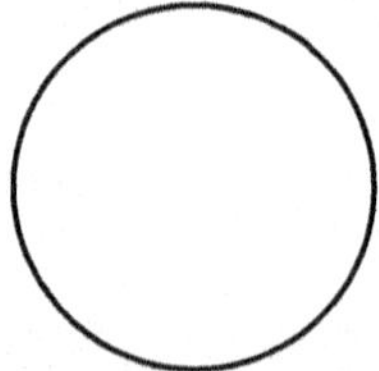

Recursive graphics. A *Koch curve* of order 0 is a straight line. To form a Koch curve of order n, draw a Koch curve of order $n-1$, turn left 60 degrees, draw a second Koch curve of order $n-1$, turn right 120 degrees (left −120 degrees), draw a third Koch curve of order $n-1$, turn left 60 degrees, and draw a fourth Koch curve of order $n-1$. These recursive instructions lead immediately to turtle client code. With appropriate modifications, recursive schemes like this have proved useful in modeling self-similar patterns found in nature, such as snowflakes.

The client code below is straightforward, except for the value of the step size. If you carefully examine the first few examples, you will see (and be able to prove by induction) that the width of the curve of order n is 3^n times the step size, so setting the step size to $1/3^n$ produces a curve of width 1. Similarly, the number of steps in a curve of order n is 4^n, so `koch.py` will not finish if you invoke it for large n.

You can find many examples of recursive patterns of this sort that have been studied and developed by mathematicians, scientists, and artists from many cultures in many contexts. Here, our interest in them is that the turtle graphics abstraction greatly simplifies the client code that draws them.

```
import sys
import stddraw
from turtle import Turtle

def koch(n, step, turtle):
    if n == 0:
        turtle.goForward(step)
        return
    koch(n-1, step, turtle)
    turtle.turnLeft(60.0)
    koch(n-1, step, turtle)
    turtle.turnLeft(-120.0)
    koch(n-1, step, turtle)
    turtle.turnLeft(60.0)
    koch(n-1, step, turtle)

n = int(sys.argv[1])
stddraw.setPenRadius(0.0)
step = 3.0 ** -n
turtle = Turtle(0.0, 0.0, 0.0)
koch(n, step, turtle)
stddraw.show()
```

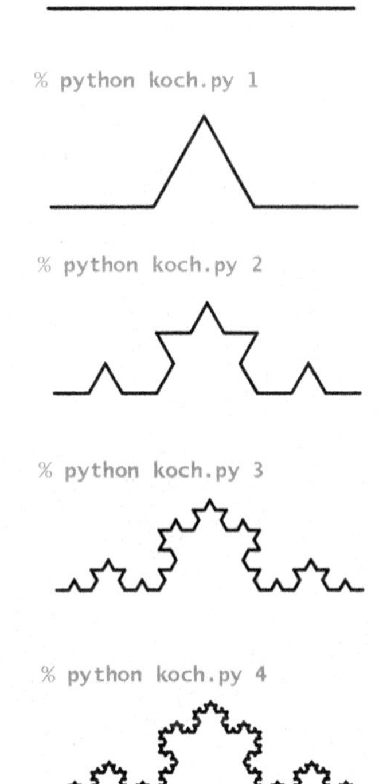

Drawing Koch curves with turtle graphics

Spira mirabilis. Perhaps the turtle is a bit tired after taking 4^n steps to draw a Koch curve (or just lazy). Accordingly, imagine that the turtle's step size decays by a tiny constant factor (close to 1) each time it takes a step. What happens to our drawings? Remarkably, modifying the polygon-drawing test client in PROGRAM 3.2.4 to answer this question leads to an image known as a *logarithmic spiral*, a curve that is found in many contexts in nature.

PROGRAM 3.2.5 (`spiral.py`) is an implementation of this curve. It instructs the turtle to alternately step and turn until it has wound around itself a given number of times, with the step size decaying by a constant factor after each step. The script takes three command-line arguments, which control the shape and nature of the spiral. As you can see from the four examples given with the program, the path spirals into the center of the drawing. You are encouraged to experiment with `spiral.py` yourself to develop an understanding of the way in which the parameters control the behavior of the spiral.

The logarithmic spiral was first described by René Descartes in 1638. Jacob Bernoulli was so amazed by its mathematical properties that he named it the *spira mirabilis* (miraculous spiral) and even asked to have it engraved on his tombstone. Many people also consider it to be "miraculous" that this precise curve is clearly present in a broad variety of natural phenomena. Three examples are depicted below: the chambers of a nautilus shell, the arms of a spiral galaxy, and the cloud formation in a tropical storm. Scientists have also observed it as the path followed by a hawk approaching its prey and the path followed by a charged particle moving perpendicular to a uniform magnetic field.

One of the goals of scientific enquiry is to provide simple but accurate models of complex natural phenomena. Our tired turtle certainly passes that test!

nautilus shell

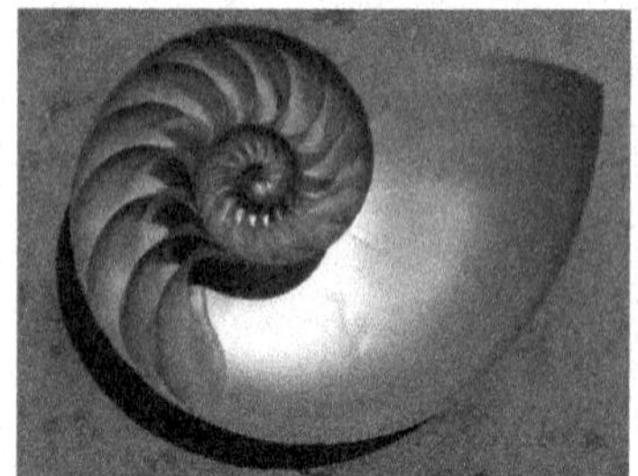

Photo: Chris 73 (CC-by-SA license)

spiral galaxy

Photo: NASA and ESA

storm clouds

Photo: NASA

Examples of the spira mirabilis in nature

Program 3.2.5 Spira mirabilis (spiral.py)

```
import math
import sys
import stddraw
from turtle import Turtle

n = int(sys.argv[1])
wraps = int(sys.argv[2])
decay = float(sys.argv[3])
angle = 360.0 / n

step = math.sin(math.radians(angle/2.0))
turtle = Turtle(0.5, 0, angle/2.0)

stddraw.setPenRadius(0)
for i in range(wraps * n):
    step /= decay
    turtle.goForward(step)
    turtle.turnLeft(angle)
stddraw.show()
```

n	*number of sides*
wraps	*wrap count*
step	*step size*
decay	*decay factor*
angle	*rotation amount*
step	*step size*
turtle	*lazy turtle*

This code is a modification of the test client in Program *3.2.4 that decreases the step size at each step and cycles around a given number of times. The value of* n *controls the shape;* wraps *controls its extent; and* decay *controls the nature of the spiral.*

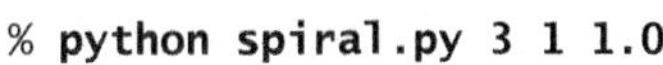

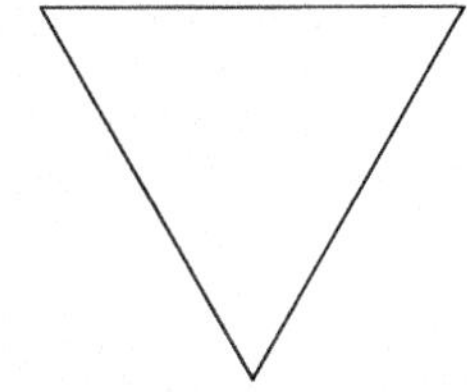

% **python spiral.py 3 10 1.2**

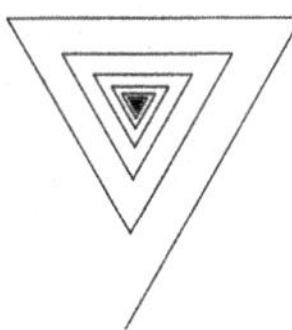

% **python spiral.py 1440 10 1.00004**

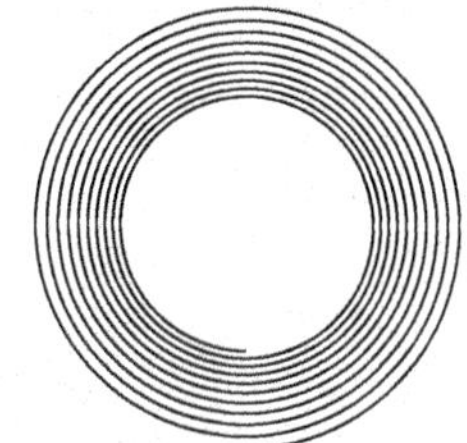

% **python spiral.py 1440 10 1.0004**

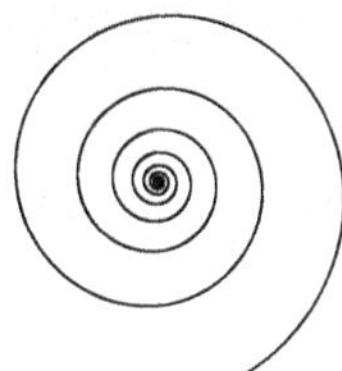

Brownian motion. Or perhaps the turtle has had one too many. Accordingly, imagine that the disoriented turtle (again following its standard alternating turn-and-step regimen) turns in a *random* direction before each step. Again, it is easy to plot the path followed by such a turtle for millions of steps, and again, such paths are found in nature in many contexts. In 1827, the botanist Robert Brown observed through a microscope that tiny particles ejected from pollen grains seemed to move about in just such a random fashion when immersed in water. This process later became known as *Brownian motion* and led to Albert Einstein's insights into the atomic nature of matter.

Or perhaps our turtle has friends, all of whom have had one too many. After they have wandered around for a sufficiently long time, their paths merge together and become indistinguishable from a single path. Astrophysicists today are using this model to understand observed properties of distant galaxies.

TURTLE GRAPHICS WAS ORIGINALLY DEVELOPED BY Seymour Papert at MIT in the 1960s as part of an educational programming language, Logo, that is still used today in toys. But turtle graphics is no toy, as we have just seen in numerous scientific examples. Turtle graphics also has numerous commercial applications. For example, it is the basis for PostScript, a programming language for creating printed pages that is used for most newspapers, magazines, and books. In the present context, `Turtle` is a quintessential object-oriented programming example, showing that a small amount of saved state (data abstraction using objects, not just functions) can vastly simplify a computation.

```
import sys
import stddraw
import stdrandom
from turtle import Turtle

trials = int(sys.argv[1])
step = float(sys.argv[2])
stddraw.setPenRadius(0.0)
turtle = Turtle(0.5, 0.5, 0.0)
for t in range(trials):
    angle = stdrandom.uniformFloat(0.0, 360.0)
    turtle.turnLeft(angle)
    turtle.goForward(step)
    stddraw.show(0)
stddraw.show()
```

% python drunk.py 10000 .01

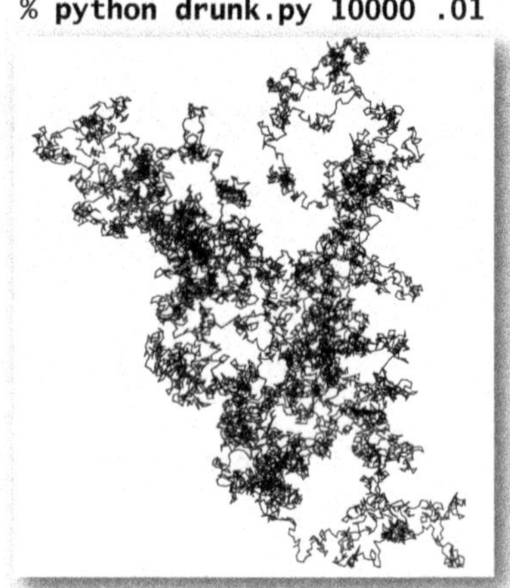

Brownian motion of a drunken turtle (moving a fixed distance in a random direction)

```
import sys
import stdarray
import stddraw
import stdrandom
from turtle import Turtle

n = int(sys.argv[1])
trials = int(sys.argv[2])
step = float(sys.argv[3])
stddraw.setPenRadius(0.0)
turtles = stdarray.create1D(n)
for i in range(n):
    x = stdrandom.uniformFloat(0.0, 1.0)
    y = stdrandom.uniformFloat(0.0, 1.0)
    turtles[i] = Turtle(x, y, 0.0)
for t in range(trials):
    for i in range(n):
        angle = stdrandom.uniformFloat(0.0, 360.0)
        turtles[i].turnLeft(angle)
        turtles[i].goForward(step)
        stddraw.show(0)
stddraw.show()
```

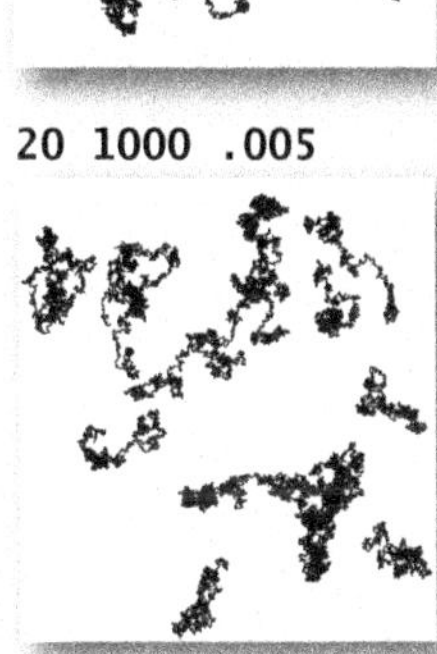

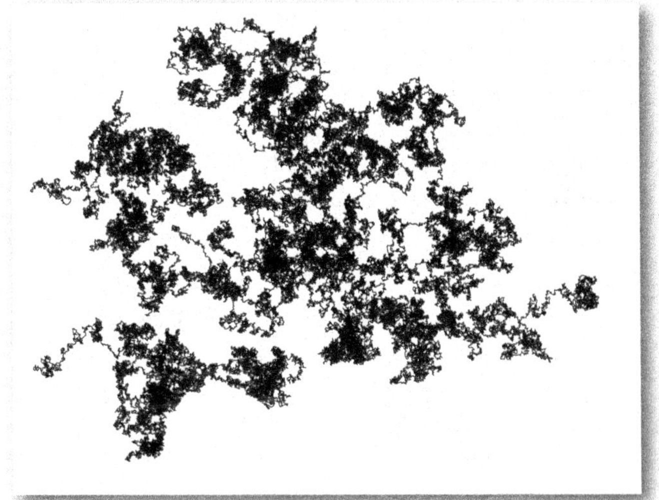

Brownian motion of a bale of drunken turtles

Complex numbers A *complex number* is a number of the form $x + yi$, where x and y are real numbers and i is the square root of -1. The number x is known as the *real* part of the complex number, and the number y is known as the *imaginary* part. This terminology stems from the idea that the square root of -1 has to be an imaginary number, because no real number can have this value. Complex numbers are a quintessential mathematical abstraction: whether or not one believes that it makes sense physically to take the square root of -1, complex numbers help us understand the natural world. They are used extensively in applied mathematics and play an essential role in many branches of science and engineering. They are used to model physical systems of all sorts, from circuits to sound waves to electromagnetic fields. These models typically require extensive computations involving manipulating complex numbers according to well-defined arithmetic operations, so we want to compose computer programs to do the computations. In short, we need a new data type.

No programming language can provide implementations of every mathematical abstraction that we might possibly need, but the ability to implement data types give us not just the ability to compose programs to easily manipulate abstractions such as complex numbers, polynomials, vectors, and matrices, but also the freedom to think in terms of new abstractions.

The Python language provides a `complex` (with a lowercase `c`) data type. However, since developing a data type for complex numbers is a prototypical exercise in object-oriented programming, we now consider our own `Complex` (with an uppercase `C`) data type. Doing so will allow us to consider a number of interesting issues surrounding data types for mathematical abstractions, in a nontrivial setting.

The operations on complex numbers that are needed for basic computations are to add and multiply them by applying the commutative, associative, and distributive laws of algebra (along with the identity $i^2 = -1$); to compute the magnitude; and to extract the real and imaginary parts, according to the following equations:

- *Addition*: $(x+yi) + (v+wi) = (x+v) + (y+w)i$
- *Multiplication*: $(x + yi) * (v + wi) = (xv - yw) + (yv + xw)\, i$
- *Magnitude*: $|x + yi| = \sqrt{x^2 + y^2}$
- *Real part*: $\mathrm{Re}(x + yi) = x$
- *Imaginary part*: $\mathrm{Im}(x + yi) = y$

For example, if $a = 3 + 4i$ and $b = -2 + 3i$, then $a + b = 1 + 7i$, $a * b = -18 + i$, $\text{Re}(a) = 3$, $\text{Im}(a) = 4$, and $|a| = 5$.

With these basic definitions, the path to implementing a data type for complex numbers is clear. As usual, we start with an API that specifies the data-type operations. For simplicity, we concentrate in the text on just the basic operations in this API, but EXERCISE 3.2.18 asks you to consider several other useful operations that might be supported. Except for the uppercase `C`, this API is also implemented by Python's built-in data type `complex`.

client operation	*special method*	*description*
`Complex(x, y)`	`__init__(self, re, im)`	*new* `Complex` *object with value* `x+yi`
`a.re()`		*real part of* `a`
`a.im()`		*imaginary part of* `a`
`a + b`	`__add__(self, other)`	*sum of* `a` *and* `b`
`a * b`	`__mul__(self, other)`	*product of* `a` *and* `b`
`abs(a)`	`__abs__(self)`	*magnitude of* `a`
`str(a)`	`__str__(self)`	`'x + yi'` *(string representation of* `a`*)*

API for a user-defined `Complex` *data type*

Special methods. How can we implement data-type operations so that clients can invoke them using arithmetic operators, such as + and *? The answer is found in another set of Python *special methods* that are specifically designed for this purpose. For example, when Python sees the expression `a + b` in client code, it replaces it with the method call `a.__add__(b)`. Similarly, Python replaces `a * b` with the method call `a.__mul__(b)`. Therefore, we need only to implement the special methods `__add__()` and `__mul__()` for addition and multiplication to operate as expected. The mechanism is the same one that we used to support Python's built-in `str()` function for `Charge`, by implementing the `__str__()` special method, except that the special methods for arithmetic operators take two arguments. The above API includes an extra column that maps the client operations to the special methods. We generally omit this column in our APIs because these names are standard, and irrelevant to clients. The list of Python special methods is extensive—we will discuss them further in SECTION 3.3.

`Complex` (Program 3.2.6) is a class that implements this API. It has all of the same components as did `Charge` (and every Python data-type implementation): instance variables (`_re` and `_im`), a constructor, methods, and a test client. The test client first sets z_0 to $1 + i$, then sets z to z_0, and then evaluates the expressions:

$$z = z^2 + z_0 = (1 + i)^2 + (1 + i) = (1 + 2i - 1) + (1 + i) = 1 + 3i$$
$$z = z^2 + z_0 = (1 + 3i)^2 + (1 + i) = (1 + 6i - 9) + (1 + i) = -7 + 7i$$

This code is straightforward and similar to code that you have seen earlier in this chapter.

Accessing instance variables in objects of this type. The implementations of both `__add__()` and `__mul__()` need to access values in *two* objects: the object passed as an argument and the object used to call the method (that is, the object referenced by `self`). When the client calls `a.__add__(b)`, the parameter variable `self` is set to reference the same object as argument `a` does, and the parameter variable `other` is set to reference the same object as argument `b` does. We can access the instance variables of `a` using `self._re` and `self._im`, as usual. To access the instance variables of `b`, we use the code `other._re` and `other._im`. Since our convention is to keep the instance variables private, we do not access directly instance variables in another class. Accessing instance variables within another object in the same class does not violate this privacy policy.

Immutability. The two instance variables in `Complex` are set for each `Complex` object when it is created and do not change during the lifetime of an object. That is, `Complex` objects are immutable. We discuss the benefits of this design decision in Section 3.3.

Complex numbers are the basis for sophisticated calculations from applied mathematics that have many applications. Our main reason for developing `Complex`—even though `complex` is built-in to Python—is to demonstrate the use of Python's special functions in a simple but authentic setting. In real applications, you certainly should take advantage of `complex` unless you find yourself wanting more operations than Python provides.

To give you a feeling for the nature of calculations involving complex numbers and the utility of the complex number abstraction, we next consider a famous example of a `complex` (or `Complex`) client.

Program 3.2.6 Complex numbers (`complex.py`)

```
import math
import stdio

class Complex:

    def __init__(self, re=0, im=0):
        self._re = re
        self._im = im

    def re(self): return self._re
    def im(self): return self._im

    def __add__(self, other):
        re = self._re + other._re
        im = self._im + other._im
        return Complex(re, im)

    def __mul__(self, other):
        re = self._re * other._re - self._im * other._im
        im = self._re * other._im + self._im * other._re
        return Complex(re, im)

    def __abs__(self):
        return math.sqrt(self._re*self._re + self._im*self._im)

    def __str__(self):
        return str(self._re) + ' + ' + str(self._im) + 'i'

def main():
    z0 = Complex(1.0, 1.0)
    z = z0
    z = z*z + z0
    z = z*z + z0
    stdio.writeln(z)

if __name__ == '__main__': main()
```

instance variables	
`_re`	*real part*
`_im`	*imaginary part*

This data type enables us to compose Python programs that manipulate complex numbers.

```
% python complex.py
-7.0 + 7.0i
```

Mandelbrot set The *Mandelbrot set* is a specific set of complex numbers discovered by Benoît Mandelbrot that has many fascinating properties. It is a fractal pattern that is related to the Barnsley fern, the Sierpinski triangle, the Brownian bridge, the Koch curve, the drunken turtle, and other recursive (self-similar) patterns and programs that we have seen in this book. Patterns of this kind are found in natural phenomena of all sorts, and these models and programs are very important in modern science.

The set of points in the Mandelbrot set cannot be described by a single mathematical equation. Instead, it is defined by an *algorithm* and, therefore, a perfect candidate for a `complex` client: we study the set by composing a program to plot it.

The rule for determining whether a complex number z_0 is in the Mandelbrot set is deceptively simple. Consider the sequence of complex numbers $z_0, z_1, z_2, \ldots, z_t, \ldots$, where $z_{t+1} = (z_t)^2 + z_0$. For example, this table shows the first few entries in the sequence corresponding to $z_0 = 1 + i$:

t	z_t	$(z_t)^2$		$(z_t)^2 + z_0$	
0	$1 + i$	$1 + 2i + i^2 =$	$2i$	$2i + (1 + i) =$	$1 + 3i$
1	$1 + 3i$	$1 + 6i + 9i^2 =$	$-8 + 6i$	$-8 + 6i + (1 + i) =$	$-7 + 7i$
2	$-7 + 7i$	$49 - 98i + 49i^2 =$	$-98i$	$-98i + (1 + i) =$	$1 - 97i$

Mandelbrot sequence computation

Now, if the sequence $|z_t|$ diverges to infinity, then z_0 is *not* in the Mandelbrot set; if the sequence is bounded, then z_0 *is* in the Mandelbrot set. For many points, the test is simple. For many other points, the test requires more computation, as indicated by the examples in this table:

z_0	$0 + 0i$	$2 + 0i$	$1 + i$	$0 + i$	$-0.5 + 0i$	$-0.10 - 0.64i$
z_1	0	6	$1 + 3i$	$-1 + i$	-0.25	$-0.30 - 0.77i$
z_2	0	36	$-7 + 7i$	$-i$	-0.44	$-0.40 - 0.18i$
z_3	0	1446	$1 - 97i$	$-1 + i$	-0.31	$0.23 - 0.50i$
z_4	0	2090918	$-9407 - 193i$	$-i$	-0.40	$-0.09 - 0.87i$
⋮	⋮	⋮	⋮	⋮	⋮	⋮
in set?	*yes*	*no*	*no*	*yes*	*yes*	*yes*

Mandelbrot sequence for several starting points

For brevity, the numbers in the rightmost two columns of this table are given to just two decimal places. In some cases, we can prove whether numbers are in the set; for example, $0 + 0i$ is certainly in the set (since the magnitude of all the numbers in its sequence is 0), and $2 + 0i$ is certainly not in the set (since its sequence dominates the powers of 2, which diverge). In other cases, the growth is readily apparent; for example, $1 + i$ does not seem to be in the set. Other sequences exhibit a periodic behavior; for example, the sequence for $0 + i$ alternates between $-1 + i$ and $-i$. And some sequences go on for a very long time before the magnitude of the numbers begins to get large.

To visualize the Mandelbrot set, we sample *complex* points, just as we sample real-valued points to plot a real-valued function. Each complex number $x + yi$ corresponds to a point (x, y) in the plane, so we can plot the results as follows: for a specified resolution n, we define a regularly spaced n-by-n pixel grid within a specified square and draw a black pixel if the corresponding point is in the Mandelbrot set and a white pixel if it is not. This plot is a strange and wondrous pattern, with all the black dots connected and falling roughly within the 2-by-2 square centered at the point $-1/2 + 0i$. Large values of n produce higher-resolution images, albeit at the cost of more computation. Looking closer reveals self-similarities throughout the plot, as shown in the example at right. For example, the same bulbous pattern with self-similar appendages appears all around the contour of the main black cardioid region, of sizes that resemble the simple ruler function of Program 1.2.1. When we zoom in near the edge of the cardioid, tiny self-similar cardioids appear!

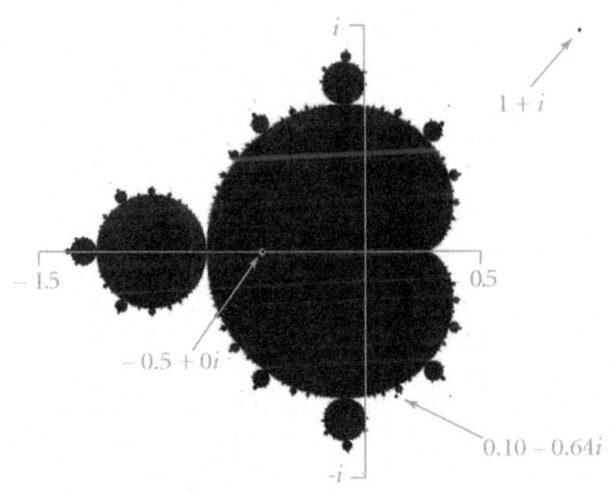

Mandelbrot set

But how, precisely, do we produce such plots? Actually, no one knows for sure, because there is no simple test that enables us to conclude that a point is surely in the set. Given a complex point, we can compute the terms at the beginning of its sequence, but may not be able to know for sure that the sequence remains bounded. There *is* a simple mathematical test that tells us for sure that a point is *not* in the set: if the magnitude of any number in the sequence ever exceeds 2 (such as $1 + 3i$), then the sequence surely will diverge.

PROGRAM 3.2.7 (`mandelbrot.py`) uses this test to plot a visual representation of the Mandelbrot set. Since our knowledge of the set is not quite black-and-white, we use grayscale in our visual representation. The basis of the computation is the function `mandel()`, which takes a complex argument `z0` and an integer argument `limit` and computes the Mandelbrot iteration sequence starting at `z0`, returning the number of iterations for which the magnitude stays less than (or equal to) 2, up to the given limit.

512 .1015 -.633 1.0

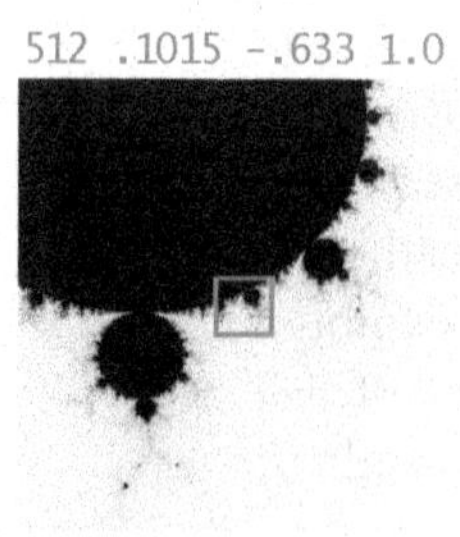

512 .1015 -.633 .10

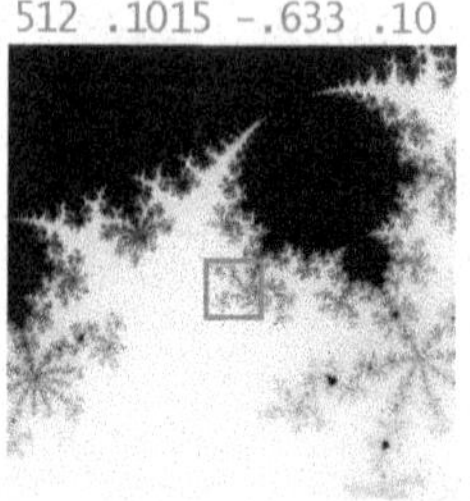

512 .1015 -.633 .01

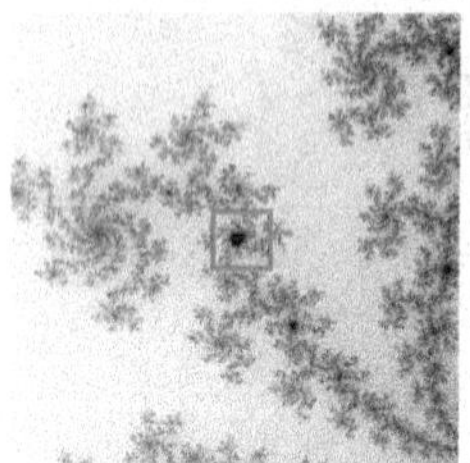

512 .1015 -.633 .001

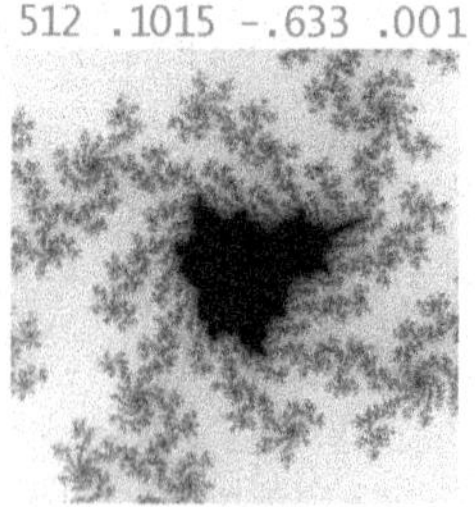

Zooming in on the set

For each pixel, the main script in `mandelbrot.py` computes the point `z0` corresponding to the pixel and then computes `255 - mandel(z0, 255)` to create a grayscale color for the pixel. Any pixel that is not black corresponds to a point that we know to be not in the Mandelbrot set because the magnitude of the numbers in its sequence exceeds 2 (and therefore will go to infinity). The black pixels (grayscale value 0) correspond to points that we assume to be in the set because the magnitude stayed less than (or equal to) 2 for 255 iterations, but we do not necessarily know for sure.

The complexity of the images that this simple program produces is remarkable, even when we zoom in on a tiny portion of the plane. For even more dramatic pictures, we can use color (see EXERCISE 3.2.32). Moreover, the Mandelbrot set is derived from iterating just one function ($z^2 + z_0$); we have a great deal to learn from studying the properties of other functions as well.

The simplicity of the code masks a substantial amount of computation. There are about 250,000 pixels in a 512-by-512 image, and all of the black ones require 255 iterations, so producing an image with `mandelbrot.py` requires hundreds of millions of operations on complex values. Accordingly, we use Python's `complex` data type, which is certain to be more efficient than the `Complex` data type that we just considered (see EXERCISE 3.2.14).

Fascinating as it is to study, our primary interest in the Mandelbrot set is to illustrate that computing with a type of data that is a pure abstraction is a natural and useful programming activity. The client code in `mandelbrot.py` is a simple and natural expression of the computation, made so by the ease of designing, implementing, and using data types in Python.

Program 3.2.7 Mandelbrot set (mandelbrot.py)

```
import sys
import stddraw
from color import Color
from picture import Picture

def mandel(z0, limit):
    z = z0
    for i in range(limit):
        if abs(z) > 2.0: return i
        z = z*z + z0
    return limit

n    = int(sys.argv[1])
xc   = float(sys.argv[2])
yc   = float(sys.argv[3])
size = float(sys.argv[4])

pic = Picture(n, n)
for col in range(n):
    for row in range(n):
        x0 = xc - size/2 + size*col/n
        y0 = yc - size/2 + size*row/n
        z0 = complex(x0, y0)
        gray = 255 - mandel(z0, 255)
        color = Color(gray, gray, gray)
        pic.set(col, n-1-row, color)

stddraw.setCanvasSize(n, n)
stddraw.picture(pic)
stddraw.show()
```

x0, y0	*point in square*
z0	*x0 + y0 i*
limit	*iteration limit*
xc, yc	*center of square*
size	*square is* size*-by-*size
n	*grid is* n*-by-*n *pixels*
pic	*image for output*
color	*pixel color for output*

% python mandelbrot.py 512 -.5 0 2

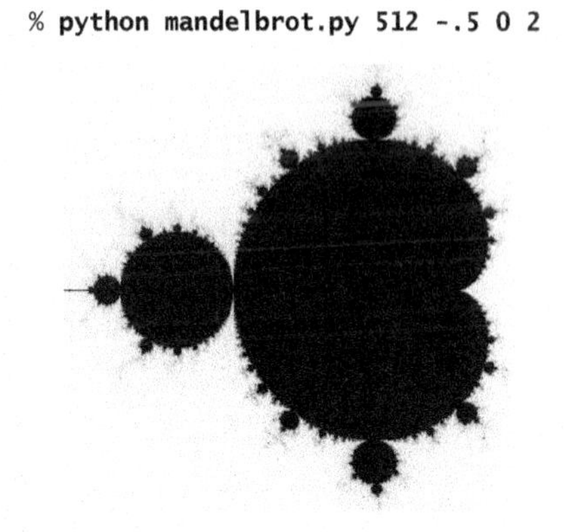

This program takes three command-line arguments that specify the n-by-n grid and the center (xc, yc) and size *of a square region of interest, and makes a digital image showing the result of sampling the Mandelbrot set in that region at a n-by-n grid of equally spaced pixels. It colors each pixel with a grayscale value that is determined by counting the number of iterations before the Mandelbrot sequence for the corresponding complex number exceeds 2.0, up to 255.*

Commercial data processing One of the driving forces behind the development of object-oriented programming has been the need for an extensive amount of reliable software for commercial data processing. As an illustration, we consider next an example of a data type that might be used by a financial institution to keep track of customer information.

Suppose that a stock broker needs to maintain customer accounts containing shares of various stocks. That is, the set of values the broker needs to process includes the customer's name, number of different stocks held, number of shares and ticker symbol for each stock, and cash on hand. To process an account, the broker needs at least the operations defined in this API:

operation	*description*
`StockAccount(filename)`	*a new account, created from data from file* `filename`
`c.valueOf()`	*total value of account* `c`
`c.buy(amount, symbol)`	*add* `amount` *shares of stock* `symbol` *to account* `c` *(and subtract cost from cash in account)*
`c.sell(amount, symbol)`	*subtract* `amount` *shares of stock* `symbol` *from account* `c` *(and add proceeds to cash in account)*
`c.write(filename)`	*write account* `c` *to file* `filename`
`c.writeReport()`	*write to standard output a detailed report for account* `c` *(cash on hand plus all stocks and their values)*

API for a user-defined `Account` *data type*

The broker certainly needs to buy, sell, and provide reports to the customer, but the first key to understanding this kind of data processing is to consider the `StockAccount()` constructor and the `write()` method in this API. The customer information has a long lifetime and needs to be saved in a *file* or *database*. To process an account, a client program needs to read information from the corresponding file; process the information as appropriate; and, if the information changes, write it back to the file, saving it for later. To enable this kind of processing, we need a *file format* and an *internal representation*, or a *data structure*, for the account information. The situation is analogous to what we saw for matrix processing in Chapter 1, where we defined a file format (numbers of rows and columns followed by the elements in row-major order) and an internal representation (Python two-dimensional arrays) to enable us to compose programs for the random surfer and other applications.

As a (whimsical) running example, we imagine that a broker is maintaining a small portfolio of stocks in leading software companies for Alan Turing, the father of computing. *As an aside*: Turing's life story is a fascinating one that is worth investigating further. Among many other things, he worked on computational cryptography that helped to bring about the end of World War II, he developed the basis for modern theoretical computer science, he designed and built one of the first computers, and he was a pioneer in artificial intelligence research. It is perhaps safe to assume that Turing, whatever his financial situation as an academic researcher in the middle of the last century, would be sufficiently optimistic about the potential impact of computing software in today's world that he would make some small investments.

File format. Modern systems often use text files, even for data, to minimize dependence on formats defined by any one program. For simplicity, we use a direct representation where we list the account holder's name (a string), cash balance (a float), and number of stocks held (an integer), followed by a line for each stock giving the number of shares and the ticker symbol, as shown in the example at right. It is also wise to use *tags* such as `<Name>` and `<Number of shares>` and so forth to label all the information, to further minimize dependencies on any one program, but we omit such tags here for brevity.

```
% more turing.txt
Turing, Alan
10.24
4
100 ADBE
 25 GOOG
 97 IBM
250 MSFT
```

Data structure. To represent information for processing by Python programs, we define a data type and use *instance variables* to organize the information. The instance variables specify the type of information and provide the structure that we need to refer to it in code. For example, to implement a `StockAccount`, we use the following instance variables:

- A string for the account name
- A float for the cash on hand
- An integer for the number of stocks
- An array of strings for stock symbols
- An array of integers for numbers of shares

We directly reflect these choices in the instance variable declarations in `StockAccount`, defined in PROGRAM 3.2.8. The arrays `_stocks[]` and `_shares[]` are known as *parallel arrays*. Given an index `i`, `_stocks[i]` gives a stock symbol and `_shares[i]` gives the number of shares of that stock in the account. An alternative design would be to define a separate data type for stocks to manipulate this information for each stock and maintain an array of objects of that type in `StockAccount`.

`StockAccount` includes a constructor, which reads a file and builds an account with this internal representation. It also includes a method `valueOf()`, which uses `stockquote.py` (PROGRAM 3.1.10) to get each stock's price from the web. To provide a periodic detailed report to customers, our broker might use the following code for `writeReport()` in `StockAccount`:

```
def writeReport(self):
    stdio.writeln(self._name)
    total = self._cash
    for i in range(self._n):
        amount = self._shares[i]
        price = stockquote.priceOf(self._stocks[i])
        total += amount * price
        stdio.writef('%4d  %4s ', amount, self._stocks[i])
        stdio.writef('  %7.2f   %9.2f\n', price, amount*price)
    stdio.writef('%21s %10.2f\n', 'Cash:', self._cash)
    stdio.writef('%21s %10.2f\n', 'Total:', total)
```

On the one hand, this client illustrates the kind of computing that was one of the primary drivers in the evolution of computing in the 1950s. Banks and other companies bought early computers precisely because of the need to do such financial reporting. For example, formatted writing was developed precisely for such applications. On the other hand, this client exemplifies modern web-centric computing, as it gets information directly from the web, without using a browser.

The implementations of `buy()` and `sell()` require the use of basic mechanisms introduced in SECTION 4.4, so we defer them to EXERCISE 4.4.39. Beyond these basic methods, an actual application of these ideas would likely use a number of other clients. For example, a broker might want to create an array of all accounts, then process a list of transactions that both modify the information in those accounts and actually carry out the transactions through the web. Of course, such code needs to be developed with great care!

Program 3.2.8 Stock account (`stockaccount.py`)

```
import sys
import stdarray
import stdio
import stockquote
from instream import InStream

class StockAccount:
    def __init__(self, filename):
        instream = InStream(filename)
        self._name = instream.readLine()
        self._cash = instream.readFloat()
        self._n = instream.readInt()
        self._shares = stdarray.create1D(self._n, 0)
        self._stocks = stdarray.create1D(self._n, 0)
        for i in range(self._n):
            self._shares[i] = instream.readInt()
            self._stocks[i] = instream.readString()

    def valueOf(self):
        total = self._cash
        for i in range(self._n):
            price = stockquote.priceOf(self._stocks[i])
            amount = self._shares[i]
            total += amount * price
        return total

def main():
    acct = StockAccount(sys.argv[1])
    acct.writeReport()

if __name__ == '__main__': main()
```

instance variables

`_name`	*customer name*
`_cash`	*cash balance*
`_n`	*number of stocks*
`_shares[]`	*numbers of shares*
`_stocks[]`	*stock symbols*

`instream`	*input stream*

```
% python stockaccount.py turing.txt
Turing, Alan
 100  ADBE      70.56     7056.00
  25  GOOG     502.30    12557.50
  97   IBM     156.54    15184.38
 250  MSFT      45.68    11420.00
                Cash:       10.24
               Total:    46228.12
```

This class for processing accounts illustrates typical usage of object-oriented programming for commercial data processing. See the text for the `writeReport()` *method; see* Exercise *3.2.20 for the* `write()` *method and* Exercise *4.4.39 for the* `buy()` *and* `sell()` *methods.*

When you learned how to define functions that can be used in multiple places in a program (or in other programs) in Chapter 2, you moved from a world where programs are simply sequences of statements in a single file to the world of modular programming, summarized in our mantra: *whenever you can clearly separate tasks within a computation, you should do so.* The analogous capability for data, introduced in this chapter, moves you from a world where data has to be one of a few elementary types of data to a world where you can define your own types of data. This profound new capability vastly extends the scope of your programming. As with the concept of a function, once you have learned to implement and use data types, you will marvel at the primitive nature of programs that do not use them.

But object-oriented programming is much more than structuring data. It enables us to associate the data relevant to a subtask with the operations that manipulate this data and to keep both separate in an independent module. With object-oriented programming, our mantra is this: *whenever you can clearly separate data and associated operations within a computation, you should do so.*

The examples that we have considered are persuasive evidence that object-oriented programming can play a useful role in a broad range of programming activities. Whether we are trying to design and build a physical artifact, develop a software system, understand the natural world, or process information, a key first step is to define an appropriate abstraction, such as a geometric description of the physical artifact, a modular design of the software system, a mathematical model of the natural world, or a data structure for the information. When we want to compose programs to manipulate instances of a well-defined abstraction, we implement the abstraction as a data type in a Python class and compose Python programs to create and manipulate objects of that type.

Each time that we develop a class that makes use of other classes by creating and manipulating objects of the type defined by the class, we are programming at a higher layer of abstraction. In the next section, we discuss some of the design challenges inherent in this kind of programming.

Q&A

Q. Can I define a class in a file whose name is unrelated to the class name? Can I define more than one class in a single `.py` file?

A. Yes and yes, but we do not do so in this chapter as a matter of style. In CHAPTER 4, we will encounter a few situations where these features are appropriate.

Q. If `__init__()` is technically not a constructor, what is?

A. Another special function, `__new__()`. To create a object, Python first calls `__new__()` and then `__init__()`. For the programs in this book, the default implementation of `__new__()` serves our purposes, so we do not discuss it.

Q. Must every class have a constructor?

A. Yes, but if you do not define a constructor, Python provides a default (no-argument) constructor automatically. With our conventions, such a data type would be useless, as it would have no instance variables.

Q. Why do I need to use `self` explicitly when referring to instance variables?

A. Syntactically, Python needs some way to know whether you are assigning to a local variable or to an instance variable. In many other programming languages (such as C++ and Java), you *declare* explicitly the data type's instance variables, so there is no ambiguity. The `self` variable also makes it easy for programmers to know whether code is referring to a local variable or an instance variable.

Q. Suppose I do not include a `__str__()` method in my data type. What happens if I call `str()` or `stdio.writeln()` with an object of that type?

A. Python provides a default implementation that returns a string containing the object's type and its identity (memory address). This is unlikely to be of much use, so you usually want to define your own.

Q. Are there other kinds of variables besides parameter, local, and instance variables in a class?

A. Yes. Recall from CHAPTER 1 that you can define *global variables* in global code, outside of the definition of any function, class, or method. The scope of global variables is the entire .py file. In modern programming, we focus on limiting scope and therefore rarely use global variables (except in tiny scripts not intended for reuse). Python also supports *class variables*, which are defined inside a class but outside any method. Each class variable is shared among all of the objects in a class; this contrasts with instance variables, where there is one per object. Class variables have some specialized uses, but we do not use them in this book.

Q. Is it just me, or are Python's conventions for naming things complicated?

A. Yes, but this is also true of many other programming languages. Here is a quick summary of the naming conventions we have encountered in the book:

- A variable name starts with lowercase letter.
- A constant variable name starts with an uppercase letter.
- An instance variable name starts with an underscore and a lowercase letter.
- A method name starts with a lowercase letter.
- A special method name starts with a double underscore and a lowercase letter and ends with a double underscore.
- A user-defined class name starts with an uppercase letter.
- A built-in class name starts with a lowercase letter.
- A script or module is stored in a file whose name consists of lowercase letters and ends with `.py`.

Most of those conventions are *not* part of the language, though many Python programmers treat them as if they are. You might wonder: If they are so important, why not make them part of the language? Good question. Still, some programmers are passionate about such conventions, and you are likely to someday encounter a teacher, supervisor, or colleague who insists that you follow a certain style, so you may as well go with the flow. Indeed, many Python programmers separate multi-word variable names with underscores instead of capital letters, preferring `is_prime` and `hurst_exponent` to `isPrime` and `hurstExponent`.

Q. How can I specify a literal for the `complex` data type?

A. Appending the character `j` to a numeric literal produces an imaginary number (whose real part is zero). You can add this character to a numeric literal to produce a complex number, as in `3 + 7j`. The choice of `j` instead of `i` is common in some engineering disciplines. Note that `j` is *not* a `complex` literal—instead, you must use `1j`.

Q. You said that `mandelbrot.py` creates hundreds of millions of `complex` objects. Doesn't all that object-creation overhead slow things down?

A. Yes, but not so much that we cannot generate our plots. Our goal is to make our programs readable and easy to compose and maintain. Limiting scope via the complex number abstraction helps us achieve that goal. If you need to speed up `mandelbrot.py` significantly for some reason, you might consider bypassing the complex number abstraction and using a lower-level language where numbers are not objects. Generally, Python is not optimized for performance. We will revisit this issue in Chapter 4.

Q. Why is it okay for the `__add__(self, other)` method in `complex.py` (Program 3.2.6) to refer to the instance variables of the parameter variable `other`? Aren't these instance variables supposed to be private?

A. Python programmers view privacy as relative to a particular class, not to a particular object. So, a method can refer to the instance variables of any object in the same class. Python has no "superprivate" naming conventions in which you can refer only to the instance variables of the invoking object. Accessing the instance variables of `other` can be a bit risky, however, because a careless client might pass an argument that is not of type `Complex`, in which case we would be (unknowingly) accessing an instance variable in another class! With a mutable type, we might even (unknowingly) modify or create instance variables in another class!

Q. If methods are really functions, can I call a method using function-call syntax?

A. Yes, you can call a function defined in a class as either a method or an ordinary function. For example, if `c` is an object of type `Charge`, then the function call `Charge.potentialAt(c, x, y)` is equivalent to the method call `c.potentialAt(x, y)`. In object-oriented programming, we prefer the method-call syntax to highlight the role of the featured object and to avoid hardwiring the name of the class into the function call.

Exercises

3.2.1 Consider the following data-type implementation for (axis-aligned) rectangles, which represents each rectangle with the coordinates of its center point and its width and height:

```
class Rectangle:
    # Create rectangle with center (x, y),
    # width w, and height h.

    def __init__(self, x, y, w, h):
        self._x = x
        self._y = y
        self._width  = w
        self._height = h

    # The area of self.
    def area(self):
        return self._width * self._height

    # The perimeter of self.
    def perimeter(self):
        ...

    # True if self intersects other; False otherwise.
    def intersects(self, other):
        ...

    # True if self contains other; False otherwise.
    def contains(self, other):
        ...

    # Draw self on stddraw.
    def draw(self):
        ...
```


Compose an API for this data type, and complete its implementation as a class by filling in the code for `perimeter()`, `intersects()`, `contains()`, and `draw()`. *Note*: Treat coincident lines as intersecting, so that, for example, `a.intersects(a)` is `True` and `a.contains(a)` is `True`.

3.2.2 Compose a test client for `Rectangle` that takes three command-line arguments `n`, `lo`, and `hi`; generates `n` random rectangles whose width and height are uniformly distributed between `lo` and `hi` in the unit square; draws those rectangles to standard drawing; and writes their average area and average perimeter to standard output.

3.2.3 Add to your test client from the previous exercise code to compute the average number of pairs of rectangles that intersect and are contained in one another.

3.2.4 Develop an implementation of your `Rectangle` API from the previous exercises that represents rectangles with the coordinates of their lower-left and upper-right corners. Do *not* change the API.

3.2.5 What is wrong with the following code?

```
class Charge:
    def __init__(self, x0, y0, q0):
        _rx = x0
        _ry = y0
        _q = q0
...
```

Solution: The assignment statements in the constructor create *local* variables `_rx`, `_ry`, and `_q`, which are assigned values from the parameter variables but are never used. They disappear when the constructor is finished executing. Instead, the constructor should create instance variables by prefixing each variable with `self` followed by the dot operator and an underscore, like this:

```
class Charge:
    def __init__(self, x0, y0, q0):
        self._rx = x0
        self._ry = y0
        self._q = q0
...
```

The underscore is not strictly required in Python, but we follow this standard Python convention throughout this book to indicate that our intent is for instance variables to be private.

3.2.6 Create a data type `Location` that represents a location on Earth using latitudes and longitudes. Include a method `distanceTo()` that computes distances using the great-circle distance (see 1.2.30).

3.2.7 Python provides a data type `Fraction`, defined in the standard module `fraction.py`, that implements rational numbers. Implement your own version of that data type. Specifically, develop an implementation of the following API for a data type for rational numbers:

client operation	*special method*	*description*
`Rational(x, y)`	`__init__(self)`	*a new* `Rational` *object with value* `x/y`
`a + b`	`__add__(self, b)`	*sum of* `a` *and* `b`
`a - b`	`__sub__(self, b)`	*difference of* `a` *and* `b`
`a * b`	`__mul__(self, b)`	*product of* `a` *and* `b`
`abs(a)`	`__abs__(self)`	*magnitude of* `a`
`str(a)`	`__str__(self)`	`'x/y'` *(string representation of* `a`*)*

API for a user-defined `Rational` *data type*

Use `euclid.gcd()` (Program 2.3.1) to ensure that the numerator and the denominator never have any common factors. Include a test client that exercises all of your methods.

3.2.8 An *interval* is defined to be the set of all points on a line greater than or equal to `left` and less than or equal to `right`. In particular, an interval with `right` less than `left` is empty. Compose a data type `Interval` that implements the API at the top of the next page. Include a test client that is a filter and takes a float `x` from the command line and writes to standard output (1) all of the intervals from standard input (each defined by a pair of floats) that contain `x` and (2) all pairs of intervals from standard input that intersect one another.

client operation	description
`Interval(left, right)`	*a new* `Interval` *object with endpoints* `left` *and* `right`
`a.contains(b)`	*does interval* `a` *contain interval* `b`*?*
`a.intersects(b)`	*does interval* `a` *intersect interval* `b`*?*
`str(a)`	`'[left, right]'` *(string representation of* `a`*)*

API for a user-defined `Interval` *data type*

3.2.9 Develop an implementation of your `Rectangle` API from Exercise 3.2.1 that takes advantage of `Interval` to simplify and clarify the code.

3.2.10 Compose a data type `Point` that implements the following API. Include a test client of your own design.

client operation	description
`Point(x, y)`	*a new* `Point` *object with value* `(x, y)`
`a.distanceTo(b)`	*Euclidean distance between* `a` *and* `b`
`str(a)`	`'(x, y)'` *(string representation of* `a`*)*

API for a user-defined `Point` *data type*

3.2.11 Add methods to `Stopwatch` that allow clients to stop and restart the stopwatch.

3.2.12 Use a `Stopwatch` to compare the cost of computing harmonic numbers with a `for` loop (see Program 1.3.5) as opposed to using the recursive method given in Section 2.3.

3.2.13 Modify the test client in `turtle.py` to produce stars with `n` points for odd `n`.

3.2.14 Compose a version of `mandelbrot.py` that uses `Complex` instead of Python's `complex`, as described in the text. Then use `Stopwatch` compute the ratio of the running times of the two programs.

3.2.15 Modify the `__str__()` method in `complex.py` so that it writes complex numbers in the traditional format. For example, it should write the value $3 - i$ as `3 - i` instead of `3.0 + -1.0i`, the value 3 as `3` instead of `3.0 + 0.0i`, and the value $3i$ as `3i` instead of `0.0 + 3.0i`.

3.2.16 Compose a `complex` client that takes three floats a, b, and c as command-line arguments and writes the complex roots of $ax^2 + bx + c$.

3.2.17 Compose a `complex` client `Roots` that takes two floats a and b and an integer n from the command line and writes the nth roots of $a + bi$. *Note*: Skip this exercise if you are not familiar with the operation of taking roots of complex numbers.

3.2.18 Implement the following additions to the `Complex` API:

client operation	*special method*	*description*
`a.theta()`		*polar angle (phase) of* `a`
`a.conjugate()`		*complex conjugate of* `a`
`a - b`	`__sub__(self, b)`	*difference of* `a` *and* `b`
`a / b`	`__truediv__(self, b)`	*quotient of* `a` *and* `b`
`a ** b`	`__pow__(self, b)`	`a` *to the* `b`*th power*

API for `Complex` *(continued)*

Include a test client that exercises all of your methods.

3.2.19 Find a `complex` number for which `mandel()` returns an iteration count greater than 100, and then zoom in on that number, as in the examples in the text.

3.2.20 Implement the method `write()` in `stockaccount.py`, which takes a file name as an argument and writes the contents of the account to the file, using the file format specified in the text.

Creative Exercises

3.2.21 *Mutable charges.* Modify `Charge` so that the charge value `q0` can change, by adding a method `increaseCharge()` that takes a float argument and adds the given value to `q0`. Then, compose a client that initializes an array with

```
a = stdarray.create1D(3)
a[0] = charge.Charge(.4, .6, 50)
a[1] = charge.Charge(.5, .5, -5)
a[2] = charge.Charge(.6, .6, 50)
```

and then displays the result of slowly decreasing the charge value of `a[1]` by wrapping the code that computes the picture in a loop like the following:

```
for t in range(100):
    # Compute the picture p.
    stddraw.clear()
    stddraw.picture(p)
    stddraw.show(0)
    a[1].increaseCharge(-2.0)
```

-5

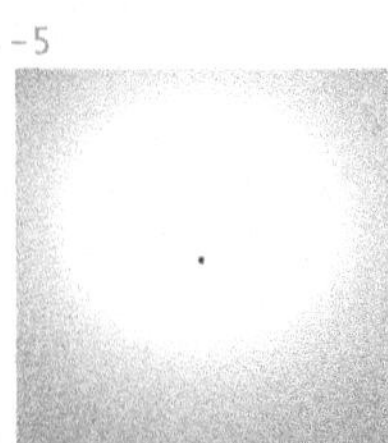

-55

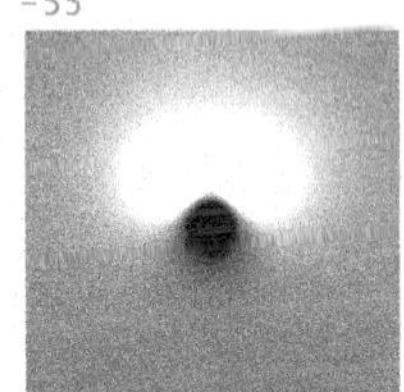

-105

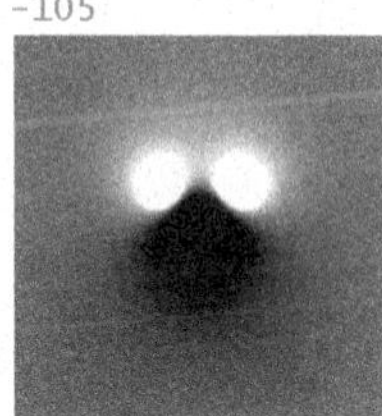

-155

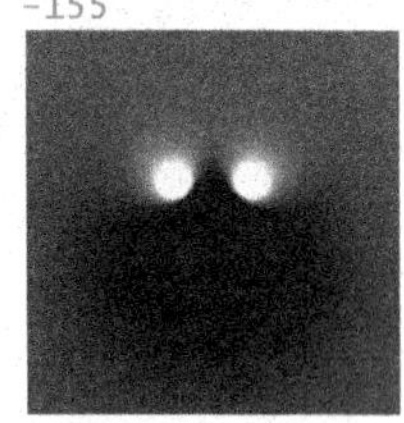

-205

Mutating a charge

3.2.22 *Complex timing.* Write a `Stopwatch` client that compares the cost of using `complex` to the cost of composing code that directly manipulates two floats, for the task of doing the calculations in `mandelbrot.py`. Specifically, create a version of `mandelbrot.py` that just does the calculations (remove the code that refers to `Picture`), then create a version of that program that does not use `complex`, and then compute the ratio of the running times.

3.2.23 *Quaternions.* In 1843, Sir William Hamilton discovered an extension to complex numbers called quaternions. A quaternion is a vector $a = (a_0, a_1, a_2, a_3)$ with the following operations:

- *Magnitude:* $|a| = \sqrt{a_0^2 + a_1^2 + a_2^2 + a_3^2}$
- *Conjugate:* the conjugate of a is $(a_0, -a_1, -a_2, -a_3)$
- *Inverse:* $a^{-1} = (a_0/|a|^2, -a_1/|a|^2, -a_2/|a|^2, -a_3/|a|^2)$

- *Sum:* $a + b = (a_0 + b_0, a_1 + b_1, a_2 + b_2, a_3 + b_3)$
- *Product:* $a * b = (a_0 b_0 - a_1 b_1 - a_2 b_2 - a_3 b_3, a_0 b_1 - a_1 b_0 + a_2 b_3 - a_3 b_2,$
  $a_0 b_2 - a_1 b_3 + a_2 b_0 + a_3 b_1, a_0 b_3 + a_1 b_2 - a_2 b_1 + a_3 b_0)$
- *Quotient:* $a / b = ab^{-1}$

Create a data type for quaternions and a test client that exercises all of your code. Quaternions extend the concept of rotation in three dimensions to four dimensions. They are used in computer graphics, control theory, signal processing, and orbital mechanics.

3.2.24 *Dragon curves.* Write a recursive `Turtle` client `Dragon` that draws dragon curves (see Exercises 1.2.32 and 1.5.9).

Solution: These curves, which were originally discovered by three NASA physicists, were popularized in the 1960s by Martin Gardner and later used by Michael Crichton in the book and movie *Jurassic Park.* This exercise can be solved with remarkably compact code, based on a pair of mutually interacting recursive functions derived directly from the definition in Exercise 1.2.32. One of them, `dragon()`, should draw the curve as you expect; the other, `nogard()`, should draw the curve in *reverse* order. See the booksite for details.

```
% python dragon.py 15
```

3.2.25 *Hilbert curves.* A *space-filling curve* is a continuous curve in the unit square that passes through every point. Write a recursive `Turtle` client that produces these recursive patterns, which approach a space-filling curve that was defined by the mathematician David Hilbert at the end of the 19th century.

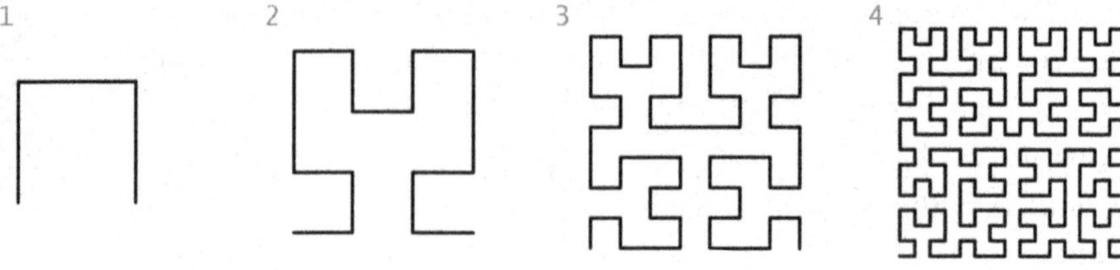

Partial solution: See the previous exercise. You need a pair of methods: `hilbert()`, which traverses a Hilbert curve, and `treblih()`, which traverses a Hilbert curve *in reverse order*. See the booksite for details.

3.2.26 *Gosper island.* Compose a recursive `Turtle` client that produces these recursive patterns.

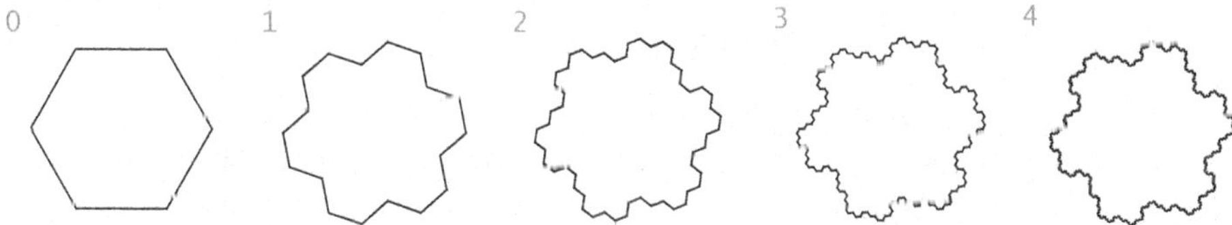

3.2.27 *Data analysis.* Compose a data type for use in running experiments where the control variable is an integer in the range [0, n) and the dependent variable is a float. For example, studying the running time of a program that takes an integer argument would involve such experiments. A *Tukey plot* is a way to visualize the statistics of such data (see EXERCISE 2.2.17). Implement the API shown below.

You can use the functions in `stdstats` to do the statistical calculations and draw the plots. Use `stddraw` so clients can use different colors for `plot()` and `plotTukey()` (for example, light gray for all the points and black for the Tukey plot). Compose a test client that plots the results (percolation probability) of running experiments with percolation (see SECTION 2.4) as the grid size increases.

client operation	*description*
`Data(n)`	*a new* `Data` *object for the* `n` *integer values in* `[0, n)`
`d.addDataPoint(i, x)`	*add to* `d` *a data point with abscissa* `i` *and ordinate* `x`
`d.plot()`	*plot* `d` *in the standard drawing window*
`d.plotTukey()`	*display a Tukey plot of* `d` *in the standard drawing window*

API for a user-defined `Data` *data type*

3.2.28 *Elements.* Compose a data type `Element` for entries in the periodic table of elements. Include data-type values for the element, atomic number, symbol, and atomic weight and accessor methods for each of these values. Then, compose a data type `PeriodicTable` that reads values from a file to create an array of `Element` objects (you can find the file and a description of its format on the booksite) and responds to queries from standard input so that a user can type a molecular formula like `H2O` and have the program respond by writing the molecular weight. Develop APIs and implementations for each data type.

3.2.29 *Stock prices.* The file `DJIA.csv` on the booksite contains all closing stock prices in the history of the Dow Jones Industrial Average, using the comma-separated-value format. Compose a data type `Entry` that can hold one entry in the table, with values for the date, opening price, daily high, daily low, closing price, and so forth. Then, compose a data type `Table` that reads the file to build an array of `Entry` objects and supports methods for computing averages over various periods of time. Finally, create interesting `Table` clients to produce plots of the data. Be creative: this path is well trodden.

3.2.30 *Chaos with Newton's method.* The polynomial $f(z) = z^4 - 1$ has four roots: at 1, -1, i, and $-i$. We can find the roots using Newton's method in the complex plane: $z_{k+1} = z_k - f(z_k) \,/\, f'(z_k)$. Here, $f(z) = z^4 - 1$ and $f'(z) = 4z^3$. The method converges to one of the four roots, depending on the starting point z_0. Compose a `Complex` client `Newton` that takes a command-line argument n and colors pixels in an n-by-n `Picture` white, red, green, or blue by mapping the pixel's complex points in a regularly spaced grid in the square of size 2 centered at the origin and by coloring each pixel according to which of the four roots the corresponding point converges on (black if no convergence occurs after 100 iterations).

3.2.31 *Equipotential surfaces.* An equipotential surface is the set of all points that have the same electric potential V. Given a group of point charges, it is useful to visualize the electric potential by plotting equipotential surfaces (also known as a *contour plot*). Compose a program `equipotential.py` that draws a line every $5V$ by computing the potential at each pixel and checking whether the potential at the corresponding point is within 1 pixel of a multiple of $5V$. *Note*: A *very easy* approximate solution to this exercise is obtained from PROGRAM 3.1.8 by scrambling the color values assigned to each pixel, rather than having them be proportional to the grayscale value. For example, the figure at left is created by inserting the code above it before creating the `Color`. Explain why it works, and experiment with your own version.

```
if (g != 255): g = g * 17 % 256
```

3.2.32 *Color Mandelbrot plot.* Create a file of 256 integer triples that represent interesting `Color` values, and then use those colors instead of grayscale values to plot each pixel in `mandelbrot.py`. Read the values to create an array of 256 `Color` values, then index into that array with the return value of `mandel()`. By experimenting with various color choices at various places in the set, you can produce astonishing images. See `mandel.txt` on the booksite for an example.

3.2.33 *Julia sets.* The *Julia set* for a given complex number c is a set of points related to the Mandelbrot function. Instead of fixing z and varying c, we fix c and vary z. Those points z for which the modified Mandelbrot function stays bounded are in the *Julia set*; those for which the sequence diverges to infinity are not in the set. All points z of interest lie in the 4-by-4 box centered at the origin. The Julia set for c is connected if and only if c is in the Mandelbrot set! Compose a program `colorjulia.py` that takes two command-line arguments a and b, and plots a color version of the Julia set for $c = a + bi$, using the color-table method described in the previous exercise.

3.2.34 *Biggest winner and biggest loser.* Compose a `StockAccount` client that builds an array of `StockAccount` objects, computes the total value of each account, and writes a report for the account with the largest value and the account with the smallest value. Assume that the data in the accounts are kept in a single file that contains the information for each of the accounts, one after the other, in the format given in the text.

3.3 Designing Data Types

THE ABILITY TO CREATE DATA TYPES turns every programmer into a language designer. We do not have to settle for the data types and associated operations that are built into the language, because we can easily create our own data types data and then compose client programs that use them. For example, Python does not have a built-in facility for charged particles, but we can define a `Charge` data type and compose client programs that take immediate advantage of this abstraction. Even when Python does have a particular facility, we can use a data type to tailor it to our needs, as we do when we use our booksite modules instead of the more extensive ones provided by Python for software developers.

Programs in this section

At this point, the first thing that we strive for when composing a program is an understanding of the data types that we will need. Developing this understanding is a *design* activity. In this section, we focus on developing APIs as a critical step in the development of any program. We need to consider various alternatives, understand their impact on both client programs and implementations, and refine the design to strike an appropriate balance between the needs of clients and the possible implementation strategies.

If you take a course in systems programming, you will learn that this design activity is critical when building large systems, and that Python and similar languages have powerful high-level mechanisms that support code reuse when composing large programs. Many of these mechanisms are intended for use by experts building large systems, but the general approach is worthwhile for every programmer, and some of these mechanisms are useful when composing small programs.

In this section we discuss encapsulation, immutability, and inheritance, with particular attention to the use of these ideas in data-type design to enable modular programming, facilitate debugging, and compose clear and correct code.

At the end of the section, we discuss Python's mechanisms for use in checking design assumptions against actual conditions at run time. Such tools are invaluable aids in developing reliable software.

Designing APIs In Section 3.1, we composed client programs that *use* APIs; in Section 3.2, we *implemented* APIs. Now we consider the challenge of *designing* APIs. Treating these topics in this order and with this focus is appropriate because most of the time that you spend programming will be composing client programs. The main purpose of designing a good API is to streamline and simplify client code.

Often the most important and most challenging step in building software is designing the APIs. This task takes practice, careful deliberation, and many iterations. However, any time spent designing a good API is certain to be repaid in time saved during debugging or with code reuse.

Articulating an API might seem to be overkill when composing a small program, but you should consider composing every program as though you will need to reuse the code someday—not because you know that you will reuse that code, but because you are quite likely to want to reuse some of your code and you cannot know which code you will need.

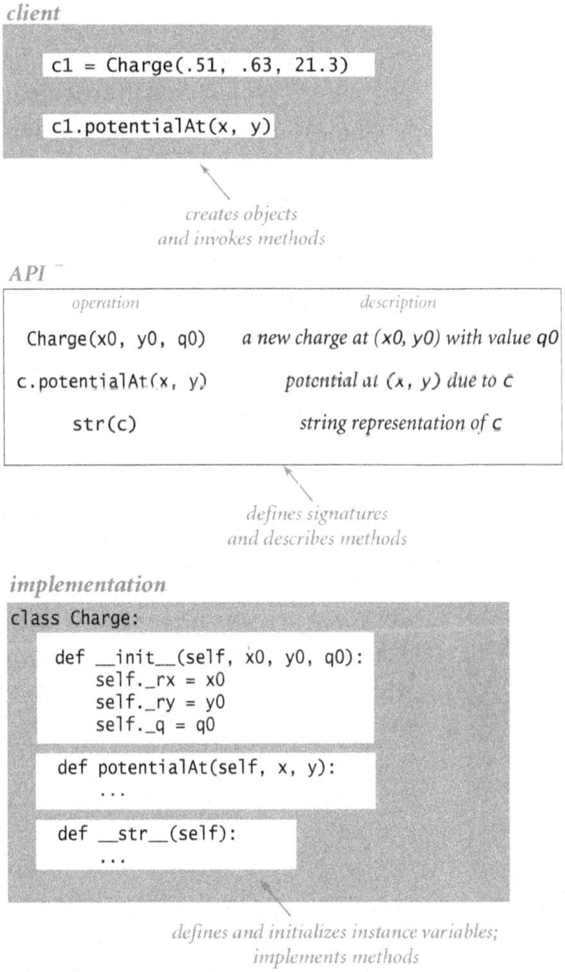

client

```
c1 = Charge(.51, .63, 21.3)

c1.potentialAt(x, y)
```

creates objects and invokes methods

API

operation	*description*
`Charge(x0, y0, q0)`	*a new charge at (x0, y0) with value q0*
`c.potentialAt(x, y)`	*potential at* `(x, y)` *due to* `c`
`str(c)`	*string representation of* `c`

defines signatures and describes methods

implementation

```
class Charge:

    def __init__(self, x0, y0, q0):
        self._rx = x0
        self._ry = y0
        self._q = q0

    def potentialAt(self, x, y):
        ...

    def __str__(self):
        ...
```

defines and initializes instance variables; implements methods

Object-oriented data-type abstraction

Standards. It is easy to understand why conforming to an API is so important by considering other domains. From railroad tracks, to threaded nuts and bolts, to MP3s and DVDs, to radio frequencies, to Internet standards, we know that using a common standard interface enables the broadest usage of a technology. Python itself is another example: your Python programs are clients of the *Python virtual machine*, which is a standard interface that is implemented on a wide variety of hardware and software platforms. By using APIs to separate clients from implementations, we reap the benefits of standard interfaces for every program that we compose.

Specification problem. Our APIs for data types are sets of methods, along with brief English-language descriptions of what the methods are supposed to do. Ideally, an API would clearly articulate behavior for all possible arguments, including side effects, and then we would have software to check that implementations meet the specification. Unfortunately, a fundamental result from theoretical computer science, known as the *specification problem*, says that this goal is actually *impossible* to achieve. Briefly, such a specification would have to be written in a formal language like a programming language, and the problem of determining whether two programs perform the same computation is known, mathematically, to be *unsolvable.* (If you are interested in this idea, you can learn much more about the nature of unsolvable problems and their role in our understanding of the nature of computation in a course in theoretical computer science.) Therefore, we resort to informal descriptions with examples, such as those in the text surrounding our APIs.

Wide interfaces. A *wide interface* is one that has an excessive number of methods. An important principle to follow in designing an API is to *avoid wide interfaces.* The size of an API naturally tends to grow over time because it is easy to add methods to an existing API, whereas it is difficult to remove methods without breaking existing clients. In certain situations, wide interfaces are justified—for example, in widely used built-in types such as `str`. Various techniques are helpful in reducing the effective width of an interface. For example, one approach is to include only methods that are orthogonal in functionality—Python's `math` module includes methods for `sin()`, `cos()`, and `tan()`, but not `sec()`.

Start with client code. One of the primary purposes of developing a data type is to simplify client code. Therefore, it makes sense to pay attention to client code from the start when designing an API. Very often, doing so is no problem at all, because a typical reason to develop a data type in the first place is to simplify client code that is becoming cumbersome. When you find yourself with some client code that you are not proud of, one way to proceed is to compose a fanciful simplified version of the code that expresses the computation in the way that you are thinking about it, at some higher level that does not involve the details of the code. Or, if you have done a good job of composing succinct comments to describe your computation, one possible starting point is to think about opportunities to convert the comments into code.

Remember the basic mantra for data types: *whenever you can clearly separate data and associated operations within a computation, you should do so.* Whatever the source, it is normally wise to compose client code (and develop the API) *before* working on an implementation. Composing two clients is even better. Starting with client code is one way of ensuring that developing an implementation will be worth the effort.

Avoid dependence on representation. Usually when developing an API, we have a representation in mind. After all, a data type is a set of values and a set of operations defined on those values, and it does not make much sense to talk about the operations without knowing the values. But that is different from knowing the *representation* of the values. One purpose of the data type is to simplify client code by allowing it to avoid details of and dependence on a particular representation. For example, our client programs for `Picture` and `stdaudio` work with simple abstract representations of pictures and sound, respectively. The primary value of the APIs for these abstraction is that they allow client code to ignore a substantial amount of detail that is found in the standard representations of those abstractions.

Pitfalls in API design. An API may be *too hard to implement*, implying implementations that are difficult or impossible to develop, or *too hard to use*, creating client code that is more complicated than without the API. An API might be *too narrow*, omitting methods that clients need, or *too wide*, including a large number of methods not needed by any client. An API may be *too general*, providing no useful abstractions, or *too specific*, providing abstractions so detailed or so diffuse as to be useless. These considerations are sometimes summarized in yet another motto: *provide to clients the methods they need and no others.*

WHEN YOU FIRST STARTED PROGRAMMING, YOU typed in `helloworld.py` without understanding much about it except the effect that it produced. From that starting point, you learned to program by mimicking the code in the book and eventually developing your own code to solve various problems. You are at a similar point with API design. There are many APIs available in the book, on the booksite, and in online Python documentation that you can study and use, to gain confidence in designing and developing APIs of your own.

Encapsulation The process of separating clients from implementations by hiding information is known as *encapsulation*. Details of the implementation are kept hidden from clients, and implementations have no way of knowing details of client code, which may even be created in the future.

As you may have surmised, we have been practicing encapsulation in our data-type implementations. In Section 3.1, we started with the mantra *you do not need to know how a data type is implemented to use it*. This statement describes one of the prime benefits of encapsulation. We consider it to be so important that we have not described to you any other way of designing a data type. Now, we discuss in more detail our three primary reasons for doing so. We use encapsulation:

- To enable modular programming
- To facilitate debugging
- To clarify program code

These reasons are tied together (well-designed modular code is easier to debug and understand than code based entirely on built-in types).

Modular programming. The modular programming style that we have been developing since learning functions in Chapter 2 has been predicated on the idea of breaking large programs into small modules that can be developed and debugged independently. This approach improves the resiliency of our software by limiting and localizing the effects of making changes, and it promotes code reuse by making it possible to substitute new implementations of a data type to improve performance, accuracy, or memory footprint. The key to success in modular programming is to maintain *independence* among modules. We do so by insisting on the API being the *only* point of dependence between client and implementation—data-type implementation code can assume that the client knows nothing *but* the API.

Changing an API. We often reap the benefits of encapsulation when we use standard modules. New versions of Python often, for example, may include new implementations of various data types or modules that define functions. There is a strong and constant motivation to improve data-type *implementations* because *all* clients can potentially benefit from an improved implementation. However, *Python APIs rarely change.* When changes do occur, they are costly throughout the Python community—everyone has to update their clients. As an extreme example, consider the change in the meaning of the / operator for integer operands from Python 2 to Python 3 (see page 27). Whatever the benefits of this change, it amounts to a change in the API for the `int` data type (changing the behavior of the / operator), *requiring all programs that use the / operator with integers to be checked and debugged!* Some people have estimated that this change might delay the widespread adoption of Python 3 for up to a decade. This situation calls for another mantra: once a significant number of clients are using a module, *do not change the API.*

Changing an implementation. Consider the class `Complex`, defined in PROGRAM 3.3.1 (`complexpolar.py`). It has the same name and API as the class `Complex` from PROGRAM 3.2.6, but uses a different representation for the complex numbers. The `Complex` class defined in `complex.py` uses the Cartesian representation, where instance variables `_re` and `_im` represent a complex number as $x + yi$. The `Complex` class defined in `complexpolar.py` uses the *polar representation*, where instance variables `_r` and `_theta` represent complex numbers as $r(\cos\theta + i\sin\theta)$. In this representation, we refer to r as the *magnitude* and θ as the *polar angle*. The polar representation is of interest because certain operations on complex numbers are easier to perform in the polar representation. Addition and subtraction are easier in the Cartesian representation; multiplication and division are easier in the polar representation. As you will learn in SECTION 4.1, it is often the case that performance differences for different approaches are dramatic. The idea of encapsulation is that we can substitute one of these programs for the other (for whatever reason) *without changing client code*, except to change the `import` statement to use `complexpolar` instead of `complex`. The choice between the two implementations depends on the client. Indeed, in principle, the *only* difference to the client should be in different performance properties. This capability is of critical importance for many reasons. One of the most important is that it allows us to improve software constantly: when we develop a better way to implement a data type, all of its clients can benefit. You take advantage of this property every time you install a new version of a software system, including Python itself.

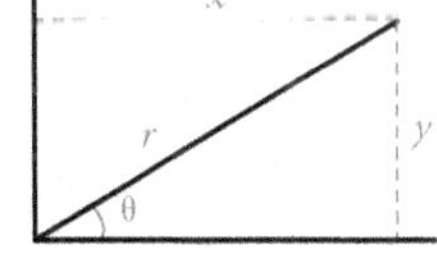

Polar representation

Private. Many programming languages provide support for enforcing encapsulation. For example, Java provides the `private` visibility modifier. When you declare an instance variable (or method) to be `private`, you are making it impossible for any client (code in another module) to directly access the instance variable (or method) that is the subject of the modifier. As a result, clients can use the class only through its public methods and constructors—that is, through its API.

Program 3.3.1 Complex numbers (`complexpolar.py`)

```
import math
import stdio

class Complex:
    def __init__(self, re=0, im=0):
        self._r     = math.hypot(im, re)
        self._theta = math.atan2(im, re)

    def re(self): return self._r * math.cos(self._theta)
    def im(self): return self._r * math.sin(self._theta)

    def __add__(self, other):
        re = self.re() + other.re()
        im = self.im() + other.im()
        return Complex(re, im)

    def __mul__(self, other):
        c = Complex()
        c._r = self._r * other._r
        c._theta = self._theta + other._theta
        return c

    def __abs__(self): return self.r

    def __str__(self):
        return str(self.re()) + ' + ' + str(self.im()) + 'i'

def main():
    z0 = Complex(1.0, 1.0)
    z = z0
    z = z*z + z0
    z = z*z + z0
    stdio.writeln(z)

if __name__ == '__main__': main()
```

instance variables

`_r`	*magnitude*
`_theta`	*polar angle*

This data type implements the same API as Program 3.2.6. *It uses the same methods but different instance variables. Since the instance variables are private, this program might be used in place of* Program 3.2.6 *without changing any client code (except for the* `import` *statement).*

```
% python complexpolar.py
-7.000000000000002 + 7.000000000000003i
```

Python does not offer a private visibility modifier, which means that clients can directly access all instance variables, methods, and functions. However the Python programming community espouses a pertinent convention: if an instance variable, method, or function has a name that begins with an underscore, then clients should consider that instance variable, method, or function to be private. Through this naming convention, clients are informed that they should not directly access the instance variable, method, or function thus named.

Programmers who conform to the underscore convention can modify the implementation of private functions or methods (or use different private instance variables) and know that no client that also conforms to the convention will be directly affected. For example, in the `Complex` class defined in `complex.py` (Program 3.2.6), if the instance variables `_re` and `_im` (note the leading underscores indicating that the variables are private) were instead named `re` and `im` (note the absence of leading underscores indicating that the variables are public), then a client might compose code that directly accesses them. If `z` is a variable that refers to a `Complex` object, then the client can use `z.re` and `z.im` to refer to its instance variables. But any client code that does so becomes dependent on that particular implementation of the API, violating a basic precept of encapsulation. A switch to a different implementation, such as the one in Program 3.3.1, could render that client useless.

To protect ourselves against such situations, in this book, we go one step further and always make *all* instance variables private in our classes. We strongly recommend that you do the same—there is no good reason to access an instance variable directly from a client. Next, we examine some ramifications of this convention.

Planning for the future. There are numerous examples where significant expense can be traced directly to programmers not encapsulating their data types.

- *Y2K problem.* In the last millennium, many programs represented the year using only two decimal digits to save storage. Such programs could not distinguish between the year 1900 and the year 2000. As January 1, 2000, approached, programmers raced to fix such rollover errors and avert the catastrophic failures that were predicted by many technologists.
- *ZIP codes.* In 1963, The United States Postal Service (USPS) began using a five-digit ZIP code to improve the sorting and delivery of mail. Programmers wrote software assuming that these codes would remain at five digits forever. In 1983, the USPS introduced an expanded ZIP code called ZIP+4, which consists of the original five-digit ZIP code plus four extra digits.

- *IPv4 versus IPv6.* The Internet Protocol (IP) is a standard used by electronic devices to exchange data over the Internet. Each device is assigned a unique integer or address. IPv4 uses 32-bit addresses and supports about 4.3 billion addresses. Due to explosive growth of the Internet, a new version, IPv6, uses 128-bit addresses and supports 2^{128} addresses.

In each of these cases, if the programmer did not properly encapsulate the data, then a change to the internal representation (to accommodate the new standard) would break a large amount of client code (that depended on the old standard). The estimated costs for the changes in each of these cases runs to hundreds of millions of dollars! That is a huge cost for failing to encapsulate a single number. These predicaments might seem distant to you, but you can be sure that every individual programmer (that's you) who does not take advantage of the protection available through encapsulation risks losing significant amounts of time and effort fixing broken code when standards change.

Our convention of always considering *all* of our instance variables to be private provides some protection against such problems. If you adopt this convention when implementing a data type for a year, ZIP code, IP address, or whatever, you can change the internal representation without affecting clients. The *data-type implementation* knows the data representation, and the *object* holds the data; the *client* holds only a reference to the object and does not know the details.

Limiting the potential for error. Encapsulation also helps programmers ensure that their code operates as intended. As an example, we consider yet another horror story: in the 2000 presidential election, Al Gore received *negative* 16,022 votes on an electronic voting machine in Volusia County, Florida. The counter variable was not properly encapsulated in the voting machine software! To understand the problem, consider `Counter` (Program 3.3.2), which implements a simple counter according to the API at the bottom of this page. This abstraction is useful in many

operation	*description*
`Counter(id, maxCount)`	*a new counter named* `id`*, initialized to* 0 *with maximum value* `maxCount`
`c.increment()`	*increment* `c`*, unless its value is* `maxCount`
`c.value()`	*value of counter* `c`
`str(c)`	`'id: value'` *(string representation of counter* `c`*)*

API for a user-defined `Counter` *data type*

Program 3.3.2 *Counter* (`counter.py`)

```
import sys
import stdarray
import stdio
import stdrandom

class Counter:
    def __init__(self, id, maxCount):
        self._name = id
        self._maxCount = maxCount
        self._count = 0

    def increment(self):
        if self._count < self._maxCount:
            self._count += 1

    def value(self):
        return self._count

    def __str__(self):
        return self._name + ': ' + str(self._count)

def main():
    n = int(sys.argv[1])
    p = float(sys.argv[2])
    heads = Counter('Heads', n)
    tails = Counter('Tails', n)
    for i in range(n):
        if stdrandom.bernoulli(p): heads.increment()
        else:                      tails.increment()
    stdio.writeln(heads)
    stdio.writeln(tails)

if __name__ == '__main__': main()
```

instance variables

`_name`	*counter name*
`_maxCount`	*maximum value*
`count`	*value*

This class encapsulates a simple integer counter, assigning it a string name and initializing it to 0, incrementing it each time the client calls `increment()`*, reporting the value when the client calls* `value()`*, and creating a string with its name and value when the client calls* `str()`*.*

```
% python counter.py 1000000 .75
Heads: 750056
Tails: 249944
```

contexts, including, for example, an electronic voting machine. It encapsulates a single integer and ensures that the only operation that can be performed on the integer is *increment by one*. Therefore, it can never go negative. The goal of data abstraction is to *restrict* the operations on the data. It also *isolates* operations on the data. For example, we could add a new implementation with a logging capability so that `counter.increment()` records a timestamp for each vote or some other information that can be used for consistency checks. But the most important problem is that Python's convention is no protection against malicious client code. For example, there could be client code like the following somewhere in the voting machine:

```
counter = Counter('Volusia', VOTERS_IN_VOLUSIA_COUNTY)
counter._count = -16022;
```

In a programming language that enforces encapsulation, code like this will not even compile; without such protection, Gore's vote count was negative. Proper encapsulation is far from a complete solution to the voting security problem, but it is a good start. For this reason, security experts generally view Python as being unsafe for such applications.

Code clarity. Precisely specifying a data type improves design because it leads to client code that can more clearly express its computation. You have seen many examples of such client code in Sections 3.1 and 3.2, from charged particles to pictures to complex numbers. One key to good design is to observe that code composed with the proper abstractions can be nearly self-documenting.

We have stressed the benefits of encapsulation throughout this book. We summarize them again here, in the context of designing data types. Encapsulation enables modular programming, allowing us to

- Independently develop client and implementation code
- Substitute improved implementations without affecting clients
- Support clients not yet composed (any client can compose code to the API)

Encapsulation also isolates data-type operations, which leads to the possibility of

- Adding consistency checks and other debugging tools in implementations
- Clarifying client code

A properly implemented data type (encapsulated) extends the Python language, allowing any client program to make use of it.

Immutability An object from a data type is *immutable* if its data-type value cannot change once created. An *immutable data type*, such as a Python string, is one in which all objects of that type are immutable. By contrast, a *mutable* data type, such as a Python list/array, is one in which objects of that type have values that are designed to change. Of the data types considered in this chapter, `Charge`, `Color`, and `Complex` are all immutable, and `Picture`, `Histogram`, `Turtle`, `StockAccount`, and `Counter` are all mutable. Whether to make a data type immutable is a fundamental design decision and depends on the application at hand.

Immutable data types. The purpose of many data types is to encapsulate values that do not change. For example, a programmer implementing a `Complex` client might reasonably expect to compose the code `z = z0`, thus setting two variables to reference the same `Complex` object, in the same way as for floats or integers. But if `Complex` were mutable and the object referenced by `z` were to change after the assignment `z = z0`, then the object referenced by `z0` would also change (they are aliases, or both references to the same object). Conceptually, changing the value of `z` would change the value of `z0`! This unexpected result, known as an *aliasing bug*, comes as a surprise to many newcomers to object-oriented programming. One very important reason to implement immutable types is that we can use immutable objects in assignment statements and as arguments and return values from functions without having to worry about their values changing.

mutable	*immutable*
`Picture`	`Charge`
`Histogram`	`Color`
`Turtle`	`Complex`
`StockAccount`	`str`
`Counter`	`int`
`list`	`float`
	`bool`
	`complex`

Mutable data types. For many other data types, the very purpose of the abstraction is to encapsulate values as they change. The `Turtle` class defined in PROGRAM 3.2.4 (`turtle.py`) is a prime example. Our reason for using `Turtle` is to relieve client programs of the responsibility of tracking the changing values. Similarly, `Picture`, `Histogram`, `StockAccount`, `Counter`, and Python lists/arrays are all types where we expect values to change. In a client where we pass a `Turtle` as an argument to a function or method, as in `koch.py`, we expect the turtle's position and orientation to change.

Arrays and strings. You have already encountered this distinction as a client programmer, when using Python lists/arrays (mutable) and Python strings (immutable). When you pass a string to a method/function, you do not need to worry about that method/function changing the sequence of characters in the string. In contrast, when you pass an array to a method/function, the method/function is free to change the elements of the array. Python strings are immutable because we generally do *not* want `str` values to change; Python arrays are mutable because we often *do* want array elements to change. There are also situations where we want to have mutable strings and where we want to have immutable arrays, which we consider later in this section.

Advantages of immutability. Generally, immutable data types are easier to use and harder to misuse because the scope of code that can change object values is far smaller than for mutable types. It is easier to debug code that uses immutable data types because it is easier to guarantee that objects remain in a consistent state. When using mutable data types, you must always be concerned about where and when object values might change.

Cost of immutability. The downside of immutability is that you must create a new object for every value. For example, when you are using the `Complex` data type, the expression `z = z*z + z0` involves creating a third object (to hold the value `z*z`), then using that object with the + operator (without saving an explicit reference to it) and creating a fourth object to hold the value `z*z + z0`, and assigning that object to `z` (thereby orphaning the original reference to `z`). A program such as `mandelbrot.py` (Program 3.2.7) creates a huge number of such intermediate objects. However, this expense is normally manageable because Python's memory management is typically optimized for such situations.

Enforcing immutability. Some languages include direct support to help enforce immutability. For example, Java supports the `final` modifier for instance variables whose values never change, which serves as documentation that the value does not change, prevents accidental changes, and makes programs easier to debug. It is possible to simulate this behavior in Python, but such code is best left for experts. In this book, the best that we can do is to state our intent to make a data type immutable and make sure not to change any object's value in our implementation code (which is not always as easy as you might think).

Defensive copies. Suppose that we wish to develop an immutable data type named `Vector`, whose constructor takes an array of floats as an argument to initialize an instance variable. Consider this attempt:

```
class Vector:
    def __init__(self, a):
        self._coords = a    # array of coordinates
    ...
```

This code makes `Vector` a *mutable* data type. A client program could create a `Vector` object by specifying the elements in an array, and then (bypassing the API) change the elements of the `Vector` after creation:

```
a = [3.0, 4.0]
v = new Vector(a)
a[0] = 17.0  # bypasses the public API
```

The instance variable `_coords` is marked as private (via its leading underscore), but `Vector` is mutable because the implementation holds a reference to the same array as does the client; if the client changes an element in that array, then the client also changes the `Vector` object.

To ensure immutability of a data type that includes an instance variable of a mutable type, the implementation needs to make a local copy, known as a *defensive copy*. Recall from Section 1.4 that the expression `a[:]` creates a copy of array `a[]`. As a consequence, this code creates a defensive copy:

```
class Vector:
    def __init__(self, a):
        self._coords = a[:]    # array of coordinates
    ...
```

Next, we consider a full implementation of such a data type.

Immutability needs to be taken into account in any data-type design. Ideally, whether a data type is immutable should be specified in the API, so that clients know that object values will not change. Implementing an immutable type can be a burden. For complicated types, making the defensive copy is one challenge; ensuring that none of the methods change object values is another.

Example: spatial vectors To illustrate these ideas in the context of a useful mathematical abstraction, we now consider a *vector* data type. Like complex numbers, the basic definition of the vector abstraction is familiar because it has played a central role in applied mathematics for over 100 years. The field of mathematics known as *linear algebra* is concerned with properties of vectors. Linear algebra is a rich and successful theory with numerous applications, and it plays an important role in all fields of social and natural science. Full treatment of linear algebra is certainly beyond the scope of this book, but several important applications are based upon elementary and familiar calculations, so we touch upon vectors and linear algebra throughout the book (for example, the random surfer example in SECTION 1.6 is based on linear algebra). Accordingly, it is worthwhile to encapsulate such an abstraction in a data type.

A *spatial vector* is an abstract entity that has a *magnitude* and a *direction*. Spatial vectors provide a natural way to describe properties of the physical world, such as force, velocity, momentum, or acceleration. One standard way to specify a vector is as an arrow from the origin to a point in a Cartesian coordinate system: the direction is the ray from the origin to the point and the magnitude is the length of the arrow (distance from the origin to the point). To specify the vector, it suffices to specify the point.

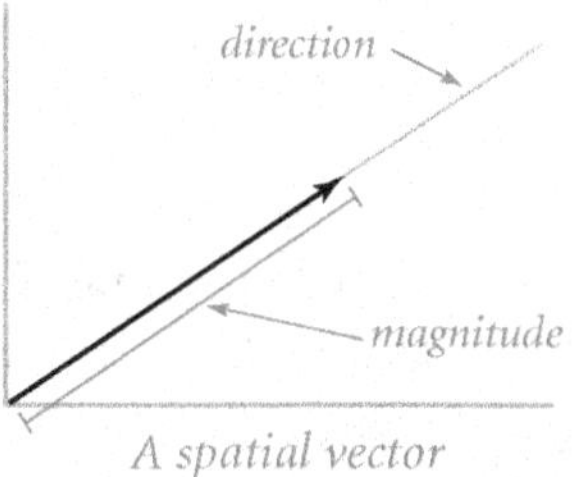

A spatial vector

This concept extends to any number of dimensions: an ordered list of n real numbers (the coordinates of an n-dimensional point) suffices to specify a vector in n-dimensional space. By convention, we use a boldface letter to refer to a vector and numbers or indexed variable names (the same letter in italics) separated by commas within parentheses to denote its value. For example, we might use $\mathbf{x}$ to denote the vector $(x_0, x_1, \ldots, x_{n-1})$ and $\mathbf{y}$ to denote the vector $(y_0, y_1, \ldots, y_{n-1})$.

API. The basic operations on vectors are to add two vectors, multiply a vector by a scalar (a real number), compute the dot product of two vectors, and compute the magnitude and direction, as follows:

- *Addition*: $\mathbf{x} + \mathbf{y} = (x_0 + y_0, x_1 + y_1, \ldots, x_{n-1} + y_{n-1})$
- *Scalar product*: $\alpha\mathbf{x} = (\alpha x_0, \alpha x_1, \ldots, \alpha x_{n-1})$
- *Dot product*: $\mathbf{x} \cdot \mathbf{y} = x_0 y_0 + x_1 y_1 + \ldots + x_{n-1} y_{n-1}$
- *Magnitude*: $|\mathbf{x}| = (x_0{}^2 + x_1{}^2 + \ldots + x_{n-1}{}^2)^{1/2}$
- *Direction*: $\mathbf{x} / |\mathbf{x}| = (x_0 / |\mathbf{x}|, x_1 / |\mathbf{x}|, \ldots, x_{n-1} / |\mathbf{x}|)$

The results of addition, scalar product, and direction are vectors, but the magnitude and the dot product are scalar quantities (floats). For example, if $\mathbf{x} = (0, 3, 4, 0)$, and $\mathbf{y} = (0, -3, 1, -4)$, then $\mathbf{x} + \mathbf{y} = (0, 0, 5, -4)$, $3\mathbf{x} = (0, 9, 12, 0)$, $\mathbf{x} \cdot \mathbf{y} = -5$, $|\mathbf{x}| = 5$, and $\mathbf{x} / |\mathbf{x}| = (0, 0.6, 0.8, 0)$. The direction vector is a *unit vector*: its magnitude is 1. These definitions lead to the API shown at the bottom of this page. As with `Complex`, this API does not explicitly specify that the data type is immutable, but we know that client programmers (who are likely to be thinking in terms of the mathematical abstraction) will certainly expect that convention, and perhaps we would rather not explain to them that we are trying to protect them from aliasing bugs!

Representation. As usual, our first choice in developing an implementation is to choose a representation for the data. Using an array to hold the Cartesian coordinates provided in the constructor is a clear choice, but not the only reasonable choice. Indeed, one of the basic tenets of linear algebra is that other sets of n vectors can be used as the basis for a coordinate system: any vector can be expressed as a linear combination of a set of n vectors, satisfying a certain condition known as *linear independence*. This ability to change coordinate systems aligns nicely with

client operation	*special method*	*description*
`Vector(a)`	`__init__(self, a)`	*a new* `Vector` *object with Cartesian coordinates taken from array* `a[]`
`x[i]`	`__getitem__(self, i)`	`i`*th Cartesian coordinate of* `x`
`x + y`	`__add__(self, other)`	*sum of* `x` *and* `y`
`x - y`	`__sub__(self, other)`	*difference of* `x` *and* `y`
`x.dot(y)`		*dot product of* `x` *and* `y`
`x.scale(alpha)`		*scalar product of float* `alpha` *and* `x`
`x.direction()`		*unit vector with same direction as* `x` *(raise an error if* `x` *is the zero vector)*
`abs(x)`	`__abs__(self)`	*magnitude of* `x`
`len(x)`	`__len__(self)`	*length of* `x`
`str(x)`	`__str__(self)`	*string representation of* `x`

API for a user-defined `Vector` *data type*

Program 3.3.3 Spatial vectors (vector.py)

```
import math
import stdarray
import stdio
class Vector:
    def __init__(self, a):
        self._coords = a[:]
        self._n = len(a)
    def __add__(self, other):
        result = stdarray.create1D(self._n, 0)
        for i in range(self._n):
            result[i] = self._coords[i] + other._coords[i]
        return Vector(result)
    def dot(self, other):
        result = 0
        for i in range(self._n):
            result += self._coords[i] * other._coords[i]
        return result
    def scale(self, alpha):
        result = stdarray.create1D(self._n, 0)
        for i in range(self._n):
            result[i] = alpha * self._coords[i]
        return Vector(result)
    def direction(self):      return self.scale(1.0 / abs(self))
    def __getitem__(self, i): return self._coords[i]
    def __abs__(self):        return math.sqrt(self.dot(self))
    def __len__(self):        return self._n
    def __str__(self):        return str(self._coords)
```

instance variables

`_coords[]`	*Cartesian coordinates*
`_n`	*dimension*

This implementation encapsulates the mathematical spatial-vector abstraction in an immutable Python data type. *Program 3.3.4 (`sketch.py`) and Program 3.4.1 (`body.py`)* *are typical clients. The test client and `__sub__()` implementations are left for* *Exercises 3.3.5 and 3.3.6.*

encapsulation. Most clients do not need to know about the representation at all and can work with `Vector` objects and operations. If warranted, the implementation can change the coordinate system without affecting client code.

Implementation. Given the representation, the code that implements all of these operations is straightforward, as you can see in the `Vector` class defined in `vector.py` (Program 3.3.3). The constructor makes a defensive copy of the client array and none of the methods assigns a value to the copy, so that `Vector` objects are immutable. Note in particular that the implementation of `x[i]` (`__getitem__(self, i)`) is easy in our Cartesian coordinate representation: return the appropriate coordinate in the array. It actually implements a mathematical function that is defined for any `Vector` representation—the geometric projection onto the `i`th Cartesian axis.

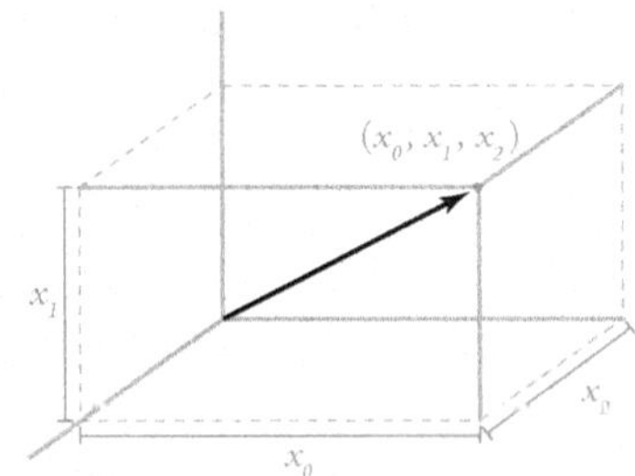

Projecting a vector (3D)

How can we ensure immutability when it seems that the client is free to compose code like `x[i] = 2.0`? The answer to this question lies in a special method that we do *not* implement in an immutable data type: in such a case, Python calls the special method `__setitem__()` instead of `__getitem__()`. Since `Vector` does not implement that method, such client code would raise an `AttributeError` at run time. Later in this section, we will survey Python's special methods so that you will have some context when faced with such issues.

Why go to the trouble of using a `Vector` data type when all of the operations are so easily implemented with arrays? By now the answer to this question should be obvious to you: to enable modular programming, facilitate debugging, and clarify code. The array is a low-level Python mechanism that admits all kinds of operations. By restricting ourselves to just the operations in the `Vector` API (which are the only ones that we need, for many clients), we simplify the process of designing, implementing, and maintaining our programs. Because the type is immutable, we can use it as we use built-in types (`int`, `float`, `bool`, and `str`). For example, when we pass a `Vector` to a function, we are assured its value will not change, but we do not have that assurance with an array. Composing programs that use `Vector` objects and operations is an easy and natural way to take advantage of the extensive amount of mathematical knowledge that has been developed around this abstract concept.

Tuples Python's built-in `tuple` data type represents an *immutable* sequence of objects. It is similar to the built-in `list` data type (which we use for arrays), except that once you create a tuple, you cannot change its items. In situations where you need to change the items in the sequence (such as reversing or shuffling an array) you must use arrays; in situations where the items do not change (such as the coordinates in our `Vector` data type), you should use tuples.

You can manipulate tuples using familiar array notation, as documented in the API at the bottom of the page. You can create tuples either using the built-in function `tuple()` or by listing a sequence of expressions, separated by commas, and (optionally) enclosed in matching parentheses.

Using tuples can improve the design of a program. For example, if we replace the first statement in the constructor of `vector.py` with

```
self._coords = tuple(a)
```

then any attempt to change a vector coordinate within the `Vector` class raises a `TypeError` at run time, helping to enforce immutability of `Vector` objects.

Python also provides a powerful tuple assignment feature known as *tuple packing* and *tuple unpacking* that lets you assign a tuple of expressions on the right-hand side of an assignment operator to a tuple of variables on the left-hand side (provided the number of variables on the left matches the number of expressions on the right). You can use this feature to assign multiple variables simultaneously. For example, the following statement exchanges the object references in variable `x` and `y`:

```
x, y = y, x
```

You can also use tuple packing and unpacking to return multiple values from a function (see Exercise 3.3.14).

`a = (1, 7, 3)`

operation	*comment*
`len(a)`	3
`a[1]`	7
`a[1] = 9`	*run-time error*
`a += [8]`	*run-time error*
`(x, y, z) = a`	*tuple unpacking*
`b = (y, z, x)`	*tuple packing*
`b[1]`	3

Examples of tuple operations

operation	*description*
`len(a)`	*length of* `a`
`a[i]`	*the* `i`*th item of* `a`
`for v in a:`	*iterate over the items in* `a`

Partial API for Python's built-in `tuple` *data type*

Polymorphism Often, when we compose methods (or functions), we intend for them to work only with objects of specific types. Sometimes, we want them to work with objects of different types. A method (or function) that can take arguments with different types is said to be *polymorphic.*

The best kind of polymorphism is the unexpected kind: when you apply an existing method/function to a new data type (for which you never planned) and discover that the method/function has exactly the behavior that you wanted. The worst kind of polymorphism is also the unexpected kind: when you apply an existing method/function to a new data type and it returns the wrong answer! Finding a bug of this sort can be an extraordinary challenge.

Duck typing. Duck typing is a programming style in which the language does not formally specify the requirements for a function's arguments; instead, it just tries to call the function if a compatible one is defined (and raises a run-time error otherwise). The name comes from an old quote attributed to the poet J. W. Riley:

When I see a bird that
walks like a duck and swims like a duck and quacks like a duck
I call that bird a duck

In Python, if an object walks like a duck, swims like a duck, and quacks like a duck, you can treat that object as a duck; you don't need to explicitly declare it to be a duck. In many languages (such as Java or C++), you *do* need to explicitly declare the types of variables, but not in Python—Python uses duck typing for all operations (function calls, method calls, and operators). It raises a `TypeError` at run time if an operation cannot be applied to an object because it is of an inappropriate type. One principle of duck typing is that a method/function should not care about the type of an object, just whether a client can perform the desired operations on that object. That is, if all of the operations within a method/function can be applied to a type, then the method/function can be applied to that type. This approach leads to simpler and more flexible client code and puts the focus on operations that are actually used rather than the type.

Disadvantages of duck typing. The primary disadvantage of duck typing is that it is difficult to know precisely what the contract is between the client and the implementation, especially when a required method is needed only indirectly. The API simply does not carry this kind of information. This lack of information can lead to run-time errors. Worse, the end result can be semantically incorrect, with no error raised at all. Next, we consider a simple example of this situation.

A case in point. We designed our `Vector` data type under the implicit assumption that the vector components would be floats and that the client would create a new vector by passing an array of `float` objects to the constructor. If the client creates two vectors `x` and `y` in this way, then both `x[i]` and `x.dot(y)` return floats and both `x + y` and `x - y` return vectors with float components, as expected.

Suppose, instead, that a client creates a `Vector` with integer components by passing an array of `int` objects to the constructor. If the client creates two vectors `x` and `y` in this manner, then both `x[i]` and `x.dot(y)` return integers and both `x + y` and `x - y` return vectors with integer components, as desired. Of course, `abs(x)` returns a float and `x.direction()` returns a vector with float components. This is the best kind of polymorphism, where duck typing works serendipitously.

Now, suppose that a client creates a `Vector` with complex components by passing an array of `complex` objects to the constructor. There is no problem with vector addition or scalar multiplication, but the implementation of the dot product operation (along with the implementations of magnitude and direction, which depend on the dot product) *fails spectacularly*. Here is an example:

```
a = [1 + 2j, 2 + 0j, 4 + 0j]
x = Vector(a)
b = abs(x)
```

This code results in a `TypeError` at run time, with `math.sqrt()` trying to take the square root of a complex number. The problem is that the dot product of two complex-valued vectors **x** and **y** requires taking the *complex conjugate* of the elements in the second vector:

$$\mathbf{x} \cdot \mathbf{y} = x_0\bar{y}_0 + x_1\bar{y}_1 + \ldots + x_{n-1}\bar{y}_{n-1}$$

In our example, the `__abs__()` special method in `Vector` calls `x.dot(x)`, which is supposed to compute the result

$$(1 + 2i)\,(1-2i) + 2 \cdot 2 + 4 \cdot 4 = 25$$

but actually computes the result

$$(1 + 2i)\,(1 + 2i) + 2 \cdot 2 + 4 \cdot 4 = 17 + 4i$$

which is the complex number that raises the TypeError for math.sqrt(). An unexpected run-time error is bad enough, but suppose that the last line of the code were b = abs(x.dot(x)). In that case, b would get assigned the integer 33 (it is supposed to be 25) with *no indication whatsoever of any problem*. Let's hope that such code is not being used to control a nuclear power plant or a surface-to-air missile somewhere. Computing with a wrong result is certain to wreak havoc.

Once we are aware of the problem, we can fix Vector to be compatible with complex numbers by making two changes, one to dot() and one to __abs__():

```
def dot(self, other):
    result = 0
    for i in range(self._length):
        result += self._coords[i] * other._coords[i].conjugate()
    return result

def __abs__(self):
    return math.sqrt(abs(self.dot(self)))
```

The modification to dot() works because Python's numeric types all include a conjugate() method that returns the complex conjugate of a number (which is the number itself if it is an integer or float). The modification to __abs__() is needed because math.sqrt() raises a TypeError if its argument is complex (even if its imaginary part is zero). The dot product of a complex number with itself is guaranteed to be a nonnegative real number, but it is a complex, so we take its magnitude (a float) using abs() before taking the square root.

In this case, duck typing is the worst kind of polymorphism. It is certainly reasonable for a client to expect the implementation of Vector to work properly when vector components are complex numbers. How can an implementation anticipate and prepare for all potential uses of a data type? This situation presents a design challenge that is impossible to meet. All we can do is caution you to check, if possible, that any data type that you use can handle the types of data that you intend to use with it.

Overloading The ability to define a data type that provides its own definitions of operators is a form of polymorphism known as *operator overloading*. In Python, you can overload almost every operator, including operators for arithmetic, comparisons, indexing, and slicing. You can also overload *built-in functions*, including absolute value, length, hashing, and type conversion. Overloading operators and built-in functions makes user-defined types behave more like built-in types.

Special methods. The Python mechanism for supporting overloading is to associate a *special method* with each operator and each built-in function. Though you have already seen the use of special methods in several data-type implementations (notably `Complex` and `Vector`), we briefly summarize the concept here.

To perform an operation, Python internally converts the expression into a call on the corresponding special method; to call a built-in function, Python internally calls the corresponding special method instead. To overload an operator or built-in function, you include an implementation of the corresponding special method with your own code. For example, whenever Python sees `x + y` in client code, it converts that expression into the special method call `x.__add__(y)`. Thus, to overload the + operator in your data type, just include an implementation of the special method `__add__()`. Similarly, whenever Python sees `str(x)` in client code, it converts that expression into the special method call `x.__str__()`. Thus, to overload the `str()` built-in function, just include an implementation of the special method `__str__()`.

Arithmetic operators. In Python, arithmetic operations like `x + y` and `x * y` are not just for integers and floats. Python associates a special method with each of its arithmetic operators, so you can overload any arithmetic operation by implementing the corresponding special method, as detailed in the table below.

client operation	*special method*	*description*
`x + y`	`__add__(self, other)`	*sum of x and y*
`x - y`	`__sub__(self, other)`	*difference of x and y*
`x * y`	`__mul__(self, other)`	*product of x and y*
`x ** y`	`__pow__(self, other)`	*x to the yth power*
`x / y`	`__truediv__(self, other)`	*quotient of x and y*
`x // y`	`__floordiv__(self, other)`	*floored quotient of x and y*
`x % y`	`__mod__(self, other)`	*remainder when dividing x by y*
`+x`	`__pos__(self)`	*x*
`-x`	`__neg__(self)`	*arithmetic negation of x*

Note: Python 2 uses `__div__` instead of `__truediv__`.

Special methods for arithmetic operators

Equality. The `==` and `!=` operators for testing equality require special attention. For example, consider the code in the diagram at right, which creates two `Charge` objects, referenced by three variables `c1`, `c2`, and `c3`. As illustrated in the diagram, `c1` and `c3` both reference the same object, which is different from the one referenced by `c2`. Clearly, `c1 == c3` is `True`, but what about `c1 == c2`? The answer to this question is unclear because there are two ways to think about equality in Python:

- *Reference equality (identity equality).* Reference equality holds when two references are equal—they refer to the same object. The built in function `id()` gives the identity of an object (its memory address); the `is` and `is not` operators test whether two variables refer to the same object. That is, the implementation of `c1 is c2` tests whether `id(c1)` and `id(c2)` are the same. In our example, `c1 is c3` is `True` as expected, but `c1 is c2` is `False` because `c1` and `c2` reside at different memory addresses.

```
c1 = Charge(.51, .63, 21.3)
c2 = Charge(.51, .63, 21.3)
c3 = c1
```

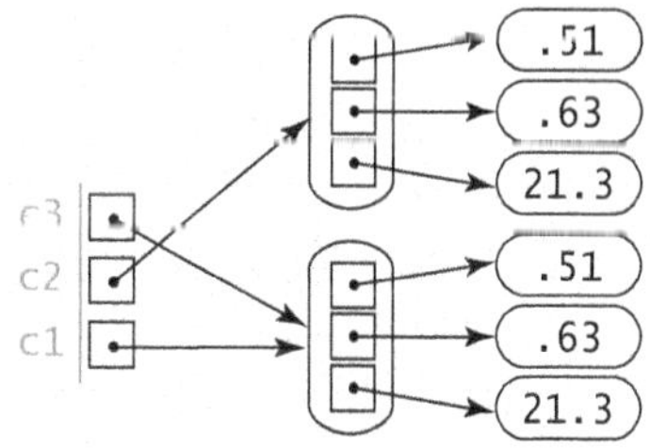

Three variables referring to two `Charge` objects

- *Object equality (value equality).* Object equality holds when two objects are equal—they have the same data-type value. You should use the `==` and `!=` operators, defined using the special methods `__eq__()` and `__ne__()`, to test for object equality. If you do not define an `__eq__()` method, then Python substitutes the `is` operator. That is, by default `==` implements reference equality. So, in our earlier example, `c1 == c2` is `False` even though `c1` and `c2` have the same position and charge value. If we want two charges with identical position and charge value to be considered equal, we can ensure this outcome by including the following code in `charge.py` (PROGRAM 3.2.1):

```
def __eq__(self, other):
    if self._rx != other._rx: return False
    if self._ry != other._ry: return False
    if self._q  != other._q:  return False
    return True

def __ne__(self, other):
     return not __eq__(self, other)
```

With this code in place, c1 == c2 is now True in our example. In this case, which is typical, it is not so clear whether clients would expect this behavior (that is why we did not include these methods in our implementation). Deciding about object equality is an important (and challenging) design decision for any data type.

To test your understanding of these ideas, study the interactive Python session diagrammed at right. In the example, a and b refer to different int objects with the same value, whereas a and c refer to the same int object.

```
>>> a = 123456789
>>> b = 123456789
>>> c = a
>>> a == b
True
>>> a == c
True
>>> id(a)
140461201279248
>>> id(b)
140461201280816
>>> id(c)
140461201279248
>>> a is b
False
>>> a is c
True
```

Hashing. We now consider a fundamental operation related to equality testing, known as *hashing*, that maps an object to an integer, known as a *hash code*. This operation is so important that it is handled by Python's special method __hash__() in support of the built-in hash() function. We refer to an object as *hashable* if it satisfies the following three properties:

- The object can be compared for equality with other objects via the == operator.
- Whenever two objects compare as equal, they have the same hash code.
- The object's hash code does not change during its lifetime.

For example, in the interactive Python session at right, a and b refer to equal str objects, so they must have the same hash code; a and c refer to different str objects, so we expect their hash codes to be different.

In typical applications, we use the hash code to map an object x to an integer in a small range, say between 0 and m-1, using the *hash function*

```
hash(x) % m
```

Then, we can use the hash function value as an integer index into an array of length m (see Program 3.3.4 and Program 4.4.3). By definition, hashable objects that are equal have the same hash code, so they also have the same hash function value. Objects that are not equal can have the same hash function value but we expect the hash function to divide the objects into m groups of roughly equal length. All of Python's immutable data types (including int, float, str, and tuple) are hashable and engineered to distribute the objects in a reasonable manner.

```
>>> a = 'Python'
>>> b = 'Python'
>>> c = 'programmer'
>>> hash(a)
-2359742753373747800
>>> hash(b)
-2359742753373747800
>>> hash(c)
7354308922443094682
```

String hash example

You can make a user-defined data types hashable by implementing the two special methods `__hash__()` and `__eq__()`. Crafting a good hash function requires a deft combination of science and engineering, and is beyond the scope of this book. Instead, we describe a simple recipe for doing so in Python that is effective in a wide variety of situations:

- Ensure that the data type is immutable.
- Implement `__eq__()` by comparing all significant instance variables.
- Implement `__hash__()` by putting the same instance variables into a tuple and calling the built-in `hash()` function on the tuple.

For example, following is a `__hash__()` implementation for the `Charge` data type (PROGRAM 3.2.1) to accompany the `__eq__()` implementation that we just considered:

```
def __hash__(self):
    a = (self._rx, self._ry, self._q)
    return hash(a)
```

client operation	*special method*	*description*
`x is y`	*[cannot be overloaded]*	*do* `x` *and* `y` *refer to the same object?*
`x is not y`	*[cannot be overloaded]*	*do* `x` *and* `y` *refer to different objects?*
`id(x)`	*[cannot be overloaded]*	*identity (memory address) of* `x`
`hash(x)`	`__hash__(self)`	*hash code of* `x`
`x == y`	`__eq__(self, other)`	*is* `x` *equal to* `y`*?*
`x != y`	`__ne__(self, other)`	*is* `x` *not equal to* `y`*?*

Operations for testing equality

Comparison operators. Similarly, comparisons like `x < y` and `x >= y` are not just for integers, floats, and strings in Python. Again, Python associates a special method with each of its comparison operators, so you can overload any comparison operator by implementing the corresponding special method, as detailed in the table on the next page. As a matter of style, if you define any one of the comparison methods, then you should define all of them, and in a consistent manner. For example, if `x < y`, then you should ensure that both `y > x` and `x <= y`. Moreover, in any data type where the client might expect to sort objects, the comparison methods must define a *total order*. Specifically, the following three properties must hold:

- *Antisymmetry*: if both `x <= y` and `y <= x`, then `x == y`.
- *Transitivity*: if both `x <= y` and `y <= z`, then `x <= z`.
- *Totality*: either `x <= y` or `y <= x` or both.

We refer to a data type as *comparable* if implements the six comparison methods and they define a total order. Python's built-in `int`, `float`, and `str` types are all comparable. You can make a user-defined type comparable by implementing the six special methods, as we do here for `Counter` (PROGRAM 3.3.2):

```
def __lt__(self, other): return self._count <  other._count
def __le__(self, other): return self._count <= other._count
def __eq__(self, other): return self._count == other._count
def __ne__(self, other): return self._count != other._count
def __gt__(self, other): return self._count >  other._count
def __ge__(self, other): return self._count >= other._count
```

We will consider several applications of comparable objects in SECTION 4.1 (sorting) and SECTION 4.3 (symbol tables).

client operation	*special method*	*description*
`x < y`	`__lt__(self, other)`	*is x less than y?*
`x <= y`	`__le__(self, other)`	*is x less than or equal to y?*
`x >= y`	`__ge__(self, other)`	*is x greater than or equal to y?*
`x > y`	`__gt__(self, other)`	*is x greater than y?*

Special methods for comparison operators

Other operators. Almost every operator in Python can be overloaded. For example, you can overload augmented assignment operators such as += and *=, and bitwise logical operators such as &, `|`, and `^`. If you want to overload such an operator, you can track down the corresponding special method on our booksite or in Python's online documentation. There are a number of operations relating to processing strings, arrays, and similar data types (like the `[]` operator and corresponding `__getitem__()` special method that we used in `Vector`) that we will consider in more detail in SECTION 4.4.

Built-in functions. We have been overloading the built-in function `str()` in every class we develop, and there are several other built-in functions that we can overload in the same way. The ones that we use in this book are summarized in the table below. We have already used all of these functions, except for `iter()`, which we defer until SECTION 4.4.

client operation	*special method*	*description*
`len(x)`	`__len__(self)`	*length of* x
`float(x)`	`__float__(self)`	*float equivalent of* x
`int(x)`	`__int__(self)`	*integer equivalent of* x
`str(x)`	`__str__(self)`	*string representation of* x
`abs(x)`	`__abs__(self)`	*absolute value of* x
`hash(x)`	`__hash__(self)`	*integer hash code for* x
`iter(x)`	`__iter__(self)`	*iterator for* x

Special methods for built-in functions

THE ABILITY TO OVERLOAD OPERATORS AND built-in functions is a powerful feature of the Python language. It enables a programmer to create user-defined types that have similar behavior to built-in types. However, with great power comes great responsibility. While it is natural to overload arithmetic operators with familiar mathematical entities (such as complex number or spatial vectors, as we have seen), sometimes it is inappropriate to overload arithmetic operators for non-mathematical data types, as doing so can lead to unclear code.

For example, a digital artist might be tempted to develop a way to compute with colors by defining `a + b` or `a * b` in insightful ways when `a` and `b` are `Color` objects, or a musician might be tempted to do something similar for tones or chords. Far be it from us to discourage such creativity, but do you really want to be adding, subtracting, and multiplying `Turtle` objects (or whatever type of object you are considering)? Using ordinary methods (with descriptive names) might be a better approach. In fact, many programming languages (such as Java) do not support operator overloading because programmers often abuse this power. Overloading operators properly can entail a significant amount of work, and is worthwhile only when it leads to natural and expected behavior.

Functions are objects In Python, "everything" is an object, including functions. This means that you can use functions as arguments to functions and return them as results. Defining so-called *higher-order functions* that manipulate other functions is common both in mathematics and in scientific computing. For example, in calculus, the *derivative* is a function that takes a function as an argument and produces another function as a result. In scientific computing, we often want to differentiate functions, integrate functions, find roots of functions, and so forth.

As an example, consider the problem of estimating the *Riemann integral* of a positive real-valued function f (the area under the curve) in an interval (a, b). This computation is known as *quadrature* or *numerical integration.* A number of methods have been developed for quadrature. Perhaps the simplest is known as the *rectangle rule*, where we approximate the value of the integral by computing the total area of n equal-width rectangles under the curve. The `integrate()` function defined below evaluates the integral of a real-valued function $f()$ in the interval (a, b), using the rectangle rule with n rectangles:

```
def square(x):
    return x*x

def integrate(f, a, b, n=1000):
    total = 0.0
    dt = 1.0 * (b - a) / n
    for i in range(n):
        total += dt * f(a + (i + 0.5) * dt)
    return total
```

Approximating an integral

The indefinite integral of x^2 is $x^3/3$, so the definite integral between 0 and 10 is 1000/3. The call to `integrate(square, 0, 10)` returns `333.33324999999996`, which is the correct answer to six significant digits of accuracy. Similarly, the call to `integrate(gaussian.pdf, -1, 1)` returns `0.6826895727940137`, which is the correct answer to seven significant digits of accuracy (recall the Gaussian probability density function and PROGRAM 2.2.1).

Quadrature is not always the most efficient or accurate way to evaluate a function. For example, the `gaussian.cdf()` function in PROGRAM 2.2.1 is a faster and more accurate way to integrate the Gaussian probability density function. However, quadrature has the advantage of being useful for any function whatsoever, subject only to certain technical conditions on smoothness.

Inheritance Python provides language support for defining relationships among classes, known as *inheritance*. Software developers use inheritance widely, so you will study it in detail if you take a course in software engineering. Effective use of inheritance is beyond the scope of this book, but we briefly describe it here because there are a few situations where you may encounter it.

When used properly, inheritance enables a form of code reuse known as *subclassing*. Subclassing is a powerful technique that enables a programmer to change the behavior of a class and add functionality without recomposing the entire class from scratch. The idea is to define a new class (*subclass*, or *derived class*) that inherits its instance variables and methods from another class (*superclass*, or *base class*). The subclass contains more methods than the superclass. Systems programmers use subclassing to build so-called *extensible* modules. The idea is that one programmer (even you) can add methods to a class built by another programmer (or, perhaps, a team of systems programmers), effectively reusing the code in a potentially huge module. This approach is widely used, particularly in the development of user interfaces, so that the large amount of code required to provide all the facilities that users expect (drop-down menus, cut-and-paste, access to files, and so forth) can be reused.

An important use of subclassing in Python is the so-called *numeric tower* that implements Python's numeric types, in the `numbers.py` module. This module includes the classes `Integral`, `Rational`, `Real`, and `Complex`, structured with subclassing relationships. For example, `Real` includes all of the methods in `Complex` plus those that work on real numbers, such as the comparison operators <, <=, >, and >=. The built-in numeric types are subclasses of these—for example, `int` is a subclass of `Integral` and `float` is a subclass of `Real`.

Despite its advantages, the use of subclassing is controversial, even among systems programmers. We do not use it in this book because it generally works against encapsulation. Subclassing makes modular programming more difficult for two reasons. First, any change in the superclass affects all subclasses. The subclass cannot be developed *independently* of the superclass; indeed, it is *completely dependent* on the superclass. This problem is known as the *fragile base class problem*. Second, the subclass code, having access to instance variables, can subvert the intention of the superclass code. For example, the designer of a class such as `Vector` may have taken great care to make the `Vector` immutable, but a subclass, with full access to the instance variables, can just change them, wreaking havoc for any client assuming the class to be immutable.

Application: data mining To illustrate some of the concepts discussed in this section in the context of an application, we next consider a software technology that is proving important in addressing the daunting challenges of *data mining*—that is, the process of searching through massive amounts of information. This technology can serve as the basis for dramatic improvements in the quality of web search results, for multimedia information retrieval, for biomedical databases, for plagiarism detection, for research in genomics, for improved scholarship in many fields, for innovation in commercial applications, for learning the plans of evildoers, and for many other purposes. Accordingly, there is intense interest and extensive ongoing research on data mining.

You have direct access to thousands of files on your computer and indirect access to billions of files on the web. As you know, these files are remarkably diverse: there are commercial web pages, music and video, email, program code, and all sorts of other information. For simplicity, we will restrict our attention to *text* documents (though the approach we will consider applies to pictures, music, and all sorts of other files as well). Even with this restriction, there is remarkable diversity in the types of documents. For reference, you can find the documents listed at the bottom of this page on the booksite.

Our interest is in finding efficient ways to search through the files using their *content* to characterize documents. One fruitful approach to this problem is to associate with each document a vector known as a *sketch*, which is an ultra-compact representation of its content. The basic idea is that the sketch should capture salient statistical features of the document, so that documents that are different have sketches that are "different" and documents that are similar have sketches that are "similar." You probably are not surprised to learn that this approach can enable us to

file name	*description*	*sample text*
`constitution.txt`	*legal document*	`... of both Houses shall be determined by ...`
`tomsawyer.txt`	*American novel*	`..."Say, Tom, let ME whitewash a little." ...`
`huckfinn.txt`	*American novel*	`...was feeling pretty good after breakfast...`
`prejudice.txt`	*English novel*	`... dared not even mention that gentleman....`
`picture.py`	*Python code*	`...import sys import color import stdarray...`
`djia.csv`	*financial data*	`...01-Oct-28,239.43,242.46,3500000,240.01 ...`
`amazon.html`	*web page source*	`...<table width="100%" border="0" cellspac...`
`actg.txt`	*virus genome*	`...GTATGGAGCAGCAGACGCGCTACTTCGAGCGGAGGCATA...`

Some text documents

distinguish among a novel, a Python program, and a genome, but you might be surprised to learn that it can tell the difference between novels written by different authors and can be effective as the basis for many other subtle search criteria.

To start, we need an abstraction for documents. What is a document? Which operations do we want to perform on documents? The answers to these questions inform our design and therefore, ultimately, the code that we compose. For our purposes, a document is the contents of any text file. As indicated, we store only a document's sketch (and not the whole document), and we use the sketches to measure the similarity between associated documents. These considerations lead to the API at the bottom of this page. The arguments of the constructor are a string and two integers that control the quality of the sketch. Clients can use `similarTo()` to determine the extent of similarity between two sketches on a scale of 0 (not similar) to 1 (similar). This simple data type provides a good separation between implementing a similarity measure and implementing clients that use the measure to search among documents.

Computing sketches. Computing a sketch of a document is the first challenge. Our first choice is to use a `Vector` to represent a document's sketch. But which information should go into the sketch and how do we compute it? Many different approaches have been studied, and researchers are still actively seeking efficient and effective algorithms for this task. Our implementation `sketch.py` (PROGRAM 3.3.4) uses a simple *frequency count* approach. In addition to the string, the constructor has two arguments, an integer k and a vector dimension d. It scans the document and examines all of the *k-grams* in the document—that is, the substrings of length k starting at each position. In its simplest form, the sketch is a vector that gives the

operation	*description*
`Sketch(text, k, d)`	*a new sketch built from the string* `text` *using* `k`*-grams and dimension* `d`
`a.similarTo(b)`	*similarity measure between sketches* `a` *and* `b` *(a float between* `0.0` *and* `1.0`*)*
`str(a)`	*string representation of sketch* `a`

API for a user-defined `Sketch` *data type*

		ATAGATGCAT AGCGCATAGC		CTTTCGGTTT GGAACCGAAG CCGCGCGTCT TGTCTGCTGC AGCATCGTTC	
2-gram	*hash*	*count*	*unit*	*count*	*unit*
AA	0	0	0	2	.137
AC	1	0	0	1	.069
AG	2	4	.508	1	.069
AT	3	3	.381	2	.137
CA	4	3	.381	3	.206
CC	5	0	0	2	.137
CG	6	0	0	4	.275
CT	7	1	.127	6	.412
GA	8	3	.381	0	0
GC	9	0	0	5	.343
GG	10	0	0	6	.412
GT	11	1	.127	4	.275
TA	12	1	.127	2	.137
TC	13	4	.508	6	.412
TG	14	0	0	4	.275
TT	15	0	0	2	.137

Profiling genomic data

relative frequency of occurrence of the k-grams in the string: an element for each possible k-gram giving the number of k-grams in the document that have that value. For example, suppose that we use $k = 2$ in genomic data, with $d = 16$ (there are 4 possible character values and therefore 16 possible 2-grams). The 2-gram `AT` occurs 4 times in the string `ATAGATGCATAGCGCATAGC`, so, for example, the element in the vector corresponding to `AT` would be 4. To build the frequency vector, we need to convert each of the k-grams into an integer between 0 and 15 (the function that maps strings to integers is known as a *hash function*). For genomic data, this is an easy exercise (see Exercise 3.3.27). Then, we can compute an array to build the frequency vector in one scan through the text, incrementing the array element corresponding to each k-gram encountered. While we lose information by disregarding the order of the k-grams, remarkably, the information content of that order is lower than that of k-grams' frequency. (A Markov model paradigm not dissimilar from the one that we studied for the random surfer in Section 1.6 can be used to take order into account—such models are effective, but more work to implement.) We encapsulate the computation into the `Sketch` class, defined in `sketch.py` (Program 3.3.4). This gives us the flexibility to experiment with various designs without needing to rewrite `Sketch` clients.

Hashing. On many systems there are 128 different possible values for each character, so there are 128^k possible k-grams, and the dimension d would have to be 128^k for the simple scheme just described. This number is prohibitively large even for moderately large k. For Unicode, with more than 65,536 characters, even 2-grams lead to huge vector sketches. To ameliorate this problem, we use *hashing*, a

Python 2 alert. *All hash functions start their computation with a numeric "seed." In Python 2, the hash seed is constant, so the hash value of any given object is the same each time you run the program. In contrast, the hash seed in Python 3 varies (by default). In Python 3, then, the hash value of any given object, although the same within any given run of the program, is very likely to differ across runs of the program. Thus,* `sketch.py` *will produce different output each time you run it using Python 3.*

Program 3.3.4 Document sketch (sketch.py)

```
import sys
import stdarray
import stdio
from vector import Vector

class Sketch:
    def __init__(self, text, k, d):
        freq = stdarray.create1D(d, 0)
        for i in range(len(text) - k):
            kgram = text[i:i+k]
            freq[hash(kgram) % d] += 1
        vector = Vector(freq)
        self._sketch = vector.direction()

    def similarTo(self, other):
        return self._sketch.dot(other._sketch)

    def __str__(self):
        return str(self._sketch)

def main():
    text = stdio.readAll()
    k = int(sys.argv[1])
    d = int(sys.argv[2])
    sketch = Sketch(text, k, d)
    stdio.writeln(sketch)

if __name__ == '__main__': main()
```

instance variable

`_sketch`	*unit vector*

`text`	*document string*
`k`	*length of gram*
`d`	*dimension*
`kgram`	*k consecutive characters in document*
`freq[]`	*hash frequencies*
`vector`	*frequencies vector*

This Vector client creates a unit vector from a document's k-grams that clients can use to measure its similarity with other documents (see text).

```
% more genome20.txt
ATAGATGCATAGCGCATAGC
% python sketch.py 2 16 < genome20.txt
[ 0.0, 0.0, 0.0, 0.0, 0.504, 0.504, ..., 0.126, 0.0, 0.0, 0.378 ]
```

fundamental operation that we considered earlier in this section to map an object to an integer. For any string `s`, `hash(s) % d` is an integer between `0` and `d - 1` that we can use as an index into an array to compute frequencies. The sketch that we use is the direction of the vector defined by frequencies of these values for all *k*-grams in the document (the unit vector with the same direction).

Comparing sketches. The second challenge is to compute a similarity measure between two sketches. Again, there are many different ways to compare two vectors. Perhaps the simplest is to compute the *Euclidean distance* between them. Given vectors **x** and **y**, this distance is defined as follows:

$$|\mathbf{x} - \mathbf{y}| = ((x_0 - y_0)^2 + (x_1 - y_1)^2 + \ldots + (x_{d-1} - y_{d-1})^2)^{1/2}$$

You are familiar with this formula for $d = 2$ or $d = 3$. With `Vector`, the distance is easy to compute. If `x` and `y` are two `Vector`s, then `abs(x - y)` is the Euclidean distance between them. If documents are similar, we expect their sketches to be similar and the distance between them to be low. Another widely used similarity measure, known as the *cosine similarity measure*, is even simpler: since our sketches are unit vectors with nonnegative coordinates, their *dot product*

$$\mathbf{x} \cdot \mathbf{y} = x_0 y_0 + x_1 y_1 + \ldots + x_{d-1} y_{d-1}$$

is a number between 0 and 1. Geometrically, this quantity is the cosine of the angle formed by the two vectors (see Exercise 3.3.9). The more similar the documents, the closer we expect this measure to be to 1. If `x` and `y` are two `Vector`s, then `x.dot(y)` is their dot product.

Comparing all pairs. Program 3.3.5 (`comparedocuments.py`) is a simple and useful `Sketch` client that provides the information needed to solve the following problem: given a set of documents, find the two that are most similar. Since this specification is a bit subjective, `comparedocuments.py` writes the cosine similarity measure for all pairs of documents. For moderate-size *k* and *d*, the sketches do a remarkably good job of characterizing our sample set of documents. The results show not only that genomic data, financial data, Python code, and web source code are quite different from legal documents and novels, but also that *Tom Sawyer* and *Huckleberry Finn* are much more similar to each other than to *Pride and Prejudice*. A researcher in comparative literature could use this program to discover relationships between texts; a teacher could use this program to detect plagiarism in a set

Program 3.3.5 Similarity detection (comparedocuments.py)

```
import sys
import stdarray
import stdio
from instream import InStream
from sketch import Sketch

k = int(sys.argv[1])
d = int(sys.argv[2])
filenames = stdio.readAllStrings()

sketches = stdarray.create1D(len(filenames))
for i in range(len(filenames)):
    text = InStream(filenames[i]).readAll()
    sketches[i] = Sketch(text, k, d)

stdio.write('    ')
for i in range(len(filenames)):
    stdio.writef('%8.4s', filenames[i])
stdio.writeln()

for i in range(len(filenames)):
    stdio.writef('%.4s', filenames[i])
    for j in range(len(filenames)):
        stdio.writef('%8.2f', sketches[i].similarTo(sketches[j]))
    stdio.writeln()
```

k	*length of gram*
d	*dimension*
filenames[]	*document names*
sketches[]	*all sketches*

```
% more documents.txt
constitution.txt
tomsawyer.txt
huckfinn.txt
prejudice.txt
picture.py
djia.csv
amazon.html
actg.txt
```

This Sketch *client reads a list of documents from standard input, computes sketches based on k-gram frequencies for all the documents, and writes a table of similarity measures between all pairs of documents. It takes the value* k *and the dimension* d *as command-line arguments.*

```
% python comparedocuments.py 5 10000 < documents.txt
        cons    toms    huck    prej    pict    djia    amaz    actg
cons    1.00    0.69    0.63    0.67    0.06    0.15    0.19    0.12
toms    0.69    1.00    0.93    0.89    0.05    0.18    0.19    0.14
huck    0.63    0.93    1.00    0.83    0.03    0.16    0.16    0.13
prej    0.67    0.89    0.83    1.00    0.04    0.20    0.20    0.14
pict    0.06    0.05    0.03    0.04    1.00    0.01    0.13    0.01
djia    0.15    0.18    0.16    0.20    0.01    1.00    0.11    0.07
amaz    0.19    0.19    0.16    0.20    0.13    0.11    1.00    0.06
actg    0.12    0.14    0.13    0.14    0.01    0.07    0.06    1.00
```

of student submissions; and a biologist could use this program to discover relationships among genomes.

Searching for similar documents. Another natural `Sketch` client is one that uses sketches to search among a large number of documents to identify those that are similar to a given document. For example, web search engines uses clients of this type to present you with pages that are similar to those you have previously visited, online book merchants use clients of this type to recommend books that are similar to ones you have purchased, and social networking websites use clients of this type to identify people whose personal interests are similar to yours. Since the `Instream` constructor can take a web address as an argument instead of a file name, it is feasible to compose a program that surfs the web, computes sketches, and returns links to pages with sketches that are similar to the ones sought. We leave this client for a challenging exercise.

THIS SOLUTION IS JUST AN OVERVIEW. Many sophisticated algorithms for efficiently computing sketches and comparing them are still being invented and studied by computer scientists. Our purpose here is to introduce you to this fundamental problem domain while at the same time illustrating the power of abstraction in addressing a computational challenge. Vectors are an essential mathematical abstraction, and we can build search solutions by developing *layers of abstraction*: `Vector` is built with an array, `Sketch` is built with `Vector`, and client code uses `Sketch`. As usual, we have spared you from a lengthy account of our many attempts to develop these APIs, but you can see that the data types are designed in response to the needs of the problem, with an eye toward the requirements of implementations. Identifying and implementing appropriate abstractions is the key to effective object-oriented programming. The power of abstraction—in mathematics, physical models, and computer programs—pervades these examples. As you become fluent in developing data types to address your own computational challenges, your appreciation for this power will surely grow.

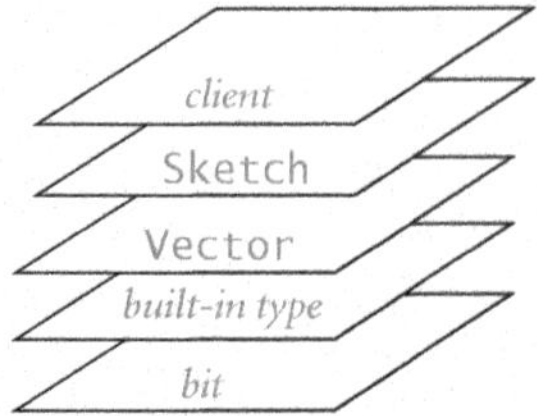

Layers of abstraction

Design-by-contract To conclude, we briefly discuss Python language mechanisms that enable you to verify assumptions about your program *while it is running*. For example, if you have a data type that represents a particle, you might assert that its mass is positive and its speed is less than the speed of light. Or if you have a method to add two vectors of the same dimension, you might assert that the dimension of the resulting vector also has the same dimension.

Exceptions. An *exception* is a disruptive event that occurs while a program is running, often to signal an error. The action taken is known as *raising an exception* (or *error*). We have already encountered exceptions raised by Python's standard modules in the course of learning to program: `IndexError` and `ZeroDivisionError` are typical examples. You can also raise your own exceptions. The simplest kind is an `Exception` that disrupts execution of the program and writes an error message:

```
raise Exception('Error message here.')
```

It is good practice to use exceptions when they can be helpful to the client. For example, in `Vector` (Program 3.3.3), we should raise an exception in `__add__()` if the two `Vector`s to be added have different dimensions. To do so, we insert the following statement at the beginning of `__add__()`:

```
if len(self) != len(other):
    raise Exception('vectors have different dimensions')
```

This leads to a more informative error message than the `IndexError` that the client otherwise would receive if the dimensions of `self` and `other` do not agree.

Assertions. An *assertion* is a boolean expression that you are affirming is `True` at that point in the program. If the expression is `False`, the program will raise an `AssertionError` at run time. Programmers uses assertions to detect bugs and gain confidence in the correctness of their programs. Assertions also serve to document the programmer's intent. For example, in `Counter` (Program 3.3.2), we might check that the counter is never negative by adding the following assertion as the last statement in `increment()`:

```
assert self._count >= 0
```

This statement would call attention to a negative count. You can also add an optional detail message, such as

```
assert self._count >= 0, 'Negative count detected!'
```

to help identify the bug.

By default, assertions are enabled, but you can disable them from the command line by using the `-O` (that's a minus sign followed by an uppercase "oh") flag with the `python` command. (The `O` stands for "optimize.") Assertions are for debugging only; your program should not rely on assertions for normal operation since they may be disabled.

When you take a course in systems programming, you will learn to use assertions to ensure that your code *never* terminates in a system error or goes into an infinite loop. One model, known as the *design-by-contract* model of programming, expresses this idea. The designer of a data type expresses a *precondition* (the condition that the client promises to satisfy when calling a method), a *postcondition* (the condition that the implementation promises to achieve when returning from a method), *invariants* (any condition that the implementation promises to satisfy while the method is executing), and *side effects* (any other change in state that the method could cause). During development, these conditions can be tested with assertions. Many programmers use assertions liberally to aid in debugging.

THE LANGUAGE MECHANISMS DISCUSSED THROUGHOUT THIS section illustrate that effective data-type design takes us into deep water in programming-language design. Experts are still debating the best ways to support some of the design ideas that we are discussing. Why does Python not enforce access control of "private" instance variables? Why are functions not first-class objects in Java? Why does Matlab pass copies of arrays and matrices to functions instead of references? As mentioned early in CHAPTER 1, it is a slippery slope from complaining about features in a programming language to becoming a programming-language designer. If you do not plan to do so, your best strategy is to use widely available languages. Most systems have extensive libraries that you certainly should use when appropriate, but you often can simplify your client code and protect yourself by building abstractions that can be easily translated to other languages. Your main goal is to develop data types so that most of your work is done at a level of abstraction that is appropriate to the problem at hand.

Q&A

Q. Why is the underscore convention not part of (and enforced by) Python?

A. Good question.

Q. Why all the leading underscores?

A. This is just one of many examples where a programming-language designer goes with a personal preference and we live with the result. Fortunately, most Python programs that you compose will be client programs, which do not directly call special methods or refer to private instance variables, so they will not need many leading underscores. The relatively few Python programmers who implement their own data types (that's you, now) need to follow the underscore conventions, but even those programmers are likely to be composing more client code than class implementations, so the underscores may not be so onerous in the long run.

Q. The `__mul__()` method in `complexpolar.py` (Program 3.3.1) is awkward because it create a `Complex` object (representing $0 + 0i$) and then immediately changes its instance variables to the desired polar coordinates. Wouldn't the design be better if I could add a second constructor that takes the polar coordinates as arguments?

A. Yes, but we already have a constructor that takes the rectangular coordinates as arguments. A better design might be to have two ordinary functions (not methods) `createRect(x, y)` and `createPolar(r, theta)` in the API that create and return new objects. This design is perhaps better because it would provide the *client* with the capability to switch to polar coordinates. This example demonstrates that it is a good idea to think about more than one implementation when developing a data type. Of course, making such a change necessitates enhancing all existing implementations and clients of the API, so this thinking should happen as early in the design process as possible.

Q. How do I specify a tuple consisting of zero items or one item?

A. You can use `()` and `(1,)`, respectively. Without the comma in the second expression, Python would treat it as an arithmetic expression enclosed in parentheses.

Q. Do I really need to overload all six comparison methods if I want to make my data type comparable?

A. Yes. This is an example where the convention is to provide maximum flexibility to clients at the expense of extra code in implementations. Often, you can use symmetries to cut down on the actual amount of implementation code. Also, Python 3 supplies a few shortcuts. For example, if you define an `__eq__()` method for a data type but do not define an `__ne__()` method, then Python automatically provides an implementation that calls `__eq__()` and negates the result. However, Python 2 does not provide these shortcuts, so it is best not to rely upon them in your code.

Q. Is there is any situation where I would not want the six comparison methods to implement a total order?

A. Yes, you might want to implement a *partial order*, where not every pair of objects can be compared. For example, you might compare people according to genealogical order, where one person is considered less than another if he or she is a descendant (child, grandchild, great-grandchild, and so forth) of the other. Not all people are related in this manner. Also, you might want to be able to compare `Counter` objects by their counts (when sorting) but you might want to consider two `Counter` objects to be equal only if they have both the same count and name.

Q. What is the range of integer values returned by the built-in `hash()` function?

A. Typically, Python uses a 64-bit integer, so the range is between -2^{63} and $2^{63} - 1$. For cryptographic applications, you should use Python's `hashlib` module, which supports "secure" hash functions that support much larger ranges.

Q. Which Python operators cannot be overloaded?

A. In Python, you cannot overload

- The boolean operators `and`, `or`, and `not`.
- The `is` and `is not` operators, which test for object identity.
- The string format operator `%`, which can be applied only to strings.
- The assignment operator `=`.

Exercises

3.3.1 Create a data type `Location` for dealing with locations on Earth using spherical coordinates (latitude/longitude). Include methods to generate a random location on the surface of the Earth, parse a location "25.344 N, 63.5532 W," and compute the great-circle distance between two locations.

3.3.2 Create a data type for a three-dimensional particle with position (r_x, r_y, r_z), mass (m), and velocity (v_x, v_y, v_z). Include a method to return its kinetic energy, which equals $1/2\ m\ (v_x^2 + v_y^2 + v_z^2)$. Use the `Vector` data type.

3.3.3 If you know your physics, develop an alternative implementation of the data type from the previous exercise based on using the *momentum* (p_x, p_y, p_z) as an instance variable.

3.3.4 Develop an implementation of `Histogram` (Program 3.2.3) that uses the `Counter` (Program 3.3.2) data type.

3.3.5 Design a test client for `Vector`.

3.3.6 Compose an implementation of `__sub__()` for `Vector` that subtracts two vectors.

3.3.7 Implement a data type `Vector2D` for two-dimensional vectors that has the same API as `Vector`, except that the constructor takes two floats as arguments. Use two floats (instead of an array) for instance variables.

3.3.8 Implement the `Vector2D` data type of the previous exercise using one `Complex` object as the only instance variable.

3.3.9 Prove that the dot product of two two-dimensional unit-vectors is the cosine of the angle between them.

3.3.10 Implement a data type `Vector3D` for three-dimensional vectors that has the same API as `Vector`, except that the constructor takes three floats as arguments. Also, add a *cross-product* method; the cross-product of two vectors is another vector, defined by the equation

$$\mathbf{a} \times \mathbf{b} = \mathbf{c}\ |\mathbf{a}|\ |\mathbf{b}|\ \sin\theta$$

where **c** is the unit normal vector perpendicular to both **a** and **b**, and θ is the angle between **a** and **b**. In Cartesian coordinates, the following equation defines the cross-product:

$$(a_0, a_1, a_2) \times (b_0, b_1, b_2) = (a_1 b_2 - a_2 b_1, a_2 b_0 - a_0 b_2, a_0 b_1 - a_1 b_0)$$

The cross-product arises in the definition of torque, angular momentum, and vector operator curl. Also, $|\mathbf{a} \times \mathbf{b}|$ is the area of the parallelogram with sides **a** and **b**.

3.3.11 Which modifications (if any) would you need to make `Vector` work with `Complex` components (see PROGRAM 3.2.6) or `Rational` components (see EXERCISE 3.2.7)?

3.3.12 Add code to `charge.py` to make `Charge` objects comparable using the value of the charge to determine the total order.

3.3.13 Compose a function `fibonacci()` that takes an integer argument `n` and computes the `n`th Fibonacci number. Use tuple packing and unpacking.

3.3.14 Revise the `gcd()` function in PROGRAM 2.3.1 so that it takes two nonnegative integer arguments `p` and `q` and returns a `tuple` of integers `(d, a, b)` such that `d` is the greatest common divisor of `p` and `q`, and the coefficients `a` and `b` satisfy Bézout's identity: `d = a*p + b*q`. Use tuple packing and unpacking.

Solution: This algorithm is known as *extended Euclid's algorithm*:

```
def gcd(p, q):
    if q == 0: return (p, 1, 0)
    (d, a, b) = gcd(q, p % q)
    return (d, b, a - (p // q) * b)
```

3.3.15 Discuss the advantages and disadvantages of Python's design in making the built-in type `bool` be a subclass of the built-in type `int`.

3.3.16 Add code to `Counter` to raise a `ValueError` at run time if the client tries to create a `Counter` object using a negative value for `maxCount`.

3.3.17 Use exceptions to develop an implementation of `Rational` (see EXERCISE 3.2.7) that raises a `ValueException` at run time if the denominator is zero.

Data-Type Design Exercises

This group of exercises is intended to give you experience in developing data types. For each problem, design one or more APIs with API implementations, testing your design decisions by implementing typical client code. Some of the exercises require either knowledge of a particular domain or a search for information about it on the web.

3.3.18 *Statistics.* Develop a data type for maintaining statistics in a set of floats. Provide a method to add data points and methods that return the number of points, the mean, the standard deviation, and the variance. Develop two implementations: one whose instance values are the number of points, the sum of the values, and the sum of the squares of the values, and another that keeps an array containing all the points. For simplicity, you may take the maximum number of points in the constructor. Your first implementation is likely to be faster and use substantially less space, but is also likely to be susceptible to round-off error. See the booksite for a well-engineered alternative.

3.3.19 *Genome.* Develop a data type to store the genome of an organism. Biologists often abstract the genome to a sequence of bases (`A`, `C`, `G`, or `T`). The data type should support the methods `addCodon(c)` and `baseAt(i)`, as well as `isPotentialGene()` (see Program 3.1.1). Develop three implementations.

- Use a string as the only instance variable; implement `addCodon()` with string concatenation.
- Use an array of single-character strings as the only instance variable; implement `addCodon()` with the += operator.
- Use a boolean array, encoding each base with two bits.

3.3.20 *Time.* Develop a data type for the time of day. Provide client methods that return the current hour, minute, and second, as well as a `__str__()` method. Develop two implementations: one that keeps the time as a single `int` value (number of seconds since midnight) and another that keeps three `int` values, one each for seconds, minutes, and hours.

3.3.21 *Vector fields.* Develop a data type for force vectors in two dimensions. Provide a constructor, a method to add two vectors, and an interesting test client.

3.3.22 *Dates.* Develop an API for dates (year, month, day). Include methods for comparing two dates chronologically, computing the number of days between two dates, determining the day of the week of a given date, and any other operations that you think a client might want. After you have designed your API, look at the Python's `datetime.date` data type.

3.3.23 *Polynomials.* Develop a data type for univariate polynomials with integer coefficients, such as $x^3 + 5x^2 + 3x + 7$. Include methods for standard operations on polynomials such as addition, subtraction, multiplication, degree, evaluation, composition, differentiation, definite integration, and testing equality.

3.3.24 *Rational polynomials.* Repeat the previous exercise, ensuring that the polynomial data type behaves correctly when provided coefficients of type `int`, `float`, `complex`, and `Fraction` (see Exercise 3.2.7).

Creative Exercises

3.3.25 *Calendar.* Develop `Appointment` and `Calendar` APIs that can be used to keep track of appointments (by day) in a calendar year. Your goal is to enable clients to schedule appointments that do not conflict and to report current appointments to clients. Use Python's `datetime` module.

3.3.26 *Vector field.* A vector field associates a vector with every point in a Euclidean space. Compose a version of `potential.py` (PROGRAM 3.1.8) that takes as input a grid size n, computes the `Vector` value of the potential due to the point charges at each point in an n-by-n grid of equally spaced points, and draws the unit vector in the direction of the accumulated field at each point.

3.3.27 *Genome sketching.* Compose a function `hash()` that takes as an argument a k-gram (string of length k) whose characters are all `A`, `C`, `G`, or `T` and returns an `int` between 0 and 4^k that corresponds to treating the string as base-4 numbers with {`A`, `C`, `G`, `T`} replaced by {0, 1, 2, 3}, respectively, as suggested by the table in the text. Next, compose a function `unhash()` that reverses the transformation. Use your methods to create a class `Genome` that is like `Sketch`, but is based on exact counting of k-grams in genomes. Finally, compose a version of `comparealldocuments.py` for `Genome` objects and use it to look for similarities among a set of genome files.

3.3.28 *Sketching.* Pick an interesting set of documents from the booksite (or use a collection of your own) and run `comparealldocuments.py` with various command-line arguments, to learn about their effect on the computation.

3.3.29 *Multimedia search.* Develop sketching strategies for sound and pictures, and use them to discover interesting similarities among songs in the music library and photos in the photo album on your computer.

3.3.30 *Data mining.* Compose a recursive program that surfs the web, starting at a page given as the first command-line argument, and looks for pages that are similar to the page given as the second command-line argument, as follows. To process a name, open an input stream, do a `readAll()`, sketch it, and write the name if its distance to the target page is greater than the threshold value given as the third command-line argument. Then scan the page for all strings that contain the substring `http://` and (recursively) process pages with those names. *Note*: This program might read a very large number of pages!

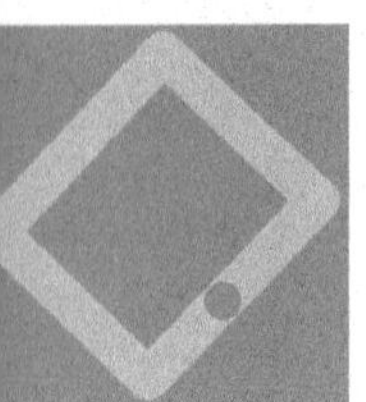

3.4 Case Study: N-Body Simulation

WE CAN EXPRESS SEVERAL OF THE examples that we considered in CHAPTERS 1 AND 2 more clearly as object-oriented programs. For example, we can implement `bouncingball.py` (PROGRAM 1.5.7) as a data type whose values are the position and the velocity of the ball and a client that calls methods to move and draw the ball. Such a data type enables, for example, clients that can simulate the motion of several balls at once (see EXERCISE 3.4.1). Similarly, our case study for percolation in SECTION 2.4 certainly makes an interesting exercise in object-oriented programming, as does our random-surfer case study in SECTION 1.6. We leave the former for an exercise (see EXERCISE 3.4.11) and will revisit the latter in SECTION 4.5. In this section, we consider a new program that exemplifies object-oriented programming.

Programs in this section

Our task is to compose a program that dynamically simulates the motion of n bodies under the influence of mutual gravitational attraction. This *n-body simulation* problem was first formulated by Isaac Newton over 350 years ago, and scientists still study it intensely today.

What is the set of values, and what are the operations on those values? One reason that this problem is a compelling example of object-oriented programming is that it presents a direct and natural correspondence between physical objects in the real world and the abstract objects that we use in programming. The shift from solving problems by putting together sequences of statements to be executed to beginning with data-type design is a difficult one for many novices. As you gain more experience, you will benefit from applying this approach to computational problem solving.

First, we revisit a few basic concepts and equations that you learned in high-school physics. Understanding these equations fully is not required to appreciate the code—because of *encapsulation*, these equations are restricted to a few methods, and because of *data abstraction*, most of the code is intuitive and will make sense to you. In a sense, this is the ultimate object-oriented program.

N-body simulation The bouncing-ball simulation of Section 1.5 is based on *Newton's first law of motion*: a body in motion remains in motion at the same velocity unless acted on by an outside force. Embellishing that example to include Newton's *second law of motion* (which explains how outside forces affect velocity) leads us to a basic problem that has fascinated scientists for ages. Given a system of n bodies, mutually affected by gravitational forces, the problem is to describe their motion. The same basic model applies to problems ranging in scale from astrophysics to molecular dynamics.

In 1687, Newton formulated the principles governing the motion of two bodies under the influence of their mutual gravitational attraction, in his famous *Principia*. However, Newton was unable to develop a mathematical description of the motion of *three* bodies. It has since been shown that not only that no such description exists in terms of elementary functions, but also that chaotic behavior is possible, depending on initial values. To study such problems, scientists have no recourse except to develop accurate simulations. In this section, we develop an object-oriented program that implements such a simulation. Scientists are interested in studying such problems for huge numbers of bodies, so our solution is only an introduction to the subject, but you are likely to be surprised at the ease with which we can develop realistic images depicting the complexity of the motion.

Body data type. In `bouncingball.py` (Program 1.5.7), we keep the displacement from the origin in the floats `rx` and `ry` and the velocity in the floats `vx` and `vy`, and displace the ball the amount it moves in one time unit with the statements:

```
rx = rx + vx
ry = ry + vy
```

With `Vector` (Program 3.3.3), we can keep the position in the `Vector` `r` and the velocity in the `Vector` `v`, and then displace the body the amount it moves in `dt` time units with a single statement:

```
r = r + v.scale(dt)
```

In n-body simulation, we have several operations of this kind, so our first design decision is to work with `Vector` objects instead of individual components. This decision leads to code that is clearer, more compact, and more flexible than

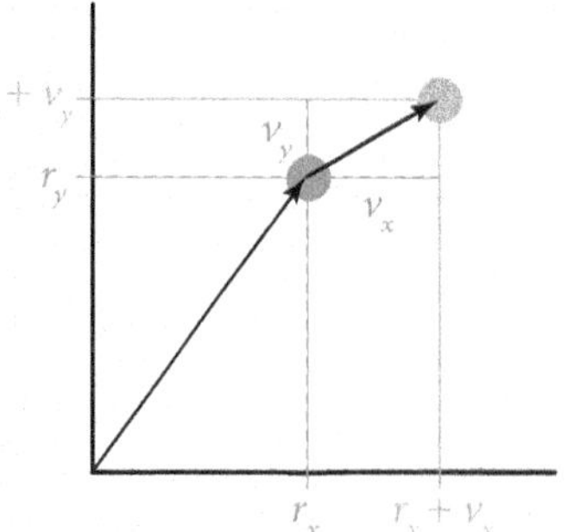

Adding vectors to move a ball

operation	description
`Body(r, v, mass)`	*a new body with mass* `mass` *at position* `r` *moving at velocity* `v`
`b.move(f, dt)`	*move* `b` *by applying force* `f` *for* `dt` *seconds*
`b.forceFrom(a)`	*force vector from body* `a` *on body* `b`
`b.draw()`	*draw body* `b` *to standard drawing*

API for a user-defined Body data type

the alternative of working with individual components. PROGRAM 3.4.1 (`body.py`) implements `Body`, a Python class for a data type for moving bodies. `Body` is a `Vector` client—the values of the data type are `Vector` objects that carry the body's position and velocity, as well as a float that carries the mass. The data-type operations allow clients to move and to draw the body (and to compute the force vector due to gravitational attraction from another body), as defined by the API at the top of this page. Technically, the body's position (displacement from the origin) is not a vector (it is a point in space, not a direction and a magnitude), but it is convenient to represent it as a `Vector` because `Vector` operations lead to compact code for the transformation that we need to move the body, as just discussed. When we move a `Body`, we need to change not just its position, but also its velocity.

Force and motion. ***Newton's second law of motion*** says that the force on a body (a vector) is equal to the scalar product of its mass and its acceleration (also a vector): $\mathbf{F} = m\,\mathbf{a}$. In other words, to compute the acceleration of a body, we compute the force, then divide by its mass. In `Body`, the force is a `Vector` argument `f` to `move()`,

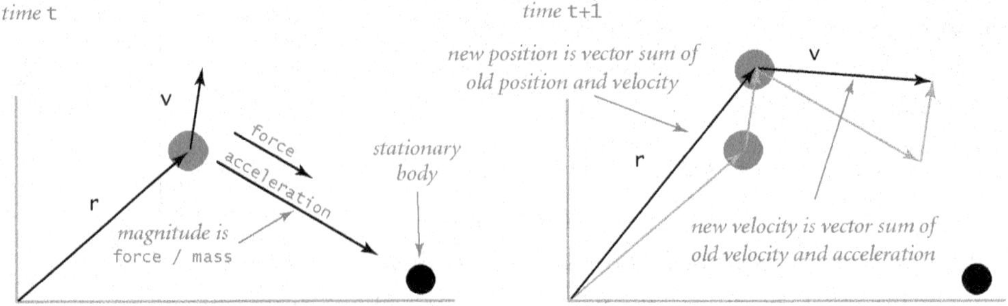

Motion near a stationary body

so that we can first compute the acceleration vector just by dividing by the mass (a scalar value that is kept as a float in an instance variable) and then compute the change in velocity by adding to it the amount this vector changes over the time interval (in the same way that we used the velocity to change the position). This law immediately translates to the following code for updating the position and velocity of a body due to a given force vector `f` and amount of time `dt`:

```
a = f.scale(1.0 / mass)
v = v + a.scale(dt)
r = r + v.scale(dt)
```

This code appears in the `move()` method in `Body`, to adjust its values to reflect the consequences of that force being applied for that amount of time: the body moves and its velocity changes. This calculation assumes that the acceleration is constant during the time interval.

Forces among bodies. The computation of the force imposed by one body on another is encapsulated in the method `forceFrom()` in `Body`, which takes a `Body` object as argument and returns a `Vector`. *Newton's law of universal gravitation* is the basis for the calculation: the magnitude of the gravitational force between two bodies is given by the product of their masses divided by the square of the distance between them (scaled by the gravitational constant G, which is 6.67×10^{-11} N m^2 / kg^2) and the direction of the force is the line between the two particles. This law translates to the following code for computing `a.forceFrom(b)`:

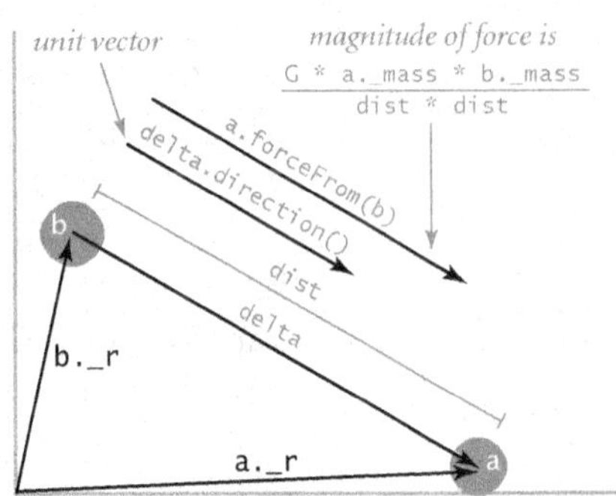

Force from one body to another

```
G = 6.67e-11
delta = b._r - a._r
dist = abs(delta)
magnitude = G * a.mass * b.mass / (dist * dist)
f = delta.direction().scale(magnitude)
```

The *magnitude* of the force vector is the float `magnitude`, and the *direction* of the force vector is the same as the direction of the difference vector between the two body's positions. The force vector `f` is the product of magnitude and direction.

Program 3.4.1 Gravitational body (body.py)

```
import stddraw
from vector import Vector

class Body:
    def __init__(self, r, v, mass):
        self._r = r
        self._v = v
        self._mass = mass

    def move(self, f, dt):
        a = f.scale(1.0 / self._mass)
        self._v = self._v + a.scale(dt)
        self._r = self._r + self._v.scale(dt)

    def forceFrom(self, other):
        G = 6.67e-11
        delta = other._r - self._r
        dist = abs(delta)
        m1 = self._mass
        m2 = other._mass
        magnitude = G * m1 * m2 / (dist * dist)
        return delta.direction().scale(magnitude)

    def draw(self):
        stddraw.setPenRadius(0.0125)
        stddraw.point(self._r[0], self._r[1])
```

instance variables

`_r`	*position*
`_v`	*velocity*
`_mass`	*mass*

`f`	*force on this body*
`dt`	*time increment*
`a`	*acceleration*

`self`	*invoking body*
`other`	*another body*
`G`	*gravitational constant*
`delta`	*vector between bodies*
`dist`	*distance between bodies*
`magnitude`	*magnitude of force*

This data type provides the operations that we need to simulate the motion of physical bodies such as planets or atomic particles. It is a mutable type whose instance variables are the position and velocity of the body, which change in the `move()` *method in response to external forces (the body's mass is not mutable). The* `forceFrom()` *method returns a force vector. The unit test is deferred to* Exercise *3.4.2.*

Universe data type. `Universe` (PROGRAM 3.4.2) is a data type that implements the following API:

operation	*description*
`Universe(file)`	*a new universe built from a description in* `file`
`u.increaseTime(dt)`	*update* `u` *by simulating the universe for* `dt` *seconds*
`u.draw()`	*draw universe* `u` *to standard drawing*

API for a user-defined `Universe` *data type*

Its data-type values define a universe (its size, the number of bodies, and an array of bodies) and two data type operations: `increaseTime()`, which adjusts the positions (and velocities) of all of the bodies, and `draw()`, which draws all of the bodies. The key to the n-body simulation is the implementation of `increaseTime()` in `Universe`. The first part of the computation is a doubly nested loop that computes the force vector describing the gravitational force of each body on each other body. It applies the *principle of superposition*, which says that we can add together the force vectors affecting a body to get a single vector representing the aggregate force. After it has computed all of the forces, it calls the `move()` method for each body to apply the computed force for a fixed time quantum.

```
% more 2body.txt
2
5.0e10
0.0e00  4.5e10  1.0e04 0.0e00 1.5e30
0.0e00 -4.5e10 -1.0e04 0.0e00 1.5e30

% more 3body.txt
3
1.25e11
0.0e00  0.0e00 0.05e04 0.0e00 5.97e24
0.0e00  4.5e10  3.0e04 0.0e00 1.989e30
0.0e00 -4.5e10 -3.0e04 0.0e00 1.989e30

% more 4body.txt
4          ← n
5.0e10     ← radius
-3.5e10 0.0e00 0.0e00  1.4e03 3.0e28
-1.0e10 0.0e00 0.0e00  1.4e04 3.0e28
 1.0e10 0.0e00 0.0e00 -1.4e04 3.0e28
 3.5e10 0.0e00 0.0e00 -1.4e03 3.0e28
```


Universe file format examples

File format. We use a data-driven design with input taken from a file. The constructor reads the universe parameters and body descriptions from a file that contains the following information:

- The number of bodies
- The radius of the universe
- The position, velocity, and mass of each body

As usual, for consistency, all measurements are in standard SI units (recall that the gravitational constant G also appears in our code). With this defined file format, the code for our `Universe` constructor is straightforward.

```
def __init__(self, filename):
    instream = InStream(filename)
    n = instream.readInt()
    radius = instream.readFloat()

    stddraw.setXscale(-radius, +radius)
    stddraw.setYscale(-radius, +radius)

    self._bodies = stdarray.create1D(n)
    for i in range(n):
        rx   = instream.readFloat()
        ry   = instream.readFloat()
        vx   = instream.readFloat()
        vy   = instream.readFloat()
        mass = instream.readFloat()
        r = Vector([rx, ry])
        v = Vector([vx, vy])
        self._bodies[i] = Body(r, v, mass)
```

Each `Body` is characterized by five floats: the x- and y-coordinates of its position, the x- and y-components of its initial velocity, and its mass.

To summarize, we have in the test client `main()` in `Universe` a data-driven program that simulates the motion of n bodies mutually attracted by gravity. The constructor creates an array of n `Body` objects, reading each body's initial position, initial velocity, and mass from the file name specified as the command-line argument. The `increaseTime()` method calculates the mutual force on the bodies and uses that information to update the acceleration, velocity, and position of each body after a time quantum `dt`. The `main()` test client invokes the constructor, then stays in a loop calling `increaseTime()` and `draw()` to simulate motion.

Program 3.4.2 N-body simulation (universe.py)

```
import sys
import stdarray
import stddraw
from body import Body
from instream import InStream
from vector import Vector

class Universe:

    def __init__(self, filename):
    // See text.

    def increaseTime(self, dt):
        n = len(self._bodies)
        f = stdarray.create1D(n, Vector([0, 0]))
        for i in range(n):
            for j in range(n):
                if i != j:
                    bodyi = self._bodies[i]
                    bodyj = self._bodies[j]
                    f[i] = f[i] + bodyi.forceFrom(bodyj)
        for i in range(n):
            self._bodies[i].move(f[i], dt)

    def draw(self):
        for body in self._bodies:
            body.draw()

def main():
    universe = Universe(sys.argv[1])
    dt = float(sys.argv[2])
    while True:
        universe.increaseTime(dt)
        stddraw.clear()
        universe.draw()
        stddraw.show(10)

if __name__ == '__main__': main()
```

instance variables

_bodies	*array of bodies*

n	*number of bodies*
f[]	*force on each body*

```
% python universe.py 3body.txt 20000
```

880 steps

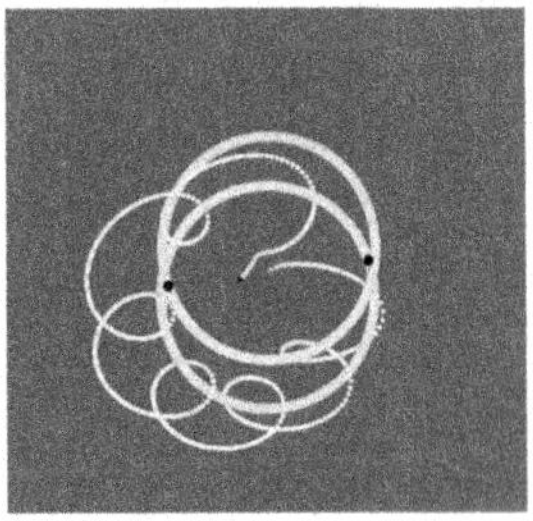

This data-driven program simulates motion in the universe defined by the data in the file specified on the command line, increasing time at the rate dt *specified on the command line. The constructor is given in the text.*

You will find on the booksite a variety of files that define "universes" of all sorts, and you are encouraged to run `universe.py` and observe their motion. When you view the motion for even a small number of bodies, you will understand why Newton had trouble deriving the equations that define their trajectories. The figures on the facing page illustrate the result of running `universe.py` for the 2-body, 3-body, and 4-body examples in the data files given earlier. The 2-body example is a mutually orbiting pair, the 3-body example is a chaotic situation with a moon jumping between two orbiting planets, and the 4-body example has two pairs of mutually orbiting bodies that are slowly rotating. (The 3-body example uses a slightly modified version of `Body` where the radius of the body drawn is proportional to its mass.) The static images on these pages were made by modifying `Universe` and `Body` to draw the bodies in white, and then black on a gray background, as in `bouncingball.py` (PROGRAM 1.5.7). By comparison, the dynamic images that you get when you run `universe.py` as it stands give a realistic feeling of the bodies orbiting one another, which is difficult to discern in the fixed pictures. When you run `universe.py` on an example with a large number of bodies, you can appreciate why simulation is such an important tool for scientists trying to understand a complex problem. The n-body simulation model is remarkably versatile, as you will see if you experiment with some of these input files.

You will certainly be tempted to design your own universe (see EXERCISE 3.4.10). The biggest challenge in creating a data file is appropriately scaling the numbers so that the radius of the universe, time scale, and the mass and velocity of the bodies lead to interesting behavior. You can study the motion of planets rotating around a sun or subatomic particles interacting with one another, but you will have no luck studying the interaction of a planet with a subatomic particle. When you work with your own data, you are likely to have some bodies that will fly off to infinity and some others that are sucked into others, but enjoy!

planetary scale

```
% more 2body.txt
2
5.0e10
0.0e00  4.5e10  1.0e04 0.0e00 1.5e30
0.0e00 -4.5e10 -1.0e04 0.0e00 1.5e30
```

subatomic scale

```
% more 2bodyTiny.txt
2
5.0e-10
0.0e00  4.5e-10  1.0e-16 0.0e00 1.5e-30
0.0e00 -4.5e-10 -1.0e-16 0.0e00 1.5e-30
```

Two input files of varying scale

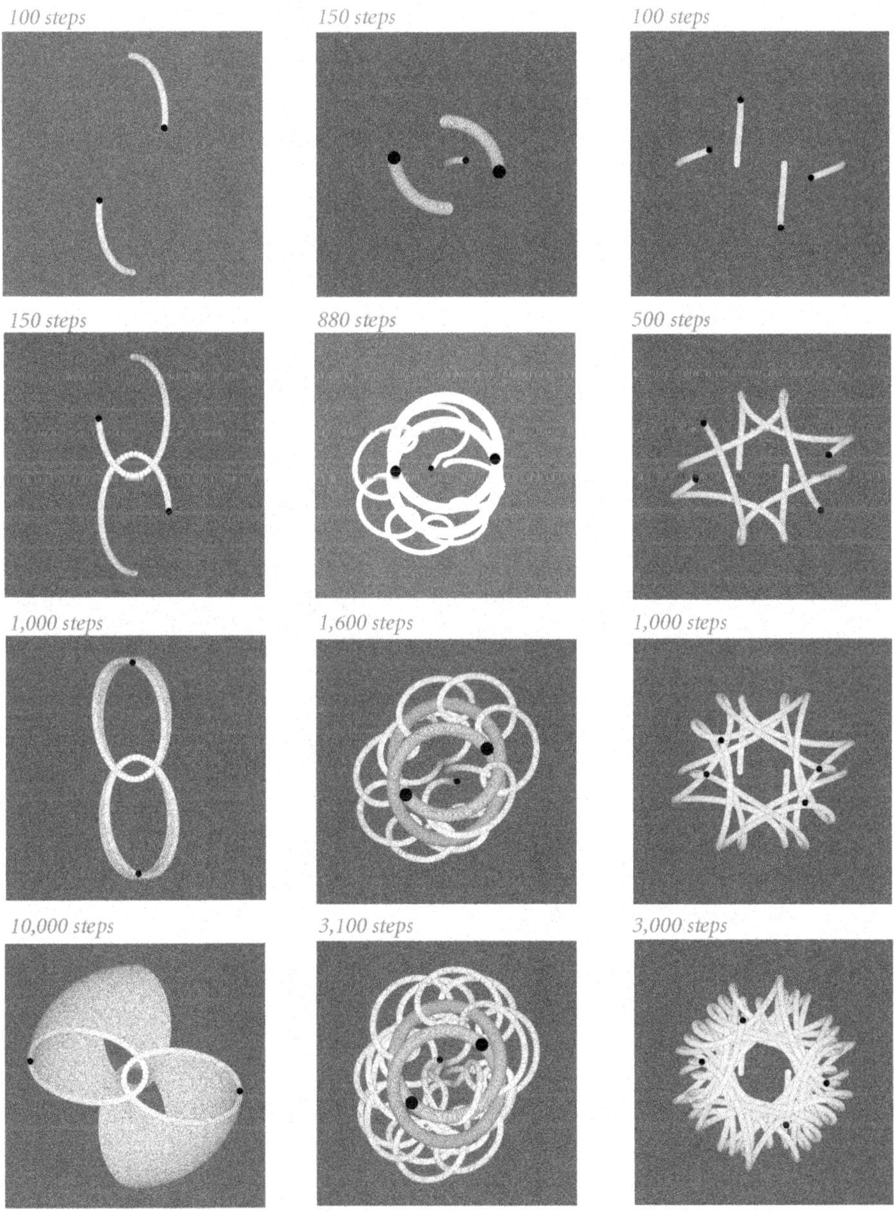

Simulating 2-, 3-, and 4-body universes

Our purpose in presenting this example is to illustrate the utility of data types, not to present simulation code for production use. There are many issues that scientists have to deal with when using this approach to study natural phenomena. One such issue is *numerical accuracy*: it is common for inaccuracies in the calculations to accumulate and yield dramatic effects in the simulation that would not be observed in nature. The technique that we use to update the positions and velocities is known as the *leapfrog* method; it produces more accurate results than many competing approaches. A second issue is *efficiency*: the `move()` method in `Universe` takes time proportional to n^2 and, therefore, is not usable for huge numbers of bodies. Our simulation also ignores other forces. For example, our code takes no special action when two (or more) bodies collide. Addressing scientific problems related to the n-body problem involves not just knowledge of the original problem domain, but also the core issues that computer scientists have been studying since the early days of computation.

For simplicity, we are working with a *two-dimensional* universe, which is realistic only when we are considering bodies in motion on a plane. But an important implication of basing the implementation of `Body` on `Vector` is that a client could use *three-dimensional* vectors to simulate the motion of moving balls in three dimensions (actually, any number of dimensions) without changing much code (see Exercise 3.4.9).

The test client in `Universe` is just one possibility; we can use the same basic model in all sorts of other situations (for example, involving different kinds of interactions among the bodies). One such possibility is to observe and measure the current motion of some existing bodies and then run the simulation backward! Astrophysicists use just such a method to try to understand the origins of the universe. In science, we try to understand the past and to predict the future; with a good simulation, we can do both.

Q&A

Q. The `Universe` API is certainly small. Why not just implement that code in a `main()` test client for `Body`?

A. Our design is an expression of what many people believe about the universe: it was created, and then time moves on. It clarifies the code and allows for maximum flexibility in simulating what goes on in the universe.

Q. Why is `forceFrom()` a method? Wouldn't it be better for it to be a function that takes two `Body` objects as arguments?

A. Implementing `forceFrom()` as a method is one of several possible alternatives, and having a function that takes two `Body` objects as arguments is certainly a reasonable choice. Some programmers prefer to completely avoid functions in data-type implementations; another option is to maintain the force acting on each `Body` as an instance variable. Our choice is a compromise between these two options.

Q. Shouldn't the `move()` method in `body.py` update the position using the *old* velocity instead of the *updated* velocity?

A. It turns out that using the updated velocity (known as the *leapfrog method*) produces more accurate results than using the old velocity (known as the *Euler method*). If you take a course in numerical analysis, you will learn why.

Exercises

3.4.1 Develop an object-oriented version of `bouncingball.py` (PROGRAM 1.5.7). Include a constructor that starts each ball moving in a random direction at a random velocity (within reasonable limits) and a test client that takes an integer `n` from the command line and simulates the motion of `n` bouncing balls.

3.4.2 Add to `body.py` (PROGRAM 3.4.1) a `main()` method that unit tests the `Body` data type.

3.4.3 Modify `body.py` so that the radius of the circle it draws for a body is proportional to its mass.

3.4.4 What happens in a universe with no gravitational force? This situation would correspond to `forceFrom()` in `Body` always returning the zero vector.

3.4.5 Create a data type `Universe3D` to model three-dimensional universes. Develop a data file to simulate the motion of the planets in our solar system around the sun.

3.4.6 Compose a test client that simulates the motion of two different universes (defined by two different files and appearing in two distinct parts of the standard drawing window). You also need to modify the `draw()` method in `Body`.

3.4.7 Compose a class `RandomBody` that initializes its instance variables with (carefully chosen) random values instead of taking them as arguments. Then compose a client that takes a single argument `n` from the command line and simulates motion in a random universe with `n` bodies.

3.4.8 Modify `Vector` to include a method `__iadd__(self, other)` to support the in-place addition operator `+=`, which enables the client to compose code like `r += v.scale(dt)`. Using this method, revise `body.py` and `universe.py`.

3.4.9 Modify the `Vector` constructor so that if passed a positive integer `d` as argument, it creates and returns the all-zero vector of dimension `d`. Using this modified constructor, revise `universe.py` so that it works with three- (or higher-) dimensional universes. For simplicity, don't worry about changing the `draw()` method in `body.py`—it projects the position onto the plane defined by the first x- and y-coordinates.

Creative Exercises

3.4.10 *New universe.* Design a new universe with interesting properties and simulate its motion with `Universe`. This exercise is truly an opportunity to be creative!

3.4.11 *Percolation.* Compose an object-oriented version of `percolation.py` (PROGRAM 2.4.6). Think carefully about the design before you begin, and be prepared to defend your design decisions.

Chapter Four

Algorithms and Data Structures

THIS CHAPTER PRESENTS FUNDAMENTAL DATA TYPES that are essential building blocks for a broad variety of applications. We present full implementations, even though some of them are built into Python, so that you can have a clear idea of how they work and why they are important.

Objects can contain references to other objects, so we can build structures known as *linked structures*, which can be arbitrarily complex. With linked structures and arrays, we can build *data structures* to organize information in such a way that we can efficiently process it with associated *algorithms*. In a data type, we use the set of values to build data structures and the methods that operate on those values to implement algorithms.

The algorithms and data structures that we consider in this chapter introduce a body of knowledge developed over the past several decades that constitutes the basis for the efficient use of computers for a broad variety of applications. From n-body simulation problems in physics to genetic sequencing problems in bioinformatics, the basic approaches we describe have become essential in scientific research; from database systems to search engines, these methods are the foundation of commercial computing. As the scope of computing applications continues to expand, so grows the impact of these basic approaches.

Algorithms and data structures themselves are valid subjects of scientific inquiry. Accordingly, we begin by describing a scientific approach for analyzing the performance of algorithms, which we use throughout the chapter to study the performance characteristics of our implementations.

4.1 Performance

IN THIS SECTION, YOU WILL LEARN to respect a principle that is succinctly expressed in yet another mantra that should live with you whenever you program: *Pay attention to the cost.* If you become an engineer, that will be your job; if you become a biologist or a physicist, the cost will dictate which scientific problems you can address; if you are in business or become an economist, this principle needs no defense; and if you become a software developer, the cost will dictate whether the software that you build will be useful to your clients.

Programs in this section

To study the cost of running them, we study our programs themselves via the *scientific method*, the commonly accepted body of techniques universally used by scientists to develop knowledge about the natural world. We also apply *mathematical analysis* to derive concise models of the cost.

Which features of the natural world are we studying? In most situations, we are interested in one fundamental characteristic: *time*. Whenever we run a program, we are performing an experiment involving the natural world, putting a complex system of electronic circuitry through series of state changes involving a huge number of discrete events that we are confident will eventually stabilize to a state with results that we want to interpret. Although developed in the abstract world of Python programming, these events most definitely are happening in the natural world. What will be the elapsed time until we see the result? It makes a great deal of difference to us whether that time is a millisecond, a second, a day, or a week. Therefore, we want to learn, through the scientific method, how to properly control the situation, just as when we launch a rocket, build a bridge, or smash an atom.

On the one hand, modern programs and programming environments are complex; on the other hand, they are developed from a simple (but powerful) set of abstractions. It is a small miracle that a program produces the same result each time we run it. To predict the time required, we take advantage of the relative simplicity of the supporting infrastructure that we use to build programs. You may be surprised at the ease with which you can develop cost estimates and predict the performance characteristics of many of the programs that you compose.

Scientific method. The following five-step approach briefly summarizes the scientific method:

- *Observe* some feature of the natural world.
- *Hypothesize* a model that is consistent with the observations.
- *Predict* events using the hypothesis.
- *Verify* the predictions by making further observations.
- *Validate* by repeating until the hypothesis and observations agree.

One of the key tenets of the scientific method is that the experiments we design must be *reproducible*, so that others can convince themselves of the validity of the hypothesis. In addition, the hypotheses we formulate must be *falsifiable*—we have the possibility of knowing for sure when a hypothesis is wrong (and thus needs revision).

Observations Our first challenge is to make quantitative measurements of the running time of our programs. Although measuring the exact running time of our program is difficult, usually we are happy with estimates. There are a number of tools available to help us obtain such approximations. Perhaps the simplest is a physical stopwatch or the `Stopwatch` data type (see Program 3.2.2). We can simply run a program on various inputs, measuring the amount of time to process each input.

```
% python threesum.py < 1Kints.txt
```

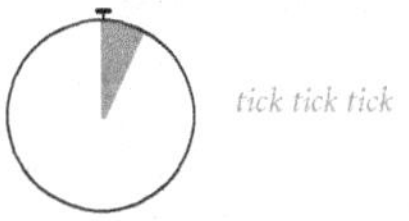

tick tick tick

```
0
% python threesum.py < 2Kints.txt
```

tick tick tick tick tick tick
tick tick tick tick tick tick
tick tick tick tick tick tick
tick tick tick tick tick tick

```
2
391930676 -763182495 371251819
-326747290 802431422 -475684132
```

Observing the running time of a program

Our first qualitative observation about most programs is that there is a *problem size* that characterizes the difficulty of the computational task. Normally, the problem size is either the size of the input or the value of a command-line argument. Intuitively, the running time should increase with the problem size, but the question of *how much* it increases naturally arises every time we develop and run a program.

Another qualitative observation for many programs is that the running time is relatively insensitive to the input itself; it depends primarily on the problem size. If this relationship does not hold, we need to run more experiments to better understand, and perhaps better control, the running time's sensitivity to the input. Since this relationship does often hold, we focus now on the goal of better quantifying the correspondence between problem size and running time.

As a concrete example, we start with threesum.py (Program 4.1.1), which counts the number of triples in an array of n numbers that sum to 0. This computation may seem contrived to you, but it is deeply related to numerous fundamental computational tasks, particularly those found in computational geometry, so it is a problem worthy of careful study. What is the relationship between the problem size n and the running time for threesum.py?

Hypotheses In the early days of computer science, Donald Knuth showed that, despite all of the complicating factors in understanding the running times of our programs, it is possible *in principle* to create accurate models that can help us predict precisely how long a particular program will take. Proper analysis of this sort involves:

- Detailed understanding of the program
- Detailed understanding of the system and the computer
- Advanced tools of mathematical analysis

Thus it is best left for experts. Every programmer, however, needs to know how to make back-of-the-envelope performance estimates. Fortunately, we can often acquire such knowledge by using a combination of empirical observations and a small set of mathematical tools.

Doubling hypotheses. For a great many programs, we can quickly formulate a hypothesis for the following question: *What is the effect on the running time of doubling the size of the input?* For clarity, we refer to this hypothesis as a *doubling hypothesis*. Perhaps the easiest way to pay attention to the cost is to ask yourself this question about your programs during development and also as you use them in practical applications. Next, we describe how to develop answers via the scientific method.

Empirical analysis. Clearly, we can get a headstart on developing a doubling hypothesis by doubling the size of the input and observing the effect on the running time. For example, doublingtest.py (Program 4.1.2) generates a sequence of random input arrays for threesum.py, doubling the array length at each step, and writes the ratio of running times of threesum.countTriples() for each input over the previous (which was one-half the size). If you run this program, you will find yourself caught in a prediction–verification cycle: It writes several lines very quickly, but then begins to slow down. Each time it writes a line, you find yourself

Program 4.1.1 3-sum problem (`threesum.py`)

```
import stdarray
import stdio

def writeTriples(a):
    # See Exercise 4.1.1.

def countTriples(a):
    n = len(a)
    count = 0
    for i in range(n):
        for j in range(i+1, n):
            for k in range(j+1, n):
                if (a[i] + a[j] + a[k]) == 0:
                    count += 1
    return count

def main():
    a = stdarray.readInt1D()
    count = countTriples(a)
    stdio.writeln(count)
    if count < 10:
        writeTriples(a)

if __name__ == '__main__': main()
```

`a[]`	*array of integers*
`n`	*length of* `a[]`
`count`	*number of triples that sum to 0*

This program reads an array of integers from standard input, and writes to standard output the number of triples in the array that sum to 0. If the number is low, then it also writes the triples. The file `1000ints.txt` *contains 1,000 random 32-bit integers (between* -2^{31} *and* $2^{31}-1$*). Such a file is not likely to have such a triple (see* Exercise *4.1.27).*

```
% more 8ints.txt
8
  30
 -30
 -20
 -10
  40
   0
  10
   5
```

```
% python threesum.py < 8ints.txt
4
  30  -30    0
  30  -20  -10
 -30  -10   40
 -10    0   10

% python threesum.py < 1000ints.txt
0
```

wondering how long it will be until it writes the next line. Checking the stopwatch as the program runs, it is easy to predict that the elapsed time increases by about a factor of 8 to write each line. This prediction is verified by the `Stopwatch` measurements that the program writes, and leads immediately to the hypothesis that the running time increases by a factor of 8 when the input size doubles. We might also plot the running times, either on a standard plot (*left*), which shows that the *rate* of increase of the running time increases with input size, or on a log-log plot. In the case of `threesum.py`, the log-log plot (*below*) is a straight line with slope 3, which clearly suggests the hypothesis that the running time satisfies a *power law* of the form cn^3 (see EXERCISE 4.1.29).

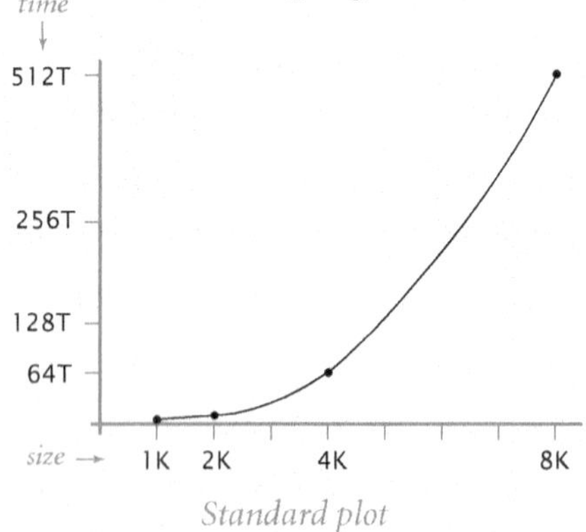

Standard plot

Mathematical analysis. Knuth's basic insight on building a mathematical model to describe the running time of a program is simple: the total running time is determined by two primary factors:

- The cost of executing each statement
- The frequency of execution of each statement

The former is a property of the system, and the latter is a property of the algorithm. If we know both for all instructions in the program, we can multiply them together and sum for all instructions in the program to get the running time.

The primary challenge is to determine the frequency of execution of the statements. Some statements are easy to analyze; for example, the statement that initializes `count` to `0` in `threesum.countTriples()` is executed only once. Others require higher-level reasoning; for example, the `if` statement in `threesum.countTriples()` is executed precisely $n(n-1)(n-2)/6$ times (that is precisely the number of ways to pick three different numbers from the input array—see EXERCISE 4.1.5).

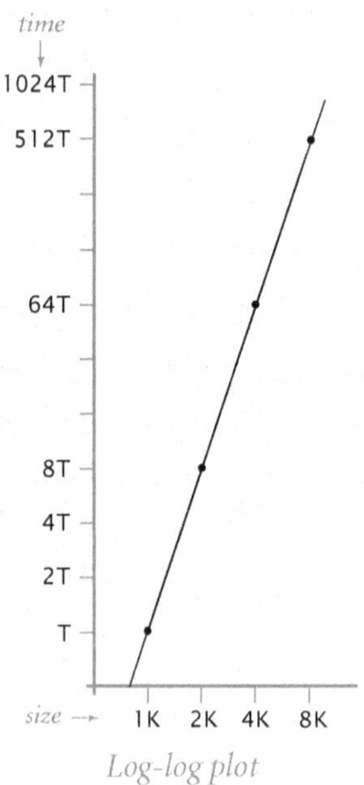

Log-log plot

Frequency analyses of this sort can lead to complicated and lengthy mathematical expressions. To substantially simplify matters in the mathematical analysis, we develop sim-

Program 4.1.2 Validating a doubling hypothesis (doublingtest.py)

```
import sys
import stdarray
import stdio
import stdrandom
import threesum
from stopwatch import Stopwatch

# Time to solve a random three-sum instance of size n.
def timeTrial(n):
    a = stdarray.create1D(n, 0)
    for i in range(n):
        a[i] = stdrandom.uniformInt(-1000000, 1000000)
    watch = Stopwatch()
    count = threesum.countTriples(a)
    return watch.elapsedTime()

n = int(sys.argv[1])
while True:
    previous = timeTrial(n // 2)
    current  = timeTrial(n)
    ratio = current / previous
    stdio.writef('%7d %4.2f\n', n, ratio)
    n *= 2
```

n	*problem size*
a[]	*random integers*
watch	*stopwatch*

n	*problem size*
previous	*running time for* n // 2
current	*running time for* n
ratio	*ratio of running times*

This program writes to standard output a table of doubling ratios for the three-sum problem. The table shows how doubling the problem size affects the running time of the function call threesum.countTriples() *for problem sizes that double for each row of the table. These experiments lead to the hypothesis that the running time increases by a factor of 8 when the input size doubles. When you run the program, note carefully that the elapsed time increases by a factor of 8 for each line written, validating the hypothesis.*

```
% python doublingtest.py 256
    256 7.52
    512 8.09
   1024 8.07
   2048 7.97
   ...
```

```
import stdarray
import stdio

def writeTriples(a):
    # See Exercise 4.1.1

def countTriples(a):
    n = len(a)
    count = 0
    for i in range(n):
        for j in range(i+1, n):
            for k in range(j+1, n):
                if (a[i] + a[j] + a[k]) == 0:
                    count += 1
    return count

def main():
    a = stdarray.readInt1D()
    count = countTriples(a)
    stdio.writeln(count)
    if count < 10:
        writeTriples(a)
if __name__ == '__main__': main()
```

Anatomy of a program's statement execution frequencies

pler *approximate* expressions in two ways. First, we work with the *leading term* of mathematical expressions by using a mathematical device known as the *tilde notation*. We write $\sim f(n)$ to represent any quantity that, when divided by $f(n)$, approaches 1 as n grows. We also write $g(n) \sim f(n)$ to indicate that $g(n) / f(n)$ approaches 1 as n grows. With this notation, we can ignore complicated parts of an expression that represent small values. For example, the `if` statement in `threesum.py` is executed $\sim n^3/6$ times because $n(n-1)(n-2) / 6 = n^3/6 - n^2/2 + n/3$, which, when divided by $n^3/6$, approaches 1 as n grows. This notation is useful when the terms after the leading term are relatively insignificant (for example, when $n =$ 1,000, this assumption amounts to saying that $-n^2/2 + n/3 \approx -499{,}667$ is relatively insignificant by comparison with $n^3/6 \approx 166{,}666{,}667$, which it is). Second, we focus on the instructions that are executed most frequently, sometimes referred to as the *inner loop* of the program. In this program it is reasonable to assume that the time devoted to the instructions outside the inner loop is relatively insignificant.

The key point in analyzing the running time of a program is this: for a great many programs, the running time satisfies the relationship

$$T(n) \sim cf(n)$$

where c is a constant and $f(n)$ is a function known as the *order of growth* of the running time. For typical programs, $f(n)$ is a function such as $\log n$, n, $n \log n$, n^2, or n^3, as you will soon see (customarily, we express order-of-growth functions without any constant coefficient). When $f(n)$ is a power of n, as is often the case, this assumption is equivalent to saying that the running time satis-

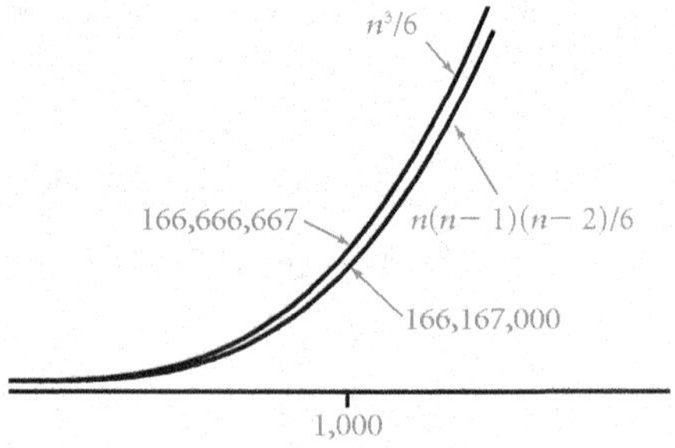

Leading-term approximation

fies a power law. In the case of `threesum.py`, it is a hypothesis already verified by our empirical observations: *the order of growth of the running time of* `threesum.py` is n^3. The value of the constant c depends both on the cost of executing instructions and on details of the frequency analysis, but we normally do not need to work out the value, as you will now see.

The order of growth is a simple but powerful model of running time. For example, knowing the order of growth typically leads immediately to a doubling hypothesis. In the case of `threesum.py`, knowing that the order of growth is n^3 tells us to expect the running time to increase by a factor of 8 when we double the size of the problem because

$$T(2n) \,/\, T(n) \;\rightarrow\; c(2n)^3 \,/\, (cn^3) = 8$$

This matches the value resulting from the empirical analysis, thus validating both the model and the experiments. *Study this example carefully, because you can use the same method to better understand the performance of any program that you compose.*

Knuth showed that it is possible to develop an accurate mathematical model of the running time of any program, and many experts have devoted much effort to developing such models. But you do not need such a detailed model to understand the performance of your programs: it is typically safe to ignore the cost of the instructions outside the inner loop (because that cost is negligible by comparison to the cost of the instruction in the inner loop) and not necessary to know the value of the constant in the running-time approximation (because it cancels out when you use a doubling hypothesis to make predictions).

number of instructions	*time per instruction in seconds*	*frequency*	*total time*
6	2×10^{-9}	$n^3/6 - n^2/2 + n/3$	$(2\,n^3 - 6\,n^2 + 4\,n) \times 10^{-9}$
4	3×10^{-9}	$n^2/2 - n/2$	$(6\,n^2 - 6\,n) \times 10^{-9}$
4	3×10^{-9}	n	$(12\,n) \times 10^{-9}$
10	1×10^{-9}	1	10×10^{-9}
		grand total:	$(2\,n^3 + 10\,n + 10) \times 10^{-9}$
		tilde notation:	$\sim 2\,n^3 \times 10^{-9}$
		order of growth:	n^3

Analyzing the running time of a program (example)

These approximations are significant because they relate the abstract world of a Python program to the real world of a computer running it. The approximations are such that characteristics of the particular machine that you are using do not play a significant role in the models—the analysis separates the *algorithm* from the *system*. The order of growth of the running time of `threesum.py` is n^3 does not depend on whether it is implemented in Python or whether it is running on your laptop, someone else's mobile phone, or a supercomputer; rather, it depends primarily on the fact that it examines all the triples. The properties of the computer and the *system* are all summarized in various assumptions about the relationship between program statements and machine instructions, and in the actual running times that we observe as the basis for the doubling hypothesis. The *algorithm* that you are using determines the order of growth. This separation is a powerful concept because it allows us to develop knowledge about the performance of algorithms and then apply that knowledge to any computer. In fact, much of the knowledge about the performance of classic algorithms was developed decades ago, but that knowledge is still relevant to today's computers.

Empirical and mathematical analyses like those we have described constitute a model (an explanation of what is going on) that might be formalized by listing all of the assumptions mentioned (each instruction takes the same amount of time each time it is executed, running time has the given form, and so forth). Not many programs are worthy of a detailed model, but you need to have an idea of the running time that you might expect for every program that you compose. *Pay attention to the cost.* Formulating a doubling hypothesis—through empirical studies, mathematical analysis, or (preferably) both—is a good way to start. This information about performance is extremely useful, and you will soon find yourself formulating and validating hypotheses every time you run a program. Indeed, doing so is a good use of your time while you wait for your program to finish!

Order of growth classifications We use just a few structural primitives (statements, conditionals, loops, and function calls) to build Python programs, so very often the order of growth of our programs is one of just a few functions of the problem size, summarized in the table on the next page. These functions immediately lead to a doubling hypothesis, which we can verify by running the programs. Indeed, you *have* been running programs that exhibit these orders of growth, as you can see in the following brief discussions.

Constant. A program whose running time's order of growth is *constant* executes a fixed number of statements to finish its job; consequently, its running time does not depend on the problem size. Our first several programs in CHAPTER 1—such as `helloworld.py` (PROGRAM 1.1.1) and `leapyear.py` (PROGRAM 1.2.5)—fall into this category: they each execute several statements just once.

All of Python's operations on standard numeric types take constant time. That is, applying an operation to a large number consumes no more time than does applying it to a small number. (One exception is that operations involving integers with a huge number of digits can consume more than constant time; see the Q&A at the end of this section for details.) The functions in Python's `math` module also take constant time. Note that we do not specify the size of the constant. For example, the constant for `math.atan2()` is somewhat larger than the constant for `math.hypot()`.

Logarithmic. A program whose running time's order of growth is *logarithmic* is barely slower than a constant-time program. The classic example of a program whose running time is logarithmic in the problem size is looking for an element in a sorted array, which we consider in the next section (see PROGRAM 4.2.3, `binarysearch.py`). The base of the logarithm is not relevant with respect to the order of growth (since all logarithms with a constant base are related by a constant factor), so we use log n when referring to the order of growth. Occasionally, we write more precise formulas using lg n (base 2, or *binary* log) or ln n (base e, or *natural* logarithm) because both arise naturally when studying computer programs. For example, lg n, rounded up, is the number of bits in the binary representation of n, and ln n arises in the analysis of binary search trees (see SECTION 4.4).

order of growth		*factor for doubling hypothesis*
description	*function*	
constant	1	1
logarithmic	log n	1
linear	n	2
linearithmic	n log n	2
quadratic	n^2	4
cubic	n^3	8
exponential	2^n	2^n

Common growth functions

Linear. Programs that spend a constant amount of time processing each piece of input data, or that are based on a single `for` loop, are quite common. The order of growth of such a program is said to be *linear*—its running time is directly proportional to the problem size. PROGRAM 1.5.3 (`average.py`), which computes the average of the numbers on standard input, is prototypical, as is our code to shuffle the elements in an array in SECTION 1.4. Filters such as `plotfilter.py` (PROGRAM 1.5.5) also fall into this category, as do the various image-processing filters that we considered in SECTION 3.2, which perform a constant number of arithmetic operations per input pixel.

Linearithmic. We use the term *linearithmic* to describe programs whose running time for a problem of size n has order of growth $n \log n$. Again, the base of the logarithm is not relevant. For example, `couponcollector.py` (PROGRAM 1.4.2) is linearithmic. The prototypical example is mergesort (see PROGRAM 4.2.6). Several important problems have natural solutions that are quadratic but clever algorithms that are linearithmic. Such algorithms (including mergesort) are critically important in practice because they enable us to address problem sizes far larger than could be addressed with quadratic solutions. In the next section, we consider a general design technique for developing linearithmic algorithms.

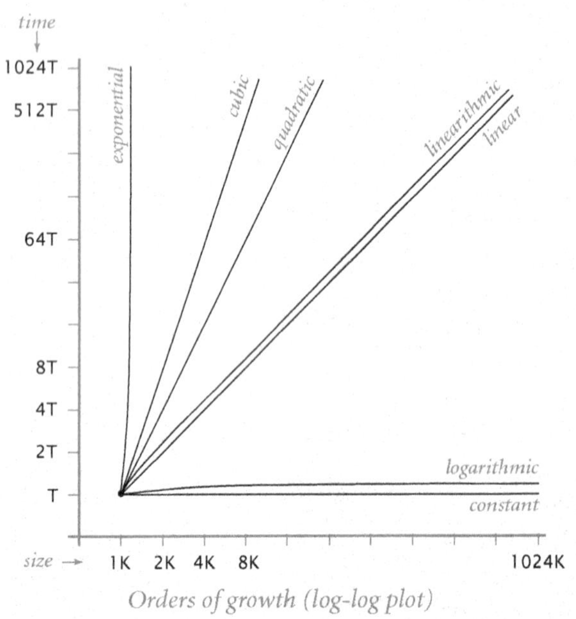

Orders of growth (log-log plot)

Quadratic. A typical program whose running time has order of growth n^2 has two nested `for` loops, used for some calculation involving all pairs of n elements. The force update double loop in `universe.py` (PROGRAM 3.4.2) is a prototype of the programs in this classification, as is the elementary sorting algorithm insertion sort (see PROGRAM 4.2.4).

Cubic. Our example for this section, `threesum.py`, is cubic (its running time has order of growth n^3) because it has *three* nested `for` loops, to process all triples of n elements. The running time of matrix multiplication, as implemented in SECTION 1.4 has order of growth m^3 to multiply two m-by-m matrices, so the basic matrix multiplication algorithm is often considered to be cubic. However, the size of the input (the number of elements in the matrices) is proportional to $n = m^2$, so the algorithm is best classified as $n^{3/2}$, not cubic.

description	*order of growth*	*example*	*framework*
constant	1	`count += 1`	*statement (increment an integer)*

logarithmic	$\log n$	`while n > 0:`
		`    n = n // 2`
		`    count += 1`
			divide in half (bits in binary representation)

linear	n	`for i in range(n):`
		`    if a[i] == 0:`
		`        count += 1`
			single loop

linearithmic	$n \log n$	[see *mergesort* (Program 4.2.6)]	*divide and conquer (mergesort)*

quadratic	n^2	`for i in range(n):`
		`    for j in range(i+1, n):`
		`        if (a[i] + a[j]) == 0:`
		`            count += 1`
			doubly nested loop (check all pairs)

cubic	n^3	`for i in range(n):`
		`    for j in range(i+1, n):`
		`        for k in range(j+1, n):`
		`            if (a[i] + a[j] + a[k]) == 0:`
		`                count += 1`
			triply nested loop (check all triples)

exponential	2^n	[see *Gray code* (Program 2.3.3)]	*exhaustive search (check all subsets)*

Summary of common order-of-growth hypotheses

Exponential. As discussed in SECTION 2.3, both `towersofhanoi.py` (PROGRAM 2.3.2) and `beckett.py` (PROGRAM 2.3.3) have running times proportional to 2^n because they process all subsets of n elements. Generally, we use the term "exponential" to refer to algorithms whose order of growth is b^n for any constant $b > 1$, even though different values of b lead to vastly different running times. Exponential algorithms are extremely slow—you should never run one of them for a large problem. They play a critical role in the theory of algorithms because there exists a large class of problems for which it seems that an exponential algorithm is the best possible choice.

THESE CLASSIFICATIONS ARE THE MOST COMMON, but certainly not a complete set. Indeed, the detailed analysis of algorithms can require the full gamut of mathematical tools that have been developed over the centuries. Understanding the running time of programs such as `factors.py` (PROGRAM 1.3.9), `primesieve.py` (PROGRAM 1.4.3), and `euclid.py` (PROGRAM 2.3.1) requires fundamental results from number theory. Classic algorithms like `hashst.py` (PROGRAM 4.4.3) and `bst.py` (PROGRAM 4.4.4) require careful mathematical analysis. The programs `sqrt.py` (PROGRAM 1.3.6) and `markov.py` (PROGRAM 1.6.3) are prototypes for numerical computation: their running time depends on the rate of convergence of a computation to a desired numerical result. Monte Carlo simulations such as `gambler.py` (PROGRAM 1.3.8) and `percolation.py` (PROGRAM 2.4.6) and variants are of interest precisely because detailed mathematical models for them are not available.

Nevertheless, a great many of the programs that you will compose have straightforward performance characteristics that can be described accurately by one of the orders of growth that we have considered, as documented in the table on the preceding page. Accordingly, we can usually work with simple higher-level hypotheses, such as *the order of growth of the running time of mergesort is linearithmic.* For economy, we abbreviate such a statement to just say *mergesort is linearithmic.* Most of our hypotheses about cost are of this form, or of the form *mergesort is faster than insertion sort.* Again, a notable feature of such hypotheses is that they are statements about algorithms, not just about programs.

Predictions You can always try to estimate the running time of a program by simply running it, but that might be a poor way to proceed when the problem size is large. In that case, it is analogous to trying to estimate where a rocket will land by launching it, how destructive a bomb will be by igniting it, or whether a bridge will stand by building it.

Knowing the order of growth of the running time allows us to make decisions about addressing large problems so that we can invest whatever resources we have to deal with the specific problems that we actually need to solve. We typically use the results of verified hypotheses about the order of growth of the running time of programs in one of the following ways.

Estimating the feasibility of solving large problems. To pay attention to the cost, you need to answer this basic question for every program that you compose: *Will this program be able to process this input data in a reasonable amount of time?* For example, a cubic algorithm that runs in a couple of seconds for a problem of size n will require a few *weeks* for a problem of size $100n$ because it will be a million (100^3) times slower, and a couple of million seconds is a few weeks. If that is the size of the problem that you need to solve, you have to find a better method. Knowing the order of growth of the running time of an algorithm provides precisely the information that you need to understand limitations on the size of the problems that you can solve. Developing such understanding is the most important reason to study performance. Without it, you are likely have no idea how much time a program will consume; with it, you can perform a back-of-the-envelope calculation to estimate costs and proceed accordingly.

order of growth	*predicted running time if problem size is increased by a factor of 100*
linear	a few minutes
linearithmic	a few minutes
quadratic	several hours
cubic	a few weeks
exponential	forever

Effect of increasing problem size for a program that runs for a few seconds

Estimating the value of using a faster computer. To pay attention to the cost, you also may be faced with this basic question: *How much faster can I solve a problem if I run it on a faster computer?* Again, knowing the order of growth of the running time provides precisely the information that you need. A famous rule of thumb known as *Moore's law* implies that you can expect to have a computer with about double the speed and double the memory 18 months from now, or a computer with about 10 times the speed and 10 times the memory in about 5 years. It is natural to think that if you buy a new computer that is 10 times faster and has 10 times more memory than your old one, you can solve a problem 10 times the size, but that is unmistakably *not* the case for quadratic or cubic algorithms. Whether it is an investment banker running daily financial models or a scientist running a program to analyze experimental data or an engineer running simulations to test a design, it is not unusual for people to regularly run programs that take several hours to complete. Suppose that you are using a program whose running time is cubic, and then buy a new computer that is 10 times faster with 10 times more memory, not just because you need a new computer, but because you face problem sizes that are 10 times larger. The rude awakening is that your program will take 100 times longer than before! This kind of situation is the primary reason that linear and linearithmic algorithms are so valuable: with such an algorithm and a new computer that is 10 times faster with 10 times more memory than the old computer, you can solve a problem that is 10 times larger than could be solved by the old computer in the same amount of time. In other words, you cannot keep pace with Moore's law if you are using a quadratic or a cubic algorithm.

order of growth	*factor of increase in running time*
linear	1
linearithmic	1
quadratic	10
cubic	100
exponential	forever

Effect of using a computer that is 10 times as fast to solve a problem that is 10 times larger

Comparing programs. We always seek ways to improve our programs, and we can often extend or modify our hypotheses to evaluate the effectiveness of various improvements. With the ability to predict performance, we can make design decisions during development that can guide us toward better, more efficient implementations. In many cases, we can determine the order of growth of the running times and develop accurate hypotheses about comparative performance. The order of growth is extremely useful in this process because it allows us to compare one particular algorithm with whole classes of algorithms. For example, once we have a linearithmic algorithm to solve a problem, we become less interested in quadratic or cubic algorithms to solve the same problem.

Caveats There are many reasons that you might get inconsistent or misleading results when trying to analyze program performance in detail. All of them have to do with the idea that one or more of the basic assumptions underlying our hypotheses might not be quite correct. We can develop new hypotheses based on new assumptions, but the more details that we take into account, the more care we need in the analysis.

Instruction time. The assumption that each instruction always takes the same amount of time is not always correct. For example, most modern computer systems use a technique known as *caching* to organize memory, in which case accessing elements in huge arrays can take much longer if they are not close together in the array. You may be able to observe the effect of caching for `threesum.py` by letting `doublingtest.py` run for a while. After seeming to converge to 8, the ratio of running times may jump to a larger value for large arrays because of caching.

Nondominant inner loop. The assumption that the inner loop dominates may not always be correct. The problem size n might not be sufficiently large to make the leading term in the mathematical description of the frequency of execution of instructions in the inner loop so much larger than lower-order terms that we can ignore them. Some programs have a significant amount of code outside the inner loop that needs to be taken into consideration.

System considerations. Typically, there are many, many things going on in your computer. Python is just one application of many competing for resources, and Python itself has many options and controls that significantly affect performance. Such considerations can interfere with the bedrock principle of the scientific method that experiments should be reproducible, since what is happening at this moment in your computer will never be reproduced again. Whatever else is going on in your system (that is beyond your control) should *in principle* be negligible.

Too close to call. Often, when we compare two different programs for the same task, one might be faster in some situations, and slower in others. One or more of the considerations just mentioned could make the difference. Again, there is a natural tendency among some programmers (and some students) to devote an extreme amount of energy running such horseraces to find the "best" implementation, but such work is best left for experts.

Strong dependence on input values. One of the first assumptions that we made to determine the order of growth of the program's running time of a program was that the running time should be relatively insensitive to the input values. When that is not the case, we may get inconsistent results or be unable to validate our hypotheses. Our running example `threesum.py` does not have this problem, but we will see several examples in this chapter of programs whose running time does depends on the input values. Often, a prime design goal is to eliminate such dependence on the input values. If we cannot do so, we need to more carefully model the kind of input to be processed in the problems that we need to solve, which may be a significant challenge. For example, if we are composing a program to process a genome, how do we know how it will perform on a different genome? But a good model describing the genomes found in nature is precisely what scientists seek, so estimating the running time of our programs on data found in nature actually makes a valuable contribution to that model!

Multiple problem parameters. We have been focusing on measuring performance as a function of a *single* parameter n, generally the value of a command-line argument or the size of the input. However, it is not unusual to measure performance using two (or more) parameters. For example, suppose that `a[]` is an array of length `m` and `b[]` is an array of length `n`. Consider the following code fragment that counts the number of pairs `i` and `j` for which `a[i] + b[j]` equals `0`:

```
for i in range(m):
    for j in range(n):
        if a[i] + b[j] == 0:
            count += 1
```

In such cases, we treat the parameters m and n separately, holding one fixed while analyzing the other. For example, the order of growth of the running time of this code fragment is mn.

DESPITE ALL THESE CAVEATS, UNDERSTANDING THE order of growth of the running time of each program is valuable knowledge for any programmer, and the methods that we have described are powerful and broadly applicable. Knuth's insight was that we can carry these methods through to the last detail *in principle* to make detailed, accurate predictions. Typical computer systems are extremely complex and close analysis is best left for experts, but the same methods are effective for developing approximate estimates of the running time of any program. A rocket scientist needs to have some idea of whether a test flight will land in the ocean or in a city; a medical researcher needs to know whether a drug trial will kill or cure all the subjects; and any scientist or engineer using a computer program needs to have some idea of whether it will run for a second or for a year.

Performance guarantees For some programs, we demand that the running time of a program is less than a certain bound for *any* input of a given size. To provide such *performance guarantees*, theoreticians take an extremely pessimistic view: what would the running time be in the *worst case*?

For example, such a conservative approach might be appropriate for the software that runs a nuclear reactor or an air traffic control system or the brakes in your car. We must guarantee that such software completes its job within the bounds that we set because the result could be catastrophic if it does not. Scientists normally do not contemplate the worst case when studying the natural world: in biology, the worst case might the extinction of the human race; in physics, the worst case might be the end of the universe. But the worst case can be a very real concern in computer systems, where the input is generated by another (potentially malicious) user, rather than by nature. For example, websites that do not use algorithms with performance guarantees are subject to *denial-of-service* attacks, where hackers flood them with pathological requests that make them run harmfully slower than planned.

Performance guarantees are difficult to verify with the scientific method, because we cannot test a hypothesis such as *mergesort is guaranteed to be linearithmic* without trying all possible inputs, which we cannot do because there are far too many of them. We might falsify such a hypothesis by providing inputs for which mergesort is slow, but how can we prove it to be true? We must do so not with experimentation, but rather with mathematical models.

It is the task of the algorithm analyst to discover as much relevant information about an algorithm as possible, and it is the task of the applications programmer to apply that knowledge to develop programs that effectively solve the problems at hand. For example, if you are using a quadratic algorithm to solve a problem but can find an algorithm that is guaranteed to be linearithmic, you will usually prefer the linearithmic one. On rare occasions, you might still prefer the quadratic algorithm because it is faster on the kinds of inputs that you need to solve or because the linearithmic algorithm is too complex to implement.

Ideally, we want algorithms that lead to clear and compact code that provides both a good worst-case guarantee and good performance on inputs of interest. Many of the classic algorithms that we consider in this chapter are of importance for a broad variety of applications precisely because they have all of these properties. Using these algorithms as models, you can develop good solutions yourself for typical problems that you face while programming.

Python lists and arrays Python's built-in `list` data type represents a mutable sequence of objects. We have been using Python lists throughout the book—recall that we use Python lists as arrays because they support the four core array operations: creation, indexed access, indexed assignment, and iteration. However, Python lists are more general than arrays because you can also insert items into and delete items from Python lists. Even though Python programmers typically do not distinguish between lists and arrays, many other programmers do make such a distinction. For example, in many programming languages, arrays are of fixed length and do not support insertions or deletions. Indeed, all of the array-processing code that we have considered in this book so far could have been done using fixed-length arrays.

The table on the facing page gives the most commonly used operations for Python lists. Note that several of these operations—indexing, slicing, concatenation, deletion, containment, and iteration—enjoy direct language support in the form of special syntax. As illustrated in the table at right, some of these operations return values while others mutate the invoking list.

```
a = [3, 1, 4, 1, 5, 9]
b = [2, 7, 1]
```

operation	*result*
`len(a)`	`6`
`a[4]`	`5`
`a[2:5]`	`[4, 1, 5, 9]`
`min(a)`	`1`
`max(a)`	`9`
`sum(a)`	`23`
`4 in a`	`True`
`b + [0]`	`[2, 7, 1, 0]`
`b += [6]`	`[2, 7, 1, 6]`
`del b[1]`	`[2, 1, 6]`
`b.insert(2, 9)`	`[2, 1, 9, 6]`
`b.reverse()`	`[6, 1, 9, 2]`
`b.sort()`	`[1, 2, 6, 9]`

Examples of list operations

We have deferred this API to this section because programmers who use Python lists without following our mantra *pay attention to the cost* are in for trouble. For example, consider these two code snippets:

```
# quadratic time
a = []
for i in range(n):
    a .insert(0, 'slow')
```

```
# linear time
a = []
for i in range(n):
    a.insert(i, 'fast')
```

The one on the left takes *quadratic* time; the one on the right takes *linear* time. To understand why Python list operations have the performance characteristics that they do, you need to learn more about Python's *resizing array* representation of lists, which we discuss next.

constant-time operations	*description*
`len(a)`	*length of* `a`
`a[i]`	*the* `i`*th item of* `a` *(indexed access)*
`a[i] = v`	*replace the* `i`*th item of* `a` *with item* `v` *(indexed assignment)*
`a += [v]`	*append item* `v` *to the end of* `a` *(in-place concatenation)*
`a.pop()`	*delete* `a[len(a)-1]` *from the list and return that item*
linear-time operations	
`a + b`	*concatenation of* `a` *and* `b`
`a[i:j]`	`[a[i], a[i+1], ..., a[j-1]]` *(slicing)*
`a[i:j] = b`	`a[i] = b[0], a[i+1] = b[1], ...` *(slice assignment)*
`v in a`	`True` *if* `a` *contains* `v`, `False` *otherwise (containment)*
`for v in a:`	*iterate over the items in* `a` *(iteration)*
`del a[i]`	*delete* `a[i]` *from the list (indexed deletion)*
`a.pop(i)`	*delete* `a[i]` *from the list and return that item*
`a.insert(i, v)`	*insert item* `v` *into* `a` *before* `a[i]`
`a.index(v)`	*index of first occurrence of item* `v` *in* `a`
`a.reverse()`	*rearrange the items of* `a` *into reverse order*
`min(a)`	*a minimal item in* `a`
`max(a)`	*a maximal item in* `a`
`sum(a)`	*sum of items in* `a`
linearithmic-time operations (see SECTION *4.2)*	
`a.sort()`	*rearrange the items of* `a` *into ascending order*

Note 1: `a += [v]` *and* `a.pop()` *are "amortized" constant-time operations (see text).*
Note 2: The `del a[i]`, `pop(i)`, *and* `insert(i, v)` *operations take "amortized" constant time if* `i` *is close to* `len(a)`.
Note 3: The slicing operations take time linear in the length of the slice.
Note 4: Items in `a` *must be of compatible types for* `min()`, `max()`, *and* `sum()`.

Partial API for Python's built-in `list` *data type*

Resizing arrays. A *resizing array* is a data structure that stores a sequence of items (not necessarily fixed in length), which can be accessed by indexing. To implement a resizing array (at the machine level), Python uses a fixed-length array (allocated as one contiguous block of memory) to store the item references. The array is divided into two logical parts: the first part of the array contains the items in the sequence; the second part of the array is unused and reserved for subsequent insertions. Thus, we can append or remove items from the end in constant time, using the reserved space. We use the term *size* to refer to the number of items in the data structure and the term *capacity* to refer to the length of the underlying array.

The main challenge is ensuring that the data structure has sufficient capacity to hold all of the items, but is not so large as to waste an excessive amount of memory. Achieving these two goals turns out to be remarkably easy.

First, if we want to append an item to the end of a resizing array, we check its capacity. If there is room, we simply insert the new item at the end. If not, we *double* its capacity by creating a new array of twice the length and copying the items from the old array into the new array.

Similarly, if we want to remove an item from the end of the resizing array, we check its capacity. If it is excessively large, we *halve* its capacity by creating a new array of half the length and copying the items from the old array into the new array. An appropriate test is to check whether the size of the resizing array is less than *one-fourth* of its capacity. That way, after the capacity is halved, the resizing array is about half full and can accommodate a substantial number of insertions before we have to change its capacity again.

The doubling-and-halving strategy guarantees that the resizing array remains between 25% and 100% full, so that space is linear in the number of items. The specific strategy is not sacrosanct. For example, typical Python implementations expand the capacity by a factor of 9/8 (instead of 2) when the resizing array is full. This wastes less space (but triggers more expansion and shrinking operations).

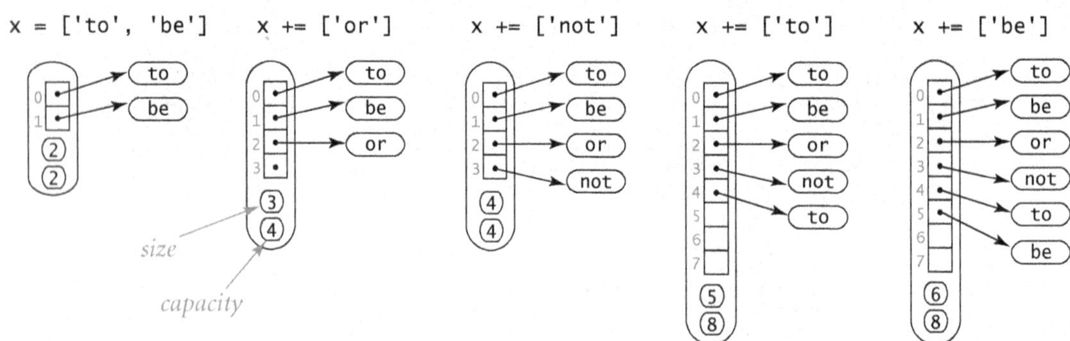

Resizing array data structure to represent a Python list

Amortized analysis. The doubling-and-halving strategy is a judicious tradeoff between wasting space (by setting the capacity to be too large and leaving much of the array unused) and wasting time (either by creating a new array or by reorganizing the existing array). More important, we can prove that the cost of doubling and halving is always absorbed (to within a constant factor) in the cost of other Python list operations.

More precisely, starting from an empty Python list, any sequence of n operations labeled as "constant time" in the API table on page 531 takes time linear in n. In other words, *the total cost of any such sequence of Python list operations divided by the number of operations is bounded by a constant.* This kind of analysis is known as *amortized analysis.* This guarantee is not as strong as saying that each operation is constant time, but it has the same implications in many applications (for example, when our primary interest is in total running time). We leave the full details as an exercise for the mathematically inclined.

For the special case where we perform a sequence of n insertions into an empty resizing array, the idea is simple: each insertion takes constant time to add the item; each insertion that triggers a resizing (when the current size is a power of 2) takes additional time proportional to n to copy the elements from the old array of length n to a new array of length $2n$. Thus, assuming n is a power of 2 for simplicity, the total cost is proportional to

$$(1 + 1 + 1 + \ldots + 1) + (1 + 2 + 4 + 8 + \ldots + n) \sim 3n$$

The first term (which sums to n) accounts for the n insertion operations; the second term (which sums to $2n - 1$) accounts for the $\lg n$ resizing operations.

UNDERSTANDING RESIZING ARRAYS IS IMPORTANT in Python programming. For example, it explains why creating a Python list of n items by repeatedly appending items to the end takes time proportional to n (and why creating a list of n items by repeatedly prepending items to the front takes time proportional to n^2). Such performance pitfalls are precisely the reason that we recommend using narrower interfaces that address performance.

Strings Python's string data type has some similarity to Python lists, with one very important exception: *strings are immutable.* When we introduced strings, we did not emphasize this fact, but it makes lists and strings quite different. For example, you may not have noticed at the time, but you cannot change a character in a string. For example, you might think that you could capitalize a string `s` having the value `'hello'` with `s[0] = 'H'`, but that will result in this run-time error:

```
TypeError: 'str' object does not support item assignment
```

If you want `'Hello'`, you need to create a completely new string. This difference reinforces the idea of immutability and has significant implications with regard to performance, which we now examine.

Internal representation. First, Python uses a much simpler internal representation for strings than for lists/arrays, as detailed in the diagram at left. Specifically, a string object contains two pieces of information:

- A reference to a place in memory where the characters in the string are stored contiguously
- The length of the string

By contrast, consider the diagram at right, which is an array of one-character strings. We will consider a more detailed analysis later in this section, but you can see that the string representation is certainly significantly simpler. It uses much less space per character and provides faster access to each character. In many applications, these characteristics are very important because strings can be very long. So, it is important both that the memory usage be not much more than is required for the characters themselves and that characters can be quickly accessed by their index, as in an array.

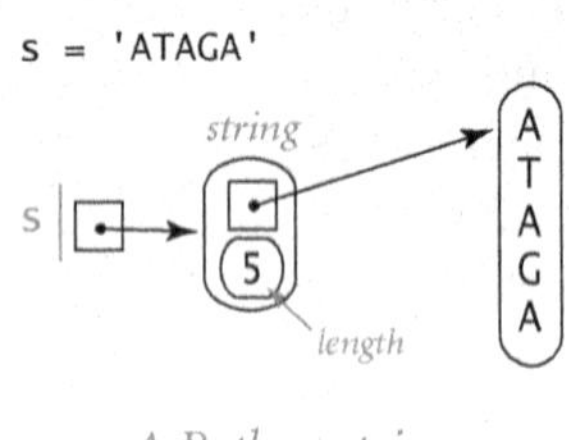

A Python string

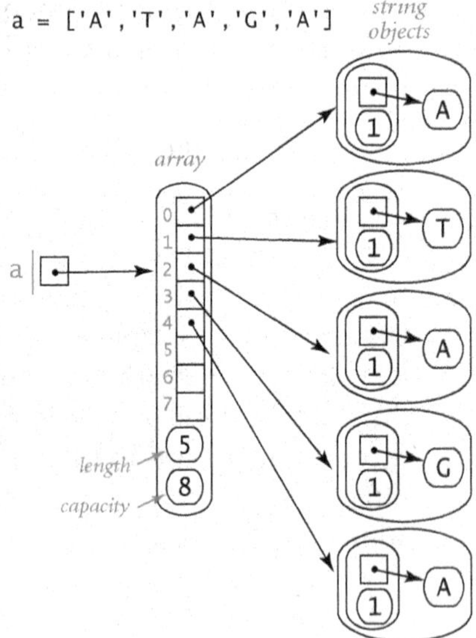

An array of one-character strings

Performance. As for arrays, indexed access and computing the length of strings are constant-time operations. It is clear from the API at the beginning of SECTION 3.1 that most other operations take linear time as a function of the length of the input string or strings, because they refer to a *copy* of the string. In particular, *concatenating a character to a string takes linear time* and *concatenating two strings takes time proportional to the length of the result.* An example is shown at right. With respect to performance, this is the most significant difference between strings and lists/arrays: Python does not have resizable strings, because strings are immutable.

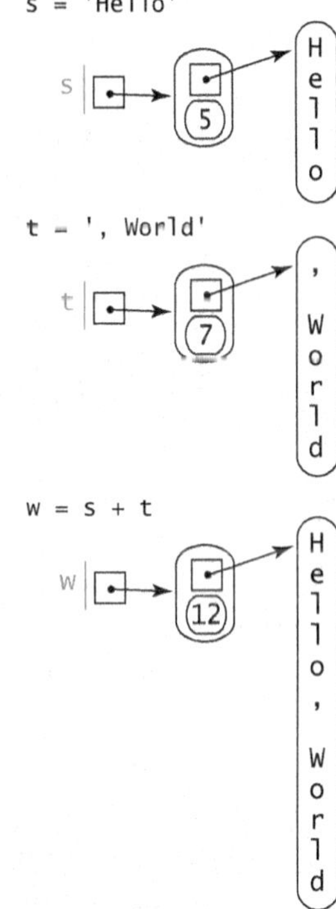

String concatenation

Example. Not understanding the performance of string concatenation often leads to performance bugs. The most common performance bug is building up a long string one character at a time. For example, consider the following code fragment to create a new string whose characters are in reverse order of the characters in a string s:

```
n = len(s)
reverse = ''
for i in range(n):
    reverse = s[i] + reverse
```

During iteration i of the for loop, the string concatenation operator produces a string of length i+1. Thus, the overall running time is proportional to $1 + 2 + \ldots + n \sim n^2 / 2$ (see EXERCISE 4.1.4). That is, the code fragment takes *quadratic* time as a function of the string length n (see EXERCISE 4.1.13 for a linear-time solution).

UNDERSTANDING DIFFERENCES BETWEEN DATA TYPES like strings and Python lists is critical in learning any programming language, and programmers must be vigilant to ensure they avoid performance bugs like the one just described. This has been the case since the early days of data abstraction. For example, the string data type in the C language that was developed in the 1970s has a linear-time length function, and countless programmers using the length in a for loop that iterates through the string have found themselves with a quadratic-time performance bug for a simple linear-time job.

Memory As with running time, a program's memory usage connects directly to the physical world: a substantial amount of your computer's circuitry enables your program to store values and later retrieve them. The more values you need to store at any given instant, the more circuitry you need. To pay attention to the cost, you need to be aware of memory usage. You probably are aware of limits on memory usage on your computer (even more so than for time) because you probably have paid extra money to get more memory.

At the outset, you should be aware that the flexibility that we get from Python's pure approach to object-oriented programming (everything is an object, even boolean values) comes with costs, and one of the most significant costs is the amount of memory consumed. This will become more clear as we examine some specific examples.

Memory usage is well defined for Python on your computer (every value will require precisely the same amount of memory each time that you run your program), but Python is implemented on a very wide range of computational devices, and memory consumption is implementation-dependent. Different versions of Python might implement the same data type in different ways. For economy, we use the word *typical* to signal values that are particularly subject to machine dependencies. Analyzing memory usage is somewhat different from analyzing time usage, primarily because one of Python's most significant features is its memory allocation system, which is supposed to relieve you of having to worry about memory. Certainly, you are well advised to take advantage of this feature when appropriate. Still, it is your responsibility to know, at least approximately, when a program's memory requirements might prevent you from solving a given problem.

Computer memory is divided into *bytes*, where each byte consists of 8 bits, and where each *bit* is a single binary digit. To determine the memory usage of a Python program, we count up the number of objects used by the program and weight them by the number of bytes that they require, according to their type. To use that approach, we must know the number of bytes consumed by an object of any given type. To determine the memory consumption of an object, we add the amount of memory used by each of its instance variables to the overhead associated with each object.

Python does not define the sizes of the built-in data types that we have been using (`int`, `float`, `bool`, `str`, and `list`); the sizes of objects of those types differ from system to system. Accordingly, the sizes of data types that you create also will differ from system to system because they are based on these built-in data types.

The function call `sys.getsizeof(x)` returns the number of bytes that a built-in object `x` consumes on your system. The numbers that we give in this section are observations gathered by using this function in interactive Python on one typical system. We encourage you to do the same on your computer!

Python 3 alert. *The numbers we give in this section are for a typical Python 2 system. Python 3 uses a more complicated memory model. For example, the memory used by the `int` object 0 is not the same as the memory used by the `int` object 1.*

Integers. To represent an `int` object whose value is in the range (-2^{63} to $2^{63} - 1$), Python uses 16 bytes for overhead and 8 bytes (that is, 64 bits) for the numeric value. So, for example, Python uses 24 bytes to represent the `int` object whose value is 0, 24 bytes to represent the `int` object whose value is 1234, and so forth. In most applications, we are not dealing with huge integers outside this range, so the memory consumption for each integer is 24 bytes. Python switches to a different internal representation for integers outside this range, which consumes memory proportional to the number of digits in the integer, as in the case with strings (see below).

Floats. To represent a `float` object, Python uses 16 bytes for overhead and 8 bytes for the numeric value (that is, the mantissa, exponent, and sign), no matter what value the object has. So a `float` object always consumes 24 bytes.

Booleans. In principle, Python could represent a boolean value using a single bit of computer memory. In practice, Python represents boolean values as integers. Specifically, Python uses 24 bytes to represent the `bool` object `True` and 24 bytes to represent the `bool` object `False`. That is a factor of 192 higher than the minimum amount needed! However, this wastefulness is partially mitigated because Python "caches" the two boolean objects, as we discuss next.

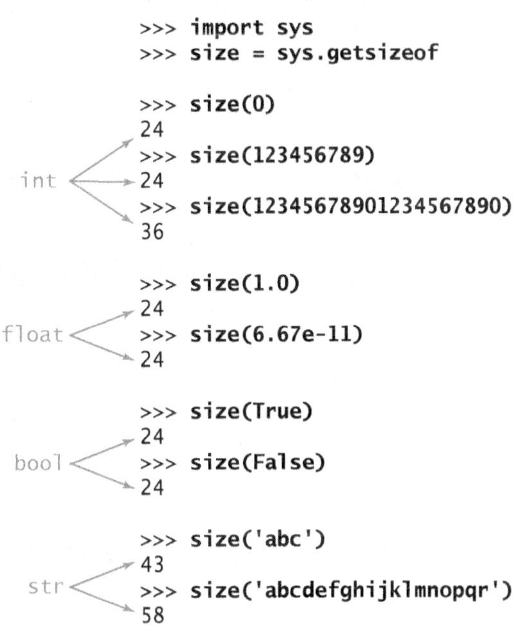

>>> import sys
>>> size = sys.getsizeof
>>> size(0)
24
>>> size(123456789)
24
>>> size(12345678901234567890)
36
>>> size(1.0)
24
>>> size(6.67e-11)
24
>>> size(True)
24
>>> size(False)
24
>>> size('abc')
43
>>> size('abcdefghijklmnopqr')
58
int
float
bool
str

Typical memory requirements of built-in types

Caching. To save memory, Python creates only one copy of objects with certain values. For example, Python creates only one `bool` object with value true and only one with value false. That is, every boolean variables holds a reference to one of these two objects. This *caching* technique is possible because the `bool` data type is immutable. On typical systems, Python also caches small `int` values (between –5 and 256), as they are the ones that programmers use most often. Python does not typically cache `float` objects.

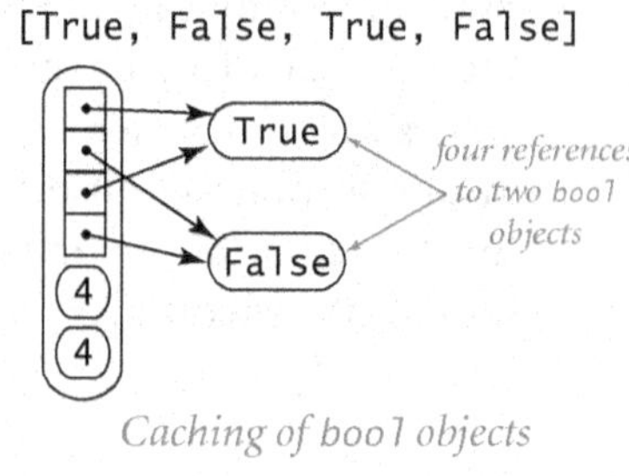

Caching of bool objects

Strings. To represent a `str` object, Python uses 40 bytes for overhead (including the string length), plus one byte for each character of the string. So, for example, Python represents the string `'abc'` using 40 + 3 = 43 bytes and represents the string `'abcdefghijklmnopqr'` using 40 + 18 = 58 bytes. Python typically caches only string literals and one-character strings.

Arrays (Python lists). To represent an array, Python uses 72 bytes for overhead (including the array length) plus 8 bytes for each object reference (one for each element in the array). So, for example, the Python representation of the array `[0.3, 0.6, 0.1]` uses 72 + 8*3 = 96 bytes. This does not include the memory for the objects that the array references, so the total memory consumption for the array `[0.3, 0.6, 0.1]` is 96 + 3*24 = 168 bytes. In general, the memory consumption for an array of n integers or floats is 72 + 32n bytes. This total is likely to be an underestimate, because the resizing array data structure that Python uses to implement arrays may consume an additional n bytes in reserved space.

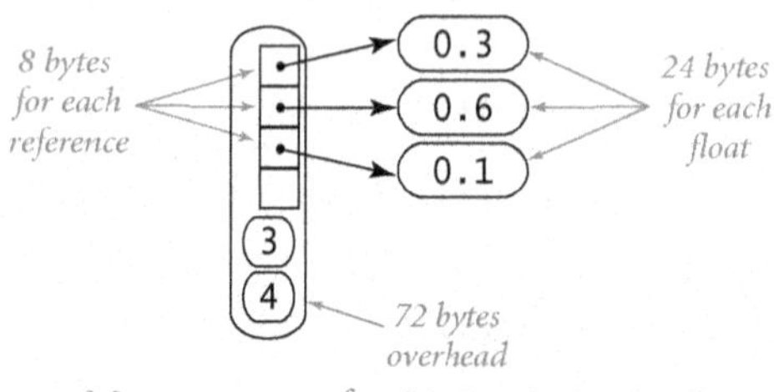

Memory usage for [0.3, 0.6, 0.1]

Two-dimensional arrays and arrays of objects. A two-dimensional array is an array of arrays, so we can calculate the memory consumption of a two-dimensional array with m rows and n columns from the information in the previous paragraph. Each row is an array that consumes 72 + 32n bytes, so the total is 72 (overhead) plus 8m (references to the rows) plus m(72 + 32n) (memory for the m rows) bytes, for a grand total of $72 + 80m + 32mn$ bytes. The same logic works for an array of any type of object: if an object uses x bytes, an array of m such objects consumes a total of $72 + m(x+8)$ bytes. Again, this is likely to be a slight underestimate because of the resizing array data structure Python uses to represent arrays. *Note*: Python's `sys.getsizeof(x)` is not much help in these calculations because it does not calculate the memory for the objects themselves—it returns $72 + 8m$ for any array of length m (or any two-dimensional array with m rows).

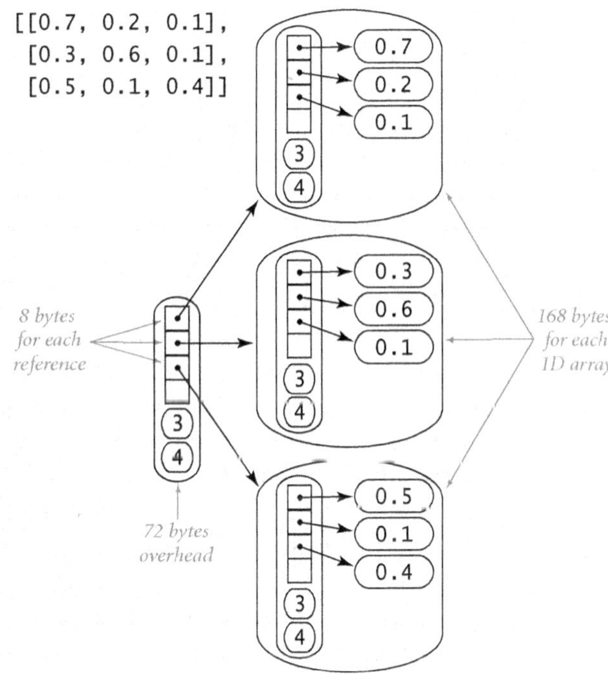

Memory usage for a two-dimensional array

Objects. A key question for Python programming is the following: How much memory is required to represent a user-defined object? The answer to this question may surprise you, but is important to know: *hundreds of bytes, at least.* Specifically, Python uses 72 bytes of overhead *plus* 280 bytes for a dictionary that binds instance variables to objects (we will discuss dictionaries in Section 4.4) *plus* 24 bytes for a reference to each instance variable *plus* memory for the instance variables themselves. For example, to represent a `Charge` object, Python uses at least 72 + 280 = 352 bytes for overhead, 8 * 3 = 24 bytes to store the object references for the three instance variables, 24 bytes to store the `float` object referenced by the `_rx` instance variable, 24 bytes to store the float object referenced by the `_ry` instance variable, and 24 bytes to store the float object referenced by the `_q` instance variable, for a grand total of (at least) 448 bytes. The total might be even higher on your system, because some implementations consume even more overhead.

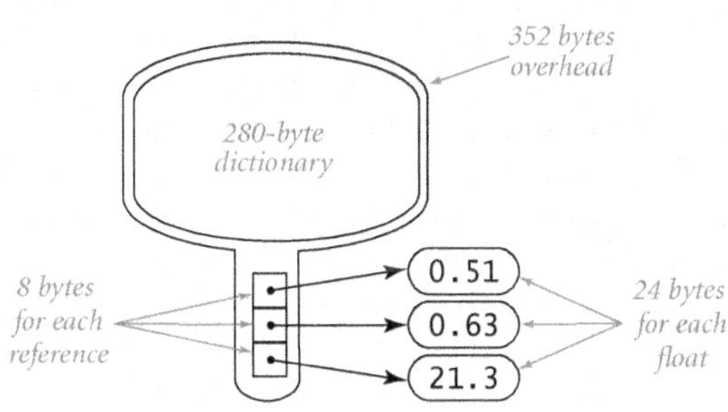

Memory usage for a Charge object

THESE BASIC MECHANISMS ARE EFFECTIVE FOR estimating the memory usage of a great many programs, but there are numerous complicating factors that can make the task significantly more difficult. For example, we have already noted the potential effect of caching. Moreover, memory consumption is a complicated dynamic process when function calls are involved because the system memory allocation mechanism plays a more important role. For example, when your program calls a function, the system allocates the memory needed for the function (for its local variables) from a special area of memory called the *stack*, and when the method returns to the caller, this memory is returned to the stack. For this reason, creating arrays or other large objects in recursive functions is dangerous, since each recursive call implies significant memory usage. When you create an object, the system allocates the memory needed for the object from another special area of memory known as the *heap*. Every object lives until no references to it remain, at which point a system process known as *garbage collection* reclaims its memory for the heap. Such dynamics can make the task of precisely estimating memory usage of a program challenging.

type	*bytes*
boolean	24
integer	24
float	24
reference	24
string of length n	$40 + n$
array of n booleans	$72 + 8n$
array of n floats	$72 + 32n$
n-by-n array of floats	$\sim 32mn$

Typical memory requirements

Despite all these caveats, it is important for every Python programmer to understand that *each object of a user-defined type is likely to consume a large amount of memory*. So, a Python program that defines a large number of objects of a user-defined type can use much more space (and time) than you might expect. That is especially true if each object contains only a few instance variables—in that case, the ratio of memory devoted to overhead versus memory devoted to instance variables is very high. For example, if you compare the performance of our `Complex` type with Python's built-in `complex` type for `mandelbrot.py`, you will certainly notice this effect. Numerous object-oriented languages have come and gone since the concept was introduced decades ago, and many of them eventually embraced *lightweight* objects for user-defined types. Python offers two advanced features for this purpose—*named tuples* and *slots*—but we will not take advantage of such memory optimizations in this book.

Perspective Good performance is important. An impossibly slow program is almost as useless as an incorrect one, so it is certainly worthwhile to *pay attention to the cost* at the outset, so as to have some idea of what sorts of problems you might feasibly address. In particular, it is always wise to have some idea of which code constitutes the inner loop of your programs.

Perhaps the most common mistake made in programming is to pay too much attention to performance characteristics. Your first priority is to make your code clear and correct. Modifying a program for the sole purpose of speeding it up is best left for experts. Indeed, doing so is often counterproductive, as it tends to create code that is complicated and difficult to understand. C. A. R. Hoare (the inventor of quicksort and a leading proponent of composing clear and correct code) once summarized this idea by saying that "*premature optimization is the root of all evil,*" to which Knuth added the qualifier "*(or at least most of it) in programming.*" Beyond that, improving the running time is not worthwhile if the available cost benefits are insignificant. For example, improving the running time of a program by a factor of 10 is inconsequential if the running time is only an instant. Even when a program takes a few minutes to run, the total time required to implement and debug an improved algorithm might be substantially longer than the time required simply to run a slightly slower one—you may as well let the computer do the work. Worse, you might spend a considerable amount of time and effort implementing ideas that do not actually make a program any faster.

Perhaps the second most common mistake made in developing an algorithm is to ignore performance characteristics. Faster algorithms are often more complicated than brute-force solutions, so you might be tempted to accept a slower algorithm to avoid having to deal with more complicated code. However, you can sometimes reap huge savings with just a few lines of good code. Users of a surprising number of computer systems lose substantial time waiting for simple quadratic algorithms to finish solving a problem, even though linear or linearithmic algorithms are available that are only slightly more complicated and could therefore solve the problem in a fraction of the time. When we are dealing with huge problem sizes, we often have no choice but to seek better algorithms.

Improving a program to make it clearer, more efficient, and elegant should be your goal every time that you work on it. If you *pay attention to the cost* all the way through the development of a program, you will reap the benefits every time you use it.

Q&A

Q. The text notes that operations on very large integers can consume more than constant time. Can you be more precise?

A. Not really. The definition of "very large" is system dependent. For most practical purposes, you can consider operations applied to 32- or 64-bit integers to work in constant time. Modern applications in cryptography involve huge numbers with hundreds or thousands of digits.

Q. How do I find out how long it takes to add or multiply two floats on my computer?

A. Run some experiments! The program `timeops.py` on the booksite uses `Stopwatch` to test the execution time of various arithmetic operations on integers and floats. This technique measures the actual elapsed time as would be observed on a wall clock. If your system is not running many other applications, it can produce accurate results. Python also includes the `timeit` module for measuring the running time of small code fragments.

Q. Is there any way to measure processor time instead of wall clock time?

A. On some systems, the function call `time.clock()` returns the current processor time as a float, expressed in seconds. When available, you should substitute `time.time()` with `time.clock()` for benchmarking Python programs.

Q. How much time do functions such as `math.sqrt()`, `math.log()`, and `math.sin()` take?

A. Run some experiments! `Stopwatch` makes it easy to compose programs such as `timeops.py` to answer questions of this sort for yourself. You will be able to use your computer much more effectively if you get in the habit of doing so.

Q. Why does allocating an array (Python list) of size n take time proportional to n?

A. Python initializes all array elements to whatever values the programmer specifies. That is, in Python there is no way to allocate memory for an array without also assigning an object reference to each element of the array. Assigning object references to each element of an array of size n takes time proportional to n.

Q. How do I find out how much memory is available for my Python programs?

A. Since Python will raise a `MemoryError` when it runs out of memory, it is not difficult to run some experiments. For example, use this program (`bigarray.py`):

```
import sys
import stdarray
import stdio

n = int(sys.argv[1])
a = stdarray.create1D(n, 0)
stdio.writeln('finished')
```

and run it like this:

```
% python bigarray.py 100000000
finished
```

to show that you have room for 100 million integers. But if you type

```
% python bigarray.py 1000000000
```

Python will hang, crash, or raise a run-time error; you can conclude that you do not have room for an array of 1 billion integers.

Q. What does it mean when someone says that the worst-case running time of an algorithm is $O(n^2)$?

A. That is an example of a notation known as *big-O* notation. We write $f(n)$ is $O(g(n))$ if there exist constants c and n_0 such that $f(n) \leq c\, g(n)$ for all $n > n_0$. In other words, the function $f(n)$ is bounded above by $g(n)$, up to constant factors and for sufficiently large values of n. For example, the function $30n^2 + 10n + 7$ is $O(n^2)$. We say that the worst-case running time of an algorithm is $O(g(n))$ if the running time as a function of the input size n is $O(g(n))$ for all possible inputs. This notation is widely used by theoretical computer scientists to prove theorems about algorithms, so you are sure to see it if you take a course in algorithms and data structures. It provides a worst-case performance guarantee.

Q. So can I use the fact that the worst-case running time of an algorithm is $O(n^3)$ or $O(n^2)$ to predict performance?

A. No, because the actual running time might be much less. For example, the function $30n^2 + 10n + 7$ is $O(n^2)$, but it is also $O(n^3)$ and $O(n^{10})$ because big-O notation provides only an upper bound on the worst-case running time. Moreover, even if there is some family of inputs for which the running time is proportional to the given function, perhaps these inputs are not encountered in practice. Consequently, you cannot use big-O notation to predict performance. The tilde notation and order-of-growth classifications that we use are more precise than big-O notation because they provide matching upper and lower bounds on the growth of the function. Many programmers incorrectly use big-O notation to indicate matching upper and lower bounds.

Q. How much memory does Python typically use to store a tuple of n items?

A. $56 + 8n$ bytes, plus whatever memory is needed for the objects themselves. This is a bit less than for arrays because Python can implement a tuple (at the machine level) using an array instead of a resizing array.

Q. Why does Python use so much memory (280 bytes) to store a dictionary that maps an object's instance variables to its values?

A. In principle, different objects from the same data type can have different instance variables. In this case, Python would need some way to manage an arbitrary number of possible instance variables for each object. But most Python code does not call for this (and, as a matter of style, we never need it in this book).

Exercises

4.1.1 Implement the function `writeAllTriples()` for `threesum.py`, which writes all of the triples that sum to zero.

4.1.2 Modify `threesum.py` to take a command-line argument `x` and find a triple of numbers on standard input whose sum is closest to `x`.

4.1.3 Compose a program `foursum.py` that reads an integer `n` from standard input, then reads `n` integers from standard input, and counts the number of distinct 4-tuples that sum to zero. Use a quadruply nested loop. What is the order of growth of the running time of your program? Estimate the largest `n` that your program can handle in an hour. Then, run your program to validate your hypothesis.

4.1.4 Prove that $1 + 2 + \ldots + n = n(n+1)/2$.

Solution: We proved this by induction at the beginning of SECTION 2.3. Here is the basis for another proof:

$$
\begin{array}{rcccccccccc}
 & 1 & + & 2 & + & \ldots & + & n-1 & + & n \\
+ & n & + & n-1 & + & \ldots & + & 2 & + & 1 \\
\hline
 & n+1 & + & n+1 & + & \ldots & + & n+1 & + & n+1
\end{array}
$$

4.1.5 Prove by induction that the number of distinct triples of integers between 0 and $n-1$ is $n(n-1)(n-2)/6$.

Solution: The formula is correct for $n = 2$. For $n > 2$, count all the triples that do not include n, which is $(n-1)(n-2)(n-3)/6$ by the inductive hypothesis, and all the triples that do include $n-1$, which is $(n-1)(n-2)/2$, to get the total

$$(n-1)(n-2)(n-3)/6 + (n-1)(n-2)/2 = n(n-1)(n-2)/6$$

4.1.6 Show by approximating with integrals that the number of distinct triples of integers between 0 and $n-1$ is about $n^3/6$.

Solution: $\Sigma_0^n \Sigma_0^i \Sigma_0^j 1 \approx \int_0^n \int_0^i \int_0^j dk\, dj\, di = \int_0^n \int_0^i j\, dj\, di = \int_0^n (i^2/2)\, di = n^3/6$.

4.1.7 What is the value of x (as a function of n) after running the following code fragment?

```
x = 0
for i in range(n):
    for j in range(i+1, n):
        for k in range(j+1, n):
            x += 1
```

Solution: $n\,(n-1)\,(n-2)\,/\,6$.

4.1.8 Use tilde notation to simplify each of the following formulas, and give the order of growth of each:

a. $n\,(n-1)\,(n-2)\,(n-3)\,/\,24$
b. $(n-2)\,(\lg n - 2)\,(\lg n + 2)$
c. $n(n+1) - n^2$
d. $n(n+1)\,/\,2 + n \lg n$
e. $\ln((n-1)(n-2)\,(n-3))^2$

4.1.9 Is the following code fragment linear, quadratic, or cubic (as a function of n)?

```
for i in range(n):
    for j in range(n):
        if i == j: c[i][j] = 1.0
        else:      c[i][j] = 0.0
```

4.1.10 Suppose the running time of an algorithm on inputs of size 1,000, 2,000, 3,000, and 4,000 is 5 seconds, 20 seconds, 45 seconds, and 80 seconds, respectively. Estimate how long it will take to solve a problem of size 5,000. Is the algorithm linear, linearithmic, quadratic, cubic, or exponential?

4.1.11 Which would you prefer: a quadratic, linearithmic, or linear algorithm?

Solution: While it is tempting to make a quick decision based on the order of growth, it is very easy to be misled by doing so. You need to have some idea of the problem size and of the relative value of the leading coefficients of the running time. For example, suppose that the running times are n^2 seconds, $100 n \log_2 n$ seconds, and $10{,}000n$ seconds. The quadratic algorithm will be fastest for n up to about 1,000, and the linear algorithm will never be faster than the linearithmic one (n would have to be greater than 2^{100}—far too large to bother considering).

4.1.12 Apply the scientific method to develop and validate a hypothesis about order of growth of the running time of the following code fragment, as a function of the argument n:

```
def f(n):
    if (n == 0): return 1
    return f(n-1) + f(n-1)
```

4.1.13 Apply the scientific method to develop and validate a hypothesis about order of growth of the running time of each of the following code fragments as a function of n:

```
s = ''
for i in range(n):
    if stdrandom.bernoulli(0.5): s += '0'
    else:                        s += '1'
```

```
s = ''
for i in range(n):
    oldS = s
    if stdrandom.bernoulli(0.5): s += '0'
    else:                        s += '1'
```

Solution: On many systems, the first is linear; the second is quadratic. You have no way of knowing why: In the first case, Python detects that s is the only variable that refers to the string, so it appends each character to the string as it would with a list (in amortized constant time) *even though the string is immutable*! A safer alternative is to create a list containing the characters and concatenate them together with by calling the join() method.

```
a = []
for i in range(n):
    if stdrandom.bernoulli(0.5): a += ['0']
    else:                        a += ['1']
s = ''.join(a)
```

4.1.14 Each of the four Python functions below returns a string of length n whose characters are all x. Determine the order of growth of the running time of each function. Recall that concatenating two strings in Python takes time proportional to the sum of their lengths.

```
def f1(n):
    if (n == 0):
        return ''
    temp = f1(n // 2)
    if (n % 2 == 0): return temp + temp
    else:            return temp + temp + 'x'

def f2(n):
    s = ''
    for i in range(n):
        s += 'x'
    return s

def f3(n):
    if (n == 0): return ''
    if (n == 1): return 'x'
    return f3(n//2) + f3(n - n//2)
```

```
def f4(n):
    temp = stdarray.create1D(n, 'x')
    return ''.join(temp)

def f5(n):
    return 'x' * n
```

4.1.15 Each of the three Python functions below returns the reverse of a string of length n. What is the order of growth of the running time of each function?

```
def reverse1(s):
    n = len(s)
    reverse = ''
    for i in range(n):
        reverse = s[i] + reverse
    return reverse

def reverse2(s):
    n = len(s)
    if (n <= 1):
        return s
    left = s[0 : n//2]
    right = s[n//2 : n]
    return reverse2(right) + reverse2(left)

def reverse3(s):
    return s[::-1]
```

The slice expression s[::-1] uses an optional third argument to specify the step size.

4.1.16 The following code fragment (adapted from a Java programming book) creates a random permutation of the integers from 0 to $n-1$. Determine the order of growth of its running time as a function of n. Compare its order of growth with the shuffling code in Section 1.4.

```
a = stdarray.create1D(n, 0)
taken = stdarray.create1D(n, False)
count = 0
while (count < n):
    r = stdrandom.uniform(0, n)
    if not taken[r]:
        a[r] = count
        taken[r] = True
        count += 1
```

4.1.17 How many times does the following code fragment execute the first `if` statement in the triply nested loop?

```
for i in range(n):
    for j in range(n):
        for k in range(n):
            if (i < j) and (j < k):
                if a[i] + a[j] + a[k] == 0:
                    count += 1
```

Use tilde notation to simply your answer.

4.1.18 Apply the scientific method to develop and validate a hypothesis about order of growth of the running time of the `collect()` method in `coupon.py` (Program 2.1.3), as a function of the argument `n`. *Note*: Doubling is not effective for distinguishing between the linear and linearithmic hypotheses—you might try *squaring* the size of the input.

4.1.19 Apply the scientific method to develop and validate a hypothesis about order of growth of the running time of `markov.py` (Program 1.6.3), as a function of the arguments `moves` and `n`.

4.1.20 Compose a program `mooreslaw.py` that takes a command-line argument n and writes the increase in processor speed over a decade if processor speed doubles every n months. How much will processor speed increase over the next decade if speeds double every $n = 15$ months? 24 months?

4.1.21 Using the memory model from the text, give the memory requirements for each object of the following data types from CHAPTER 3:

a. `Stopwatch`
b. `Turtle`
c. `Vector`
d. `Body`
e. `Universe`

4.1.22 Estimate, as a function of the grid size n, the amount of memory used by `visualizev.py` (PROGRAM 2.4.4) with vertical percolation detection (PROGRAM 2.4.2). *Extra credit*: Answer the same question for the case where the recursive percolation detection method `percolation.py` (PROGRAM 2.4.6) is used.

4.1.23 Estimate the size of the largest n-by-n array of integers that your computer can hold, and then try to allocate such an array.

4.1.24 Estimate, as a function of the number of documents n and the dimension d, the amount of space used by `comparedocuments.py` (PROGRAM 3.3.5).

4.1.25 Compose a version of `primesieve.py` (PROGRAM 1.4.3) that uses an array of integers instead of an array of booleans and uses 32 bits in each integer, to raise the largest value of `n` that it can handle by a factor of 32.

4.1.26 The following table gives running times for various programs for various values of n. Fill in the blanks with estimates that you think are reasonable on the basis of the information given.

program	*1,000*	*10,000*	*100,000*	*1,000,000*
A	0.001 second	0.012 second	0.16 second	? seconds
B	1 minute	10 minutes	1.7 hours	? hours
C	1 second	1.7 minutes	2.8 hours	? days

Give hypotheses for the order of growth of the running time of each program.

Creative Exercises

4.1.27 *Three-sum analysis.* Calculate the probability that no triple among n random 32-bit integers sums to 0, and give an approximate estimate for n equal to 1,000, 2,000, and 4,000. *Extra credit*: Give an approximate formula for the expected number of such triples (as a function of n), and run experiments to validate your hypothesis.

4.1.28 *Closest pair.* Design a quadratic algorithm that finds the pair of integers that are closest to each other. (In the next section you will be asked to find a linearithmic algorithm.)

4.1.29 *Power law.* Show that a log-log plot of the function cn^b has slope b and x-intercept $\log c$. What are the slope and x-intercept for $4\, n^3 (\log n)^2$?

4.1.30 *Sum furthest from zero.* Design an algorithm that finds the pair of integers whose sum is furthest from zero. Can you discover a linear-time algorithm?

4.1.31 *The "beck" exploit.* A popular web server supports a function `no2slash()` whose purpose is to collapse multiple / characters. For example, the string `/d1///d2////d3/test.html` becomes `/d1/d2/d3/test.html`. The original algorithm was to repeatedly search for a / and copy the remainder of the string:

```
def no2slash(name):
    for x in range(1, len(name)):
        if x > 0:
            if (name[x-1] == '/') and (name[x] == '/'):
                for y in range(x+1, len(name)):
                    name[y-1] = name[y]
            else:
                x += 1
```

Unfortunately, the running time of this code is quadratic in the number of / characters in the input. By sending multiple simultaneous requests with large numbers of / characters, a hacker can deluge a server and starve other processes for CPU time, thereby creating a denial-of-service attack. Develop a version of `no2slash()` that runs in linear time and does not allow for this type of attack.

4.1.32 *Young tableaux.* Suppose you have in memory an n-by-n array of integers `a[][]` such that `a[i][j] < a[i+1][j]` and `a[i][j] < a[i][j+1]` for all `i` and `j`, like the table below:

```
 5  23  54  67  89
 6  69  73  74  90
10  71  83  84  91
60  73  84  86  92
99  91  92  93  94
```

Devise an algorithm whose order of growth is linear in n to determine whether a given integer x is in a given Young tableaux.

4.1.33 *Subset sum.* Compose a program `anysum.py` that takes an integer n from standard input, then reads n integers from standard input, and counts the number of subsets that sum to 0. Give the order of growth of the running time of your program.

4.1.34 *Array rotation.* Given an array of n elements, give a linear-time algorithm to rotate the array by k positions. That is, if the array contains $a_0, a_1, \ldots, a_{n-1}$, the rotated array is $a_k, a_{k+1}, \ldots, a_{n-1}, a_0, \ldots, a_{k-1}$. Use at most a constant amount of extra space (array indices and array values). *Hint*: Reverse three subarrays.

4.1.35 *Finding a duplicated integer.* (*a*) Given an array of n integers from 1 to n with one value repeated twice and one missing, give an algorithm that finds the missing integer, in linear time and constant extra space. (*b*) Given a read-only array of n integers, where each value from 1 to $n-1$ occurs once and one occurs twice, give an algorithm that finds the duplicated value, in linear time and constant extra space. (*c*) Given a read-only array of n integers with values between 1 and $n-1$, give an algorithm that finds a duplicated value, in linear time and constant extra space.

4.1.36 *Factorial.* Design a fast algorithm to compute $n!$ for large values of n. Use your program to compute the longest run of consecutive 9s in 1000000!. Develop and validate a hypothesis for the order of growth of the running time of your algorithm.

4.1.37 *Maximum sum.* Design a linear-time algorithm that finds a contiguous subsequence of at most m in a sequence of n integers that has the highest sum among all such subsequences. Implement your algorithm, and confirm that the order of growth of its running time is linear.

4.1.38 *Pattern matching.* Given an n-by-n array of black (`1`) and white (`0`) pixels, design a linear algorithm that finds the largest square subarray that consists of entirely black pixels. As an example, the following 8-by-8 array contains a 3-by-3 subarray entirely of black pixels:

```
1 0 1 1 1 0 0 0
0 0 0 1 0 1 0 0
0 0 1 1 1 0 0 0
0 0 1 1 1 0 1 0
0 0 1 1 1 1 1 1
0 1 0 1 1 1 1 0
0 1 0 1 1 0 1 0
0 0 0 1 1 1 1 0
```

Implement your algorithm and confirm that the order of growth of its running time is linear in the number of pixels. *Extra credit*: Design an algorithm to find the largest *rectangular* black subarray.

4.1.39 *Maximum average.* Compose a program that finds a contiguous subarray of at most m elements in an array of n integers that has the highest average value among all such subarrays, by trying all subarrays. Use the scientific method to confirm that the order of growth of the running time of your program is mn^2. Next, compose a program that solves the problem by first computing `prefix[i] = a[0] + ... + a[i]` for each `i`, then computing the average in the interval from `a[i]` to `a[j]` with the expression `(prefix[j] - prefix[i]) / (j - i + 1)`. Use the scientific method to confirm that this method reduces the order of growth by a factor of n.

4.1.40 *Sub-exponential function.* Find a function whose order of growth is larger than any polynomial function, but smaller than any exponential function. *Extra credit*: Compose a program whose running time has that order of growth.

4.1.41 *Resizing arrays.* For each of the following strategies, either show that each resizing array operation takes constant amortized time or find a sequence of n operations (starting from an empty data structure) that takes quadratic time.

a. Double the capacity of the resizing array when it is full and halve the capacity when it is half full.

b. Double the capacity of the resizing array when it is full and halve the capacity when it is one-third full.

c. Increase the capacity of the resizing array by a factor of 9/8 when it is full and decrease it by a factor of 9/8 when it is 80% full.

4.2 Sorting and Searching

THE SORTING PROBLEM SEEKS TO REARRANGE an array of elements in ascending order. It is a familiar and critical task in many computational applications: the songs in your music library are in alphabetical order, your email messages are in reverse order of the time received, and so forth. Keeping things in some kind of order is a natural desire. One reason that it is so useful is that it is much easier to *search* for something in a sorted list than an unsorted one. This need is particularly acute in computing, where the list of things to search can be huge and an efficient search can be an important factor in a problem's solution.

Programs in this section

Sorting and searching are important for commercial applications (businesses keep customer files in order) and scientific applications (to organize data and computation), and have all manner of applications in fields that may appear to have little to do with keeping things in order, including data compression, computer graphics, computational biology, numerical computing, combinatorial optimization, cryptography, and many others.

We use these fundamental problems to illustrate the idea that *efficient algorithms* are one key to effective solutions for computational problems. Indeed, many different sorting and searching algorithms have been proposed. Which should we use to address a given task? This question is important because different algorithms can have vastly differing performance characteristics, enough to make the difference between success in a practical situation and not coming close to doing so, even on the fastest available computer.

In this section, we will consider in detail two classical algorithms for sorting and searching, along with several applications in which their efficiency plays a critical role. With these examples, you will be convinced not just of the utility of these algorithms, but also of the need to *pay attention to the cost* whenever you address a problem that requires a significant amount of computation.

Binary search The game of "twenty questions" (see PROGRAM 1.5.2, `twentyquestions.py`) provides an important and useful lesson in the idea of designing and using efficient algorithms for computational problems. The setup is simple: your task is to guess the value of a secret number that is one of the n integers between 0 and $n - 1$. Each time that you make a guess, you are told whether your guess is equal to the secret number, too high, or too low. As we discussed in SECTION 1.5, an effective strategy is to guess the number in the middle of the interval, then use the answer to halve the length of the interval that can contain the secret number. For reasons that will become clear later, we begin by slightly modifying the game to make the questions of the form "Is the number greater than or equal to m?" with only *true* or *false* answers, and assume for the moment that n is a power of 2. Now, the basis of an effective algorithm that always gets to the secret number in a minimal number of questions (in the worst case) is to maintain an interval that contains the secret number and shrink it by half at each step. More precisely, we use a *half-open interval*, which contains the left endpoint but not the right one. We use the notation $[lo, hi)$ to denote all of the integers greater than or equal to lo and less than (but not equal to) hi. We start with $lo = 0$ and $hi = n$ and use the following recursive strategy:

interval	*length*	*Q*	*A*
0 128	128	≥ 64 ?	*true*
0 64 128	64	≥ 96 ?	*false*
0 64 96	32	≥ 80 ?	*false*
0 64 80	16	≥ 72 ?	*true*
0 72 80	8	≥ 76 ?	*true*
0 76 80	4	≥ 78 ?	*false*
0 76 78	2	≥ 77 ?	*true*
0 77	1	$= 77$	

Finding a hidden number with binary search

- *Base case*: If $hi - lo$ equals 1, then the secret number is lo.
- *Recursive step*: Otherwise, ask whether the secret number is greater than or equal to the number $mid = (hi + lo) / 2$. If so, look for the number in $[mid, hi)$; if not, look for the number in $[lo, mid)$.

This strategy is an example of the general problem-solving algorithm known as *binary search*, which has many applications. PROGRAM 4.2.1 (`questions.py`) is an implementation.

Program 4.2.1 Binary search (20 questions) (questions.py)

```
import sys
import stdio

def search(lo, hi):
    if (hi - lo) == 1:
        return lo
    mid = (hi + lo) // 2
    stdio.write('Greater than or equal to ' + str(mid) + '?  ')
    if stdio.readBool():
        return search(mid, hi)
    else:
        return search(lo, mid)

k = int(sys.argv[1])
n = 2 ** k
stdio.write('Think of a number ')
stdio.writeln('between 0 and ' + str(n - 1))
guess = search(0, n)
stdio.writeln('Your number is ' + str(guess))
```

`lo`	*smallest possible integer*
`hi - 1`	*largest possible integer*
`mid`	*midpoint*
`n`	*number of possible integers*
`k`	*number of questions*

This script uses binary search to play the same game as Program *1.5.2, but with the roles reversed: you choose the secret number and the program guesses its value. It takes a command-line argument k, asks you to think of a number between 0 and $2^k - 1$, and always guesses the answer with k questions.*

```
% python questions.py 7
Think of a number between 0 and 127
Greater than or equal to 64?  True
Greater than or equal to 96?  False
Greater than or equal to 80?  False
Greater than or equal to 72?  True
Greater than or equal to 76?  True
Greater than or equal to 78?  False
Greater than or equal to 77?  True
Your number is 77
```

Correctness proof. First, we have to convince ourselves that the strategy is *correct*—in other words, that it always leads us to the secret number. We do so by establishing the following facts:

- The interval always contains the secret number.
- The interval lengths are the powers of 2, decreasing from 2^k.

The first of these facts is enforced by the code; the second follows by noting that if $(hi - lo)$ is a power of 2, then $(hi - lo) / 2$ is the next smaller power of 2 and also the length of both halved intervals. These facts are the basis of an induction proof that the algorithm operates as intended. Eventually, the interval length becomes 1, so we are guaranteed to find the number.

Analysis of running time. Let n be the number of possible values. In `questions.py`, we have $n = 2^k$, where $k = \lg n$. Now, let $T(n)$ be the number of questions. The recursive strategy immediately implies that $T(n)$ must satisfy the following recurrence relation:

$$T(n) = T(n/2) + 1$$

with $T(1) = 0$. Substituting 2^k for n, we can telescope the recurrence (apply it to itself) to immediately get a closed-form expression:

$$T(2^k) = T(2^{k-1}) + 1 = T(2^{k-2}) + 2 = \ldots = T(1) + k = k$$

Substituting back n for 2^k (and $\lg n$ for k) gives the result

$$T(n) = \lg n$$

We normally use this equation to justify a hypothesis that the running time of a program that uses binary search is logarithmic. *Note*: Binary search and `questions.search()` work even when n is not a power of 2 (see Exercise 4.2.1).

Linear–logarithmic chasm. The alternative to using binary search is to guess 0, then 1, then 2, then 3, and so forth, until we hit the secret number. We refer to such an algorithm as a *brute-force* algorithm: it seems to get the job done, but without much regard to the cost (which might prevent it from actually getting the job done for large problems). In this case, the running time of the brute-force algorithm is sensitive to the secret number, but could take as many as n questions in the worst case. Meanwhile, binary search guarantees to take no more than $\lg n$ questions (or, more precisely, $\lceil \lg n \rceil$ if n is not a power of 2). As you will learn to appreciate, the difference between n and $\lg n$ makes a huge difference in practical applications. *Understanding the enormity of this difference is a critical step to understanding the importance of algorithm design and analysis.* In the present context, suppose that it takes 1 second to process a question. With binary search, you can guess the value of any number less than 1 million in 20 seconds; with the brute-force algorithm, it might take 1 million seconds, which is more than 1 week. We will see many examples where such a cost difference is the determining factor in whether a practical problem can be feasibly solved.

Binary representation. If you look back to PROGRAM 1.3.7 (`binary.py`), you will immediately recognize that binary search is nearly the same computation as converting a number to binary! Each question determines one bit of the answer. In our example, the information that the number is between 0 and 127 says that the number of bits in its binary representation is 7, the answer to the first question (Is the number greater than or equal to than 64?) tells us the value of the leading bit, the answer to the second question tells us the value of the next bit, and so forth. For example, if the number is 77, the sequence of answers `True False False True True False True` immediately yields 1001101, the binary representation of 77.

Thinking in terms of the binary representation is another way to understand the linear–logarithmic chasm: when we have a program whose running time is linear in a parameter n, its running time is proportional to the *value* of n, whereas a logarithmic running time is just proportional to the *number of digits* in n. In a context that is perhaps slightly more familiar to you, think about the following question, which illustrates the same point: would you rather earn \$6 or a six-figure salary?

Inverting a function. As an example of the utility of binary search in scientific computing, we revisit a problem that we first encountered in SECTION 2.1: inverting an increasing function (see EXERCISE 2.1.26). Given an increasing function f and a value y, and an open interval (lo, hi), our task is to find a value x within the interval such that $f(x) = y$. In this situation, we use real numbers as the endpoints of our interval, not integers, but we use the same essential approach that we used for guessing a hidden integer with the "twenty questions" problem: we halve the length of the interval at each step, keeping x in the interval, until the interval is sufficiently small that we know the value of x to within a desired precision δ, which we take as an argument to the function. The figure at the top of the next page illustrates the first step.

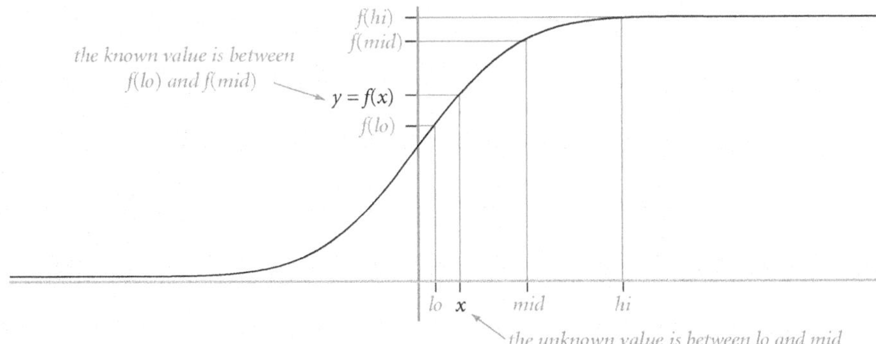

Binary search (bisection) to invert an increasing function (one step)

PROGRAM 4.2.2 (`bisection.py`) implements this strategy. We start with an interval (*lo* , *hi*) known to contain *x* and use the following recursive procedure:

- Compute *mid* = (*hi* + *lo*) / 2.
- *Base case*: If *hi* − *lo* is less than δ, then return *mid* as an estimate of *x*.
- *Recursive step*: Otherwise, test whether *f*(*mid*) > *y*. If so, look for *x* in (*lo* , *mid*); if not, look for *x* in (*mid* , *hi*).

The key to this approach is the idea that the function is increasing—for any values *a* and *b*, knowing that *f*(*a*) < *f*(*b*) tells us that *a* < *b*, and vice versa. The recursive step just applies this knowledge: knowing that *y* = *f*(*x*) < *f*(*mid*) tells us that *x* < *mid*, so that *x* must be in the interval (*lo*, *mid*), and knowing that *y* = *f*(*x*) > *f*(*mid*) tells us that *x* > *mid*, so that *x* must be in the interval (*mid*, *hi*). You can think of the problem as determining which of the *n* = (*hi*−*lo*) / δ tiny intervals of length δ within (*lo*, *hi*) contains *x*, with running time logarithmic in *n*. As with converting an integer to binary, we determine one bit of *x* in each iteration. In this context, binary search is often called *bisection search* because we bisect the interval at each stage.

Weighing an object. Binary search has been known since antiquity, perhaps partly because of the following application. Suppose that you need to determine the weight of a given object using only a balancing scale. With binary search, you can do so with weights that are powers of 2 (and just one weight of each type). Put the object on the right side of the balance and try the weights in decreasing order on the left side. If a weight causes the balance to tilt to the left, remove it; otherwise, leave it. This process is precisely analogous to determining the binary representation of a number by subtracting decreasing powers of 2, as in PROGRAM 1.3.7.

Program 4.2.2 Bisection search (bisection.py)

```
import sys
import stdio
import gaussian

def invert(f, y, lo, hi, delta=0.00000001):
    mid = (lo + hi) / 2.0
    if (hi - lo) < delta:
        return mid
    if f(mid) > y:
        return invert(f, y, lo, mid, delta)
    else:
        return invert(f, y, mid, hi, delta)

def main():
    y = float(sys.argv[1])
    x = invert(gaussian.cdf, y, -8.0, 8.0)
    stdio.writef('%.3f\n', x)

if __name__ == '__main__': main()
```

f	*function*
y	*given value*
delta	*precision*
lo	*left endpoint*
mid	*midpoint*
hi	*right endpoint*

The function invert() *in this program uses binary search to compute a float x within the interval* (lo, hi) *for which* f(x) *is equal to a given value y, within a given precision* delta, *for any function f that is increasing in the interval. It is a recursive function that halves the interval containing the given value, evaluates the function at the midpoint of the interval, and decides whether the desired float x is in the left half or the right half, continuing until the interval length is less than the given precision.*

```
% python bisection.py .5
0.000

% python bisection.py .95
1.645

% python bisection.py .975
1.960
```

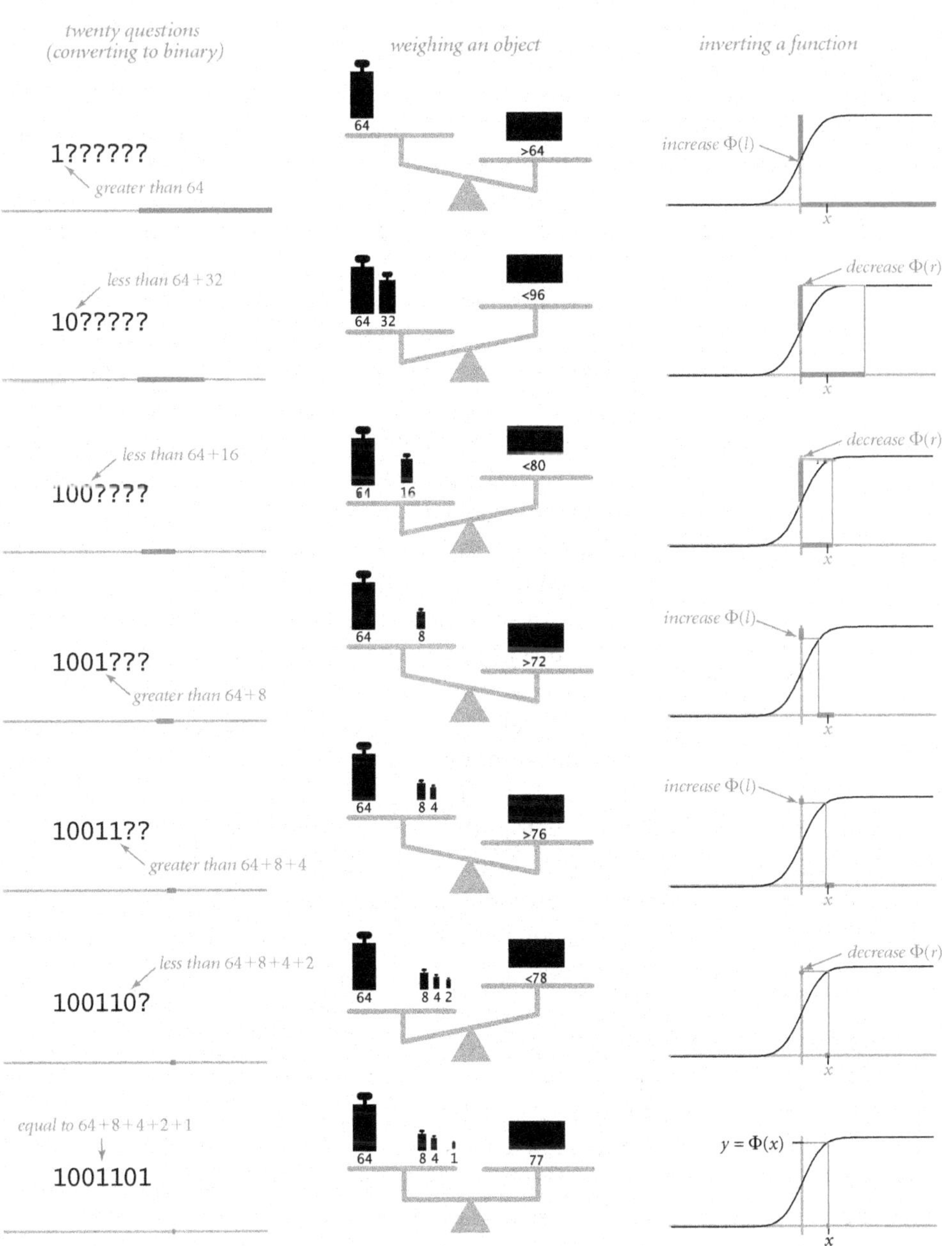

Three applications of binary search

Binary search in a sorted array. One of the most important uses of binary search is to find a piece of information using a key to guide the search. This usage is ubiquitous in modern computing, to the extent that printed artifacts that depend on the same concepts are well on their way to becoming obsolete. For example, during the last few centuries, people would use a publication known as a *dictionary* to look up the definition of a word, and during much of the last century people would use a publication known as a *phone book* to look up a person's phone number. In both cases, the basic mechanism is the same: entries appear in order, sorted by a key that identifies it (the word in the case of the dictionary, and the person's name in the case of the phone book, sorted in alphabetical order in both cases). You probably use your computer to reference such information, but think about how you would look up a word in a dictionary. A brute-force solution known as *sequential search* is to start at the beginning, examine each key one at a time, and continue until you find the word. No one uses that approach: instead, you open the book to some interior page and look for the word on that page. If it is there, you are done; otherwise, you eliminate either the part of the book before the current page or the part of the book after the current page from consideration, and then repeat. We now recognize this approach as binary search. Whether you look exactly in the middle is immaterial; as long as you eliminate at least a constant fraction of the keys each time that you look, your search will be logarithmic.

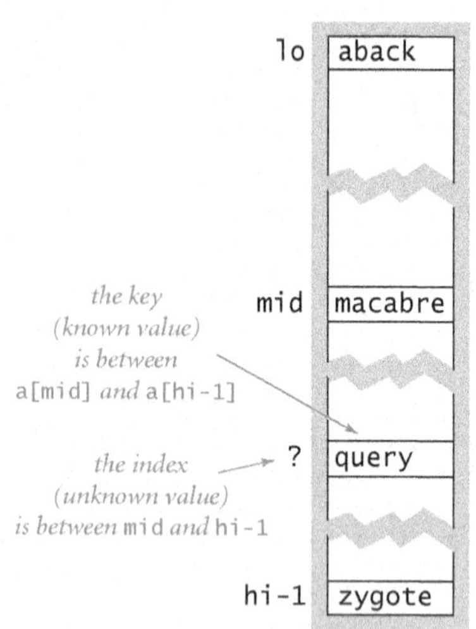

Binary search in a sorted array (one step)

Exception filter. We will consider in Section 4.3 the details of implementing the kind of computer program that you use in place of a dictionary or a phone book. Program 4.2.3 (`binarysearch.py`) uses binary search to solve the simpler *existence problem*: is a given key in a sorted array of keys, in any location? For example, when checking the spelling of a word, you need to know only whether your word is in the dictionary and are not interested in the definition. In a computer search, we keep the information in an array, sorted in order of the key (for some applications, the information comes in sorted order; for others, we have to sort it first, using one

Program 4.2.3 Binary search (in a sorted array) (binarysearch.py)

```
import sys
import stdio
from instream import InStream

def _search(key, a, lo, hi):
    if hi <= lo: return -1  # Not found.
    mid = (lo + hi) // 2
    if a[mid] > key:
        return _search(key, a, lo, mid)
    elif a[mid] < key:
        return _search(key, a, mid+1, hi)
    else:
        return mid

def search(key, a):
    return _search(key, a, 0, len(a))

def main():
    instream = InStream(sys.argv[1])
    a = instream.readAllStrings()
    while not stdio.isEmpty():
        key = stdio.readString()
        if search(key, a) < 0: stdio.writeln(key)

if __name__ == '__main__': main()
```

`key`	*key sought*
`a[]`	*sorted array*
`lo`	*smallest possible index*
`mid`	*midpoint*
`hi`	*largest possible index*

The `search()` *method uses binary search to find the index of a key in a sorted array (or returns -1 if the key is not in the array). The test client is an exception filter that reads a sorted array of strings from the whitelist file given on the command line and writes the words from standard input that are not in the whitelist.*

```
% more emails.txt
bob@office
carl@beach
marvin@spam
bob@office
bob@office
mallory@spam
dave@boat
eve@airport
alice@home
```

```
% more white.txt
alice@home
bob@office
carl@beach
dave@boat

% python binarysearch.py white.txt < emails.txt
marvin@spam
mallory@spam
eve@airport
```

of the algorithms discussed later in this section). The binary search in `binarysearch.py` differs from our other applications in two details. First, the array length n need not be a power of 2. Second, it has to allow for the possibility that the key sought is not in the array. Coding binary search to account for these details requires some care, as discussed in this section's Q&A and exercises.

The test client in `binarysearch.py` is known as an *exception filter*: it reads in a sorted array of strings from a file (which we refer to as the *whitelist*) and an arbitrary sequence of strings from standard input, and writes those in the sequence that are not in the whitelist. Exception filters have many direct applications. For example, if the whitelist is the words from a dictionary and standard input is a text document, the exception filter will write the misspelled words. Another example arises in web applications: your email application might use an exception filter to reject any messages that are not on a whitelist that contains the email addresses of your friends, or your operating system might have an exception filter that disallows network connections to your computer from any device having an IP address that is not on a preapproved whitelist.

FAST ALGORITHMS ARE AN ESSENTIAL ELEMENT of the modern world, and binary search is a prototypical example that illustrates the impact of fast algorithms. Whether it be extensive experimental data or detailed representations of some aspect of the physical world, modern scientists are awash in vast amounts of data. With a few quick calculations, you can convince yourself that problems like finding all the misspelled words in a document or protecting your computer from intruders using an exception filter *require* a fast algorithm like binary search. *Take the time to do so*—a fast algorithm can certainly make the difference between being able to solve a problem easily and spending substantial resources trying to do so (and failing). You can find the exceptions in a million-word document to a million-entry whitelist in an instant, whereas that task might take days or weeks using the brute-force algorithm. Nowadays, web companies routinely provide services that are based on using binary search *billions* of times in arrays with *billions* of elements—without a fast algorithm like binary search, we could not contemplate such services.

Insertion sort Binary search requires that the array be sorted, and sorting has many other direct applications, so we now turn to sorting algorithms. We consider first a brute-force algorithm, then a sophisticated algorithm that we can use for huge arrays.

The brute-force algorithm we consider is known as *insertion sort.* It is based on a simple approach that people often use to arrange hands of playing cards—that is, consider the cards one at a time and insert each into its proper place among those already considered (keeping them sorted).

PROGRAM 4.2.4 (`insertion.py`) contains an implementation of a `sort()` function that mimics this process to sort elements in an array `a[]` of length `n`. The test client reads all the strings from standard input, puts them into the array, calls the `sort()` function to sort them, and then writes the sorted result to standard output.

In `insertion.sort()`, the outer `for` loop sorts the first `i` elements in the array. The inner `while` loop completes the sort by putting `a[i]` into its proper position in the array, as in the following example when `i` is `6`:

i	j	a							
		0	1	2	3	4	5	6	7
6	6	and	had	him	his	was	you	the	but
6	5	and	had	him	his	was	the	you	but
6	4	and	had	him	his	the	was	you	but
		and	had	him	his	the	was	you	but

Inserting `a[6]` into position by exchanging it with larger elements to its left

Element `a[i]` is put in its place among the sorted elements to its left by exchanging it (using a tuple-packing variant of the `exchange()` function that we first encountered in SECTION 2.1) with each larger element to its left, moving from right to left, until it reaches its proper position. The black elements in the three bottom rows in this trace are the ones that are compared (and exchanged, on all but the final iteration).

The insertion process just described is executed first with `i` equal to `1`, then `2`, then `3`, and so forth, as illustrated in the trace at the top of the next page. When `i` reaches the end of the array, the whole array is sorted.

i	j	a[0]	a[1]	a[2]	a[3]	a[4]	a[5]	a[6]	a[7]
		was	had	him	and	you	his	the	but
1	0	had	was	him	and	you	his	the	but
2	1	had	him	was	and	you	his	the	but
3	0	and	had	him	was	you	his	the	but
4	4	and	had	him	was	you	his	the	but
5	3	and	had	him	his	was	you	the	but
6	4	and	had	him	his	the	was	you	but
7	1	and	but	had	him	his	the	was	you
		and	but	had	him	his	the	was	you

Inserting a[1] through a[n-1] into position (insertion sort)

This trace displays the contents of the array each time the outer `for` loop completes, along with the value of `j` at that time. The highlighted element is the one that was in `a[i]` at the beginning of the loop, and the other elements printed in black are the other ones that were involved in exchanges and moved to the right one position within the loop. Since the elements `a[0]` through `a[i-1]` are in sorted order when the loop completes for each value of `i`, they are, in particular, in sorted order the final time the loop completes, when the value of `i` is `len(a)`. This discussion again illustrates the first thing that you need to do when studying or developing a new algorithm: convince yourself that it is correct. Doing so provides the basic understanding that you need to study its performance and use it effectively.

Analysis of running time. The `sort()` function contains a `while` loop nested inside a `for` loop, which suggests that the running time is quadratic. However, we cannot immediately draw this conclusion because the `while` loop terminates as soon as `a[j]` is greater than or equal to `a[j-1]`. For example, in the best case, when the argument array is already in sorted order, the `while` loop amounts to nothing more than a comparison (to learn that `a[j]` is greater than or equal to `a[j-1]` for each `j` from `1` to `n-1`), so the total running time is linear. On the other hand, if the argument array is in reverse-sorted order, the `while` loop does not terminate until `j` equals 0. So, the frequency of execution of the instructions in the inner loop is

$$1 + 2 + \ldots + n-1 \sim n^2/2$$

Program 4.2.4 Insertion sort (insertion.py)

```
import sys
import stdio

def exchange(a, i, j):
    a[i], a[j] = a[j], a[i]

def sort(a):
    n = len(a)
    for i in range(1, n):
        j = i
        while (j > 0) and (a[j] < a[j-1]):
            exchange(a, j, j-1)
            j -= 1

def main():
    a = stdio.readAllStrings()
    sort(a)
    for s in a:
        stdio.write(s + ' ')
    stdio.writeln()

if __name__ == '__main__': main()
```

a[]	*array to sort*
n	*number of elements*

This program reads strings from standard input, sorts them into increasing order, and writes them to standard output. The `sort()` *function is an implementation of insertion sort. It sorts arrays of any type of data that supports < (implements a* `__lt__()` *method). Insertion sort is appropriate for small arrays or for large arrays that are nearly in order, but is too slow to use for large arrays that are out of order.*

```
% more tiny.txt
was had him and you his the but

% python insertion.py < tiny.txt
and but had him his the was you

% python insertion.py < TomSawyer.txt
```

tick tick tick tick tick tick tick tick tick tick tick tick tick tick tick tick tick tick tick tick tick tick tick tick
tick tick tick tick tick tick tick tick tick tick tick tick tick tick tick tick tick tick tick tick tick tick tick tick tick

and the running time is quadratic (see EXERCISE 4.1.4). To understand the performance of insertion sort for *randomly* ordered arrays, take a careful look at the trace: it is an n-by-n array with one black element corresponding to each exchange. That is, the number of black elements is the frequency of execution of instructions in the inner loop. We expect that each new element to be inserted is equally likely to fall into any position, so that element will move halfway to the left on average. Thus, on the average, we expect only about one-half the elements below the diagonal (about $n^2/4$ in total) to be black. This observation leads immediately to the hypothesis that the expected running time of insertion sort for a randomly ordered array is quadratic.

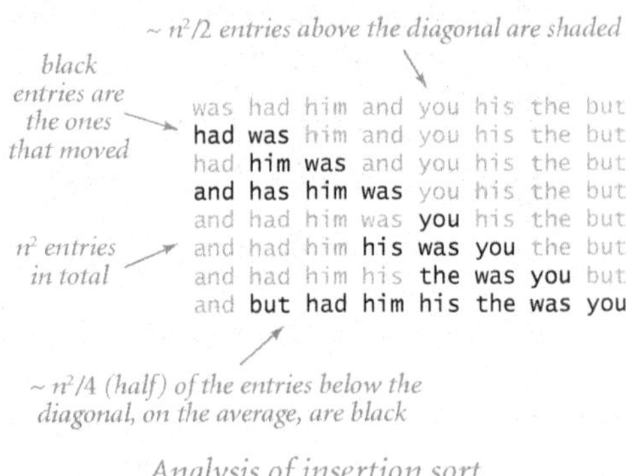

Analysis of insertion sort

Empirical analysis. PROGRAM 4.2.5 (`timesort.py`) provides the functions that we need to test our hypothesis that insertion sort is quadratic for randomly ordered arrays by running a doubling test (see SECTION 4.1). The module includes two function: `timeTrials()`, which runs experiments for a given problem size n, and `doublingTest()`, which computes the ratios of running times between problems of size $n/2$ and n. We can also use these functions for other sorting algorithms. For insertion sort, the interactive Python session ratio converges to 4, which validates the hypothesis that the running time is quadratic, as discussed in the last section. You are encouraged to run `timesort.py` on your own computer. As usual, you might notice the effect of caching or some other system characteristic for some values of n, but the quadratic running time should be quite evident, and you will be quickly convinced that insertion sort is too slow to be useful for large inputs.

Sensitivity to input. Note that each function in `timesort.py` takes an argument `trials` and runs `trials` experiments for each problem size, not just one. As we have just observed, one reason for doing so is that *the running time of insertion sort is sensitive to its input values.* This behavior is quite different from (for example) `threesum.py`, and it means that we have to carefully interpret the results of our analysis. It is not correct to flatly predict that the running time of insertion sort will

Program 4.2.5 Doubling test for sorts (`timesort.py`)

```
import stdio
import stdrandom
import stdarray
from stopwatch import Stopwatch

def timeTrials(f, n, trials):
    total = 0.0
    a = stdarray.create1D(n, 0.0)
    for t in range(trials):
        for i in range(n):
            a[i] = stdrandom.uniformFloat(0.0, 1.0)
        watch = Stopwatch()
        f(a)
        total += watch.elapsedTime()
    return total

def doublingTest(f, n, trials):
    while True:
        prev = timeTrials(f, n // 2, trials)
        curr = timeTrials(f, n,      trials)
        ratio = curr / prev
        stdio.writef('%7d %4.2f\n', n, ratio)
        n *= 2
```

`f()`	*function to test*
`n`	*problem size*
`trials`	*number of trials*
`total`	*total elapsed time*
`a[]`	*array to sort*
`watch`	*stopwatch*

`n`	*problem size*
`prev`	*running time for* `n // 2`
`curr`	*running time for* `n`
`ratio`	*ratio of running times*

The function `timeTrials()` *runs the function* `f()` *for arrays of* n *random floats, performing this experiment* `trials` *times. Multiple trials produce more accurate results because they dampen system effects and dependence on the input. The function* `doublingTest()` *performs a doubling test starting at* n*, doubling* n*, and writing the ratio of the time for the current* n *and the time for the previous* n *each time through the loop.*

```
% python
>>> import insertion
>>> import timesort
>>> timesort.doublingTest(insertion.sort, 128, 100)
    128 3.90
    256 3.93
    512 3.98
   1024 4.12
   2048 4.13
```

be quadratic, because your application might involve input for which the running time is linear. When an algorithm's performance is sensitive to input values, you might not be able to make accurate predictions without taking the input values into account. We will return to this issue often as we face real applications. Are the strings that we need to sort in random order? Indeed, that is often not the case. In particular, if only a few elements in a large array are out of position, then insertion sort is the method of choice.

Comparable keys. We want to be able to sort any type of data that has a natural order. In a scientific application, we may wish to sort experimental results by numeric values; in a commercial application, we may wish to use monetary amounts, times, or dates; in systems software, we might wish to use IP addresses or account numbers.

Happily, our insertion sort and binary search functions work not only with strings but also with any data type that is *comparable*. Recall from SECTION 3.3 that a data type is comparable if it implements the six comparison methods and they define a *total order*. Python's built-in `int`, `float`, and `str` types are all comparable.

You can make a user-defined type comparable by implementing the six special methods corresponding to the <, <=, ==, !=, >=, and > operators. In fact, our insertion sort and binary search functions rely on only the < operator, but it is better style to implement all six special methods.

A more general design is sometimes appropriate for user-defined types. For example, a teacher might wish to sort a file of student grade records by name on some occasions and by grade on some other occasions. One solution that is often used to handle such situations is to pass the function that is to be used to compare keys as an argument to the sort function.

IT IS MORE LIKELY THAN NOT in natural applications that the running time of insertion sort *is* quadratic, so we need to consider faster sorting algorithms. As we know from SECTION 4.1, a back-of-the-envelope calculation can tell us that having a faster computer is not much help. A dictionary, a scientific database, or a commercial database can contain billions of elements; how can we sort such a large array? Next, we turn to a classic algorithm for addressing this question.

Mergesort To develop a faster sorting method, we use recursion (as we did for binary search) and a *divide-and-conquer* approach to algorithm design that every programmer needs to understand. This nomenclature refers to the idea that one way to solve a problem is to *divide* it into independent parts, *conquer* them independently, and then use the solutions for the parts to develop a solution for the full problem. To sort an array of comparable keys with this strategy, we divide it into two halves, sort the two halves independently, and then *merge* the results to sort the full array. This method is known as *mergesort*.

input
`was had him and you his the but`
sort left
`and had him was you his the but`
sort right
`and had him was but his the you`
merge
`and but had him his the was you`

Mergesort overview

We process contiguous subarrays of a given array, using the notation $a[lo, hi)$ to refer to $a[lo]$, $a[lo+1]$, ..., $a[hi-1]$, (adopting the same convention as we used for binary search to denote a half-open interval that excludes $a[hi]$). To sort $a[lo, hi)$, we use the following recursive strategy:

- *Base case*: If the length of the subarray is 0 or 1, it is already sorted.
- *Recursive step*: Otherwise, compute $mid = (hi + lo) / 2$, sort (recursively) the two subarrays $a[lo, mid)$ and $a[mid, hi)$, and merge them.

Program 4.2.6 (`merge.py`) is an implementation of this algorithm. The array elements are rearranged by the code that follows the recursive calls, which *merges* the two halves of the array that were sorted by the recursive calls. As usual, the easiest way to understand the merge process is to study a trace of the contents of the array during the merge. The code maintains one index `i` into the first half, another index

i	j	k	aux[k]	a[]							
				0	1	2	3	4	5	6	7
				and	had	him	was	but	his	the	you
0	4	0	and	and	had	him	was	but	his	the	you
1	4	1	but	and	had	him	was	but	his	the	you
1	5	2	had	and	had	him	was	but	his	the	you
2	5	3	him	and	had	him	was	but	his	the	you
3	5	4	his	and	had	him	was	but	his	the	you
3	6	5	the	and	had	him	was	but	his	the	you
3	7	6	was	and	had	him	was	but	his	the	you
4	7	7	you	and	had	him	was	but	his	the	you

Trace of the merge of the sorted left half with the sorted right half

Program 4.2.6 Mergesort (merge.py)

```
import sys
import stdio
import stdarray

def _merge(a, lo, mid, hi, aux):
    n = hi - lo
    i = lo
    j = mid
    for k in range(n):
        if   i == mid:    aux[k] = a[j]; j += 1
        elif j == hi:     aux[k] = a[i]; i += 1
        elif a[j] < a[i]: aux[k] = a[j]; j += 1
        else:             aux[k] = a[i]; i += 1
    a[lo:hi] = aux[0:n]

def _sort(a, lo, hi, aux):
    n = hi - lo
    if n <= 1: return

    mid = (lo + hi) // 2
    _sort(a, lo, mid, aux)
    _sort(a, mid, hi, aux)
    _merge(a, lo, mid, hi, aux)

def sort(a):
    n = len(a)
    aux = stdarray.create1D(n)
    _sort(a, 0, n, aux)
```

`a[lo, hi)`	*subarray to sort*
`n`	*length of subarray*
`mid`	*midpoint*
`aux[]`	*extra array for merge*

```
% python merge.py < tiny.txt
was had him and you his the but
had was
        and him
and had him was
                his you
                        but the
                but his the you
and but had him his the was you
```

The `sort()` *function in this module is a fast function that you can use to sort arrays of any comparable data type. It is based on a recursive* `sort()` *that sorts* `a[lo, hi)` *by sorting its two halves recursively, then merging together the two halves to create the sorted result. The output at right is a trace of the sorted subarray for each call to* `sort()` *(see Exercise 4.2.8). In contrast to* `insertion.sort()`*,* `merge.sort()` *is suitable for sorting huge arrays.*

j into the second half, and a third index k into an auxiliary array aux[] that holds the result. The merge implementation is a single loop that sets aux[k] to either a[i] or a[j] (and then increments k and the index for the value that is used). If either i or j has reached the end of its subarray, aux[k] is set from the other; otherwise, it is set to the smaller of a[i] or a[j]. After all of the elements from the two halves have been copied to aux[], the sorted result is copied back to the original array. Take a moment to study the trace just given to convince yourself that this code always properly combines the two sorted subarrays to sort the full array.

The recursive method ensures that the two halves of the array are put into sorted order before the merge. Again, the best way to gain an understanding of this process is to study a trace of the contents of the array each time the recursive sort() method returns. Such a trace for our example is shown next. First a[0] and a[1] are merged to make a sorted subarray in a[0, 2), then a[2] and a[3] are merged to make a sorted subarray in a[2, 4), then these two subarrays of size 2 are merged to make a sorted subarray in a[0, 4), and so forth. If you are convinced that the merge works properly, you need only convince yourself that the code properly divides the array to be convinced that the sort works correctly. Note that when the number of elements is not even, the left half will have one fewer element than the right half.

	a[]							
	0	1	2	3	4	5	6	7
	was	had	him	and	you	his	the	but
_sort(a, 0, 8, aux)								
_sort(a, 0, 4, aux)								
_sort(a, 0, 2, aux)								
return	had	was	him	and	you	his	the	but
_sort(a, 2, 4, aux)								
return	had	was	and	him	you	his	the	but
return	and	had	him	was	you	his	the	but
_sort(a, 4, 8, aux)								
_sort(a, 4, 6, aux)								
return	and	had	him	was	his	you	the	but
_sort(a, 6, 8, aux)								
return	and	had	him	was	his	you	but	the
return	and	had	him	was	but	his	the	you
return	and	but	had	him	his	the	was	you

Trace of recursive mergesort calls

Analysis of running time. The inner loop of mergesort is centered on the auxiliary array. The `for` loop involves n iterations, so the frequency of execution of the instructions in the inner loop is proportional to the sum of the subarray lengths over all calls to the recursive function. The value of this quantity emerges when we arrange the calls on levels according to their size. For simplicity, suppose that n is a power of 2, with $n = 2^k$. On the first level, we have one call for size n; on the second level, we have two calls for size $n/2$; on the third level, we have four calls for size $n/4$; and so forth, down to the last level with $n/2$ calls of size 2. There are precisely $k = \lg n$ levels, giving the grand total $n \lg n$ for the frequency of execution of the instructions in the inner loop of mergesort. This equation justifies a hypothesis that the running time of mergesort is linearithmic. *Note*: When n is not a power of 2, the subarrays on each level are not necessarily all the same size, but the number of levels is still logarithmic, so the linearithmic hypothesis is justified for all n (see EXERCISES 4.2.14 and 4.2.15). The interactive Python script at left uses `timesort.doublingTest()` (see PROGRAM 4.2.5) to validate this hypotheses.

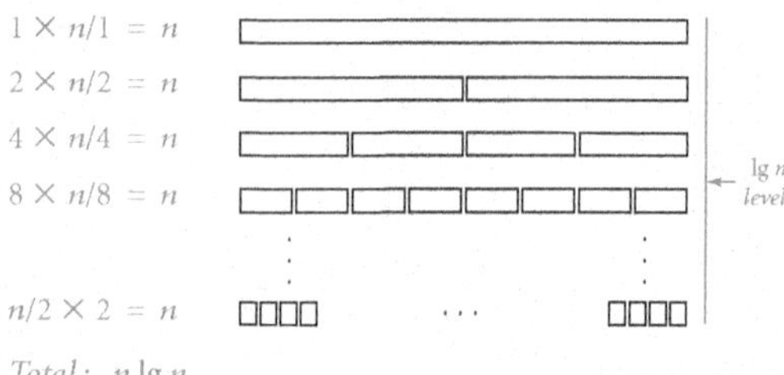

Mergesort inner loop count (when n is a power of 2)

```
% python
...
>>> import merge
>>> import timesort
>>> timesort.doublingTest(
... merge.sort, 1024, 100)
   1024 1.92
   2048 2.19
   4096 2.07
   8192 2.13
  16384 2.13
  32768 2.11
  65536 2.31
 131072 2.14
 262144 2.29
 524288 2.13
1048576 2.17
```

You are encouraged to run these tests on your computer. If you do so, you certainly will appreciate that `merge.sort()` is much faster for large arrays than is `insertion.sort()` and that you can sort huge arrays with relative ease. Validating the hypothesis that the running time is linearithmic (and not linear) is a bit more work, but you certainly can see that mergesort scales, making it possible for us to address sorting problems that we could not contemplate solving with a brute-force algorithm such as insertion sort.

Quadratic–linearithmic chasm. The difference between n^2 and $n \log n$ makes a huge difference in practical applications, just as with the linear–logarithmic chasm that is overcome by binary search. *Understanding the enormity of this difference is another critical step to understanding the importance of the design and analysis of algorithms.* For a great many important computational problems, a speedup from quadratic to linearithmic—such as we achieve with mergesort over insertion sort—makes the difference between the ability to solve a problem involving a huge amount of data and not being able to effectively address it at all.

Python system sort Python includes two operations for sorting. The method `sort()` in the built-in `list` data type rearranges the items in the underlying list into ascending order, much like `merge.sort()`. In contrast, the built-in function `sorted()` leaves the underlying list alone; instead, it returns a new list containing the items in ascending order. The interactive Python script at right illustrates both techniques. The Python system sort uses a version of mergesort:. It is likely to be substantially faster (10–20×) than `merge.py` because it uses a low-level implementation that is not composed in Python, thereby avoiding the substantial overhead that Python imposes on itself. As with our sorting implementations, you can use the system sort with any comparable data type, such as Python's built-in `str`, `int`, and `float` data types.

```
% python
...
>>> a = [3, 1, 4, 1, 5]
>>> b = sorted(a)
>>> a
[3, 1, 4, 1, 5]
>>> b
[1, 1, 3, 4, 5]

>>> a.sort()
>>> a
[1, 1, 3, 4, 5]
```

Mergesort traces back to John von Neumann, an accomplished physicist, who was among the first to recognize the importance of computation in scientific research. Von Neumann made many contributions to computer science, including a basic conception of the computer architecture that has been used since the 1950s. When it came to applications programming, von Neumann recognized that:

- Sorting is an essential ingredient in many applications.
- Quadratic algorithms are too slow for practical purposes.
- A divide-and-conquer approach is effective.
- Proving programs correct and knowing their cost is important.

Computers are many orders of magnitude faster and have many orders of magnitude more memory, but these basic concepts remain important today. People who use computers effectively and successfully know, as did von Neumann, that brute-force algorithms are often only a start. That Python and other modern systems still use von Neumann's method is testimony to the power of these ideas.

Application: frequency counts PROGRAM 4.2.7 (`frequencycount.py`) reads a sequence of strings from standard input and writes to standard output a table of the distinct strings found and the number of times each was found, in decreasing order of frequency. This computation is useful in numerous applications: a linguist might be studying patterns of word usage in long texts, a scientist might be looking for frequently occurring events in experimental data, a merchant might be looking for the customers who appear most frequently in a long list of transactions, or a network analyst might be looking for the heaviest users. Each of these applications might involve millions of strings or more, so we need a linearithmic algorithm (or better). PROGRAM 4.2.7 accomplishes this by performing *two* sorts.

Computing the frequencies. Our first step is to read the strings from standard input and sort them. In this case, we are not so much interested in the fact that the strings are put into sorted order, but in the fact that *sorting brings equal strings together.* If the input is

```
to be or not to be to
```

then the result of the sort is

```
be be not or to to to
```

with equal strings, such as the two occurrences of `be` and the three occurrences of `to`, brought together in the array. Now, with equal strings all together in the array, we can make a single pass through the array to compute all of the frequencies. The `Counter` data type (PROGRAM 3.3.2) is the perfect tool for the job. Recall that a `Counter` has a string instance variable (initialized to the constructor argument), a count instance variable (initialized to 0), and an `increment()` method, which increments the counter by 1. We maintain a Python list `zipf[]` of `Counter` objects and do the following for each string:

- If the string is not equal to the previous one, create a new `Counter` and append it to the end of `zipf[]`.
- Increment the most recently created `Counter`.

At the end of this process, `zipf[i]` contains the `i`th string and its frequency.

i	M	a[i]	zipf[i].value() 0	1	2	3
	0					
0	1	be	1			
1	1	be	2			
2	2	not	2	1		
3	3	or	2	1	1	
4	4	to	2	1	1	1
5	4	to	2	1	1	2
6	4	to	2	1	1	3
			2	1	1	3

Computing the frequencies

Program 4.2.7 Frequency counts (frequencycount.py)

```
import sys
import stdio
from counter import Counter

words = stdio.readAllStrings()
words.sort()    # or merge.sort(words)
zipf = []
for i in range(len(words)):
    if (i == 0) or (words[i] != words[i-1]):
        entry = Counter(words[i], len(words))
        zipf += [entry]
    zipf[len(zipf) - 1].increment()
zipf.sort()     # or merge.sort(zipf)
zipf.reverse()
for entry in zipf:
    stdio.writeln(entry)
```

words	*strings in input*
zipf[]	*counter array*

This program sorts the words on standard input, uses the sorted array to count the frequency of occurrence of each, and then sorts the frequencies. The test file used below has over 20 million words. The plot compares the i*th frequency relative to the first (bars) with* 1/i *(blue). This program assumes that the* Counter *data type is comparable (see* Program 3.3.2 *and page 476).*

```
% python frequencycount.py < leipzig.txt
1160105 the
593492 of
560945 to
472819 a
435866 and
430484 in
205531 for
192296 The
188971 that
172225 is
148915 said
147024 on
...
```

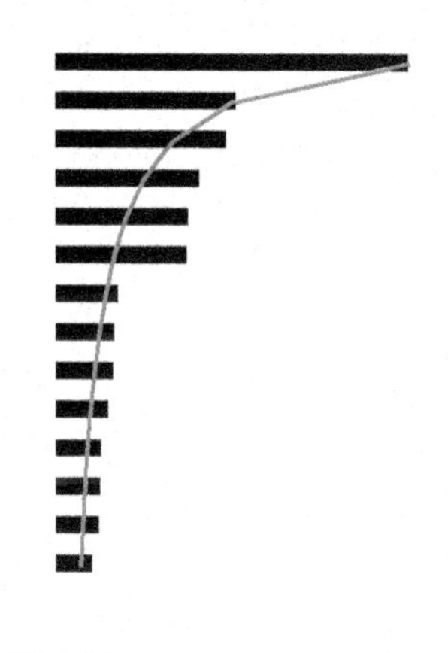

Sorting the frequencies. Next, we sort the `Counter` objects by frequency. We can do so in client code by augmenting the `Counter` data type to include the six comparison methods for comparing `Counter` objects by their counts, as on page 476. Thus, we simply sort the array of `Counter` objects to rearrange them in ascending order of frequency! Next, we reverse the array so that the elements are in descending order of frequency. Finally, we write each `Counter` object to standard output. As usual, Python automatically calls the built-in `str()` function to do so, which, for `Counter` objects, writes the count followed by the string.

	i	zipf[i]	
before			
	0	2	be
	1	1	not
	2	1	or
	3	3	to
after			
	0	1	not
	1	1	or
	2	2	be
	3	3	to

Sorting the frequencies

Zipf's law. The application highlighted in `frequencycount.py` is elementary linguistic analysis: which words appear most frequently in a text? A phenomenon known as *Zipf's law* says that the frequency of the ith most frequent word in a text of m distinct words is proportional to $1/i$ (with its constant of proportionality being the mth harmonic number). For example, the second most common word should appear about half as often as the first. This is an empirical hypothesis that holds in a surprising variety of situations, ranging from financial data to web usage statistics. The test client run in PROGRAM 4.2.7 validates Zipf's law for a database containing 1 million sentences drawn from the web (see the booksite).

YOU ARE LIKELY TO FIND YOURSELF composing a program sometime in the future for a simple task that could easily be solved by first using a sort. With a linearithmic sorting algorithm such as mergesort, you can address such problems even for huge data sets. PROGRAM 4.2.7 (`frequencycount.py`), which uses two different sorts, is a prime example. Without a good algorithm (and an understanding of its performance characteristics), you might find yourself frustrated by the idea that your fast and expensive computer cannot solve a problem that seems to be a simple one. With an ever-increasing set of problems that you know how to solve efficiently, you will find that your computer can be a much more effective tool than you now imagine.

Lessons The vast majority of programs that we compose involve managing the complexity of addressing a new practical problem by developing a clear and correct solution, breaking the program into modules of manageable size, and making use of the basic available resources. From the very start, our approach in this book has been to develop programs along these lines. But as you become involved in ever more complex applications, you will find that a clear and correct solution is not always sufficient, because the cost of computation can be a limiting factor. The examples in this section are a basic illustration of this fact.

Respect the cost of computation. If you can quickly solve a small problem with a simple algorithm, fine. But if you need to address a problem that involves a large amount of data or a substantial amount of computation, you need to take into account the cost. For insertion sort, we did a quick analysis to determine that the brute-force method is infeasible for large arrays.

Divide-and-conquer algorithms. It is worthwhile for you to reflect a bit on the power of the divide-and-conquer paradigm, as illustrated by developing a logarithmic search algorithm (binary search) and a linearithmic sorting algorithm (mergesort). The same basic approach is effective for many important problems, as you will learn if you take a course on algorithm design. For the moment, you are particularly encouraged to study the exercises at the end of this section, which describe problems for which divide-and-conquer algorithms provide feasible solutions and which could not be addressed without such algorithms.

Reduction to sorting. We say that problem A *reduces to* problem B if we can use a solution to B to solve A. Designing a new divide-and-conquer algorithm from scratch is sometimes akin to solving a puzzle that requires some experience and ingenuity, so you may not feel confident that you can do so at first. But it is often the case that a simpler approach is effective: given a new problem that lends itself to a quadratic brute-force solution, ask yourself how you would solve it if the data were sorted. Often, a relatively simple linear pass through the sorted data will do the job. Thus, we get a linearithmic algorithm, with the ingenuity hidden in the mergesort implementation. For example, consider the problem of determining whether every element in an array has a distinct value. This problem reduces to sorting because we can sort the array, and then pass through the sorted array to check whether the value of any element is equal to the next—if not, they are all distinct.

Know your underlying tools. Our ability to count word frequencies for huge texts using `frequencycount.py` (Program 4.2.7) depends on the performance characteristics of the particular operations that we use on arrays and lists. First, its efficiency depends on the fact that mergesort can sort an array in linearithmic time. Second, the efficiency of creating `zipf[]` depends on the fact that building a list in Python by repeatedly appending items one at time takes time and space linear in the length of the resulting list. This is made possible by the resizing array data structure that Python uses (which we examined in Section 4.1). As an applications programmer you must be vigilant, because not all programming languages support such an efficient implementation of appending an item to a list (and performance characteristics are rarely stated in APIs).

Since the advent of computing, people have been developing algorithms such as binary search and mergesort that can efficiently solve practical problems. The field of study known as *design and analysis of algorithms* encompasses the study of design paradigms like divide-and-conquer, techniques to develop hypotheses about algorithms' performance, and algorithms for solving fundamental problems like sorting and searching that can be put to use for practical applications of all kinds. Implementations of many of these algorithms are found in Python libraries or other specialized libraries, but understanding these basic tools of computation is like understanding the basic tools of mathematics or science. You can use a matrix-processing package to find the eigenvalues of a matrix, but you still need a course in linear algebra to apply the concepts and interpret the results. Now that you *know* that a fast algorithm can make the difference between spinning your wheels and properly addressing a practical problem, you can be on the lookout for situations where efficient algorithms like binary search and mergesort can do the job or opportunities where algorithm design and analysis can make the difference.

Q&A

Q. Why do we need to go to such lengths to prove a program correct?

A. To spare ourselves considerable pain. Binary search is a notable example. For example, you now understand binary search; a classic programming exercise is to compose a version that uses a `while` loop instead of recursion. Try solving EXERCISES 4.2.1–3 without looking back at the code in the book. In a famous experiment, Jon Bentley once asked several professional programmers to do so, and most of their solutions were *not* correct.

Q. Why introduce the mergesort algorithm when Python provides an efficient `sort()` method defined in the `list` data type?

A. As with many topics we have studied, you will be able to use such tools more effectively if you understand the background behind them.

Q. What is the running time of the following version of insertion sort on an array that is already sorted?

```
def sort(a):
    n = len(a)
    for i in range(1, n):
        for j in range(i, 0, -1):
            if a[j] < a[j-1]: exchange(a, j, j-1)
            else:             break
```

A. *Quadratic* time in Python 2; *linear* time in Python 3. The reason is that, in Python 2, `range()` is a function that returns an array of integers of length equal to the length of the range (which can be wasteful if the loop terminates early because of a `break` or `return` statement). In Python 3, `range()` returns an iterator, which generates only as many integers as needed.

Q. What happens if I try to sort an array of elements that are not all of the same type?

A. If the elements are of compatible types (such as `int` and `float`), everything works fine. For example, mixed numeric types are compared according to their numeric value, so `0` and `0.0` are treated as equal. If the elements are of incompatible types (such as `str` and `int`), then Python 3 raises a `TypeError` at run time. Python 2 supports some mixed-type comparisons, using the name of the class to determine which object is smaller. For example, Python 2 treats all integers as less than all strings because `'int'` is lexicographically less than `'str'`.

Q. Which order is used when comparing strings with operators such as == and < ?

A. Informally, Python uses *lexicographic order* to compare two strings, as words in a book index or dictionary. For example `'hello'` and `'hello'` are equal, `'hello'` and `'goodbye'` are unequal, and `'goodbye'` is less than `'hello'`. More formally, Python first compares the first character of each string. If those characters differ, then the strings as a whole compare as those two characters compare. Otherwise, Python compares the second character of each string. If those characters differ, then the strings as a whole compare as those two characters compare. Continuing in this manner, if Python reaches the ends of the two strings simultaneously, then it considers them to be equal. Otherwise, it considers the shorter string to be the smaller one. Python uses Unicode for character-by-character comparisons. We list a few of the most important properties:

- `'0'` is less than `'1'`, and so forth.
- `'A'` is less than `'B'`, and so forth.
- `'a'` is less than `'b'`, and so forth.
- Decimal digits (`'0'` to `'9'`) are less than the uppercase letters (`'A'` to `'Z'`).
- Uppercase letters (`'A'` to `'Z'`) are less than lowercase letters (`'a'` to `'z'`).

Exercises

4.2.1 Develop an implementation of `questions.py` (Program 4.2.1) that takes the maximum number `n` as a command-line argument (it need not be a power of 2). Prove that your implementation is correct.

4.2.2 Compose a nonrecursive version of binary search (Program 4.2.3).

4.2.3 Modify `binarysearch.py` so that if the search key is in the array, it returns the smallest index `i` for which `a[i]` is equal to `key`, and otherwise it returns the largest index `i` for which `a[i]` is smaller than `key` (or -1 if no such index exists).

4.2.4 Describe what happens if you apply binary search to an unordered array. Why shouldn't you check whether the array is sorted before each call to binary search? Could you check that the elements binary search examines are in ascending order?

4.2.5 Describe why it is desirable to use immutable keys with binary search.

4.2.6 Let $f()$ be a monotonically increasing function with $f(a) < 0$ and $f(b) > 0$. Compose a program that computes a value x such that $f(x) = 0$ (up to a given error tolerance).

4.2.7 Add code to `insertion.py` to produce the trace given in the text.

4.2.8 Add code to `merge.py` to produce the trace given in the text.

4.2.9 Give traces of insertion sort and mergesort in the style of the traces in the text, for the input `it was the best of times it was`.

4.2.10 Compose a program `dedup.py` that reads strings from standard input and writes them to standard output with all duplicates removed (and in sorted order).

4.2.11 Compose a version of mergesort (Program 4.2.6) that creates an auxiliary array in each recursive call to `_merge()` instead of creating only one auxiliary array in `sort()` and passing it as an argument. What impact does this change have on performance?

4.2.12 Compose a nonrecursive version of mergesort (Program 4.2.6).

4.2.13 Find the frequency distribution of words in your favorite book. Does it obey Zipf's law?

4.2.14 Analyze mergesort mathematically when n is a power of 2, as we did for binary search.

Solution: Let $M(n)$ be the frequency of execution of the instructions in the inner loop. Then $M(n)$ must satisfy the following recurrence relation:

$$M(n) = 2M(n/2) + n$$

with $M(1) = 0$. Substituting 2^k for n gives

$$M(2^k) = 2M(2^{k-1}) + 2^k$$

which is similar to but more complicated than the recurrence that we considered for binary search. But if we divide both sides by 2^k, we get

$$M(2^k)/ 2^k = M(2^{k-1})/ 2^{k-1} + 1$$

which is *precisely* the recurrence that we had for binary search. That, is $M(2^k)/ 2^k = T(2^k) = k$. Substituting back n for 2^k (and $\lg n$ for k) gives the result $M(n) = n \lg n$.

4.2.15 Analyze mergesort for the case when n is not a power of 2.

Partial solution: When n is an odd number, one subarray has to have one more element than the other, so when n is not a power of 2, the subarrays on each level are not necessarily all the same size. Still, every element appears in some subarray, and the number of levels is still logarithmic, so the linearithmic hypothesis is justified for all n.

Creative Exercises

The following exercises are intended to give you experience in developing fast solutions to typical problems. Think about using binary search or mergesort, or devising your own divide-and-conquer algorithm. Implement and test your algorithm.

4.2.16 *Median.* Implement the function `median()` in `stdstats.py` so that it computes the median in linearithmic time. *Hint*: Reduce to sorting.

4.2.17 *Mode.* Add to `stdstats.py` a function `mode()` that computes in linearithmic time the mode (the value that occurs most frequently) of a sequence of n integers. *Hint*: Reduce to sorting.

4.2.18 *Integer sort.* Compose a *linear*-time filter that reads from standard input a sequence of integers that are between 0 and 99 and writes the integers in sorted order to standard output. For example, presented with the input sequence

```
98 2 3 1 0 0 0 3 98 98 2 2 2 0 0 0 2
```

your program should write the output sequence

```
0 0 0 0 0 0 1 2 2 2 2 2 3 3 98 98 98
```

4.2.19 *Floor and ceiling.* Given a sorted array of n comparable keys, compose functions `floor()` and `ceiling()` that return the index of the largest (or smallest) key not larger (or smaller) than an argument key in logarithmic time.

4.2.20 *Bitonic maximum.* An array is bitonic if it consists of an increasing sequence of keys followed immediately by a decreasing sequence of keys. Given a bitonic array, design a logarithmic algorithm to find the index of a maximum key.

4.2.21 *Search in a bitonic array.* Given a bitonic array of n distinct integers, design a logarithmic-time algorithm to determine whether a given integer is in the array.

4.2.22 *Closest pair.* Given an array of n floats, compose a function to find in linearithmic time the pair of integers that are closest in value.

4.2.23 *Furthest pair.* Given an array of n floats, compose a function to find in linear time the pair of integers that are furthest apart in value.

4.2.24 *Two sum.* Compose a function that takes as an argument an array of n integers and determines in linearithmic time whether any *two* of them sum to 0.

4.2.25 *Three sum.* Compose a function that takes as an argument an array of n integers and determines whether any *three* of them sum to 0. Your program should run in time proportional to $n^2 \log n$. *Extra credit*: Develop a program that solves the problem in quadratic time.

4.2.26 *Majority.* Given an array of n elements, an element is a *majority* if it appears more than $n/2$ times. Compose a function that takes an array of n strings as an argument and identifies a majority (if it exists) in linear time.

4.2.27 *Common element.* Compose a function that takes as an argument three arrays of strings, determines whether there is any string common to all three arrays, and if so, returns one such string. The running time of your method should be linearithmic in the total number of strings.

4.2.28 *Largest empty interval.* Given n timestamps for when a file is requested from web server, find the largest interval of time in which no file is requested. Compose a program to solve this problem in linearithmic time.

4.2.29 *Prefix-free codes.* In data compression, a set of strings is *prefix-free* if no string is a prefix of another. For example, the set of strings `01`, `10`, `0010`, and `1111` is prefix-free, but the set of strings `01`, `10`, `0010`, `1010` is not prefix-free because `10` is a prefix of `1010`. Compose a program that reads in a set of strings from standard input and determines whether the set is prefix-free.

4.2.30 *Partitioning.* Compose a function that sorts an array that is known to have at most two different values. *Hint*: Maintain two pointers, one starting at the left end and moving right, and the other starting at the right end and moving left. Maintain the invariant that all elements to the left of the left pointer are equal to the smaller of the two values and all elements to the right of the right pointer are equal to the larger of the two values.

4.2.31 *Dutch national flag.* Compose a function that sorts an array that is known to have at most three different values. (Edsgar Dijkstra named this the *Dutch-*

national-flag problem because the result is three "stripes" of values like the three stripes in the flag.)

4.2.32 *Quicksort.* Compose a recursive program that sorts an array of randomly ordered distinct values. *Hint*: Use a method like the one described in EXERCISE 4.2.31. First, partition the array into a left part with all elements less than v, followed by v, followed by a right part with all elements greater than v. Then, recursively sort the two parts. *Extra credit*: Modify your method (if necessary) to work properly when the values are not necessarily distinct.

4.2.33 *Reverse domain.* Compose a program to read in a list of domain names from standard input and write the reverse domain names in sorted order. For example, the reverse domain of `cs.princeton.edu` is `edu.princeton.cs`. This computation is useful for web log analysis. To do so, create a data type `Domain` that implements the special comparison methods, using reverse domain name order.

4.2.34 *Local minimum in an array.* Given an array of n floats, compose a function to find in logarithmic time a *local minimum* (an index `i` such that `a[i]` < `a[i-1]` and `a[i] < a[i+1]`).

4.2.35 *Discrete distribution.* Design a fast algorithm to repeatedly generate numbers from the discrete distribution. Given an array `p[]` of nonnegative floats that sum to 1, the goal is to return index `i` with probability `p[i]`. Form an array `s[]` of cumulated sums such that `s[i]` is the sum of the first `i` elements of `p[]`. Now, generate a random float `s` between 0 and 1, and use binary search to return the index `i` for which `s[i] <= r < s[i+1]`.

4.2.36 *Rhyming words.* Tabulate a list that you can use to find words that rhyme. Use the following approach:

- Read in a dictionary of words into an array of strings.
- Reverse the letters in each word (`confound` becomes `dnuofnoc`, for example).
- Sort the resulting array.
- Reverse the letters in each word back to their original order.

For example, `confound` is adjacent to words such as `astound` and `surround` in the resulting list.

4.3 Stacks and Queues

IN THIS SECTION, WE introduce two closely related data types for manipulating arbitrarily large collections of items: the *stack* and the *queue*. Stacks and queues are special cases of the idea of a *collection*. A collection of items is characterized by five operations: *create* the collection, *insert* an item, *remove* an item, and test whether the collection *is empty*, and determine its *size* or number of items.

Programs in this section

When we insert an item, our intent is clear. But when we remove an item, which one do we choose? You have encountered different ways to answer this question in various real-world situations, perhaps without thinking about it.

Each kind of collection is characterized by the rule used for *remove*. Moreover, depending on the removal rule each kind of collection is amenable to various implementations with differing performance characteristics. For example, the rule used for a *queue* is to always remove the item that has been in the collection the *most* amount of time. This policy is known as *first-in first-out*, or *FIFO*. People waiting in line to buy a ticket follow this discipline: the line is arranged in the order of arrival, so the person who leaves the line is the one who has been there longer than any other person in the line.

A policy with quite different behavior is the rule used for a *stack*: always remove the item that has been in the collection the *least* amount of time. This policy is known as *last-in first-out*, or *LIFO*. For example, you follow a policy closer to LIFO when you enter and leave the coach cabin in an airplane: people near the front of the cabin board last and exit before those who boarded earlier.

Stacks and queues are broadly useful, so it is important for you to be familiar with their basic properties and the kind of situation where each might be appropriate. They are excellent examples of fundamental data types that we can use to address higher-level programming tasks. They are widely used in systems and applications programming, as we will see in several examples in this section. The implementations and data structures that we consider also serve as models for other removal rules, some of which we examine in the exercises at the end of this section.

Pushdown stacks A *pushdown stack* (or just a *stack*) is a collection that is based on the *last-in-first-out* (*LIFO*) policy.

When you keep your mail in a pile on your desk, you are using a stack. You pile pieces of new mail on the top when they arrive and take each piece of mail from the top when you are ready to read it. People do not process as much paper mail as they did in the past, but the same organizing principle underlies several of the applications that you use regularly on your computer. For example, many people organize their email as a stack, where messages go on the top when they are received and are taken from the top, with most recently received first (last in, first out). The advantage of this strategy is that we see interesting email as soon as possible; the disadvantage is that some old email might never get read if we never empty the stack.

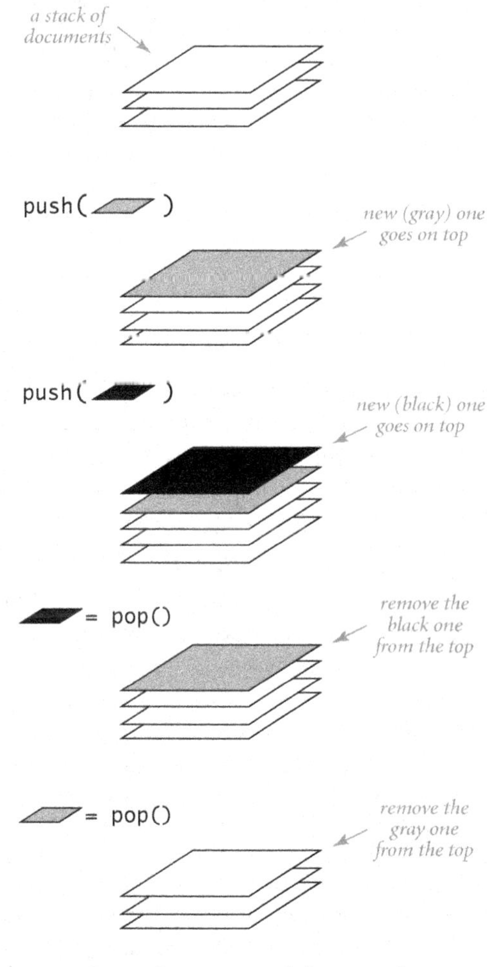

Operations on a pushdown stack

You have likely encountered another common example of a stack when surfing the web. When you click a link, your browser displays the new page (and inserts it onto a stack). You can keep clicking on links to visit new pages, but you can always revisit the previous page by clicking the back button (remove it from a stack). The last-in-first-out policy offered by a stack provides just the behavior that you expect.

Such uses of stacks are intuitive, but perhaps not persuasive. In fact, the importance of stacks in computing is fundamental and profound, but we defer further discussions of applications to later in this section. For the moment, our goal is to make sure that you understand how stacks work and how to implement them.

Programmers have been using stacks since the earliest days of computing. By tradition, we name the stack insert operation *push* and the stack remove operation *pop*, as indicated in the API at the top of the next page:

constant-time operation	*description*
`Stack()`	*a new stack*
`s.isEmpty()`	*is s empty?*
`len(s)`	*number of items in s*
`s.push(item)`	*push* `item` *onto s*
`s.pop()`	*remove and return the item most recently added to s*

Note: Space used must be linear in the number of items in the stack.

API for a `Stack` *data type*

The API includes the core `push()` and `pop()` methods, along with a method `isEmpty()` to test whether the stack is empty and the built-in function `len()` to get the number of items on the stack. The `pop()` method raises a run-time error if it is called when the stack is empty. It is the client's responsibility to call `isEmpty()` to avoid doing so. Next we consider two implementations of this API: `arraystack.py` and `linkedstack.py`.

Important note: When we include performance specifications in an API, as we have in `Stack`, we consider them to be *requirements*. An implementation that does not meet them might implement a `SlowStack` or a `SpaceWastingStack`, but not a `Stack`. We want clients to be able to depend on the performance guarantees.

Python list (resizing array) implementation of a stack Representing a stack with a Python list is a natural idea, but before reading further, it is worthwhile for you to think for a moment about how you would do so.

Naturally, you need an instance variable `a[]` to hold the stack items in a Python list. Should you maintain the items in order of their insertion, with the least recently inserted item in `a[0]`, the second in `a[1]`, and so forth? Or should you maintain the items in *reverse* order of their insertion? For efficiency, we store the items in order of their insertion because inserting and deleting from the end of a Python list takes constant amortized time per operation (whereas inserting and deleting from the front takes linear time per operation).

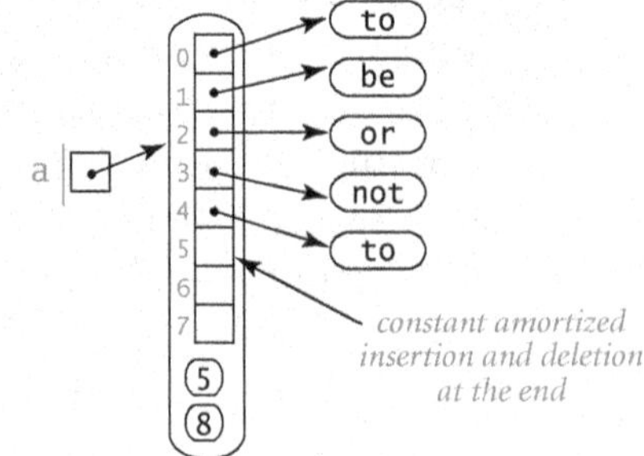

Using a Python list to represent a stack

We could hardly hope for a simpler implementation of the stack API than `stack.py` (Program 4.3.1)—all of the methods are one-liners! The instance variable is a Python list `_a[]` that holds the items in the stack in order of their insertion. To push an item, we append it to the end of the list using the += operator; to pop an item, we call the `pop()` method, which removes and returns the item from the end of the list; to determine the size of the stack, we call the built-in `len()` function. These operations preserve the following properties:

- That stack contains `len(_a)` items.
- The stack is empty when `len(_a)` is 0.
- The list `_a[]` contains the stack items, in order of their insertion.
- The item most recently inserted onto the stack (if nonempty) is `_a[len(_a) - 1]`.

As usual, thinking in terms of invariants of this sort is the easiest way to verify that an implementation operates as intended.

Be sure that you fully understand this implementation. Perhaps the best way to do so is to carefully examine a trace of the list contents for a sequence of `push()` and `pop()` operations. The test client in `stack.py` allows for testing with an arbitrary sequence of operations: it does a `push()` for each string on standard input except the string consisting of a minus sign, for which it does a `pop()`. The diagram at right is a trace for the test input shown.

The primary characteristics of this implementation are that it uses space linear in the number of items in the stack and that *the push and pop operations take constant amortized time.* These properties follow immediately from the corresponding properties for Python lists that we discussed at the end of Section 3.1, which, in turn, depend on Python's resizing array implementation of Python lists. If your programming language provides fixed-size arrays as a built-in data type (but not resizing arrays), you can implement a stack by implementing your own resizing array (see Exercise 4.3.45).

stdin	*stdout*	*n*	*a[]*				
			0	*1*	*2*	*3*	*4*
		0					
to		1	to				
be		2	to	be			
or		3	to	be	or		
not		4	to	be	or	not	
to		5	to	be	or	not	to
-	to	4	to	be	or	not	
be		5	to	be	or	not	be
-	be	4	to	be	or	not	
-	not	3	to	be	or		
that		4	to	be	or	that	
-	that	3	to	be	or		
-	or	2	to	be			
-	be	1	to				
is		2	to	is			

Trace of `arraystack.py` test client

Program 4.3.1 *Stack (resizing array)* (arraystack.py)

```
import sys
import stdio

class Stack:

    def __init__(self):
        self._a = []

    def isEmpty(self):
        return len(self._a) == 0

    def __len__(self):
        return len(self._a)

    def push(self, item):
        self._a += [item]

    def pop(self):
        return self._a.pop()

def main():
    stack = Stack()
    while not stdio.isEmpty():
        item = stdio.readString()
        if item != '-': stack.push(item)
        else:           stdio.write(stack.pop() + ' ')
    stdio.writeln()

if __name__ == '__main__': main()
```

instance variables

`_a[]`	*stack items*

This program defines a Stack *class implemented as a Python list (which, in turn, is implemented using a resizing array). The test client reads strings from standard input, popping and writing to standard output when an input string is a minus sign and pushing otherwise.*

```
% more tobe.txt
to be or not to - be - - that - - - is
% python arraystack.py < tobe.txt
to be not that or be
```

Linked-list implementation of a stack Next, we consider a completely different way to implement a stack, using a fundamental data structure known as a *linked list*. Reuse of the word "list" here is a bit confusing, but we have no choice—linked lists have been around much longer than Python.

A linked list is a recursive data structure defined as follows: *it is either empty (null) or a reference to a node having a reference to a linked list.* The *node* in this definition is an abstract entity that might hold any kind of data, in addition to the node reference that characterizes its role in building linked lists. As with a recursive program, the concept of a recursive data structure can be a bit mind bending at first, but is of great value because of its simplicity.

With object-oriented programming, implementing linked lists is not difficult. We start with a class for the node abstraction:

```
class Node:
    def __init__(self, item, next):
        self.item = item
        self.next = next
```

An object of type `Node` has two instance variables: `item` (a reference to an item) and `next` (a reference to another `Node` object). The `next` instance variable characterizes the linked nature of the data structure. To emphasize that we are just using the `Node` class to structure the data, we define no methods other than the constructor. We also omit leading underscores from the names of the instance variables, thus indicating that it is permissible for code external to the data type (but still within our `Stack` implementation) to access those instance variables.

Now, from the recursive definition, we can represent a linked list with a reference to a `Node` object, which contains a reference to an item and a reference to another `Node` object, which contains a reference to an item and a reference to another `Node` object, and so forth. The final `Node` object in the linked list must indicate that it is, indeed, the final `Node` object. In Python, we accomplish that by assigning `None` to the `next` instance variable of the final `Node` object. Recall that `None` is a Python keyword—a variable assigned the value `None` references no object.

Note that our definition of the `Node` class conforms to our recursive definition of a linked list. With our `Node` class we can represent a linked list as a variable whose value is either (1) `None` or (2) a reference to a `Node` object whose `next` field is a reference to a linked list. We create an object of type `Node` by calling the constructor with two arguments: a reference to an item and a reference to the next `Node` object in the linked list.

For example, to build a linked list that contains the items `'to'`, `'be'`, and `'or'`, we execute this code:

```
third  = Node('or', None)
second = Node('be', third)
first  = Node('to', second)
```

The end result of these operations is actually to create three linked lists:

- `third` is a linked list—it is a reference to a `Node` object that contains `'or'` and `None`, which is the reference to an empty linked list.
- `second` is a linked list—it is a reference to a `Node` object that contains `'be'` and a reference to `third`, which is a linked list.
- `first` is a linked list—it is a reference to a `Node` object that contains `'to'` and a reference to `second`, which is a linked list.

A linked list represents a sequence of items. In this example, `first` represents the sequence `'to', 'be', 'or'`.

We might also use an ordinary array (or Python list) to represent a sequence. For example, we could use the array `['to', 'be', 'or']` to represent the same sequence of strings. One key difference is that linked lists enable efficient insertion of items into (or deletion of items from) either the *front* or *back* of the sequence. Next, we consider code to accomplish these tasks.

When tracing code that uses linked lists and other linked structures, we use a visual representation where:

- We draw a rectangle to represent each object.
- We put the values of instance variables within the rectangle.
- We use arrows that point to the referenced objects to depict references.

This visual representation captures the essential characteristic of linked lists. For economy, we use the term *link* to refer to a `Node` reference. For simplicity, when the item is a string (as in our examples), we put it within the node

save a link to the first node in the linked list

```
Node oldFirst = first
```

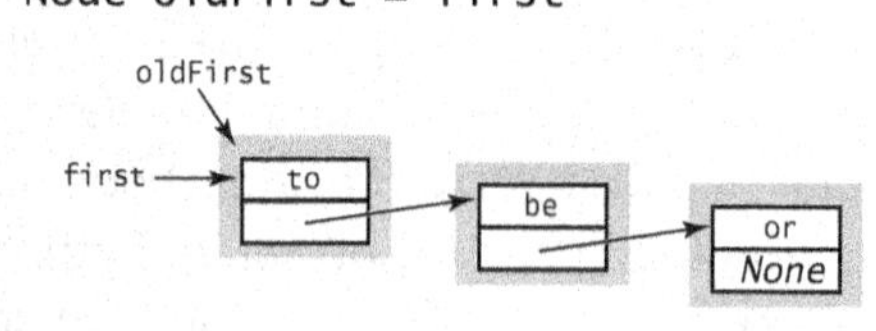

create a new node and set its instance variables

```
first = Node('not', oldFirst)
```

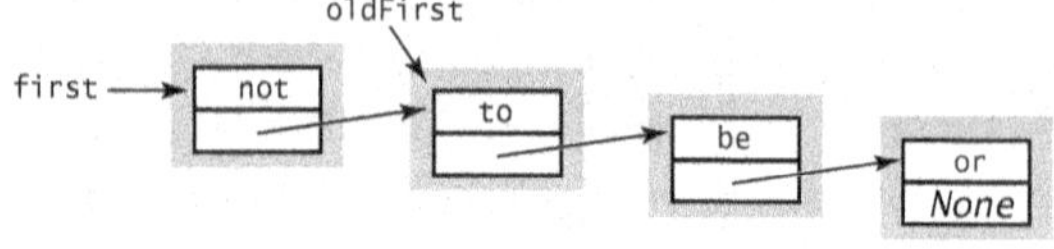

Inserting a new node at the beginning of a linked list

rectangle (rather than using the more accurate rendition in which the node holds a reference to a string object, which is external to the node). This visual representation allows us to focus on the links.

Suppose that you want to *remove* the first node from a linked list. This operation is easy: simply assign to `first` the value `first.next`. Normally, you would retrieve the item (by assigning it to some variable) before doing this assignment, because once you change the variable `first`, you may lose any access to the node to which it was referring previously. Typically, the `Node` object becomes an orphan, and Python's memory management system eventually reclaims it.

```
first = first.next
```

Removing the first node in a linked list

Now, suppose that you want to *insert* a new node into a linked list. The easiest place to do so is at the beginning of the linked list. For example, to insert the string `'not'` at the beginning of a given linked list whose first node is `first`, we save `first` in a variable `oldFirst`; create a new `Node` whose `item` instance variable is `'not'` and whose `next` instance variable is `oldFirst`; and assign `first` to refer to that new `Node`.

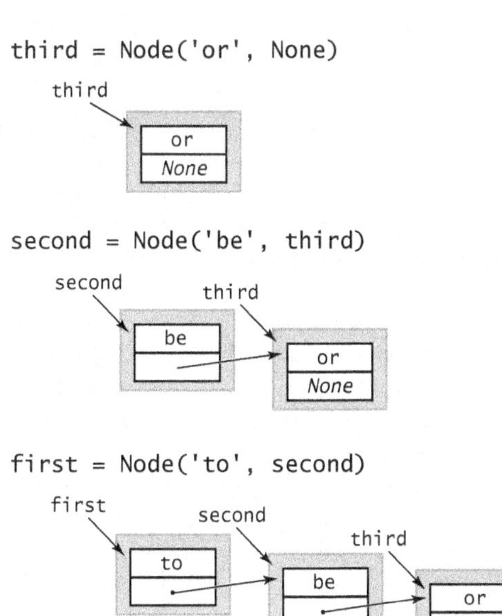

Linking together a linked list

This code for inserting and removing a node from the beginning of a linked list involves just a few assignment statements and thus takes *constant* time (independent of the length of the list). If you hold a reference to a node at an arbitrary position in a list, you can use similar (but more complicated) code to remove the node after it or to insert a node after it, also in constant time, no matter how long the list. We leave those implementations as exercises (see Exercises 4.3.22 and 4.3.24) because inserting and removing at the beginning are the only linked-list operations that we need to implement stacks.

Program 4.3.2 Stack (linked list) (`linkedstack.py`)

```
import stdio

class Stack:
    def __init__(self):
        self._first = None

    def isEmpty(self):
        return self._first is None

    def push(self, item):
        self._first = _Node(item, self._first)

    def pop(self):
        item = self._first.item
        self._first = self._first.next
        return item

class _Node:
    def __init__(self, item, next):
        self.item = item
        self.next = next

def main():
    stack = Stack()
    while not stdio.isEmpty():
        item = stdio.readString()
        if item != '-': stack.push(item)
        else:           stdio.write(stack.pop() + ' ')
    stdio.writeln()

if __name__ == '__main__': main()
```

instance variable for `Stack`

`_first`	*first node on list*

instance variables for Node

`item`	*list item*
`next`	*next node on list*

This program defines a `Stack` *class implemented as a linked list, using a private class _Node as the basis for representing the stack as a linked list of _Node objects. The instance variable* `first` *refers to the most recently inserted _Node in the linked list. The instance variable* `next` *in each _Node refers to the next _Node (the value of* `next` *in the final node is None). The test client is the same as in* `arraystack.py`*. We defer the* `__len__()` *method to* Exercise *4.3.4.*

```
% python linkedstack.py < tobe.txt
to be not that or be
```

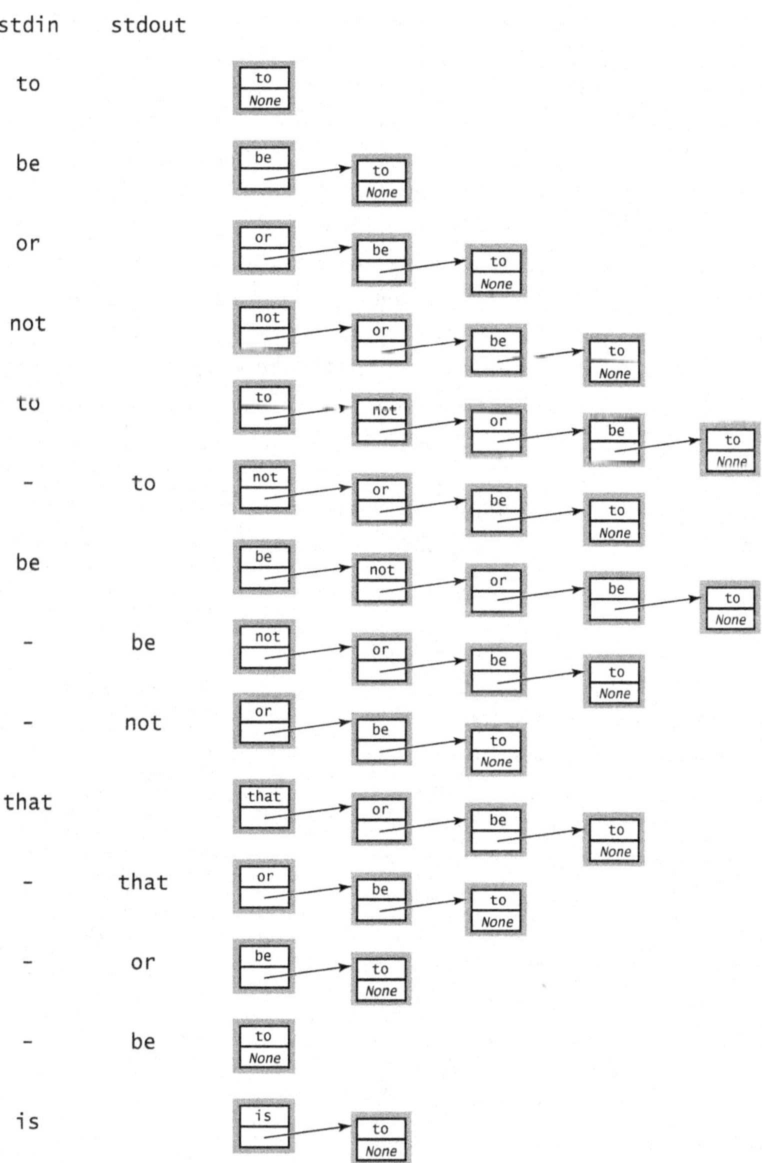

Trace of `linkedstack.py` *test client*

Implementing stacks with linked lists. Program 4.3.2 (`linkedstack.py`) uses a linked list to implement a stack, using little more code than the elementary solution that uses a Python list. The implementation is based on a *private* `_Node` class that is identical to the `Node` class that we have been using. Python allows us to define more than one class in a module and use it in this natural way. We make the class private because *clients* of the `Stack` data type do not need to know any of the details of the linked lists. As usual, we give the class a name that begins with a leading underscore (that is, we name it `_Node` instead of `Node`) to emphasize to `Stack` clients that they should not access the `_Node` class directly.

The `Stack` class defined in `linkedstack.py` itself has just one instance variable: a reference to the linked list that represents the stack, with the item most recently inserted in the first node. That single link suffices to directly access the item at the top of the stack and also provides access to the rest of the items in the stack for `push()` and `pop()`.

Again, *be sure that you understand this implementation*—it is the prototype for several implementations using linked structures that we will examine later in this chapter.

Linked list traversal. While we do not do so in `linkedstack.py`, many linked-list applications need to iterate over the items in a linked list. To do so, we first initialize a loop index variable `x` that references the first `Node` of the linked list. Next, we get the item associated with `x` by accessing `x.item`, and then update `x` to refer to the next `Node` in the linked list, assigning to it the value of `x.next` and repeating this process until `x` is `None` (which indicates that we have reached the end of the linked list). This process is known as *traversing* the list.

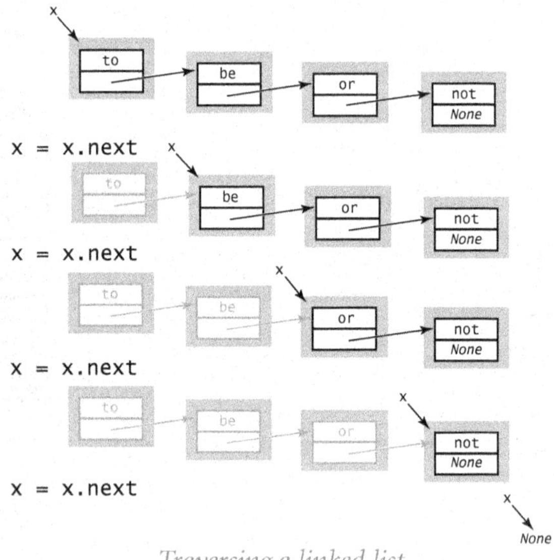

Traversing a linked list

With a linked-list implementation we can implement collections of all sorts without having to worry much about space usage, so linked lists are widely used in programming. Indeed, typical implementations of the Python memory management system are based on maintaining linked lists corresponding to blocks of memory of various sizes. Before the widespread use of high-level languages like Python, the details of memory management and programming with linked lists were critical parts of any programmer's arsenal. In modern systems, most of these details are encapsulated in the implementations of a few data types like the pushdown stack, including the queue, the symbol table, and the set, which we will consider later in this chapter. If you take a course in algorithms and data structures, you will learn several others and gain expertise in creating and debugging programs that manipulate linked lists. Otherwise, you can focus your attention on understanding the role played by linked lists in implementing these fundamental data types.

For stacks, linked lists are significant because they allow us to implement the `push()` and `pop()` methods in constant time in the worst case, while using only a small constant factor of extra space (for the links). If you are uncertain about the value of linked structures, you might think about how you might achieve the same performance specifications for our stack API without using them.

Specifically, `arraystack.py` does not implement performance specifications in the API, because resizing arrays do not provide a constant-time guarantee for every operation. In many practical situations, the distinction between amortized and guaranteed worst-case performance is a minor one, but you might want to think about whether there might be some huge Python list being resized the next time your phone does not respond to a swipe, the next time your plane is readying for takeoff, or the next time you step on the brakes in your car.

Still, Python programmers usually prefer Python lists (resizing arrays), primarily because of the substantial Python overhead for user-defined types like our linked-list `Node`. The same principles apply to collections of any sort. For some data types that are more complicated than stacks, resizing arrays are also preferred over linked lists because the ability to access any item in the array in constant time (through indexing) is critical for implementing certain operations (see, for example, `RandomQueue` in Exercise 4.3.40). For some other data types, linked structures are easier to manipulate, as we will see in Section 4.4.

Stack applications Pushdown stacks play an essential role in computation. If you study operating systems, programming languages, and other advanced topics in computer science, you will learn that not only are stacks used explicitly in many applications, but they also serve as the basis for executing programs composed in high-level languages such as Python.

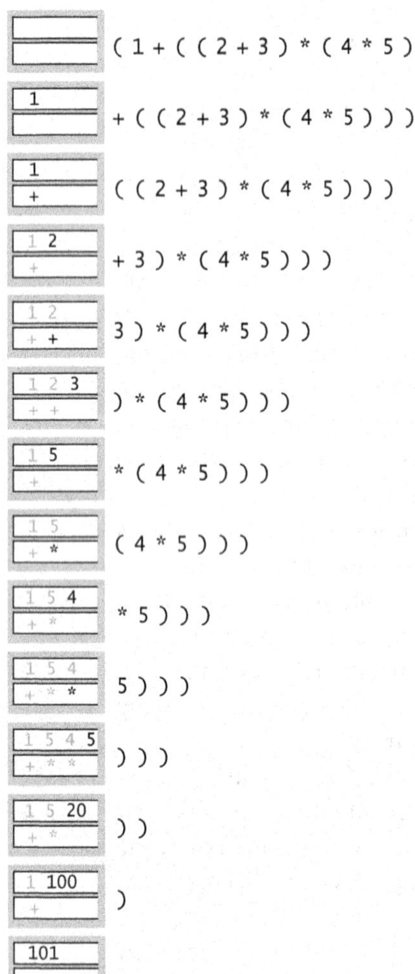

Trace of expression evaluation

Arithmetic expressions. Some of the first programs that we considered in Chapter 1 involved computing the value of arithmetic expressions like this one:

```
( 1 + ( ( 2 + 3 ) * ( 4 * 5 ) ) )
```

If you multiply `4` by `5`, add `3` to `2`, multiply the result, and then add `1`, you get the value `101`. But how does Python do this calculation? Without going into the details of how Python is built, we can address the essential ideas just by composing a Python program that can take a string as input (the expression) and produce the number represented by the expression as output. For simplicity, we begin with the following explicit recursive definition: an *arithmetic expression* is either a number or a left parenthesis followed by an arithmetic expression followed by an operator followed by another arithmetic expression followed by a right parenthesis. For simplicity, this definition applies to *fully parenthesized* arithmetic expressions, which specifies precisely which operators apply to which operands. With a bit more work, we could also handle expressions like `1 + 2 * 3`, which use precedence rules instead of parentheses, but we avoid that complication here. For specificity, we support the familiar binary operators `*`, `+`, and `-`, as well as a square-root operator `sqrt` that takes only one argument. We could easily allow more operators and more kinds of operators to embrace a large class of familiar mathematical expressions, involving trigonometric, exponential, and logarithmic functions and whatever other operators we might wish to include. Our focus here, however, is on understanding how to interpret the string of parentheses, operators, and numbers to enable performing in the proper order the low-level arithmetic operations that are available on any computer.

Arithmetic expression evaluation. Precisely how can we convert an arithmetic expression—a string of characters—to the value that it represents? A remarkably simple algorithm that was developed by Edsgar Dijkstra in the 1960s uses two pushdown stacks (one for operands and one for operators) to do this job. An expression consists of parentheses, operators, and operands (numbers). Proceeding from left to right and taking these entities one at a time, we manipulate the stacks according to four possible cases, as follows:

- Push *operands* onto the operand stack.
- Push *operators* onto the operator stack.
- Ignore *left* parentheses.
- On encountering a *right* parenthesis, pop an operator, pop the requisite number of operands, and push onto the operand stack the result of applying that operator to those operands.

After the final right parenthesis has been processed, there is one value on the stack, which is the value of the expression. This method may seem mysterious at first, but it is easy to convince yourself that it computes the proper value: anytime the algorithm encounters a subexpression consisting of two operands separated by an operator, all surrounded by parentheses, it leaves the result of performing that operation on those operands on the operand stack. The result is the same as if that value had appeared in the input instead of the subexpression, so we can think of replacing the subexpression by the value to get an expression that would yield the same result. We can apply this argument again and again until we get a single value. For example, the algorithm computes the same value of all of these expressions:

```
( 1 + ( ( 2 + 3 ) * ( 4 * 5 ) ) )
( 1 + ( 5 * ( 4 * 5 ) ) )
( 1 + ( 5 * 20 ) )
( 1 + 100 )
101
```

Program 4.3.3 (`evaluate.py`) is an implementation of this algorithm. This code is a simple example of an *interpreter*: a program that interprets the computation specified by a given string and performs the computation to arrive at the result. A *compiler* is a program that converts the string into code on a lower-level machine that can do the job. This conversion is a more complicated process than the step-by-step conversion used by an interpreter, but it is based on the same underlying mechanism. Initially, Python was based on using an interpreter. Now, however, it includes a compiler that converts arithmetic expressions (and, more generally, Python programs) into code for the *Python virtual machine*, an imaginary machine that is easy to simulate on an actual computer.

Stack-based programming languages. Remarkably, Dijkstra's two-stack algorithm also computes the same value as in our example for this expression:

```
( 1 ( ( 2 3 + ) ( 4 5 * ) * ) + )
```

In other words, we can put each operator *after* its two operands instead of *between* them. In such an expression, each right parenthesis immediately follows an operator so we can ignore *both* kinds of parentheses, writing the expressions as follows:

```
1 2 3 + 4 5 * * +
```

This notation is known as *reverse Polish notation*, or *postfix*. To evaluate a postfix expression, we use one stack (see Exercise 4.3.13). Proceeding from left to right, taking these entities one at a time, we manipulate the stacks according to just two possible cases:

- Push operands onto the operand stack.
- On encountering an operator, pop the requisite number of operands and push onto the operand stack the result of applying the operator to those operands.

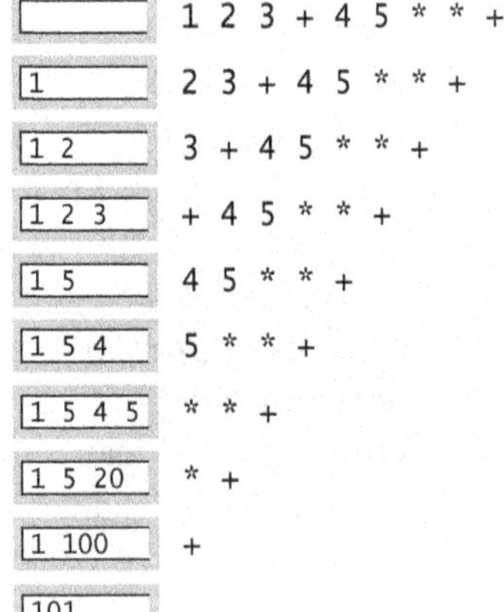

Trace of postfix evaluation

Again, this process leaves one value on the stack, which is the value of the expression. This representation is so simple that some programming languages, such as Forth (a scientific programming language) and PostScript (a page description language that is used on most printers) use explicit stacks. For example, the string `1 2 3 + 4 5 * * +` is a legal program in both Forth and

Program 4.3.3 Expression evaluation (evaluate.py)

```
import stdio
import math
from arraystack import Stack

ops = Stack()
values = Stack()

while not stdio.isEmpty():
    token = stdio.readString()
    if   token == '+':    ops.push(token)
    elif token == '-':    ops.push(token)
    elif token == '*':    ops.push(token)
    elif token == 'sqrt': ops.push(token)
    elif token == ')':
        op = ops.pop()
        value = values.pop()
        if   op == '+':    value = values.pop() + value
        elif op == '-':    value = values.pop() - value
        elif op == '*':    value = values.pop() * value
        elif op == 'sqrt': value = math.sqrt(value)
        values.push(value)
    elif token != '(':
        values.push(float(token))
stdio.writeln(values.pop())
```

`ops`	*operator stack*
`values`	*operand stack*
`token`	*current token*
`value`	*current value*

This Stack client reads a fully parenthesized numeric expression from standard input, uses Dijkstra's two-stack algorithm to evaluate it, and writes the resulting number to standard output. It illustrates an essential computational process: interpreting a string as a program and executing that program to compute the desired result. Executing a Python program is nothing other than a more complicated version of this same process.

```
% python evaluate.py
( 1 + ( ( 2 + 3 ) * ( 4 * 5 ) ) )
101.0
```

```
% python evaluate.py
( ( 1 + sqrt ( 5.0 ) ) * 0.5 )
1.618033988749895
```

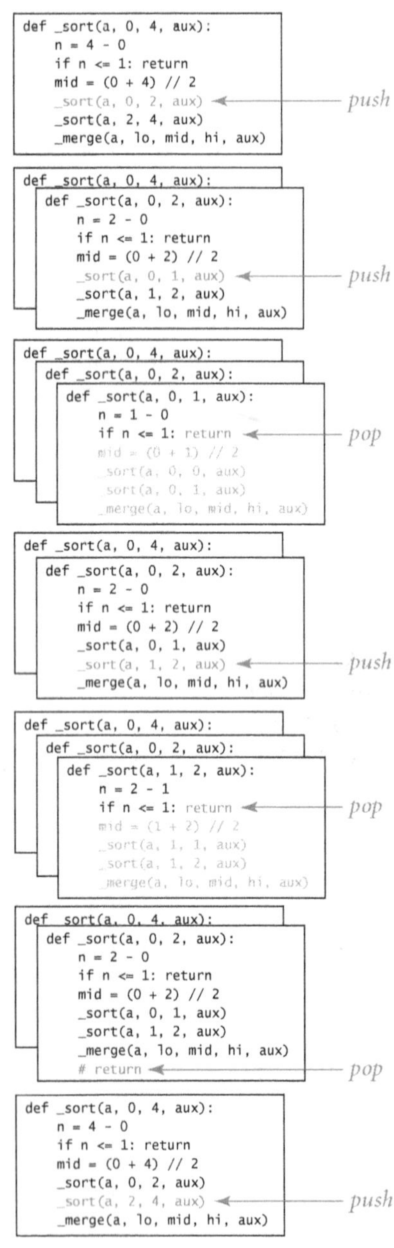

def _sort(a, 0, 4, aux):
n = 4 - 0
if n <= 1: return
mid = (0 + 4) // 2
_sort(a, 0, 2, aux)
_sort(a, 2, 4, aux)
_merge(a, lo, mid, hi, aux)
push
def _sort(a, 0, 2, aux):
n = 2 - 0
mid = (0 + 2) // 2
_sort(a, 0, 1, aux)
_sort(a, 1, 2, aux)
push
def _sort(a, 0, 1, aux):
n = 1 - 0
pop
push
def _sort(a, 1, 2, aux):
n = 2 - 1
pop
return
pop
push

Using a stack to support function calls

PostScript that leaves the value 101 on the execution stack. Aficionados of these and similar stack-based programming languages prefer them because they are simpler for many types of computation. Indeed, the Python virtual machine itself is stack-based.

Function-call abstraction. You may have noticed a pattern in the formal traces that we have shown throughout this book. When the flow of control enters a function, Python creates the function's parameter variables on top of the other variables that might already exist. As the function executes, Python creates the function's local variables—again on top of the other variables that might already exist. When flow of control returns from a function, Python destroys that function's local and parameter variables. In that sense Python creates and destroys parameter and local variables in stack-like fashion: the variables that were created most recently are the first to be destroyed.

Indeed, most programs use stacks implicitly because they support a natural way to implement function calls, as follows: at any point during the execution of a function, define its state to be the values of all of its variables and a pointer to the next instruction to be executed. One of the fundamental characteristics of computing environments is that every computation is fully determined by its state (and the value of its inputs). In particular, the system can suspend a computation by saving away its state, then restart it by restoring the state. If you take a course about operating systems, you will learn the details of this process, because it is critical to much of the behavior of computers that we take for granted (for example, switching from one application to another is simply a matter of saving and restoring state). Now, the natural way to implement the function-call abstraction, which is used by almost all modern programming environments, is to use a stack. To call a function, push the state on a stack. To return from a function call, pop the state from the stack to restore all variables to their values before the function call, substitute the function return value (if there is one) in the expression containing the function call (if there is one), and resume execution at the next instruction to be executed (whose location was saved as part of the state of the computation). This mechanism works whenever functions call one another, even recursively. Indeed, if you think about the process carefully, you will see that it is essentially the same process that we just examined in detail for expression evaluation. A program is a sophisticated expression.

THE PUSHDOWN STACK IS A FUNDAMENTAL computational abstraction. Stacks have been used for expression evaluation, implementing the function-call abstraction, and other basic tasks since the earliest days of computing. We will examine another (tree traversal) in SECTION 4.4. Stacks are used explicitly and extensively in many areas of computer science, including algorithm design, operating systems, compilers, and numerous other computational applications.

FIFO queues A *FIFO queue* (or just a *queue*) is a collection that is based on the first-in first-out (FIFO) policy.

The policy of doing tasks in the same order that they arrive is one that we encounter frequently in everyday life, from people waiting in line at a theater, to cars waiting in line at a toll booth, to tasks waiting to be serviced by an application on your computer.

One bedrock principle of any service policy is the perception of fairness. The first idea that comes to mind when most people think about fairness is that whoever has been waiting the longest should be served first. That is precisely the FIFO discipline, so queues play a central role in numerous applications. Queues are a natural model for so many everyday phenomena—their properties were studied in detail even before the advent of computers.

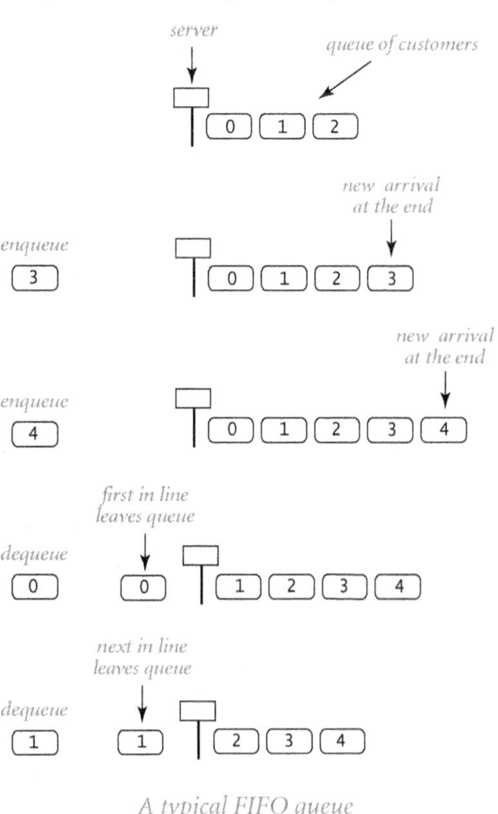

A typical FIFO queue

As usual, we begin by articulating an API. Again by tradition, we name the queue insert operation *enqueue* and the remove operation *dequeue*, as indicated in the API below.

constant-time operation	*description*
`Queue()`	*a new queue*
`q.isEmpty()`	*is q empty?*
`len(q)`	*number of items in q*
`q.enqueue(item)`	*enqueue* `item` *onto q*
`q.dequeue()`	*remove and return the item least recently added to q*

Note: Space used must be linear in the number of items in the queue.

API for a Queue data type

Applying our knowledge from stacks, we can use either Python lists (resizing arrays) or linked lists to develop implementations where the operations take constant time and the memory associated with the queue grows and shrinks with the number of elements in the queue. As with stacks, each of these implementations represents a classic programming exercise. You may wish to think about how you might achieve these goals in an implementation before reading further.

Linked-list implementation. To implement a queue with a linked list, we keep the items in order of their arrival (the reverse of the order that we used in `linkedstack.py`). The implementation of `dequeue()` is the same as the `pop()` implementation in `linkedstack.py` (save the item in the first node, remove the first node from the queue, and return the saved item). Implementing `enqueue()`, however, is a bit more challenging: how do we add a node to the *end* of a linked list? To do so, we need a link to the last node in the list, because that node's link has to be changed to reference a new node containing the item to be inserted. In `Stack`, the only instance variable is a reference to the *first* node in the linked list; with just that information available, our only recourse is to traverse all the nodes in the linked list to get to the end. That solution is unattractive when lists might be lengthy. A reasonable alternative is to maintain a second instance variable that always refer-

Program 4.3.4 FIFO queue (linked list) (`linkedqueue.py`)

```
class Queue:

    def __init__(self):
        self._first = None
        self._last = None
        self._n = 0

    def isEmpty(self):
        return self._first is None

    def enqueue(self, item):
        oldLast = self._last
        self._last = _Node(item, None)
        if self.isEmpty(): self._first = self._last
        else:              oldLast.next = self._last
        self._n += 1

    def dequeue(self):
        item = self._first.item
        self._first = self._first.next
        if self.isEmpty(): self._last = None
        self._n -= 1
        return item

    def __len__(self):
        return self._n

class _Node:
    def __init__(self, item, next):
        self.item = item
        self.next = next
```

instance variables for Queue

`_first`	*first node on list*
`_last`	*last node on list*
`_n`	*number of items*

instance variables for Node

`item`	*list item*
`next`	*next node on list*

This program defines a `Queue` *class implemented as a linked list. The implementation is very similar to our linked-list stack implementation (Program 4.3.2):* `dequeue()` *is almost the same as* `pop()`*, but* `enqueue()` *links the new item onto the end of the list, not the beginning as in* `push()`*. To do so, it maintains an instance variable that references the last node on the list. The test client is similar to the ones we have been using (it reads strings from standard input, dequeuing and writing to standard output when an input string is a minus sign, enqueuing the string otherwise) and is omitted.*

```
% python linkedqueue.py < tobe.txt
to be or not to be
```

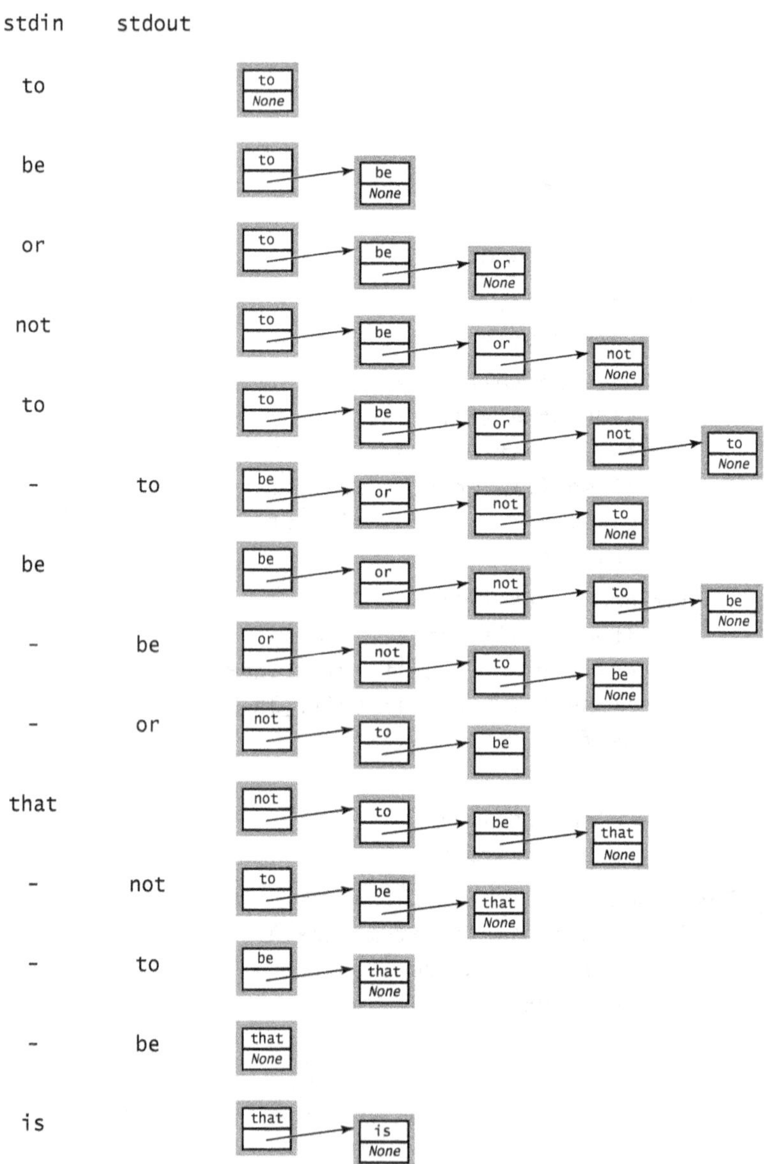

Trace of `linkedqueue.py` *test client*

ences the *last* node in the linked list. Adding an extra instance variable that needs to be maintained is not something that should be taken lightly, particularly in linked-list code, because every method that modifies the linked list needs code to check whether that variable needs to be modified (and to make the necessary modifications). For example, removing the first node in the linked list might involve changing the reference to the last node in the linked list, since when there is only one node in the linked list, it is both the first one and the last one! Similarly, we need an extra check when adding a new node to an empty linked list. Details like these make linked-list code notoriously difficult to debug.

save a link to the last node in the linked list

```
oldLast = last
```

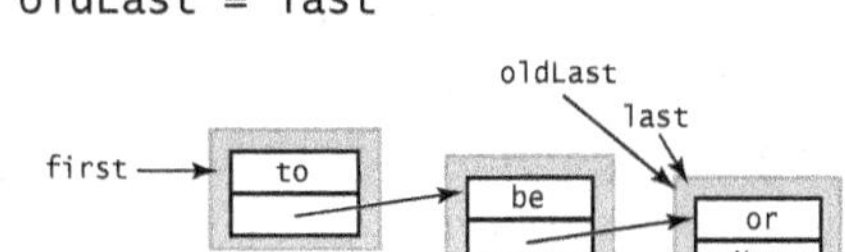

create a new node for the end

```
last = Node('not', None)
```

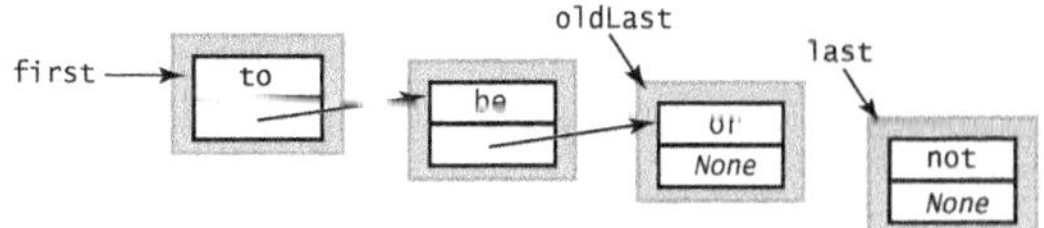

link the new node to the end of the linked list

```
oldLast.next = last
```

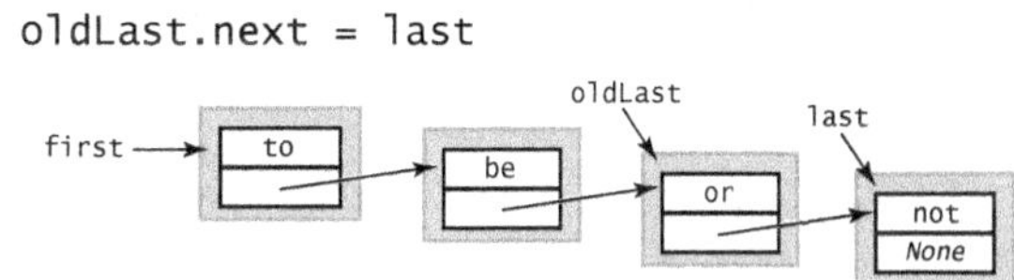

Inserting a new node at the end of a linked list

Program 4.3.4 (`linkedqueue.py`) is a linked-list implementation of `Queue` that has the same performance properties as `Stack`: all of the methods are constant-time operations, and space usage is linear in the number of items on the queue.

Resizing array implementation. It is also possible to develop a FIFO queue implementation that is based on an explicit resizing array representation that has the same performance characteristics as those that we developed for a stack in `arraystack.py` (Program 4.3.1). This implementation is a worthy and classic programming exercise that you are encouraged to pursue further (see Exercise 4.3.46). It might be tempting to use one-line calls on Python list methods, as in Program 4.3.1. However, the methods for inserting or deleting items at the front of a Python list will not fill the bill, as they take linear time (see Exercises 4.3.16 and 4.3.17). For example, if `a` is a list with n items, then operations such as `a.pop(0)` and `a.insert(0, item)` take time proportional to n (and not constant amortized time). Again, an implementation that does not provide the specified performance guarantees might implement a `SlowQueue`, but not a `Queue`.

Random queues. Even though they are widely applicable, there is nothing sacred about the FIFO and LIFO disciplines. It makes perfect sense to consider other rules for removing items. One of the most important to consider is a data type for which `dequeue()` removes a *random* item (sampling without replacement) and `sample()` returns a random item without removing it from the queue (sampling with replacement). Such actions are precisely called for in numerous applications, some of which we have already considered, starting with `sample.py` (PROGRAM 1.4.1). With a Python list (resizing array) representation, implementing `sample()` is straightforward, and we can use the same idea as in PROGRAM 1.4.1 to implement `dequeue()` (exchange a random item with the last item before removing it). We use the name `RandomQueue` to refer to this data type (see EXERCISE 4.3.40). Note that this solution depends on using a resizing-array representation (Python list): it is not possible to access a random item in a linked list in constant time because we have to start from the beginning of the list and traverse links one at a time to access it. With a Python list (resizing array), all of the operations take constant amortized time.

THE STACK, QUEUE, AND RANDOM QUEUE APIs are essentially *identical*—they differ only in the choice of class and method names (which are chosen arbitrarily). Thinking about this situation is a good way to cement your understanding of the basic issues surrounding data types that we introduced in SECTION 3.3. The true differences among these data types are in the semantics of the *remove* operation—which item is to be removed? The differences between stacks and queues are embodied in the English-language descriptions of what they do. These differences are akin to the differences between `math.sin(x)` and `math.log(x)`, but we might want to articulate them with a formal description of stacks and queues (in the same way as we have mathematical descriptions of the sine and logarithm functions). But precisely describing what we mean by first-in-first-out or last-in-first-out or random-out is not so simple. For starters, which language would you use for such a description? English? Python? Mathematical logic? The problem of describing how a program behaves is known as the *specification problem*, and it leads immediately to deep issues in computer science. One reason for our emphasis on clear and concise code is that the code itself can serve as the specification for simple data types such as stacks and queues.

Queue applications In the past century, FIFO queues proved to be accurate and useful models in a broad variety of applications, ranging from manufacturing processes to telephone networks to traffic simulations. A field of mathematics known as *queuing theory* has been used with great success to help understand and control complex systems of all kinds. FIFO queues also play an important role in computing. You often encounter queues when you use your computer: a queue might hold songs on a playlist, documents to be printed, or events in a game.

Perhaps the ultimate queue application is the Internet itself, which is based on huge numbers of messages moving through huge numbers of queues that have all sorts of different properties and are interconnected in all sorts of complicated ways. Understanding and controlling such a complex system involves solid implementations of the queue abstraction, application of mathematical results of queueing theory, and simulation studies involving both. We consider next a classic example to give a flavor of this process.

M/M/1 queue. One of the most important queueing models is known as an *M/M/*1 queue, which has been shown to accurately model many real-world situations, such as a single line of cars entering a toll booth or patients entering an emergency room. The *M* stands for *Markovian* or *memoryless* and indicates that both arrivals and services are *Poisson processes*: both the interarrival times and service times obey an *exponential distribution* (see Exercise 2.2.12) and the 1 indicates that there is one server. An *M/M/*1 queue is parameterized by its *arrival rate* λ (for example, the number of cars per minute arriving at the toll booth) and its *service rate* μ (for example, the number of cars per minute that can pass through the toll booth) and is characterized by three properties:

- There is one server—a FIFO queue.
- Interarrival times to a queue obey an exponential distribution with rate λ per minute.
- Service times from a nonempty queue obey an exponential distribution with rate μ per minute.

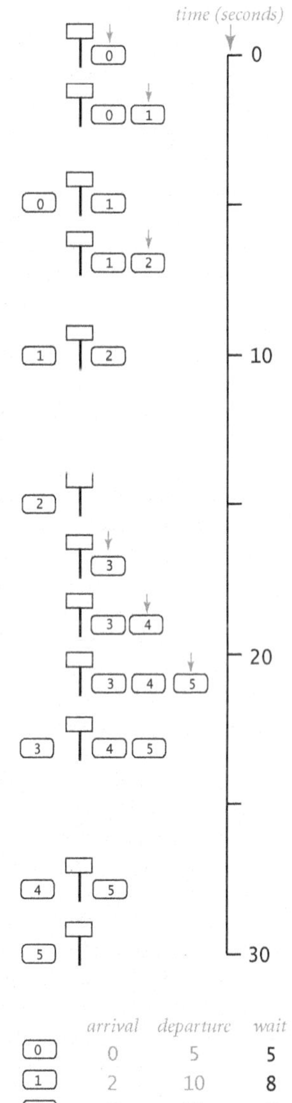

	arrival	departure	wait
0	0	5	5
1	2	10	8
2	7	15	8
3	17	23	6
4	19	28	9
5	21	30	9

An M/M/1 queue

The average time between arrivals is $1/\lambda$ minutes and the average time between services (when the queue is nonempty) is $1/\mu$ minutes. So, the queue will grow without bound unless $\mu > \lambda$; otherwise, customers enter and leave the queue in an interesting dynamic process.

Analysis. In practical applications, people are interested in the effect of the parameters λ and μ on various properties of the queue. If you are a customer, you may want to know the expected amount of time you will spend in the system; if you are designing the system, you might want to know how many customers are likely to be in the system, or something more complicated, such as the likelihood that the queue size will exceed a given maximum size. For simple models, probability theory yields formulas expressing these quantities as functions of λ and μ. For *M*/*M*/1 queues, it is known that:

- The average number of customers in the system L is $\lambda / (\mu - \lambda)$.
- The average time a customer spends in the system W is $1 / (\mu - \lambda)$.

For example, if the cars arrive at a rate of $\lambda = 10$ per minute and the service rate is $\mu = 15$ per minute, then the average number of cars in the system will be 2 and the average time that a customer spends in the system will be 1/5 minutes or 12 seconds. These formulas confirm that the wait time (and queue length) grows without bound as λ approaches μ. They also obey a general rule known as *Little's law*: the average number of customers in the system is λ times the average time a customer spends in the system ($L = \lambda W$) for many types of queues.

Simulation. PROGRAM 4.3.5 (`mm1queue.py`) is a `Queue` client that you can use to validate these sorts of mathematical results. It is a simple example of an *event-based simulation*: we generate *events* that take place at particular times and adjust our data structures accordingly for the events, simulating what happens at the time they occur. In an *M*/*M*/1 queue, there are two kinds of events: we either have a customer *arrival* or a customer *service*. In turn, we maintain two variables:

- `nextService` is the time of the next service.
- `nextArrival` is the time of the next arrival.

To simulate an arrival event, we enqueue a float `nextArrival` (the time of arrival); to simulate a service, we dequeue a float, compute the wait time `wait` (which is the time that the service is completed minus the time that the customer arrived and entered the queue), and add the wait time to a histogram (see PROGRAM 3.2.3).

Program 4.3.5 M/M/1 queue simulation (mm1queue.py)

```
import sys
import stddraw
import stdrandom
from linkedqueue import Queue
from histogram import Histogram

lambd = float(sys.argv[1])
mu    = float(sys.argv[2])

histogram = Histogram(60 + 1)
queue = Queue()
stddraw.setCanvasSize(700, 500)

nextArrival = stdrandom.exp(lambd)
nextService = nextArrival + stdrandom.exp(mu)

while True:

    while nextArrival < nextService:
        queue.enqueue(nextArrival)
        nextArrival += stdrandom.exp(lambd)

    arrival = queue.dequeue()
    wait = nextService - arrival

    stddraw.clear()
    histogram.addDataPoint(min(60, int(round(wait))))
    histogram.draw()
    stddraw.show(20.0)

    if queue.isEmpty():
        nextService = nextArrival + stdrandom.exp(mu)
    else:
        nextService = nextService + stdrandom.exp(mu)
```

`lambd`	*arrival rate* λ
`mu`	*service rate* μ
`histogram`	*histogram*
`queue`	*M/M/1 queue*
`nextArrival`	*time of next arrival*
`nextService`	*time of next service completion*
`arrival`	*arrival time of next customer to be serviced*
`wait`	*time on queue*

This program accepts float command-line arguments `lambd` *and* `mu` *and simulates an M/M/1 queue with arrival rate* `lambd` *and service rate* `mu`*, producing a dynamic* `Histogram` *of the wait times. Time is tracked with two variables* `nextArrival` *and* `nextService` *and a single* `Queue` *of floats. The value of each item on the queue is the (simulated) time it entered the queue. Example plots produced by the program are shown and discussed on the next page.*

The shape that results after a large number of trials is characteristic of the *M/M/*1 queueing system. From a practical point of view, one of the most important characteristics of the process, which you can discover for yourself by running `mm1queue.py` for various values of the parameters λ and μ, is that the average time a customer spends in the system (and the average number of customers in the system) can increase dramatically when the service rate approaches the arrival rate. When the service rate is high, the histogram has a visible tail where the frequency of customers having a given wait time decreases to a negligible duration as the wait time increases. But when the service rate is close to the arrival rate, the tail of the histogram stretches to the point that most values are in the tail, so the frequency of customers having at least the highest wait time displayed dominates.

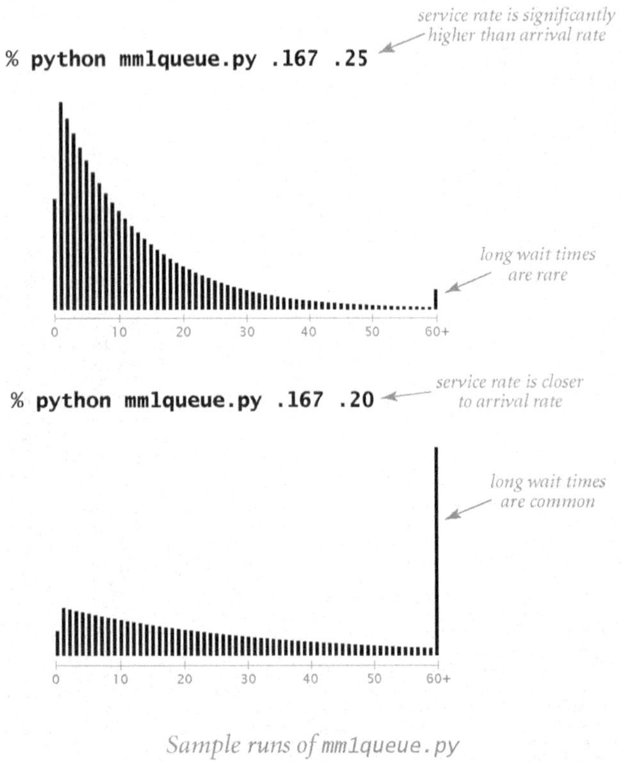

Sample runs of `mm1queue.py`

As in many other applications that we have studied, the use of simulation to validate a well-understood mathematical model is a starting point for studying more complex situations. In practical applications of queues, we may have multiple queues, multiple servers, multistage servers, limits on queue length, and many other restrictions. Moreover, the distributions of interarrival and service times may not be possible to characterize mathematically. In such situations, we may have no recourse but to use simulations. It is quite common for a system designer to build a computational model of a queuing system (such as `mm1queue.py`) and to use it to adjust design parameters (such as the service rate) to properly respond to the outside environment (such as the arrival rate).

Resource allocation Next, we examine another application that illustrates the data structures that we have been considering. A *resource-sharing* system involves a large number of loosely cooperating *servers* that want to share resources. Each server agrees to maintain a queue of items for sharing, and a central authority distributes the items to the servers (and informs users where they may be found). For example, the items might be songs, photos, or videos to be shared by a large number of users. To fix ideas, we will think in terms of millions of items and thousands of servers.

We will consider the kind of program that the central authority might use to distribute the items, ignoring the dynamics of deleting items from the systems, adding and deleting servers, and so forth.

If we use a *round-robin* policy, cycling through the servers to make the assignments, we get a balanced allocation, but it is rarely possible for a distributor to have such complete control over the situation. For example, there might be a large number of independent distributors, so none of them could have up-to-date information about the servers. Accordingly, such systems often use a *random* policy, where the assignments are based on random choice. An even better policy is to choose a random *sample* of servers and assign a new item to the one that has smallest number of items. For small queues, differences among these policies is immaterial, but in a system with millions of items on thousands of servers, the differences can be quite significant, since each server has a fixed amount of resources to devote to this process. Indeed, similar systems are used in Internet hardware, where some queues might be implemented in special-purpose hardware, so queue length translates directly to extra equipment cost. But how big a sample should we take?

Program 4.3.6 (`loadbalance.py`) is a simulation of the sampling policy, which we can use to study this question. This program makes good use of the `RandomQueue` data type that we have been considering to provide an easily understood program that we can use for experimentation. The simulation maintains a random queue of queues and builds the computation around an inner loop where each new request for service goes on the smallest of a sample of queues, using the `sample()` method from `RandomQueue` to randomly sample queues. The surprising end result is that samples of size 2 lead to near-perfect balancing, so there is no point in taking larger samples.

Program 4.3.6 Load-balancing simulation (`loadbalance.py`)

```
import sys
import stddraw
import stdstats
from linkedqueue import Queue
from randomqueue import RandomQueue

m = int(sys.argv[1])
n = int(sys.argv[2])
t = int(sys.argv[3])

servers = RandomQueue()
for i in range(m):
    servers.enqueue(Queue())

for j in range(n):
    best = servers.sample()
    for k in range(1, t):
        queue = servers.sample()
        if len(queue) < len(best):
            best = queue
    best.enqueue(j)

lengths = []
while not servers.isEmpty():
    lengths += [len(servers.dequeue())]

stddraw.setYscale(0, 2.0*n/m)
stdstats.plotBars(lengths)
stddraw.show()
```

`m`	*number of servers*
`n`	*number of items*
`t`	*sample size*
`servers`	*queues*
`best`	*shortest in sample*
`lengths`	*queue lengths*

This `Queue` and `RandomQueue` client simulates the process of assigning `n` items to a set of `m` servers. Requests are put on the shortest of a sample of `t` queues chosen at random.

% python loadbalance.py 50 500 1

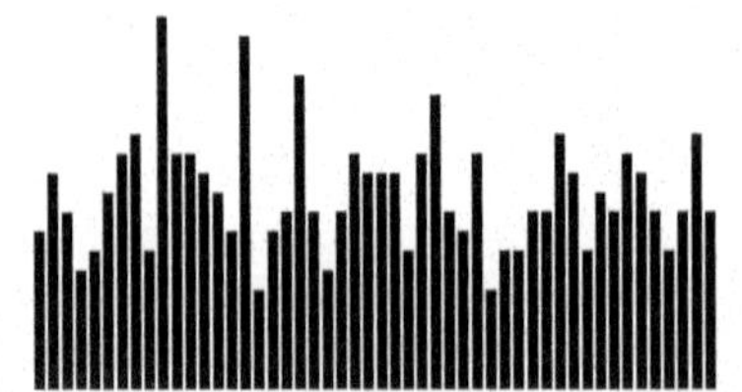

% python loadbalance.py 50 500 2

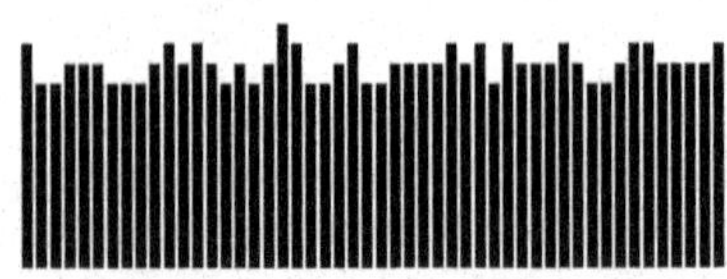

We have considered in detail the issues surrounding the time and memory usage of basic implementations of the stack and queue APIs not just because these data types are important and useful, but also because you are likely to encounter the very same issues in the context of your own data-type implementations.

Should you use a pushdown stack, a FIFO queue, or a random queue when developing a client that maintains collections of data? The answer to this question depends on a high-level analysis of the client to determine which of the LIFO, FIFO, or random disciplines is appropriate.

Should you use a linked list or a resizing array to structure your data? The answer to this question depends on low-level analysis of performance characteristics. A *linked list* has the advantage that you can add items at either end but the disadvantage that you cannot access an arbitrary item in constant time. A *resizing array* has the advantage that you can access any item in constant time but the disadvantage that the constant running time is only for insertions and deletions at one end (and it is constant time only in the amortized sense). Each data structure is appropriate in various different situations; you are likely to encounter both in most programming environments.

The careful attention to performance guarantees that we have emphasized in our `Stack` and `Queue` APIs are not to be taken for granted. They are just the first in a progression of data types that provide the underpinnings of our computational infrastructure. The next section is devoted to an even more important one, the *symbol table*, and you will learn about others when you take a course on data structures and algorithms. By now, you know that learning to use a new data type is not so different from learning to ride a bicycle or implement `helloworld.py`: it seems completely mysterious until you have done it for the first time, but quickly becomes second nature. And learning to design and implement a new data type by developing a new data structure is a challenging, fruitful, and satisfying activity. As you will see in the exercises that follow, stacks, queues, linked lists, and resizing arrays raise a host of fascinating questions, but they are also just the beginning.

Q&A

Q. When should I call the _Node constructor?

A. Just as with any other class, you should call the _Node constructor when you want to create a new _Node object (a new node in the linked list). You should not use it to create a new reference to an existing _Node object. For example, the code

```
oldfirst = _Node(item, next)
oldfirst = first
```

creates a new _Node object, then immediately loses track of the only reference to it. This code does not result in an error, but it is a bit untidy to create orphans for no reason.

Q. Why not define Node as a stand-alone class in a separate file named node.py?

A. By defining _Node in the same file as linkedstack.py or linkedqueue.py and giving it a name that begins with an underscore, we encourage clients of the Stack or Queue classes not to use the _Node class directly. Our intention is that the _Node objects be used only in the linkedstack.py or linkedqueue.py implementations, not in other clients.

Q. Should a client be allowed to insert the item None onto a stack or queue?

A. This question arises frequently when implementing collections in Python. Our implementations do permit the insertion of any object, including None.

Q. Are there standard Python modules for stacks and queues?

A. Not really. As noted earlier in this section, Python's built-in list data type has operations that make it is easy to efficiently implement a stack using a list. But the list data type also needs many additional methods that are not normally associated with a stack, such as indexed access and deleting an arbitrary item. The prime advantage of restricting ourselves to the set of operations that we need (and only those operations) is that it makes it easier to develop an implementation that can provide the best possible performance guarantees for those operations. Python also includes a data type collections.deque that implements a mutable sequence of items with efficient insertion and deletion to either the front or the back.

Q. Why not have a single data type that implements methods to insert an item, remove the most recently inserted item, remove the least recently inserted item, remove a random item, iterate over the items, return the number of items in the collection, and whatever other operations we might desire? Then we could get them all implemented in a single class that could be used by many clients.

A. This is an example of a *wide interface*, which, as we pointed out in SECTION 3.3, should be avoided. As just mentioned, one reason to avoid wide interfaces is that it is difficult to construct implementations that are efficient for all operations. A more important reason is that narrow interfaces enforce a certain discipline on your programs, which makes client code much easier to understand. If one client uses `Stack` and another uses `Queue`, we have a good idea that the LIFO discipline is important to the first and the FIFO discipline is important to the second. Another approach is to use inheritance to try to encapsulate operations that are common to all collections. However, such implementations are best left for experts, whereas any programmer can learn to build implementations such as `Stack` and `Queue`.

Q. Is there any way that I can compose a client that uses both `arraystack.py` and `linkedstack.py` in the same program?

A. Yes, the easiest way is to add an `as` clause to the `import` statement, as below. In effect, this kind of `import` statement creates an alias for the name of the class and your code can then use that alias instead of the name of the class.

```
from arraystack  import Stack as ArrayStack
from linkedstack import Stack as LinkedStack
...
stack1 = ArrayStack()
stack2 = LinkedStack()
```

Exercises

4.3.1 Give the output written by `python arraystack.py` for the following input:

```
it was - the best - of times - - - it was - the - -
```

4.3.2 Give the contents and length of the array for `arraystack.py` after each operation for the following input:

```
it was - the best - of times - - - it was - the - -
```

4.3.3 Suppose that a client performs an intermixed sequence of *push* and *pop* operations on a `Stack`. The push operations put the integers 0 through 9 in order onto the stack; the pop operations write the return value. Which of the following sequence(s) could *not* occur?

a. 4 3 2 1 0 9 8 7 6 5
b. 4 6 8 7 5 3 2 9 0 1
c. 2 5 6 7 4 8 9 3 1 0
d. 4 3 2 1 0 5 6 7 8 9
e. 1 2 3 4 5 6 9 8 7 0
f. 0 4 6 5 3 8 1 7 2 9
g. 1 4 7 9 8 6 5 3 0 2
h. 2 1 4 3 6 5 8 7 9 0

4.3.4 Compose a stack client `reverse.py` that reads in strings from standard input and writes them in reverse order to standard output.

4.3.5 Compose a stack client `parentheses.py` that reads in a text stream from standard input and uses a stack to determine whether its parentheses are properly balanced. For example, your program should write `True` for `[()]{}{[()()]()}` and `False` for `[(])`.

4.3.6 Add the method `__len__()` to the `Stack` class in `linkedstack.py` (Program 4.3.2).

4.3.7 Add a method `peek()` to the `Stack` class in `arraystack.py` that returns the most recently inserted item on the stack (without popping it).

4.3.8 What does the following code fragment write when n is 50? Give a high-level description of what the code fragment does for a given positive integer n.

```
stack = Stack()
while n > 0:
    stack.push(n % 2)
    n /= 2
while not stack.isEmpty():
    stdio.write(stack.pop())
stdio.writeln()
```

Solution: It writes the binary representation of n (110010 when n is 50).

4.3.9 What does the following code fragment do to the queue queue?

```
stack = Stack()
while not queue.isEmpty(): stack.push(queue.dequeue())
while not stack.isEmpty(): queue.enqueue(stack.pop())
```

4.3.10 Draw an object-level trace diagram for the three-node example used to introduce linked lists in this section.

4.3.11 Compose a program that takes from standard input an expression without left parentheses and writes the equivalent infix expression with the parentheses inserted. For example, given the input

```
1 + 2 ) * 3 - 4 ) * 5 - 6 ) ) )
```

your program should write

```
( ( 1 + 2 ) * ( ( 3 - 4 ) * ( 5 - 6 ) )
```

4.3.12 Compose a filter infixtopostfix.py that converts a fully parenthesized arithmetic expression from infix to postfix.

4.3.13 Compose a program evaluatepostfix.py that reads a postfix expression from standard input, evaluates it, and writes the value to standard output. (Piping the output of your program from the previous exercise to this program gives equivalent behavior to evaluate.py.)

4.3.14 Suppose that a client performs an intermixed sequence of *enqueue* and *dequeue* operations on a Queue. The enqueue operations put the integers 0 through 9 in order onto the queue; the dequeue operations write the return value. Which of the following sequence(s) could *not* occur?

a. 0 1 2 3 4 5 6 7 8 9

b. 4 6 8 7 5 3 2 9 0 1

c. 2 5 6 7 4 8 9 3 1 0

d. 4 3 2 1 0 5 6 7 8 9

4.3.15 Compose a Queue client that takes a command-line argument k writes the kth from the last string found on standard input.

4.3.16 Give the running time of each operation in the following Queue class, where the item least recently inserted is at _a[0].

```
class Queue:
    def __init__(self):       self._a = []
    def isEmpty(self):        return len(self._a) == 0
    def __len__(self):        return len(self._a)
    def enqueue(self, item): self._a += [item]
    def dequeue(self):        return self._a.pop(0)
```

4.3.17 Give the running time of each operation in the following Queue class, where the item most recently inserted is at _a[0].

```
class Queue:
    def __init__(self):       self._a = []
    def isEmpty(self):        return len(self._a) == 0
    def __len__(self):        return len(self._a)
    def enqueue(self, item): self._a.insert(0, item)
    def dequeue(self):        return self._a.pop()
```

4.3.18 Modify mm1queue.py to make a program md1queue.py that simulates a queue for which the service times are fixed (deterministic) at rate of μ. Verify Little's law empirically for this model.

Linked-List Exercises

The following exercises are intended to give you experience in working with linked lists. The easiest way to work them is to make drawings using the visual representation described in the text.

4.3.19 Suppose `x` is a linked-list node. What is the effect of the following code fragment?

```
x.next = x.next.next
```

Solution: Deletes from the list the node immediately following `x`.

4.3.20 Compose a function `find()` that takes the first node in a linked list and an object `key` as arguments and returns `True` if some node in the list has `key` as its item field, and `False` otherwise.

4.3.21 Compose a function `delete()` that takes the first node in a linked list and an integer `k` as arguments and deletes the `k`th element in a linked list, if it exists.

4.3.22 Suppose that `x` is a linked-list node. What is the effect of the following code fragment?

```
t.next = x.next
x.next = t
```

Solution: Inserts node `t` immediately after node `x`.

4.3.23 Why does the following code fragment not have the same effect as the code fragment in the previous question?

```
x.next = t
t.next = x.next
```

Solution: When it comes time to update `t.next`, `x.next` is no longer the original node following `x`, but is instead `t` itself!

4.3.24 Compose a function `removeAfter()` that takes a linked-list node as an argument and removes the node following the given one (and does nothing if the argument or the `next` field in the argument node is `None`).

4.3.25 Compose a function copy() that takes a linked-list node as an argument and creates a new linked list with the same sequence of items, without destroying the original linked list.

4.3.26 Compose a function remove() that takes a linked-list node and an object item as arguments and removes every node in the list whose item is item.

4.3.27 Compose a function listmax() that takes the first node in a linked list as an argument and returns the value of the maximum item in the list. Assume that the items are comparable, and return None if the list is empty.

4.3.28 Develop a recursive solution to the previous question.

4.3.29 Compose a function that takes the first node in a linked list as an argument and reverses the list, returning the first node in the result.

Iterative solution: To accomplish this task, we maintain references to three consecutive nodes in the linked list: reverse, first, and second. At each iteration, we extract the node first from the original linked list and insert it at the beginning of the reversed list. We maintain the invariant that first is the first node of what's left of the original list, second is the second node of what's left of the original list, and reverse is the first node of the resulting reversed list.

```
def reverse(first):
    reverse = None
    while first is not None:
        second = first.next
        first.next = reverse
        reverse = first
        first = second
    return reverse
```

When composing code involving linked lists, we must always be careful to properly handle the exceptional cases (when the linked list is empty, when the list has only one or two nodes) and the boundary cases (dealing with the first or last items). This is usually much trickier than handling the normal cases.

4.3.30 Compose a recursive function to write the elements of a linked list in reverse order. Do not modify any of the links. *Easy*: Use quadratic time, constant extra space. *Also easy*: Use linear time, linear extra space. *Not so easy*: Develop a divide-and-conquer algorithm that uses linearithmic time and logarithmic extra space.

Quadratic time, constant space solution: We recursively reverse the part of the list starting at the second node, and then carefully append the first element to the end.

```
def reverse(first):
    if first is None:
        return None
    if first.next is None:
        return first
    second = first.next
    rest = reverse(second)
    second.next = first
    first.next = None
    return rest
```

4.3.31 Compose a recursive function to randomly shuffle the elements of a linked list by modifying the links. *Easy*: Use quadratic time, constant extra space. *Not so easy*: Develop a divide-and-conquer algorithm that takes linearithmic time and uses logarithmic extra memory. For the "merging" step, see Exercise 1.4.38.

Creative Exercises

4.3.32 *Deque.* A double-ended queue or *deque* (pronounced "deck") is a combination of a stack and a queue. Compose a class `Deque` that uses a linked list to implement this API:

constant-time operation	*description*
`Deque()`	*a new deque*
`d.isEmpty()`	*is q empty?*
`d.enqueue(item)`	*enqueue* `item` *(at the end) of* `d`
`d.dequeue()`	*remove and return the item (from the end) of* `d`
`d.push(item)`	*push* `item` *(from the beginning) of* `d`
`d.pop(item)`	*remove and return the item (from the beginning) of* `d`

Note: Space used must be linear in the number of items in the deque.

API for a double-ended queue

4.3.33 *Josephus problem.* In the Josephus problem from antiquity, n people are in dire straits and agree to the following strategy to reduce the population. They arrange themselves in a circle (at positions numbered from 0 to n) and proceed around the circle, eliminating every m person until only one person is left. Legend has it that Josephus figured out where to sit to avoid being eliminated. Compose a `Queue` client `josephus.py` that takes n and m from the command line and writes the order in which people are eliminated (and thus would show Josephus where to sit in the circle).

```
% python josephus.py 7 2
1 3 5 0 4 2 6
```

4.3.34 *Merging two sorted queues.* Given two queues with strings in ascending order, move all of the strings to a third queue so that the third queue ends up with the strings in ascending order.

4.3.35 *Nonrecursive mergesort.* Given n strings, create n queues, each containing one of the strings. Create a queue of the n queues. Then, repeatedly apply the sorted merging operation to the first two queues and reinsert the merged queue at the end. Repeat until the queue of queues contains only one queue.

4.3.36 *Delete ith element.* Implement a class that supports the following API:

operation	*description*
`GeneralizedQueue()`	*a new queue*
`q.isEmpty()`	*is q empty?*
`q.insert(item)`	*add an* `item` *to q*
`q.delete(i)`	*remove and return the item that was the* `i`*th least recently inserted on q*

Note: Space used must be linear in the number of items in the queue.

API for a generalized queue

First, develop an implementation that uses a Python list (resizing array) implementation, and then develop one that uses a linked-list implementation. (See EXERCISE 4.4.69 for a more efficient implementation that uses a binary search tree.)

4.3.37 *Queue with two stacks.* Show how to implement a queue using two stacks (and only a constant amount of extra memory) so that each queue operations uses a constant amortized number of stack operations.

4.3.38 *Ring buffer.* A ring buffer, or circular queue, is a FIFO data structure of a fixed capacity n. It is useful for transferring data between asynchronous processes or for storing log files. When the buffer is empty, the consumer waits until data is deposited; when the buffer is full, the producer waits to deposit data. Develop an API for a ring buffer and an implementation that uses an array representation (with circular wrap-around).

4.3.39 *Move-to-front.* Read in a sequence of characters from standard input and maintain the characters in a linked list with no duplicates. When you read in a previously unseen character, insert it at the front of the list. When you read in a duplicate character, delete it from the list and reinsert it at the beginning. Name your program MoveToFront: it implements the well known *move-to-front* strategy, which is useful for caching, data compression, and many other applications where items that have been recently accessed are more likely to be reaccessed.

4.3.40 *Random queue.* A *random queue* stores a collection of items as per this API:

constant-time operation	*description*
`RandomQueue()`	*a new random queue*
`q.isEmpty()`	*is q empty?*
`q.enqueue(item)`	*enqueue* `item` *onto q*
`q.dequeue()`	*remove and return a random item from q (sample without replacement)*
`q.sample()`	*return but do not remove a random item from q (sample with replacement)*
`len(q)`	*number of items in q*

Note: Space used must be linear in the number of items in the randomized queue.

API for a random queue

Compose a class RandomQueue that implements this API. *Hint*: Use a Python list (resizing array) representation, as in PROGRAM 4.3.1. To remove an item, swap one at a random position (indexed 0 through n-1) with the one at the last position (index n-1). Then delete and return the last object. Compose a client that writes a deck of cards in random order using RandomQueue.

4.3.41 *Topological sort.* You have to sequence the order of n jobs that are numbered from 0 to n-1 on a server. Some of the jobs must complete before others can begin. Compose a program topologicalsorter.py that takes n as a command-line argument and a sequence on standard input of ordered pairs of jobs i j, and then writes a sequence of integers such that for each pair i j in the input, job i appears before job j. Use the following algorithm: First, from the input, build, for each job, (1) a queue of the jobs that must follow it and (2) its *indegree* (the number of jobs that must come before it). Then, build a queue of all nodes whose indegree is 0 and repeatedly delete some job with zero indegree, maintaining all the data structures. This process has many applications; for example, you can use it to model course prerequisites for your major so that you can find a sequence of courses to take so that you can graduate.

4.3.42 *Text editor buffer.* Develop a data type for a buffer in a text editor that implements the following API:

constant-time operation	*description*
`Buffer()`	*a new buffer*
`buf.insert(c)`	*insert character* `c` *just before the cursor in* `buf`
`buf.delete()`	*delete and return the character at the cursor in* `buf`
`buf.left(k)`	*move the cursor* `k` *positions to the left in* `buf`
`buf.right(k)`	*move the cursor* `k` *positions to the right in* `buf`

API for a text buffer

Hint: Use two stacks.

4.3.43 *Copy a stack.* Create a `copy()` method for the linked-list implementation of `Stack` so that

```
stack2 = stack1.copy()
```

makes `stack2` a reference to a new and independent copy of the stack `stack1`. You should be able to push and pop from either `stack1` or `stack2` without influencing the other.

4.3.44 *Copy a queue.* Create a `copy()` method for the linked-list implementation of `Queue` so that

```
queue2 = queue1.copy()
```

makes `queue2` a reference to a new and independent copy of the queue `queue1`. *Hint*: Delete all of the items from `queue1` and add these items to both `queue1` and `queue2`.

4.3.45 *Stack with explicit resizing array.* Implement a stack using an explicit resizing array: initialize an empty stack by using an array of length 1 as an instance variable; double the length of the array when it becomes full and halve the length of the array when it becomes one-fourth full.

Solution:

```
class Stack:

    def __init__(self):
        self._a = [None]
        self._n = 0

    def isEmpty(self):
        return self._n == 0

    def __len__(self):
        return self._n

    def _resize(self, capacity):
        temp = stdarray.create1D(capacity)
        for i in range(self._n):
            temp[i] = self._a[i]
        self._a = temp

    def push(self, item):
        if self._n == len(self._a):
            self._resize(2 * self._n)
        self._a[self._n] = item
        self._n += 1

    def pop(self):
        self._n -= 1
        item = self._a[self._n]
        self._a[self._n] = None
        if (self._n > 0) and (self._n == len(self._a) // 4):
            self._resize(self._n // 2)
        return item
```

4.3.46 *Queue with explicit resizing array.* Implement a queue using an explicit resizing array so that all operations take constant amortized time. *Hint*: The challenge is that the items will "crawl across" the array as items are added to and removed from the queue. Use modular arithmetic to maintain the array indices of the items at the front and back of the queue.

stdin	stdout	n	lo	hi	a[]							
					0	1	2	3	4	5	6	7
		0	0	0	None							
to		1	0	1	to	None						
be		2	0	2	to	be						
or		3	0	3	to	be	or	None				
not		4	0	4	to	be	or	not				
to		5	0	5	to	be	or	not	to	None	None	None
-	to	4	1	4	None	be	or	not	to	None	None	None
be		5	1	6	None	be	or	not	to	be	None	None
-	be	4	2	6	None	None	or	not	to	be	None	None
-	or	3	3	6	None	None	None	not	to	not	None	None
that		4	3	7	None	None	None	not	to	not	that	None

4.3.47 *Queue simulations.* Study what happens when you modify `mm1queue.py` to use a stack instead of a queue. Does Little's law hold? Answer the same question for a random queue. Plot histograms and compare the standard deviations of the waiting times.

4.3.48 *Load-balancing simulations.* Revise `loadbalance.py` to write the average queue length and the maximum queue length instead of plotting the histogram, and use it to run simulations for 1 million items on 100,000 queues. Write the average value of the maximum queue length for 100 trials each with sample sizes 1, 2, 3, and 4. Do your experiments validate the conclusion drawn in the text about using a sample of size 2?

4.3.49 *Listing files.* A folder is a list of files and subfolders. Compose a program that takes the name of a folder as a command-line argument and writes all of the file names contained in that folder, with the contents of each folder recursively listed (indented) under that folder's name. *Hint*: Use a queue, and see the `listdir()` function defined in Python's os module.

4.4 Symbol Tables

A SYMBOL TABLE IS A DATA type that we use to associate *values* with *keys*. Clients can store (*put*) an entry into the symbol table by specifying a key–value pair and then can retrieve (*get*) the value corresponding to a particular key from the symbol table. For example, a university might associate information such as a student's name, home address, and grades (the value) with that student's Social Security number (the key), so that each student's record can be accessed by specifying a Social Security number. The same approach might be appropriate for a scientist who needs to organize data, a business that needs to keep track of customer transactions, an Internet search engine that has to associate keywords with web pages, or in countless other ways.

Programs in this section

Because of their fundamental importance, symbol tables have been heavily used and studied since the early days of computing. The development of implementations that guarantee good performance continues to be an active area of research. Several other operations on symbol tables beyond the characteristic *put* and *get* operations naturally arise, and guaranteeing good performance for richer sets of operations can be quite challenging.

In this chapter we consider a basic API for the symbol-table data type. Our API adds to the *put* and *get* operations the abilities to test whether any value has been associated with a given key (*contains*) and to *iterate* over the keys. We also consider an extension to the API for the case where keys are comparable, which admits a number of useful operations.

We also consider two classic implementations. The first uses an operation known as *hashing*, which transforms keys into array indices that we can use to access values. The second is based on a data structure known as the *binary search tree (BST)*. Both are remarkably simple solutions that perform well in many practical situations and also serve as the basis for the industrial-strength symbol-table implementations that are found in modern programming environments. The code that we consider for symbol tables is only slightly more complicated than the resizing array and linked-list code that we considered for stacks and queues, but it will introduce you to new dimensions in structuring data that have far-reaching impact.

API A *symbol table* is a collection of key–value pairs—every symbol-table entry associates a value with a key, as follows:

logarithmic or constant-time operation	*description*
`SymbolTable()`	*a new symbol table*
`st[key] = val`	*associate* `key` *with* `val` *in* `st`
`st[key]`	*the value associated with* `key` *in* `st`
`key in st`	*is there a value associated with* `key` *in* `st`*?*
linear-time operation	
`for key in st:`	*iterate over the keys in* `st`

Note: Space used must be linear in the number of keys in the symbol table.

API for a symbol table

In this section, we discuss this API, clients, implementations, and extensions. The API is consistent with the API for Python's built-in `dict` data type, which we consider later in this section. The API already reflects several design decisions, which we now enumerate.

Associative arrays. We overload the `[]` operator for the two basic operations *put* and *get*. In client code this means that we can think of a symbol table as an *associative array*, where we can use standard array syntax with any type of data inside the square brackets instead of an integer between 0 and the length, as for an array. Thus, we can associate a codon with an amino acid name with client code like

```
amino['TTA'] = 'Leucine'
```

and we can later access the name associated with a given codon with client code like

```
stdio.writeln(amino['TTA'])
```

That is, an associative array reference is a *get* operation, unless it is on the left side of an assignment statement, when it is a *put* operation. We can support these operations by implementing the special methods `__getitem__()` and `__setitem__()`. Thinking in terms of associative arrays is a good way to understand the basic purpose of symbol tables.

Replace-the-old-value policy. If a value is to be associated with a key that already has an associated value, we adopt the convention that the new value replaces the old one (just as with an array assignment statement). Again, this is what one would expect from the associative-array abstraction. The `key in st` operation, supported by the special method `__contains__()`, gives the client the flexibility to avoid doing so, if desired.

Not found. The call `st[key]` raises a `KeyError` if no value has been associated with `key` in the table. An alternative design would be to return `None` in such cases.

None keys and values. Clients may use `None` as a key or value, though they typically do not do so. An alternative design would be to disallow either `None` keys and/or values.

Iterable. To support the `for key in st:` construct, Python's convention is that we need to implement a special method `__iter__()` that returns an *iterator*, a special data type that includes methods that are called at the beginning and for each iteration of the `for` loop. We consider Python's mechanism for iteration at the end of this section.

Remove. Our basic API does not include a method for removing keys from the symbol table. Some applications do require such a method, and Python provides the special syntax `del st[key]` that can be supported by implementing the special method `__delitem__()`. We leave implementations as exercises or for a more advanced course in algorithms.

Immutable keys. We assume the keys do not change their value while in the symbol table. The simplest and most commonly used types of keys (integers, floats, and strings) are immutable. If you think about it, you will see that is a very reasonable assumption! If a client changes a key, how could the symbol table implementation keep track of that fact?

Variations. Computer scientists have identified numerous other useful operations on symbol tables, and APIs based on various subsets of them have been widely studied. We consider several of these operations throughout this section, and particularly in the exercises at the end.

Comparable keys. In many applications, the keys may be integers, floats, strings, or other data types of data that have a natural order. In Python, as discussed in SECTION 3.3, we expect such keys to be *comparable.* Symbol tables with comparable keys are important for two reasons. First, we can take advantage of key ordering to develop implementations of *put* and *get* that can *guarantee* the performance specifications in the API. Second, a whole host of new operations come to mind (and can be supported) with comparable keys. A client might want the smallest key, or the largest, or the median, or to iterate over the keys in sorted order. Full coverage of this topic is more appropriate for a book on algorithms and data structures, but we examine a typical client and an implementation of such a data type later in this section. A partial API is shown at the bottom of this page.

SYMBOL TABLES ARE AMONG THE MOST widely studied data structures in computer science, so the impact of these and many alternative design decisions has been carefully studied, as you will learn if you take later courses in computer science. In this section, our approach is to introduce you to the most important properties of symbol tables by considering two prototypical client programs, developing two classic and efficient implementations, and studying the performance characteristics of those implementations, to show you that they can meet the needs of typical clients, even when the symbol tables are huge.

logarithmic or constant-time operation	*description*
`OrderedSymbolTable()`	*a new ordered symbol table*
`st[key] = val`	*associate* `key` *with* `val` *in* `st`
`st[key]`	*the value associated with* `key` *in* `st`
`key in st`	*is there a value associated with* `key` *in* `st`?
`st.rank(key)`	*number of keys less than* `key` *in* `st`
`st.select(k)`	*kth smallest key in* `st` *(key in* `st` *of rank* `k`*)*
linear-time operation	
`for key in st:`	*iterate over the keys in* `st`*, in sorted order*

Note: Space used must be linear in the number of keys in the symbol table.

Partial API for an ordered symbol table of comparable keys

Symbol table clients Once you gain some experience with the idea, you will realize that symbol tables are broadly useful. To convince you of this fact, we start with two prototypical examples, each of which arises in a large number of important and familiar practical applications.

Dictionary lookup. The most basic kind of symbol-table client builds a symbol table with successive *put* operations to support *get* requests. We maintain a collection of data so that we can quickly access the data we need. Most applications also take advantage of the idea that a symbol table is a *dynamic* dictionary, where it is easy both to look up information *and* to update the information in the table. The following list of familiar examples illustrates the utility of this approach.

- *Phone book.* When keys are people's names and values are their phone numbers, a symbol table models a phone book. A very significant difference from a printed phone book is that we can add new names or change existing phone numbers. We could also use the phone number as the key and the name as the value. If you have never done so, try typing your phone number (with area code) into the search field in your browser.
- *Dictionary.* Associating a word with its definition is a familiar concept that gives us the name "dictionary." For centuries people kept printed dictionaries in their homes and offices so that they could check the definitions and spellings (values) of words (keys). Now, because of good symbol-table implementations, people expect built-in spell checkers and immediate access to word definitions on their computers.
- *Account information.* People who own stock now regularly check the current price on the web. Several services on the web associate a ticker symbol (key) with the current price (value), usually along with a great deal of other information. Commercial applications of this sort abound, including financial institutions associating account information with a name or account

	key	*value*
phone book	name	phone number
dictionary	word	definition
account	account number	balance
genomics	codon	amino acid
data	data/time	results
compiler	variable name	memory location
file share	song name	machine
Internet DNS	website	IP address

Typical dictionary applications

number or educational institutions associating grades with a student name or identification number.

- *Genomics.* Symbols play a central role in modern genomics, as we have already seen (see PROGRAM 3.1.1). The simplest example is the use of the letters A, C, T, and G to represent the nucleotides found in the DNA of living organisms. The next simplest is the correspondence between codons (nucleotide triplets) and amino acids (TTA corresponds to leucine, TCT to cycstine, and so forth), then the correspondence between sequences of amino acids and proteins, and so forth. Researchers in genomics routinely use various types of symbol tables to organize this knowledge.
- *Experimental data.* From astrophysics to zoology, modern scientists are awash in experimental data, and organizing and efficiently accessing this data is vital to understanding what it means. Symbol tables are a critical starting point, and advanced data structures and algorithms that are based on symbol tables are now an important part of scientific research.
- *Programming languages.* One of the earliest uses of symbol tables was to organize information for programming. At first, programs were simply sequences of numbers, but programmers very quickly found that using symbolic names for operations and memory locations (variable names) was far more convenient. Associating the names with the numbers requires a symbol table. As the size of programs grew, the cost of the symbol-table operations became a bottleneck in program development time, which led to the development of data structures and algorithms like the ones we consider in this section.
- *Files.* We use symbol tables regularly to organize data on computer systems. Perhaps the most prominent example is the *file system*, where we associate a file name (key) with the location of its contents (value). Your music player uses the same system to associate song titles (keys) with the location of the music itself (value).
- *Internet DNS.* The domain name system (DNS) that is the basis for organizing information on the Internet associates URLs (keys) that humans understand (such as `www.princeton.edu` or `www.wikipedia.org`) with IP addresses (values) that computer network routers understand (such as `208.216.181.15` or `207.142.131.206`). This system is the next-generation "phone book." Thus, humans can use names that are easy to remember and machines can efficiently process the numbers. The number of symbol-table

```
% more amino.csv
TTT,Phe,F,Phenylalanine
TTC,Phe,F,Phenylalanine
TTA,Leu,L,Leucine
TTG,Leu,L,Leucine
TCT,Ser,S,Serine
TCC,Ser,S,Serine
TCA,Ser,S,Serine
TCG,Ser,S,Serine
TAT,Tyr,Y,Tyrosine
TAC,Tyr,Y,Tyrosine
TAA,Stop,Stop,Stop
...
GCA,Ala,A,Alanine
GCG,Ala,A,Alanine
GAT,Asp,D,Aspartic Acid
GAC,Asp,D,Aspartic Acid
GAA,Gly,G,Glutamic Acid
GAG,Gly,G,Glutamic Acid
GGT,Gly,G,Glycine
GGC,Gly,G,Glycine
GGA,Gly,G,Glycine
GGG,Gly,G,Glycine

% more djia.csv
...
20-Oct-87,1738.74,608099968,1841.01
19-Oct-87,2164.16,604300032,1738.74
16-Oct-87,2355.09,338500000,2246.73
15-Oct-87,2412.70,263200000,2355.09
...
30-Oct-29,230.98,10730000,258.47
29-Oct-29,252.38,16410000,230.07
28-Oct-29,295.18,9210000,260.64
25-Oct-29,299.47,5920000,301.22
...

% more ip.csv
...
www.ebay.com,66.135.192.87
www.princeton.edu,128.112.128.15
www.cs.princeton.edu,128.112.136.35
www.harvard.edu,128.103.60.24
www.yale.edu,130.132.51.8
www.cnn.com,64.236.16.20
www.google.com,216.239.41.99
www.nytimes.com,199.239.136.200
www.apple.com,17.112.152.32
www.slashdot.org,66.35.250.151
www.espn.com,199.181.135.201
www.weather.com,63.111.66.11
www.yahoo.com,216.109.118.65
...
```

Typical comma-separated-value (CSV) files

lookups done each second for this purpose on Internet routers around the world is huge, so performance is of obvious importance. Millions of new computers and other devices are put onto the Internet each year, so these symbol tables on Internet routers need to be dynamic.

Despite its scope, this list is still just a representative sample, intended to give you a flavor of the scope of applicability of the symbol-table abstraction. Whenever you specify something by name, there is a symbol table at work. Your computer's file system or the web might do the work for you, but there is still a symbol table there somewhere.

Program 4.4.1 (`lookup.py`) builds a set of key–value pairs from a file of comma-separated values (see Section 3.1) as specified on the command line and then writes values corresponding to the keys read from standard input. The command-line arguments are the file name and two integers, one specifying the field to serve as the key and the other specifying the field to serve as the value. Examples of similar but slightly more sophisticated test clients are described in the exercises. For instance, we could make the dictionary dynamic by also allowing standard-input commands to change the value associated with a key (see Exercise 4.4.1).

Your first step in understanding symbol tables is to download `lookup.py` and `hashst.py` (the symbol-table implementation that we consider next) from the booksite to do some symbol-table searches. You can find numerous comma-separated-value (`.csv`) files that are related to various applications that we have described, including `amino.csv` (codon-to-amino-acid encodings), `djia.csv` (opening price, volume, and closing price of the stock market average, for every day in its history), and `ip.csv` (a selection of entries from

Program 4.4.1 Dictionary lookup (lookup.py)

```
import sys
import stdio
from instream import InStream
from hashst import SymbolTable

instream = InStream(sys.argv[1])
keyField = int(sys.argv[2])
valField = int(sys.argv[3])

database = instream.readAllLines()

st = SymbolTable()
for line in database:
    tokens = line.split(',')
    key = tokens[keyField]
    val = tokens[valField]
    st[key] = val

while not stdio.isEmpty():
    query = stdio.readString()
    if query in st: stdio.writeln(st[query])
    else:           stdio.writeln('Not found')
```

`instream`	*input stream (.csv)*
`keyField`	*key position*
`valField`	*value position*
`database[]`	*lines in input*
`st`	*symbol table*
`tokens`	*values on a line*
`key`	*key*
`val`	*value*
`query`	*query string*

This data-driven symbol table client reads key–value pairs from a comma-separated file, then writes values corresponding to keys on standard input. Both keys and values are strings.

```
% python lookup.py amino.csv 0 3
TTA
Leucine
ABC
Not found
TCT
Serine

% python lookup.py amino.csv 3 0
Glycine
GGG
```

```
% python lookup.py ip.csv 0 1
www.google.com
216.239.41.99

% python lookup.py ip.csv 1 0
216.239.41.99
www.google.com

% python lookup.py djia.csv 0 1
29-Oct-29
252.38
```

the DNS database). When choosing which field to use as the key, remember that *each key must uniquely determine a value.* If there are multiple *put* operations to associate values with a key, the table will remember only the most recent one (think about associative arrays). We will consider next the case where we want to associate multiple values with a key.

Later in this chapter, we will see that the cost of associative array references in `lookup.py` can be linear or logarithmic. This fact implies that you may experience a small delay getting the answer to your first request (for all the *put* operations to build the table), but you get immediate response for all the others.

Indexing. Program 4.4.2 (`index.py`) is a prototypical example of a symbol-table client for comparable keys. It reads in a list of strings from standard input and writes a sorted table of all the different strings along with a list of integers for each string specifying the positions where it appears in the input. In this case, we seem to be associating multiple values with each key, but we actually associating just one: a Python list. Again, this problem has familiar applications:

	key	*value*
book	term	page numbers
genomics	DNA substring	locations
web search	keyword	websites
business	customer name	transactions

Typical indexing applications

- *Book index.* Every textbook has an index where you look up a word and get the page numbers containing that word. While no reader wants to see every word in the book in an index, a program like `index.py` can provide a starting point for creating a good index.
- *Programming languages.* In a large program that uses a large number of symbols, it is useful to know where each name is used. A program like `index.py` can be a valuable tool to help programmers keep track of where symbols are used in their programs. Historically, an explicit printed symbol table was one of the most important tools used by programmers to manage large programs. In modern systems, symbol tables are the basis of software tools that programmers use to manage names of modules in systems.
- *Genomics.* In a typical (if oversimplified) scenario in genomics research, a scientist wants to know the positions of a given genetic sequence in an existing genome or set of genomes. Existence or proximity of certain sequences may be of scientific significance. The starting point for such research is an

Program 4.4.2 Indexing (index.py)

```
import sys
import stdio
from bst import OrderedSymbolTable

minLength = int(sys.argv[1])
minCount  = int(sys.argv[2])

words = stdio.readAllStrings()

bst = OrderedSymbolTable()
for i in range(len(words)):
    word = words[i]
    if len(word) >= minLength:
        if word not in bst: bst[word] = []
        bst[word] += [i]

for word in bst:
    if len(bst[word]) >= minCount:
        stdio.write(word + ': ')
        for i in bst[word]:
            stdio.write(str(i) + ' ')
        stdio.writeln()
```

minLength	*minimum length*
minCount	*count threshold*
bst	*ordered symbol table*
word	*current word*
bst[word]	*array of positions for current word*

This program accepts integers minLength *and* minCount *as command-line arguments, reads all of the words from standard input and creates a sorted index indicating where each word appears within standard input. It considers only words that have at least* minLength *characters and it writes only words that occur at least* minCount *times. The computation is based on a symbol table of comparables, where each key is a word and each corresponding value is an array of positions where the word occurs in standard input.*

```
% python index.py 9 30 < tale.txt
confidence: 2794 23064 25031 34249 47907 48268 48577 ...
courtyard: 11885 12062 17303 17451 32404 32522 38663 ...
evremonde: 86211 90791 90798 90802 90814 90822 90856 ...
expression: 3777 5575 6574 7116 7195 8509 8928 15015 ...
gentleman: 2521 5290 5337 5698 6235 6301 6326 6338   ...
influence: 27809 36881 43141 43150 48308 54049 54067 ...
monseigneur: 85 90 36587 36590 36611 36636 36643     ...
...
```

index like the one produced by `index.py`, modified to take into account the fact that genomes are not separated into words.

- *Web search.* When you type a keyword and get a list of websites containing that keyword, you are using an index created by your web search engine. There is one value (the list of pages) associated with each key (the query), although the reality is a bit more dynamic and complicated because we often specify multiple keys and the pages are spread through the web, not kept in a table on a single computer.
- *Account information.* One way for a company that maintains customer accounts to keep track of a day's transactions is to keep an index of the list of the transactions. The key is the account number; the value is the list of occurrences of that account number in the transaction list.

To cut down on the amount of output, `index.py` takes three command-line arguments: a file name and two integers. The first integer is the minimum string length to include in the symbol table, and the second is the minimum number of occurrences (among the words that appear in the text) to include in the printed index. Again, several similar clients for various useful tasks are discussed in the exercises. For example, one common scenario is to build multiple indices on the same data, using different keys. In our account example, one index might use customer account numbers for keys and another might use vendor account numbers.

As with `lookup.py`, you are certainly encouraged to download `index.py` and `bst.py` (the symbol-table implementation for comparable keys that we consider later) from the booksite and run them on various input files to gain further appreciation for the utility of symbol tables for comparable keys. If you do so, you will find that the programs can build large indices for huge files with little delay, because each symbol-table operation is taken care of immediately.

One reason for the proliferation of algorithms and implementations is that the needs of symbol-table clients can vary widely. On the one hand, when the symbol table or the number of operations to be performed is small, any implementation will do. On the other hand, symbol tables for some applications are so huge that they are organized as databases that reside on external storage or the web. In this section, we focus on the huge class of clients like `index.py` and `lookup.py` whose needs fall between these extremes, where we need to be able to use associative assignments to build and maintain large tables dynamically while also responding immediately to a large number of associative lookups. Providing this immediate response for huge dynamic tables is one of the classic contributions of algorithmic technology.

Elementary symbol-table implementations All of these examples are persuasive evidence of the importance of symbol tables. Symbol-table implementations have been heavily studied, many different algorithms and data structures have been invented for this purpose, and modern programming environments (including Python) provide direct support. As usual, knowing how a basic implementation works will help you appreciate, choose among, and more effectively use the advanced ones, or help implement your own version for some specialized situation that you might encounter.

To begin, we briefly consider four different elementary implementations, based on the two basic data structures that we have encountered: resizing arrays and linked lists. Our purpose in doing so is to establish that we need a more sophisticated data structure, as none of these achieve the performance requirements in our API. Each implementation uses linear time for one of the operations, which makes each of them unsuitable for large practical applications.

Perhaps the simplest implementation is to use *sequential search* with two *parallel (resizing) arrays*, one for keys and one for values, as follows (see Exercise 4.4.10 and Exercise 4.4.33 for implementations of `__contains__()` and `__iter__()`, respectively):

```
# sequential search implementation of a symbol table
class SymbolTable:

    def __init__(self):
        self._keys = []
        self._vals = []

    def __getitem__(self, key):
        for i in range(len(self._keys)):
            if self._keys[i] == key:
                return self._vals[i]
        raise KeyError

    def __setitem__(self, key, val):
        for i in range(len(self._keys)):
            if self._keys[i] == key:
                self._vals[i] = val
                return
        self._keys += [key]
        self._vals += [val]
```

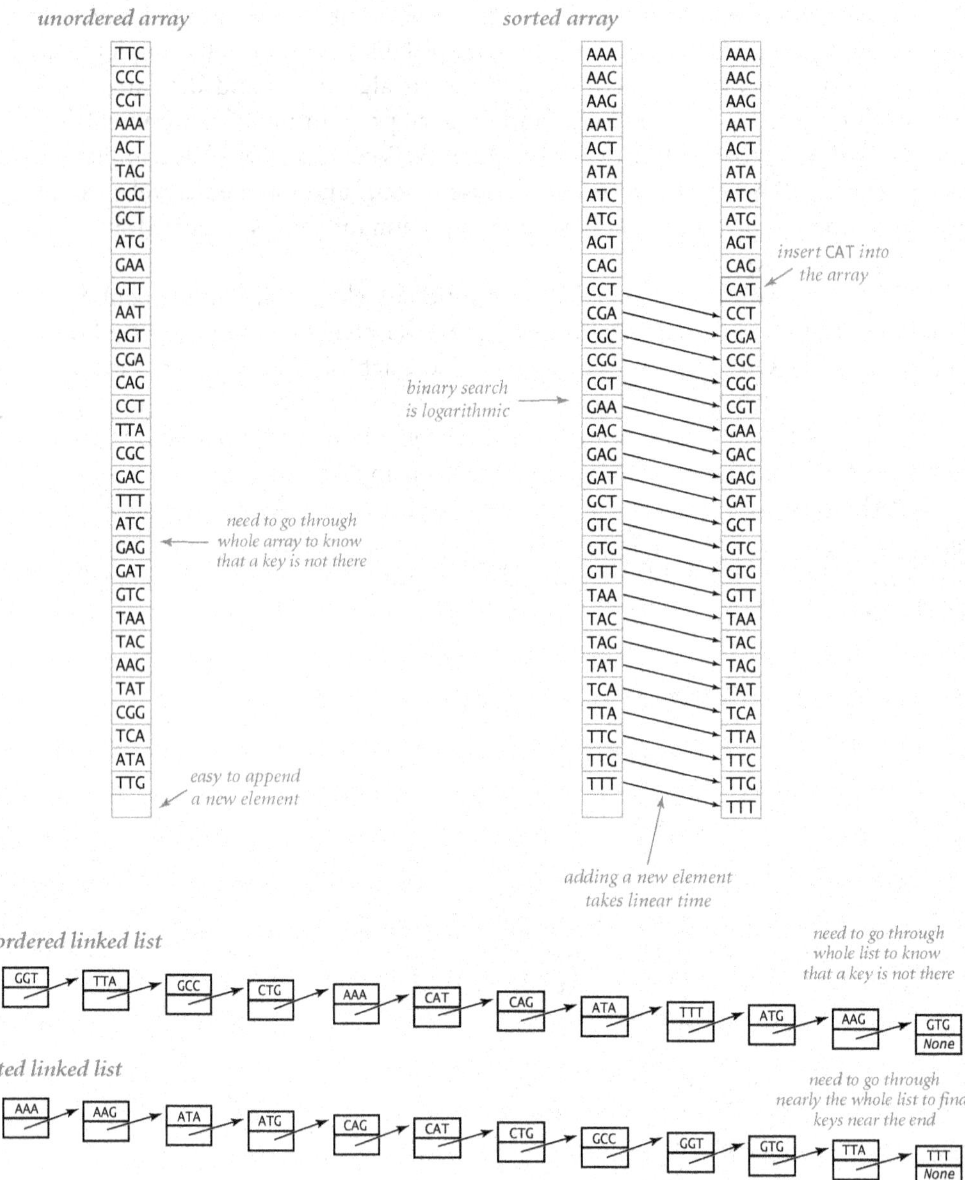

Elementary symbol-table implementations (only the keys are shown)

The key array is *unordered*—we just append new keys at the end. As usual, this is an (amortized) constant-time operation for Python lists. But a search for a key in the symbol table is typically a *linear*-time operation: For example, if we are looking for a key that is not in the table, we have to examine all of the keys.

To respond to the linear-time search cost, we might use a *sorted (resizing) array* for the keys. Actually, we already considered the idea of a dictionary when we considered binary search in Section 4.2. It is not difficult to build a symbol-table implementation that is based on binary search (see Exercise 4.4.5) but such an implementation is not feasible for use with a client like `index.py`, because it depends on maintaining a resizing array sorted in order of the keys. Each time a new key is added, larger keys have to be shifted one position higher in the array, which implies that the total time required to build the table is *quadratic* in the size of the table.

Alternatively, we might consider basing an implementation on an *unordered linked list*, because we can quickly add new key–value pairs at the beginning. But such an implementation is also not feasible for use by typical clients, because the only way to search for a key in a linked list is to traverse its links, so the total time required for searches is the product of the number of searches and the size of the table, which again is prohibitive. Associating a key with a value is also slow because we have to search first to avoid putting duplicate keys in the symbol table. Even keeping the linked list in sorted order does not help much—for example, traversing all the links is still required to add a new node to the end of the linked list.

To implement a symbol table that is feasible for use with clients such as `lookup.py` and `index.py`, we need data structures that are more flexible and efficient than these elementary examples. Next, we consider two examples of such data structures: the hash table and the binary search tree.

Hash tables A *hash table* is a data structure in which we divide the keys into small groups that can be quickly searched. The basic idea is simple. We choose a parameter m and divide the keys into m groups, which we expect to be about equal in size. For each group, we keep the keys in a list and use sequential search, as in the elementary implementation we just considered.

To divide the keys into small groups, we use a function called a *hash function* that maps every possible key into a *hash value*—an integer between 0 and $m - 1$. This enables us to model the symbol table as a *fixed-length array of lists* and use the hash value as an array index to access the desired list. In Python, we can implement both the fixed-length array and the lists using the built-in `list` data type.

Hashing is widely useful, so many programming languages include direct support for it. As we saw in SECTION 3.3, Python provides the built-in `hash()` function for this purpose, which takes a hashable object as an argument returns an integer *hash code*. To convert that to a hash value between 0 and $m-1$, we use the expression

```
hash(x) % m
```

Recall that an object is *hashable* if it satisfies the following three properties:

- The object can be compared for equality with other objects.
- Whenever two objects compare as equal, they have the same hash code.
- The object's hash code does not change during its lifetime.

Objects that are not equal may have the same hash code. However, for good performance, we expect the hash function to divide our keys into m groups of roughly equal length.

At right are hash codes and hash values for 12 representative string keys, with $m = 5$. The hash codes and hash values on your system may differ, due to a different or randomized `hash()` implementation.

With this preparation, implementing an efficient symbol table with hashing is a straightforward extension of the sequential search code that we have already considered. For the keys, we maintain an array of m lists, with element `i` containing a Python list of keys whose hash value is `i`. For the values, we maintain a parallel array of m lists, so that when we have located a key, we can access the corresponding value using the same indices. PROGRAM 4.4.3 (`hashst.py`) is a full implementation, using a fixed number of m lists (1,024 by default).

The efficiency of `hashst.py` depends on the value of m and the quality of the hash function. Assuming the hash function reasonably distributes the keys, performance is about m times faster than that for sequential search, at the cost of m extra references and lists. This is a classic *space–time tradeoff*: the higher the value of m, the more space we use, but the less time we spend.

key	*hash code*	*hash value*
GGT	-6162965092945700575	0
TTA	-2354942681944301382	3
GCC	-6162965092941700414	1
CTG	-1658743042903269101	4
AAA	5933679820854465332	2
CAT	-1658743042924269169	1
CAG	-1658743042924269156	4
ATA	5933679821064465599	4
TTT	-2354942681944301393	2
ATG	5933679821064465593	3
AAG	5933679820854465330	0
GTG	-6162965092962700473	2

Program 4.4.3 **Hash table** (hashst.py)

```
import stdio
import stdarray

class SymbolTable:

    def __init__(self, m=1024):
        self._m = m
        self._keys = stdarray.create2D(m, 0)
        self._vals = stdarray.create2D(m, 0)

    def __getitem__(self, key):
        i = hash(key) % self._m
        for j in range(len(self._keys[i])):
            if self._keys[i][j] == key:
                return self._vals[i][j]
        raise KeyError

    def __setitem__(self, key, val):
        i = hash(key) % self._m
        for j in range(len(self._keys[i])):
            if self._keys[i][j] == key:
                self._vals[i][j] = val
                return
        self._keys[i] += [key]
        self._vals[i] += [val]
```

instance variables

`_m`	*number of lists*
`_keys`	*array of lists (keys)*
`_vals`	*array of lists (values)*

This program uses two parallel arrays of lists to implement a hash table. Each list is represented as a Python `list` *of varying length. The hash function selects one of the* `m` *lists. When there are* `n` *keys in the table, the average cost of a put or get operation is* `n/m`*, for suitable* `hash()` *functions. This cost per operation is constant if we use a resizing array to ensure that the average number of keys per list is between 1 and 8 (see* Exercise *4.4.12). We defer implementations of* `__contains__()` *to* Exercise *4.4.11 and* `__iter__()` *to* Exercise *4.4.34.*

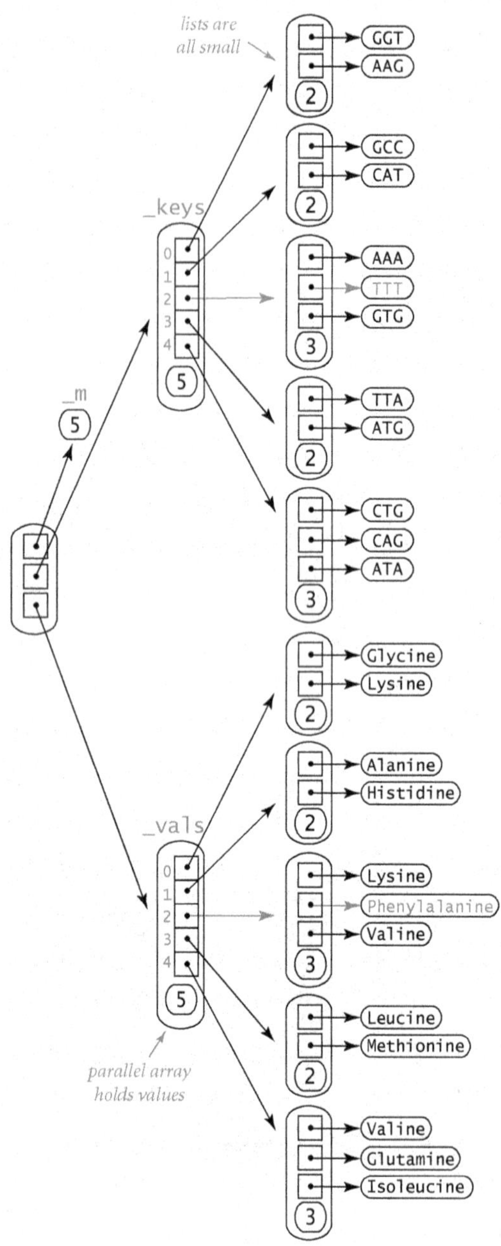

A hash table (m = 5)

The figure at left shows the symbol table built for our sample keys, inserted in the order given on page 648. (To save space, we omit the resizing array capacities in the Python lists in this diagram.) First, GGT is inserted in list 0, then TTA is inserted in list 3, then GCC is inserted in list 1, and so forth. After the table is built, a search for TTT starts by computing its hash value and then searching through `_keys[2]`. After finding the key TTT at `_keys[2][1]`, `__getitem__()` returns the entry `_vals[2][1]`, or `Phenylalnine`.

Typically, programmers choose a large fixed value of *m* (like the 1,024 default we have chosen) based on a rough estimate of the number of keys to be handled. With more care, we can arrange things so that the average number of keys per list is a constant, using resizing arrays for `_keys[]` and `_vals[]`. For example, EXERCISE 4.4.12 shows how to ensure that the average number of keys per list is always between 1 and 8, which leads to constant (amortized) time performance for both *put* and *get*. There is certainly opportunity to adjust these parameters to best fit a given practical situation.

The primary disadvantage of hash tables is that they do not take advantage of order in the keys and therefore cannot provide the keys in sorted order or support efficient implementations of operations like finding the minimum or maximum. For example, the keys will come out in arbitrary order in `index.py`, not the sorted order that is called for. Next, we consider a symbol table implementation that can support such operations when keys are comparable, without sacrificing much performance.

Binary search trees The *binary tree* is a mathematical abstraction that plays a central role in the efficient organization of information. As with arrays, linked lists, and hash tables, we use binary trees to store collections of data. Binary trees play an important role in computer programming because they strike an efficient balance between flexibility and ease of implementation.

For symbol-table implementations, we use a special type of binary tree to organize the data and to provide a basis for efficient implementations of the symbol-table *put* operations and *get* requests. A *binary search tree (BST)* associates comparable keys with values, in a structure defined recursively. A BST is one of the following:

- Empty (`None`)
- A node having a key–value pair and two references to BSTs, a *left* BST with smaller keys and a *right* BST with larger keys

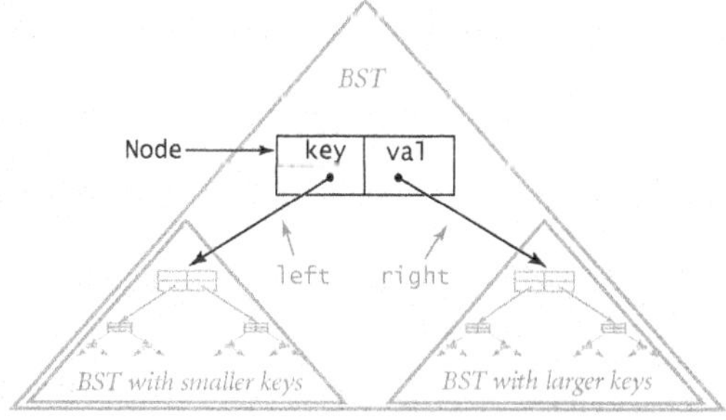

Binary search tree

The keys must be *comparable* via the < operator. The type of the value is not specified, so a BST node can hold any kind of data in addition to the key and the (characteristic) references to BSTs. As with our linked-list definition in SECTION 4.3, the idea of a recursive data structure can be a bit mind bending, but all we are doing is adding a second link to our linked-list definition (and imposing an ordering restriction).

To implement BSTs, we start with a class for the *node* abstraction, which has references to a key, a value, and left and right BSTs:

```
class Node:
    def __init__(self, key, val):
        self.key   = key
        self.val   = val
        self.left  = None
        self.right = None
```

This definition is like our definition of nodes for linked lists, except that it has *two* links, not just one. From the recursive definition of BSTs, we can represent a BST with a variable of type `Node` by ensuring that its value is either `None` or a reference to a `Node` whose `left` and `right` instance variables are references to BSTs, and by ensuring that the ordering condition is satisfied (keys in the left BST are smaller than `key` and keys in the right BST are larger than `key`).

The result of Node(key, val) is a reference to a Node object whose key and val instance variables are set to the given values and whose left and right instance variables are both initialized to None.

As with linked lists, when tracing code that uses BSTs, we can use a visual representation of the changes:

- We draw a rectangle to represent each object.
- We put the values of instance variables within the rectangle.
- We depict references as arrows that point to the referenced object.

Most often, we use an even simpler abstract representation where we draw rectangles containing keys to represent nodes (suppressing the values) and connect the nodes with arrows that represent links. This abstract representation allows us to focus on the structure.

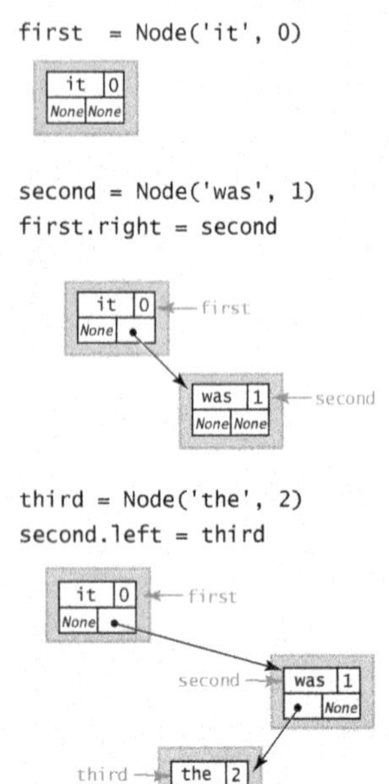

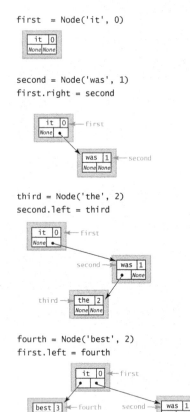

Linking together a BST

For example, to build a one-node BST that associates the string key 'it' with the integer value 0, we just create a Node:

```
first = Node('it', 0)
```

Since the left and right links are both None, both refer to BSTs, so this node is a BST. To add a node that associates the key 'was' with the value 1, we create another Node:

```
second = Node('was', 1)
```

(which itself is a BST) and link to it from the right field of the first Node

```
first.right = second
```

The second node has to go to the right of the first because 'it' compares as less than 'was' (or we could have chosen to set second.left to first). Now we can add a third node that associates the key 'the' with the value 2 with the code:

```
third = Node('the', 2)
second.left = third
```

and a fourth node that associates the key 'best' with the value 3 with the code

```
fourth = new Node('best', 3)
first.left = fourth
```

Note that each of our links—`first`, `second`, `third`, and `fourth`—are, by definition, BSTs (each is either `None` or refers to BSTs, and the ordering condition is satisfied at each node).

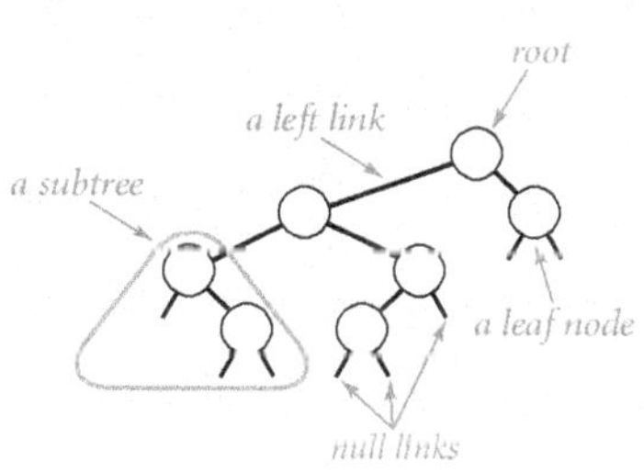

Anatomy of a binary tree

We often use tree-based terminology when discussing BSTs. We refer to the node at the top as the *root* of the tree, the BST referenced by its left link as the *left subtree*, and the BST referenced by its right link as the *right subtree*. Traditionally, computer scientists draw trees upside down, with the root at the top. Nodes whose links are both *null* are called *leaf* nodes. The *height* of a tree is the maximum number of links on any path from the root node to a leaf node. Trees have many applications in science, mathematics, and computational applications, so you are certain to encounter this model on many occasions.

In the present context, we take care to ensure that we always link together nodes such that *every* `Node` that we create is the root of a BST (has a key, a value, a link to a left BST with smaller values, and a link to a right BST with a larger value). From the standpoint of the BST data structure, the value is immaterial, so we often ignore it in our diagrams. We also intentionally confuse our nomenclature, using `st` to signify both "symbol table" and "search tree" because search trees play such a central role in symbol-table implementations.

A BST represents an *ordered* sequence of items. In the example considered on the previous page, `first` represents the sequence `best it the was`. As we have seen, we might also use an array to represent an ordered sequence. For example, we could use

```
a = ['best', 'it', 'the', 'was']
```

to represent the same ordered sequence of strings. Given a set of distinct keys, there is only one way to represent the set as an ordered array, but there are many

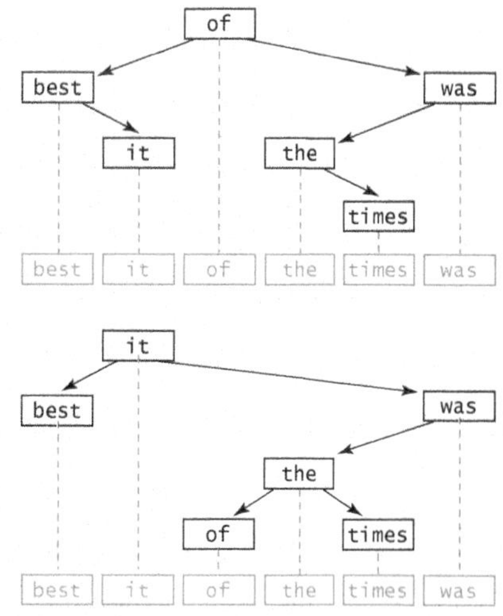

Two BSTs representing the same sequence

ways to represent the set as a BST (see EXERCISE 4.4.14). This flexibility allows us to develop efficient symbol-table implementations. For instance, in our example we were able to insert each new item by creating a new node and changing just one link. As it turns out, it is always possible to do so. Equally important, we can easily find a given key in the tree and find the place where we need to add a link to a new node with a given key. Next, we consider symbol-table code that accomplishes these tasks.

Suppose that you want to *search* for a node with a given key in a BST (or to *get* a value with a given key in a symbol table). There are two possible outcomes: the search might be *successful* (we find the key in the BST; in a symbol-table implementation, we return the associated value) or it might be *unsuccessful* (there is no key in the BST with the given key; in a symbol-table implementation, we raise a run-time error).

A recursive searching algorithm is immediate: Given a BST (a reference to a `Node`), first check whether the tree is empty (the reference is `None`). If so, then terminate the search as unsuccessful (in a symbol-table implementation, raise a run-time error). If the tree is nonempty, check whether the key in the node is equal

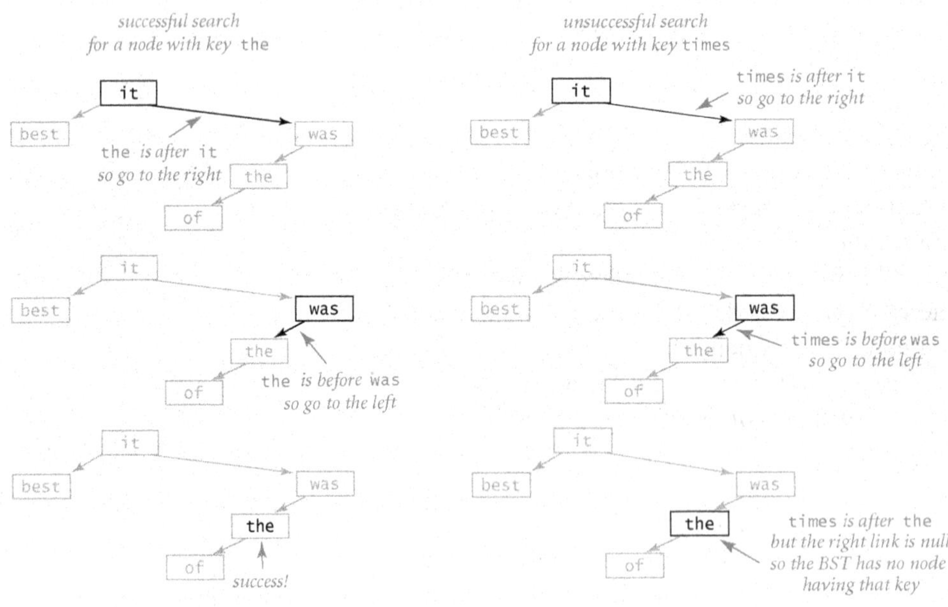

Searching in a BST

to the search key. If so, then terminate the search as successful (in a symbol-table implementation, return the value associated with the key). If not, compare the search key with the key in the node. If it is smaller, search (recursively) in the left subtree; if it is greater, search (recursively) in the right subtree.

Thinking recursively, it is not difficult to become convinced that this method behaves as intended, based on the invariant that the key is in the BST if and only if it is in the current subtree. The key property of the recursive method is that we always have just one node to examine to decide what to do next. Moreover, we typically examine only a small number of the nodes in the tree: whenever we go to one of the subtrees at a node, we will never examine any of the nodes in the other subtree.

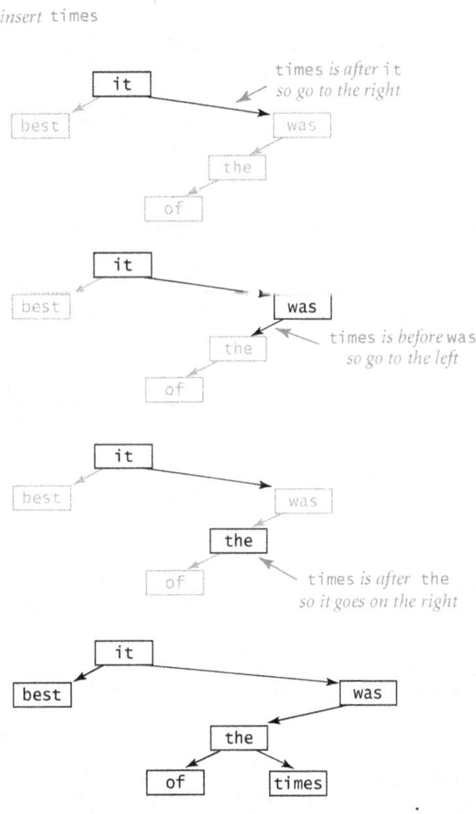

Inserting a new node into a BST

Suppose that you want to *insert* a new node into a BST (in a symbol-table implementation, *put* a new key–value pair into the data structure). The logic is similar to searching for a key, but the implementation is trickier. The key to understanding it is to realize that only one link must be changed to point to the new node, and that link is precisely the link that would be found to be `None` in an unsuccessful search for the key in that node.

If the BST is empty, we create and return a new `Node` containing the key–value pair; if the search key is less than the key at the root, we set the left link to the result of inserting the key–value pair into the left subtree; if the search key is greater, we set the right link to the result of inserting the key–value pair into the right subtree; otherwise, if the search key is equal, we overwrite the existing value with the new value. Resetting the left or right link after the recursive call in this way is usually unnecessary, because the link changes only if the subtree is empty, but it is as easy to set the link as it is to test to avoid setting it.

Program 4.4.4 Binary search tree (bst.py)

```
class OrderedSymbolTable:
    def __init__(self):
        self._root = None

    def _get(self, x, key):
        if x is None: raise KeyError
        if   key < x.key: return self._get(x.left,  key)
        elif x.key < key: return self._get(x.right, key)
        else:             return x.val

    def __getitem__(self, key):
        return self._get(self._root, key)

    def _set(self, x, key, val):
        if x is None: return _Node(key, val)
        if   key < x.key: x.left  = self._set(x.left,  key, val)
        elif x.key < key: x.right = self._set(x.right, key, val)
        else:             x.val   = val
        return x

    def __setitem__(self, key, val):
        self._root = self._set(self._root, key, val)

class _Node:
    def __init__(self, key, val):
        self.key   = key
        self.val   = val
        self.left  = None
        self.right = None
```

instance variable for BST

`_root`	*BST root*

instance variables for Node

`key`	*key*
`val`	*value*
`left`	*left subtree*
`right`	*right subtree*

This implementation of the symbol-table data type is centered on the recursive BST data structure and recursive methods for traversing it. We defer implementations of `__contains__()` *to* Exercise *4.4.13 and* `__iter__()` *to page 661.*

PROGRAM 4.4.4 (`bst.py`) is a symbol-table implementation based on these two recursive algorithms. As with `linkedstack.py` and `linkedqueue.py`, we use a *private* `_Node` class to emphasize that clients of `OrderedSymbolTable` do not need to know any of the details of the binary search tree representation.

If you compare `bst.py` with our binary search implementation `binarysearch.py` (PROGRAM 4.2.3) and our stack and queue implementations `linkedstack.py` (PROGRAM 4.3.2) and `linkedqueue.py` (PROGRAM 4.3.4), you will appreciate the elegance and simplicity of this code. *Take the time to think recursively and convince yourself that this code behaves as intended.* Perhaps the simplest way to do so is to trace the construction of an initially empty BST from a sample sequence of keys (see the diagram at right). Your ability to do so is a sure test of your understanding of this fundamental data structure.

Moreover, the *put* and *get* implementations in BST are remarkably efficient; typically, each accesses a small number of the nodes in the BST (those on the path from the root to the node sought or to the null link that is replaced by a link to the new node). Next, we show that *put* operations and *get* requests take logarithmic time (under certain assumptions). Also, to add a new key–value pair to the symbol table, only one new node is created and linked onto the bottom of the tree. If you make a drawing of a BST built by inserting some keys into an initially empty tree, you certainly will be convinced of this fact—you can just draw each new node at its unique position at the bottom of the tree.

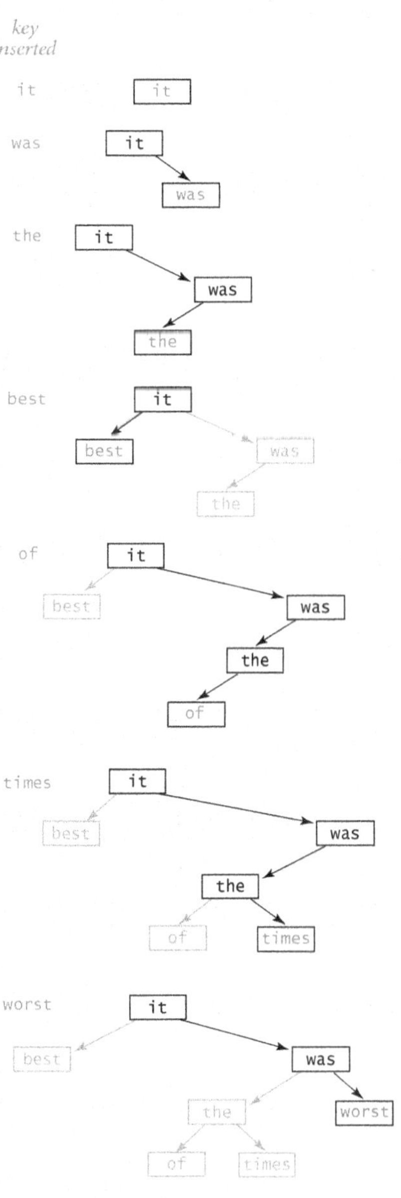

Constructing a BST

Performance characteristics of BSTs The running times of BST algorithms are ultimately dependent on the shape of the trees, and the shape of the trees is dependent on the order in which the keys are inserted. Understanding this dependence is a critical factor in being able to use BSTs effectively in practical situations.

Best case. In the best case, the tree is perfectly balanced (each `Node` has exactly two children that are not `None`, except the nodes at the bottom, which have exactly two children that *are* `None`), with lg n nodes between the root node and each leaf node. In such a tree, it is easy to see that the cost of an unsuccessful search is logarithmic,

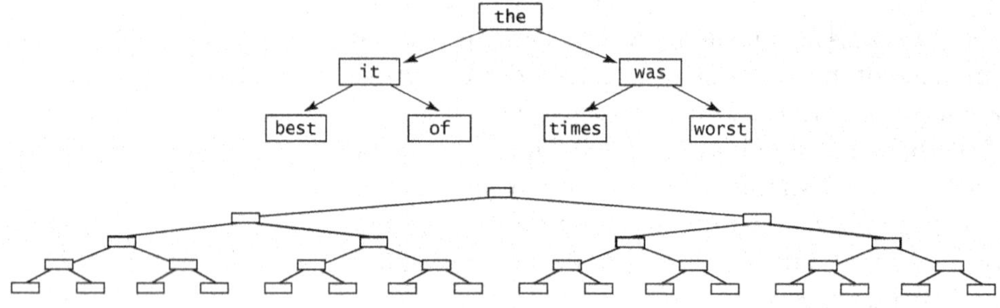

Best-case (perfectly balanced) BSTs

because that cost satisfies the same recurrence relation as the cost of binary search (see Section 4.2) so that the cost of every *put* operation and *get* request is proportional to lg n or less. You would have to be quite lucky to get a perfectly balanced tree like this by inserting keys one by one in practice, but it is worthwhile to know the best possible performance characteristics.

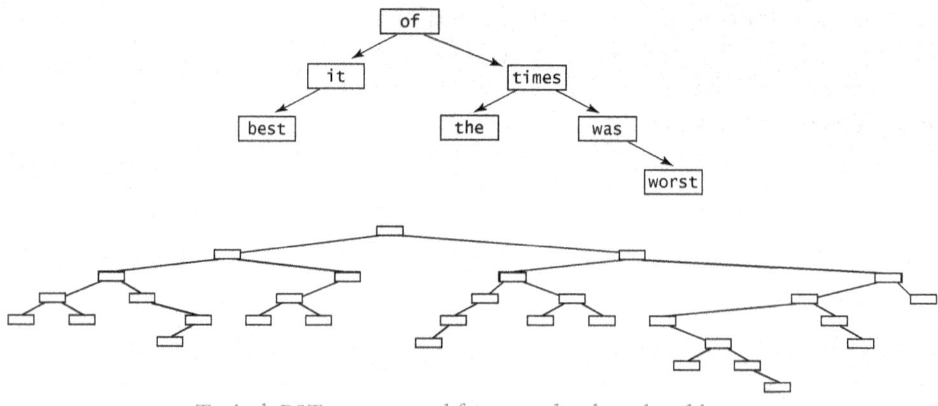

Typical BSTs constructed from randomly ordered keys

Average case. If we insert random keys, we might expect the search times to be logarithmic as well, because the first key becomes the root of the tree and should divide the keys roughly in half. Applying the same argument to the subtrees, we expect to get about the same result as for the best case. This intuition is, indeed, validated by careful analysis: a classic mathematical derivation shows that the time required for *put* and *get* in a tree constructed from randomly ordered keys is logarithmic (see the booksite for references). More precisely, *the expected number of key comparisons is ~2 ln n for a random put or get in a tree built from n randomly ordered keys.* In a practical application such as `lookup.py`, when we can explicitly randomize the order of the keys, this result suffices to (probabilistically) guarantee logarithmic performance. Indeed, since 2 ln *n* is about 1.39 lg *n*, the *average* case is only about 39% greater than the *best* case. In an application like `index.py`, where we have no control over the order of insertion, there is no guarantee, but typical data gives logarithmic performance (see Exercise 4.4.26). As with binary search, this fact is very significant because of the enormousness of the logarithmic–linear chasm: with a BST-based symbol table implementation, we can perform millions of operations per second (or more), even in a huge symbol table.

Worst case. In the worst case, each node has exactly one null link, so the BST is like a linked list with an extra wasted link, where *put* operations and *get* requests take linear time. Unfortunately, this worst case is not rare in practice—it arises, for example, when we insert the keys in order.

Thus, good performance of the basic BST implementation is dependent on the keys being sufficiently similar to random keys that the tree is not likely to contain many long paths. If you are not sure that assumption is justified, *do not use a simple BST.* Your only clue that something is amiss will be slow response time as the problem size increases. (*Note*: It is not unusual to encounter software of this sort!) Remarkably, there are BST variants that eliminate this worst case and guarantee logarithmic performance per operation, by making all trees nearly perfectly balanced. One popular variant is known as a *red-black tree*.

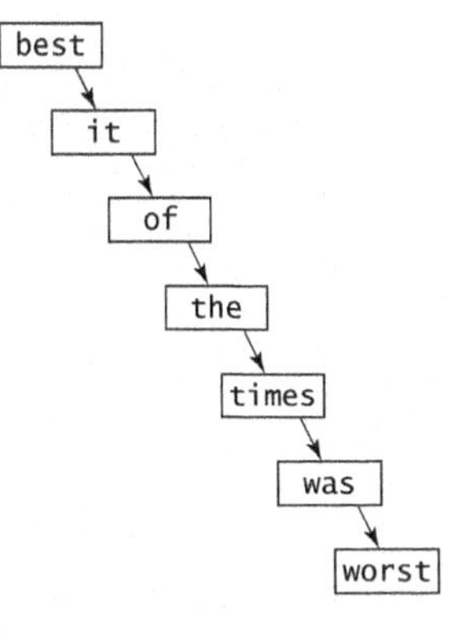

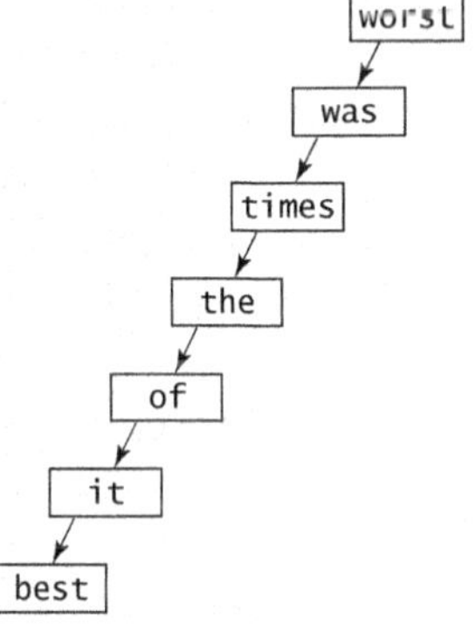

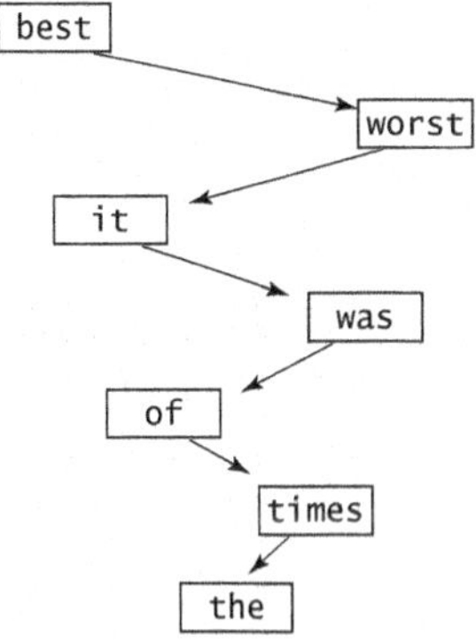

Worst-case BSTs

Traversing a BST Perhaps the most basic tree-processing function is known as *tree traversal*: given a (reference to) a tree, we want to systematically process every key–value pair in the tree. For linked lists, we accomplish this task by following the single link to move from one node to the next. For binary trees, however, we have decisions to make, because there are generally *two* links to follow. Recursion comes immediately to the rescue. To process every key in a BST:

- Process every key in the left subtree.
- Process the key at the root.
- Process every key in the right subtree.

This approach is known as *inorder* tree traversal, to distinguish it from *preorder* (do the root first) and *postorder* (do the root last), which arise in other applications. Given a BST, it is easy to convince yourself with mathematical induction that not only does this approach process every key in the BST, but that it processes them in *key-sorted order*. For example, the following method writes the keys in the BST rooted at its argument in key-sorted order:

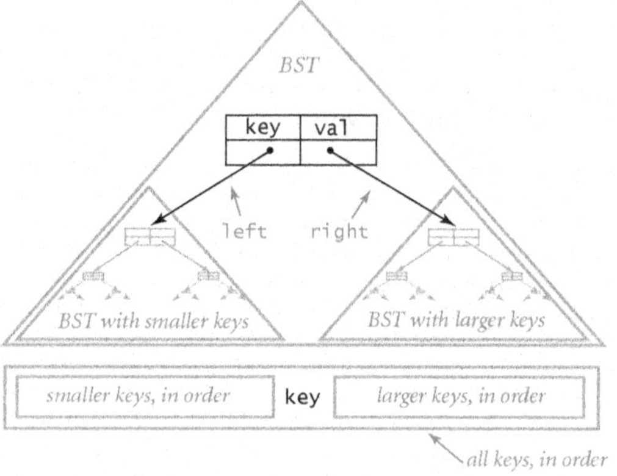

Recursive inorder traversal of a binary search tree

```
def inorder(x):
    if x is None: return
    inorder(x.left)
    stdio.writeln(x.key)
    inorder(x.right)
```

This remarkably simple method is worthy of careful study. It can be used as a basis for a `str()` implementation for BSTs (see Exercise 4.4.23) and as a starting point for developing the iterator that we need to provide clients with the ability to use a `for` loop to process the keys in key-sorted order. Indeed, one of the fundamental operations on a collection is to iterate over its items. The paradigm that we consider next leads to clear and compact code that is largely separate from the details of the collection's implementation. In the case of BSTs, it takes advantage of this natural procedure for traversing a tree.

Iterables As you learned in SECTION 1.3 and SECTION 1.4, you can use a `for` loop to iterate over either integers in a range or elements in an array `a[]`.

```
for i in range(n):          for v in a:
    stdio.writeln(i)            stdio.writeln(v)
```

The `for` loop is not just for integer ranges and arrays—you can use it with any *iterable* object. An iterable object is an object that is capable of returning its *items* one at a time. All of Python's sequence types—including `list`, `tuple`, `dict`, `set`, and `str`—are iterable, as is the object returned by the built-in `range()` function.

Now, our goal is to make `SymbolTable` iterable, so that we can use a `for` loop to iterate over its keys (and use indexing to *get* the corresponding values):

```
st = SymbolTable()
...
for key in st:
    stdio.writeln(str(key) + ' ' + str(st[key]))
```

To make a user-defined date type iterable, you must implement the special method `__iter__()`, in support of the built-in function `iter()`. The `iter()` function creates and returns an *iterator*, which is a data type that includes a special method `__next__()` that Python calls at the beginning of each iteration of a `for` loop.

While this appears complicated, we can use a shortcut based on the fact that Python lists are iterable: if a is a Python list, then `iter(a)` returns an iterator over its items. With this in mind, making our sequential-search symbol table (from page 645) iterable is a one-liner:

```
def __iter__():
    return iter(_keys)
```

Similarly, we can make our hash table and binary search tree implementations iterable by collecting the keys in a Python list and returning an iterator for that list. For example, to make `bst.py` iterable, we modify the recursive `inorder()` method from the previous page to collect the keys in a Python list instead of writing them. Then we can return an iterator for that list, as follows:

```
def __iter__(self):
    a = []
    self._inorder(self._root, a)
    return iter(a)
```

```
def _inorder(self, x, a):
    if x is None: return
    self._inorder(x.left, a)
    a += [x.key]
    self._inorder(x.right, a)
```

Python includes several built-in functions that either take iterables as arguments or return iterables, as documented in the API table below.

Python 2 alert. *In Python 3, `range()` returns an iterable of integers; in Python 2, `range()` returns an array of integers.*

Most of these built-in operations take linear time because the default implementation scans through all of the items in the iterable to compute the result. Of course, for performance-critical applications, we would use a symbol table instead of the built-in `in` construct to test whether an item is in a collection.

Next, we will see that it is also possible to develop implementations of *minimum* and *maximum* that are much more efficient than `min()` and `max()` when the underlying data structure is a BST, and we can support a broad range of other useful operations as well.

operation	*description*
`for v in a:`	*iterate over the items in* `a`
`v in a`	*is item* `v` *in* `a`*?*
`range(i, j)`	*an iterable containing the integers* `i`, `i+1`, `i+2`, ..., `j-1` (`i` *defaults to* `0`)
`iter(a)`	*a new iterator over the items in* `a`
`list(a)`	*a new* `list`*, created from the items in* `a`
`tuple(a)`	*a new* `tuple`*, created from the items in* `a`
`sum(a)`	*sum of items in* `a`
`min(a)`	*a minimum item in* `a`
`max(a)`	*a maximum item in* `a`
`reversed(a)`	*an iterable containing the items of sequence* `a` *in reverse order*

Note: Iterable items must be numeric for `sum()` *and comparable for* `min()` *and* `max()`*.*

Iterable operations and built-in functions

Ordered symbol table operations The flexibility of BSTs and the ability to compare keys enables the implementation of many useful operations beyond those that can be supported efficiently in hash tables. We leave implementations of these operations for exercises and leave further study of their performance characteristics and applications for a course in algorithms and data structures.

Minimum and maximum. To find the smallest key in a BST, follow left links from the root until reaching `None`. The last key encountered is the smallest in the BST. The same procedure following right links leads to the largest key in the BST (see Exercise 4.4.27).

Size and subtree sizes. To keep track of the number of nodes in a BST, keep an extra instance variable `n` in `OrderedSymbolTable` that counts the number of nodes in the tree. Initialize it to 0 and increment it whenever creating a new `_Node`. Alternatively, keep an extra instance variable `n` in each `_Node` that counts the number of nodes in the subtree rooted at that node (see Exercise 4.4.29).

Range search and range count. With a recursive method like `_inorder()`, we can return an iterator for keys falling between two given values in time proportional to the height of the BST plus the number of keys in the range (see Exercise 4.4.30). If we maintain an instance variable in each node having the size of the subtree rooted at each node, we can *count* the number of keys falling between two given values in time proportional to the height of the BST (see Exercise 4.4.31).

Order statistics and ranks. If we maintain an instance variable in each node having the size of the subtree rooted at each node, we can implement a recursive method that returns the *k*th smallest key in time proportional to the height of the BST (see Exercise 4.4.64). Similarly, we can compute the *rank* of a key, which is the number of keys in the BST that are strictly smaller than the key (see Exercise 4.4.65).

Remove. Many applications demand the ability to remove a key–value pair with a given key. You can find code for removing a node from a BST on the booksite or in a book on algorithms and data structures (see Exercise 4.4.32).

This list is representative; numerous other important operations have been invented for BSTs that are broadly useful in applications.

Dictionary data type Now that you understand how a symbol table works, you are ready to use Python's industrial-strength version. The built-in `dict` data type follows the same basic API as `SymbolTable`, but with a richer set of operations, including *deletion*; a version of *get* that returns a default value if the key is not in the dictionary; and *iteration* over the key–value pairs. The underlying implementation is a hash table, so ordered operations are not supported. As usual, since Python uses a lower-level language and does not impose on itself the overhead it imposes on all its users, that implementation will be more efficient and is preferred if ordered operations are not important.

As a simple example, the following `dict` client reads a sequence of strings from standard input, counts the number of times each string appears, and writes the strings and their frequencies. The strings do *not* come out in sorted order.

```
import stdio
while not stdio.isEmpty():
    word = stdio.readString()
    st[word] = 1 + st.get(word, 0)
for word, frequency in st.iteritems():
    stdio.writef('%4d %s\n', word, frequency)
```

Several examples of `dict` clients appear in the exercises at the end of this section.

constant-time operation	*description*
`dict()`	*a new empty dictionary*
`st[key] = val`	*associate* `key` *with* `val` *in* `st`
`st[key]`	*the value associated with* `key` *in* `st` *(raises* `KeyError` *if no such* `key` *in* `st`*)*
`st.get(key, x)`	`st[key]` *if* `key` *is in* `st`*; otherwise, x (x defaults to* `None`*)*
`key in st`	*is* `key` *in* `st`*?*
`len(st)`	*number of key–value pairs in* `st`
`del st[key]`	*remove* `key` *(and its associated value) from* `st`
linear-time operation	
`for key in st:`	*iterate over the keys in* `st`

Partial API for Python's built-in `dict` *data type*

Set data type As a final example, we consider a data type that is simpler than a symbol table, still broadly useful, and easy to implement with hashing or with BSTs. A *set* is a collection of distinct keys, like a symbol table with no values. For example, we could implement a set by deleting references to values in `hashst.py` or `bst.py` (see Exercises 4.4.20 and 4.4.21). Again, Python provides a `set` data type that is implemented in a lower-level language. A partial API is given at the bottom of this page.

For example, consider the task of reading a sequence of strings from standard input and writing the first occurrence of each string (thereby removing duplicates). We might use a `set`, as in the following client code:

```
import stdio
distinct = set()
while not stdio.isEmpty():
    key = stdio.readString()
    if key not in distinct:
        distinct.add(key)
        stdio.writeln(key)
```

You can find several other examples of `set` clients in the exercises at the end of this section.

constant-time operation	*description*
`set()`	*a new empty set*
`s.add(item)`	*add* `item` *to* `s` *(if not already in set)*
`item in s`	*is* `item` *in* `s`*?*
`len(s)`	*number of items in* `s`
`s.remove(item)`	*remove* `item` *from* `s`
linear-time operation	
`for item in s:`	*iterate over the items in* `s`
`s.intersection(t)`	*intersection of* `s` *and* `t`
`s.union(t)`	*union of* `s` *and* `t`
`s.issubset(t)`	*is* `s` *a subset of* `t`*?*

Partial API for Python's built-in `set` *data type*

Perspective Symbol-table implementations are a prime topic of further study in algorithms and data structures. Different APIs and different assumptions about keys call for different implementations. Methods are available that have even better performance than hashing and BSTs under various circumstances. Examples include balanced BSTs and tries. Implementations of many of these algorithms and data structures are found in Python and most other computational environments. Researchers in algorithms and data structures still study symbol-table implementations of all sorts.

Which symbol-table implementation is better, hashing or BSTs? The first point to consider is whether the client has comparable keys and needs symbol-table operations that involve ordered operations such as selection and rank. If so, then you need to use BSTs. If not, most programmers are likely to use hashing, though that choice requires caution in two respects: (1) you need check that you have a good hash function for the key data type, and (2) you need to make sure that the hash table is appropriately sized, either through resizing arrays or an appropriate application-dependent choice.

Should you use Python's built-in `dict` and `set` data types? Of course, if they support the operations that you need, because they are written in a lower-level language, not subject to the overhead Python imposes on user code, and therefore are likely to be faster than anything that you could implement yourself. But if your application needs order-based operations like finding the minimum or maximum, you may wish to consider BSTs.

People use dictionaries, indexes, and other kinds of symbol tables every day. Applications based on symbol tables have completely replaced phone books, encyclopedias, and all sorts of physical artifacts that served us well in the last millennium. Without symbol-table implementations based on data structures such as hash tables and BSTs, such applications would not be feasible; with them, we have the feeling that anything that we need is instantly accessible online.

Q&A

Q. Can I use an array (or Python list) as a key in a `dict` or `set`?

A. No, the built-in `list` data type is mutable, so you should not use arrays as keys in a symbol table or set. In fact, Python lists are not hashable, so you cannot use them as keys in a `dict` or `set`. The built-in `tuple` data type is immutable (and hashable), so you can that instead.

Q. Why doesn't my user-defined data type work with `dict` or `set`?

A. By default, user-defined types are hashable, with `hash(x)` returning `id(x)` and `==` testing reference equality. While these default implementations satisfy the hashable requirements, they rarely provide the behavior you want.

Q. Why can't I return a Python list directly in the special method `__iter__()`? Why must I instead call the built-in `iter()` function with the Python list as an argument?

A. A Python list is an iterable object (because it has an `__iter__()` method that returns an iterator) but it is not an iterator.

Q. Which data structure does Python use to implement `dict` and `set`?

A. Python uses an *open-addressing* hash table, which is a cousin of the *separate-chaining* hash table we considered in this section. Python's implementation is highly optimized and written in a low-level programming language.

Q. Does Python provide language support for specifying `set` and `dict` objects?

A. Yes, you can specify a `set` by enclosing in curly braces a comma-separated list of its items. You can specify a `dict` by enclosing in curly braces a comma-separated list of its key–value pairs, with a colon between each key and its associated value.

```
stopwords = {'and', 'at', 'of', 'or', on', 'the', 'to'}
grades = {'A+':4.33, 'A':4.0, 'A-':3.67, 'B+':3.33, 'B':3.0}
```

Q. Does Python provide a built-in data type for an ordered symbol table (or ordered set) that supports ordered iteration, order statistics, and range search?

A. No. If you need only ordered iteration (with comparable keys), you could use Python's `dict` data type and sort the keys (and pay a performance hit for sorting). For example, if you use a `dict` instead of a binary search tree in `index.py`, you can arrange to write the keys in sorted order by using code like

```
for word in sorted(st):
```

If you need other ordered symbol table operations (such as range search or order statistics), you can use our binary search tree implementation (and pay a performance hit for using a data type that is implemented in Python).

Exercises

4.4.1 Modify `lookup.py` to make a program `lookupandput.py` that allows *put* operations to be specified on standard input. Use the convention that a plus sign indicates that the next two strings typed are the key–value pair to be inserted.

4.4.2 Modify `lookup.py` to make a program `lookupmultiple.py` that handles multiple values having the same key by collecting the values in an array, as in `index.py`, and then writing them all out on a *get* request, as follows:

```
% python lookupmultiple.py amino.csv 3 0
Leucine
TTA TTG CTT CTC CTA CTG
```

4.4.3 Modify `index.py` to make a program `indexbykeyword.py` that takes a file name from the command line and makes an index from standard input using only the keywords in that file. *Note*: Using the same file for indexing and keywords should give the same result as `index.py`.

4.4.4 Modify `index.py` to make a program `indexlines.py` that considers only consecutive sequences of letters as keys (no punctuation or numbers) and uses line numbers instead of word position as the value. This functionality is useful for programs: When given a Python program as input, `indexlines.py` should write an index showing each keyword or identifier in the program (in sorted order), along with the line numbers on which it occurs.

4.4.5 Develop an implementation `OrderedSymbolTable` of the symbol-table API that maintains parallel arrays of keys and values, keeping them in key-sorted order. Use binary search for *get*, and move larger elements to the right by one position for *put* (using resizing arrays to keep the array length linear in the number of key–value pairs in the table). Test your implementation with `index.py`, and validate the hypothesis that using such an implementation for `index.py` takes time proportional to the product of the number of strings and the number of distinct strings in the input.

4.4.6 Develop an implementation `LinkedSymbolTable` of the symbol-table API that maintains a linked list of nodes containing keys and values, keeping them in arbitrary order. Test your implementation with `index.py`, and validate the hypothesis that using such an implementation for `index.py` takes time proportional to the product of the number of strings and the number of distinct strings in the input.

4.4.7 Compute `hash(x) % 5` for the single-character keys

`E A S Y Q U E S T I O N`

In the style of the drawing in the text, draw the hash table created when the `i`th key in this sequence is associated with the value `i`, for `i` from 0 to 11.

4.4.8 What is wrong with the following `__hash__()` implementation?

```
def __hash__(self):
    return -17
```

Solution: While technically it satisfies the conditions needed for a data type to be hashable (if two objects are equal, they have the same hash value), it will lead to poor performance because we expect `hash(x) % m` to divide keys into `m` groups of roughly equal size.

4.4.9 Extend `Complex` (Program 3.2.6) and `Vector` (Program 3.3.3) to make them hashable by implementing the special methods `__hash__()` and `__eq__()`.

4.4.10 Implement the special method `__contains__()` for the sequential-search symbol table on page 645.

4.4.11 Implement the special method `__contains__()` for `hashst.py`.

4.4.12 Modify `hashst.py` to use a resizing array so that the average length of the list associated with each hash value is between 1 and 8.

4.4.13 Implement the special method `__contains__()` for `bst.py`.

4.4.14 Draw all the different BSTs that can represent the key sequence

`best of it the time was`

4.4.15 Draw the BST that results when you insert items with keys

`E A S Y Q U E S T I O N`

in that order into an initially empty tree. What is the height of the resulting BST?

4.4.16 Suppose we have integer keys between `1` and `1000` in a BST and search for `363`. Which of the following *cannot* be the sequence of keys examined?

a. `2 252 401 398 330 363`
b. `399 387 219 266 382 381 278 363`
c. `3 923 220 911 244 898 258 362 363`
d. `4 924 278 347 621 299 392 358 363`
e. `5 925 202 910 245 363`

4.4.17 Suppose that the following 31 keys appear (in some order) in a BST of height 5:

```
10 15 18 21 23 24 30 30 38 41 42 45 50 55 59
60 61 63 71 77 78 83 84 85 86 88 91 92 93 94 98
```

Draw the top three nodes of the tree (the root and its two children).

4.4.18 Describe the effect on performance if you replaced `hashst` with `bst` in `lookup.py`. To protect against the worst case, call `stdrandom.shuffle(database)` before processing client queries.

4.4.19 True or false: Given a BST, let *x* be a leaf node, and let *p* be its parent. Then either (i) the key of *p* is the smallest key in the BST larger than the key of *x* or (ii) the key of *p* is the largest key in the BST smaller than the key of *x*.

4.4.20 Modify the class `SymbolTable` in `hashst.py` to make a class `Set` that implements the constant-time operations in the partial API given in the text for Python's built-in `set` data type.

4.4.21 Modify the class `OrderedSymbolTable` in `bst.py` to make a class `OrderedSet` that implements the constant-time operations in the partial API given in the text for Python's built-in `set` data type, assuming that the keys are comparable.

4.4.22 Modify `hashst.py` to support the client code `del st[key]` by adding a method `__delitem__()` that takes a `key` argument and removes that `key` (and the corresponding value) from the symbol table, if it exists. As in Exercise 4.4.12, use a resizing array to ensure that the average length of the list associated with each hash value is between 1 and 8.

4.4.23 Implement `__str__()` for `bst.py`, using a recursive helper method like `traverse()`. As usual, you can accept quadratic performance because of the cost of string concatenation. *Extra credit*: Compose a linear-time `__str__()` method for `bst.py` that uses an array and the `join()` method of Python's built-in `str` data type.

4.4.24 A *concordance* is an alphabetical list of the words in a text that gives all word positions where each word appears. Thus, `python index.py 0 0` produces a concordance. In a famous incident, one group of researchers tried to establish credibility while keeping details of the Dead Sea Scrolls secret from others by making public a concordance. Compose a program `invertconcordance.py` that takes a command-line argument `n`, reads a concordance from standard input, and writes the first `n` words of the corresponding text on standard output.

4.4.25 Run experiments to validate the claims in the text that the *put* operations and *get* requests for `lookup.py` are constant-time operations when using `hashst.py` with resizing arrays, as described in Exercise 4.4.12. Develop test clients that generate random keys and also run tests for various data sets, either from the booksite or of your own choosing.

4.4.26 Run experiments to validate the claims in the text that the *put* operations and *get* requests for `index.py` are logarithmic in the size of the symbol table when using `bst.py`. Develop test clients that generate random keys and also run tests for various data sets, either from the booksite or of your own choosing.

4.4.27 Modify `bst.py` to add methods `min()` and `max()` that return the smallest (or largest) key in the table (or `None` if the table is empty).

4.4.28 Modify `bst.py` to add methods `floor()` and `ceiling()` that take as an argument a key and return the largest (smallest) key in the set that is no larger (no smaller) than the given key.

4.4.29 Modify `bst.py` to support the special `len()` function by implementing a special method `__len__()` that returns the number of key–value pairs in the symbol table. Use the approach of storing within each `_Node` the number of nodes in the subtree rooted there.

4.4.30 Modify `bst.py` to add a method `rangeSearch()` that take two keys `lo` and `hi` as arguments and return an iterator over all keys that are between `lo` and `hi`. The running time should be proportional to the height plus the number of keys in the range.

4.4.31 Modify `bst.py` to add a method `rangeCount()` that takes keys as arguments and returns the number of keys in a BST between the two given keys. Your method should take time proportional to the height of the tree. *Hint*: First complete the previous exercise.

4.4.32 Modify `bst.py` to support the client code `del st[key]` by adding a method `__delitem__()` that takes a `key` argument and removes that `key` (and the corresponding value) from the symbol table, if it exists. *Hint*: This operation is more difficult than it might seem. Replace the key and its associated value with the next largest key in the BST and its associated value; then remove from the BST the node that contained the next largest key.

4.4.33 Implement the special method `__iter__()` for the sequential-search symbol table on page 645.

4.4.34 Implement the special method `__iter__()` for `hashst.py` to support iteration.

Solution: Collect all the keys in a list.

```
def __iter__(self):
    a = []
    for i in range(self._m):
        a += self._keys[i]
    return iter(a)
```

4.4.35 Modify the symbol-table API to handle values with duplicate keys by having `get()` return an *iterator* for the values having a given key. Reimplement `hashst.py` and `bst.py` as dictated by this API. Discuss the pros and cons of this approach versus the one given in the text.

4.4.36 Suppose that `a[]` is an array of hashable objects. What is the effect of the following statement?

```
a = list(set(a))
```

4.4.37 Recompose `lookup.py` and `index.py` using a `dict` instead of using `hashst.py` and `bst.py`, respectively. Compare performance.

4.4.38 Compose a `dict` client that creates a symbol table mapping letter grades to numerical scores, as in the table below, and then reads from standard input a list of letter grades and computes their average (GPA).

A+	A	A-	B+	B	B-	C+	C	C-	D	F
4.33	4.00	3.67	3.33	3.00	2.67	2.33	2.00	1.67	1.00	0.00

4.4.39 Implement the methods `buy()` and `sell()` methods in `stockaccount.py` (Program 3.2.8). Use a `dict` to store the number of shares of each stock.

Binary Tree Exercises

The following exercises are intended to give you experience in working with binary trees that are not necessarily BSTs. They all assume a `Node` *class with three instance variables: a positive* `double` *value and two* `Node` *references. As with linked lists, you will find it helpful to make drawings using the visual representation shown in the text.*

4.4.40 Implement the following functions, each of which takes as an argument a `Node` that is the root of a binary tree.

`size(node)`	*number of nodes in the tree rooted at* `node`
`leaves(node)`	*number of nodes in the tree rooted at* `node` *whose links are both* `None`
`total(node)`	*sum of the key values in all nodes in the tree rooted at* `node`

Your methods should all run in linear time.

4.4.41 Implement a linear-time function `height()` that returns the maximum number of nodes on any path from the root to a leaf node (the height of the empty tree is 0; the height of a one-node tree is 1).

4.4.42 A binary tree is *heap-ordered* if the key at the root is larger than the keys in all of its descendants. Implement a linear-time function `heapOrdered()` that returns `True` if the tree is heap-ordered, and `False` otherwise.

4.4.43 Given a binary tree, a *single-value* subtree is a maximal subtree that contains the same value. Design a linear-time algorithm that counts the number of single-value subtrees in a binary tree.

4.4.44 A binary tree is *balanced* if both its subtrees are balanced and the height of its two subtrees differ by at most 1. Implement a linear-time method `balanced()` that returns `True` if the tree is balanced, and `False` otherwise.

4.4.45 Two binary trees are *isomorphic* if only their key values differ (that is, they have the same shape). Implement a linear-time function `isomorphic()` that takes two tree references as arguments and returns `True` if they refer to isomorphic trees, and `False` otherwise. Then, implement a linear-time function `eq()` that takes two tree references as arguments and returns `True` if they refer to identical trees (isomorphic with the same key values), and `False` otherwise.

4.4.46 Compose a function `levelOrder()` that writes BST keys in *level order*: first write the root; then the nodes one level below the root, from left to right; then the nodes two levels below the root, from left to right; and so forth. *Hint*: Use a `Queue`.

4.4.47 Implement a linear-time function `isBST()` that returns `True` if the binary tree is a BST, and `False` otherwise.

Solution: This task is a bit more difficult than it might seem. Use a recursive helper function `_inRange()` that takes two additional arguments `lo` and `hi` and returns `True` if the binary tree is a BST and all its values are between `lo` and `hi`, and use `None` to represent both the smallest possible key and the largest possible key.

```
def _inRange(node, lo, hi):
    if node is None: return True
    if (lo is not None) and (node.item <= lo):  return False
    if (hi is not None) and (hi <= node.item):  return False
    if not _inRange(node.left, lo, node.item):  return False
    if not _inRange(node.right, node.item, hi): return False
    return True
def _isBST(node):
    return _inRange(node, None, None)
```

We note that this implementation uses both the < and <= operators, whereas our binary search tree code uses only the < operator.

4.4.48 Compute the value returned by `mystery()` on some sample binary trees, and then formulate a hypothesis about the value and prove it.

```
def mystery(node):
    if node is None: return 1
    return mystery(node.left) + mystery(node.right)
```

Creative Exercises

4.4.49 *Spell checking.* Compose a `set` client `spellchecker.py` that takes as a command-line argument the name of a file containing a dictionary of words, and then reads strings from standard input and writes any string that is not in the dictionary. You can find a dictionary file on the booksite. *Extra credit*: Augment your program to handle common suffixes such as *-ing* or *-ed*.

4.4.50 *Spell correction.* Compose a `dict` client `spellcorrector.py` that serves as a filter that replaces commonly misspelled words on standard input with a suggested replacement, writing the result to standard output. Take as a command-line argument a file that contains common misspellings and corrections. You can find an example on the booksite.

4.4.51 *Web filter.* Compose a `set` client `webblocker.py` that takes as a command-line argument the name of a file containing a list of objectionable websites, and then reads strings from standard input and writes only those websites not on the list.

4.4.52 *Set operations.* Add the methods `union()` and `intersection()` to `OrderedSet` (Exercise 4.4.21), each of which takes two sets as arguments and that return the union and intersection, respectively, of those two sets.

4.4.53 *Frequency symbol table.* Develop a data type `FrequencyTable` that supports the following operations: `click()` and `count()`, both of which take string arguments. The data-type value is an integer that keeps track of the number of times the `click()` operation has been called with the given string as an argument. The `click()` operation increments the count by 1, and the `count()` operation returns the value, possibly 0. Clients of this data type might include a web traffic analyzer, a music player that counts the number of times each song has been played, phone software for counting calls, and so forth.

4.4.54 *1D range searching.* Develop a data type that supports the following operations: insert a date, search for a date, and count the number of dates in the data structure that lie in a particular interval. Use Python's `datetime.Date` data type.

4.4.55 *Non-overlapping interval search.* Given a list of non-overlapping intervals of integers, compose a function that takes an integer argument and determines in which, if any, interval that value lies. For example, if the intervals are 1643–2033, 5532–7643, 8999–10332, and 5666653–5669321, then the query point 9122 lies in the third interval and 8122 lies in no interval.

4.4.56 *IP lookup by country.* Compose a `dict` client that uses the data file `ip-to-country.csv` found on the booksite to determine from which country a given IP address is coming. The data file has five fields: beginning of IP address range, end of IP address range, two-character country code, three-character country code, and country name. The IP addresses are non-overlapping. Such a database tool can be used for credit card fraud detection, spam filtering, auto-selection of language on a website, and web server log analysis.

4.4.57 *Inverted index of web pages with single-word queries.* Given a list of web pages, create a symbol table of words contained in the web pages. Associate with each word a list of web pages in which that word appears. Compose a program that reads in a list of web pages, creates the symbol table, and supports single-word queries by returning the list of web pages in which that query word appears.

4.4.58 *Inverted index of web pages with multi-word queries.* Extend the previous exercise so that it supports multi-word queries. In this case, output the list of web pages that contain at least one occurrence of each of the query words.

4.4.59 *Multiple-word search (unordered).* Compose a program that takes `k` keywords from the command line, reads in a sequence of words from standard input, and identifies the smallest interval of text that contains all of the `k` keywords (not necessarily in the same order). You do not need to consider partial words.

4.4.60 *Multiple-word search (ordered).* Repeat the previous exercise, but now assume the keywords must appear in the same order as specified.

4.4.61 *Repetition draw in chess.* In the game of chess, if a board position is repeated three times with the same side to move, the side to move can declare a draw. Describe how you could test this condition using a computer program.

4.4.62 *Registrar scheduling.* The registrar at a prominent Northeastern university recently scheduled an instructor to teach two different classes at the same exact time. Help the registrar prevent future mistakes by describing a method to check for such conflicts. For simplicity, assume all classes run for 50 minutes and start at 9, 10, 11, 1, 2, or 3.

4.4.63 *Entropy.* We define the *relative entropy* of a text corpus with n words, k of which are distinct as

$$E = 1 \,/\, (n \lg n)\ (p_0 \lg(k/p_0) + p_1 \lg(k/p_1) + \ldots + p_{k-1} \lg(k/p_{k-1}))$$

where p_i is the fraction of times that word i appears. Compose a program that reads in a text corpus and writes the relative entropy. Convert all letters to lowercase and treat punctuation marks as whitespace.

4.4.64 *Order statistics.* Add to `bst.py` a method `select()` that takes an integer argument k and returns the kth smallest key in the BST. Maintain subtree sizes in each node (see Exercise 4.4.29). The running time should be proportional to the height of the tree.

4.4.65 *Rank query.* Add to `bst.py` a method `rank()` that takes a `key` as an argument and returns the number of keys in the BST that are strictly smaller than `key`. Maintain subtree sizes in each node (see Exercise 4.4.29). The running time should be proportional to the height of the tree.

4.4.66 *Random element.* Add to `bst.py` a method `random()` that returns a random key. Maintain subtree sizes in each node (see Exercise 4.4.29). The running time should be proportional to the height of the tree.

4.4.67 *Queue with no duplicates.* Create a data type that is a queue, except that an element may appear on the queue at most once at any given time. Ignore requests to insert an item if it is already on the queue.

4.4.68 *Unique substrings of a given length.* Compose a program that reads in text from standard input and calculates the number of unique substrings of a given length `k` that it contains. For example, if the input is `CGCGGGCGCG`, then there are five unique substrings of length 3: `CGC`, `CGG`, `GCG`, `GGC`, and `GGG`. This calculation is useful in data compression. *Hint*: Use the string slice `s[i:i+k]` to extract the `i`th substring and insert into a symbol table. Test your program on a large genome from the booksite and on the first 10 million digits of π.

4.4.69 *Generalized queue.* Implement a class that supports the following API:

operation	*description*
`GeneralizedQueue()`	*a new generalized queue*
`isEmpty()`	*is the queue empty?*
`q.enqueue(item)`	*enqueue* `item` *on* `q`
`q.dequeue(i)`	*remove and return the* `i`*th least recently inserted item*

API for a generalized queue

Use a BST that associates the *k*th element inserted with the key *k* and maintains in each node the total number of nodes in the subtree rooted at that node. To find the `i`th least recently added item, search for the *i*th smallest element in the BST.

4.4.70 *Dynamic discrete distribution.* Create a data type that supports the following two operations: `add()` and `random()`. The `add()` method should insert a new item into the data structure if it has not been seen before; otherwise, it should increase its frequency count by 1. The `random()` method should return an element at random, where the probabilities are weighted by the frequency of each element. Use space proportional to the number of items.

4.4.71 *Password checker.* Compose a program that takes a string as a command-line argument and a dictionary of words from standard input, and checks whether the string is a "good" password. Here, assume "good" means that it (1) is at least eight characters long, (2) is not a word in the dictionary, (3) is not a word in the dictionary followed by a digit `0-9` (e.g., `hello5`), (4) is not two words in the dictionary concatenated together (e.g., `helloworld`), and (5) none of (2) through (4) hold for reverses of words in the dictionary.

4.4.72 *Random phone numbers.* Compose a program that takes a command-line argument *n* and writes *n* random phone numbers of the form `(xxx) xxx-xxxx`. Use a `set` to avoid choosing the same number more than once. Use only legal area codes (you can find a file of such codes on the booksite).

4.4.73 *Sparse vectors.* An n-dimensional vector is *sparse* if its number of nonzero values is small. Your goal is to represent a vector with space proportional to its number of nonzeros, and to be able to add two sparse vectors in time proportional to the total number of nonzeros. Implement a class that supports the following API:

operation	*description*
`SparseVector()`	*a new sparse vector*
`a[i] = v`	*set the* `i`*th element in* `a` *to* `v`
`a[i]`	*the* `i`*th element in* `a`
`a + b`	*vector sum of* `a` *and* `b`
`a.dot(b)`	*dot product of* `a` *and* `b`

API for a sparse vector

4.4.74 *Sparse matrices.* An n-by-n matrix is *sparse* if its number of nonzeros is proportional to n (or less). Your goal is to represent a matrix with space proportional to n, and to be able to add and multiply two sparse matrices in time proportional to the total number of nonzeros (perhaps with an extra $\log n$ factor). Implement a class that supports the following API:

operation	*description*
`SparseMatrix()`	*a new sparse matrix*
`a[i][j] = v`	*set the element in row* `i` *and column* `j` *of* `a` *to* `v`
`a[i][j]`	*the element in row* `i` *and column* `j` *of* `a`
`a + b`	*matrix sum of* `a` *and* `b`
`a * b`	*matrix product of* `a` *and* `b`

API for a sparse matrix

4.4.75 *Mutable string.* Create a data type that supports the following API on a string. Use a BST to implement all operations in logarithmic time.

4.4.76 *Assignment statements.* Compose a program to parse and evaluate programs consisting of assignment and write statements with fully parenthesized arithmetic expressions (see PROGRAM 4.3.3). For example, given the input

```
A = 5
B = 10
C = A + B
D = C * C
write(D)
```

your program should write the value 225. Assume that all variables and values are floats. Use a symbol table to keep track of variable names.

4.4.77 *Codon usage table.* Compose a program that uses a symbol table to write summary statistics for each codon in a genome taken from standard input (frequency per thousand), like the following:

```
UUU 13.2  UCU 19.6  UAU 16.5  UGU 12.4
UUC 23.5  UCC 10.6  UAC 14.7  UGC  8.0
UUA  5.8  UCA 16.1  UAA  0.7  UGA  0.3
UUG 17.6  UCG 11.8  UAG  0.2  UGG  9.5
CUU 21.2  CCU 10.4  CAU 13.3  CGU 10.5
CUC 13.5  CCC  4.9  CAC  8.2  CGC  4.2
CUA  6.5  CCA 41.0  CAA 24.9  CGA 10.7
CUG 10.7  CCG 10.1  CAG 11.4  CGG  3.7
AUU 27.1  ACU 25.6  AAU 27.2  AGU 11.9
AUC 23.3  ACC 13.3  AAC 21.0  AGC  6.8
AUA  5.9  ACA 17.1  AAA 32.7  AGA 14.2
AUG 22.3  ACG  9.2  AAG 23.9  AGG  2.8
GUU 25.7  GCU 24.2  GAU 49.4  GGU 11.8
GUC 15.3  GCC 12.6  GAC 22.1  GGC  7.0
GUA  8.7  GCA 16.8  GAA 39.8  GGA 47.2
```

4.5 Case Study: Small-World Phenomenon

THE MATHEMATICAL MODEL THAT WE USE for studying the nature of pairwise connections among entities is known as the *graph*. Graphs are important for studying the natural world and for helping us to better understand and refine the networks that we create. From models of the nervous system in neurobiology, to the study of the spread of infectious diseases in medical science, to the development of the telephone system, graphs have played a critical role in science and engineering over the past century, including the development of the Internet itself.

Programs in this section

Some graphs exhibit a specific property known as the *small-world phenomenon*. You may be familiar with this property, which is sometimes known as *six degrees of separation*. It is the basic idea that, even though each of us has relatively few acquaintances, there is a relatively short chain of acquaintances (the six degrees of separation) separating us from one another. This hypothesis was validated experimentally by Stanley Milgram in the 1960s and modeled mathematically by Duncan Watts and Stephen Strogatz in the 1990s. In recent years, the principle has proved important in a remarkable variety of applications. Scientists are interested in small-world graphs because they model natural phenomena, and engineers are interested in building networks that take advantage of the natural properties of small-world graphs.

In this section, we address basic computational questions surrounding the study of small-world graphs. Indeed, the simple question

Does a given graph exhibit the small-world phenomenon?

can present a significant computational burden. To address this question, we will consider a graph-processing data type and several useful graph-processing clients. In particular, we will examine a client for computing *shortest paths*, a computation that has a vast number of important applications in its own right.

A persistent theme of this section is that the algorithms and data structures that we have been studying play a central role in graph processing. Indeed, you will see that several of the fundamental data types introduced earlier in this chapter help us to develop elegant and efficient code for studying the properties of graphs.

Graphs We begin with some basic definitions. A *graph* is composed of a set of *vertices* and a set of *edges*. Each edge represents a connection between two vertices. Two vertices are *neighbors* if they are connected by an edge, and the *degree* of a vertex is its number of neighbors. Note that there is no relationship between a graph and the idea of a function graph (a plot of a function values) or the idea of graphics (drawings). We often visualize graphs by drawing labeled geometric shapes (vertices) connected by lines (edges), but it is always important to remember that it is the connections that are essential, not the way we depict them.

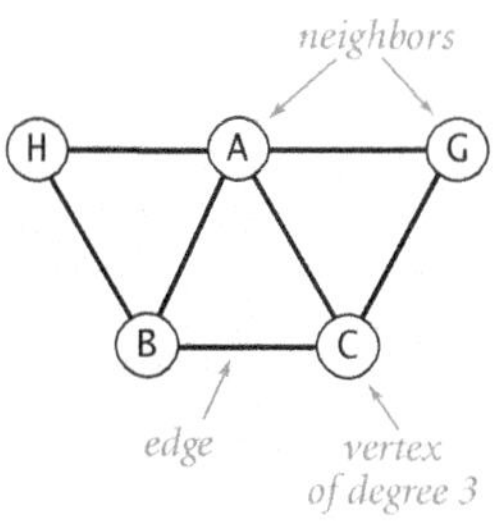

Graph terminology

The following list suggests the diverse range of systems where graphs are appropriate starting points for understanding structure.

Transportation systems. Train tracks connect stations, roads connect intersections, and airline routes connect airports, so all of these systems naturally admit a simple graph model. No doubt you have used applications that are based on such models when getting directions from an interactive mapping program or a GPS device, or using an online service to make travel reservations. What is the best way to get from here to there?

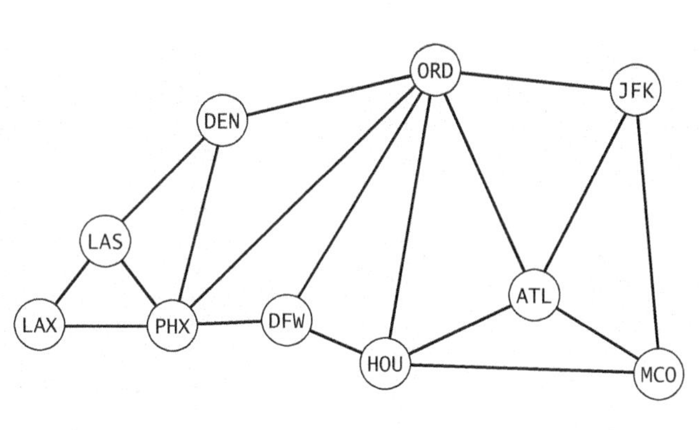

vertices	*edges*
JFK	JFK MCO
MCO	ORD DEN
ATL	ORD HOU
ORD	DFW PHX
HOU	JFK ATL
DFW	ORD DFW
PHX	ORD PHX
DEN	ATL HOU
LAX	DEN PHX
LAS	PHX LAX
	JFK ORD
	DEN LAS
	DFW HOU
	ORD ATL
	LAS LAX
	ATL MCO
	HOU MCO
	LAS PHX

Graph model of a transportation system

Human biology. Arteries and veins connect organs, synapses connect neurons, and joints connect bones, so an understanding of the human biology depends on understanding appropriate graph models. Perhaps the largest and most important such modeling challenge in this arena is the human brain. How do local connections among neurons translate to consciousness, memory, and intelligence?

Social networks. People have relationships with other people. From the study of infectious diseases to the study of political trends, graph models of these relationships are critical to our understanding of their implications. Hoes does information propagate in online networks?

Physical systems. Atoms connect to form molecules; molecules connect to form a material or a crystal; and particles are connected by mutual forces such as gravity or magnetism. Graph models are appropriate for studying the percolation problem that we considered in Section 2.4, the interacting charges that we considered in Section 3.1, and the n-body problem that we considered in Section 3.4. How do local interactions propagate through such systems as they evolve?

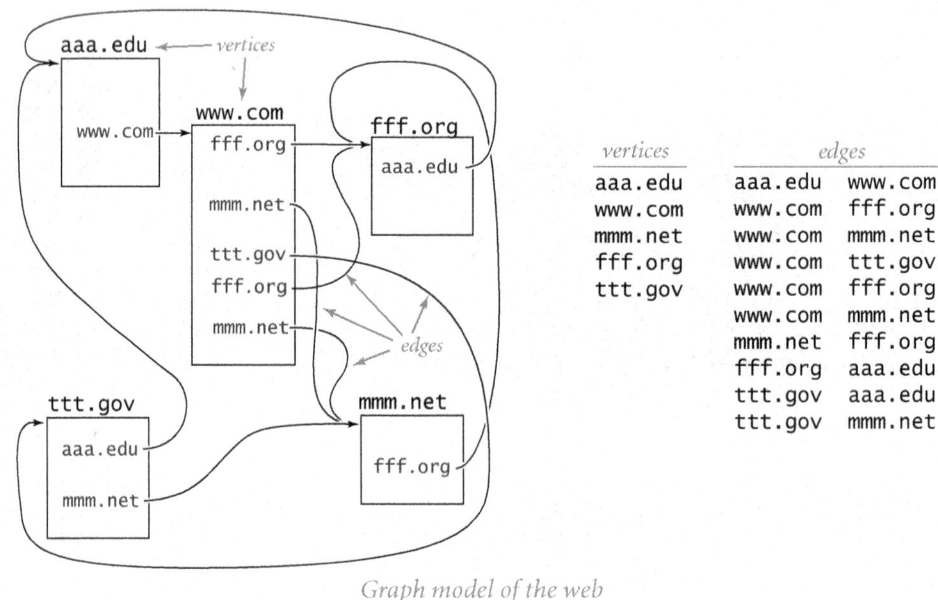

vertices	edges	
aaa.edu	aaa.edu	www.com
www.com	www.com	fff.org
mmm.net	www.com	mmm.net
fff.org	www.com	ttt.gov
ttt.gov	www.com	fff.org
	www.com	mmm.net
	mmm.net	fff.org
	fff.org	aaa.edu
	ttt.gov	aaa.edu
	ttt.gov	mmm.net

Graph model of the web

Communications systems. From electric circuits, to the telephone system, to the Internet, to wireless services, communications systems are all based on the idea of connecting devices. For at least the past century, graph models have played a critical role in the development of such systems. What is the best way to connect the devices?

Resource distribution. Power lines connect power stations and home electrical systems, pipes connect reservoirs and home plumbing, and truck routes connect warehouses and retail outlets. The study of effective and reliable means of distributing resources depends on accurate graph models. Where are the bottlenecks in a distribution system?

Mechanical systems. Trusses or steel beams connect joints in a bridge or a building. Graph models help us to design these systems and to understand their properties. Which forces must a joint or a beam withstand?

Software systems. Methods in one program module invoke methods in other modules. As we have seen throughout this book, understanding relationships of this sort is a key to success in software design. Which modules will be affected by a change in an API?

Financial systems. Transactions connect accounts, and accounts connect customers to financial institutions. These are but a few of the graph models that people use to study complex financial transactions, and to profit from better understanding them. Which transactions are routine and which are indicative of a significant event that might translate into profits?

system	*vertex*	*edge*
natural phenomena		
circulatory	organ	blood vessel
skeletal	joint	bone
nervous	neuron	synapse
social	person	relationship
epidemiological	person	infection
chemical	molecule	bond
n-body	particle	force
genetic	gene	mutation
biochemical	protein	interaction
engineered systems		
transportation	airport	route
	intersection	road
communication	telephone	wire
	computer	cable
	web page	link
distribution	power station home	power line
	reservoir home	pipe
	warehouse retail outlet	truck route
mechanical	joint	beam
software	module	call
financial	account	transaction

Typical graph models

Some of these graphs are models of natural phenomena, where our goal is to gain a better understanding of the natural world by developing simple models and then using them to formulate hypotheses that we can test. Other graph models are of networks that we engineer, where our goal is to build a better network or to better maintain a network by understanding its basic characteristics.

Graphs are useful models whether they are small or massive. A graph having just dozens of vertices and edges (for example, one modeling a chemical compound, where vertices are molecules and edges are bonds) is already a complicated combinatorial object because there are a huge number of possible graphs, so understanding the structures of the particular ones at hand is important. A graph having billions or trillions of vertices and edges (for example, a government database containing all phone calls or a graph model of the human nervous system) is vastly more complex, and presents significant computational challenges.

Processing graphs typically involves building a graph from information in a database and then answering questions about the graph. Beyond the application-specific questions in the examples just cited, we often need to ask basic questions about graphs. How many vertices and edges does the graph have? What are the neighbors of a given vertex? Some questions depend on an understanding of the structure of a graph. For example, a *path* in a graph is a sequence of vertices connected by edges. Is there a path connecting two given vertices? What is the shortest such path? What is the maximum length of a shortest path in the graph (the graph's *diameter*)? We have already seen in this book several examples of questions from scientific applications that are much more complicated than these. What is the probability that a random surfer will land on each vertex? What is the probability that a system represented by a certain graph percolates?

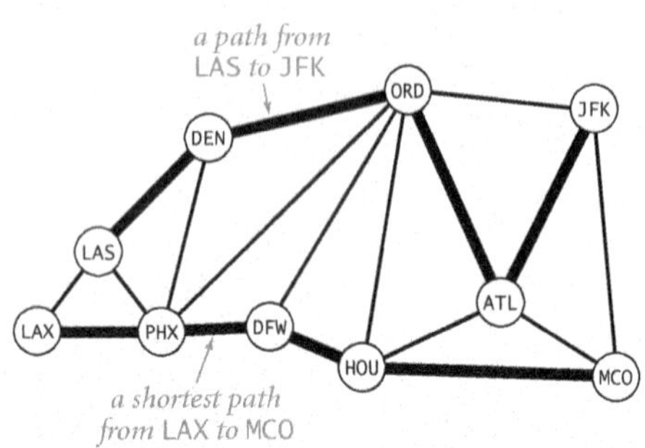

Paths in a graph

As you encounter complex systems in later courses, you are certain to encounter graphs in many different contexts. You may also study their properties in detail in later courses in mathematics, operations research, or computer science. Some graph-processing problems present insurmountable computational challenges; others can be solved with relative ease with data-type implementations of the sort we have been considering.

Graph data type Graph-processing algorithms generally first build an internal representation of a graph by adding edges, then process it by iterating through the vertices and through the edges that are adjacent to a vertex. The API at the bottom of this page supports such processing. As usual, this API reflects several design choices, each made from among various alternatives, some of which we now briefly discuss.

Undirected graph. Edges are *undirected*: an edge that connects `v` to `w` is the same as one that connects `w` to `v`. Our interest is in the connection, not the direction. Directed edges (for example, one-way streets in road maps) require a slightly different data type (see Exercise 4.5.38).

String vertex type. We assume that vertices are strings. We might use a more general vertex type, to allow clients to build graphs with objects of any comparable or hashable type. We leave such implementations to Exercise 4.5.10 because string vertices suffice for the applications that we consider here.

constant-time operations	*description*
`g.addEdge(v, w)`	*add edge* `v-w` *to* `g`
`g.countV()`	*the number of vertices in* `g`
`g.countE()`	*the number of edges in* `g`
`g.degree(v)`	*the number of neighbors of* `v` *in* `g`
`g.hasVertex(v)`	*is* `v` *a vertex in* `g`*?*
`g.hasEdge(v, w)`	*is* `v-w` *an edge in* `g`*?*
linear-time operations	
`Graph(file, delimiter)`	*a new graph from* `file` *using* `delimiter` (`file` *defaults to* `None`, *an empty graph*) (`delimiter` *defaults to whitespace*)
`g.vertices()`	*an iterable for the vertices of* `g`
`g.adjacentTo(v)`	*an iterable for the neighbors of vertex* `v` *in* `g`
`str(g)`	*string representation of* `g`

Note: Space used must be linear in the number of vertices plus the number of edges.

API for a `Graph` *data type*

Implicit vertex creation. When an object is used as an argument to `addEdge()`, we assume that it is a (string) vertex name. If no edge using that name has yet been added, our implementation creates a vertex with that name. The alternative design of having an `addVertex()` method requires more client code (to create the vertices) and more cumbersome implementation code (to check that edges connect vertices that have previously been created).

Self-loops and parallel edges. Although the API does not explicitly address the issue, we assume that implementations *do* allow self-loops (edges connecting a vertex to itself) but *do not* allow parallel edges (two copies of the same edge). Checking for self-loops and parallel edges is easy; our choice is to omit both checks.

Client query methods. We also include the methods `countV()` and `countE()` in our API to provide to the client the number of vertices and edges in the graph. Similarly, the methods `degree()`, `hasVertex()`, and `hasEdge()` are useful in client code. All of these implementations are constant-time one-liners.

None of these design decisions is sacrosanct; they are simply the choices that we have made for the code in this book. Some other choices might be appropriate in various situations, and some decisions are still left to implementations. It is wise to carefully consider the choices that you make for design decisions like this *and to be prepared to defend them.*

Program 4.5.1 (`graph.py`) implements this API. Its internal representation is a *symbol table of sets*: the keys are vertices and the values are the sets of neighbors—the vertices adjacent to the key. A small example is illustrated at right. To implement this representation, we use the two built-in data types `dict` and `set` that we introduced in Section 4.4. This choice leads to three important properties:

- Clients can efficiently iterate over the graph vertices.
- Clients can efficiently iterate over a vertex's neighbors.
- Space used is proportional to the number of vertices plus the number of edges.

These properties follow from basic properties of `dict` and `set`. As you will see, the two iterators are at the heart of graph processing.

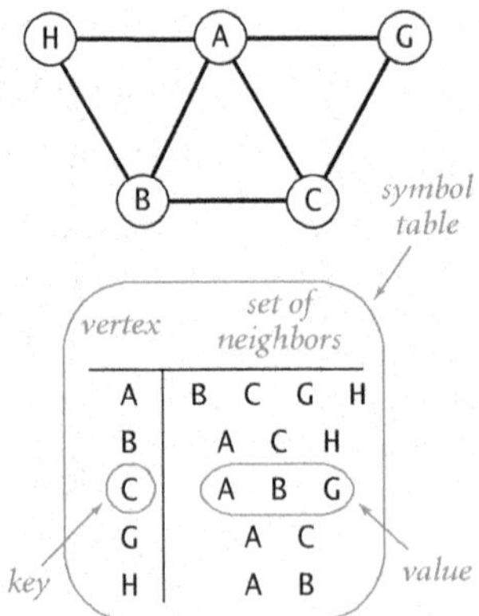

Symbol-table-of-sets graph representation

Program 4.5.1 Graph data type (graph.py)

```
import sys
import stdio
from instream import InStream

class Graph:
    # See text for __str__() and __init__()

    def addEdge(self, v, w):
        if not self.hasVertex(v): self._adj[v] = set()
        if not self.hasVertex(w): self._adj[w] = set()
        if not self.hasEdge(v, w):
            self._e += 1
            self._adj[v].add(w)
            self._adj[w].add(v)

    def adjacentTo(self, v): return iter(self._adj[v])
    def vertices(self):      return iter(self._adj)
    def hasVertex(self, v):  return v in self._adj
    def hasEdge(self, v, w): return w in self._adj[v]
    def countV(self):        return len(self._adj)
    def countE(self):        return self._e
    def degree(self, v):     return len(self._adj[v])

def main():
    file = sys.argv[1]
    graph = Graph(file)
    stdio.writeln(graph)
if __name__ == '__main__': main()
```

instance variables	
`_e`	*# of edges*
`_adj`	*adjacency lists*

This implementation uses the built-in types `dict` and `set` (see Section 4.4) to implement the graph data type. Clients can build graphs by adding edges one at a time or by reading from a file; they can process graphs by iterating over the set of all vertices or over the set of vertices adjacent to a given vertex. The test client builds a graph from the file specified on the command line.

```
% more tinygraph.txt
A B
A C
C G
A G
H A
B C
B H
```

```
% python graph.py tinygraph.txt
A  B C G H
B  A C H
C  A B G
G  A C
H  A B
```

A natural way to write a Graph is to put the vertices one per line, each followed by a list of its immediate neighbors. Accordingly, we support the built-in function str() by implementing __str__() as follows:

```
def __str__(self):
    s = ''
    for v in self.vertices():
        s += v + '  '
        for w in self.adjacentTo(v):
            s += w + ' '
        s += '\n'
    return s
```

The resulting string includes two representations of each edge, one for the case in which we discover that w is a neighbor of v and one for the case in which we discover that v is a neighbor of w. Many graph algorithms are based on this basic paradigm of processing each edge in the graph (twice). This implementation is intended for use only for small graphs, as the running time is quadratic in the string length on some systems (see Exercise 4.5.3).

The output format for str() also defines a reasonable input file format. The __init__() method supports creating a graph from a file in this format (each line is a vertex name followed by the names of neighbors of that vertex, separated by whitespace). For flexibility, we allow for the use of delimiters besides whitespace (so that, for example, vertex names may contain spaces), as follows:

```
def __init__(self, filename=None, delimiter=None):
    self._e = 0
    self._adj = dict()
    if filename is not None:
        instream = InStream(filename)
        while instream.hasNextLine():
            line = instream.readLine()
            names = line.split(delimiter)
            for i in range(1, len(names)):
                self.addEdge(names[0], names[i])
```

Note that the constructor (with the default whitespace delimiter) works properly even when the input is a list of edges, one per line, as in the test client for Program

4.5.1. Also, the constructor, with the default file name and delimiter, creates an empty graph. Adding `__init__()` and `__str__()` to `Graph` provides a complete data type suitable for a broad variety of applications, as we will now see.

Graph client example As a first graph-processing client, we consider an example of social relationships—one that is certainly familiar to you and for which extensive data is readily available.

On the booksite you can find the file `movies.txt` (and many similar *movie-cast files*), which contains a list of movies and the performers who appeared in them. Each line gives the name of a movie followed by the cast (a list of the names of the performers who appeared in that movie). Since names have spaces and commas in them, we use the `'/'` character as a delimiter. Now you can see why we provided graph clients with a way to specify the delimiter.

If you study `movies.txt`, you will notice a number of characteristics that, though minor, need attention when working with the database:

- Cast lists are not in alphabetical order.
- Movie titles and performer names are Unicode strings.
- Movies have the year in parentheses after the title.
- Multiple performers with the same name are differentiated by Roman numerals within parentheses.

Depending on your terminal and operating system settings, special characters may be replaced by blanks or question marks. These types of anomalies are common when working with large amounts of real-world data. If you experience problems, consult the booksite for details on how to configure your environment to work with Unicode characters properly.

```
% more movies.txt
...
Tin Men (1987)/DeBoy, David/Blumenfeld, Alan/... /Geppi, Cindy/Hershey, Barbara
Tirez sur le pianiste (1960)/Heymann, Claude/.../Berger, Nicole (I)
Titanic (1997)/Mazin, Stan/...DiCaprio, Leonardo/.../Winslet, Kate/...
Titus (1999)/Weisskopf, Hermann/Rhys, Matthew/.../McEwan, Geraldine
To Be or Not to Be (1942)/Verebes, Ernö (I)/.../Lombard, Carole (I)
To Be or Not to Be (1983)/.../Brooks, Mel (I)/.../Bancroft, Anne/...
To Catch a Thief (1955)/París, Manuel/.../Grant, Cary/.../Kelly, Grace/...
To Die For (1995)/Smith, Kurtwood/.../Kidman, Nicole/.../ Tucci, Maria
...
```

Movie database example

Using `Graph`, we can compose a simple and convenient client for extracting information from `movies.txt`. We begin by building a `Graph` to better structure the information. What should the vertices and edges model? Should the vertices be movies, with edges connecting two movies if a performer has appeared in both? Should the vertices be performers, with edges connecting two performers if both have appeared in the same movie? These choices are both plausible, but which should we use? This decision affects both the client and the implementation code. Another way to proceed (which we choose because it leads to simple implementation code) is to have vertices for *both* the movies and the performers, with an edge connecting each movie to each performer in that movie. As you will see, programs that process this graph can answer a great variety of interesting questions for us.

PROGRAM 4.5.2 (`invert.py`) is a first example. It is a `Graph` client that takes a query, such as the name of a movie, and writes the list of performers who appear in that movie.

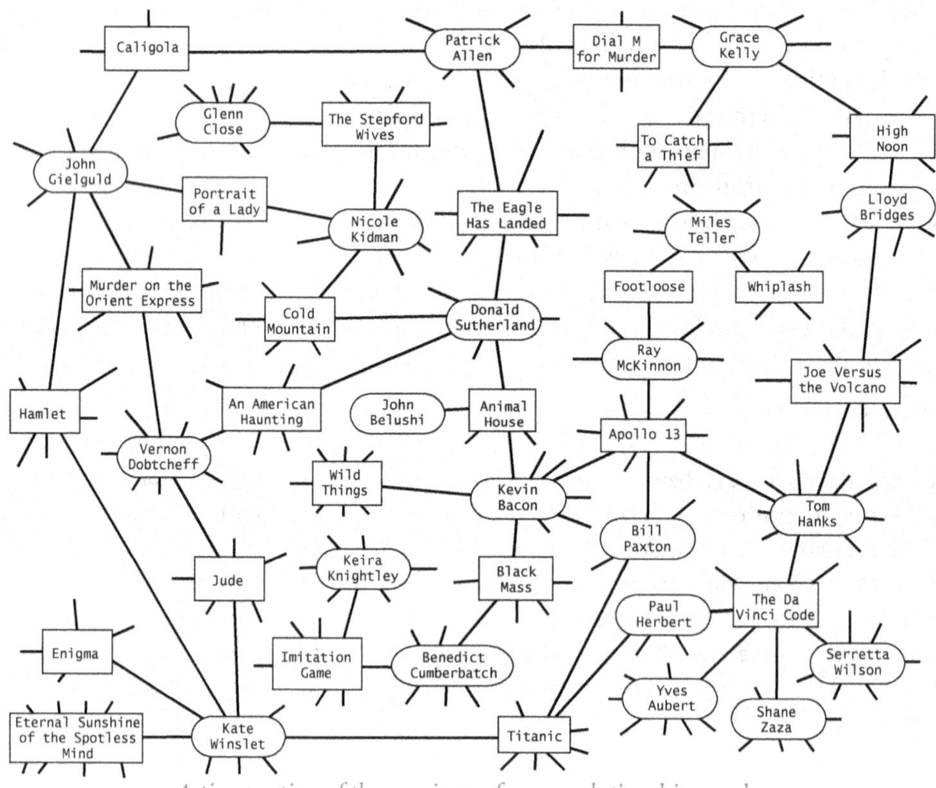

A tiny portion of the movie–performer relationship graph

Program 4.5.2 Using a graph to invert an index (invert.py)

```
import sys
import stdio
from graph import Graph

file = sys.argv[1]
delimiter = sys.argv[2]
graph = Graph(file, delimiter)

while stdio.hasNextLine():
    v = stdio.readLine()
    if graph.hasVertex(v):
        for w in graph.adjacentTo(v):
            stdio.writeln('  ' + w)
```

file	*input file*
delimiter	*vertex delimiter*
graph	*graph*
v	*query*
w	*neighbor of* v

This Graph client takes the name of a graph file and a delimiter as command-line arguments, builds a graph from the file, and then repeatedly reads a vertex name from standard input and writes the neighbors of that vertex. When the file is a movie-cast file (such as movies.txt) index, it creates a bipartite graph and amounts to an interactive inverted index.

```
% python invert.py tinygraph.txt " "
C
  A
  B
  G
A
  B
  C
  G
  H
```

```
% python invert.py movies.txt "/"
Da Vinci Code, The (2006)
  Fosh, Christopher
  Sciarappa, Fausto Maria
  Zaza, Shane
  L'Abidine, Dhaffer
  Bettany, Paul
  ...
Bacon, Kevin
  Murder in the First (1995)
  JFK (1991)
  Novocaine (2001)
  In the Cut (2003)
  Where the Truth Lies (2005)
  ...
```

Typing a movie name and getting its cast does not entail much more than regurgitating the corresponding line in `movies.txt`. (Note that the cast list appears in arbitrary order because we use a `set` to represent each adjacency list.) A more interesting feature of `invert.py` is that you can type the name of a *performer* and get the list of *movies* in which that performer has appeared. Why does this work? Even though the database seems to connect movies to performers and not the other way around, the edges in the graph are *connections* that also connect performers to movies.

A graph in which connections all connect one kind of vertex to another kind of vertex is known as a *bipartite* graph. As this example illustrates, bipartite graphs have many natural properties that we can often exploit in interesting ways.

As we saw at the beginning of SECTION 4.4, the indexing paradigm is general and very familiar. It is worth reflecting on the fact that building a bipartite graph provides a simple way to automatically invert *any* index! The `movies.txt` database is indexed by movie, but we can query it by performer. You could use `invert.py` in precisely the same way to write the index words appearing on a given page or the codons corresponding to a given amino acid (see the example shown at right), or to invert any of the other indices discussed at the beginning of SECTION 4.2. Since `invert.py` takes the delimiter as a command-line argument, you can use it to create an interactive inverted index for a `.csv` file or a test file with space delimiters.

```
% more amino.csv
TTT,Phe,F,Phenylalanine
TTC,Phe,F,Phenylalanine
TTA,Leu,L,Leucine
TTG,Leu,L,Leucine
TCT,Ser,S,Serine
TCC,Ser,S,Serine
TCA,Ser,S,Serine
TCG,Ser,S,Serine
TAT,Tyr,Y,Tyrosine
...
GGA,Gly,G,Glycine
GGG,Gly,G,Glycine

% python invert.py amino.csv ","
TTA
  Lue
  L
  Leucine
Serine
  TCT
  TCC
  TCA
  TCG
```

Inverting an index

This inverted-index functionality is a direct benefit of the graph *data structure*. Next, we examine some of the added benefits to be derived from *algorithms* that process the data structure.

Shortest paths in graphs Given two vertices in a graph, a *path* is a sequence of vertices connected by edges. A *shortest path* is one with the minimal number of edges over all such paths (there may be multiple shortest paths). Finding a shortest path connecting two vertices in a graph is a fundamental problem in computer science. Shortest paths have been famously and successfully applied to solve large-scale problems in a broad variety of applications, from routing the Internet to financial arbitrage transactions to studying the dynamics of neurons in the brain.

As an example, imagine that you are a customer of an imaginary no-frills airline that serves a limited number of cities with a limited number of routes. Assume that best way to get from one place to another is to minimize your number of flight segments, because delays in transferring from one flight to another are likely to be lengthy (or perhaps the best thing to do is to consider paying more for a direct flight on another airline!). A shortest-path algorithm is just what you need to plan a trip. Such an application appeals to intuition in understanding the basic problem and our approach to solving it. After covering these topics in the context of this example, we will consider an application where the graph model is more abstract.

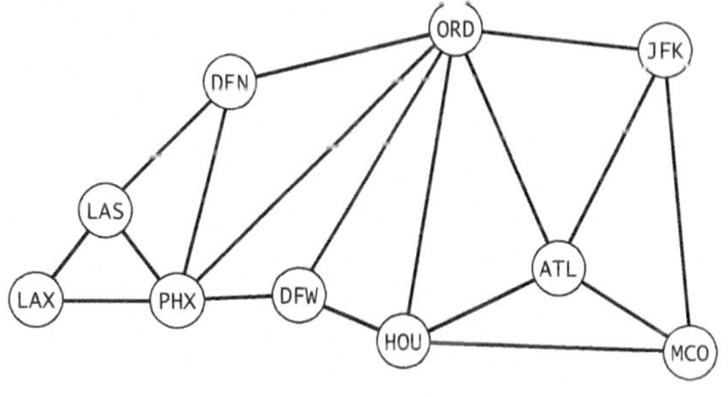

source	*destination*	*distance*	*a shortest path*
JFK	LAX	3	JFK-ORD-PHX-LAX
LAS	MCO	4	LAS-PHX-DFW-HOU-MCO
HOU	JFK	2	HOU-ATL-JFK

Examples of shortest paths in a graph

Depending on the application, clients have various needs with regard to shortest paths. Do we want the shortest path connecting two given vertices? Just the length of such a path? Will we have a large number of such queries? Is one particular vertex of interest? Our choice is to start with the following API:

operation	*description*
`PathFinder(graph, s)`	*find all shortest paths from* s *in* graph
`pf.distanceTo(v)`	*distance between* s *and* v
`pf.hasPathTo(v)`	*is there a path between* s *and* v*?*
`pf.pathTo(v)`	*an iterable for the path from* s *to* v

API for a `PathFinder` *data type*

In huge graphs or for huge numbers of queries, we have to pay particular attention to API design because the cost of computing paths might prove to be prohibitive. With this design, clients can create a `PathFinder` object for a given graph and a given vertex, and then use that object either to find the length of the shortest path or to iterate over the vertices on a shortest path to any other vertex in the graph. An implementation of these methods is known as a *single-source shortest-path algorithm.* A classic algorithm known as *breadth-first search* provides a direct and elegant solution where the constructor takes linear time, `distanceTo()` takes constant time, and `pathTo()` takes time proportional to the length of the path. Before examining our implementation, we will consider some clients.

Single-source client. Suppose that you have available to you the graph of vertices and connections for your no-frills airline's route map. Then, using your home city as a source, you can compose a client that writes your route anytime you want to go on a trip. PROGRAM 4.5.3 (`separation.py`) is a `PathFinder` client that provides this functionality for any graph. This sort of client is particularly useful in applications where we anticipate numerous queries from the same source. In this situation, the cost of building a `PathFinder` is amortized over the cost of all the queries. You are encouraged to explore the properties of shortest paths by running `PathFinder` on our sample input `routes.txt` or any input model that you choose. In fact, many people frequently use an algorithm like this, in the map application on their phone.

Degrees of separation. One of the classic applications of shortest-paths algorithms is to find the *degrees of separation* between individuals in a social network. To fix ideas, we discuss this application in terms of a recently popularized pastime known as the *Kevin Bacon game*, which uses the movie–performer graph that we just considered. Kevin Bacon is a prolific actor who has appeared in many movies. We assign every performer who has appeared in a movie a *Kevin Bacon number*: Bacon himself is 0, any performer who has been in the same cast as Bacon has a Kevin Bacon number of 1, any other performer (except Bacon) who has been in the same cast as a performer whose number is 1 has a Kevin Bacon number of 2, and so forth. For example, Meryl Streep has a Kevin Bacon number of 1 because she appeared in *The River Wild* with Kevin Bacon. Nicole Kidman's number is 2: although she did not appear in any movie with Kevin Bacon, she was in *Cold Mountain* with Donald Sutherland, and Sutherland appeared in *Animal House* with Kevin Bacon. Given the name of a performer, the simplest version of the game is to find some alternating sequence of movies and performers that leads back to Kevin Bacon. For ex-

Program 4.5.3 *Shortest-paths client* (separation.py)

```
import sys
import stdio
from graph import Graph
from pathfinder import PathFinder

file = sys.argv[1]
delimiter = sys.argv[2]
graph = Graph(file, delimiter)

s = sys.argv[3]
pf = PathFinder(graph, s)

while stdio.hasNextLine():
    t = stdio.readLine()
    if pf.hasPathTo(t):
        distance = pf.distanceTo(t)
        for v in pf.pathTo(t):
            stdio.writeln('   ' + v)
        stdio.writeln('distance: ' + str(distance))
```

`file`	*name of graph file*
`delimiter`	*delimiter of vertex names*
`graph`	*graph*
`pf`	`PathFinder` *from* `s`
`s`	*source vertex*
`t`	*destination vertex*
`v`	*vertex on path from* `s` *to* `t`

This `PathFinder` *test client takes a file name, a delimiter, and a source vertex as command-line arguments. It builds a Graph from the file, assuming that each line of the file specifies a vertex and a list of vertices connected to that vertex, separated by the delimiter. When you type a destination vertex* `t` *on standard input, you get the shortest path from the source to that destination.*

```
% more routes.txt
JFK MCO
ORD DEN
ORD HOU
DFW PHX
JFK ATL
ORD DFW
ORD PHX
ATL HOU
DEN PHX
...
```

```
% python separation.py routes.txt " " JFK
LAX
    JFK
    ORD
    PHX
    LAX
distance 3
DFW
    JFK
    ORD
    DFW
distance 2
```

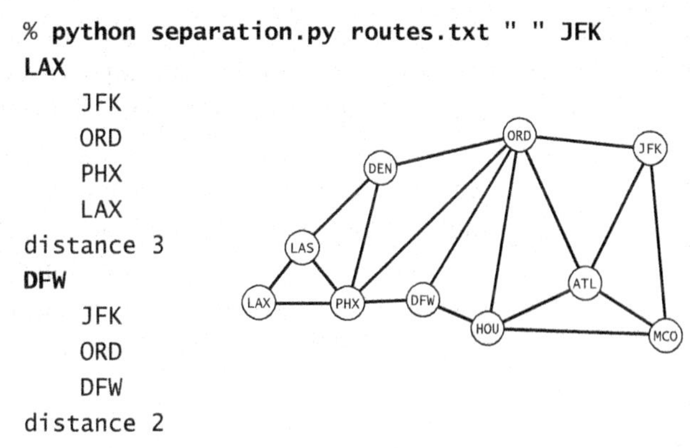

ample, a movie buff might know that Tom Hanks was in *Joe Versus the Volcano* with Lloyd Bridges, who was in *High Noon* with Grace Kelly, who was in *Dial M for Murder* with Patrick Allen, who was in *The Eagle Has Landed* with Donald Sutherland, who we know was in *Animal House* with Kevin Bacon. But this knowledge does not suffice to establish Tom Hanks's Bacon number (it is actually 1 because he was in *Apollo 13* with Kevin Bacon). You can see that the Kevin Bacon number is defined by counting the movies in a *shortest* such sequence, so it is hard to be sure whether someone wins the game without using a computer. Remarkably, `separation.py` (PROGRAM 4.5.3 is just the program you need to find a shortest path that establishes the Kevin Bacon number of any performer in `movies.txt`—the number is precisely half the distance. You might enjoy using this program, or extending it to answer some entertaining questions about the movie business or in one of many other domains. For example, mathematicians play this same game with the graph defined by paper co-authorship and their connection to Paul Erdös, a prolific 20th-century mathematician. Similarly, everyone in New Jersey seems to have a Bruce Springsteen number of 2, because everyone in the state seems to know someone who claims to know Bruce.

```
% python separation.py movies.txt "/" "Bacon, Kevin"
Kidman, Nicole
   Bacon, Kevin
   Animal House (1978)
   Sutherland, Donald (I)
   Cold Mountain (2003)
   Kidman, Nicole
distance 4
Hanks, Tom
   Bacon, Kevin
   Apollo 13 (1995)
   Hanks, Tom
distance 2
```

Degrees of separation from Kevin Bacon

Other clients. `PathFinder` is a versatile data type that can be put to many practical uses. For example, it is easy to develop a client that handles pairwise source–destination requests on standard input, by building a `PathFinder` for each vertex (see EXERCISE 4.5.11). Travel services use precisely this approach to handle requests at a very high service rate. Since this client builds a `PathFinder` for each vertex (each of which might consume space proportional to the number of vertices), space usage might be a limiting factor in using it for huge graphs. For an even more performance-critical application that is conceptually the same, consider an Internet router that has a graph of connections among machines available and must decide the best next stop for packets heading to a given destination. To do so, it can build a PathFinder with itself as the source, then send a packet heading to the first vertex in pf.pathTo(w)—that is, the next stop on the shortest path to w. Or a central authority might build a PathFinder for each of several dependent routers and use them to issue routing instructions. The ability to handle such requests at a high service rate is one of the prime responsibilities of Internet routers, and shortest-paths algorithms are a critical part of the process.

Shortest-path distances. We define the *distance* between two vertices to be the length of the shortest path between them. The first step in understanding breadth-first search is to consider the problem of computing distances between the source and each vertex (the implementation of distanceTo() in PathFinder). Our approach is to compute and store away all the distances in the constructor, and then just return the requested value when a client invokes distanceTo(). To associate an integer distance with each vertex name, we use a symbol table:

```
_distTo = dict()
```

The purpose of this symbol table is to associate with each vertex the length of the shortest path (the distance) between that vertex and s. We begin by giving s the distance 0 with _distTo[s] = 0, and we assign to s's neighbors the distance 1 with the following code:

```
for v in g.adjacentTo(s)
   self._distTo[v] = 1
```

But then what do we do? If we blindly set the distances to all the neighbors of each of those neighbors to 2, then not only would we face the prospect of unnecessarily setting many values twice (neighbors may have many common neighbors), but we would also set s's distance to 2 (it is a neighbor of each of its neighbors)—and we clearly do not want that outcome. The solution to these difficulties is simple:

- Consider the vertices in order of their distance from s.
- Ignore vertices whose distance to s is already known.

To organize the computation, we use a FIFO queue. Starting with s on the queue, we perform the following operations until the queue is empty:

- Dequeue a vertex v.
- Assign all of v's unknown neighbors a distance 1 greater than v's distance.
- Enqueue all of the unknown neighbors.

This method dequeues the vertices in nondecreasing order of their distance from the source s. Following a trace of this method on a sample graph will help persuade you that it is correct. Showing that this method labels each vertex v with its distance to s is an exercise in mathematical induction (see EXERCISE 4.5.13).

Shortest-paths tree. We need not only distances from the source, but also paths. To implement `pathTo()`, we use a subgraph known as the *shortest-paths tree*, defined as follows:

- Put the source vertex s at the root of the tree.
- Put vertex v's neighbors in the tree if they are added to the queue, with an edge connecting each to v.

Since we enqueue each vertex only once, this structure is a proper tree: it consists of a root (the source) connected to one subtree for each neighbor of the source. Studying such a tree, you can see immediately that the distance from each vertex to the root in the tree is the same as the shortest-path distance to the source in the graph. More importantly, each path in the tree is a shortest path in the graph. This observation is important because it gives us an easy way to provide clients with the shortest paths themselves (implement `pathTo()` in `PathFinder`).

First, we maintain a symbol table associating each vertex with the vertex one step nearer to the source on the shortest path:

```
_edgeTo = dict()
```

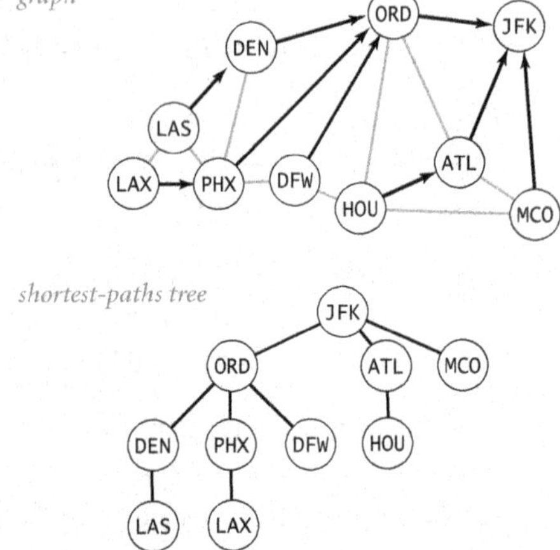

parent-link representation

w	ATL	DEN	DFW	HOU	JFK	LAS	LAX	MCO	ORD	PHX
prev[w]	JFK	ORF	ORD	ATL		DEN	PHX	JFK	JFK	ORD

Shortest-paths tree

To each vertex w, we want to associate the previous stop on the shortest path from the source to w. Augmenting the shortest-distances method to also compute this information is easy: when we enqueue w because we first discover it as a neighbor of v, we do so precisely because v is the previous stop on the shortest path from the source to w, so we can assign `_edgeTo[w] = v`. The `_prev` data structure is nothing more than a representation of the shortest-paths tree: it provides a link from each node to its parent in the tree. Then, to respond to a client request for the path from the source to `v` (a call to `pathTo(v)` in `PathFinder`), we follow these links *up* the tree from `v`, which traverses the path in reverse order. We collect the vertices in an array as we encounter them, then reverse the array, so the client gets the path from `s` to `v` when using the iterator returned from `pathTo()`.

Breadth-first search. Program 4.5.4 (`pathfinder.py`) is an implementation of the single-source shortest-paths API, based on the ideas just discussed. It maintains two symbol tables. One symbol table stores the distance between the source vertex and each vertex; the other symbol table stores the previous stop on a shortest path from the source vertex to each vertex. The constructor uses a queue to keep track of vertices that have been encountered (neighbors of vertices for which the shortest paths have been found but whose neighbors have not yet been examined). This process is known as *breadth-first search* (BFS) because it searches broadly in the graph.

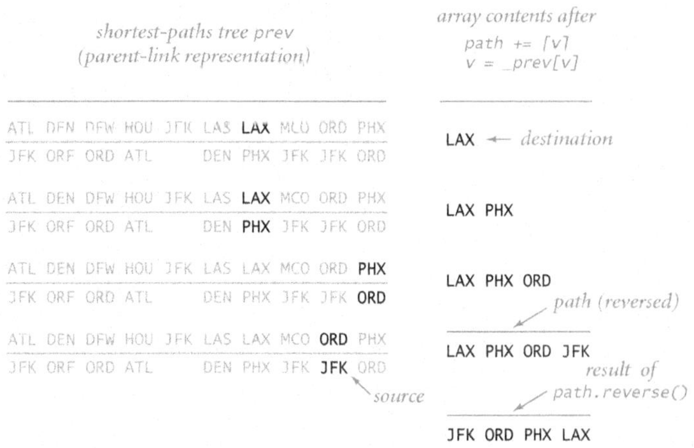

Recovering a path from the tree

By contrast, another important graph-search method known as *depth-first search* is based on a recursive method like the one we used for percolation in Program 2.4.6 and searches deeply into the graph. Depth-first search tends to find long paths; breadth-first search is guaranteed to find shortest paths.

Performance. The cost of graph-processing algorithms typically depends on two graph parameters: the number of vertices V and the number of edges E. For simplicity, we assume that there is a path between the source vertex and each other vertex. Then, as implemented in `PathFinder`, *the time required for breadth-first search is linear in the size of the input*—proportional to $E + V$—under suitable technical assumptions about the hash function. To convince yourself of this fact, first

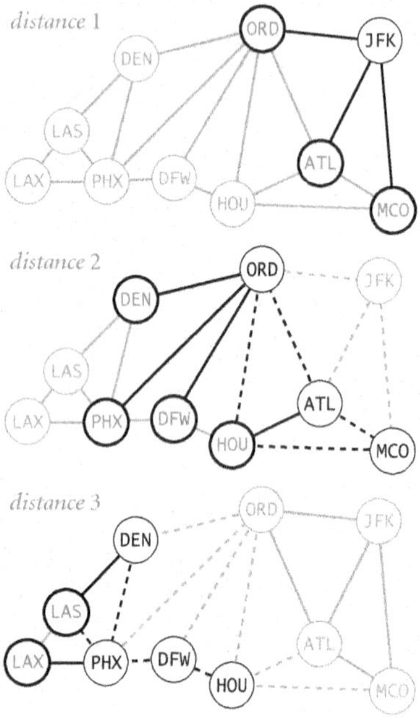

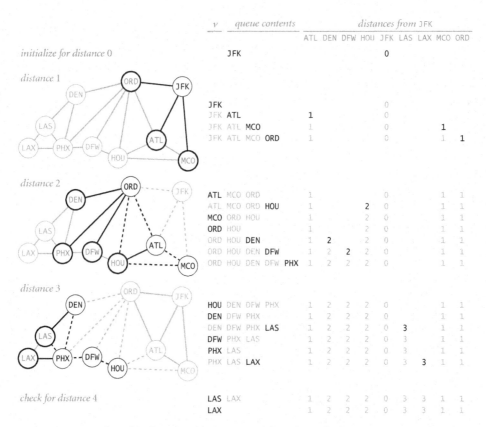

	v	*queue contents*	*distances from* JFK								
			ATL	DEN	DFW	HOU	JFK	LAS	LAX	MCO	ORD
initialize for distance 0		JFK					0				
distance 1	JFK						0				
	JFK	ATL	1				0				
	JFK	ATL MCO	1				0			1	
	JFK	ATL MCO ORD	1				0			1	1
distance 2	ATL	MCO ORD	1				0			1	1
	ATL	MCO ORD HOU	1			2	0			1	1
	MCO	ORD HOU	1			2	0			1	1
	ORD	HOU	1			2	0			1	1
	ORD	HOU DEN	1	2		2	0			1	1
	ORD	HOU DEN DFW	1	2	2	2	0			1	1
	ORD	HOU DEN DFW PHX	1	2	2	2	0			1	1
distance 3	HOU	DEN DFW PHX	1	2	2	2	0			1	1
	DEN	DFW PHX	1	2	2	2	0			1	1
	DEN	DFW PHX LAS	1	2	2	2	0	3		1	1
	DFW	PHX LAS	1	2	2	2	0	3		1	1
	PHX	LAS	1	2	2	2	0	3		1	1
	PHX	LAS LAX	1	2	2	2	0	3	3	1	1
check for distance 4	LAS	LAX	1	2	2	2	0	3	3	1	1
	LAX		1	2	2	2	0	3	3	1	1

Using breadth-first search to compute shortest-path distances in a graph

observe that the outer (`while`) loop iterates exactly V times, once for each vertex, because we are careful to ensure that a vertex is not enqueued more than once. Next, observe that the inner (`for`) loop iterates $2E$ times over all iterations, because it examines each edge exactly twice—once for each of the two vertices it connects. The body of the inner (`for`) loop requires at least one *search* operation (to determine if the vertex has been previously encountered) and perhaps one *get* and two *put* operations (to update the distance and path information) on symbol tables of size at most V. Thus, the overall running time is proportional to $E + V$ (under suitable technical assumptions about the hash function). If we were to use binary search trees instead of hash tables, then the overall running time would be linearithmic—proportional to $E \log V$.

Program 4.5.4 Shortest-paths implementation (pathfinder.py)

```
import stdio
import graph
from linkedqueue import Queue

class PathFinder:
    def __init__(self, graph, s):
        self._distTo = dict()
        self._edgeTo = dict()

        queue = Queue()
        queue.enqueue(s)
        self._distTo[s] = 0
        self._edgeTo[s] = None
        while not queue.isEmpty():
            v = queue.dequeue()
            for w in graph.adjacentTo(v):
                if w not in self._distTo:
                    queue.enqueue(w)
                    self._distTo[w] = 1 + self._distTo[v]
                    self._edgeTo[w] = v

    def distanceTo(self, v):
        return self._distTo[v]

    def hasPathTo(self, v):
        return v in self._distTo

    def pathTo(self, v):
        path = []
        while v is not None:
            path += [v]
            v = self._edgeTo[v]
        return reversed(path)
```

instance variables

_distTo	*distance to s*
_prevTo	*previous vertex on shortest path from s*

graph	*graph*
s	*source*
queue	*queue of vertices to visit*
v	*current vertex*
w	*neighbors of v*

This class allows clients to find (shortest) paths connecting a specified vertex to other vertices in a graph. See Program *4.5.3 and* Exercise *4.5.17 for sample clients.*

Adjacency-matrix representation. Without proper data structures, fast performance for graph-processing algorithms is sometimes not easy to achieve, and so should not be taken for granted. For example, another graph representation that programmers often implement, known as the *adjacency-matrix representation*, uses a symbol table to map vertex names to integers between 0 and $V-1$, then maintains a V-by-V array of booleans with `True` in the element in row `i` and column `j` (and, symmetrically, the element in row `j` and column `i`) if there is an edge connecting the vertex corresponding to `i` with the vertex corresponding to `j`, and `False` if there is no such edge. We have already used similar representations in this book, when studying the random-surfer model for ranking web pages in Section 1.6. The adjacency-matrix representation is simple, but infeasible for use with huge graphs—a graph with a million vertices would require an adjacency matrix with a *trillion* elements. Understanding this distinction for graph-processing problems makes the difference between solving a problem that arises in a practical situation and not being able to address it at all.

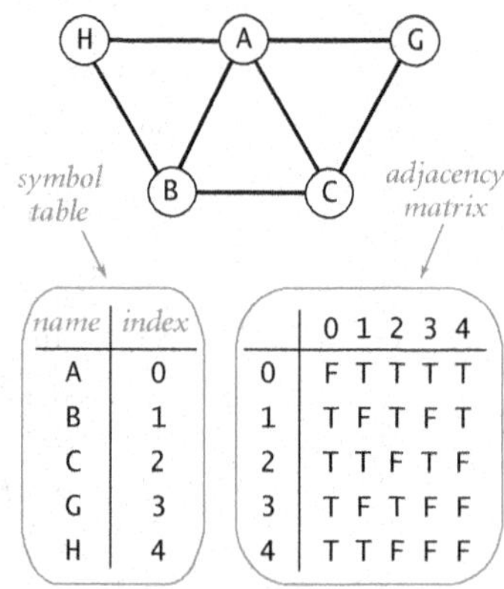

name	*index*
A	0
B	1
C	2
G	3
H	4

	0	1	2	3	4
0	F	T	T	T	T
1	T	F	T	F	T
2	T	T	F	T	F
3	T	F	T	F	F
4	T	T	F	F	F

Adjacency-matrix graph representation

Breadth-first search is a fundamental algorithm that you use in applications on your mobile device to find your way around an airline route map or a city subway or in numerous similar situations. As indicated by our degrees-of-separation example, it is used for countless other applications as well, from crawling the web or routing packets on the Internet, to studying infectious disease, models of the brain, or relationships among genomic sequences. Many of these applications involve huge graphs, so an efficient algorithm is absolutely essential.

An important generalization of the shortest-paths model is to associate a positive weight (which may represent distance or time) with each edge and seek to find a path that minimizes the sum of the edge weights. If you take later courses in algorithms or in operations research, you will learn a generalization of breadth-first search known as *Dijkstra's algorithm* that solves this problem in linearithmic time. When you get directions from a GPS device or a map application on your phone, Dijkstra's algorithm is the basis for solving the associated shortest-path problems. These important and omnipresent applications are just the tip of an iceberg, because graph models are much more general than maps.

Small-world graphs Scientists have identified a particularly interesting class of graphs that arise in numerous applications in the natural and social sciences. Small-world graphs are characterized by the following three properties:

- They are *sparse*: the number of vertices is much smaller than the number of edges.
- They have *short average path lengths*: if you pick two random vertices, the length of the shortest path between them is short.
- They exhibit *local clustering*: if two vertices are neighbors of a third vertex, then the two vertices are likely to be neighbors of each other.

We refer to graphs having these three properties collectively as exhibiting the *small-world phenomenon*. The term *small world* refers to the idea that the preponderance of vertices have both local clustering and short paths to other vertices. The modifier *phenomenon* refers to the unexpected fact that so many graphs that arise in practice are sparse, exhibit local clustering, and have short paths. Beyond the social-relationships applications just considered, small-world graphs have been used to study the marketing of products or ideas, the formation and spread of fame and fads, the analysis of the Internet, the construction of secure peer-to-peer networks, the development of routing algorithms and wireless networks, the design of electrical power grids, modeling information processing in the human brain, the study of phase transitions in oscillators, the spread of infectious viruses (in both living organisms and computers), and many other applications. Starting with the seminal work of Watts and Strogatz in the 1990s, an intensive amount of research has gone into quantifying the small-world phenomenon.

A key question in such research is the following: *Given a graph, how can we tell whether it is a small-world graph?* To answer this question, we begin by imposing the conditions that the graph is not small (say, 1,000 vertices or more) and that it is connected (there exists *some* path connecting each pair of vertices). Then, we need to settle on specific thresholds for each of the small-world properties:

- By *sparse*, we mean the average vertex degree is less than $20 \lg V$.
- By *short average path length*, we mean the average length of the shortest path between two vertices is less than $10 \lg V$.
- By *locally clustered*, we mean that a certain quantity known as the *clustering coefficient* should be greater than 10%.

The definition of locally clustered is a bit more complicated than the definitions of sparsity and average path length. Intuitively, the clustering coefficient of a vertex represents the probability that if you pick two of its neighbors at random, they will also be connected by an edge. More precisely, if a vertex has t neighbors, then there are $t(t-1)/2$ possible edges that connect those neighbors; its *local clustering coefficient* is the fraction of those edges that are in the graph (or 0 if the vertex has degree 0 or 1). The *clustering coefficient of a graph* is the average of the local clustering coefficients of its vertices. If that average is greater than 10%, we say that the graph is locally clustered. The diagram below calculates these three quantities for a tiny graph.

average vertex degree

vertex	degree
A	4
B	3
C	3
G	2
H	2
total	14

average degree = 14/5 = 2.8

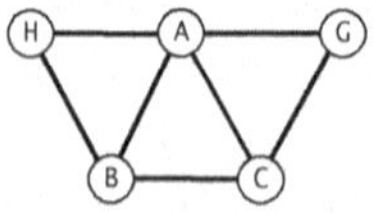

average path length

vertex pair	shortest path	length
A B	A-B	1
A C	A-C	1
A G	A-G	1
A H	A-H	1
B C	B-C	1
B G	B-A-G	2
B H	B-H	1
C G	C-G	1
C H	C-A-H	2
G H	G-A-H	2
	total	13

$\frac{\textit{total of lengths}}{\textit{number of pairs}} = 13/10 = 1.3$

cluster coefficient

vertex	degree	edges in neighborhood possible	actual
A	4	6	3
B	3	3	2
C	3	3	2
G	2	1	1
H	2	1	1

$\frac{3/6 + 2/3 + 2/3 + 1/1 + 1/1}{5} \approx .767$

Calculating small-world graph characteristics

To better familiarize you with these definitions, we next define some simple graph models, and consider whether they describe small-world graphs by checking whether they exhibit the three requisite properties.

Complete graphs. A ***complete graph*** with V vertices has $V\,(V-1)\,/\,2$ edges, one connecting each pair of vertices. Complete graphs are *not* small-world graphs. They have short average path length (every shortest path has length is 1) and they exhibit local clustering (the cluster coefficient is 1), but they are *not* sparse (the average vertex degree is $V-1$, which is much greater than 20 lg V for large V).

Ring graphs. A ***ring graph*** is a set of V vertices equally spaced on the circumference of a circle, with each vertex connected to its neighbor on either side. In a *k-ring graph*, each vertex is connected to its k nearest neighbors on either side.

The diagram at right illustrates a 2-ring graph with 16 vertices. Ring graphs are also *not* small-world graphs. For example, 2-ring graphs are sparse (every vertex has degree 4) and exhibit local clustering (the cluster coefficient is 1/2), but their average path length is not short (see Exercise 4.5.17).

Three graph models

Random graphs. The *Erdös-Renyi model* is a well studied model for generating random graphs. In this model, we build a *random graph* on V vertices by including each possible edge with probability p. Random graphs with a sufficient number of edges are very likely to be connected and have short average path lengths but they are *not* small-world graphs, because they are not locally clustered (see Exercise 4.5.43).

These examples illustrate that developing a graph model that satisfies all three properties simultaneously is a puzzling challenge. Take a moment to try to design a graph model that you think might do so. After you have thought about this problem, you will realize that you are likely to need a program to help with calculations. Also, you may agree that it is quite surprising that they are found so often in practice. Indeed, you might be wondering if *any* graph is a small-world graph!

Choosing 10% for the clustering threshold instead of some other fixed percentage is somewhat arbitrary, as is the choice of 20 lg V for the sparsity threshold and 10 lg V for the short paths threshold, but we often do not come close to these borderline values. For example, consider the *web graph*, which has a vertex for each web page and an edge connecting two web pages if they are connected by a link. Scientists estimate that the number of clicks to get from one web page to another is rarely more than about 30. Since there are billions of web pages, this estimate implies that the average length of a path between two vertices is very short, much lower than our 10 lg V threshold (which would be about 300 for 1 billion vertices).

model	sparse?	short paths?	locally clustered?
complete	○	●	●
2-ring	●	○	●
random	●	●	○

Small-world properties of graph models

Having settled on the definitions, testing whether a graph is a small-world graph can still

Program 4.5.5 Small-world test (smallworld.py)

```
from pathfinder import PathFinder

def averageDegree(graph):
    return 2.0 * graph.countE() / graph.countV()

def averagePathLength(graph):
    total = 0
    for v in graph.vertices():
        pf = PathFinder(graph, v)
        for w in graph.vertices():
            total += pf.distanceTo(w)
    return 1.0 * total / (graph.countV() * (graph.countV() - 1))

def clusteringCoefficient(graph):
    total = 0
    for v in graph.vertices():
        possible = graph.degree(v) * (graph.degree(v) - 1)
        actual = 0
        for u in graph.adjacentTo(v):
            for w in graph.adjacentTo(v):
                if graph.hasEdge(u, w):
                    actual += 1
        if possible > 0:
            total += 1.0 * actual / possible
    return total / graph.countV()

# See Exercise 4.5.21 for a test client.
```

This Graph and PathFinder client computes the values of various graph parameters to test whether the graph exhibits the small-world phenomenon.

```
% python smallworld.py tinygraph.txt " "
5 vertices, 7 edges
average degree         =   2.800
average path length    =   1.300
clustering coefficient =   0.767
```

be a significant computational burden. As you probably have suspected, the graph-processing data types that we have been considering provide precisely the tools that we need. PROGRAM 4.5.5 (`smallworld.py`) is a `Graph` and `PathFinder` client that implements these tests. Without the efficient data structures and algorithms that we have been considering, the cost of this computation would be prohibitive. Even so, for large graphs (such as `movies.txt`), we must resort to statistical sampling to estimate the average path length and the cluster coefficient in a reasonable amount of time (see EXERCISE 4.5.41) because the functions `averagePathLength()` and `clusteringCoefficient()` take quadratic time.

A classic small-world graph. Our movie–performer graph is not a small-world graph, because it is bipartite and therefore has a clustering coefficient of 0. Also, some pairs of performers are not connected to each other by any paths. However, the simpler *performer–performer* graph defined by connecting two performers by an edge if they appeared in the same movie is a classic example of a small-world graph (after discarding performers not connected to Kevin Bacon). The diagram below illustrates the movie–performer and performer–performer graphs associated with a tiny movie-cast file.

PROGRAM 4.5.6 (`performer.py`) is a script that creates a performer–performer graph from a file in our movie-cast input format. Recall that each line in a movie-cast file consists of a movie followed by all of the performers who appeared in that movie, delimited by slashes. The script connects all pairs of performers in that movie by adding an edge connecting each pair. Doing so for each movie in the input produces a graph that connects the performers, as desired.

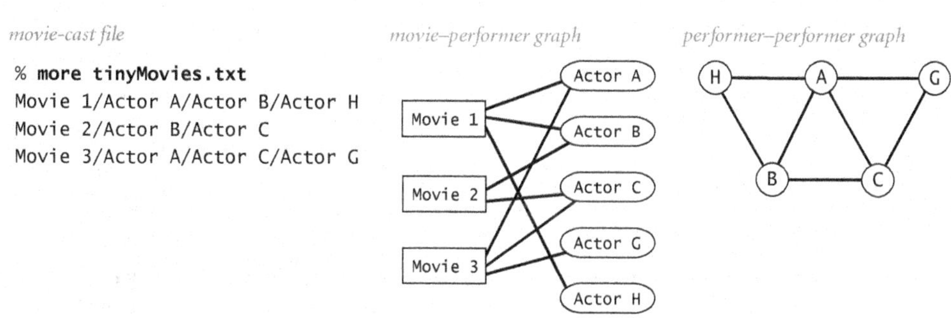

Two different graph representations of a movie-cast file

Program 4.5.6 Performer–performer graph (performer.py)

```
import sys
import stdio
import smallworld
from graph import Graph
from instream import InStream

file      = sys.argv[1]
delimiter = sys.argv[2]
graph = Graph()
instream = InStream(file)
while instream.hasNextLine():
    line = instream.readLine()
    names = line.split(delimiter)
    for i in range(1, len(names)):
        for j in range(i+1, len(names)):
            graph.addEdge(names[i], names[j])

degree  = smallworld.averageDegree(graph)
length  = smallworld.averagePathLength(graph)
cluster = smallworld.clusteringCoefficient(graph)
stdio.writef('number of vertices     = %d\n', graph.countV())
stdio.writef('average degree         = %7.3f\n', degree)
stdio.writef('average path length    = %7.3f\n', length)
stdio.writef('clustering coefficient = %7.3f\n', cluster)
```

This script is a `smallworld.py` client takes the name of a movie-cast file and a delimiter as command-line arguments and creates the associated performer–performer graph. It writes to standard output the number of vertices, the average degree, the average path length, and the clustering coefficient of this graph. It assumes that the performer–performer graph is connected (see Exercise 4.5.22) so that the average page length is defined.

```
% python performer.py tinymovies.txt "/"
number of vertices     = 5
average degree         =   2.800
average path length    =   1.300
clustering coefficient =   0.767
```

```
% python performer.py moviesg.txt "/"
number of vertices     = 19044
average degree         = 148.688
average path length    =   3.494
clustering coefficient =   0.911
```

Since a performer–performer graph typically has many more edges than the corresponding movie–performer graph, we will work for the moment with the smaller performer–performer graph derived from the file `moviesg.txt`, which contains 1,261 G-rated movies and 19,044 performers (all of which are connected to Kevin Bacon). Now, `performer.py` tells us that the performer–performer graph associated with `moviesg.txt` has 19,044 vertices and 1,415,808 edges, so the average vertex degree is 148.7 (about half of 20 lg V = 284.3), which means it is sparse; its average path length is 3.494 (much less than 10 lg V = 142.2), so it has short paths; and its clustering coefficient is 0.911, so it has local clustering. We have found a small-world graph! These calculations validate the hypothesis that social relationship graphs of this sort exhibit the small-world phenomenon. You are encouraged to find other real-world graphs and to test them with `smallworld.py`. You will find many suggestions in the exercises at the end of this section.

One approach to understanding something like the small-world phenomenon is to develop a mathematical model that we can use to test hypotheses and to make predictions. We conclude by returning to the problem of developing a graph model that can help us to better understand the small-world phenomenon. The trick to developing such a model is to combine two sparse graphs: a 2-ring graph (which has a high cluster coefficient) and a random graph (which has small average path length).

Ring graphs with random shortcuts. One of the most surprising facts to emerge from the work of Watts and Strogatz is that adding a relatively small number of random edges to a sparse graph with local clustering produces a small-world graph. To gain some insight into why this is the case, consider a 2-ring graph, where the diameter (length of path between farthest pair of vertices) is ~ $V/4$ (see the figure at right). Adding a single edge connecting antipodal vertices decreases the diameter to ~ $V/8$ (see Exercise 4.5.18). Adding $V/2$ *random* "shortcut" edges to a 2-ring graph is extremely likely to significantly lower the average path length, making it logarithmic (see Exercise 4.5.25). Moreover, it does so while increasing the average degree by only 1 and without lowering the cluster coefficient much below 1/2. That is, a 2-ring graph with $V/2$ random shortcut edges is extremely likely to be a small-world graph!

2-ring with antipodal edge

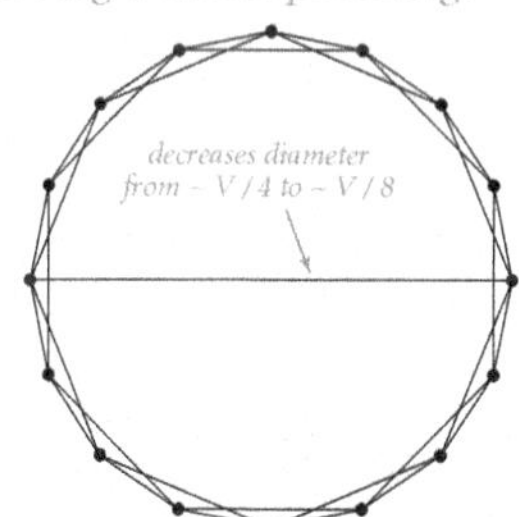

2-ring with random shortcuts

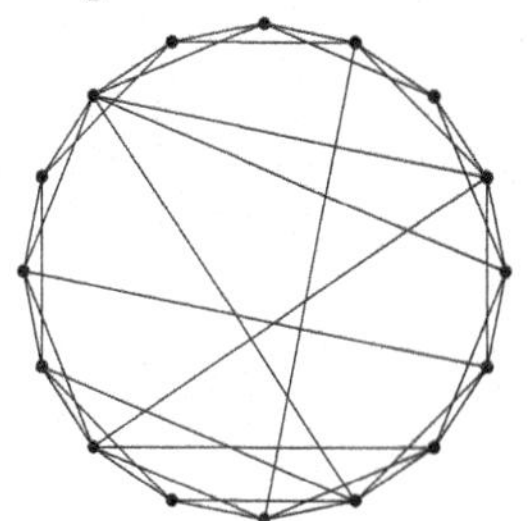

A new graph model

GENERATORS THAT CREATE GRAPHS DRAWN FROM such models are simple to develop, and we can use `smallworld.py` to determine whether the graphs exhibit the small-world phenomenon (see EXERCISE 4.5.22). We also can verify the analytic results that we derived for simple graphs such as `tinygraph.txt`, complete graphs, and ring graphs. As with most scientific research, new questions arise as quickly as we answer old ones. How many random shortcuts do we need to add to get a short average path length? What is the average path length and the clustering coefficient in a random connected graph? Which other graph models might be appropriate for study? How many samples do we need to accurately estimate the clustering coefficient or the average path length in a huge graph? You can find in the exercises many suggestions for addressing such questions and for further investigations of the small-world phenomenon. With the basic tools and the approach to programming developed in this book, you are well equipped to address this and many other scientific questions.

model	*average degree*	*average path length*	*clustering coefficient*
complete	999 ○	1 ●	1.0 ●
2-ring	4 ●	125.38 ○	0.5 ●
random connected graph with p = 10/V	10 ●	3.26 ●	0.010 ○
2-ring with V/2 random shortcuts	5 ●	5.71 ●	0.343 ●

Small-world parameters for various 1,000-vertex graphs

Lessons This case study illustrates the importance of algorithms and data structures in scientific research. It also reinforces several of the lessons that we have learned throughout this book, which are worth repeating.

Carefully design your data type. One of our most persistent messages throughout this book is that effective programming is based on a precise understanding of the possible set of data-type values and the operations on them. Using a modern object-oriented programming language such as Python provides a path to this understanding because we design, build, and use our own data types. Our `Graph` data type is a fundamental one, the product of many iterations and experience with the design choices that we have discussed. The clarity and simplicity of our client code are testimony to the value of taking seriously the design and implementation of basic data types in any program.

Develop code incrementally. As with all of our other case studies, we build software one module at a time, testing and learning about each module before moving to the next.

Solve problems that you understand before addressing the unknown. Our shortest-paths example involving air routes between a few cities is a simple one that is easy to understand. It is just complicated enough to hold our interest while debugging and following through a trace, but not so complicated as to make these tasks unnecessarily laborious.

Keep testing and check results. When working with complex programs that process huge amounts of data, you cannot be too careful in checking your results. Use common sense to evaluate every bit of output that your program produces. Novice programmers have an optimistic mindset ("If the program produces an answer, it must be correct"); experienced programmers know that a pessimistic mindset ("There must be something wrong with this result") is far better.

Use real-world data. The `movies.txt` file from the *Internet Movie Database* is just one example of the data files that are now omnipresent on the web. In past years, such data was often cloaked behind private or parochial formats, but most people are now realizing that simple text formats are much preferred. The various methods in Python's `str` data type make it easy to work with real data, which is the best way to formulate hypotheses about real-world phenomena. Start working with small files in the real-world format, so that you can test and learn about performance before attacking huge files.

Reuse software. Another of our most persistent messages is that effective programming is based on an understanding of the fundamental data types available for our use, so that we do not have to rewrite code for basic functions. Our use of `dict` and `set` in `Graph` is a prime example—most programmers still use lower-level representations and implementations that use linked lists or arrays for graphs, which means, inevitably, that they are recomposing code for simple operations such as maintaining and traversing linked lists. Our shortest-paths class `PathFinder` uses `dict`, `list`, `Graph`, and `Queue`—an all-star lineup of fundamental data structures.

Performance matters. Without good algorithms and data structures, many of the problems that we have addressed in this chapter would go unsolved, because naïve methods require an impossible amount of time or space. Maintaining an awareness of the approximate resource needs of our programs is essential.

THIS CASE STUDY IS AN APPROPRIATE place to end the book because the programs that we have considered are a starting point, not a complete study. This book is a starting point, too, for your further study in science, mathematics, or engineering. The approach to programming and the tools that you have learned here should prepare you well for addressing any computational problem whatsoever.

Q&A

Q. How many different graphs are there with V given vertices?

A. With no self-loops or parallel edges, there are $V(V-1)/2$ possible edges, each of which can be present or not present, so the grand total is $2^{V(V-1)/2}$. The number grows to be huge quite quickly, as shown in the following table:

V	1	2	3	4	5	6	7	8	9
$2^{V(V-1)/2}$	1	2	8	64	1,024	32,768	2,097,152	268,435,456	68,719,476,736

These huge numbers provide some insight into the complexities of social relationships. For example, if you just consider the next nine people that you see on the street, there are over 68 *trillion* mutual-acquaintance possibilities!

Q. Can a graph have a vertex that is not connected to any other vertex by an edge?

A. Good question. Such vertices are known as *isolated vertices*. Our implementation disallows them. Another implementation might choose to allow isolated vertices by including an explicit `addVertex()` method for the *add a vertex* operation.

Q. Why do the `countV()` and `countE()` query methods need to have constant-time implementations. Won't most clients would call such methods only once?

A. It might seem so, but code like this

```
while i < g.countE():
    ...
    i += 1
```

would take quadratic time if you were to use a lazy implementation that counts the edges instead of maintaining an instance variable with the number of edges.

Q. Why are `Graph` and `PathFinder` in separate classes? Wouldn't it make more sense to include the `PathFinder` methods in the `Graph` API?

A. Finding shortest paths is just one of many graph-processing algorithms. It would be poor software design to include all of them in a single interface. Please reread the discussion of wide interfaces in SECTION 3.3.

Exercises

4.5.1 Find the performer in `movies.txt` who has appeared in the most movies.

4.5.2 Modify the `__str__()` method in `Graph` so that it returns the vertices in sorted order (assuming the vertices are comparable). *Hint*: Use the built-in `sorted()` function.

4.5.3 Modify the `__str__()` method in `Graph` so that it runs in time linear in the number of vertices and the number of edges in the worst case. *Hint*: Use the `join()` method in the `str` data type. (See Exercise 4.1.13.)

4.5.4 Add to `Graph` a method `copy()` that creates and return a new, independent copy of the graph. Any future changes to the original graph should not affect the newly created graph (and vice versa!).

4.5.5 Compose a version of `Graph` that supports explicit vertex creation and allows self-loops, parallel edges, and *isolated vertices* (vertices of degree 0).

4.5.6 Add to `Graph` a method `removeEdge()` that takes two string arguments and deletes the specified edge from the graph, if present.

4.5.7 Add to `Graph` a method `subgraph()` that takes a `set` of strings as an argument and returns the *induced subgraph* (the graph consisting of only those vertices and only those edges from the original graph that connect any two of them).

4.5.8 Describe the advantages and disadvantages of using an array or a linked list to represent the neighbors of a vertex instead of using a `set`.

4.5.9 Compose a `Graph` client that reads a `Graph` from a file, then writes the edges in the graph, one per line.

4.5.10 Modify `Graph` so that it supports vertices of any hashable type.

4.5.11 Implement a `PathFinder` client `allshortestpaths.py` that takes the name of a graph file and a delimiter as command-line arguments, builds a `PathFinder` for each vertex, and then repeatedly takes from standard input the names of two vertices (on one line, separated by the delimiter) and writes the shortest path connecting them. *Note*: For `movies.txt`, the vertex names may both be performers, both be movies, or be a performer and a movie.

4.5.12 *True or false*: At some point during breadth-first search, the queue can contain two vertices, one whose distance from the source is 7 and one whose distance from the source is 9.

Solution: False. The queue can contain vertices of at most two distinct distances d and $d+1$. Breadth-first search examines the vertices in increasing order of distance from the source. When examining a vertex at distance d, only vertices of distance $d+1$ can be enqueued.

4.5.13 Prove by induction on the set of vertices visited that `PathFinder` finds the shortest path distances from the source to each vertex.

4.5.14 Suppose you use a stack instead of a queue for breadth-first search in `PathFinder`. Does it still find a path? Does it still correctly compute shortest paths? In each case, prove that it does or give a counterexample.

4.5.15 Compose a program that plots average path length versus the number of random edges as random shortcuts are added to a 2-ring graph on 1,000 vertices.

4.5.16 Add an optional argument `k` to `clusterCoefficient()` in the module `smallworld.py` so that it computes a local cluster coefficient for the graph based on the total edges present and the total edges possible among the set of vertices within distance `k` of each vertex. Use the default value `k=1` so that your function produces results identical to the function with the same name in `smallworld.py`.

4.5.17 Show that the cluster coefficient in a k-ring graph is $(2k-2) / (2k-1)$. Derive a formula for the average path length in a k-ring graph on V vertices as a function of both V and k.

4.5.18 Show that the diameter in a 2-ring graph on V vertices is $\sim V/4$. Show that if you add one edge connecting two antipodal vertices, then the diameter decreases to $\sim V/8$.

4.5.19 Perform computational experiments to verify that the average path length in a ring graph on V vertices is $\sim$ 1/4 V. Repeat, but add one random edge to the ring graph and verify that the average path length decreases to $\sim$3/16 V.

4.5.20 Add to `smallworld.py` a function `isSmallWorld()` that takes a graph as an argument and returns `True` if the graph exhibits the small-world phenomenon (as defined by the specific thresholds given in the text) and `False` otherwise.

4.5.21 Implement a test client `main()` for `smallworld.py` (PROGRAM 4.5.5) that produces the output given in the sample runs. Your program should take the name of a graph file and a delimiter as command-line arguments; write the number of vertices and edges, the average degree, the average path length, and the clustering coefficient for the graph; and indicate whether the values are too large or too small for the graph to exhibit the small-world phenomenon.

4.5.22 Compose a program to generate random connected graphs and 2-ring graphs with random shortcuts. Using `smallworld.py`, generate 500 random graphs from both models (with 1,000 vertices each) and compute their average degree, average path length, and clustering coefficient. Compare your results to the corresponding values in the table on page 714.

4.5.23 Compose a `smallworld.py` and `Graph` client that generates k-ring graphs and tests whether they exhibit the small-world phenomenon (first do EXERCISE 4.5.20).

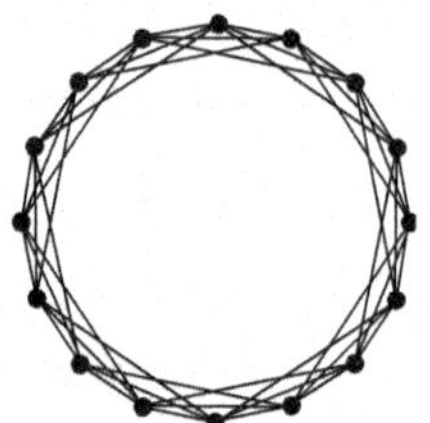

3-ring graph

4.5.24 In a *grid graph*, vertices are arranged in an n-by-n grid, with edges connecting each vertex to its neighbors above, below, to the left, and to the right in the grid. Compose a `smallworld.py` and `Graph` client that generates grid graphs and tests whether they exhibit the small-world phenomenon (first do EXERCISE 4.5.20).

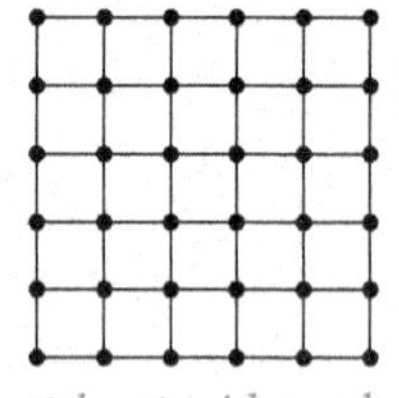

6-by-6 grid graph

4.5.25 Extend your solutions to the previous two exercises to also take a command-line argument m and to add m random edges to the graph. Experiment with your programs for graphs with approximately 1,000 vertices to find small-world graphs with relatively few edges.

4.5.26 Compose a `Graph` and `PathFinder` that takes the name of a movie-cast file and a delimiter as arguments and writes a new movie-cast file, but with all movies not connected to Kevin Bacon removed.

Creative Exercises

4.5.27 *Large Bacon numbers.* Find the performers in `movies.txt` with the largest, but finite, Kevin Bacon number.

4.5.28 *Histogram.* Compose a program `baconhistorgram.py` that writes a histogram of Kevin Bacon numbers, indicating how many performers from `movies.txt` have a Bacon number of 0, 1, 2, 3, ... Include a category for those who have an infinite number (not connected at all to Kevin Bacon).

4.5.29 *Performer–performer graph.* As mentioned in the text, an alternative way to compute Kevin Bacon numbers is to build a graph where there is a vertex for each performer (but not for each movie), and where two performers are connected by an edge if they appear in a movie together. Calculate Kevin Bacon numbers by running breadth-first search on the performer–performer graph. Compare the running time with the running time on `movies.txt`. Explain why this approach is so much slower. Also explain what you would need to do to include the movies along the path, as happens automatically with our implementation.

4.5.30 *Connected components.* A *connected component* in an undirected graph is a maximal set of vertices that are mutually reachable. Compose a data type `ConnectedComponents` that computes the connected components of a graph. Include a constructor that takes a `Graph` as an argument and computes all of the connected components using breadth-first search. Include a method `areConnected(v, w)` that returns `True` if `v` and `w` are in the same connected component and `False` otherwise. Also add a method `components()` that returns the number of connected components.

4.5.31 *Flood fill.* A `Picture` is a two-dimensional array of `Color` values (see Section 3.1) that represent pixels. A *blob* is a collection of neighboring pixels of the same color. Compose a `Graph` client whose constructor builds a grid graph (see Exercise 4.5.24) from a given image and supports the *flood fill* operation. Given pixel coordinates `col` and `row` and a color `c`, change the color of that pixel and all the pixels in the same blob to `c`.

4.5.32 *Word ladders.* Compose a program `wordladder.py` that takes two 5-letter strings from the command line, reads in a list of 5-letter words from standard input, and writes a shortest word ladder using the words on standard input connecting the two strings (if it exists). Two words can be connected in a word ladder chain if they differ in exactly one letter. As an example, the following word ladder connects `green` and `brown`:

```
green greet great groat groan grown brown
```

Compose a simple filter to get the 5-letter words from a system dictionary for standard input or download a list from the booksite. (This game, originally known as *doublet*, was invented by Lewis Carroll.)

4.5.33 *All paths.* Compose a `Graph` client class `AllPaths` whose constructor takes a `Graph` as an argument and supports operations to count or write all simple paths between two given vertices `s` and `t` in the graph. A *simple* path does not revisit any vertex more than once. In two-dimensional grids, such paths are referred to as self-avoiding walks (see SECTION 1.4). It is a fundamental problem in statistical physics and theoretical chemistry, for example, to model the spatial arrangement of linear polymer molecules in a solution. *Warning*: There might be exponentially many paths.

4.5.34 *Percolation threshold.* Develop a graph model for percolation, and compose a `Graph` client that performs the same computation as `percolation.py` (PROGRAM 2.4.6). Estimate the percolation threshold for triangular, square, and hexagonal grids.

4.5.35 *Subway graphs.* In the Tokyo subway system, routes are labeled by letters and stops by numbers, such as `G-8` or `A-3`. Stations allowing transfers are sets of stops. Find a Tokyo subway map on the web, develop a simple database format, and compose a `Graph` client that reads a file and can answer shortest-path queries for the Tokyo subway system. If you prefer, do the Paris subway system, where routes are sequences of names and transfers are possible when two stations have the same name.

4.5.36 *Center of the Hollywood universe.* We can measure how good a center Kevin Bacon is by computing each performer's *Hollywood number* or average path length. The Hollywood number of Kevin Bacon is the average Bacon number of all the performers (in its connected component). The Hollywood number of another performer is computed the same way, making that performer the source instead of Kevin Bacon. Compute Kevin Bacon's Hollywood number and find a performer with a better Hollywood number than Kevin Bacon. Find the performers (in the same connected component as Kevin Bacon) with the best and worst Hollywood numbers.

4.5.37 *Diameter.* The *eccentricity* of a vertex is the greatest distance between it and any other vertex. The *diameter* of a graph is the greatest distance between any two vertices (the maximum eccentricity of any vertex). Compose a `Graph` client `diameter.py` that can compute the eccentricity of a vertex and the diameter of a graph. Use it to find the diameter of the graph represented by `movies.txt`.

4.5.38 *Directed graphs.* Implement a `Digraph` data type that represents *directed* graphs, where the direction of edges is significant: `addEdge(v, w)` means to add an edge from `v` to `w` but *not* from `w` to `v`. Replace `adjacentTo()` with two methods: `adjacentFrom()`, to give the set of vertices having edges directed to them *from* the argument vertex, and `adjacentTo()`, to give the set of vertices having edges directed from them *to* the argument vertex. Explain how to modify `PathFinder` to find shortest paths in directed graphs.

4.5.39 *Random surfer.* Modify your `Digraph` class of the previous exercise to make a `MultiDigraph` class that allows parallel edges. For a test client, run a random surfer simulation that matches `randomsurfer.py` (Program 1.6.2).

4.5.40 *Transitive closure.* Compose a `Digraph` client class `TransitiveClosure` whose constructor takes a `Digraph` as an argument and whose method `isReachable(v, w)` returns `True` if `w` is reachable from `v` along a directed path in the digraph and `False` otherwise. *Hint*: Run breadth-first search from each vertex, as in `allshortestpaths.py` (Exercise 4.5.11).

4.5.41 *Statistical sampling.* Use statistical sampling to estimate the average path length and clustering coefficient of a graph. For example, to estimate the clustering coefficient, pick t random vertices and compute the average of the clustering coefficients of those vertices. The running time of your functions should be orders of magnitude faster than the corresponding functions from `smallworld.py`.

4.5.42 *Cover time.* A *random walk* in a connected undirected graph moves from a vertex to one of its neighbors, each chosen with equal probability. (This process is the random surfer analog for undirected graphs.) Write programs to run experiments that support the development of hypotheses on the number of steps used to visit every vertex in the graph. What is the cover time for a complete graph with V vertices? A ring graph? A 2-ring graph? Can you find a family of graphs where the cover time grows proportionally to V^3 or 2^V?

4.5.43 *Erdös-Renyi random graph model.* In the classical random graph model, we build a random graph on V vertices by including each possible edge with probability p, independently of the other edges. Compose a `Graph` client to verify the following properties:

- *Connectivity thresholds*: If $p < 1/V$ and V is large, then most of the connected components are small, with the largest being logarithmic in size. If $p > 1/V$, then there is almost surely a giant component containing almost all vertices. If $p < \ln V / V$, the graph is disconnected with high probability; if $p > \ln V / V$, the graph is connected with high probability.
- *Distribution of degrees*: The distribution of degrees follows a binomial distribution, centered on the average, so most vertices have similar degrees. The probability that a vertex is connected to k other vertices decreases exponentially in k.
- *No hubs*: The maximum vertex degree when p is a constant is at most logarithmic in V.
- *No local clustering*: The cluster coefficient is close to 0 if the graph is sparse and connected. Random graphs are not small-world graphs.
- *Short path lengths*: If $p > \ln V / V$, then the diameter of the graph (see Exercise 4.5.37) is logarithmic.

4.5.44 *Power law of web links.* The indegrees and outdegrees of pages in the web obey a power law that can be modeled by a *preferred attachment* process. Suppose that each web page has exactly one outgoing link. Each page is created one at a time, starting with a single page that points to itself. With probability $p < 1$, it links to one of the existing pages, chosen uniformly at random. With probability $1-p$, it links to an existing page with probability proportional to the number of incoming links of that page. This rule reflects the common tendency for new web pages to point to popular pages. Compose a program to simulate this process and plot a histogram of the number of incoming links.

Partial solution: The fraction of pages with indegree k is proportional to $k^{-1/(1-p)}$.

4.5.45 *Global clustering coefficient.* Add a function to `smallworld.py` that computes the global clustering coefficient of a graph. The *global clustering coefficient* is the conditional probability that two random vertices that are neighbors of a common vertex are neighbors of each other. Find graphs for which the local and global clustering coefficients are different.

4.5.46 *Watts–Strogatz graph model.* (See Exercises 4.5.24 and 4.5.25.) Watts and Strogatz proposed a hybrid model that contains typical links of vertices near each other (people know their geographic neighbors), plus some random long-range connection links. Plot the effect of adding random edges to an n-by-n grid graph on the average path length and on the cluster coefficient, for $n = 100$. Do the same for k-ring graphs on V vertices, for $V = 10{,}000$ and various values of k up to $10 \log V$.

4.5.47 *Bollobás–Chung graph model.* Bollobás and Chung proposed a hybrid model that combines a 2-ring on V vertices (V is even), plus a *random matching*. A *matching* is a graph in which every vertex has degree 1. To generate a random matching, shuffle the V vertices and add an edge between vertex i and vertex $i+1$ in the shuffled order. Determine the degree of each vertex for graphs in this model. Using `smallworld.py`, estimate the average path length and cluster coefficient for random graphs generated according to this model for $V = 1{,}000$.

4.5.48 *Kleinberg graph model.* There is no way for participants in the Watts-Strogatz model to find short paths in a decentralized network. But Milgram's experiment also had a striking algorithmic component—individuals can find short paths! Jon Kleinberg proposed making the distribution of shortcuts obey a power law, with probability proportional to the dth power of the distance (in d dimensions). Each vertex has *one* long-range neighbor. Compose a program to generate graphs according to this model, with a test client that uses `smallworld.py` to test whether they exhibit the small-world phenomenon. Plot histograms to show that the graphs are uniform over all distance scales (same number of links at distances 1–10 as at distances 10–100 or 100–1000). Compose a program to compute the average lengths of paths obtained by taking the edge that brings the path as close to the target as possible in terms of lattice distance, and test the hypothesis that this average is proportional to $(\log V)^2$.

Context

IN THIS CLOSING SECTION, WE PLACE your newly acquired knowledge of programming in a broader context by briefly describing some of the basic elements of the world of computation that you are likely to encounter. It is our hope that this information will whet your appetite to use your knowledge of programming as a platform for learning more about the role of computation in the world around you.

You now know how to program. Just as learning to drive an SUV is not difficult when you know how to drive a car, so learning to program in a different language will not be difficult for you. Many scientists regularly use several different languages, for different purposes. The built-in data types, conditionals, loops, and functional abstraction of CHAPTERS 1 AND 2 (which served programmers well for the first couple of decades of computing) and the object-oriented programming approach of CHAPTER 3 (which is used by modern programmers) are basic models found in many programming languages. Your skill in using them and the fundamental data types of CHAPTER 4 will prepare you to cope with libraries, program development environments, and specialized applications of all sorts. You are also well positioned to appreciate the power of abstraction in designing complex systems and understanding how they work.

The study of *computer science* is much more than learning to program. Now that you are familiar with programming and conversant with computing, you are well prepared to learn about some of the outstanding intellectual achievements of the past century, some of the most important unsolved problems of our time, and their role in the evolution of the computational infrastructure that surrounds us. Perhaps even more significant, as we have hinted throughout the book, is that computation is playing an ever-increasing role in our understanding of nature, from genomics to molecular dynamics to astrophysics. Further study of the basic precepts of computer science is certain to pay dividends for you.

Standard Python modules. The Python system provides a wide range of resources for your use. We have made extensive use of some Python standard modules, such as `math`, but have ignored most of them. A great deal of information about the standard modules is readily available online. If you have not yet browsed through the Python standard modules, now is the time to do so. You will find that much of this code is intended for use by professional developers, but there are a number of modules that you are likely to find interesting. Perhaps the most important thing to keep in mind when studying modules is that you may not *need* to use them, but you *can* use them. When you find an API that seems to meet your needs, take advantage of it, by all means.

Programming environments. You will certainly find yourself using other programming environments besides Python in the future. Many programmers, even experienced professionals, are caught between the past, because of huge amounts of legacy code in old languages such as C, C++, and Fortran, and the future, because of the availability of modern tools like JavaScript, Ruby, Java, Python, and Scala. Again, perhaps the most important thing to keep in mind when using a programming language is that you do not *need* to use it, but you *can* use it. If some other language might better meet your needs, take advantage of it, by all means. People who insist on staying within a single programming environment, for whatever reason, are missing opportunities.

Scientific computing. In particular, computing with numbers can be very tricky because of issues related to accuracy and precision, so the use of libraries of mathematical functions is certainly justified. Many scientists use Fortran, an old scientific language; many others use Matlab, a language that was developed specifically for computing with matrices. The combination of good libraries and built-in matrix operations makes Matlab an attractive choice for many problems. However, since Matlab lacks support for mutable types and other modern facilities, Python is a better choice for many other problems. *You* can use both! The same mathematical libraries used by Matlab and Fortran programmers are accessible from Python. Indeed, the Python community has extensive ties to this software in the *NumPy* (numerical Python) and *SciPy* (scientific Python) libraries. If you are engaged in scientific computing, you should make use of these libraries. You can find information on the booksite about how to do so.

Computer systems. Properties of specific computer systems once completely determined the nature and extent of problems that could be solved, but now they hardly intrude on these considerations. You can still count on having a faster machine with much more memory next year at this time. Strive to keep your code machine-independent, so that you can easily make the switch. More importantly, the web is playing an increasingly critical role in commercial and scientific computing, as you have seen in many examples in this book. You can compose programs that process data that is maintained elsewhere, compose programs that interact with programs executing elsewhere, and take advantage of many other properties of the extensive and evolving computational infrastructure. Do not hesitate to do so. People who invest significant effort in writing programs for specific machines, even high-powered supercomputers, are missing opportunities.

Theoretical computer science. By contrast, fundamental limits on computation have been apparent from the start and continue to play an important role in determining the kinds of problems that we can address. You might be surprised to learn that there are some problems that no computer program can solve and many other problems, which arise commonly in practice, that are thought to be too difficult to solve on any conceivable computer. Everyone who depends on computation for problem solving, creative work, or research needs to respect these facts.

You have certainly come a long way since you tentatively created, compiled, and ran `helloworld.py`, but you also still have a great deal to learn. Keep programming, and keep learning about programming environments, scientific computing, computer systems, and theoretical computer science, and you will open opportunities for yourself that people who do not program cannot even conceive.

Glossary

algorithm A step-by-step procedure for solving a problem, such as Euclid's algorithm.

alias Two (or more) variables that refer to the same object.

API (application programming interface) Specification of the set of operations that characterize how a client can use a data type.

array A data structure that stores a sequence of elements, with support for creation, indexed access, indexed assignment, and iteration.

argument An object reference passed to a function.

assignment statement A Python statement consisting of a variable name followed by = followed by an expression, which directs Python to evaluate the expression and to bind the variable to an object holding the resulting value.

binding Association between a variable and an object holding a data-type value.

bit Either of the two binary digits (0 or 1).

booksite module Module created by the authors for use in the book.

built-in function A function built into the Python language, such as `max()`, `abs()`, `int()`, `str()`, and `hash()`.

built-in type A data type built into the Python language, such as `str`, `float`, `int`, `bool`, `list`, `tuple`, `dict`, and `set`.

class The Python construct to implement a user-defined data type, providing a template to create and manipulate objects holding values of the type, as specified by an API.

client A program that uses an implementation via an API.

command line The active line in the terminal application; used to invoke system commands and to run programs.

command-line argument A string passed to a program at the command line.

comment Explanatory text (ignored by the compiler) to help a reader understand the purpose of code.

comparable data type A Python data type that defines a total order using the six comparison operators <, <=, >, >=, ==, and !=, such as `int`, `str`, `float`, and `bool`.

compile-time (syntax) error An error found by the compiler.

compiler A program that translates a program from a high-level language into a low-level language, such as from the Python programming language to Python bytecode.

constant variable A variable whose associated data-type value does not change during execution of the program (or from one execution of the program to the next).

constructor A special data-type method for creating and initializing a new object.

data structure A way to organize data in a computer (usually to save time or space), such as an array, a resizing array, a linked list, and a binary search tree.

data type A set of values and a set of operations defined on those values.

default value The object assigned to a parameter variable if the function call does not include the corresponding argument.

defining and initializing a variable Binding a variable to an object for the first time in a program.

element One of the objects in an array.

evaluate an expression Simplify an expression to a value by applying operators to the operands in the expression, using precedence rules.

exception An exceptional condition or error at run time.

expression A combination of literals, variables, operators, and function calls (perhaps parenthesized) that can be simplified to produce a value.

function A named sequence of statements that performs a computation.

function call An expression that executes a function and returns a value.

garbage collection The process of automatically identifying and freeing memory when it is no longer in use.

global code Code not inside any function or class definition.

global variable A variable defined outside of any function or class.

hashable data type A data type that defines the built-in function `hash()` and is suitable for use with `dict` and `set`, such as `int`, `str`, `float`, `bool`, and `tuple` (but not `list`).

identifier The name used to identify a variable, function, class, module, or other object.

immutable object An object whose value cannot change.

immutable data type A data type for which the value of any instance cannot change.

implementation A program that implements a set of methods defined in API, for use by a client.

import statement A Python statement that enables you to refer to code in another module.

instance An object of a particular class.

(instance) method The implementation of a data-type operation (a function that is invoked with respect to a particular object).

instance variable A variable defined inside a class (but outside any method) that represents a data-type value (data associated with each instance of the class).

interpreter A program that executes a program written in a high-level language, one line at a time.

item One of the objects in a collection.

iterable data type A data type that returns an iterator over its items, such as `list`, `tuple`, `str`, `dict`, and `set`.

iterator A data type that supports the built-in function `next()`, which Python calls at the beginning of each iteration of a `for` loop.

literal Source-code representation of a data-type value for built-in number and string types, such as `123`, `'Hello'`, and `True`.

local variable A variable defined within a function, with scope limited to that function.

modular programming A style of programming that emphasizes using separate, independent modules to address a task.

module A `.py` file structured so that its features can be reused in other Python programs.

none object A special object `None` that represents no object.

object An in-computer-memory representation of a value from a particular data type, characterized by its identity, type, and value.

object-oriented programming A style of programming that emphasizes modeling real-world or abstract entities using data types and objects.

object reference A concrete representation of the object's identity (the memory address where the object is stored).

operand An object on which an operator operates.

operating system The program on your computer that manages resources and provides common services for programs and applications.

operator A special symbol (or sequence of symbols) that represents a built-in data-type operation, such as +, -, *, and `[]`.

overloading a function Defining the behavior of a built-in function—such as `len()`, `max()`, and `abs()`—for a data type.

overloading an operator Defining the behavior of an operator—such as +, *, <=, and `[]`—for a data type.

parameter variable A variable specified in the definition of a function, initialized to the corresponding argument when the function is called.

pass by object reference Python's style of passing an object to a function (by passing a reference to the object).

polymorphism Using the same API (or partial API) for different types of data.

precedence rules Rules that determine in which order the operators in an expression are applied.

private Data-type implementation code that is not to be referenced by clients.

program A sequence of instructions to be executed on a computer.

pure function A function that, given the same arguments, always returns the same value, without producing any observable side effect.

raise an error Signal a compile-time or run-time error.

return value The object (reference) provided as the result of a function call.

run-time error An error that occurs while the program is executing (an exception).

script A short program, usually implemented as global code and not intended for reuse.

scope The region of a program where a variable or name is directly accessible.

self parameter variable The first parameter variable in a method, which is bound to the object that calls the method. By convention, this variable is named `self`.

sequence An iterable data type which supports indexed access `a[i]` and `len(a)`, such as `list`, `str`, and `tuple` (but not `dict`).

side effect A change in state, such as writing output, reading input, raising an error, or modifying the value of some persistent object (instance variable, parameter variable, or global variable).

slice A subsequence of an array, string, or other sequence.

source code A program or program fragment in a high-level programming language.

special method One of a set of built-in methods that Python calls implicitly when a corresponding data-type operation is invoked, such as `__plus__()`, `__eq__()`, and `__len__()`.

standard input, output, drawing, and audio Our input/output modules for Python.

statement An instruction that Python can execute, such as an assignment statement, an `if` statement, a `while` statement, and a `return` statement.

terminal An application for your operating system that accepts commands.

unit testing The practice of including code in every module that tests the code in that module.

variable A container that stores a reference to an object.

Index

F

H

I

S

V

W

Y

Z

APIs

function call	*description*
`math.sin(x)`	*sine of* x *(expressed in radians)*
`math.cos(x)`	*cosine of* x *(expressed in radians)*
`math.tan(x)`	*tangent of* x *(expressed in radians)*
`math.atan2(y, x)`	*polar angle of the point* (x, y)
`math.hypot(x, y)`	*Euclidean distance between the origin and* (x, y)
`math.radians(x)`	*conversion of* x *(expressed in degrees) to radians*
`math.degrees(x)`	*conversion of* x *(expressed in radians) to degrees*
`math.exp(x)`	*exponential function of* x *(e^x)*
`math.log(x, b)`	*base-*b *logarithm of* x *($\log_b x$)* *(the base* b *defaults to e—the natural logarithm)*
`math.sqrt(x)`	*square root of* x
`math.erf(x)`	*error function of* x
`math.gamma(x)`	*gamma function of* x
`math.factorial(x)`	*factorial of integer* x

Note: The `math` *module also includes the inverse trigonometric functions* `asin()`, `acos()`, *and* `atan()`; *the hyperbolic functions* `sinh()`, `cosh()`, `tanh()`, `asinh()`, `acosh()`, *and* `atanh()`; *and the constant variables* `e` (`2.718281828459045`) *and* `pi` (`3.141592653589793`).

Python's `math` *module (partial API)*

function call	*description*
functions that read individual tokens from standard input	
`stdio.isEmpty()`	*is standard input empty (or only whitespace)?*
`stdio.readInt()`	*read a token, convert it to an integer, and return it*
`stdio.readFloat()`	*read a token, convert it to a float, and return it*
`stdio.readBool()`	*read a token, convert it to a boolean, and return it*
`stdio.readString()`	*read a token and return it as a string*
functions that read lines from standard input	
`stdio.hasNextLine()`	*does standard input have a next line?*
`stdio.readLine()`	*read the next line and return it as a string*
functions that read a sequence of values of the same type until standard input is empty	
`stdio.readAll()`	*read all remaining input and return it as a string*
`stdio.readAllInts()`	*read all remaining tokens and return as an array of integers*
`stdio.readAllFloats()`	*read all remaining tokens and return as an array of floats*
`stdio.readAllBools()`	*read all remaining tokens and return as an array of booleans*
`stdio.readAllStrings()`	*read all remaining tokens and return as an array of strings*
`stdio.readAllLines()`	*read all remaining lines and return as an array of strings*
functions that write to standard output	
`stdio.write(x)`	*write* `x` *to standard output*
`stdio.writeln(x)`	*write* `x` *and a newline to standard output (*`x` *defaults to the empty string)*
`stdio.writef(fmt, arg1, ...)`	*write the arguments* `arg1, ...` *to standard output as specified by the format string* `fmt`

Note 1: A token is a maximal sequence of non-whitespace characters.
Note 2: Before reading a token, any leading whitespace is discarded.
Note 3: Each function that reads input raises a run-time error if it cannot read in the next value, either because there is no more input or because the input does not match the expected type.

Our `stdio` *module*

function call	*description*
basic functions for drawing	
`stddraw.line(x0, y0, x1, y1)`	*draw a line from* `(x0, y0)` *to* `(x1, y1)`
`stddraw.point(x, y)`	*draw a point at* `(x, y)`
`stddraw.show()`	*show the drawing in the standard drawing window (and wait until it is closed by the user)*
control functions for setting drawing parameters	
`stddraw.setCanvasSize(w, h)`	*set the size of the canvas to* `w`*-by-*`h` *pixels (*`w` *and* `h` *default to* `512`*)*
`stddraw.setXscale(x0, x1)`	*set the x-range of the canvas to* `(x0, x1)` *(*`x0` *defaults to* `0` *and* `y0` *defaults to* `1`*)*
`stddraw.setYscale(y0, y1)`	*set the y-range of the canvas to* `(y0, y1)` *(*`y0` *defaults to* `0` *and* `y1` *defaults to* `1`*)*
`stddraw.setPenRadius(r)`	*set the pen radius to* `r` *(defaults to* `0.005`*)*

Note: If the pen radius is `0`*, then points and line widths will be the minimum possible size.*

functions for drawing shapes	
`stddraw.circle(x, y, r)`	*draw a circle of radius* `r` *centered at* `(x, y)`
`stddraw.square(x, y, r)`	*draw a 2*`r`*-by-2*`r` *square centered at* `(x, y)`
`stddraw.rectangle(x, y, w, h)`	*draw a w-by-h rectangle with lower-left endpoint* `(x, y)`
`stddraw.polygon(x, y)`	*draw a polygon that connects* `(x[i], y[i])`

Note: `filledCircle()`*,* `filledSquare()`*,* `filledRectangle()`*, and* `filledPolygon()` *correspond to these and draw filled shapes, not just outlines.*

functions for drawing shapes	
`stddraw.text(x, y, s)`	*draw string* `s`*, centered at* `(x, y)`
`stddraw.setPenColor(color)`	*set the pen color to* `color` *(defaults to* `stddraw.BLACK`*)*
`stddraw.setFontFamily(font)`	*set the font family to* `font` *(defaults to* `'Helvetica'`*)*
`stddraw.setFontSize(size)`	*set the font size to* `size` *(defaults to* `12`*)*
functions for animation	
`stddraw.clear(color)`	*clear the background canvas (color every pixel* `color`*)*
`stddraw.show(t)`	*show the drawing in the standard drawing window and wait for* `t` *milliseconds*

Our `stddraw` module

function call	*description*
`stdaudio.playFile(filename)`	*play all sound samples in the file* `filename.wav`
`stdaudio.playSamples(a)`	*play all sound samples in the float array* `a[]`
`stdaudio.playSample(x)`	*play the sound sample in the float* `x`
`stdaudio.save(filename, a)`	*save all sound samples in the float array* `a[]` *to the file* `filename.wav`
`stdaudio.read(filename)`	*read all sound samples from the file* `filename.wav` *and return as a float array*
`stdaudio.wait()`	*wait for the currently playing sound to finish (must be the last call to* `stdaudio` *in each program)*

Our `stdaudio` *module*

function call	*description*
`create1D(n, val)`	*array of length* `n`*, each element initialized to* `val`
`create2D(m, n, val)`	`m`*-by-*`n` *array, each element initialized to* `val`
`readInt1D()`	*array of integers, read from standard input*
`readInt2D()`	*two-dimensional array of integers, read from standard input*
`readFloat1D()`	*array of floats, read from standard input*
`readFloat2D()`	*two-dimensional array of floats, read from standard input*
`readBool1D()`	*array of booleans, read from standard input*
`readBool2D()`	*two-dimensional array of booleans, read from standard input*
`write1D(a)`	*write array* `a[]` *to standard output*
`write2D(a)`	*write two-dimensional array* `a[]` *to standard output*

Note 1: 1D format is an integer `n` *followed by* `n` *elements.*
2D format is two integers `m` *and* `n` *followed by* `m × n` *elements in row-major order.*
Note 2: Booleans are written as `0` *and* `1` *instead of* `False` *and* `True`*.*

Our `stdarray` *module*

function call	*description*
`uniformInt(lo, hi)`	*uniformly random integer in the range [`lo`, `hi`)*
`uniformFloat(lo, hi)`	*uniformly random float in the range [`lo`, `hi`)*
`bernoulli(p)`	`True` *with probability* `p` *(*`p` *defaults to* `0.5`*)*
`binomial(n, p)`	*number of heads in* `n` *coin flips, each of which is heads with probability* `p` *(*`p` *defaults to* `0.5`*)*
`gaussian(mu, sigma)`	*normal, mean* `mu`*, standard deviation* `sigma` *(*`mu` *defaults to* `0.0`*,* `sigma` *defaults to* `1.0`*)*
`discrete(a)`	`i` *with probability proportional to* `a[i]`
`shuffle(a)`	*randomly shuffle the array* `a[]`

Our `stdrandom` *module*

function call	*description*
`mean(a)`	*average of the values in the numeric array* `a[]`
`var(a)`	*sample variance of the values in the numeric array* `a[]`
`stddev(a)`	*sample standard deviation of the values in the numeric array* `a[]`
`median(a)`	*median of the values in the numeric array* `a[]`
`plotPoints(a)`	*point plot of the values in the numeric array* `a[]`
`plotLines(a)`	*line plot of the values in the numeric array* `a[]`
`plotBars(a)`	*bar plot of the values in the numeric array* `a[]`

Our `stdstats` *module*

operation	*description*
`len(s)`	*length of* `s`
`s + t`	*a new string that is the concatenation of* `s` *and* `t`
`s += t`	*assign to* `s` *a new string that is the concatenation of* `s` *and* `t`
`s[i]`	*the* `i`*th character of* `s` *(a string)*
`s[i:j]`	*the* `i`*th through* `(j-1)`*st characters of* `s` *(*`i` *defaults to* `0`*;* `j` *defaults to* `len(s)`*)*
`s < t`	*is* `s` *less than* `t`*?*
`s <= t`	*is* `s` *less than or equal to* `t`*?*
`s == t`	*is* `s` *equal to* `t`*?*
`s != t`	*is* `s` *not equal to* `t`*?*
`s >= t`	*is* `s` *greater than or equal to* `t`*?*
`s > t`	*is* `s` *greater than* `t`*?*
`s in t`	*does* `s` *appear as a substring in* `t`*?*
`s not in t`	*does* `s` *not appear as a substring in* `t`*?*
`s.count(t)`	*number of occurrences of substring* `t` *in* `s`
`s.find(t, start)`	*the first index in* `s` *where* `t` *appears (*`-1` *if not found)* *starting at* `start` *(default* `0`*)*
`s.upper()`	*a copy of* `s` *with lowercase letters replaced with uppercase ones*
`s.lower()`	*a copy of* `s` *with uppercase letters replaced with lowercase ones*
`s.startswith(t)`	*does* `s` *start with* `t`*?*
`s.endswith(t)`	*does* `s` *end with* `t`*?*
`s.strip()`	*a copy of* `s` *with leading and trailing whitespace removed*
`s.replace(old, new)`	*a copy of* `s` *with all occurrences of* `old` *replaced by* `new`
`s.split(delimiter)`	*an array of substrings of* `s`*, separated by* `delimiter` *(default whitespace)*
`delimiter.join(a)`	*concatenation of strings in* `a[]`*, separated by* `delimiter`

Python's built-in `str` *data type (partial API)*

operation	description
`Color(r, g, b)`	*a new color with red, green, and blue components* `r`*,* `g`*, and* `b`*, all integers between 0 and 255*
`c.getRed()`	*the red component of* `c`
`c.getGreen()`	*the green component of* `c`
`c.getBlue()`	*the blue component of* `c`
`str(c)`	`'(R, G, B)'` *(string representation of* `c`*)*

Our `Color` *data type (*`color.py`*)*

operation	description
`Picture(w, h)`	*a new* `w`*-by-*`h` *array of pixels, initially all black*
`Picture(filename)`	*a new picture, initialized from* `filename`
`pic.save(filename)`	*save* `pic` *to* `filename`
`pic.width()`	*the width of the* `pic`
`pic.height()`	*the height of the* `pic`
`pic.get(col, row)`	*the* `Color` *of pixel* `(col, row)` *in* `pic`
`pic.set(col, row, c)`	*set the* `Color` *of pixel* `(col, row)` *in* `pic` *to* `c`

Note: Filename must end in `.png` *or* `.jpg`*, which denotes the file format.*

Our `Picture` *data type (*`picture.py`*)*

operation	description
`stddraw.picture(pic, x, y)`	*display* `pic` *in* `stddraw`*, centered at* `(x, y)`

Note: Both `x` *and* `y` *default to the center of the standard drawing canvas.*

Displaying a `Picture` *object*

operation	*description*
`InStream(filename)`	*a new input stream, initialized from* `filename` *(defaults to standard input if no argument)*
methods that read tokens from standard input	
`s.isEmpty()`	*is* `s` *empty? (does it consist solely of whitespace?)*
`s.readInt()`	*read a token from* `s`*, convert it to an integer, and return it*
`s.readFloat()`	*read a token from* `s`*, convert it to a float, and return it*
`s.readBool()`	*read a token from* `s`*, convert it to a boolean, and return it*
`s.readString()`	*read a token from* `s`*, convert it to a string, and return it*
methods that read lines from standard input	
`s.hasNextLine()`	*does* `s` *have another line?*
`s.readLine()`	*read the next line from* `s` *and return it as a string*

Note 1: A token is a maximal sequence of non-whitespace characters.
Note 2: Behaves like standard input; `readAll()` *methods are also supported.*

Our `InStream` *data type (*`instream.py`*)*

operation	*description*
`OutStream(filename)`	*a new output stream that will write to* `filename` *(default standard output if no argument)*
`out.write(x)`	*write* `x` *to* `out`
`out.writeln(x)`	*write* `x` *to* `out`*, followed by a newline (*`x` *default to empty string)*
`out.writef(fmt, arg1, ...)`	*write the arguments* `arg1`*, ... to* `out` *as specified by the format string* `fmt`

Our `OutStream` *data type (*`outstream.py`*)*

operation	description
`x + y`	*sum of x and y*
`x - y`	*difference of x and y*
`x * y`	*product of x and y*
`x / y`	*quotient of x and y*
`x // y`	*floored quotient of x and y*
`x % y`	*remainder from division of x by y*
`x ** y`	*x to the power y*
`-x`	*x negated*
`+x`	*x unchanged*
`x < y`	*is x less than y?*
`x <= y`	*is x less than or equal to y?*
`x == y`	*is x equal to y?*
`x != y`	*is x not equal to y?*
`x >= y`	*is x greater than or equal to y?*
`x > y`	*is x greater than y?*
`abs(x)`	*absolute value of x*
`min(x, y, ...)`	*minimum of x, y, ...*
`max(x, y, ...)`	*maximum of x, y, ...*

Note: The quotient operator (/) operator performs floating-point division in Python 3 but floored division in Python 2. We do not use the quotient operator with two `int` operands in this book.

Python's built-in `int` data type (partial API)

operation	description
`x and y`	`True` *if both x and y are* `True`*, and* `False` *otherwise*
`x or y`	`True` *if either x or y are* `True`*, and* `False` *otherwise*
`not x`	`True` *if x is* `True`*, and* `False` *otherwise*

Python's built-in `bool` data type (partial API)

operation	description
`x + y`	*sum of x and y*
`x - y`	*difference of x and y*
`x * y`	*product of x and y*
`x / y`	*quotient of x and y*
`x // y`	*floored quotient of x and y*
`x % y`	*remainder from division of x by y*
`x ** y`	*x to the power y*
`-x`	*x negated*
`+x`	*x unchanged*
`x < y`	*is x less than y?*
`x <= y`	*is x less than or equal to y?*
`x == y`	*is x equal to y?*
`x != y`	*is x not equal to y?*
`x >= y`	*is x greater than or equal to y?*
`x > y`	*is x greater than y?*
`abs(x)`	*absolute value of x*
`min(x, y, ...)`	*minimum of x, y, ...*
`max(x, y, ...)`	*maximum of x, y, ...*

Note: We do not use the floored quotient operator (//) or remainder operator (%) with floats in this book.

Python's built-in `float` *data type (partial API)*

operation	description
`len(a)`	*length of a*
`a[i]`	*the* `i`*th item of a*
`for v in a:`	*iterate over the items in a*
`v in a`	`True` *if a contains v,* `False` *otherwise*

Python's built-in `tuple` *data type (partial API)*

constant-time operations	*description*
`len(a)`	*length of* `a`
`a[i]`	*the* `i`*th item of* `a`
`a[i] = v`	*replace the* `i`*th item of* `a` *with item* `v`
`a += [v]`	*append item* `v` *to the end of* `a`
`a.pop()`	*delete* `a[len(a)-1]` *from the list and return that item*
linear-time operations	
`a + b`	*concatenation of* `a` *and* `b`
`a[i:j]`	`[a[i], a[i+1], ..., a[j-1]]`
`a[i:j] = b`	`a[i] = b[0], a[i+1] = b[1], ...`
`v in a`	`True` *if* `a` *contains* `v`, `False` *otherwise*
`v not in a`	`False` *if* `a` *contains* `v`, `True` *otherwise*
`for v in a:`	*iterate over the items in* `a`
`del a[i]`	*delete* `a[i]` *from the list*
`a.pop(i)`	*delete* `a[i]` *from the list and return that item*
`a.insert(i, v)`	*insert item* `v` *into* `a` *before* `a[i]`
`a.index(v)`	*index of first occurrence of item* `v` *in* `a`
`a.reverse()`	*rearrange the items of* `a` *into reverse order*
linearithmic-time operations	
`a.sort()`	*rearrange the items of* `a` *into ascending order*

Note 1: `a += [v]` *and* `a.pop()` *are "amortized" constant-time operations.*
Note 2: The `del a[i]`, `pop(i)`, *and* `insert(i, v)` *operations take "amortized" constant time if* `i` *is close to* `len(a)`.
Note 3: The slicing operations take time linear in the length of the slice.

Python's built-in `list` *data type (partial API)*

constant-time operation	*description*
`dict()`	*a new empty dictionary*
`st[key] = val`	*associate* `key` *with* `val` *in* `st`
`st[key]`	*the value associated with* `key` *in* `st` *(raises* `KeyError` *if no such* `key` *in* `st`*)*
`st.get(key, x)`	`st[key]` *if* `key` *is in* `st`*; otherwise x (x defaults to* `None`*)*
`key in st`	*is* `key` *in* `st`*?*
`len(st)`	*number of key–value pairs in* `st`
`del st[key]`	*remove* `key` *(and its associated value) from* `st`
linear-time operation	
`for key in st:`	*iterate over the keys in* `st`

Note : The keys must be hashable.

Python's built-in `dict` *data type (partial API)*

constant-time operation	*description*
`set()`	*a new empty set*
`s.add(item)`	*add* `item` *to* `s` *(if not already in set)*
`item in s`	*is* `item` *in* `s`*?*
`len(s)`	*number of items in* `s`
`s.remove(item)`	*remove* `item` *from* `s`
linear-time operation	
`for item in s:`	*iterate over the items in* `s`
`s.intersection(t)`	*intersection of* `s` *and* `t`
`s.union(t)`	*union of* `s` *and* `t`

Note : The items must be hashable.

Python's built-in `set` *data type (partial API)*